Longman Dictionary of

LANGUAGE TEACHING AND APPLIED LINGUISTICS

Jack C. Richards · John Platt · Heidi Platt

Consultant
Professor C. N. Candlin

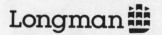

Longman Group UK Limited
Longman House, Burnt Mill, Harlow,
Essex CM20 2JE, England
and Associated Companies throughout the world.

© Longman Group UK Limited 1992 (Second Edition)

First edition published 1985
This edition published 1992
Third impression 1993

British Library Cataloguing-in-Publication Data
A catalogue record for this book is available from
the British Library
ISBN 0 582 07244 1

Set in IBX, Plantin 9/10pt

Produced by Longman Singapore Publishers Pte Ltd
Printed in Singapore

PRONUNCIATION TABLE

Consonants

Symbol	Key word
b	back
d	day
ð	then
dʒ	jump
f	few
g	gay
h	hot
j	yet
k	key
l	led
m	sum
n	sun
ŋ	sung
p	pen
r	red
s	soon
ʃ	fishing
t	tea
tʃ	cheer
θ	thing
v	view
w	wet
z	zero
ʒ	pleasure

Vowels

Symbol	Key word
æ	bad
ɑː	calm
ɒ	pot *British English*
aɪ	bite
aʊ	now
aɪə	tire
aʊə	tower
ɔː	caught
ɔɪ	boy
ɔɪə	employer
e	bed
eə	there
eɪ	make
eɪə	player
ə	about
əʊ	note
əʊə	lower
ɜː	bird
i	pretty
iː	sheep
ɪ	ship
ɪə	here
iə	alien
uː	boot
u	actuality
ʊ	put
ʊə	poor
ʌ	cut

‖   separates British and American pronunciations: British on the left, American on the right

/'/   shows main stress

/ˌ/   shows secondary stress

/r/   at the end of a word means that /r/ is usually pronounced in American English and is pronounced in British English when the next word begins with a vowel sound

/ᵻ/   means that some speakers use /ɪ/ and others use /ə/

iii

Pronunciation Table

/ʊ̯/   means that some speakers use /ʊ/ and others use /ə/

/i/   means many American speakers use /iː/ but many British speakers use /ɪ/

/u/   represents a sound somewhere between /uː/ and /ʊ/

/ə/   means that /ə/ may or may not be used

/◄/   shows stress shift

GUIDE TO THE DICTIONARY

pronunciation
(see table on p iii)

related word

part of speech

less common
alternative

aphasia /əˈfeɪʒə/ n **aphasic** /əˈfeɪzɪk/ adj
also **dysphasia** n
loss of the ability to use and understand language, usually caused by
damage to the brain. The loss may be total or partial, and may affect
spoken and/or written language ability.
There are different types of aphasia: **agraphia** is difficulty in writing;
alexia is difficulty in reading; **anomia** is difficulty in using proper
nouns; and **agrammatism** is difficulty in using grammatical words like
prepositions, articles, etc.
Aphasia can be studied in order to discover how the brain processes
language.

terms explained
within the entry

ther related
atries it may be
seful to look up

see also BRAIN, NEUROLINGUISTICS
Further reading Dalton & Hardcastle 1977

breviation for
rm

computer assisted language learning /kəmˈpjuːtər əˈsɪstd ˈlæŋ
gwɪdʒ ˌlɜːnɪŋ‖ ˈlɜːr-/ n
also **CALL**
the use of a computer in the teaching or learning of a second or foreign
language. CALL may take the form of
a activities which parallel learning through other media but which use
   the facilities of the computer (e.g. using the computer to present a
   reading text)
b activities which are extensions or adaptations of print-based or
   classroom based activities (e.g. computer programs that teach writing
   skills by helping the student develop a topic and THESIS STATEMENT
   and by checking a composition for vocabulary, grammar, and topic
   development), and
c activities which are unique to CALL.

American form of
pronunciation shown
after the ‖

term explained
at its own
alphabetical
entry

see also INTERACTIVE VIDEO
Further reading Flint Smith 1989; Hope, Taylor & Pusack 1984; Ahmad
et al 1985

books where
further information/
discussion will be
found

ntry for a
ss common
ternative

dysphasia /dɪsˈfeɪʒə/ n
another term for APHASIA

ntry for an
bbreviation

CALL /kɔːl/ n
an abbreviation for COMPUTER ASSISTED LANGUAGE LEARNING

ntry for a word
xplained
sewhere

agrammatism /eɪˈgræmətɪzəm/ n
see APHASIA

INTRODUCTION

Who is this dictionary for?

This dictionary is intended for:

- students taking undergraduate or graduate courses in language teaching or applied linguistics, particularly those planning to take up a career in the teaching of English as a Second or Foreign Language or in foreign language teaching
- language teachers doing in-service or pre-service courses, such as the RSA Certificate for Overseas Teachers of English, Diplomas in Applied Linguistics, TESL/TEFL and similar programmes
- students doing introductory courses in linguistics and related areas
- teachers and others interested in the practical applications of language study

Why this dictionary?

Language teaching and applied linguistics are fields which draw on a number of different disciplines. These include both the language based disciplines such as linguistics, sociolinguistics, and psycholinguistics, as well as the education based disciplines such as curriculum development, testing, teacher education, and evaluation. The result is that students taking courses in language teaching and applied linguistics encounter a large number of specialized terms which frequently occur in articles, books and lectures. This dictionary attempts to clarify the meanings and uses of these terms.

The scope of the dictionary

The dictionary was written for those with little or no background in linguistics, whose mother tongue is English or who use English as a second or foreign language. We have given special attention to English, and the majority of the examples in the dictionary are from English, but the dictionary will also be helpful to those interested in other languages. Although the dictionary is not intended primarily for those who already have a specialized training in language teaching or applied linguistics, it will serve as a reference book in areas with which they are less familiar. It should also be useful to general readers who need further information about the terms which occur in the fields of language teaching and applied linguistics.

Language teaching and applied linguistics

This dictionary includes the core vocabulary of both language teaching and applied linguistics. The field of language teaching is concerned with the development of language programmes and courses, teaching methodology, materials development, testing, teacher training and related areas. The dictionary includes terms from the following areas of study in the field of language teaching:

- teaching methods and approaches in language teaching
- curriculum development and syllabus design
- the teaching of listening, speaking, reading and writing
- computer assisted language learning
- teacher education in language teaching
- English grammar and pronunciation
- language testing and basic statistics

The dictionary also includes terms from the field of applied linguistics. For the purposes of this book, "applied linguistics" refers to the practical applications of linguistics and language theory, and includes terms from the following areas of study:

- introductory linguistics, including phonology, phonetics, syntax, semantics and morphology
- discourse analysis
- sociolinguistics, including the sociology of language and communicative competence
- psycholinguistics, including first and second language acquisition, contrastive analysis, error analysis and learning theories

What the dictionary contains

This dictionary contains 2000 entries which define, in as simple and precise a way as possible, the most frequently occurring terms found in the areas listed above. Many of these terms were included in the Longman Dictionary of Applied Linguistics (LDAL), but the present dictionary includes over 500 terms not included in LDAL as well as revisions of a number of the entries in LDAL. Each term was selected on the basis of its importance within an area and reflects the fact that the term has a particular meaning when used within that area, a meaning unlikely to be listed in other dictionaries. Only words which are in common usage in language teaching and applied linguistics have been included. Words used only by an individual scholar and which have not passed into more general usage have not been included.

During the preparation of the dictionary, definitions were written in consultation with experts in each field. Our aim has been to produce clear and simple definitions which communicate the basic and essential meanings of a term in non-technical language. Definitions are self-contained as far as possible, but cross references show links to other terms and concepts, and references provide information where a fuller discussion of a term or concept can be found.

Acknowledgements

We would like to thank those colleagues from institutions around the world who contributed to the preparation of the first edition of this dictionary, giving advice on inclusion and providing comments on individual entries.

For this new edition, special thanks are also due to:

Christopher Candlin, who has been associated with the dictionary in an advisory capacity since its inception and who has given valuable advice on all aspects of the project.

Susan Maingay, Adam Gadsby, Andrew Delahunty and Alison Steadman of the Longman Dictionary Division.

A

ability group /ə'bɪlɪ̯ti ˌgruːp/ n

see GROUPING

absolute /'æbsəluːt/ n

an adjective or adverb that cannot have a comparative or superlative form. For example *perfectly* and *unique* already express the idea of "to a maximum degree" and cannot therefore be used with comparative forms as in * *most perfectly*, or * *more unique*.

abstract noun /'æbstrækt 'naʊn/ n

see CONCRETE NOUN

accent¹ /'æksənt‖ 'æksent/ n

greater emphasis on a syllable so that it stands out from the other syllables in a word.

For example, in English the noun 'import has the accent on the first syllable *im-* while the verb im'port has the accent on the second syllable *-port*:

> *This car is a foreign import.*
> *We import all our coffee.*

see also PROMINENCE, STRESS

Further reading Gimson 1989; Wells 1982

accent² n

in the written form of some languages, particularly in French, a mark which is placed over a vowel. An accent may show:

a a difference in pronunciation (see DIACRITIC).

For example, in the French word *prés* "meadows", the **acute accent** on the *e* indicates a different vowel sound from that in *près* "near" with a **grave accent**.

b a difference in meaning without any change in pronunciation, e.g. French *ou* "or" and *où* "where".

accent³ n

a particular way of speaking which tells the listener something about the speaker's background.

A person's pronunciation may show:

a the region or country they come from, e.g.

> *a northern accent*
> *an American accent*

b what social class they belong to, e.g.

> *a lower middle class accent*

c whether or not the speaker is a native speaker of the language, e.g.

> *She speaks English with an accent/with a German accent.*

see also DIALECT, SOCIOLECT
Further reading Rivers 1981; Wells 1982

acceptable /ək'septəbəl/ *adj*

(in linguistics) the judgment by the native speakers/users of a speech variety that a certain linguistic item is possible in their variety. The linguistic item could be a written sentence, a spoken utterance, a particular syntactic structure, a word or a way of pronouncing a certain sound. The speech community where such an item is considered acceptable need not be large. It could be all the speakers of a particular region or social class or, alternatively, just the members of an in-group, for example teenagers belonging to a rock club who have created their own in-language. A linguistic item which is acceptable to one group or variety need not be acceptable to another, for example, speakers of some varieties of English accept such expressions as:

I want for him to come.

and

We were visiting with (meaning "calling on") *Aunt Lizzie.*

but speakers of other varieties would not accept these expressions and use instead:

I want him to come.

and

We were visiting Aunt Lizzie.

Sometimes linguistic items are acceptable in certain situations and not in others. For example a teenage girl may tell her friend:

I nearly freaked out when I saw that jerk.

and in that situation it would be acceptable. It would usually be unacceptable if she used this utterance in a formal address at a special function (except, of course, if she quoted it jokingly).

The terms acceptable and unacceptable are different from *grammatical* (see GRAMMATICAL[1]) as they cover a wider range of linguistic units and situations. And because they do not have prescriptive overtones (see PRESCRIPTIVE GRAMMAR) they are also preferred to expressions such as CORRECT/INCORRECT, SUBSTANDARD, right/wrong.

see also APPROPRIATENESS, CONVERSATIONAL RULES

acceptable alternative method /ək'septəbəl ɔːl'tɜːnətɪv ˌmeθəd‖ɔːl'tɜːr-, æl-/ *n*

see CLOZE PROCEDURE

acceptable word method /ək'septəbəl 'wɜːd ˌmeθəd‖-ɜːr-/ *n*

see CLOZE PROCEDURE

access /'æksəs/ *n, v*

locating or obtaining information or data.

In COMPUTER ASSISTED LANGUAGE LEARNING, an important consideration is the speed or ease with which learners can access information on an audio cassette, video, or videodisc. **Sequential access** means locating information in sequence. For example, in order to find something on an audiocassette, it is necessary to fast forward and check for its location a number of times. **Direct access** or **random access** means locating information directly in such a way that access time is not dependent on its location. For example with a phonographic record the needle can be placed directly and at random at the beginning of the desired location on the record.

In computer assisted language learning, linking a computer to an audiocassette recorder means that the user has direct access to any part of a prerecorded program.

Further reading Flint Smith 1989

accommodation /əˌkɒməˈdeɪʃən‖əˌkɑː-/ *n*

when a person changes their way of speaking to make it sound more like or less like the speech of the person they are talking to. For example, a teacher may use simpler words and sentence structures when he/she is talking to a class of young children. This is called **convergence**.

A person may exaggerate their rural accent because they are annoyed by the attitude of someone from the city. This is called **divergence**.

see also ACCENT³

Further reading Thakerar, Giles, and Cheshire 1982

acculturation /əˌkʌltʃəˈreɪʃən/ *n*

a process in which changes in the language, culture, and system of values of a group happen through interaction with another group with a different language, culture, and system of values.

For example, in second language learning, acculturation may affect how well one group (e.g. a group of immigrants in a country) learn the language of another (e.g. the dominant group).

see also ASSIMILATION², SOCIAL DISTANCE

Further reading Schumann 1978; Brown 1987

accuracy /ˈækjɵrəsi/ *n*

see FLUENCY

accusative case /əˈkjuːzətɪv ˈkeɪs/ *n*

the form of a noun or noun phrase which shows that it functions as the direct object of the verb in a sentence.

For example, in the German sentence:

Ursula kaufte einen neuen Tisch.
Ursula bought a new table.

in the noun phrase *einen neuen Tisch*, the article *ein* and the adjective *neu* have the inflectional ending *-en* to show that the noun phrase is in the accusative case because it is the direct object of the verb.

see also CASE¹

achievement test /əˈtʃiːvmənt ˌtest/ *n*

a test which measures how much of a language someone has learned with reference to a particular course of study or programme of instruction.

The difference between this and a more general type of test called a PROFICIENCY TEST is that the latter is not linked to any particular course of instruction.

For example, an achievement test might be a listening comprehension test based on a particular set of dialogues in a textbook. The test helps the teacher to judge the success of his or her teaching and to identify the weaknesses of his or her students. A proficiency test might use similar test items but would not be linked to any particular textbook or language SYLLABUS.

Language achievement tests and language proficiency tests differ mainly in the way they are prepared and interpreted.

Further reading Hughes 1989

acoustic cue /əˈkuːstɪk ˈkjuː/ n

an aspect of the acoustic signal in speech which is used to distinguish between phonetic features. For example VOICE ONSET TIME is an acoustic cue which is used to distinguish between the sounds /t/ and /d/.

acoustic filtering /əˈkuːstɪk ˈfɪltərɪŋ/ n

(in listening comprehension) when someone is able to hear and identify only some of the sounds that are being spoken, this is called acoustic filtering.

For example, when someone is learning a foreign language, the speech sounds of their native language may act as a filter, making it difficult for them to hear and identify new or unfamiliar sounds in the foreign language.

Further reading Rivers 1972

acoustic phonetics /əˈkuːstɪk fəˈnetɪks/ n

see PHONETICS

acquisition /ˌækwɪˈzɪʃən/ n

see FIRST LANGUAGE ACQUISITION, LANGUAGE ACQUISITION, SECOND LANGUAGE ACQUISITION

acquisition order /ˌækwɪˈzɪʃən ˌɔːdər‖ˌɔːr-/ n

another term for ORDER OF ACQUISITION

acrolect /ˈækrəʊlekt/ n

see POST-CREOLE CONTINUUM, SPEECH CONTINUUM

action research /ˈækʃən rɪˈsɜːtʃ, ˈriːsɜːtʃ‖-ɜːr-/ n

1 research which has the primary goal of finding ways of solving problems, bringing about social change or practical action, in comparison with research which seeks to discover scientific principles or develop general laws and theories.

2 (in teacher education) teacher-initiated classroom research which seeks to increase the teacher's understanding of classroom teaching

and learning and to bring about improvements in classroom practices. Action research typically involves small-scale investigative projects in the teacher's own classroom, and consists of the following cycle of activities:

The teacher (or a group of teachers)

a selects an aspect of classroom behaviour to examine in more detail (e.g. the teacher's use of questions)

b selects a suitable research technique (e.g. recording classroom lessons)

c collects data and analyzes it

d develops an action plan to help bring about a change in classroom behaviour (e.g. to reduce the frequency of questions which the teacher answers himself or herself)

e acts to implement the plan

f observes the effects of the action plan on behaviour

Further reading Kemmis & McTaggart 1988; Nunan 1989a

active/passive language knowledge /'æktɪv 'pæsɪv 'læŋgwɪdʒ ˌnɒlɪdʒ‖ˌnɑː-/ n

also **productive/receptive language knowledge**

The ability of a person to actively produce their own speech and writing is called their **active language knowledge**. This is compared to their ability to understand the speech and writing of other people, their **passive language knowledge**.

Native speakers of a language can understand many more words than they actively use. Some people have a **passive vocabulary** (i.e. words they understand) of up to 100,000 words, but an **active vocabulary** (i.e. words they use) of between 10,000 and 20,000 words.

In foreign language learning, an active vocabulary of about 3000 to 5000 words, and a passive vocabulary of about 5000 to 10,000 words is regarded as the intermediate to upper intermediate level of proficiency.

Further reading Nation 1990; Mackey 1965

active teaching /'æktɪv 'tiːtʃɪŋ/ n

another term for DIRECT TEACHING

active vocabulary /'æktɪv vəˈkæbjʊləri, vəʊ-‖-eri/ n

see ACTIVE/PASSIVE LANGUAGE KNOWLEDGE

active voice /'æktɪv 'vɔɪs/ n

see VOICE[1]

acute accent /əˈkjuːt 'æksənt‖'æksent/ n

the accent ´, e.g. on French *prés* "meadows".

see also ACCENT[2]

adaptation /ˌædæpˈteɪʃən/ n

When a teacher makes changes to published texts or materials to make

5

additive bilingual education

them more suitable or appropriate for a particular group of learners or a particular teaching need, this is called adaptation.

Further reading Madson & Bowen 1978

additive bilingual education /ˈædɪtɪv baɪˈlɪŋgwəl ˌedjʊˈkeɪʃən‖ˌedʒə-/ n

also **additive bilingualism** /ˈædɪtɪv baɪˈlɪŋgwəlɪzəm/

a form of BILINGUAL EDUCATION in which the language of instruction is not the mother tongue or home language of the children, and is not intended to replace it. In an additive bilingual education programme the first language is maintained and supported.

For example, the bilingual programmes in French for English-speaking Canadians are intended to give the children a second language, not to replace English with French.

When the language of instruction is likely to replace the children's first language, this is called **subtractive bilingualism**.

see also IMMERSION PROGRAMME

Further reading Swain 1978; Appel & Musken 1987

address form /əˈdres ˌfɔːm‖ˌfɔːrm/ n

also **address term, form/term of address**

the word or words used to address somebody in speech or writing. The way in which people address one another usually depends on their age, sex, social group, and personal relationship.

For example, many languages have different second person pronoun forms which are used according to whether the speaker wants to address someone politely or more informally, e.g. in German *Sie – du*, in French *vous – tu*, in Spanish *usted – tu* and in Mandarin Chinese *nín – nǐ* (you).

If a language has only one second person pronoun form, eg English *you*, other address forms are used to show formality or informality, e.g. *Sir, Mr Brown, Brown, Bill*. In some languages, such as Chinese dialects and Japanese, words expressing relationship, e.g. father, mother, aunt, or position, e.g. teacher, lecturer, are used as address forms to show respect and/or signal the formality of the situation, for example:

Mandarin Chinese: *bàba   qǐng   chī*
father please eat!

Japanese: *sensei   dozo!* (a polite request)
teacher/sir please!

The address forms of a language are arranged into a complex **address system** with its own rules which need to be acquired if a person wants to communicate appropriately.

see also COMMUNICATIVE COMPETENCE

Further reading Brown & Gilman 1972; Wardhaugh 1986

address system /əˈdres ˌsɪstɪm/ n

see ADDRESS FORM

address term /əˈdres ˌtɜːm‖ˌtɜːrm/ n

see ADDRESS FORM

6

adjacency pair /əˈdʒeɪsənsi ˌpeəʳ/ *n*

a sequence of two related utterances by two different speakers. The second utterance is always a response to the first.

In the following example, speaker A makes a complaint, and speaker B replies with a denial:

A: *You left the light on.*

B: *It wasn't me!*

The sequence of *complaint – denial* is an adjacency pair. Other examples of adjacency pairs are *greeting – greeting, question – answer, invitation – acceptance/non-acceptance, offer – acceptance/non-acceptance, complaint – apology.*

Adjacency pairs are part of the structure of conversation and are studied in CONVERSATIONAL ANALYSIS.

Further reading Coulthard 1985

adjacency parameter /əˈdʒeɪsənsiː pəˈræmɪtəʳ/ *n*

(in GOVERNMENT/BINDING THEORY) one of the conditions (PARAMETERS) which may vary from one language to another.

For example, English requires that the element in the sentence which "assigns" the case (see CASE ASSIGNER) has to be next (adjacent) to the noun phrase that receives the case, e.g.:

She	*liked*	*him*	*very much.*
	verb	noun phrase	
	(case assigner)	(object case)	

but not:

*She liked very much him.

Other languages, such as French, do not have this restriction:

J'aime beaucoup la France.

In second language acquisition research, investigations have been made into this variation of the adjacency condition. For example, how do native speakers of French, which has a [–adjacency] parameter, deal with a language which has a [+adjacency] parameter, such as English? Do they transfer their native [–adjacency] condition into English or not?

see also PRO-DROP PARAMETER

Further reading Cook 1988; White 1989b

adjacency principle /əˈdʒeɪsənsi ˌprɪnsɪpəl/ *n*

in some linguistic theories, the concept that two syntactic constituents must be next (adjacent) to each other and cannot be separated by other constituents.

For example, in English, a noun phrase (NP) complement must be adjacent to its verb, e.g.:

She threw the parcel into the car

verb NP complement

but not:

* She threw into the car the parcel

verb NP complement

see also ADJACENCY PARAMETER
Further reading Radford 1988

adjectival noun /ˌædʒɪk'taɪvəl 'naʊn/ *n*
an adjective used as a noun, e.g. *the poor, the rich, the sick, the old.*
see also SUBSTANTIVE

adjective /'ædʒɪktɪv/ *n*
a word that describes the thing, quality, state, or action which a noun
refers to. For example *black* in *a black hat* is an adjective. In English,
adjectives usually have the following properties:
a they can be used before a noun, e.g. *a heavy bag*
b they can be used after *be, become, seem,* etc. as complements, e.g. *the
 bag is heavy*
c they can be used after a noun as a complement, e.g. *these books make
 the bag heavy*
d they can be modified by an adverb, e.g. *a very heavy bag*
e they can be used in a comparative or superlative form, e.g. *the bag
 seems heavier now*
see also COMPLEMENT, COMPARATIVE, ATTRIBUTIVE ADJECTIVE
Further reading Quirk et al 1985

adjective complement /'ædʒɪktɪv 'kɒmplɪmənt‖'kɑːm-/ *n*
see COMPLEMENT

adjective phrase /'ædʒɪktɪv 'freɪz/ *n*
a phrase that functions as an adjective. For example,
 The woman in the corner is from Italy.

adjunct /'ædʒʌŋkt/ *n*
ADVERBIALS may be classified as adjuncts, conjuncts, or disjuncts.
An **adjunct** is part of the basic structure of the clause or sentence
in which it occurs, and modifies the verb. Adverbs of time, place,
frequency, degree, and manner, are examples of adjuncts.
 He died in England.
 I have almost finished.
Conjuncts are not part of the basic structure of a clause or sentence.
They show how what is said in the sentence containing the conjunct
connects with what is said in another sentence or sentences.
 Altogether, it was a happy week.
 However the weather was not good.
Disjuncts (also called **sentential adverbs**) are adverbs which show the
speaker's attitude to or evaluation of what is said in the rest of the
sentence.
 Naturally, I paid for my own meal.
 I had to pay for my own meal, unfortunately.
see also ADVERB
Further reading Quirk et al 1985

8

adjunction /ə'dʒʌŋkʃən/ *n*

(in TRANSFORMATIONAL GENERATIVE GRAMMAR) a kind of movement of elements within a sentence. EXTRAPOSITION, the movement of an element to another part of the sentence, is an adjunction movement. For example:

A good article on waste recycling is in the paper.
A good article is in the paper on waste recycling.

Here a prepositional phrase *on waste recycling* which was part of the noun phrase *a good article on waste recycling* has been extracted and attached to the end of the sentence. In the terms of Transformational Grammar: it is now attached to a higher NODE.

Adjunction is governed by rules which may vary from one language to another.

Further reading Radford 1988

adnominal /əd'nɒmɪ̩nəl‖æd'nɑː-/ *n, adj*

a word or phrase which occurs next to a noun and which gives further information about it.

For example, an adnominal may be:
a an adjective,
  e.g. *blue* in *the blue sea*
b another noun,
  e.g. *jade* in *the jade statue*
c a phrase,
  e.g. *at the corner* in *the shop at the corner*
An adnominal is a type of MODIFIER.

advance organizer /əd'vɑːns 'ɔːgənaɪzəʳ‖əd'væns 'ɔːr-/ *n*

(in teaching) an activity which helps students organize their thoughts and ideas as a preparation for learning or studying something. For example, a discussion which takes place before students listen to a lecture and which is intended to help them follow the lecture more easily, or a preview of the main ideas covered in a reading passage before reading it.

Further reading Omaggio 1986

adverb /'ædvɜːb‖-ɜːrb/ *n*

a word that describes or adds to the meaning of a verb, an adjective, another adverb, or a sentence, and which answers such questions as *how?*, *where?*, or *when?*. In English many adverbs have an *-ly* ending.

For example, **adverbs of manner** e.g. *carefully, slowly*, **adverbs of place** e.g. *here, there, locally*, and **adverbs of time** e.g. *now, hourly, yesterday*.

A phrase or clause which functions as an adverb is called an **adverb phrase/adverb clause**.

see also ADVERBIAL, ADVERB PARTICLE, ADVERBIAL CLAUSE, ADJUNCT

adverbial /əd'vɜːbiəl‖-ɜːr-/ *adj*

any word, phrase, or clause that functions like an ADVERB. An adverb is a single-word adverbial.

9

adverbial clause /əd'vɜːbiəl 'klɔːz‖-ɜːr-/ *n*
a clause which functions as an adverb.
For example:
> *When I arrived I went straight to my room.* (adverbial clause of time)
> <u>*Wherever we looked*</u> *there was dust.* (adverbial clause of place)
> *We painted the walls yellow* <u>*to brighten the room*</u>. (adverbial clause of purpose)

see also ADVERB, PREPOSITION
Further reading Quirk et al 1985

adverbial phrase /əd'vɜːbiəl 'freɪz‖-ɜːr-/ *n*
a phrase that functions as an adverb. For example,
After dinner, we went to the movies.

adverb particle /'ædvɜːb 'pɑːtɪkəl‖'ædvɜːrb 'pɑːr-/ *n*
also **prepositional adverb**
a word such as *in, on, back*, when it modifies a verb rather than a noun. Words like *in, out, up, down, on*, may belong grammatically with both nouns (e.g. *in the box, on the wall*) and verbs (e.g. *come in, eat up, wake up, die away*). When they are linked with nouns they are known as PREPOSITIONS and when they are linked with verbs they are known as adverb particles. The combination of verb+adverb particle is known as a PHRASAL VERB.

Further reading Quirk et al 1985

affected object /ə'fektɪd 'ɒbdʒɪkt‖'ɑːb-/ *n*
see OBJECT OF RESULT

affective domain /æ'fektɪv də'meɪn, dəʊ-/ *n*
see DOMAIN[3]

affective filter hypothesis /æ'fektɪv 'fɪltəʳ haɪ,pɒθəsɪs‖-,pɑː-/ *n*
a hypothesis proposed by Krashen and associated with his monitor model of second language development (see MONITOR HYPOTHESIS). The hypothesis is based on the theory of an **affective filter**, which states that successful second language acquisition depends on the learner's feelings. Negative attitudes (including a lack of motivation or self-confidence and anxiety) are said to act as a filter, preventing the learner from making use of INPUT, and thus hindering success in language learning.

Further reading Krashen 1985

affective filtering /æ'fektɪv 'fɪltərɪŋ/ *n*
When someone selects one variety of speech as a model for learning the language, this is called affective filtering.
For example, learners will hear English spoken by many different groups (e.g. parents, teachers, different social and ethnic groups) but will often model their own speech on only one of these, such as the speech of their friends of the same group (= their PEER GROUP).

Further reading Dulay, Burt, & Krashen 1982

affective meaning /æ'fektɪv 'miːnɪŋ/ *n*
another term for CONNOTATION

affective variable /æ'fektɪv 'veərɪəbəl/ *n*
see COGNITIVE VARIABLE

affix /'æfɪks/ *n*
a letter or sound, or group of letters or sounds, (= a MORPHEME)
which is added to a word, and which changes the meaning or function
of the word.
Affixes are BOUND FORMS that can be added:

a to the beginning of a word (= a **prefix**), e.g. English *un-* which
usually changes the meaning of a word to its opposite: *kind – unkind*

b to the end of a word (= a **suffix**), e.g. English *-ness* which usually
changes an adjective into a noun: *kind – kindness*

c within a word (= an *infix*), e.g. Tagalog *-um-* which shows that a verb
is in the past tense: *sulat* "to write" – *sumulat* "wrote"

see also COMBINING FORM
Further reading Lyons 1981

affricate /'æfrɪkᵻt/ *n* **affricated** /'æfrɪkeɪtᵻd/ *adj*
a speech sound (a CONSONANT) which is produced by stopping the
airstream from the lungs, and then slowly releasing it with friction.
The first part of an affricate is similar to a STOP, the second part is
similar to a FRICATIVE.
For example, in English the /tʃ/ in /tʃaɪld/ *child*, and the /dʒ/ in /dʒæm/
jam are affricates.

see also MANNER OF ARTICULATION, PLACE OF ARTICULATION
Further reading Gimson 1989

agent /'eɪdʒənt/ *n*
(in some grammars) the noun or noun' phrase which refers to the
person or animal which performs the action of the verb.
For example, in the English sentences:
Anthea cut the grass.
The grass was cut by Anthea.
Anthea is the agent.
The term agent is sometimes used only for the noun or noun phrase
which follows *by* in passive sentences, even if it does not refer to the
performer of an action, e.g. *everyone* in *She was admired by everyone.*

see also SUBJECT, AGENTIVE CASE, AGENTIVE OBJECT
Further reading Brown & Miller 1980

agent θ-role /'eɪdʒənt 'θiːtə ˌrəʊl/
see under θ-THEORY/THETA THEORY

agentive case /'eɪdʒəntɪv ˌkeɪs/ *n*
(In CASE GRAMMAR) the noun or noun phrase that refers to the person
or animal who performs or initiates the action of the verb is in the
agentive case.

11

For example, in:
>*Tom pruned the roses.*

Tom is in the agentive case.
But the subject of the verb is not necessarily always in the agentive case. In the sentence:
>*Tom loves roses.*

Tom does not perform an action, but his attitude to roses is mentioned. *Tom* in this sentence is therefore not agentive but dative (see DATIVE CASE²).

see also CASE GRAMMAR
Further reading Fillmore 1968

agentive object /'eɪdʒəntɪv 'ɒbdʒɪkt||'ɑːb-/ *n*

the object of a verb which itself performs the action of the verb.
For example, in the sentence:
>*Fred galloped the horse.*

Fred initiates the action, but it is *the horse* which actually gallops.

see also AGENT, AGENTIVE CASE
Further reading Lyons 1981

agglutinating language /ə'gluːtɬneɪtɪŋ 'læŋgwɪdʒ/
also **agglutinative language** /ə'gluːtɬnətɪv 'læŋgwɪdʒ||-neɪtɪv/

a language in which various AFFIX*ES* may be added to the stem of a word to add to its meaning or to show its grammatical function.
For example, in Swahili *wametulipa* "they have paid us" consists of:

wa	*me*	*tu*	*lipa*

they + perfective marker + us + pay
Languages which are highly agglutinating include Finnish,
Hungarian, Swahili, and Turkish, although there is no clear-cut distinction between agglutinating languages, INFLECTING LANGUAGES, and ISOLATING LANGUAGES.
Sometimes agglutinating languages and inflecting languages are called **synthetic languages**.

Further reading Fromkin & Rodman 1983

AGR
also **agreement**

(in GOVERNMENT/BINDING THEORY) an abstract feature that shows whether singular or plural is required, e.g.:
>*The guards* (plural *stand*) *near the gate.*
>*The guard* (singular *stand*) *near the gate.*

where *plural* and *singular* are the possible choices for AGR
Further reading Cook 1988

agrammatism /eɪ'græmətɪzəm/ *n*

see APHASIA

agraphia /eɪ'græfɪə/ *n*

see APHASIA

agreement /əˈgriːmənt/ *n*
another term for CONCORD

AI /ˌeɪ ˈaɪ/ *n*
an abbreviation for ARTIFICIAL INTELLIGENCE

aim /eɪm/ *n*
see OBJECTIVE

alexia /eɪˈleksiə/ *n*
see APHASIA

alienable possession /ˈeɪliənəbəl pəˈzeʃən/ *n*
see INALIENABLE POSSESSION

alliteration /əˌlɪtəˈreɪʃən/ *n*
the repetition of an initial sound, usually a consonant, in two or more words that occur close together. For example:
_D_own the _d_rive _d_ashed _d_ashing _D_an.

allomorph /ˈæləmɔːf‖-mɔːrf/ *n*
any of the different forms of a MORPHEME.
For example, in English the plural morpheme is often shown in writing by adding -*s* to the end of a word, e.g. *cat* /kæt/ – *cats* /kæts/. Sometimes this plural morpheme is pronounced /z/, e.g. *dog* /dɒg/ – *dogs* /dɒgz/, and sometimes it is pronounced /ɪz/, e.g. *class* /klɑːs/ – *classes* /ˈklɑːsɪz/.
/s/, /z/, and /ɪz/ all have the same grammatical function in these examples, they all show plural; they are all allomorphs of the plural morpheme.
Further reading Fromkin & Rodman 1983

allophone /ˈæləfəʊn/ *n* **allophonic** /ˌæləˈfɒnɪk◄‖-ˈfɑː-/ *adj*
any of the different forms of a PHONEME.
For example, in English, when the phoneme /p/ occurs at the beginning of words like *put* /pʊt/ and *pair* /peəʳ/, it is said with a little puff of air (i.e. it is **aspirated** see ASPIRATION). But when /p/ occurs in words like *span* /spæn/ and *spare* /speəʳ/ it is said without the puff of air, it is **unaspirated**. Both the unaspirated /p/ (or [p]) in *span* and the aspirated /p/ (or [pʰ]) in *put* have the same phonemic function, i.e. they are both heard and identified as /p/ and not as /b/; they are both allophones of the phoneme /p/.
Further reading Gimson 1989

alphabet /ˈælfəbet/ *n* **alphabetic** /ˌælfəˈbetɪk◄/ *adj*
a set of letters which are used to write a language.
The English alphabet uses roman script and consists of 26 letters – a, b, c, etc.
The Russian alphabet uses cyrillic script and consists of 31 letters – а, б, в, etc.

The Arabic alphabet uses arabic script and consists of 29 letters – ا, ب, ت, etc.

see also ALPHABETIC WRITING

alphabetic method /ˈælfəbetɪk ˈmeθəd/ n

a method of teaching children to read. It is used in teaching reading in the mother tongue.

Children are taught the names of the letters of the alphabet – *a* "ay", *b* "bee", *c* "see", etc. – and when they see a new or unfamiliar word, e.g. *bag*, they repeat the letter names – "bee ay gee". It is thought that this "spelling" of the word helps the child to recognize it.

see also PHONICS
Further reading Goodacre 1978

alphabetic writing /ˈælfəbetɪk ˈraɪtɪŋ/ n

a writing system made up of separate letters which represent sounds (see ALPHABET).

Some examples of alphabetic writing systems are:

a Roman (or Latin) script, used for many European languages including English. It has also been adopted for many non-European languages, e.g. Swahili, Indonesian and Turkish.

b Arabic script, used for Arabic and languages such as Persian, Urdu and Malay, which also uses Roman script.

c Cyrillic script, used for Russian and languages such as Ukrainian and Bulgarian.

see also IDIOGRAPHIC WRITING, SYLLABIC WRITING

alternate form reliability /ɔːlˈtɜːnɪ�ჳt fɔːm rɪˌlaɪəˈbɪlჳti‖ˈɔːltɜːr-, ˈæl-fɔːrm rɪˌlaɪəˈbɪlჳti/ n

also parallel form reliability, equivalent form reliability

(in testing) an estimate of the RELIABILITY of a test, usually employing a correlation between two or more forms of a test which are equivalent in content and difficulty.

see also CORRELATION
Further reading Ebel 1972

alternate forms /ɔːlˈtɜːnɪ̳t ˈfɔːmz‖ˈɔːltɜːr-, ˈæl- ˈfɔːrmz/ n

another term for PARALLEL FORMS

alternate response item /ɔːlˈtɜːnɪ̳t rɪˈspɒns ˌaɪtəm‖ˈɔːltɜːr-, ˈæl--ˈspɑːns/ n

see TEST ITEM

alternation /ˌɔːltəˈneɪʃən‖ˌɔːltər-, ˌæltər-/ n alternant /ɔːlˈtɜːnənt‖ˈɔːltɜːr-, ˈæl-/ n

The relationship between the different forms of a linguistic unit is called alternation. The term is used especially in MORPHOLOGY and in PHONOLOGY.

For example, the related vowels /iː/ and /e/ in:
 deceive /dɪˈsiːv/ *deception* /dɪˈsepʃən/
 receive /rɪˈsiːv/ *reception* /rɪˈsepʃən/
are in alternation.

The ALLOPHONES of a PHONEME and the ALLOMORPHS of a MORPHEME are also in alternation, or alternants.

Further reading Hyman 1975

alternation rules /ˌɔːltəˈneɪʃən ruːlz||ˌɔːltər-, ˌæl-/ *n*

see SPEECH STYLES

alternative /ɔːlˈtɜːnətɪv||ɔːlˈtɜːr-, æl-/ *n*

see MULTIPLE-CHOICE ITEM

alveolar /ˌælviˈəʊləʳ◄, ælˈvɪələʳ/ *adj*

describes a speech sound (a CONSONANT) which is produced by the front of the tongue touching or nearly touching the gum ridge behind the upper teeth (the **alveolar ridge**).

For example, in English the /t/ in /tɪn/ *tin*, and the /d/ in /dɪn/ *din* are alveolar STOPS.

In English alveolar stops are made with the tip of the tongue, but alveolar FRICATIVES – the /s/ in /sɪp/ *sip*, and the /z/ in /zuː/ *zoo* – are made with the part of the tongue which is just behind the tip, the blade.

see also LAMINAL, PLACE OF ARTICULATION, MANNER OF ARTICULATION
Further reading Gimson 1989

alveolar ridge /ˈælviəʊləʳ ˈrɪdʒ, ælˈvɪələʳ/ *n*
also alveolum /ˌælviˈəʊləm, ælˈvɪələm/

see PLACE OF ARTICULATION

ambiguous /æmˈbɪgjuəs/ *adj* ambiguity /ˌæmbɪˈgjuːⁱti/ *n*

A word, phrase, or sentence which has more than one meaning is said to be ambiguous.

An example of **grammatical ambiguity** is the sentence:
 The lamb is too hot to eat.
which can mean either:
a the lamb is so hot that it cannot eat anything
or:
b the cooked lamb is too hot for someone to eat it
There are several types of **lexical ambiguity**:
a a word can have several meanings, e.g. *face* meaning "human face", "face of a clock", "cliff face" (see also POLYSEMY)
b two or more words can sound the same but have different meanings, e.g. *bank* in *to put money in a bank, the bank of a river* (see also HOMONYMS³)
Usually, additional information either from the speaker or writer or from the situation indicates which meaning is intended.
Ambiguity is used extensively in creative writing, especially in poetry.

15

see also DISAMBIGUATION
Further reading Fromkin & Rodman 1983; Burton-Roberts 1986

Ameslan /'æmɪ̩zlæn/ *n*
an acronym for American Sign Language
see SIGN LANGUAGE

analogue data /'ænəlɒg 'deɪtə, 'dɑːtə||-lɔːg, -lɑːg/ *n*
(in sound recording) data which is represented in continuous form, as contrasted with **digital data** which is represented in discrete or discontinuous form. A record or audiocassette is an analogue recording because the sound patterns are analogous to the actual sound waves. In a digital recording, a periodic sampling of sound wave forms is taken and recorded as binary digital data, a form which can be understood by a computer. This process is known as analogue-to-digital conversion. The reverse process is used to convert the data back into a sound signal.

analogy /ə'næləʤi/ *n*
another term for OVERGENERALIZATION

analysis of covariance /ə'nælɪ̩sɪ̩s əv ˌkəʊ'veəriəns/ *n*
also **ancova**
(in statistics) a procedure similar to ANALYSIS OF VARIANCE, used to statistically equate groups in order to control the effects of one or more variables. For example if we were comparing the effect of a teaching method on three groups of subjects, and one group had a higher MEAN IQ than the others, analysis of covariance could be used to make the groups equivalent by adjusting the effects of IQ.
Further reading Hardyck & Petrinovich 1976

analysis of variance /ə'nælɪ̩sɪ̩s əv 'veəriəns/ *n*
also **anova**
(in statistics) a procedure for testing whether the difference among the MEANs of two or more groups is significant, for example to compare the effectiveness of a teaching method on three different age groups.
see also ANALYSIS OF COVARIANCE
Further reading Hardyck & Petrinovich 1976

analytic approach /'ænəlɪtɪk ə'prəʊtʃ/ *n*
see SYNTHETIC APPROACH

analytic language /'ænəlɪtɪk 'læŋgwɪʤ/ *n*
another term for ISOLATING LANGUAGE

analytic style /'ænəlɪtɪk 'staɪl/ *n*
see GLOBAL LEARNING

anaphora /ə'næfərə/ *n* **anaphor** /'ænəfɔːʳ/ *n* **anaphoric** /ˌænə'fɒrɪk◄|| -'fɔːr-, -'fɑːr-/ *adj*

a process where a word or phrase (**anaphor**) refers back to another word or phrase which was used earlier in a text or conversation.
For example, in:
    Tom likes ice cream but Bill can't eat it
the word *it* refers back to *ice cream*: it is a substitute for *ice cream*, which is called the ANTECEDENT of *it*.
Some verbs may be anaphoric, for example the verb *do* in:
    Mary works hard and so does Doris
does is anaphoric and is a substitute for *works*.
In BINDING THEORY the term *anaphor* refers to a somewhat different concept and is subject to certain restrictions (see under BINDING PRINCIPLE).

Further reading Quirk et al 1985

ancova /æŋ'kəʊvə/ *n*

another term for ANALYSIS OF COVARIANCE

animate noun /'ænɪ̞mɪ̞t 'naʊn/ *n*

a noun which refers to a living being, for example persons, animals, fish, etc.
For example, the English nouns *woman* and *fish* are animate nouns.
Nouns like *stone* and *water* are called *inanimate nouns*.

see also SEMANTIC FEATURES
Further reading Quirk et al 1985

anomia /eɪ'nəʊmiə/ *n*

see APHASIA

anomie (also **anomy**) /'ænəmi/ *n*

feelings of social uncertainty or dissatisfaction which people who do not have strong attachments to a particular social group may have. Anomie has been studied as an affective variable (see COGNITIVE VARIABLE) in second/foreign language learning. In learning a new language people may begin to move away from their own language and culture, and have feelings of insecurity. At the same time they may not be sure about their feelings towards the new language group. Feelings of anomie may be highest when a high level of language ability is reached. This may lead a person to look for chances to speak their own language as a relief.

Further reading Lambert 1967

anova /'ænəʊvə/ *n*

another term for ANALYSIS OF VARIANCE

antecedent /ˌæntɪ̞'siːdənt/ *n*

see ANAPHORA

anthropological linguistics /ˌænθrəpə'lɒdʒɪkəl lɪŋ'gwɪstɪks‖-'lɑː-/ *n*

a branch of linguistics which studies the relationship between language and culture in a community, e.g. its traditions, beliefs, and family structure.

For example, anthropological linguists have studied the ways in which relationships within the family are expressed in different cultures (kinship terminology), and they have studied how people communicate with one another at certain social and cultural events, e.g. ceremonies, rituals, and meetings, and then related this to the overall structure of the particular community.

Some areas of anthropological linguistics are closely related to areas of SOCIOLINGUISTICS and the ETHNOGRAPHY OF COMMUNICATION.

Further reading Ardener 1971

anticipation error /æn͵tɪsɪˈpeɪʃən ͵erəʳ/ *n*

see SPEECH ERRORS

anticipatory subject /æn͵tɪsɪˈpeɪtəri ˈsʌbdʒɪkt‖ænˈtɪsɪpeɪtəri, -əpətɔːri/ *n*

see EXTRAPOSITION

antonym /ˈæntənɪm/ *n* **antonymy** /ænˈtɒnɪmi‖-ˈtɑː-/ *n*

a word which is opposite in meaning to another word.

For example, in English *male* and *female*, and *big* and *small* are antonyms.

A distinction is sometimes made between pairs like *male* and *female*, and pairs like *big* and *small*, according to whether or not the words are gradable (see GRADABLE).

A person who is not *male* must be *female*, but something which is not *big* is not necessarily *small*, it may be somewhere between the two sizes.

Male and *female* are called **complementaries** (or ungradable antonyms); *big* and *small* are called gradable antonyms or a **gradable pair**.

Some linguists use the term antonym to mean only gradable pairs.

see also SYNONYM

Further reading Fromkin & Rodman 1983; Lyons 1981

apex /ˈeɪpeks/ *n*

the tip of the tongue

see also APICAL, PLACE OF ARTICULATION

aphasia /əˈfeɪʒə/ *n* **aphasic** /əˈfeɪzɪk/ *adj*
also **dysphasia** *n*

loss of the ability to use and understand language, usually caused by damage to the brain. The loss may be total or partial, and may affect spoken and/or written language ability.

There are different types of aphasia: **agraphia** is difficulty in writing; **alexia** is difficulty in reading; **anomia** is difficulty in using proper nouns; and **agrammatism** is difficulty in using grammatical words like prepositions, articles, etc.

Aphasia can be studied in order to discover how the brain processes language.

see also BRAIN, NEUROLINGUISTICS
Further reading Dalton & Hardcastle 1977

apical /'eɪpɪkəl, 'æp-/ *adj*

describes a speech sound (a CONSONANT) which is produced by the tip
of the tongue (the **apex**) touching some part of the mouth.
For example, in English the /t/ in /tɪn / *tin* is an apical STOP.
If the tongue touches the upper teeth, the sounds are sometimes called
apico-dental, e.g. French and German /t/ and /d/.
If the tongue touches the gum ridge behind the upper teeth (the
alveolar ridge), the sounds are sometimes called **apico-alveolar**, e.g.
English /t/ and /d/.

see also PLACE OF ARTICULATION, MANNER OF ARTICULATION
Further reading Gimson 1989

a posteriori syllabus /ˌeɪ pɒstɪəri'ɔːraɪ 'sɪləbəs, ˌɑː pɒstɪəri'ɔːriː‖ pɑː-/ *n*

SEE A PRIORI SYLLABUS

apostrophe s /ə'pɒstrəfi 'es‖ə'pɑː-/ *n*

the ending *'s* which is added to nouns in English to indicate
possession. For example:
Michael's son
The director's car

applications program /æplɪ'keɪʃənz ˌprəʊgræm/ *n*

a *computer program* that has been developed to meet a specific set of
needs, such as those used in word processing (see WORD PROCESSOR).
Applications programs are distinct from programs which control the
operation of the computer itself, i.e. systems programs.

applied linguistics /ə'plaɪd lɪŋ'gwɪstɪks/ *n*

1 the study of second and foreign language learning and teaching.
2 the study of language and linguistics in relation to practical
problems, such as LEXICOGRAPHY, TRANSLATION, SPEECH PATHOLOGY,
etc. Applied linguistics uses information from sociology, psychology,
anthropology, and INFORMATION THEORY as well as from linguistics in
order to develop its own theoretical models of language and language
use, and then uses this information and theory in practical areas such
as syllabus design, SPEECH THERAPY, LANGUAGE PLANNING, STYLISTICS,
etc.

see also ETHNOGRAPHY OF COMMUNICATION
Further reading Stern 1983

apposition /ˌæpə'zɪʃən/ *n* appositive /ə'pɒzɪtɪv‖-'pɑː-/ *n, adj*

When two words, phrases, or clauses in a sentence have the same
REFERENCE, they are said to be in apposition.
For example, in the sentence:
My sister, Helen Wilson, will travel with me.

My sister and *Helen Wilson* refer to the same person, and are called appositives.

The sentence can be rewritten with either of the two appositives missing, and still make sense:

My sister will travel with me.

Helen Wilson will travel with me.

Further reading Quirk et al 1985

appreciative comprehension /ə'priːʃətɪv ˌkɒmprɪ'henʃən‖ˌkɑːm-/ *n*
see READING

approach /ə'prəutʃ/ *n*
Language teaching is sometimes discussed in terms of three related aspects: approach, METHOD, and **technique**.

Different theories about the nature of language and how languages are learned (the approach) imply different ways of teaching language (the method), and different methods make use of different kinds of classroom activity (the technique).

Examples of different approaches are the aural-oral approach (see AUDIOLINGUAL METHOD), the COGNITIVE CODE APPROACH, the COMMUNICATIVE APPROACH, etc. Examples of different methods which are based on a particular approach are the AUDIOLINGUAL METHOD, the DIRECT METHOD, etc. Examples of techniques used in particular methods are DRILLS, DIALOGUES, ROLE-PLAYS, sentence completion, etc.

Further reading Anthony 1963; Richards & Rodgers 1986

appropriateness /ə'prəupri-ɪ̯tnɪ̯s/ *n* appropriate /ə'prəupri-ɪ̯t/ *adj*
When producing an utterance, a speaker needs to know that it is grammatical, and also that it is suitable (appropriate) for the particular situation.

For example:

Give me a glass of water!

is grammatical, but it would not be appropriate if the speaker wanted to be polite. A request such as:

May I have a glass of water, please?

would be more appropriate.

see also GRAMMATICAL[1,2], CORRECT, COMMUNICATIVE COMPETENCE
Further reading Hymes 1977

appropriate word method /ə'prəupri-ɪ̯t 'wɜːd ˌmeθəd‖'wɜːrd/ *n*
see CLOZE PROCEDURE

approximative system /ə'prɒksɪ̯mətɪv 'sɪstɪ̯m‖ə'prɑːksɪ̯meɪtɪv/ *n*
see INTERLANGUAGE

a priori syllabus /ˌeɪ praɪ'ɔːraɪ 'sɪləbəs, ˌɑː priː'ɔːriː/ *n*
In language teaching, a distinction is sometimes made between two kinds of syllabuses. A syllabus prepared in advance of a course, and

used as a basis for developing classroom activities, may be referred to as an a priori syllabus. This may be contrasted with a syllabus which is not developed in advance but which is prepared after a course is taught, as a "record" of the language and activities used in the course (an **a posteriori syllabus**). An a posteriori syllabus is sometimes called a **retrospective syllabus.**

see also SYLLABUS

aptitude /'æptɪtjuːd||-tuːd/ *n*
 see LANGUAGE APTITUDE

aptitude test /'æptɪtjuːd ˌtest||-tuːd/ *n*
 see LANGUAGE APTITUDE TEST

areal linguistics /'eəriəl lɪŋ'gwɪstɪks/ *n*
 the study of the languages or dialects which are spoken in a particular area.
 An example is a study of two neighbouring languages to see how they influence each other in terms of grammar, vocabulary, pronunciation, etc.

see also DIALECTOLOGY

argument /'ɑːgjʊmənt||'ɑːr-/ *n*
 see PROPOSITION

argumentation /ˌɑːgjʊmen'teɪʃən||ˌɑːr-/
 see ESSAY

article /'ɑːtɪkəl||'ɑːr-/ *n*
 a word which is used with a noun, and which shows whether the noun refers to something definite or something indefinite.
 For example, English has two articles: the **definite article** *the*, and the **indefinite article** *a* or *an*.
 The main use of the definite article in English is to show that the noun refers to a particular example of something, e.g.:
 a by referring to something which is known to both the speaker and the hearer:
 She is in the garden.
 He is at the post office.
 b by referring backwards to something already mentioned:
 There is a man waiting outside. Who, the man in the brown coat?
 c by referring forward to something:
 The chair in the living room is broken.
 d by referring to something as a group or class:
 The lion is a dangerous animal.
 The main use of the indefinite article in English is to show that the noun refers to something general or to something which has not been identified by the speaker, e.g.:

a by referring to one example of a group or class:
   Pass me a pencil, please.
b by referring to something as an example of a group or class:
   A dog is a friendly animal.
When nouns are used without an article in English, this is sometimes called **zero article**. For example:
   Cats like sleeping.
   Silver is a precious metal.

see also DETERMINER
Further reading Quirk et al 1985

articulation /ɑːˌtɪkjʊˈleɪʃən‖ɑːr-/ *n* **articulate** /ɑːˈtɪkjʊleɪt‖ɑːr-/ *v*
the production of speech sounds in the mouth and throat (see VOCAL TRACT). In describing and analysing speech sounds a distinction is made between the MANNER OF ARTICULATION and the PLACE OF ARTICULATION.
Further reading Gimson 1989

articulator /ɑːˈtɪkjʊleɪtəʳ‖ɑːr-/ *n*
a part of the mouth, nose, or throat which is used in producing speech, e.g. the tongue, lips, alveolar ridge, etc.
see also PLACE OF ARTICULATION

articulatory phonetics /ɑːˈtɪkjʊlətəri fəˈnetɪks‖ɑːrˈtɪkjʊlətɔːri/ *n*
see PHONETICS

artificial intelligence /ˈɑːtɪfɪʃəl ɪnˈtelɪdʒəns‖ˈɑːr-/ *n*
also **AI**
the ability of machines to carry out functions that are normally associated with human intelligence, such as reasoning, correcting, making self-improvements and learning through experience. Computer programmers try to create programs which have this capacity.

artificial language /ˈɑːtɪfɪʃəl ˈlæŋgwɪdʒ‖ˈɑːr-/ *n*
also **auxiliary language**
a language which has been invented for a particular purpose, and which has no NATIVE SPEAKERS.
For example, Esperanto was invented by L. L. Zamenhof and was intended to be learned as a second language and used for international communication.
Artificial languages are also invented for experiments on aspects of natural language use.
see also NATURAL LANGUAGE

aspect /ˈæspekt/ *n*
a grammatical category which deals with how the event described by a verb is viewed, such as whether it is in progress, habitual, repeated, momentary, etc. Aspect may be indicated by PREFIXES, SUFFIXES or other changes to the verb, or by AUXILIARY VERBS, as in English. English has two aspects: PROGRESSIVE and PERFECT.

see also TENSE[1]
Further reading Comrie 1976

Aspects Model /ˈæspekts ˌmɒdl‖ˌmɑː-/ *n*

see TRANSFORMATIONAL GENERATIVE GRAMMAR

aspiration /ˌæspɪˈreɪʃn/ *n* aspirate /ˈæspɪreɪt/ *v* aspirated /ˈæspɪreɪtɪd/ *adj*

the little puff of air that sometimes follows a speech sound.
For example, in English the /p/ is aspirated at the beginning of the word /pæn/ *pan*, but when it is preceded by an /s/, e.g. in /spæn/ *span* there is no puff of air. The /p/ in *span* is **unaspirated**.
In phonetic notation, aspiration is shown by the symbol [ʰ] or ['], e.g. [pʰɪn] or [pʹɪn] *pin*.
Aspiration increases when a word or syllable is stressed, e.g.:
 Ouch! I stepped on a PIN.
Further reading Gimson 1989

assessment /əˈsesmənt/ *n* assess /əˈses/ *v*

the measurement of the ability of a person or the quality or success of a teaching course, etc.
Assessment may be by test, interview, questionnaire, observation, etc.
For example, assessment of the comprehension of an immigrant child may be necessary to discover if the child is able to follow a course of study in a school, or whether extra language teaching is needed.
Students may be tested at the beginning and again at the end of a course of study to assess the quality of the teaching on the course.
Further reading Hughes 1989

assimilation[1] /əˌsɪmɪˈleɪʃn/ *n* assimilate /əˈsɪmɪleɪt/ *v*

When a speech sound changes, and becomes more like another sound which follows it or precedes it, this is called assimilation. For example, in English the negative PREFIX appears as *im-* before words such as *possible*: *impossible*. As *possible* starts with a BILABIAL sound, the prefix *im-* ends in a bilabial sound. Before words like *tolerant*, however, the prefix is *in-*: *intolerant*. As *tolerant* starts with an ALVEOLAR sound, the prefix *in-* ends in an alveolar sound. As the following sounds bring about the change, this process is called **regressive assimilation**.
On the other hand, the difference between the /s/ in the English word *cats* and the /z/ in the English word *dogs* is an example of **progressive assimilation** because the preceding sounds bring about the change.
Further reading Gimson 1980

assimilation[2] *n*

a process in which a group gradually gives up its own language, culture, and system of values and takes on those of another group with a different language, culture, and system of values, through a period of interaction.

see also ACCULTURATION, SOCIAL DISTANCE
Further reading Schumann 1978

associative learning /əˈsəʊʃi̩ətɪv ˈlɜːnɪŋ, -ʃtɪv‖ˈlɜːr-/ *n*

learning which happens when a connection or association is made, usually between two things.

For example:

a When someone hears the word *table*, they may think of the word *food*, because this word is often used with or near *table*. This is called **association by contiguity**.

b When someone hears the word *delicate*, they may think of the word *fragile*, because it has a similar meaning. This is called **association by similarity**.

c When someone hears the word *happy*, they may think of the word *sad*, because it has the opposite meaning. This is called **association by contrast**.

Associative learning theory has been used in studies of memory, learning, and verbal learning.

see also VERBAL LEARNING, WORD ASSOCIATION, PAIRED-ASSOCIATE LEARNING

Further reading Gagné 1970

associative meaning /əˈsəʊʃi̩ətɪv ˈmiːnɪŋ, -ʃtɪv/ *n*

The associative meaning of a word is the total of all the meanings a person thinks of when they hear the word.

For example, in a word association test a person might be given a word (a **stimulus**) and then asked to list all the things they think of (the **response**).

For example:

stimulus	response
puppy	*warm*
	young
	furry
	lively
	kitten

warm, young, furry, lively, kitten make up the associative meaning of *puppy* for that person.

Associative meaning has been used in studies of memory and thought.

see also WORD ASSOCIATION, STIMULUS-RESPONSE THEORY

Further reading Deese 1965

asyllabic /ˌeɪsɨˈlæbɪk◄/ *adj*

see SYLLABLE

atomistic approach /ˌætəˈmɪstɪk əˈprəʊtʃ/ *n*

see GESTALT PSYCHOLOGY

attention /əˈtenʃən/ *n*

the ability a person has to concentrate on something, or part of something, while ignoring other things. The length of time a person can attend to a single event or activity is sometimes called the

attention span. In learning theory the attention phase is regarded as the first stage in learning.

Further reading Gagné 1970

attitude /'ætɪtjuːd||-tuːd/ *n*

see LANGUAGE ATTITUDES

attitude scale /'ætɪtjuːd ˌskeɪl||-tuːd/ *n*

a technique for measuring a person's reaction to something.

A common scale is the **Likert Scale**. With this a statement of belief or attitude is shown to someone, and they are asked to show how strongly they agree or disagree with the statement by marking a scale like the one shown below:

Foreign languages are important for all educated adults.

1	2	3	4	5	6	7
strongly disagree		disagree		agree		strongly agree

Attitude scales have been used to study MOTIVATION in second and foreign language learning.

Further reading Oller 1979

attributive adjective /əˈtrɪbjʊtɪv ˈædʒɪktɪv/ *n*

an adjective which is used before a noun.

For example, *good* in *a good book* is an attributive adjective.

An adjective which is used after a verb, especially after the verbs *be, become, seem,* etc. is called a **predicative adjective**. For example, *good* in *The book was very good.*

Many adjectives in English are like *good,* and can be used both attributively and predicatively, but some, like *main* and *utter,* can only be used attributively, e.g. *a busy main road, an utter fool,* and some, like *afraid* and *asleep,* can only be used predicatively e.g. *The boy was asleep, The dog seems afraid.*

Many nouns in English can also be used attributively, e.g. *paper* in *a paper cup.*

see also ADJECTIVE

Further reading Quirk et al 1985

audiolingual method /ˌɔːdi-əʊˈlɪŋgwəl ˌmeθəd/ *n*
also **aural-oral method, mim-mem method**

a method of foreign or second language teaching which (a) emphasizes the teaching of speaking and listening before reading and writing (b) uses DIALOGUES and DRILLS (c) discourages use of the mother tongue in the classroom (d) often makes use of CONTRASTIVE ANALYSIS. The audiolingual method was prominent in the 1950s and 1960s, especially in the United States, and has been widely used in many other parts of the world.

The theory behind the audiolingual method is the **aural-oral approach** to language teaching, which contains the following beliefs about language and language learning: (a) speaking and listening are the most basic language skills (b) each language has its own unique structure and rule system (c) a language is learned through forming habits. These ideas were based partly on the theory of STRUCTURAL LINGUISTICS and partly on BEHAVIOURISM.

Criticism of the audiolingual method is based on criticism of its theory and its techniques (see COGNITIVE CODE APPROACH, COMMUNICATIVE APPROACH).

see also APPROACH, MIM-MEM METHOD
Further reading Rivers 1964, 1981; Richards & Rogers 1986

audio booth /ˈɔːdi-əu ˌbuːð‖buːθ/ n

see CARREL

audiology /ˌɔːdiˈɒlədʒi‖-ˈɑːl-/ n

the study of hearing and hearing disorders, particularly the nature of hearing loss and the treatment of people suffering from hearing disorders.

Further reading Boone 1987

audio-visual aid /ˈɔːdi-əuˌvɪʒuəl ˈeɪd/ n

an audio or visual device used by a teacher to help learning. For example, pictures, charts, and flashcards are visual aids; radio, records, and tape-recorders are auditory aids. Film, television, and video are audio-visual aids.

audio-visual method /ˈɔːdi-əuˌvɪʒuəl ˈmeθəd/ n
also structural global method

a method of foreign language teaching which
a teaches speaking and listening before reading and writing
b does not use the mother tongue in the classroom
c uses recorded dialogues with film-strip picture sequences to present language items
d uses drills to teach basic grammar and vocabulary.

The audio-visual method was developed in France in the 1950s, and is based on the belief that
a language is learned through communication
b translation can be avoided if new language items are taught in situations
c choice of items for teaching should be based on a careful analysis of the language being taught.

see also AUDIOLINGUAL METHOD
Further reading Gougenheim et al 1964

auditory /ˈɔːdɪ̯təri‖-tɔːri/ adj

of or related to hearing

26

auditory discrimination /'ɔːdʒtəri dɪˌskrɪmɪ̩'neɪʃən‖-tɔːri/ *n*
the ability to hear and recognize the different sounds in a language. In particular the ability to recognize the different PHONEMES, and the different STRESS and INTONATION patterns.
see also PERCEPTION

auditory feedback /'ɔːdʒtəri 'fiːdbæk‖-tɔːri/ *n*
When a person speaks, they can hear what they are saying, and can use this information to monitor their speech and to correct any mistakes. This is called auditory feedback.
For example, in the following utterance the speaker uses auditory feedback to correct his/her pronunciation:
Would you like a cup of cea or toffee – I mean tea or coffee?
see also FEEDBACK, DELAYED AUDITORY FEEDBACK, KINESTHETIC FEEDBACK
Further reading Dalton & Hardcastle 1977

auditory perception /'ɔːdʒtəri pə'sepʃən‖-tɔːri pər-/ *n*
see PERCEPTION

auditory phonetics /'ɔːdʒtəri fə'netɪks‖-tɔːri/ *n*
see PHONETICS

auditory/oral method /'ɔːdɪtəri 'ɔːrəl ˌmeθəd‖-tɔːri/ *n*
a method for educating deaf or HEARING-IMPAIRED children which relies on using their remaining or **residual hearing** and hearing aids. Best results are achieved through early diagnosis of the hearing loss and the use of normal language input. This is said to allow children to acquire normal language rules, and to maximize the opportunity for the learning of PROSODIC and SUPRASEGMENTAL FEATURES of speech.

aural language /'ɔːrəl 'læŋgwɪdʒ, 'aʊrəl/ *n*
also **oral language**
language that has been spoken, as compared to written language.

aural-oral approach /ˌaʊrəl 'ɔːrəl əˌprəʊtʃ/ *n*
see AUDIOLINGUAL METHOD

aural-oral method /ˌaʊrəl 'ɔːrəl ˌmeθəd/ *n*
another term for AUDIOLINGUAL METHOD

authenticity /ˌɔːθen'tɪsɪ̩ti/ *n* **authentic** /ɔː'θentɪk/ *adj*
the degree to which language teaching materials have the qualities of natural speech or writing.
Texts which are taken from newspapers, magazines, etc., and tapes of natural speech taken from ordinary radio or television programmes, etc., are called authentic materials.
When a teacher prepares texts or tapes for use in the classroom, he/she often has to use simplified examples.

authoring system /'ɔːθərɪŋ ˌsɪstɬm/ *n*
(in COMPUTER ASSISTED LEARNING) a computer program which is designed to allow teachers to write a computer lesson without requiring them to learn how to write a PROGRAM. The teacher concentrates on creating the lesson material, while the authoring system handles such things as the exercise format and the processing of answers.
Further reading Flint Smith 1989

automaticity /ˌɔːtəʊmə'tɪsɬti/ *n*
the ability to use a language using AUTOMATIC PROCESSING.

automatic processing /'ɔːtəmætɪk 'prəʊsesɪŋ‖'prɑː-/ *n*
the performance of a task without conscious or deliberate processing. In cognitive psychology, two different kinds of processing employed in carrying out tasks are distinguished. **Controlled processing** is involved when conscious effort and attention is required to perform a task. This places demands on short-term memory (see MEMORY). For example a learner driver may operate a car using controlled processing, consciously thinking about many of the decisions and operations involved while driving. **Automatic processing** is involved when the learner carries out the task without awareness or attention, making more use of information in long-term memory (see MEMORY). Many skills are considered to be 'learned' when they can be performed with automatic processing.
In language learning, the distinction between controlled and automatic processing has been used to explain why learners sometimes perform differently under different conditions. For example, a learner may speak a foreign language with relatively few grammatical errors in situations where automatic processing is being used (e.g. when talking in relaxed situations among friends). The same learner may speak less fluently and make more grammatical errors when controlled processing is being used (e.g. when speaking in public before an audience). The presence of the audience distracts the speaker, who uses more controlled processing and this interferes with his or her accuracy and fluency.
Further reading O'Malley & Chamot 1989; Shiffrin & Schneider 1977; MᶜLaughlin 1987

automatic translation /'ɔːtəmætɪk træns'leɪʃən, trænz-/ *n*
see under COMPUTATIONAL LINGUISTICS

auxiliary /ɔːg'zɪljəri ɔːk-‖ɔːg'zɪljəri, -'zɪləri/ *n*
another term for AUXILIARY VERB

auxiliary language /ɔːg'zɪljəri 'læŋgwɪdʒ, ɔːk-‖ɔːg'zɪljəri, -'zɪləri/ *n*
another term for LINGUA FRANCA and ARTIFICIAL LANGUAGE

28

auxiliary verb /ɔːgˈzɪljəri ˈvɜːb, ɔːk-‖ɔːgˈzɪljəri, -ˈzɪləri ˈvɜːrb/ *n*
also **auxiliary**

a verb which is used with another verb in a sentence, and which shows grammatical functions such as ASPECT, VOICE[1], MOOD, TENSE[1], and PERSON.

In English *be*, *do*, and *have* and the MODAL verbs like *may*, *can*, and *will* are all auxiliaries. For example:

She is working.
He didn't come.
They have finished.
You may go now.
Can you manage?
They will arrive tomorrow.

The verbs *working*, *come*, *finished*, *go*, *manage*, and *arrive* in these sentences are called **lexical verbs**, or **full verbs**. Lexical verbs can be used as the only verb in a sentence, e.g. *She works at the factory*. *Be*, *do*, and *have* can also be used as lexical verbs, e.g. *He is happy*, *She does computer studies at university*, and *They have three children*.

Further reading Quirk et al 1985

availability /əˌveɪləˈbɪləti/ *n* **available** /əˈveɪləbəl/ *adj*

When students are asked to think of the words that can be used to talk about a particular topic, they will be able to think of some words immediately. Those words which they remember first and most easily are said to have a high availability.

For example, when a group of secondary school children were asked to list words for *parts of the body*, they included *leg*, *hand*, *eye*, *nose*, and *ears*. These were the five most available words.

Available words are not always the most frequently occurring words in a language. Lists of available words have been used to choose vocabulary for language teaching.

Further reading Savard & Richards 1969

avoidance strategy /əˈvɔɪdəns ˌstrætʃdʒi/ *n*

When speaking or writing a second/foreign language, a speaker will often try to avoid using a difficult word or structure, and will use a simpler word or structure instead. This is called an avoidance strategy. For example, a student who is not sure of the use of the relative clause in English may avoid using it and use two simpler sentences instead. e.g.:

That's my building. I live there.

instead of:

That's the building where I live.

Further reading Faerch & Kasper 1983; Schachter 1974

B

babbling /'bæblɪŋ/ n

speech-like sounds produced by very young children.
Babies begin to produce babbling sounds like /dæ/, /mæ/, /næ/, /bæ/, at the age of about three or four months. At around 9–12 months, real words begin to be produced.
Further reading de Villiers & de Villiers 1978

baby talk /'beɪbi ˌtɔːk/ n

another term for CARETAKER SPEECH

backchaining /'bæk,tʃeɪnɪŋ/ n

another term for BACKWARD BUILD-UP

back channel cue /'bæk 'tʃænl 'kjuː/ n

see FEEDBACK

back formation /'bæk fɔːˌmeɪʃn‖fɔːr-/ n

When a new word is made by the removal of an AFFIX from an existing word, this is called back formation.
For example, the verb *televise* was formed from the noun *television*, and the verb *peddle* was formed from the noun *peddler*.
New words are usually formed by adding affixes to existing words (see DERIVATION).

background /'bækgraʊnd/ n

see FUNCTIONAL SENTENCE PERSPECTIVE

background information /'bækgraʊnd ˌɪnfə'meɪʃn‖ ˌɪnfər-/ n

see GROUNDING

back-shift /'bækʃɪft/ n

see DIRECT SPEECH

backsliding /'bækslaɪdɪŋ/ n

(in *second language acquisition*) the regular reappearance of features of a learner's INTERLANGUAGE which were thought to have disappeared.
Sometimes a learner who appears to have control of an area of grammar or phonology will have difficulty with particular linguistic features in situations which are stressful or which present the learner with some kind of communicative difficulty. Errors may then temporarily reappear.
Research into backsliding suggests that such errors are not random but

reflect the linguistic system the learner had learned at an earlier stage of his or her language development.

Further reading Hyltenstam 1977

back vowel /'bæk 'vauəl/ *n*

see VOWEL

backward build-up /'bækwəd 'bɪldʌp|| -wərd/ *n*
also backchaining

a language teaching technique in which an utterance is divided into parts, and then the students are taught to say it by repeating the last part, and then the last two parts, etc., until they can repeat the whole utterance.

For example:

Teacher	Students
some letters	*some letters*
to post some letters	*to post some letters*
to the post office to post some letters	*to the post office to post some letters*
I'm going to the post office to post some letters.	*I'm going to the post office to post some letters.*

Further reading Rivers 1981

backwash effect /'bækwɒʃ ɪˌfekt|| -wɔːʃ, -wɑːʃ/ *n*

(in testing) the effect of a test on teaching. In some countries, for example, national language examinations have a major impact on teaching and teachers often "teach to the tests". In order to bring about changes in teaching, changes may have to be made in the tests. For example if the education department in a country wanted schools to spend more time teaching listening skills, one way to bring this about would be to introduce a listening test into state examinations. The backwash effect would be that teachers would then spend more time teaching listening skills.

balanced bilingual/'bælənst baɪ'lɪŋgwəl/ *n*

see BILINGUAL

bare infinitive /'beəʳ ɪn'fɪnᵻtɪv/ *n*

see INFINITIVE

bar notation /'bɑːʳ nəuˌteɪʃən/ *n*

(in some linguistic theories) a device used to give a more detailed and consistent analysis of constituents.

For example, the noun phrase:

the mayor of Casterbridge

can be shown as:

N – mayor
N' (called **N-bar**) – mayor of Casterbridge
N'' (called **N-double-bar**) – the mayor of Casterbridge

In a diagrammatic representation it would be:

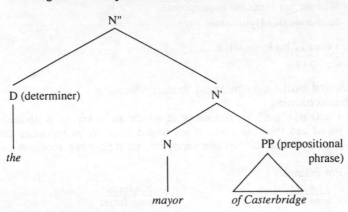

see also X-BAR THEORY
Further reading Radford 1988

basal /ˈbeɪsəl/ *adj*

When a course to teach reading has a number of graded parts, the first or most basic part is called the **basal reading programme**, and uses basic reading textbooks called **basal readers**.

base component /ˈbeɪs kəmˈpəʊnənt/ *n*
also **phrase structure component**

(In TRANSFORMATIONAL GENERATIVE GRAMMAR) the part dealing with syntax is divided into two components: the base component and the TRANSFORMATIONAL COMPONENT. The base component generates the basic sentence patterns of a language; the transformational component transforms these into sentences.

The base component consists of a set of rules and a vocabulary list **(lexicon)** which contains morphemes and idioms (see under LEXICAL ENTRY). The main rules are called **phrase structure rules** or **rewrite rules**.

For example, the rule

S → NP + VP

means that a sentence (S) can be analysed (rewritten) as consisting of a noun phrase (NP) and a verb phrase (VP).

The rule

VP → V (+NP)

means that a verb phrase can be further rewritten as simply a verb or as a verb and a noun phrase.

The lexicon gives information about the class that a word belongs to, e.g. N for nouns, V for verbs, and information about the grammatical structures with which the word may occur. For example, the English verb *sleep* cannot have an object after it. The simplified table below shows the rules and lexicon which are necessary to form the basic sentence structure for *the baby slept*.

Phrase Structure Rules	Lexicon
1. S → NP + VP 2. NP → DET(erminer) + N(oun) 3. VP → T(ense) + V(erb) 4. T(ense) → PAST	baby: N sleep: V – Object the: DET

A diagram, called a **tree diagram**, may show the way the rules are applied and how the words from the lexicon are fitted in for a particular sentence.

This simplified diagram shows the basic DEEP STRUCTURE for the sentence *The baby slept.*

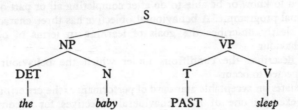

The rules of the transformational component change the above structure into the sentence *The baby slept* **(surface structure)**. see also PHRASE MARKER, PHRASE-STRUCTURE GRAMMAR, TRANSFORMATIONAL COMPONENT

Further reading Aitchison 1978; Chomsky 1965

base form /'beɪs ˌfɔːm‖ ˌfɔːrm/ *n*

another term for ROOT OR STEM[1].

For example, the English word *helpful* has the base form *help*.

Basic English /'beɪsɪk 'ɪŋglɪʃ/ *n*

Basic English is a simplified type of English developed by C. K. Ogden and I. A. Richards in 1929. It was intended to be used as a second language for international communication.

Basic English uses only 850 words and fewer grammatical rules than normal English, but it is claimed that anything that can be said in ordinary English can also be said in Basic English.

see also LINGUA FRANCA
Further reading Ogden 1930

basic interpersonal communication skills /'beɪsɪk ˌɪntə'pɜːsənəl kəˌmjuːnɪ'keɪʃən ˌskɪlz‖ˌɪntər'pɜːr-/ *n*

see COGNITIVE ACADEMIC LANGUAGE PROFICIENCY

basic skills /'beɪsɪk 'skɪlz/ *n*

(in education) skills which are considered to be an essential basis for further learning and for learning other school subjects. Reading, writing and arithmetic are often considered the basic skills in mother-tongue education.

basilect /'bæsɪlekt, 'beɪs-/ *n*

see POST-CREOLE CONTINUUM, SPEECH CONTINUUM

battery of tests /'bætəri əv 'tests/ *n*
also **test battery**

a group of tests which are given together to a student or group of students.

behavioural objective /bɪ'heɪvjərəl əb'dʒektɪv/ *n*
also **performance objective, instructional objective**

(in developing a CURRICULUM[1]) a statement of what a learner is expected to know or be able to do after completing all or part of an educational programme. A behavioural objective has three characteristics:
a it clearly describes the goals of learning in terms of observable behaviour
b it describes the conditions under which the behaviour will be expected to occur
c it states an acceptable standard of performance (the **criterion**).
For example one of the behavioural objectives for a conversation course might be:
"Given an oral request, the learner will say his/her name, address and telephone number to a native speaker of English and spell his/her name, street, city, so that an interviewer can write down the data with 100 per cent accuracy."
"Given an oral request" and "to a native speaker" describe the conditions, and "with 100 per cent accuracy" describes the criterion, in this objective.

see also OBJECTIVE
Further reading White 1988

behaviourism /bɪ'heɪvjərɪzəm/ *n*
also **behaviourist theory, behaviourist psychology**

a theory of psychology which states that human and animal behaviour can and should be studied in terms of physical processes only. It led to theories of learning which explained how an external event (a **stimulus**) caused a change in the behaviour of an individual (a **response**) without using concepts like "mind" or "ideas", or any kind of mental behaviour.
Behaviourism was an important influence on psychology, education, and language teaching, especially in the United States, and was used by psychologists like Skinner, Osgood, and Staats to explain first language learning.

see also STIMULUS-RESPONSE THEORY, COGNITIVE PSYCHOLOGY
Further reading Skinner 1957; Stern 1983

behaviourist psychology /bɪ'heɪvjərɪst saɪ'kɒlədʒi||-'kɑː-/ *n*
another term for BEHAVIOURISM

behaviourist theory /bɪˈheɪvjərɪst ˈθɪəri/ *n*
another term for BEHAVIOURISM

benefactive case /benɪˈfæktɪv ˌkeɪs/ *n*
(In CASE GRAMMAR) the noun or noun phrase that refers to the person or animal who benefits, or is meant to benefit, from the action of the verb is in the benefactive case.
For example, in the sentences:
Joan baked a cake for Louise.
Joan baked Louise a cake.
Louise is in the benefactive case.
Further reading Fillmore 1968

bicultural /baɪˈkʌltʃərəl/ *adj* **biculturalism** /baɪˈkʌltʃərəlɪzəm/ *n*
A person who knows the social habits, beliefs, customs, etc. of two different social groups can be described as bicultural.
A distinction is made between biculturalism and BILINGUALISM. For example, a person may be able to speak two languages, but may not know how to act according to the social patterns of the second or foreign language community. This person can be described as bilingual, but not as bicultural.
Further reading Romaine 1989

bidialectal /ˌbaɪdaɪəˈlektəl/ *adj* **bidialectalism** /ˌbaɪdaɪəˈlektəlɪzəm/ *n*
A person who knows and can use two different DIALECTS can be described as bidialectal. The two dialects are often a prestige dialect, which may be used at school or at work and is often the STANDARD VARIETY, and a non-prestige dialect, which may be used only at home or with friends.
see also BILINGUAL, BILINGUAL EDUCATION, DIGLOSSIA

bidialectal education /ˌbaɪdaɪəˈlektəl ˌedjʊˈkeɪʃən‖ˌedʒə-/ *n*
see BILINGUAL EDUCATION

bilabial /ˌbaɪˈleɪbiəl/ *adj*
describes a speech sound (a CONSONANT) which is produced by the two lips.
For example, in English the /p/ in /pɪn/ *pin*, and the /b/ in /bɪn/ *bin* are bilabial STOPS.
see also PLACE OF ARTICULATION, MANNER OF ARTICULATION
Further reading Gimson 1989

bilingual /baɪˈlɪŋgwəl/ *n, adj*
a person who knows and uses two languages.
In everyday use the word bilingual usually means a person who speaks, reads, or understands two languages equally well (a **balanced bilingual**), but a bilingual person usually has a better knowledge of one language than of the other.
For example, he/she may:
a be able to read and write in only one language

35

b use each language in different types of situation (domains –see DOMAIN[1]), e.g. one language at home and the other at work

c use each language for different communicative purposes, e.g. one language for talking about school life and the other for talking about personal feelings

see also BILINGUALISM, DIGLOSSIA, MULTILINGUAL

Further reading Baetens Beardsmore 1986; Romaine 1989

bilingual education /baɪˈlɪŋgwəl ˌedjʊˈkeɪʃən‖ˌedʒə-/ *n*

the use of a second or foreign language in school for the teaching of content subjects.

Bilingual education programmes may be of different types and include:

a the use of a single school language which is not the child's home language. This is sometimes called an IMMERSION PROGRAMME.

b the use of the child's home language when the child enters school but later a gradual change to the use of the school language for teaching some subjects and the home language for teaching others. This is sometimes called **maintenance bilingual education**.

c the partial or total use of the child's home language when the child enters school, and a later change to the use of the school language only. This is sometimes called **transitional bilingual education**.

When the school language is a STANDARD DIALECT and the child's home language a different dialect (e.g. Hawaiian Creole, Black English) this is sometimes called **bidialectal** or **biloquial education**.

see also BILINGUALISM, ADDITIVE BILINGUAL EDUCATION

Further reading Swain 1978; Parker 1977; Genesee 1987

bilingualism /baɪˈlɪŋgwəlɪzəm/ *n*

the use of at least two languages either by an individual (see BILINGUAL) or by a group of speakers, such as the inhabitants of a particular region or a nation.

Bilingualism is common in, for example, the Province of Quebec in Canada where both English and French are spoken, and parts of Wales, where both Welsh and English are spoken.

see also COMPOUND BILINGUALISM, DIGLOSSIA, MULTILINGUALISM

Further reading Baetens Beardsmore 1986; Romaine 1989; Wardhaugh 1986

bilingual syntax measure /baɪˈlɪŋgwəl ˈsɪntæks ˌmeʒəʳ/ *n*

a published language test which measures a child's use of grammatical structures.

In the test, the child is shown a colourful picture or set of pictures by an examiner, and is then asked questions about them. The pictures and questions are designed to make the child respond with a certain kind of grammatical structure.

Further reading Burt, Dulay, & Hernández-Chávez 1975

biliterate /baɪˈlɪtərɪt/ *n*

see LITERACY

bimodal distribution /baɪˈməʊdl ˌdɪstrɪˈbjuːʃən/ n
see MODE

binary digit /ˈbaɪnəri ˈdɪdʒɪt/ n
another term for BIT

binary feature /ˈbaɪnəri ˈfiːtʃəʳ/ n
a property of a phoneme or a word which can be used to describe the phoneme or word.
A binary feature is either present or absent.
For example, in English a /t/ sounds different from a /d/ because a /d/ is pronounced with the vocal cords vibrating (is voiced), and a /t/ is pronounced with the vocal cords not vibrating (is voiceless). VOICE is therefore one of the features which describe /d/ and /t/. This is usually shown like this:
/d/ [+voice] (= voice present)
/t/ [−voice] (= voice absent)
When a binary feature can be used to distinguish between two phonemes, like voice with /d/ and /t/, the phonemes are in **binary opposition** (see also DISTINCTIVE FEATURE.)
Binary features are also used to describe the semantic properties of words (see also SEMANTIC FEATURES).
Further reading Hyman 1975

binary opposition /ˈbaɪnəri ˌɒpəˈzɪʃən‖ˌɑː-/ n
see BINARY FEATURE

binary system /ˈbaɪnəri ˈsɪstɪm/ n
a system of expressing numbers which has only two digits, 1 and 0.
Computers use a binary system because the electronic circuits used in a computer have only two states – on and off.

binding principle /ˈbaɪndɪŋ ˌprɪnsɪpəl/ n
(in Government/Binding Theory) a principle which states whether or not expressions in a sentence refer to someone or something outside their clause or sentence or whether they are 'bound' within it.
For example, in:
Ann hurt herself.
Ann is a REFERRING EXPRESSION referring to someone in the real world and *herself* is an ANAPHOR referring to *Ann*. It is said to be 'bound' to *Ann*.
In the sentence:
Ann hurt her.
the *her* is a pronominal (see PRONOUN) which refers to another person in the real world who may or may not have been mentioned in a previous sentence or utterance. It is not 'bound' to *Ann*.
In second language research, investigations have been made into the Binding Principle in languages other than English, e.g. Korean, and how this may affect the acquisition of English.

see also BOUNDING THEORY
Further reading Bley-Vroman 1989; Cook 1988

binding theory /ˈbaɪndɪŋ ˌθɪəri/ *n*

part of the GOVERNMENT/BINDING THEORY. It examines connections between noun phrases in sentences and explores the way they relate and refer to each other (see BINDING PRINCIPLE)

bioprogram hypothesis /ˈbaɪəʊˌprəʊɡræm haɪˌpɒθ¦sɪs||-ˌpɑː-/ *n*

a theory which was proposed by Bickerton (1981) to explain the development of new languages and language development in the individual. It is suggested that people have inborn abilities to make certain basic semantic distinctions which equip them to construct a particular type of grammar. Some of the semantic distinctions which form part of the bioprogram are:

whether something is *specific* or *non-specific*
whether an occurrence is *static* or *dynamic* and
whether it is *punctual* or *non-punctual*

The first distinction relates to noun phrases, the others to verb phrases (see STATIC-DYNAMIC DISTINCTION, PUNCTUAL-NONPUNCTUAL DISTINCTION)

According to the bioprogram hypothesis, some creole languages show the underlying structures of the bioprogram, as do some of the early features used by children when they acquire their first language. It has been claimed that the closer the grammar of a child's first language is to that of the bioprogram, the faster the process of language acquisition would be. However, this claim has attracted a good deal of criticism from some applied linguists.

see also COMPETENCE, UNIVERSAL GRAMMAR
Further reading Bickerton 1981, Romaine 1988

bi-polar adjective /ˈbaɪpəʊləʳ ˈædʒ¦ktɪv/ *n*

see SEMANTIC DIFFERENTIAL

bit /bɪt/ *n*
also binary digit /ˈbaɪnəri ˈdɪdʒ¦t/

(in INFORMATION THEORY) a unit of information.

A bit is the amount of information given by a choice between two alternatives, e.g. on or off. Computers and other electronic systems measure information in bits.

Further reading Lyons 1981

black box model /ˈblæk ˈbɒks ˌmɒdl||ˈbɑːks ˌmɑː-/ *n*

A term derived from physics and used to refer to a system that can be represented in terms of observable inputs to the system and observable outputs from it, although precisely what the system is and how it works cannot be observed. The system is thus contained in a "black box". Language learning is sometimes described as a black box problem because although we can observe the language which learners hear and see and the sentences they produce, we cannot observe what goes on inside the black box, i.e., how they actually learn language.

black English /'blæk 'ɪŋglɪʃ/ *n*

the variety of English spoken by some black Americans in the United States, particularly in the inner areas of cities like New York, Chicago and Detroit. This variety is in many ways similar to the type of English spoken by Black Americans in the southern states of the USA and developed as a result of waves of migration of blacks from the south to the northern states. There are conflicting views on the origin of Black English. Some claim that it is similar to the variety of English spoken by whites in the southern states, others consider it to be a CREOLE, developed independently from Standard English (see STANDARD VARIETY)

In American schools, Black English was slow to be recognized as a variety in its own right and children speaking it were considered to be uneducated and illiterate. But researchers have shown that Black English has a structure and system of its own.

Some characteristics of Black English are:

a final consonants are sometimes deleted, for example:
   /hæn/ *hand*
b the verb is not always marked for third person singular, for example:
   He know something
c the verb *to be* is not always used as a COPULA, particularly if it can be contracted in Standard English, for example:
   We on tape (We're on tape)

see also VARIABLE[1]
Further reading Labov 1972; Wardhaugh 1986

blend / blend /*n*

another term for PORTMANTEAU WORD

Bloom's taxonomy /'bluːmz tæk'sɒnəmi‖-'saː-/ *n*

a taxonomy of OBJECTIVES for the cognitive domain (see DOMAIN) developed by the American educationalist, B. S. Bloom, and widely referred to in education and educational planning. Bloom's taxonomy consists of 6 levels, ranging from **knowledge** (which focuses on reproduction of facts) to **evaluation** (which represents higher level thinking). The six levels in Bloom's taxonomy are:

Level	Characteristic Student Behaviours
Knowledge	Remembering, memorizing, recognizing, recalling
Comprehension	Interpreting, translating from one medium to another, describing in one's own words
Application	Problem-solving, applying information to produce some result
Analysis	Subdividing something to show how it is put together, finding the underlying structure of a communication, identifying motives

| Synthesis | Creating a unique, original product that may be in verbal form or may be a physical object |
| Evaluation | Making value decisions about issues, resolving controversies or differences of opinion |

Further reading Bloom 1956

body /'bɒdi‖'baːdi/ *n*

(in composition) those sections of an ESSAY which come between the introduction and the conclusion and which support and develop the THESIS STATEMENT.

body language /'bɒdi ˌlæŋgwɪdʒ‖'baːdi/ *n*

the use of facial expressions, body movements, etc. to communicate meaning from one person to another.

In linguistics, this type of meaning is studied in PARALINGUISTICS.

see also PROXEMICS

borrowing /'bɒrəʊɪŋ‖ 'baː-,'bɔː-/ *n* borrow /'bɒrəʊ‖'baː-,'bɔː-/ *v*

a word or phrase which has been taken from one language and used in another language.

For example, English has taken *coup d'état* (the sudden seizure of government power) from French, *al fresco* (in the open air) from Italian and *moccasin* (a type of shoe) from an American Indian language.

When a borrowing is a single word, it is called a **loan word**.

Sometimes, speakers try to pronounce borrowings as they are pronounced in the original language. However, if a borrowed word or phrase is widely used, most speakers will pronounce it according to the sound system of their own language.

For example, French /garaʒ/ *garage* has become in British English /'gæ raːʒ/ or /'gærɪdʒ/, though American English keeps something like the French pronunciation.

borrowing transfer /'bɒrəʊɪŋ 'trænsfəʳ‖'baː-,'bɔː-/ *n*

see SUBSTRATUM TRANSFER

bottom-up process /ˌbɒtəm 'ʌp ˌprəʊses‖ˌbaː- ˌpraː-/ *n*

see TOP-DOWN PROCESS

boundaries /'baʊndəriz/ *n*

divisions between linguistic units. There are different types of boundaries.

For example, boundaries may be
a between words, e.g. *the##child*
b between the parts of a word such as STEM[1] and AFFIX, e.g. *kind#ness*
c between SYLLABLES, e.g. /beɪ + bi/ *baby*

see also JUNCTURE
Further reading Hyman 1975

bound form /ˈbaʊnd ˌfɔːm‖fɔːrm/ *n*
also **bound morpheme**

> a linguistic form (a MORPHEME) which is never used alone but must be used with another morpheme, e.g. as an AFFIX or COMBINING FORM. For example, the English suffix *-ing* must be used with a verb stem, e.g. *writing, loving, driving.*
>
> A form which can be used on its own is called a **free form**, e.g. *Betty, horse, red, write, love, drive.*
>
> *Further reading* Fromkin & Rodman 1983

bounding nodes /ˈbaʊndɪŋ ˌnəʊdz/ *n*

> (in BOUNDING THEORY) points (NODES) in a labelled diagram which are important for the movement of elements in a sentence.

Bounding Theory /ˈbaʊndɪŋ ˌθɪəri/ *n*

> in a Government/Binding Framework (see GOVERNMENT), a theory which is concerned with how far a constituent can move within a sentence. In a labelled diagram of a sentence structure, certain NODES have been called BOUNDING NODES, e.g. S', S, NP, and the rule is that:
>
> > A movement may not cross more than one BOUNDING NODE
>
> The rule is sometimes called the **principle of subjacency**.
>
> According to the Bounding Theory, the construction of wh- sentences in English follows the principle of subjacency. For example, the sentence in *b* below is derived from the S-STRUCTURE representation in *a*:
>
> *a* What [ₛ did Anita paint t]
>
> *b* What did Anita paint?
>
> In (a) the [ₛ stands for 'Sentence' and the t stands for 'trace' and shows the place from which the wh- word was extracted.
>
> Tests have been conducted with BILINGUAL speakers, e.g. Korean/English, Indonesian/English and Chinese/English, to determine whether the subjacency principle is in the mind of the speakers even if their own language does not make use of it. But so far the tests have not been conclusive.
>
> *Further reading* Cook 1988; Schachter 1989; White 1989

bound morpheme /ˈbaʊnd ˈmɔːfiːm‖ˈmɔːr-/ *n*

> another term for BOUND FORM

brain /breɪn/ *n*

> the organ of the body, in the upper part of the head, which controls thought and feeling.
>
> The brain consists of two main parts, the **left hemisphere** and the **right hemisphere**. As the brain develops, it is thought that different bodily functions (e.g. speech, hearing, sensations, actions) are gradually brought under the control of different areas of the brain. The development of control over different functions in different parts of the brain is known as **cerebral dominance** or **lateralization**. Those parts of the brain which control language are usually in the left hemisphere. One area in the left hemisphere is known as **Broca's area**, or the

speech centre, because it is an important area involved in speech. Damage to this area of the brain leads to different types of APHASIA. Another area called **Wernicke's area** is thought to be involved in understanding language. The exact role of these two areas in language is not yet fully understood however.

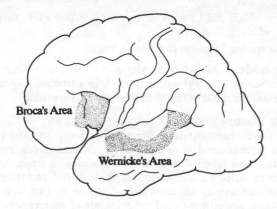

Further reading Lenneberg 1967; Penfield & Lamar Roberts 1959

brainstorming /ˈbreɪnstɔːmɪŋ‖-ɔːr-/ *n* **brainstorm** /ˈbreɪnstɔːm‖ -ɔːr-/ *v*

1 (in language teaching) a group activity in which learners have a free and relatively unstructured discussion on an assigned topic as a way of generating ideas. Brainstorming often serves as preparation for another activity.

2 (in teaching writing) a form of prewriting (see COMPOSING PROCESSES) in which a student or group of students write down as many thoughts as possible on a topic without paying attention to organization, sentence structure or spelling. Brainstorming serves to gather ideas, viewpoints, or ideas related to a writing topic and is said to help the writer produce ideas. Other writing activities sometimes included under brainstorming are:

clustering: the student writes a topic or concept in the middle of a page and gathers ideas into clusters around the topic.

word bank: the student lists words that come to mind about a topic and then arranges them into categories.

mapping: the student prepares a graphic representation of key words to be used in a composition.

Further reading Proett & Gill 1986

branching /ˈbrɑːntʃɪŋ‖ˈbræn-/ *n*

(in COMPUTER ASSISTED LEARNING) moving from one place to another within a lesson, usually on the basis of how well a student has performed on a task. The process of deciding which of several alternative paths through lesson material is best suited to the student using the program, based on previous performance, is known as **selective branching**.

Further reading Hope, Taylor & Pusack 1984

branching direction /ˈbrɑːntʃɪŋ dɪ̹ˌrekʃən,daɪ-‖ˈbræn-/ *n*

the tendency for relative clauses to follow a particular order in relation to the noun they modify. In some languages, such as English, relative clauses usually precede the noun they modify.
For example:
   The cheese that the rat ate was rotten.
English is thus said to favour a **right branching direction**. Japanese, however, primarily makes use of a **left branching direction**, because the modifying clause typically appears to the left of the head noun. For example:
   Nezumi ga tabeta cheese wa kusatte ita.
   rat   ate   cheese   rotten was
In second language learning the difficulty of learning relative clauses may be influenced by whether the learner's first language and the TARGET LANGUAGE have the same branching direction.

Further reading Odlin 1989

branching programme /ˈbrɑːntʃɪŋ ˌprəʊgræm‖ˈbræn-/ *n*

see PROGRAMMED LEARNING

breath group /ˈbreθ ˌgruːp/ *n*

a stretch of speech which is uttered during one period of breathing out.

see also SPEECH RHYTHM

broad notation /ˈbrɔːd nəʊˈteɪʃən/ *n*
also broad transcription /ˈbrɔːd trænˈskrɪpʃən/ *n*

see NOTATION

Broca's area /ˈbrəʊkəz ˌeəriə/ *n*

see BRAIN

buzz groups /ˈbʌz ˌgruːps/ *n*

(in teaching) a group activity in which groups of students have a brief discussion (for example, five minutes) to generate ideas or answer specific questions. Buzz groups may be used as preparation for a lecture, or as an activity during a lecture.

C

CA /ˌsiː'eɪ/ n

an abbreviation for CONTRASTIVE ANALYSIS

CAI /ˌsiː ˌeɪ 'aɪ/ n

an abbreviation for COMPUTER ASSISTED INSTRUCTION

CAL /kɔːl/ n

see COMPUTER ASSISTED LEARNING

CALL /kɔːl/ n

an abbreviation for COMPUTER ASSISTED LANGUAGE LEARNING

call-word /'kɔːl ˌwɜːd‖ˌwɜːrd/ n

see DRILL

CALP /kælp/ n

an abbreviation for COGNITIVE ACADEMIC LANGUAGE PROFICIENCY

calque /kælk/ n

see LOAN TRANSLATION

canonical form /kə'nɒnɪkəl 'fɔːm‖kə'nɑː-'fɔːrm/ n

the form of a linguistic item which is usually shown as the standard form.

For example, the plural morpheme in English is usually shown as -s, even though it may appear as -s, -es, -en, etc., -s is the canonical form.

cardinal number /'kɑːdɪ̩nəl 'nʌmbəʳ‖'kɑːr-/ n

also **cardinal**

see NUMBER²

cardinal vowel /'kɑːdɪ̩nəl 'vaʊəl‖'kɑːr-/ n

any of the VOWELS in the cardinal vowel system. The cardinal vowel system was invented by Daniel Jones as a means of describing the vowels in any language. The cardinal vowels themselves do not belong to any particular language, but are possible vowels to be used as reference points.

The cardinal vowel [i] is made with the front of the tongue as high as possible in the mouth without touching the roof of the mouth. It is a **front vowel**. By gradually lowering the tongue, three more front vowels were established: [e], [ɛ] and [a]. The difference in tongue position for [i] and [e], for [e] and [ɛ] and for [ɛ] and [a] is approximately equal and the difference in sound between each vowel and the next one is also similar. All these front vowels are made with fairly spread lips.

Cardinal vowel [ɑ] is made with the back of the tongue as low as possible in the mouth. It is a **back vowel**. By gradually raising the back of the tongue from the [ɑ] position, three other cardinal vowels were established: [ɔ], [o] and [u]. These three are made with the lips gradually more rounded.

These eight vowels are known as the **primary cardinal vowels**. The five vowels: [i], [e], [ɛ], [a] and [ɑ] are **unrounded vowels** and [ɔ], [o] and [u] are **rounded vowels**.

With the tongue in these eight positions, a secondary series of cardinal vowels was established. Where the primary cardinal vowels are unrounded, the **secondary cardinal vowels** are rounded. Where the primary cardinal vowels are rounded, the secondary cardinal vowels are unrounded.

	unrounded	rounded
primary	i e ɛ a ɑ	ɔ o u
	rounded	**unrounded**
secondary	y ø œ Œ ɒ	ʌ ɣ ɯ

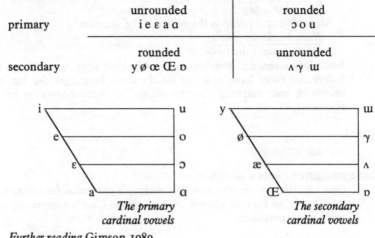

The primary cardinal vowels   *The secondary cardinal vowels*

Further reading Gimson 1989

caretaker speech /ˈkeə̯teɪkəʳ ˌspiːtʃ‖ˈkeər-/ *n*
also **motherese, mother talk, baby talk**

the simple speech used by mothers, fathers, babysitters, etc. when they talk to young children who are learning to talk.

Caretaker speech usually has:

a shorter utterances than speech to other adults
b grammatically simple utterances
c few abstract or difficult words, with a lot of repetition
d clearer pronunciation, sometimes with exaggerated INTONATION patterns

Caretaker speech is easier for children to understand, and many people believe that it helps children to learn language.

see also FOREIGNER TALK

Further reading Snow & Ferguson 1977

carrel /ˈkærəl/ *n*

in a LANGUAGE LABORATORY or video viewing station, an installation containing individual recording decks and headphones, or a video and tv monitor for student use. Carrels may be arranged in rows or other layouts. In a language laboratory, a carrel is also known as an **audio booth**.

case[1] /keɪs/ *n*

(in some languages) a grammatical category that shows the function of the noun or noun phrase in a sentence. The form of the noun or noun phrase changes (by INFLECTION) to show the different functions or cases. For example, German has four cases, NOMINATIVE, ACCUSATIVE, DATIVE, GENETIVE. Endings on the article change to show the case (the function) of the noun, e.g.:

Nominative case (table is the subject of the sentence)
Der Tisch ist gross.
The table is big.
Accusative case (table is the object of the sentence)
Karin kaufte den Tisch.
Karin bought the table.

Some languages, e.g. Russian, have more than four cases, others have fewer, and some have none at all. In these languages the functions shown by case marking may be shown by WORD ORDER or by PREPOSITIONS.

case[2]

see CASE GRAMMAR

case assigner /ˈkeɪs əˌsaɪnəʳ/ *n*

(in CASE THEORY) an element that assigns a particular function, a case (see CASE[1]), to a noun phrase in a sentence. Case assigners are often verbs or prepositions.

case grammar /ˈkeɪs ˌɡræməʳ/ *n*

an approach to grammar which stresses the semantic relationships in a sentence.

Case grammar is a type of GENERATIVE GRAMMAR developed by Fillmore.

In case grammar, the verb is regarded as the most important part of the sentence, and has a number of semantic relationships with various noun phrases. These relationships are called **cases**.

For example, in the sentences:
Smith killed the policeman with a revolver.
This revolver killed the policeman.

with a revolver and *This revolver* have different syntactic functions, but their semantic relationship with the verb *kill* is the same in both sentences. The revolver is the instrument with which the action of the verb is performed. *with a revolver* and *This revolver* are said to be in the INSTRUMENTAL CASE.

The instrumental case is just one of the cases associated with the verb *kill*. Other cases are AGENTIVE (the performer of the action – *Smith*), and DATIVE (the receiver of the action – *the policeman*).

As the examples show, case relationships can be shown in different syntactic structures. Case grammar is thus DEEP STRUCTURE..

Case grammar has been used for the grammatical description of languages, and also for the description of child language acquisition.

see also AGENTIVE CASE, BENEFACTIVE CASE, DATIVE CASE², FACTITIVE CASE, INSTRUMENTAL CASE, LOCATIVE CASE, OBJECTIVE CASE

Further reading Brown & Miller 1980; Fillmore 1968

case study /ˈkeɪs ˌstʌdi/ *n*

the intensive study of an aspect of behaviour, either at one period in time or over a long period of time, e.g. the language development of a child over one year. The case study method provides an opportunity to collect detailed information which may not be observable using other research techniques (compare CROSS-SECTION(AL) METHOD), and is usually based on the assumption that the information gathered on a particular individual, group, community etc., will also be true of the other individuals, groups or communities.

case theory /ˈkeɪs ˌθɪəri/ *n*

This theory, which is part of Chomsky's UNIVERSAL GRAMMAR, stipulates that each noun phrase in a sentence is assigned a case which shows its function in the sentence.

These cases (see CASE¹) may be shown by morphological endings; for example, in:

Monica's car

Monica is in the GENETIVE CASE. She is the possessor of the car. But in many instances the case of a noun phrase is an abstract concept which is not evident in the surface sentence. For example, in:

You should ask Paul.

Paul is in the ACCUSATIVE CASE because he is the OBJECT of *asked* but this fact is not shown by any ending. However, it becomes obvious when a pronoun is used instead of *Paul*:

You should ask him (object pronoun)

not **You should ask he*

see also θ–THEORY/THETA THEORY

Further reading Cook 1988

cataphora /ˌkəˈtæfərə/ *n* cataphoric /ˌkætəˈfɒrɪk◄||-ˈfɔːrɪk/ *adj*

The use of a word or phrase which refers forward to another word or phrase which will be used later in the text or conversation is called cataphora.

For example, in the sentence:

When I met her, Mary looked ill.

the word *her* refers forward to *Mary*.

Examples of cataphoric sentences are:

My reasons are as follows: One, I don't . . .

Here is the news. The Prime Minister. . .

see also ANAPHORA

categorize /'kætɬgəraɪz/ **categorization** /ˌkætɬgəraɪ'zeɪʃən, ˌkætɬgərɪ-/ n

to put items into groups (**categories**) according to their nature or use. For example:

a nouns may be categorized into ANIMATE and inanimate nouns.

b verbs may be categorized into TRANSITIVE and intransitive verbs.

category /'kætɬgəri‖-gɔːri/ n

see GRAMMATICAL CATEGORY

category symbol /'kætɬgəri ˌsɪmbəl‖-gɔːri/ n

see GRAMMATICAL CATEGORY[2]

category system /'kætɬgəri ˌsɪstɬm‖-gɔːri/ n

(in classroom observation and classroom research) an observation system used to code and classify different classroom behaviours. Several different category systems have been used for observing and describing language classes, including COLT (the Communicative Orientation of Language Teaching – Spada 1990), and FOCUS (Foci on Communication Used in Settings – Fanslow, 1987). Category systems attempt to provide a set of categories which can be used to objectively describe different dimensions of classroom behaviour, such as the purpose of a communicative event, the media used for communicating content, the manner in which the media are used, and the areas of content that are communicated.

see also INTERACTION ANALYSIS, HIGH INFERENCE CATEGORY

catenation /ˌkætə'neɪʃən/ n **catenate** /'kætəneɪt/ v

the linking of sounds together in speech, such as the grouping of phonemes into SYLLABLES, and the grouping of syllables and words through ASSIMILATION[1], ELISION, and JUNCTURE. Languages differ in the way they combine sounds. Two languages may share many sounds, but combine them in different ways. Spanish learners of English for example may pronounce *steak* as /estek/, because although Spanish has the combination /-st/ after a stressed vowel it does not have it before one.

causative verb /'kɔːzətɪv 'vɜːb‖'vɜːrb/ n

a verb which shows that someone or something brings about or causes an action or a state.

For example, in:

Peter killed the rabbit.

killed is a causative verb, but in:

The rabbit died.

died is not.

Some languages often form causative verbs from non-causative verbs by adding affixes, e.g. in Malay:

Gelas itu jatuh ke lantai

glass the fall to floor

"The glass fell to the floor."

> *Dia menjatuhkan gelas itu*
> He cause to fall glass the
> "He dropped the glass."

Causative verbs are always TRANSITIVE.

see also INCHOATIVE VERB

cause-effect method /'kɔːz ɪ'fekt ˌmeθəd/ *n*

see METHODS OF DEVELOPMENT

CELT /selt/ *n*

an abbreviation for **continuing education for language teachers**

see PRESERVICE EDUCATION

central nervous system /'sentrəl 'nɜːvəs ˌsɪstᵻm‖'nɜːr-/ *n*

the part of the nervous system which consists of the brain and the spinal cord.

central processing unit /'sentrəl 'prəʊsesɪŋ ˌjuːnᵻt‖'prɑː-/ *n*

the unit at the centre of a COMPUTER system which controls all the devices which do the actual work of computing.

central tendency /'sentrəl 'tendənsi/ *n*

(in statistics) any estimate of the central point around which scores tend to cluster. The most common measures of central tendency are the MODE, the MEDIAN, and the MEAN.

central vowel /'sentrəl 'vaʊəl/ *n*

see VOWEL

cerebral dominance /'serᵻbrəl 'dɒmᵻnəns‖sə'riː, 'serᵻ- 'dɑː-/ *n*

see BRAIN

channel /'tʃænl/ *n*

1 (in SOCIOLINGUISTICS) the way in which a MESSAGE is conveyed from one person to another.
The two most common channels of communication are speech and writing. Other examples are the use of drum beats, smoke signals, or flags.
2 (in INFORMATION THEORY) the path along which information is sent.
In telephone communication, for example, the message is changed into electrical signals by the telephone and the channel of communication is the telephone wire.

Further reading Hymes 1977

charged words /'tʃɑːdʒd 'wɜːdz‖'tʃɑːrdʒd 'wɜːrdz/ *n*
also **loaded words**

words which have a degree of CONNOTATION (i.e. which carry either positive or negative as opposed to neutral meaning). For example:

charged word	*neutral word*
crazy	eccentric
jock	athlete
fag	homosexual

child language /'tʃaɪld 'læŋgwɪdʒ/ n

the type of language spoken by young children who are still learning their mother tongue.
Child language is different from adult language in many ways. For example:
a different sentence structures, e.g. *Why not you coming?* instead of *Why aren't you coming?*
b different word forms, e.g. *goed* instead of *went, mouses* instead of *mice*
Differences like these show that children have their own set of rules, and do not learn language by simply imitating adults.

see also FIRST LANGUAGE ACQUISITION
Further reading Bennett-Kastor 1988; Fletcher & Garman 1979

Chi-square /'kaɪ 'skweəʳ/ n
also χ^2

(in statistics) a procedure which is used to determine whether the relationship between two or more different variables is independent. For example if we wanted to find out if there is a relationship between ability to write and belonging to a particular social or economic group, Chi-square could be used. It measures whether a particular distribution of observed values is sufficiently different from an expected distribution to indicate that it cannot be explained as a chance occurrence.

Further reading Brown 1988

choral repetition /'kɔːrəl ˌrepɪ'tɪʃən/ n
also **chorus repetition** /'kɔːrəs ˌrepɪ'tɪʃən/

When a teacher asks a whole group or class of students to repeat an example together, this is called choral repetition.

chronological order /'krɒnəlɒdʒɪkəl 'ɔːdəʳ||'krɑːnəlɑːdʒɪkəl 'ɔːr-/ n

(in composition) a paragraph in which the information is arranged according to a sequence in time. For example:
    First .... after that ... later ...

see also SPATIAL ORDER

chunking /'tʃʌŋkɪŋ/ n

the division of utterances into parts, as part of the process of learning or comprehension. The different parts of the utterance are called **chunks**.
For example, the sentence:
It was because of the rain that I was late.

might be divided into two parts – *It was because of the rain* and *that I was late* – and then the meaning of each part worked out separately.

These chunks are sometimes called **constituents**, and the process of chunking is sometimes called **constituent identification**.

In sentence production, chunks are sometimes called ROUTINEs.

Further reading Clark & Clark 1977

class /klɑːs‖klæs/ *n* **classify** /ˈklæsᵻfaɪ/ *v*

(in linguistics) a group of items which have something in common. For example, in English words can be grouped (classified) into WORD CLASS*ES* according to how they combine with other words to form phrases and sentences, how they change their form, etc. So *horse, child, tree* belong to the word class noun, and *beautiful, noisy, hard* belong to the word class adjective.

see also FORM CLASS, OPEN CLASS, TAXONOMIC

classification methods /ˌklæsᵻfᵻˈkeɪʃən ˌmeθədz/ *n*

see METHODS OF DEVELOPMENT

classifier[1] /ˈklæsᵻfaɪəʳ/ *n*

a word or affix used with a noun, which shows the sub-class to which the noun belongs.

For example, in Malay *ekor* "tail" is a classifier for animals and is used with numerals:

> *lima ekor lembu*   "five oxen"
> five   ox

Some languages such as Malay, Chinese, and various African languages have an extensive system of classifiers. In English, a few classifiers are still used, e.g. *head of* in:

> *five head of cattle*

In languages such as Swahili, the affix classifying a noun is also added to its MODIFIERS, PREDICATE, etc.

classifier[2] *n*

(in SYSTEMIC LINGUISTICS) a word in a NOUN PHRASE[1] which shows the sub-class to which a person or thing belongs.

For example, nouns and adjectives can function as classifiers:

classifier	noun classified
electric	*trains*
steam	*trains*

see also MODIFIER, HEAD

Further reading Halliday 1982

classroom-centered research /ˈklɑːsrʊm ˈsentəd rɪˈsɜːtʃ, -ruːm, ˈrɪːsɜːtʃ‖ˈklæs-, ˈsentərd, -ɜːr-/ *n*

also **classroom-process research**

a branch of second language acquisition research which focusses on language acquisition in relation to the classroom behaviours of teachers and learners. CCR may be compared with research which studies naturalistic second language acquisition outside of classrooms (such as when a person learns a language through informal contacts with native speakers of the language). CCR has focussed on such things as the linguistic features of classroom language, (see CLASSROOM DISCOURSE), teacher talk, patterns of teacher-student interaction, teacher treatment of errors, communication strategies, turn-taking patterns in the language classroom, code switching, and other factors that are believed to influence second language acquisition. CCR uses research techniques derived from INTERACTION ANALYSIS and ETHNOGRAPHY.

Further reading Long 1980; Chaudron 1988

classroom discourse /'klɑːsrʊm 'dɪskɔːs, -ruːm‖'klæs- -kɔːrs/ *n*

the type of language used in classroom situations. Classroom discourse is often different in form and function from language used in other situations because of the particular social roles students and teachers have in classrooms and the kinds of activities they usually carry out there. For example, teachers tend to rely on a discourse structure with the following pattern:

initiation – response – evaluation

In this typical three-part structure, the teacher initiates a question in order to check a student's knowledge, a student responds, and the student's response is evaluated with FEEDBACK from the teacher.

The restricted kind of discourse students encounter in classrooms is thought to influence their rate of language development.

see also QUESTIONING TECHNIQUES
Further reading Chaudron 1988

classroom interaction /'klɑːsrʊm ɪntər'ækʃən, -ruːm‖'klæs-/ *n*

the patterns of verbal and non-verbal communication and the types of social relationships which occur within classrooms. The study of classroom interaction may be a part of studies of classroom DISCOURSE, TEACHER TALK, and SECOND LANGUAGE ACQUISITION.

see also INTERACTION ANALYSIS

classroom management /'klɑːsrʊm 'mænɪdʒmənt, -ruːm‖'klæs-/ *n*

(in language teaching) the ways in which student behaviour, movement, interaction, etc. during a class is organized and controlled by the teacher (or sometimes by the learners themselves) to enable teaching to take place most effectively. Classroom management includes procedures for grouping students for different types of classroom activities, use of LESSON PLANS, handling of equipment, aids, etc., and the direction and management of student behaviour and activity.

classroom-process research /'klɑːsrʊm 'prəʊses rɪ'sɜːtʃ, -ruːm, 'riːsɜːtʃ‖'klæs- 'prɑː- -ɜːr-/ *n*

another term for CLASSROOM-CENTERED RESEARCH

clause /klɔːz/ *n*

a group of words which form a grammatical unit and which contain

a subject and a FINITE VERB. A clause forms a sentence or part of a sentence and often functions as a noun, adjective, or adverb.
For example:
I hurried home.
Because I was late, they went without me.
Clauses are classified as **dependent** or **independent**, e.g.:

I hurried	*because I was late.*
independent	dependent
clause	clause

A clause is different from a **phrase**.
A phrase is a group of words which form a grammatical unit. A phrase does not contain a finite verb and does not have a subject-predicate structure:
For example:
I liked her expensive new car.
George hates working in the garden.
Phrases are usually classified according to their central word or HEAD, e.g. NOUN PHRASE[1], VERB PHRASE, etc.

see also DEPENDENT CLAUSE, RELATIVE CLAUSE
Further reading Quirk et al 1985

cleft sentence /ˈkleft ˈsentəns/ *n*

a sentence which has been divided into two parts, each with its own verb, to emphasize a particular piece of information. Cleft sentences usually begin with *It* plus a form of the verb *be*, followed by the element which is being emphasized.
For example, the sentence *Mrs Smith gave Mary a dress* can be turned into the following cleft sentences:
It was Mrs Smith who gave Mary a dress.
It was Mary that Mrs Smith gave the dress to.
It was a dress that Mrs Smith gave to Mary.
In English a sentence with a *wh-clause* (e.g. *what I want*) as subject or complement is known as a **pseudo-cleft sentence**. For example:
A good holiday is what I need.
What I need is a good holiday.
Further reading Quirk et al 1985

cliché /ˈkliːʃeɪ‖kliːˈʃeɪ/ *n*

a word or expression which has lost its originality or effectiveness because it has been used too often. For example:
It's a crying shame.

climate /ˈklaɪmɪt/ *n*

(in teaching) the affective aspects of the classroom, such as the feelings generated by and about the teacher, the students or the subject matter, along with aspects of the classroom itself that contribute positively or negatively to the learning atmosphere. An effective teacher is said to create a suitable climate for learning by influencing students' attitudes

and perceptions in a positive way. Proponents of EFFECTIVE SCHOOLING suggest that the teacher does this by:
1 establishing an atmosphere in which academic goals are emphasized
2 promoting high standards and by monitoring and rewarding achievement
3 maintaining an orderly environment
4 building expectations for success
Further reading Kindsvatter, Wilen & Ishler 1988

clinical supervision /'klɪnɪkəl ˌsuːpə'vɪʒən, ˌsjuːpə-‖ˌsuːpər-/ *n*
(in teacher education) an approach to teacher supervision which focusses upon the improvement of teaching by means of systematic observation of teaching performance and focussed feedback by the supervisor. Clinical supervision involves:
1 a close face-to-face relationship between a teacher and a supervisor
2 a focus on the teacher's actual behaviour in the classroom, with the goal of improving the teacher's skill as a teacher
3 a three-stage strategy consisting of:
  a a planning conference, in which the teacher discusses his or her goals, methodology, problems etc. with the supervisor and they decide on what the supervisor should observe and what kind of information about the lesson he or she should collect.
  b classroom observation, in which the supervisor observes the teacher in his or her classroom.
  c feedback conference, in which the teacher and the supervisor review the data the supervisor has collected, discuss the effectiveness of the lesson, and decide on strategies for improvement, if necessary.
Further reading Acheson & Gall 1987

clitic /'klɪtɪk/ *n*
a grammatical form which cannot stand on its own in an utterance. It needs to co-occur with another form which either precedes or follows it. Some languages have clitic pronoun forms which are attached to the verb. In English, *n't* the contracted form of *not* in *couldn't*, *isn't*, and *don't* can be considered a clitic.

CLL /ˌsiː el 'el/ *n*
an abbreviation for COMMUNITY LANGUAGE LEARNING

closed class /'kləʊzd 'klɑːs‖'klæs/ *n*
see OPEN CLASS

closed-ended response /'kləʊzd ˌendɪd rɪ'spɒns‖-'spaːns/ *n*
see TEST ITEM

closed set /'kləʊzd 'set/ *n*
see OPEN CLASS

closed syllable /ˈkləʊzd ˈsɪləbəl/ *n*

see SYLLABLE

close vowel /ˈkləʊs ˈvaʊəl/ *n*
also **high vowel**

see VOWEL

closure /ˈkləʊʒəʳ/ *n*

(in teaching) that part of the lesson which brings it to an end. An effective lesson closure is said to reinforce the key teaching points of the lesson and help students transfer learning to the next lesson.

see also ENTRY

clozentropy /ˌkləʊˈzentrəpi/ *n*

a method of scoring cloze tests, based on the acceptable word method.
A cloze test is first given to a group of native speakers, and their responses are listed in frequency order.
When the test is given to non-native speakers, someone who responds with a high frequency word scores more than someone who responds with a low frequency word.

see also CLOZE PROCEDURE

cloze passage /ˈkləʊz ˈpæsɪdʒ/ *n*

see CLOZE PROCEDURE

cloze procedure/ˈkləʊz prəˈsiːdʒəʳ/ *n*

a technique for measuring reading comprehension. In a **cloze test**, words are removed from a reading passage at regular intervals, leaving blanks. For example every fifth word may be removed. The reader must then read the passage and try to guess the missing words.
For example, a **cloze passage** looks like this:

A passage used in _____ cloze test is a _____ of written material in _____ words have been regularly _____. The subjects must then _____ to reconstruct the passage _____ filling in the missing _____.

Here, the reader has to guess *a, passage, which, removed, try, by, words*. The cloze procedure can also be used to judge the difficulty of reading materials.
If the cloze procedure is being used for language testing, the reader is given a score according to how well the words guessed matched the original words, or whether or not they made sense. Two types of scoring procedure are used:

a the reader must guess the exact word which was used in the original (as in the example above). This is called the **exact word method**.

b the reader can guess any word that is appropriate or acceptable in the context. This is called the **acceptable word method** (also the **appropriate word method**, the **acceptable alternative method**, and the **contextually appropriate method**).

55

see also CLOZENTROPY
Further reading Hughes 1988; Oller 1979

cloze test /ˈkləʊz ˌtest/ *n*
see CLOZE PROCEDURE

cluster /ˈklʌstəʳ/ *n*
see CONSONANT CLUSTER

clustering /ˈklʌstərɪŋ/ *n*
see BRAINSTORMING

cluster reduction /ˈklʌstəʳ rɪˌdʌkʃən/ *n*
When a speaker leaves out one or more of the CONSONANTS in a group of consonants (CONSONANT CLUSTER), this is called cluster reduction. This can occur at the beginning, the middle or the end of a word and is found in the speech of both native speakers and language learners.
For example, a learner of English whose native language has no final consonant clusters may reduce the cluster /nts/ to /ns/ or /n/, and pronounce *wants* as /wɒns/ or /wɒn/.

cocktail-party phenomenon /ˈkɒkteɪl ˌpɑːti fɪˌnɒmɪ̩nən‖ˈkɑːkteɪl ˌpɑːrti fɪˌnɑːmɪ̩nɑːn, -nən/ *n*
a term which refers to the ability to listen selectively to speech coming from one source (e.g. while listening to one of the guests at a cocktail-party) and to ignore speech coming from other sources (e.g. the conversations of other guests nearby). The cocktail-party phenomenon is sometimes referred to in discussing the importance of REDUNDANCY in conversation.

coda /ˈkəʊdə/ *n*
see SYLLABLE

codability /ˌkəʊdəˈbɪlɪ̩ti/ *n*
the degree to which an aspect of experience can be described by the vocabulary of a language.
Languages differ in the degree to which they provide words for the description or naming of particular things, events, experiences, and states. For example, English makes a distinction between *blue* and *green* whereas some languages have a single word for this colour range.
Further reading Miller & Johnson-Laird 1976

code[1] /kəʊd/ *n*
a term which is used instead of LANGUAGE, SPEECH VARIETY, or DIALECT. It is sometimes considered to be a more neutral term than the others. People also use "code" when they want to stress the uses of a language or language variety in a particular community. For example, a

Puerto Rican in New York City may have two codes: English and Spanish. He or she may use one code (English) at work and the other code (Spanish) at home or when talking to neighbours.

see also CODE SELECTION, CODE SWITCHING
Further reading Hymes 1977; Wardhaugh 1986

code² *n*

a term used by the British educational sociologist Bernstein for different ways of conveying meaning in a social context. Bernstein distinguished between **elaborated code** and **restricted code**. The restricted code is said to have a more reduced vocabulary range, to use more question tags, to use PRONOUNS like *he* and *she* instead of nouns and to use gestures such as hand movements to help give meaning to what is said. It is claimed that speakers using a restricted code assume that their addressees share a great many of their attitudes and expectations.

On the other hand, persons using an elaborated code are said to make greater use of adjectives, more complicated sentence structures and the pronoun *I*. The elaborated code is claimed to be more explicit and speakers using it do not assume the same degree of shared attitudes and expectations on the part of the addressee. It has been claimed that while middle-class children have access to both codes, working-class children have access only to the restricted code.

There has been a great deal of controversy over Bernstein's codes as they have been linked to theories which relate language learning to social class and educational policies.

see also DEFICIT HYPOTHESIS
Further reading Bernstein 1971

code³ *n*

any system of signals which çan be used for sending a MESSAGE. A natural language is an example of a code, as are Morse code, braille, and SIGN LANGUAGE.

The medium through which the signals are sent (e.g. by telephone, in writing) is called the CHANNEL (b).

code mixing /'kəʊd ˌmɪksɪŋ/ *n*

a mixing of two codes (see CODE¹) or languages, usually without a change of topic. This is quite common in bilingual or multilingual communities and is often a mark of solidarity, e.g. between bilingual friends or colleagues in an informal situation. Code mixing can involve various levels of language, e.g. phonology, morphology, grammatical structures or lexical items.

Bilingual or multilingual speakers, for example, may think that one of their languages, e.g. English, has more appropriate lexical items for something they want to express in a particular situation and they incorporate these into the grammatical structure of the other language, in this case Mandarin Chinese:

A: Zuótiān de party zěnmeyàng?
   Yesterday's party how
   How was yesterday's party?
B: Bié tí party bù party le!
   Don't mention party no party no longer
   Don't talk to me about the party!

Sometimes a type of code mixing even acquires a special name, e.g. *Ugewa* (the mixing of English and Cantonese by Hong Kong university students).

see also CODE SELECTION, CODE SWITCHING
Further reading Wardhaugh 1986

code selection /ˈkəʊd sɪˌlekʃən/ *n*

the selection of a particular language or language variety for a given situation.

If someone uses more than one code when communicating with others, they usually select one code for certain purposes (in certain places and with certain people) and use another code for other purposes (in other places and with other people). This code selection is often quite regular and its patterns can be investigated.

For example, a Chinese in Singapore may use Hokkien (a Southern Chinese dialect) at home, Singapore English at work, and Bazaar Malay to Indian or Malay stallholders at the market.

The code a person selects may often depend on the ethnic background, sex, age, and level of education of the speaker and of the person with whom he/she is speaking.

see also CODE SWITCHING, DIGLOSSIA, DOMAIN[1]
Further reading Platt & Weber 1980; Wardhaugh 1986

code switching /ˈkəʊd ˌswɪtʃɪŋ/ *n*

a change by a speaker (or writer) from one language or language variety to another one. Code switching can take place in a conversation when one speaker uses one language and the other speaker answers in a different language. A person may start speaking one language and then change to another one in the middle of their speech, or sometimes even in the middle of a sentence.

For example, from the speech of a German immigrant in Australia:
   Das handelt von einem secondhand dealer and his son.
   "That is about a . . ."   [from Clyne 1972]

see also CODE SELECTION
Further reading Clyne 1972, 1987; Wardhaugh 1986

coding /ˈkəʊdɪŋ/ *n*

a research technique in which data that have been collected are turned into classes or categories (i.e. **codes**) for the purpose of counting or tabulation. For example in conducting a NEEDS ANALYSIS, students' responses to questions on a questionnaire may be classified into different classes or codes. The questionnaires can then be analyzed automatically by a computer.

coefficient of determination /ˌkəʊ̯ɪ'fɪʃənt əv dɪˌtɜːmɪ̯'neɪʃən||-ɜːr-/ *n*
also **r²**

a measure of the amount of variability shared or predicted by two variables (VARIABLE[1]). It is equal to the square of r (r = coefficient of CORRELATION). For example a correlation coefficient of + .70 indicates that 49% (i.e. + .70²) of the variability is shared by the two variables, i. e., 51% of the variability is not shared or predicted by the variables.

Further reading Hardyck & Petrinovich 1976

cognate /'kɒgneɪt||'kɑːg-/ *n, adj*

a word in one language which is similar in form and meaning to a word in another language because both languages are related. For example English *brother* and German *Bruder*.

Sometimes words in two languages are similar in form and meaning but are BORROWING*s* and not cognate forms.

For example, *kampuni* in the African language Swahili, is a borrowing from English *company*.

see also FALSE COGNATE

cognition /kɒg'nɪʃən||kɑːg-/ *n* **cognitive** /'kɒgnᵻtɪv||'kɑːg-/ *adj*

the various mental processes used in thinking, remembering, perceiving, recognizing, classifying, etc.

see also COGNITIVE PSYCHOLOGY

cognitive academic language proficiency /'kɒgnᵻtɪv ækə'demɪk 'læŋgwɪdʒ prəˌfɪʃənsi||'kɑːg-/ *n*
also **CALP**

a hypothesis proposed by Cummins which describes the special kind of second language proficiency which students need in order to perform school learning tasks. Cummins suggests that many classroom tasks are cognitively demanding and often have to be solved independently by the learner without support from the context. The ability to carry out such tasks in a second language is known as CALP. Cummins contrasts this kind of language proficiency with **Basic Interpersonal Communication Skills (BICS)**. This refers to the language profiency needed to perform other kinds of tasks which are not directly related to learning academic content, such as interpersonal communication. Interpersonal and social communication is relatively undemanding cognitively and relies on context to clarify meaning. According to Cummins, different kinds of tests are needed to measure CALP and BICS, and a learner's skill in BICS does not predict performance on CALP.

Further reading Cummins 1980

cognitive code approach /'kɒgnᵻtɪv 'kəʊd əˌprəʊtʃ||'kɑːg-/ *n*

an approach to second and foreign language teaching which is based on the belief that language learning is a process which involves active mental processes and not simply the forming of habits. It gives importance to the learner's active part in the process of using and learning language, particularly in the learning of grammatical rules. Although it has not led to any particular method of language teaching, the COMMUNICATIVE APPROACH makes some use of cognitive code principles.

Further reading Rivers 1981

cognitive domain /ˈkɒgnᵻtɪv dəˈmeɪn‖ˈkɑːg-/ *n*
see DOMAIN

cognitive meaning /ˈkɒgnᵻtɪv ˈmiːnɪŋ‖ˈkɑːg-/ *n*
another term for DENOTATION

cognitive process /ˈkɒgnᵻtɪv ˈprəʊses‖ˈkɑːg-, ˈprɑː-/ *n*
also **cognitive strategy**

any mental process which learners make use of in language learning, such as INFERENCING, GENERALIZATION, DEDUCTIVE LEARNING, MONITORING, and MEMORIZING.

cognitive psychology /ˈkɒgnᵻtɪv saɪˈkɒlədʒi‖ˈkɑːg-, saɪˈkɑː-/ *n*
a branch of psychology which deals with the study of the nature and learning of systems of knowledge, particularly those processes involved in thought, perception, comprehension, memory, and learning.

In recent years cognitive psychology has been related to mentalistic approaches to linguistics, especially Chomsky's TRANSFORMATIONAL GENERATIVE GRAMMAR, which links language structure to the nature of human cognitive processes.

see also BEHAVIOURISM
Further reading Neisser 1967

cognitive science /ˈkɒgnᵻtɪv ˈsaɪəns‖ˈkɑːg-/ *n*
a discipline which draws on research in LINGUISTICS, PSYCHOLINGUISTICS, COGNITIVE PSYCHOLOGY and ARTIFICIAL INTELLIGENCE. Cognitive science deals with the scientific study of thinking, reasoning and the intellectual processes of the mind; it is concerned with how knowledge is represented in the mind, how language is understood, how images are understood, and with what the mental processes underlying INFERENCING, learning, problem solving, and planning, are.

Further reading Johnson-Laird & Wason 1977

cognitive strategy /ˈkɒgnᵻtɪv ˈstrætᵻdʒi‖ˈkɑːg-/ *n*
One of two general kinds of learning strategies (LEARNING STRATEGY) employed by learners in carrying out language learning tasks, the other being **metacognitive strategies**. Cognitive strategies refer to processes and **behaviour** which learners use to help them improve their ability to learn or remember something, particularly those which learners use with specific classroom tasks and activities. For example, cognitive strategies which learners may use to assist them in listening or reading comprehension activities include:

a repeating key words or phrases silently or aloud

b summarizing to make sure the important information will be remembered

c creating visual images to help them remember new information

see also COGNITIVE PROCESS, COGNITIVE STYLE

Further reading O'Malley & Chamot 1989; Oxford 1990

cognitive style /'kɒgnˌtɪv 'staɪl‖'kaːg-/ *n*

also **cognitive strategy, learning style**

the particular way in which a learner tries to learn something. In second or foreign language learning, different learners may prefer different solutions to learning problems. For example, some may want explanations for grammatical rules; others may not need explanations. Some may feel writing down words or sentences helps them to remember them. Others may find they remember things better if they are associated with pictures. These are called differences of cognitive style.

see also FIELD DEPENDENCE, GLOBAL LEARNING

Further reading Brown 1987

cognitive variable /'kɒgnˌtɪv 'veəriəbəl‖'kaːg-/ *n*

When a person tries to learn something, his/her success is partly governed by intelligence, memory, and the ability to analyse and evaluate. These are called cognitive variables.

But attitudes, emotions, motivation, personality, etc. may also influence learning. These are called **affective variables**.

For example, the attitude a learner has towards a foreign language may affect his/her success in learning it.

One technique for measuring this aspect of learning is the SEMANTIC DIFFERENTIAL.

see also EMPATHY, LANGUAGE ATTITUDES, MOTIVATION

Further reading Brown 1987; Jakobovits 1970

coherence /kəʊˈhɪərəns/ *n* coherent /kəʊˈhɪərənt/ *adj*

the relationships which link the meanings of UTTERANCES in a DISCOURSE or of the sentences in a text.

These links may be based on the speakers' shared knowledge. For example:

A: *Could you give me a lift home?*

B: *Sorry, I'm visiting my sister.*

There is no grammatical or lexical link between A's question and B's reply (see COHESION) but the exchange has coherence because both A and B know that B's sister lives in the opposite direction to A's home.

Generally a PARAGRAPH has coherence if it is a series of sentences that develop a main idea (i.e. with a TOPIC SENTENCE and supporting sentences which relate to it).

see also SCHEME, TEXT LINGUISTICS, CONVERSATIONAL MAXIM

Further reading Coulthard 1985

cohesion /kəʊˈhiːʒən/ n

the grammatical and/or lexical relationships between the different elements of a text. This may be the relationship between different sentences or between different parts of a sentence. For example:

a A: *Is Jenny coming to the party?*
   B: *Yes, she is.*
There is a link between *Jenny* and *she* and also between *is ... coming* and *is*.

b In the sentence:
   If you are going to London, I can give you the address of a good hotel there.
the link is between *London* and *there* (see ANAPHORA).

see also COHERENCE
Further reading Halliday & Hasan 1976

cohort /ˈkəʊhɔːt‖-hɔːrt/ n

(in experimental research) a group of people who have some feature in common (e.g. age, IQ, or number of months they have studied a foreign language).

collaborative research /kəˈlæbərətɪv rɪˈsɜːtʃ, ˈriːsɜːtʃ‖-ɜːr- n

(in teacher development programmes) research which is carried out by a teacher in collaboration with others, such as another teacher or teachers, a school consultant, a university researcher, or between a teacher and learners. Collaborative research is an essential component of some models of ACTION RESEARCH.

Further reading Nunan 1989a

collective noun /kəˈlektɪv ˈnaʊn/ n

a noun which refers to a collection of people, animals, or things as a group. For example *school, family, government* are collective nouns. When collective nouns are used in the singular, they may be used with either a singular verb or a plural verb. For example:

   The government is going to look into this matter.
   The government are looking into this matter.

The use of the plural verb suggests that the noun refers to something which is seen as a group of individuals, whereas the use of the singular verb suggests something seen as a single whole.

see also NOUN
Further reading Quirk et al 1985

collocation /ˌkɒləˈkeɪʃən‖ˌkɑː-/ n **collocate** /ˈkɒləkeɪt‖ˈkɑː-/ v

the way in which words are used together regularly.

Collocation refers to the restrictions on how words can be used together, for example which prepositions are used with particular verbs, or which verbs and nouns are used together.

For example, in English the verb *perform* is used with *operation*, but not with *discussion*:

   The doctor performed the operation.
   *The committee performed a discussion.

instead we say:
The committee held/had a discussion.
perform is used with (collocates with) *operation*, and *hold* and *have* collocate with *discussion.*
high collocates with *probability*, but not with *chance*:
   a high probability   but   *a good chance*
do collocates with *damage*, *duty*, and *wrong*, but not with *trouble*, *noise*, and *excuse*:
   do a lot of damage   *do one's duty*   *do wrong*
   make trouble   *make a lot of noise*   *make an excuse*

see also IDIOM
Further reading Bolinger 1975

colloquialism /kəˈləʊkwiəlɪzəm/ *n*

a word or phrase that is more commonly used in informal speech and writing. For example *boss* is a colloquialism for *employer*.

see also COLLOQUIAL SPEECH

colloquial speech /kəˈləʊkwiəl ˈspiːtʃ/ *n*
also **informal speech**

the type of speech used in everyday, informal situations when the speaker is not paying particular attention to pronunciation, choice of words, or sentence structure. Colloquial speech is not necessarily non-prestige speech and should not be considered as SUBSTANDARD. Educated native speakers of a language normally use colloquial speech in informal situations with friends, fellow workers, and members of the family.
For example, they might say:
Why don't you come around this evening?
rather than the more formal
We should be delighted if you would pay us a visit this evening.
It is often difficult for language learners to realize that in certain situations colloquial speech is more appropriate than extremely formal speech.

see also STYLE

combining form /kəmˈbaɪnɪŋ ˌfɔːm‖ˌfɔːrm/ *n*

a BOUND FORM that can form a new word by combining with another combining form, a word, or sometimes and AFFIX. For example, the combining form *astr(o)-*, 'star', can form the word *astrology* with the combining form *-(o)logy*, the word *astrophysics* with the word *physics*, and the word *astral* with the suffix *-al*. Groups of MORPHEMES like the *-blooded* of *warm-blooded* or the *-making* of *trouble-making* are also sometimes regarded as combining forms.

see also WORD FORMATION

comment /ˈkɒment‖ˈkɑː-/ *n*
see TOPIC[2]

comment clause

comment clause /'kɒment ˌklɔːz‖'kɑː-/ *n*
a clause which comments on another clause in a sentence. For example:
She is, I believe, a New Zealander.
Coming from you, that sounds surprising.
Comment clauses function as ADJUNCTS or disjuncts, and are optional in the sentence structure.
Further reading Quirk et al 1985

commissive /kə'mɪsɪv/ *n*
see SPEECH ACT CLASSIFICATION

common core /'kɒmən 'kɔːʳ‖'kɑː-/ *n*
(in language teaching) those basic aspects of a language (e.g. vocabulary and grammar) which a learner needs to know whatever his or her purpose is in learning the language. When designing a language SYLLABUS a teacher must decide how much of the language content of the course must be common core and how much must be directed to the learner's particular needs, e.g. for science or business.

see also ENGLISH FOR SPECIAL PURPOSES

common noun /'kɒmən 'naʊn‖'kɑː-/ *n*
see PROPER NOUN

communication /kəˌmjuːnᵻ'keɪʃən/ *n* **communicate** /kə'mjuːnᵻkeɪt/ *v*
the exchange of ideas, information, etc. between two or more persons. In an act of communication there is usually at least one speaker or **sender,** a MESSAGE which is transmitted, and a person or persons for whom this message is intended (the **receiver**). The study of communication is central to SOCIOLINGUISTICS, PSYCHOLINGUISTICS, and INFORMATION THEORY.

see also COMMUNICATIVE COMPETENCE, SPEECH EVENT
Further reading Coulthard 1985; Hymes 1977

communication network /kəˌmjuːnᵻ'keɪʃən ˌnetwɜːk‖-wɜːrk/ *n*
the range of **persons** that members of a group communicate with. In any group (e.g. students in a class or members of a school staff), some members communicate more frequently with one another than with others, depending on their relationships, frequency of contact etc. Communication networks may be studied as part of the study of BILINGUALISM and DIGLOSSIA as well as in studies of second language acquisition, since language learning and language use may depend upon both the frequency of use of a language as well as on whom one uses it to communicate with.

communication strategy /kəˌmjuːnᵻ'keɪʃən ˌstrætᵻdʒi/ *n*
a way used to express a meaning in a second or foreign language, by a learner who has a limited command of the language. In trying to

communicate, a learner may have to make up for a lack of knowledge of grammar or vocabulary.

For example the learner may not be able to say *It's against the law to park here* and so he/she may say *This place, cannot park*. For *handkerchief* a learner could say *a cloth for my nose*, and for *apartment complex* the learner could say *building*. The use of PARAPHRASE and other communication strategies (e.g. gesture and mime) characterize the INTER-LANGUAGE of some language learners.

see also ACCOMMODATION, FOREIGNER TALK

Further reading Faerch & Kasper 1983; Tarone 1977

communication theory /kə,mjuːnᵻ'keɪʃən ,θɪəri/ *n*
another term for INFORMATION THEORY

communicative approach /kə'mjuːnᵻkətɪv ə'prəʊtʃ||-keɪtɪv/ *n*
also **communicative language teaching**

an APPROACH to foreign or second language teaching which emphasizes that the goal of language learning is COMMUNICATIVE COMPETENCE.

The communicative approach has been developed particularly by British applied linguists as a reaction away from grammar-based approaches such as the aural-oral approach (see under AUDIOLINGUAL METHOD). Teaching materials used with a communicative approach often

a teach the language needed to express and understand different kinds of functions, such as requesting, describing, expressing likes and dislikes, etc.

b are based on a NOTIONAL SYLLLABUS or some other communicatively organized syllabus

c emphasize the processes of communication, such as using language appropriately in different types of situations; using language to perform different kinds of tasks, e.g. to solve puzzles, to get information, etc.; using language for social interaction with other people.

Further reading Littlewood 1981; Richards & Rogers 1986

communicative competence /kə'mjuːnᵻkətɪv 'kɒmpᵻtəns||-keɪtɪv 'kɑːm-/ *n*
the ability not only to apply the grammatical rules of a language in order to form grammatically correct sentences but also to know when and where to use these sentences and to whom.

Communicative competence includes:

a knowledge of the grammar and vocabulary of the LANGUAGE[2] (see COMPETENCE)

b knowledge of rules of speaking (e.g. knowing how to begin and end conversations, knowing what topics may be talked about in different types of SPEECH EVENTS, knowing which ADDRESS FORMS should be used with different persons one speaks to and in different situations

c knowing how to use and respond to different types of SPEECH ACTS, such as requests, apologies, thanks, and invitations

d knowing how to use language appropriately (see APPROPRIATENESS)

65

When someone wishes to communicate with others, they must recognize the social setting, their relationship to the other person(s) (see ROLE RELATIONSHIP), and the types of language that can be used for a particular occasion. They must also be able to interpret written or spoken sentences within the total context in which they are used.

For example, the English statement *It's rather cold in here* could be a request, particularly to someone in a lower role relationship, to close a window or door or to turn on the heating.

see also STYLE, PRAGMATICS
Further reading Coulthard 1985; Hymes 1977

communicative drill /kə'mjuːnɪ̱kətɪv 'drɪl||-keɪtɪv/ *n*

see MEANINGFUL DRILL

communicative function /kə'mjuːnɪ̱kətɪv 'fʌŋkʃən||-keɪtɪv/ *n*

the extent to which a language is used in a community. Some languages may be used for very specific purposes, such as the language called *Pali*, which is used only for religious purposes in Buddhism. Other languages are used for almost all the communicative needs of a community, e.g. Japanese in Japan.

communicative interference /kə'mjuːnɪ̱kətɪv ˌɪntə'fɪərəns||-keɪtɪv ˌɪntər-/ *n*

interference (see LANGUAGE TRANSFER) which is caused by the use of rules of speaking (e.g. greetings, ways of opening or closing conversations, address systems – see ADDRESS FORM) from one language when speaking another. For example, conversations in English often open with a health question (*How are you?*) but in other languages, such as Malay, open with a food question (*Have you eaten yet?*). A Malay-speaking student learning English who opened a conversation in English with *Have you eaten yet?* would be speaking with communicative interference from Malay to English.

communicative language teaching /kə'mjuːnɪ̱kətɪv 'læŋgwɪdʒ ˌtiːtʃɪŋ||-keɪtɪv/ *n*

another term for COMMUNICATIVE APPROACH

community language /kə'mjuːnɪ̱ti ˌlæŋgwɪdʒ/ *n*

a language used within a particular community, including languages spoken by ethnic minority groups.

For example, in Australia, apart from English, languages such as Italian, Greek, Polish, Arabic, and Australian Aboriginal languages are community languages.

Community languages should not be confused with COMMUNITY LANGUAGE LEARNING.

Further reading Clyne 1985

Community Language Learning /kə'mjuːnɪ̱ti 'læŋgwɪdʒ ˌlɜːnɪŋ|| ˌlɜːr-/ *n*

also CLL

a METHOD of second and foreign language teaching developed by Charles Curran. Community Language Learning is an application of **counselling learning** to second and foreign language teaching and learning. It uses techniques developed in group counselling to help people with psychological and emotional problems. The method makes use of group learning in small or large groups. These groups are the "community". The method places emphasis on the learners' personal feelings and their reactions to language learning. Learners say things which they want to talk about, in their native language.

The teacher (known as "Counselor") translates the learner's sentences into the foreign language, and the learner then repeats this to other members of the group.

Further reading Curran 1976; Richards & Rogers 1986

comparative /kəm'pærətɪv/ *n*
also comparative degree

the form of an adjective or adverb which is used to show comparison between two things. In English, the comparative is formed with the suffix -*er*, or with *more*:

This is better / more useful *than that.*

The **superlative** is the form of an adjective or adverb which shows the most or the least in quality, quantity, or intensity. In English, the superlative is formed with the suffix -*est* or with *most*:

She is the tallest / the most beautiful *in the class.*

comparative clause /kəm'pærətɪv 'klɔːz/ *n*
also comparative sentence

a clause which contains a standard with which someone or something referred to in an INDEPENDENT CLAUSE is compared. In English, comparative clauses are often introduced with *than* or *as*:

Tom is much taller than John is.
Jane doesn't write as neatly as Fiona does.

Further reading Quirk et al 1985

comparative degree /kəm'pærətɪv dɪ'griː/ *n*

another term for COMPARATIVE

comparative historical linguistics /kəm'pærətɪv hɪ'stɒrɪkəl lɪŋ 'gwɪstɪks||-'stɔː-, -'staː-/ *n*
also comparative philology, philology, historical linguistics

a branch of linguistics which studies language change and language relationships. By comparing earlier and later forms of a language and by comparing different languages, it has been possible to show that certain languages are related, e.g. the INDO-EUROPEAN LANGUAGES. It has also been possible to reconstruct forms which are believed to have occurred in a particular language before written records were available. For example **p* in an ancestor language to all the Indo-European languages is said to be related to /p/ in Sanskrit as in *pita* "father" and /f/ in English as in *father*.

see also DIACHRONIC LINGUISTICS
Further reading Aitchison 1981

comparative linguistics /kəm'pærətɪv lɪŋ'gwɪstɪks/ *n*

a branch of linguistics which studies two or more languages in order to compare their structures and to show whether they are similar or different. Comparative linguistics is used in the study of language types (see TYPOLOGY) and in COMPARATIVE HISTORICAL LINGUISTICS. It is also used by some applied linguists for establishing differences between the learner's native language and the TARGET LANGUAGE[1] in the areas of syntax, vocabulary, and sound systems.

see also CONTRASTIVE ANALYSIS
Further reading Bolinger 1975

comparative philology /kəm'pærətɪv fɪ'lɒlədʒi‖-'lɑː-/ *n*

another term for COMPARATIVE HISTORICAL LINGUISTICS

comparative sentence /kəm'pærətɪv 'sentəns/

another term for COMPARATIVE CLAUSE

comparison and contrast method /kəm'pærɪsən ənd 'kɒntrɑːst ˌmeθəd‖'kɑːntræst/ *n*

see METHODS OF DEVELOPMENT

compensatory instruction /'kɒmpənseɪtəri ɪn'strʌkʃən, kəm'pensə təri‖kəm'pensətɔːri/ *n*

also **compensatory education** /'kɒmpənseɪtəri ˌedjʊ'keɪʃən, kəm'pen sətəri‖kəm'pensətɔːri ˌedʒə-/

a special education programme for children whose home background is said to lack certain kinds of language experience. For example, children who are not read to at home or who do not have story books at home.

see also CULTURAL DEPRIVATION

competence /'kɒmpɪtəns‖'kɑːm-/ *n*

(in TRANSFORMATIONAL GENERATIVE GRAMMAR) a person's internalized grammar of a language. This means a person's ability to create and understand sentences, including sentences they have never heard before. It also includes a person's knowledge of what are and what are not sentences of a particular language.

For example, a speaker of English would recognize *I want to go home* as an English sentence but would not accept a sentence such as *I want going home* even though all the words in it are English words.

Competence often refers to the ideal speaker/hearer, that is an idealized but not a real person who would have a complete knowledge of the whole language. A distinction is made between competence and PERFORMANCE, which is the actual use of the language by individuals in speech and writing.

see also COMMUNICATIVE COMPETENCE
Further reading Chomsky 1965

competency based teacher education /ˈkɒmpɫtənsi ˈbeɪst ˈtiːtʃəʳ edjʲʊ̩keɪʃən||ˈkɑːm-, edʒə-/ *n*

an approach to teacher education which focusses on the skills and competencies which are thought to constitute effective teaching.

competency based teaching /ˈkɒmpɫtənsi ˈbeɪst ˈtiːtʃɪŋ||ˈkɑːm-/ *n*

an approach to teaching which focuses on the mastery of the skills or competencies needed in different domains. In competency-based teaching, students at various levels in their schooling must pass competence tests on selected performance OBJECTIVES in basic skill areas such as reading or mathematics.

complement /ˈkɒmplɫmənt||ˈkɑːm-/ *n* **complementation** /ˌkɒmplɫmən'teɪʃən||ˌkɑːm-/ *n*

(in grammar) that part of the sentence which follows the verb and which thus *completes* the sentence. The commonest complements are:

a **subject complement**: the complement linked to a subject by *be* or a linking verb:
  She is a doctor.
b **object complement**: the complement linked to an object:
  We made her the chairperson.
c **adjective complement**: the complement linked to an adjective:
  I am glad that you can come.
d **prepositional complement**: the complement linked to a preposition:
  They argued about what to do.

While ADJUNCTS are optional parts of sentences, complements are often obligatory parts of the sentences in which they occur.

A clause which functions as a complement is called a **complement(ary) clause**. For example:
  The question is why you did it.

Further reading Quirk et al 1985

complement(ary) clause /ˌkɒmplɫmentəri ˈklɔːz||ˌkɑːm-/ *n*

see COMPLEMENT

complementaries /ˌkɒmplɫ'mentəriz||ˌkɑːm-/ *n*

see ANTONYM

complex sentence /ˈkɒmpleks ˈsentəns||ˈkɑːm-/ *n*

a sentence which contains one or more DEPENDENT CLAUSES, in addition to its independent, or main, clause. For example:
  When it rained, we went inside.
  (dep cl)   (ind cl)

A sentence which contains two or more independent clauses which are jointed by co-ordination is called a **compound sentence**. For example:

He is a small boy but he is very strong.
(ind cl)   (ind cl)
I'll either phone you or I will send you a note.
(ind cl)   (ind cl)

A sentence which contains only one PREDICATE is called a **simple sentence**. For example:

I like milk.
(pred)

complex transitive verb /ˈkɒmpleks ˈtrænsɪtɪv ˈvɜːb‖ˈkɑːm-, ˈvɜːrb/ *n*

see TRANSITIVE VERB

componential analysis /ˌkɒmpənenʃəl əˈnælɪsɪs‖ˌkɑːm-/ *n*

1 (in semantics) an approach to the study of meaning which analyses a word into a set of meaning **components** or semantic features. For example, the meaning of the English word *boy* may be shown as:

⟨+human⟩ ⟨+male⟩ ⟨–adult⟩

Usually, componential analysis is applied to a group of related words which may differ from one another only by one or two components.

This approach was developed in ANTHROPOLOGICAL LINGUISTICS for the study of kinship and other terms in various languages.

2 any approach to linguistics which analyses linguistic units, usually words or sounds, into smaller parts or components. This approach has been used in phonology and semantics.

see also DISTINCTIVE FEATURE, SEMANTIC FEATURES
Further reading Lyons 1981

components /kəmˈpəʊnənts/ *n*

see COMPONENTIAL ANALYSIS

composing processes /kəmˈpəʊzɪŋ ˌprəʊsesɪz‖ˌprɑː-/ *n*

In composition and writing, the different stages employed by writers. Three stages are often recognized in the writing process:

1 **rehearsing** (also known as **prewriting**): activities in which writers look for a topic or for ideas and language related to a topic before beginning writing.

2 **writing** (also known as **planning, drafting, composing**): activities in which writers note down ideas in rough form.

3 **revising** (also known as **editing, postwriting**): activities in which writers check, revise and rewrite what they have written.

These stages in writing do not necessarily occur in sequence but may recur throughout the composing process. A PROCESS APPROACH to the teaching of writing focusses on encouraging the development of these composing processes.

Further reading Murray 1980; Koch and Brazil 1978

composition /ˌkɒmpəˈzɪʃən‖ˌkɑːm-/ *n*

1 writing as an activity which is intended to increase a person's skills or effectiveness as writer.

2 the name for such an activity or subject in school.

3 a piece of written work produced to practice the skills and techniques of writing or to demonstrate a person's skill as a writer.

In language teaching, two types of writing activities are sometimes distinguished:

a *free composition*, in which the student's writing is not controlled or limited in any way, such as essay questions, or writing about a particular topic.

b *controlled composition*, in which the student's writing is controlled by various means, such as by providing questions to be answered, sentences to be completed, or words or pictures to describe.

compound adjective /'kɒmpaʊnd 'ædʒ‚ktɪv||'kɑːm-/ *n*

see COMPOUND WORD

compound bilingualism /'kɒmpaʊnd baɪ'lɪŋgwəlɪzəm||'kɑːm-/ *n*

There is a theory that a bilingual person relates words to their meanings in one of two ways.

Compound bilingualism means that the bilingual has one system of word meanings, which is used for both the first and the second language. For a French/English bilingual, the French word *pain* ("bread") and the English word *bread* have the same meaning.

Co-ordinate bilingualism means that the bilingual has two systems of meanings for words; one system is for the words the person knows in the first language and the other is for the words he or she knows in the second language.

For a French/English bilingual the French word *pain* and the English word *bread* would not have exactly the same meanings. This theory was an attempt to show how the different conditions under which people become bilingual could lead to different systems of meaning. The distinction between compound and co-ordinate bilingualism has been used in studies of vocabulary learning, but has not been found useful as a general model of bilingualism.

Further reading Ervin & Osgood 1954; Romaine 1989

compound noun /'kɒmpaʊnd 'naʊn||'kɑːm-/ *n*

see COMPOUND WORD

compound predicate /'kɒmpaʊnd 'predɪk‚t||'kɑːm-/ *n*

a PREDICATE containing two or more verbs sharing a single SUBJECT. For example:

Spring came and went too quickly.

compound sentence /'kɒmpaʊnd 'sentəns||'kɑːm-/ *n*

see COMPLEX SENTENCE

compound subject /'kɒmpaʊnd 'sʌbdʒɪkt||'kɑːm-/ *n*

a subject which consists of two or more elements joined by *and* and normally taking a plural verb. For example:

Beer and wine do not mix.

compound word /'kɒmpaʊnd 'wɜːd||'kɑːm- 'wɜːrd/ *n*

a combination of two or more words which functions as a single word. For example *self-made* (a **compound adjective**) as in *He was a self-made man* and *flower shop* (a **compound noun**) as in *They went to the flower shop*. Compound words are written either as a single word (e.g. *headache*), as hyphenated words (e.g. *self-government*), or as two words (e.g. *police station*).

see also PHRASAL VERB

comprehensible input /ˌkɒmprɪhensᵻbəl 'ɪnpʊt||ˌkɑːm-/ *n*

INPUT language which contains linguistic items that are slightly beyond the learner's present linguistic COMPETENCE.

see also INPUT HYPOTHESIS
Further reading Krashen 1985

comprehension approach /ˌkɒmprɪ'henʃən ə,prəʊtʃ||ˌkɑːm-/ *n*

(in language teaching) an APPROACH to second and foreign language teaching which emphasizes that:

a before learners are taught speaking, there should be a period of training in listening comprehension
b comprehension should be taught by teaching learners to understand meaning in the TARGET LANGUAGE[1]
c the learners' level of comprehension should always exceed their ability to produce language
d productive language skills will emerge more naturally when learners have well developed comprehension skills
e such an approach reflects how children learn their first language.
Although this approach has not led to a specific METHOD of language teaching, similar principles are found in the TOTAL PHYSICAL RESPONSE METHOD and the NATURAL APPROACH (2).

Further reading Winitz 1981

computational linguistics /ˌkɒmpjᵿ'teɪʃənəl lɪŋ'gwɪstɪks||ˌkɑːm-/ *n*

an approach to linguistics which uses mathematical techniques, often with the aid of a computer. Computational linguistics includes the analysis of language data, e.g. in order to establish the order in which learners acquire various grammatical rules or the frequency of occurrence of some particular item. It also includes research on **automatic translation**, electronic production of artificial speech (SPEECH SYNTHESIS) and the automatic recognition of human speech.

computer /kəm'pjuːtəʳ/ *n*

an electronic machine that can be used to manipulate data according to a series of instructions stored in its memory (see PROGRAM) and which can perform complex tasks in a very short time. The machine itself together with a keyboard, printer, screen, disk drives, programs etc., is known as a **computer system**.

see also MICROCOMPUTER, MAINFRAME COMPUTER

computer-administered test /kəmˈpjuːtər ədˈmɪnⱼstəd ˈtest‖-stərd/ *n*

a test that has been prepared or adapted so that it can be administered and scored by a computer.

computer assisted composition /kəmˈpjuːtər əˈsɪstⱼd kɒmpəˈzɪʃən‖ kɑːm-/ *n*

the use of a computer in teaching composition

computer assisted instruction /kəmˈpjuːtəʳ əˈsɪstⱼd ɪnˈstrʌkʃən/ *n* also **CAI, computer assisted language learning (CALL), computer based instruction** /kəmˈpjuːtəʳ beɪst ɪnˈstrʌkʃən/

the use of a computer in a teaching programme. This may include:

a a teaching programme which is presented by a computer in a sequence. The student responds on the computer, and the computer indicates whether the responses are correct or incorrect (see PRO-GRAMMED LEARNING).

b the use of computers to monitor student progress, to direct students into appropriate lessons, material, etc. This is also called **computer-managed instruction**.

see also INTERACTIVE

computer assisted language learning /kəmˈpjuːtər əˈsɪstⱼd ˈlæŋ gwɪdʒ ˌlɜːnɪŋ‖ˌlɜːr-/ *n* also **CALL**

the use of a computer in the teaching or learning of a second or foreign language. CALL may take the form of

a activities which parallel learning through other media but which use the facilities of the computer (e.g. using the computer to present a reading text)

b activities which are extensions or adaptations of print-based or classroom based activities (e.g. computer programs that teach writing skills by helping the student develop a topic and THESIS STATEMENT and by checking a composition for vocabulary, grammar, and topic development), and

c activities which are unique to CALL.

see also INTERACTIVE VIDEO
Further reading Flint Smith 1989; Hope, Taylor & Pusack 1984; Ahmad et al 1985

computer assisted learning /kəmˈpjuːtər əˈsɪstⱼd ˈlɜːnɪŋ‖-ɜːr-/ **(CAL)**
also **computer assisted instruction (CAI), computer aided learning** /kəmˈpjuːtər ˈeɪdⱼd ˈlɜːnɪŋ‖-ɜːr-/

the use of a computer in teaching and learning and in order to help achieve educational *objectives*. The first kinds of CAL programs which were developed reflected principles similar to programmed instruction (see PROGRAMMED LEARNING). The computer leads the student through a learning task step-by-step, asking questions to check comprehension.

Depending on the student's response, the computer gives the student further practice or progresses to new material (see BRANCHING). In more recent CAL COURSEWARE students are able to interact with the computer and perform higher level tasks while exploring a subject or problem.

see also INTERACTIVE VIDEO

computer language /kəmˈpjuːtəʳ ˈlæŋgwɪdʒ/ *n*

a programming system (see PROGRAM) used to write computer programs which are intended for particular purposes, such as **COBOL** (the name for a computer language used to write business programs) or **FOR-TRAN** (a computer language used to write engineering and scientific programs). A computer language consists of elements such as symbols, commands and functions which are combined according to specific rules to perform operations on specific types of data.

computer literacy /kəmˈpjuːtəʳ ˈlɪtərəsi/ *n* **computer literate** /kəmˈpjuːtəʳ ˈlɪtərl̩t/ *adj*

having sufficient knowledge and skill in the use of computers and computer software to be able to live in a computer-oriented society.

computer program /kəmˈpjuːtəʳ ˈprəʊgræm/ *n*

see PROGRAM

concept /ˈkɒnsept‖ˈkɑːn-/ *n*

the general idea or meaning which is associated with a word or symbol in a person's mind. Concepts are the abstract meanings which words and other linguistic items represent. Linguists believe all languages can express the same concepts, although some languages may have fewer names for some concepts than are found in other languages, or may distinguish between concepts differently. The forming of concepts is closely related to language ACQUISITION, and the use of concepts to form PROPOSITIONS is basic to human thought and communication.

concept formation /ˈkɒnsept fɔːˌmeɪʃən‖ˈkɑːn- fɔːr-/ *n*

(in child development) the process of forming CONCEPTS, and an important part of the development of thought.

conceptual meaning /kənˈseptʃuəl ˈmiːnɪŋ/ *n*

another term for DENOTATION

concessive clause /kənˈsesɪv ˈklɔːz/ *n*

a dependent clause giving information which contrasts with information contained in an independent clause, and which is usually introduced by *although* or *while*. For example,
Although she is only 13, Tina is an excellent pianist.

conclusion /kənˈkluːʒən/ *n*

see ESSAY

concord /ˈkɒŋkɔːd‖ˈkɑːŋkɔːrd/ *n*
also agreement
a type of grammatical relationship between two or more elements in a sentence, in which both or all elements show a particular feature. For example, in English a third person singular subject occurs with a singular verb, and a plural subject occurs with a plural verb (**number concord**):

> *He walks   They walk*

Concord may affect CASE, GENDER, NUMBER, and PERSON.

see also GOVERNMENT

concordance /kənˈkɔːdəns‖-ˈkɔːr-/ *n* **concordancing** /kənˈkɔːdənsɪŋ‖-ˈkɔːr-/ *v*
a list of all the words which are used in a particular text or in the works of a particular author, together with a list of the contexts in which each word occurs (usually not including highly frequent grammatical words such as articles and prepositions). Concordances have been used in the study of word frequencies, grammar, discourse and stylistics.
In recent years the preparation of concordances by computers has been used to analyze individual texts, large samples of writing by a particular author, or different genres and registers. A collection of texts for such purposes is called a **corpus**. Computer concordances are now often used in the preparation of dictionaries, since they enable lexicographers to study how words are used in a wide range of contexts.
Further reading Tribble and Jones 1990

concrete noun /ˈkɒŋkriːt ˈnaʊn‖ˈkɑːŋ-/ *n*
a noun which refers to a physical thing, rather than a quality, state, or action. For example *book, house,* and *machine* are concrete nouns. A noun which refers to a quality, state, or action is called an **abstract noun**. For example *happiness, idea,* and *punishment* are abstract nouns.
see also NOUN

concrete operational stage /ˈkɒŋkriːt ɒpəˈreɪʃənəl ˈsteɪdʒ‖ˈkɑːŋ-ɑːpə-/ *n*
see GENETIC EPISTEMOLOGY

concurrent validity /kənˈkʌrənt vəˈlɪdᵻti‖-ˈkɜːr-/ *n*
the degree to which a test correlates with some other test which is aimed at measuring the same skill, or with some other comparable measure of the skill being tested. For example to determine the concurrent validity of a listening comprehension test one could determine the correlation between scores of a group of learners on this test with their scores on an existing valid and reliable test of listening comprehension. The resulting **coefficient of correlation** would provide a measure of the concurrent VALIDITY of the test.
Further reading Brown 1988; Oller 1979

conditional /kənˈdɪʃənəl/ n

a grammatical MOOD which describes an imaginary or hypothetical situation or event. In some languages it is expressed by adding an AFFIX to the verb, e.g. *je donnerais* ("I would give") in French, where *ais* is the conditional affix added to the verb infinitive *donner* ("to give"). In English, *should* and *would* are also sometimes described as the conditional in sentences such as:

We should like to meet her.   I would go if I could.

conditional clause /kənˈdɪʃənəl ˈklɔːz/ n

(in English) ADVERBIAL CLAUSES beginning with *if, unless* or conjunctions with similar meanings, where a state or situation in one clause is dependent on something that may or will happen, and which is described in another clause. For example:

If it rains, we will go home.
If you worked harder, you would succeed.
You won't be able to drive unless you have a licence.

Further reading Close 1975

conditioned response /kənˈdɪʃənd rɪˈspɒns‖-ˈspɑːns/ n

(in behaviourist psychology (see BEHAVIOURISM)) a response which is not a normal or automatic response to a STIMULUS but which has been learned through the formation of a chain of associations (see STIMULUS-RESPONSE THEORY). For example, the Russian psychologist Pavlov noted that dogs produce saliva in the mouth when they see or smell food. This is an unconditioned response to a stimulus, the food. By ringing a bell as the dog sees the food, it is possible to train the dog to salivate when it hears the bell, even when food is absent. The salivation is now a conditioned response. Behavioural psychologists believe that people are conditioned to learn many forms of behaviour, including language, through the process of training or **conditioning**, and that learning consists of stimulus-response connections.

see also OPERANT CONDITIONING
Further reading Gagné 1970

conditioning /kənˈdɪʃənɪŋ/ n

see CONDITIONED RESPONSE

conjoining /kənˈdʒɔɪnɪŋ/ n conjoin /kənˈdʒɔɪn/ v

(in TRANSFORMATIONAL GENERATIVE GRAMMAR), a term used for the linking together of words, phrases, or clauses, etc. which are of equal status. For example:

John likes apples and pears.
Betty went to the butcher's and to the supermarket.

see also CONJUNCTION, EMBEDDING

conjugation[1] /ˌkɒndʒʊˈɡeɪʃən‖ˌkɑːn-/ n

a class of verbs which follow the same pattern for changes in TENSE, PERSON, or NUMBER. For example, in French there are four regular conjugations as well as irregular verbs. The verbs *donner* "to give", *parler* "to speak", *chercher* "to look for", etc. are described as belonging to the -*er* (or 1st) conjugation.

conjugation[2] *n* **conjugate** /ˈkɒndʒʒ̩geɪt||ˈkɑːn-/ *v*
the way in which a particular verb changes (conjugates) for TENSE, PERSON, or NUMBER. For example, the French verb *donner* "to give": *je donne* "I give", *nous donnons* "we give", *je donnerai "I shall give", j' ai donné* "I have given, I gave".

conjunct /ˈkɒndʒʌŋkt||ˈkɑːn-/ *n*
see ADJUNCT

conjunction /kənˈdʒʌŋkʃən/ *n*
also **connective**
   1 a word which joins words, phrases, or clauses together, such as *but, and, when*:
   John and Mary went.
   She sings but I don't.
Units larger than single words which function as conjunctions are sometimes known as **conjunctives**, for example *so that, as long as, as if*:
   She ran fast so that she could catch the bus.
Adverbs which are used to introduce or connect clauses are sometimes known as **conjunctive adverbs**, for example *however, nevertheless*:
   She is 86, nevertheless she enjoys good health.
   2 the process by which such joining takes place.
There are two types of conjunction:
   a **Co-ordination**, through the use of **co-ordinating conjunctions** (also known as **co-ordinators**) such as *and, or, but*. These join linguistic units which are equivalent or of the same rank.
   For example:
      It rained, but I went for a walk anyway.
      Shall we go home or go to a movie?
   The two clauses are **co-ordinate clauses**.
   b **Subordination**, through the use of **subordinating conjunctions** (also known as **subordinators**) such as *because, when, unless, that*. These join an INDEPENDENT CLAUSE and a DEPENDENT CLAUSE
   For example:
      I knew that he was lying.
      Unless it rains, we'll play tennis at 4.

conjunctive /kənˈdʒʌŋktɪv/ *n*
see CONJUNCTION

conjunctive adverb /kənˈdʒʌŋktɪv ˈædvɜːb||-vɜːrb/ *n*
see CONJUNCTION

connective /kəˈnektɪv/ *n*
another term for CONJUNCTION

connotation

connotation /ˌkɒnəˈteɪʃən||ˌkɑː-/ *n* **connotative** /ˈkɒnəteɪtɪv, kəˈnəʊ
ətɪv||ˈkɑːnə-/ *adj*
the additional meanings that a word or phrase has beyond its central
meaning (see DENOTATION). These meanings show people's emotions
and attitudes towards what the word or phrase refers to. For example,
child could be defined as a *young human being* but there are many other
characteristics which different people associate with *child*, e.g. *affec-
tionate, amusing, lovable, sweet, mischievous, noisy, irritating, grubby*.
Some connotations may be shared by a group of people of the same
cultural or social background, sex, or age; others may be restricted to
one or several individuals and depend on their personal experience.
In a meaning system, that part of the meaning which is covered by
connotation is sometimes referred to as **affective meaning, conno-
tative meaning**, or **emotive meaning**.
Further reading Leech 1981; Lyons 1977

connotative meaning /ˈkɒnəteɪtɪv ˈmiːnɪŋ, kəˈnəʊtətɪv||ˈkɑːnə-/ *n*
another term for CONNOTATION

consciousness raising /ˈkɒnʃəsnɨs ˌreɪzɪŋ||ˈkɑːn-/ *n*
an approach to the teaching of grammar in which instruction in
grammar (through drills, grammar explanation and other form –
focussed activities) is viewed as a way of raising the learner's awareness
of grammatical features of the language. This is thought to indirectly
facilitate second language acquisition. A consciousness-raising
approach is contrasted with traditional approaches to the teaching of
grammar, in which the goal is to instill correct grammatical patterns
and habits directly.
Further reading Rutherford 1987

consecutive interpretation /kənˈsekjᵿtɪv ɪnˌtɜːprɨˈteɪʃən||-ˌtɜːr-/ *n*
see INTERPRETATION

consonant /ˈkɒnsənənt||ˈkɑːn-/ *n*
a speech sound where the airstream from the lungs is either completely
blocked (STOP), partially blocked (LATERAL) or where the opening is so
narrow that the air escapes with audible friction (FRICATIVE). With
some consonants (NASALS) the airstream is blocked in the mouth but
allowed to escape through the nose.
With the other group of speech sounds, the VOWELS, the air from the
lungs is not blocked.
There are a number of cases where the distinction is not clear-cut, such
as the /j/ at the beginning of the English word *yes* where there is
only very slight friction, and linguists have sometimes called these
semi-vowels or **semi-consonants**.
see also MANNER OF ARTICULATION, PLACE OF ARTICULATION
Further reading Gimson 1989

78

consonant cluster /ˈkɒnsənənt ˈklʌstəʳ‖ˈkɑːn-/ *n*

a sequence of two or more consonants. Consonant clusters may occur at the beginning of a word (an **initial cluster**), at the end of a word (a **final cluster**), or within a word (a **medial cluster**). For example, in English:

initial cluster: /spl/ in /splæʃ/ *splash*

final cluster: /st/ in /test/ *test*

medial cluster: /str/ in /ˈpeɪstri/ *pastry*

Languages differ greatly in the ways in which consonants can form clusters, and in which positions in the word the clusters can occur. For example, in Serbo-Croatian, there are many three-consonant clusters in initial position which do not occur in English, e.g. /smr/, /zdr/, /zgr/, /zdv/. Other languages, for example Polynesian languages, do not have any consonant clusters at all.

see also CLUSTER REDUCTION

consonant system /ˈkɒnsənənt ˈsɪstm̩‖ˈkɑːn-/ *n*

The CONSONANTS of a language form systems. For example, English has, among other consonants, two parallel series of STOPS:

	bilabial	alveolar	velar
voiceless	p	t	k
voiced	b	d	g

Maori, a Polynesian language, has only one series: /p/, /t/, /k/ with no voiceless/voiced contrast (see VOICE[2]).

constative /ˈkɒnstətɪv‖ˈkɑːn-/ *n*

see PERFORMATIVE

constituent /kənˈstɪtʃuənt/ *n*

a linguistic unit, (usually in sentence analysis) which is part of a larger construction (see CONSTITUENT STRUCTURE)

see also DISCONTINUOUS CONSTITUENT, CHUNKING

constituent identification /kənˈstɪtʃuənt aɪˌdentɪfɪˈkeɪʃən/ *n*

see CHUNKING

constituent structure /kənˈstɪtʃuənt ˈstrʌktʃəʳ/ *n*

the arrangement of linguistic units (CONSTITUENTS) in a phrase, clause, sentence, etc., in order to show their relationship to one another. A constituent structure can be represented in various ways. A popular way is to use a **tree diagram**.

For example, the constituent structure of the sentence *The penguin swallowed the fish* can be shown as:

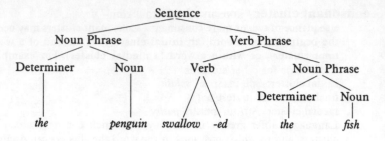

see also PHRASE-STRUCTURE GRAMMAR

constriction /kən'strɪkʃən/ *n* **constricted** /kən'strɪktɪd/ *adj*
(in the production of speech sounds) the narrowing of any part of the mouth or the throat (the VOCAL TRACT) to restrict the passage of the airstream from the lungs.

see also MANNER OF ARTICULATION

construct /'kɒnstrʌkt||'kɑːn-/ *n*
(in research) a concept that is inferred on the basis of observable phenomena and which can help in the analysis and understanding of events and phenomenon. Examples of constructs used in the study of language are ROLE and STATUS.

construct validity /'kɒnstrʌkt və'lɪdɪti||'kɑːn-/ *n*
(in testing) a form of VALIDITY which is based on the degree to which the items in a test reflect the essential aspects of the theory on which the test is based (the **construct**). For example, the greater the relationship which can be demonstrated between a test of COMMUNICATIVE COMPETENCE in a language and the theory of communicative competence, the greater the construct validity of the test.

Further reading Brown 1988; Oller 1979

contact language /'kɒntækt ˌlæŋgwɪdʒ||'kɑːn-/ *n*
see PIDGIN

content analysis /'kɒntent əˌnælɪsɪs||'kɑːn-/ *n*
(in research) a method used for analyzing and tabulating the frequency of occurrence of topics, ideas, opinions and other aspects of the content of written or spoken communication. For example, content analysis could be used to determine the frequency of occurrence of references to males, females, adults, children, caucasians, non-caucasians etc. in a set of language teaching materials, in order to discover if any particular attitudes or themes were unintentionally being communicated in the materials.

content areas /'kɒntent ˌeəriəz||'kɑːn-/ *n*
also **content fields**

the subjects other than language which are taught in a school curriculum. In countries with immigrant populations, particularly in the United States, a contrast is made between the teaching of English to non-native speakers of English and teaching in the regular school programme for other students where the focus is on the content areas, i.e. maths, science, social studies, geography etc. A course which teaches immigrant students the writing skills they need in the content areas may be known as **writing in the content areas**.

see also CONTENT BASED INSTRUCTION

content based instruction /ˈkɒntent beɪst ɪnˈstrʌkʃən‖ˈkɑːn-/ *n*

a programme in English as a second language in which the focus is on teaching students the skills they will need in regular classrooms, i.e. for learning in the CONTENT AREAS such as maths, geography, or biology. Such a programme teaches students the language skills they will need when they are MAINSTREAM*ED*.

see also LANGUAGE ACROSS THE CURRICULUM

content reading /ˈkɒntent ˌriːdɪŋ‖ˈkɑːn-/ *n*

the reading of books and other printed materials that contain information needed for learning in the CONTENT AREAS, such as text-books or other study materials, in contrast with reading which is for pleasure or relaxation.

content validity /ˈkɒntent vəˈlɪdɪ̥ti‖ˈkɑːn-/ *n*

(in testing) a form of VALIDITY which is based on the degree to which a test adequately and sufficiently measures the particular skills or behaviour it sets out to measure. For example, a test of pronunciation skills in a language would have low content validity if it tested only some of the skills which are required for accurate pronunciation, such as a test which tested the ability to pronounce isolated sounds, but not STRESS, INTONATION, or the pronunciation of sounds within words. Content validity is of particular importance in CRITERION REFERENCED TEST*S*, where the test content must represent the content of what has been taught in a course.

Futher reading Brown 1988; Oller 1979

content word /ˈkɒntent ˌwɜːd‖ˈkɑːn- ˌwɜːrd/ *n*

Words can be divided into two classes: **content words** and **function words**.

Content words are words which refer to a thing, quality, state, or action and which have meaning (**lexical meaning**) when the words are used alone. Content words are mainly nouns, verbs, adjectives, and adverbs, e.g. *book, run, musical, quickly*.

Function words are words which have little meaning on their own, but which show grammatical relationships in and between sentences (**grammatical meaning**). Conjunctions, prepositions, articles, e.g. *and, to, the*, are function words.

Function words are also called **form words, empty words, functors**,

grammatical words, **structural words**, **structure words**. Content words are also called **full words**, **lexical words**.

see also WORD CLASS

context /'kɒntekst‖'kɑːn-/ *n* **contextual** /kən'tekstʃuəl/ *adj*

that which occurs before and/or after a word, a phrase or even a longer UTTERANCE or a TEXT. The context often helps in understanding the particular meaning of the word, phrase, etc. For example, the word *loud* in *loud music* is usually understood as meaning "noisy" whereas in *a tie with a loud pattern* it is understood as "unpleasantly colourful". The context may also be the broader social situation in which a linguistic item is used. For example, in ordinary usage, *spinster* refers to an older unmarried woman but in a legal context it refers to *any* unmarried woman.

see also CONTEXTUAL MEANING

contextually appropriate method /kən'tekstʃuəli ə'prəʊprɪ-ɪ̯t 'me θəd/ *n*

see CLOZE PROCEDURE

contextual meaning /kən'tekstʃuəl 'miːnɪŋ/ *n*

the meaning a linguistic item has in context, for example the meaning a word has within a particular sentence, or a sentence has in a particular paragraph. The question *Do you know the meaning of war?* for example, may have two different contextual meanings:

a it may mean *Do you know the meaning of the word war?*, when said by a language teacher to a class of students.

b it may mean *War produces death, injury, and suffering*, when said by an injured soldier to a politician who favours war.

contingency table /kən'tɪndʒənsi ˌteɪbəl/ *n*

a table which displays data concerning two VARIABLES[2]. For example, if we wanted to determine the relationship between the scores students obtained on a grammar test and the number of hours spent in preparation for the test, a contingency table could be used to show the number of students obtaining different test scores according to the amount of time they spent in preparation. The CHI-SQUARE test can be used to test the STATISTICAL SIGNIFICANCE of the relationship between the two variables (i.e. between the scores and the preparation time).

	Test scores			
	0→10	11→20	21→30	total
hours spent in preparation	10 2	6 5	4 9	20 16
total	12	11	13	36

a contingency table

continuing education /kənˈtɪnju-ɪŋ edjˈ̩ʊkeɪʃən‖edʒə-/ *n*
in the US, educational programmes provided for adults, apart from the K-12 school system, which often include basic skills, recreational, advanced and technical studies.

continuous /kənˈtɪnjuəs/ *n*
another term for PROGRESSIVE

continuous assessment /kənˈtɪnjuəs əˈsesmənt/ *n*
(in a language programme) an approach to assessment in which students are assessed regularly throughout the programme rather than being given a single assessment at the end. This is thought to give a more accurate picture of student achievement.

continuum /kənˈtɪnjuəm/ *n*
see SPEECH CONTINUUM

contraction /kənˈtrækʃən/ *n*
the reduction of a linguistic form and often its combination with another form. For example:
I shall into *I'll*
they are into *they're*
did not into *didn't*

contrastive analysis /kənˈtrɑːstɪv əˈnæl̩s̩s‖-ˈtræ-/ *n*
also **CA**
the comparison of the linguistic systems of two languages, for example the sound system or the grammatical system. Contrastive analysis was developed and practised in the 1950s and 1960s, as an application of STRUCTURAL LINGUISTICS to language teaching, and is based on the following assumptions:
a the main difficulties in learning a new language are caused by interference from the first language (see LANGUAGE TRANSFER).
b these difficulties can be predicted by contrastive analysis.
c teaching materials can make use of contrastive analysis to reduce the effects of interference.
Contrastive analysis was more successful in PHONOLOGY than in other areas of language, and declined in the 1970s as interference was replaced by other explanations of learning difficulties (see ERROR ANALYSIS, INTERLANGUAGE). In recent years contrastive analysis has been applied to other areas of language, for example the discourse systems (see DISCOURSE ANALYSIS). This is called **contrastive discourse analysis**.
see also COMPARATIVE LINGUISTICS
Further reading James 1980; Odlin 1989

contrastive discourse analysis /kənˈtrɑːstɪv ˈdɪskɔːs ə͵næl̩s̩s‖ -ˈtræ- -ɔːrs/ *n*
see CONTRASTIVE ANALYSIS

contrastive rhetoric /kənˈtrɑːstɪv ˈretərɪk‖-ˈtræ-/ *n*
the study of similarities and differences between writing in a first and second language or between two languages, in order to understand how writing conventions in one language influence how a person writes in another. Writing in a second language is though to be influenced to some extent by the linguistic and cultural conventions of the writer's first language, and this may influence how the writer organizes written discourse (DISCOURSE STRUCTURE), the kind of SCRIPT or SCHEME the writer uses, as well as such factors as TOPIC[1], audience, paragraph organization, and choice of VOCABULARY or REGISTER.
see also CONTRASTIVE ANALYSIS
Further reading Grabe & Kaplan 1989

contrastive stress /kənˈtrɑːstɪv ˈstres‖-ˈtræ-/ *n*
stronger emphasis (STRESS) on a word in order to contrast it with another word or phrase. For example:
Q: *Did you speak to Mr Brown?*
A: *No, I spoke to Mŕs Brown.*
where the stress is on *Mrs*.
Sometimes, contrastive stress is used because the speaker wants to emphasize a particular point. For example:
Joan is studying French ańd German.
as a reply to the question:
Is Joan studying French or German?

control group /kənˈtrəʊl ˌgruːp/ *n*
one of two groups used in certain kinds of experimental research, the other being the **experimental group**. For example if we wanted to study the effectiveness of a new teaching method, one group (the experimental group) may be taught using the new method, and another group, the control group, by using the usual teaching method. The control group is chosen because of its equivalence to the experimental group (e.g. by assigning students to the two groups at random). In studying the effects of the new method, the experimental group is compared with the control group.

controlled composition /kənˈtrəʊld kɒmpəˈzɪʃən‖kɑːm-/ *n*
see COMPOSITION

controlled processing /kənˈtrəʊld ˈprəʊsesɪŋ‖ˈprɑː-/ *n*
see AUTOMATIC PROCESSING

conventionalized speech /kənˈvenʃənəlaɪzd ˈspiːtʃ/ *n*
another term for ROUTINE

convergence[1] /kənˈvɜːdʒəns‖-ɜːr-/ *n*
the process of two or more languages or language varieties becoming more similar to one another. For example:
a if one language variety gains status, then the speakers of another

variety may change their pronunciation to be more like it, and use words and grammatical structures from it.

b if speakers of two language varieties mix together, by moving to the same area for example, both varieties may change to become more like each other.

see also DIVERGENCE[1]

convergence[2] n

see ACCOMMODATION

convergent question /kən'vɜːdʒənt 'kwestʃən||-ɜːr-/ n

a question that encourages student responses to converge or focus on a central theme. Convergent questions typically require a single correct answer and elicit short responses from students. Convergent questions may be useful when the teacher wants to focus on specific skills or information or requires short responses, such as when attempting to find out whether students can locate a specific piece of information in a reading passage.

see also CLASSROOM DISCOURSE, DIVERGENT QUESTION, EVALUATIVE QUESTION, QUESTIONING TECHNIQUES

conversational analysis /ˌkɒnvə'seɪʃənəl ə'næləsɪs||ˌkɑːnvər-/ n

the analysis of natural conversation in order to discover what the linguistic characteristics of conversation are and how conversation is used in ordinary life.

Conversational analysis includes the study of:

a how speakers decide when to speak during a conversation (i.e. rules of TURN-TAKING)

b how the sentences of two or more speakers are related (see ADJACENCY PAIR, CONVERSATIONAL MAXIM)

c the different functions that conversation is used for (for example to establish ROLES, and to communicate politeness or intimacy)

see also DISCOURSE ANALYSIS, ETHNOMETHODOLOGY, SPEECH ACT
Further reading Coulthard 1985

conversational implicature /ˌkɒnvə'seɪʃənəl 'ɪmplɪkətʃʊər||ˌkɑːnvər- -tʃər/ n

see CONVERSATIONAL MAXIM

conversational maxim /ˌkɒnvə'seɪʃənəl 'mæksɪm||ˌkɑːnvər-/ n

an unwritten rule about conversation which people know and which influences the form of conversational exchanges. For example in the following exchange

A: *Let's go to the movies.*

B: *I have an examination in the morning.*

B's reply might appear not to be connected to A's remark. However, since A has made an invitation and since a reply to an invitation is usually either an acceptance or a refusal, B's reply is here understood as an excuse for not accepting the invitation (i.e. a refusal). B has used the "maxim" that speakers normally give replies which are relevant to the question that has been asked. The philosopher Grice has suggested that there are four conversational maxims:

a The maxim of quantity: give as much information as is needed.

b The maxim of quality: speak truthfully.

c The maxim of relevance: say things that are relevant.

d The maxim of manner: say things clearly and briefly.

The use of conversational maxims to imply meaning during conversation is called **conversational implicature,** and the "co-operation" between speakers in using the maxims is sometimes called the **co-operative principle**.

see also ADJACENCY PAIR, COHERENCE, REALITY PRINCIPLE
Further reading Grice 1967; Clark & Clark 1977

conversational openings /ˌkɒnvəˈseɪʃənəl ˈəʊpənɪŋz||ˌkɑːnvər-/

(in conversational interaction) the strategies a person uses to begin a conversation. These include clearing the throat, body movement, eye movement, and repeating a previous part of the conversation.

see also TURN TAKING
Further reading Wardhaugh 1985

conversational routine /ˌkɒnvəˈseɪʃənəl ruːˈtiːn||ˌkɑːnvər-/ *n*

see ROUTINE

conversational rules /ˌkɒnvəˈseɪʃənəl ˈruːlz||ˌkɑːnvər-/ *n*
also **rules of speaking**

rules shared by a group of people which govern their spoken conversational behaviour. Conversational rules may, for instance, regulate when to speak or not to speak in a conversation, what to say in a particular situation, and how to start and end a conversation. These rules vary not only between different languages (LANGUAGE[1]) but also between different social groups speaking the same language.

see also CONVERSATIONAL ANALYSIS, CONVERSATIONAL MAXIM
Further reading Hymes 1972; Wardhaugh 1986

co-occurrence restriction /ˌkəʊəˈkʌrəns rɪˌstrɪkʃənz||-əˈkɜːr-/ *n*

in some models of syntactic analysis, restrictions on the elements in the sentence so that they can only occur with certain elements and not with others.

For example, the sentence:

   *Anita laughed the baby

would be ungrammatical as the verb *laugh* cannot co-occur with an OBJECT; it is **intransitive**.

Further reading Fromkin and Rodman 1983

co-occurrence rule /ˌkəʊəˈkʌrəns ˌruːl||-əˈkɜːr-/ *n*

see SPEECH STYLES

co-operative principle /kəʊˈɒpərətɪv ˈprɪnsḷpəl||-ˈɑːp-/ *n*

see CONVERSATIONAL MAXIM

co-operating teacher /kəʊˈɒpəreɪtɪŋ ˈtiːtʃəʳ||-ˈɑːp-/ *n*
also **master teacher**

(in teacher education) an experienced teacher in whose class a student teacher does his or her practice teaching. The role of the co-operating teacher is to help the student teacher acquire teaching skills and to give feedback on his or her teaching.

co-operation /kəʊˌɒpəˈreɪʃən||-ˌɑːp-/ *n*

(in learning) working together with one or more peer(s) to solve a problem, complete a learning task, share information or get FEEDBACK on performance.

co-operative learning /kəʊˈɒpərətɪv ˈlɜːnɪŋ||-ˈɑːp- ˈlɜːr-/ *n*
also **collaborative learning**

an approach to teaching and learning in which classrooms are organized so that students work together in small co-operative teams. Such an approach to learning is said to increase students' learning since a) it is less threatening for many students, b) it increases the amount of student participation in the classroom, c) it reduces the need for competitiveness, and d) it reduces the teacher's dominance in the classroom.

Five distinct types of co-operative learning activities are often distinguished:

1 **Peer Tutoring**: students help each other learn, taking turns tutoring or drilling each other.
2 **Jigsaw**: Each member of a group has a piece of information needed to complete a group task.
3 **Co-operative Projects**: Students work together to produce a product, such as a written paper or group presentation.
4 **Co-operative/Individualized**: Students progress at their own rate through individualized learning materials but their progress contributes to a team grade so that each pupil is rewarded by the achievements of his or her teammates.
5 **Co-operative Interaction**: Students work together as a team to complete a learning unit, such as a laboratory experiment.

Co-operative-learning activities are often used in COMMUNICATIVE LANGUAGE TEACHING.

Further reading Kagan 1987

co-ordinate bilingualism /kəʊˈɔːdɪn̩t baɪˈlɪŋgwəlɪzəm||-ˈɔːr-/ *n*
see COMPOUND BILINGUALISM

co-ordinate clause /kəʊˈɔːdɪn̩t ˈklɔːz||-ˈɔːr-/ *n*
see CONJUNCTION

co-ordinating conjunction /kəʊˈɔːdɪneɪtɪŋ kənˈdʒʌŋkʃən||-ˈɔːr-/ *n*
see CONJUNCTION

co-ordination /kəʊˌɔːdɪˈneɪʃən||-ˌɔːr-/ *n*
see CONJUNCTION

co-ordinator /kəʊˈɔːdɪneɪtəʳ‖-ˈɔːr-/ n

see CONJUNCTION

copula /ˈkɒpjŭlə‖ˈkɑːp-/ n **copulative** /ˈkɒpjŭlətɪv‖ˈkɑːpjŭleɪ-/ adj
also **linking verb**

a verb that links a SUBJECT to a COMPLEMENT. For example:
He is sick. She looked afraid.
The very *be* is sometimes known as **the copula** since this is its main
function in English. The following are copulative verbs, i.e. they can
be used copulatively: *feel, look, prove, remain, resemble, sound, stay,
become, grow, turn, smell, taste.*

see also TRANSITIVE VERB
Further reading Quirk et al 1985

core grammar /ˈkɔːʳ ˌgræməʳ/ n

within the framework of Chomsky's UNIVERSAL GRAMMAR, a grammar
which contains all the universal principles of language as well as
special conditions or rules (PARAMETERS) which can be "set" for
particular languages.
Parameters may vary from one language to another. For example, in
some languages, e.g. English, the HEAD of a phrase is first, in Japanese
the head is last. Aspects of a language which are not predictable from
the Universal Grammar are considered not to belong to the core
grammar but to the **periphery** or **peripheral grammar**.
It is claimed that, in first language acquisition, the initial universal
grammar of a child consists of fixed principles and open (that is
'unset') parameters. As the child receives input from his or her first
language, the open parameters are fixed for a particular language and
the child's L1 core grammar results.
Researchers have investigated the role of core grammars in second
language acquisition.

Further reading Cook 1988; White 1989a, 1989b

corpus /ˈkɔːpəs‖ˈkɔːr-/ n (plural **corpora** /ˈkɔːpərə‖ˈkɔːr-/)

a collection of materials that has been made for a particular purpose,
such as a set of textbooks which are being analyzed and compared or a
sample of sentences or UTTERANCES which are being analyzed for their
linguistic features.

see also CONCORDANCE

corpus planning /ˈkɔːpəs ˈplænɪŋ‖ˈkɔːr-/ n

a type of LANGUAGE PLANNING
a deliberate restructuring of a language, often by government
authorities. This may be done by giving it, for example, an increased
range of vocabulary, new grammatical structures, sometimes even a
new or more standardized writing system.
For example, in Malaysia, where Bahasa Malaysia (Malay) has become
the national language, attempts have been made to construct new
vocabulary in areas such as business, education and research. Similar
efforts have been made for Swahili in East Africa.

correct /kə'rekt/ *adj* **correctness** /kə'rektn⅟s/ *n*

a term which is used to state that particular language usage, e.g. the pronunciation of a word is *right* as opposed to *wrong*. For example:

This is the correct pronunciation.

The term often expresses a particular attitude to language usage (see PRESCRIPTIVE GRAMMAR). It has become more common to abandon absolute judgments of *right* and *wrong* and to consider a usage as being more or less appropriate (APPROPRIATENESS) in a particular social setting.

see also ERROR

Further reading Hughes & Trudgill 1987

correlation /ˌkɒrɨ'leɪʃən‖ˌkɔː-, ˌkɑː-/ *n*

a measure of the strength of the relationship between two sets of data. For example we may wish to determine the **relationship** between the scores of a group of students on a mathematics test and on a language test. A common coefficient of correlation used is known as *Pearson Product Moment Coefficient* symbolized by r. Its value varies from -1.00 to $+1.00$, with the value of zero indicating the absence of any correlation and either a minus or plus one indicating perfect correspondence of scores. For example if students received quite similar scores on two tests their scores would have a high positive correlation. If their scores on one test were the reverse of their scores on the other, their scores would have a high negative correlation. If their scores on the two tests were not related in any predicable way their scores would have a zero correlation.

Further reading Brown 1988; Hardyck & Petrinovich 1976

correlative conjunction /kə'relətɪv kən'dʒʌŋkʃən/ *n*

coordinating CONJUNCTIONS used in pairs in a parallel construction. For example:

> both . . . *and*
> either . . . *or*
> neither . . . *nor*

counselling learning /'kaʊnsəlɪŋ 'lɜːnɪŋ‖'lɜːr-/ *n*

see COMMUNITY LANGUAGE LEARNING

countable noun /'kaʊntəbəl 'naʊn/ *n*
also **count noun** /'kaʊnt ˌnaʊn/

a noun which has both singular and plural forms. For example:

word – words, machine – machines, bridge – bridges

A noun which does not usually occur in the plural is called an **uncountable noun** or a **mass noun**. For example:

education, homework, harm.

see also NOUN

course density /'kɔːs 'densɨti‖'kɔːrs/ *n*

(in course design and syllabus design (see COURSE DESIGN)) the rate at which new teaching points are introduced and reintroduced in a course or syllabus in order to achieve a satisfactory rate of learning. In language courses where the main emphasis is on grammar and vocabulary, learners can generally learn four or five items per hour for active use and another four or five for passive use. Targets of 2000 items for active use and a further 2000 for passive recognition are commonly set for a 400 hour course of instruction.

Further reading Sager, Dungworth, & McDonald 1980

course design /'kɔːs dɪ'zaɪn‖'kɔːrs/ *n*
also language programme design, programme design

(in language teaching) the development of a language programme or set of teaching materials. Whereas **syllabus design** generally refers to procedures for deciding what will be taught in a language programme, course design includes how a syllabus will be carried out. For example:

a what teaching METHOD and materials will be needed to achieve the OBJECTIVES

b how much time will be required

c how classroom activities will be sequenced and organized

d what sort of PLACEMENT TESTS, ACHIEVEMENT TESTS and other sorts of tests will be used

e how the programme will be evaluated (see EVALUATION)

Course design is part of the broader process of CURRICULUM DEVELOPMENT.

see also COURSE DENSITY
Further reading White 1988

courseware /'kɔːsweəʳ‖'kɔːrs-/ *n*

computer programs used in COMPUTER ASSISTED LEARNING.

coverage /'kʌvərɪdʒ/ *n*

the degree to which words and structures can be used to replace other words and structures, because they have a similar meaning. For example *seat* includes the meanings of *chair*, *bench*, and *stool*, and *What time is it please?* can replace *Could you kindly tell me the time?* Coverage is a principle used to help select language items for language teaching, since items with a high degree of coverage are likely to be most useful to language learners.

see also SELECTION
Further reading Mackey 1965; West 1953

creative construction hypothesis /kri'eɪtɪv kən'strʌkʃən haɪˌpɒθɪˈsɪs‖-ˌpɑː-/ *n*

a theory about how second and foreign language learners work out language rules. The theory was proposed by Dulay and Burt, who claim that learners work out the rules of their TARGET LANGUAGE[1] by:

a using natural mental processes, such as GENERALIZATION

b using similar processes to first language learners

c not relying very much on the rules of the first language

d using processes which lead to the creation of new forms and structures which are not found in the target language. For example:

*She goed to school. (instead of *She went to school*)

*What you are doing? (instead of *What are you doing?*)

Further reading Dulay & Burt 1974; Dulay, Burt, & Krashen 1982

creole /ˈkriːəʊl/ n

a PIDGIN language which has become the native language of a group of speakers, being used for all or many of their daily communicative needs. Usually, the sentence structures and vocabulary range of a creole are far more complex than those of a pidgin language.

Creoles are usually classified according to the language from which most of their vocabulary comes, e.g. English-based, French-based, Portuguese-based, and Swahili-based creoles.

Examples of English-based creoles are Jamaican Creole, Hawaiian Creole and Krio in Sierra Leone, West Africa.

see also CREOLIZATION, POST-CREOLE CONTINUUM

creolization /ˌkriːəʊlaɪˈzeɪʃən‖-lə-/ n

the process by which a PIDGIN becomes a CREOLE.

Creolization involves the expansion of the vocabulary and the grammatical system.

criterion /kraɪˈtɪəriən/ n

see BEHAVIOURAL OBJECTIVE

criterion measure /kraɪˈtɪəriən ˌmeʒəʳ/ n

(in testing) a standard against which a test can be compared as a measure of its VALIDITY. A criterion measure may be another test which is known to be valid, or another valid indicator of performance.

see also CRITERION-RELATED VALIDITY

Further reading Hughes 1989

criterion referenced test /kraɪˈtɪəriən ˌrefərənst ˈtest/ n

a test which measures a student's performance according to a particular standard or criterion which has been agreed upon. The student must reach this level of performance to pass the test, and a student's score is therefore interpreted with reference to the criterion score, rather than to the scores of other students. This may be contrasted with a **norm referenced test**. This is a test which is designed to measure how the performance of a particular student or group of students compares with the performance of another student or group of students whose scores are given as the norm. A student's score is therefore interpreted with reference to the scores of other students or groups of students, rather than to an agreed criterion score.

Further reading Ebel 1972

criterion-related validity /kraɪˈtɪəriən rɪˈleɪt̬d vəˈlɪd̬ti/ *n*
(in testing) a form of VALIDITY in which a test is compared or correlated with an outside CRITERION MEASURE.

critical comprehension /ˈkrɪtɪkəl ˌkɒmprɪˈhenʃən||ˌkɑːm-/ *n*
see READING

critical period hypothesis /ˈkrɪtɪkəl ˈpɪəriəd haɪˈpɒ̩s̩s||-ˈpɑː-/ *n*
the theory that in child development there is a period during which language can be acquired more easily than at any other time. According to the biologist Lenneberg, the critical period lasts until puberty (around age 12 or 13 years), and is due to biological development. Lenneberg suggested that language learning may be more difficult after puberty because the brain lacks the ability for adaptation. This, he believed, was because the language functions of the brain have already been established in a particular part of the brain; that is, because **lateralization** (see BRAIN) has already occurred by this time.
Further reading Lenneberg 1967

critical reading /ˈkrɪtɪkəl ˈriːdɪŋ/ *n*
reading in which the reader reacts critically to what he or she is reading, through relating the content of the reading material to personal standards, values, attitudes or beliefs.

cross-cultural analysis /ˈkrɒs ˈkʌltʃərəl əˈnæl̩s̩s||ˈkrɔːs-/ *n*
analysis of data from two or more different cultural groups, in order to determine if generalizations made about members of one culture are also true of the members of other cultures. Cross-cultural research is an important part of sociolinguistics, since it is often important to know if generalizations made about one language group reflect the culture of that group or are universal.

cross-cultural communication /ˈkrɒs ˈkʌltʃərəl kəˌmjuːn̩ˈkeɪʃən|| ˈkrɔːs-/ *n*
an exchange of ideas, information, etc. between person from different cultural backgrounds.
There are often more problems in cross-cultural communication than in communication between people of the same cultural background. Each participant may interpret the other's speech according to his or her own cultural conventions and expectations (see CONVERSATIONAL RULES). If the cultural conventions of the speakers are widely different, misinterpretations and misunderstandings can easily arise, even resulting in a total breakdown of communication. This has been shown by research into real-life situations, such as job interviews, doctor-patient encounters and legal communication.
see also CONVERSATIONAL MAXIM
Further reading Gumperz 1982

cross-over groups /ˈkrɒs əʊvəʳ ˌgruːps||ˈkrɔːs-/ *n*
(in teaching) a group activity in which the class is initially divided into groups for discussion. After a period of time, one or more member(s) of each group move to join other groups, and the discussion continues. This allows for ideas to be shared without the need for a whole-class feedback session.

cross-section(al) method /ˈkrɒs ˈsekʃənəl ˈmeθəd||ˈkrɔːs/ *n*
also **cross-section(al) study** /ˈkrɒs ˈsekʃənəl ˈstʌdi||ˈkrɔːs/
a study of a group of different individuals or subjects at a single point in time, in order to measure or study a particular topic or aspect of language (for example use of the tense system of a language). This can be contrasted with a **longitudinal method** or **longitudinal study**, in which an individual or group is studied over a period of time (for example, to study how the use of the tense system changes and develops with age). This approach has been used to study first language learning.

cue /kjuː/ *n*
(in language teaching) a signal given by the teacher in order to produce a **response** by the students. For example in practising questions:

cue	response
time	*What time is it?*
day	*What day is it?*

Cues may be words, signals, actions, etc.
see also DRILL

cultural deprivation /ˈkʌltʃərəl ˌdeprɪˈveɪʃən/ *n*
also **cultural disadvantage** /ˈkʌltʃərəl ˌdɪsədˈvɑːntɪdʒ||-ˈvæn-/
the theory that some children, particularly those from lower social and economic backgrounds, lack certain home experiences and that this may lead to learning difficulties in school. For example, children from homes which lack books or educational games and activities to stimulate thought and language development may not perform well in school. Since many other factors could explain why some children do not perform well in school, this theory is an insufficient explanation for differences in children's learning abilities.

see also COMPENSATORY INSTRUCTION, CULTURAL RELATIVISM
Further reading Edwards 1979

cultural pluralism /ˈkʌltʃərəl ˈpluərəlɪzəm/ *n*
a situation in which an individual or group has more than one set of cultural beliefs, values, and attitudes. The teaching of a foreign language or programmes in BILINGUAL EDUCATION are sometimes said to encourage cultural pluralism. An educational programme which aims to develop cultural pluralism is sometimes referred to as **multicultural education**, for example a programme designed to teach about different ethnic groups in a country.

93

cultural relativism /ˈkʌltʃərəl ˈrelətɪvɪzəm/ *n*

the theory that a culture can only be understood on its own terms. This means that standards, attitudes, and beliefs from one culture should not be used in the study or description of another culture. According to this theory there are no universal cultural beliefs or values, or these are not regarded as important. Cultural relativism has been part of the discussions of LINGUISTIC RELATIVITY and CULTURAL DEPRIVATION.

Further reading Hymes 1964

culture /ˈkʌltʃərˀ/ *n*

the total set of beliefs, attitudes, customs, behaviour, social habits, etc. of the members of a particular society.

see also BICULTURAL

culture fair /ˌkʌltʃərˀ ˈfeərˀ◄/ *adj*
also **culture free** /ˌkʌltʃərˀ ˈfriː ◄/

(in language testing) a test which does not favour members of a particular cultural group, because it is based on assumptions, beliefs, and knowledge which are common to all the groups being tested, is called culture fair. For example, the following test item is not culture fair:

Bananas are _____ (a) *brown*, (b) *green*, (c) *yellow*.

The item is culturally biased because for some people bananas are thought of as yellow, but for others green bananas are eaten, and cooked bananas are brown. If only one of these answers is marked as correct, the test favours a particular cultural group.

culture shock /ˈkʌltʃərˀ ʃɒk‖ˈʃɑːk/ *n*

strong feelings of discomfort, fear, or insecurity which a person may have when they enter another culture. For example, when a person moves to live in a foreign country, they may have a period of culture shock until they become familiar with the new culture.

curriculum[1] /kəˈrɪkjǔləm/ *n*

an educational programme which states:

a the educational purpose of the programme (the **ends**)

b the content, teaching procedures and learning experiences which will be necessary to achieve this purpose (the **means**)

c some means for assessing whether or not the educational ends have been achieved.

see also EVALUATION
Further reading Nunan 1988; Pratt 1980; White 1988

curriculum[2]

another term for SYLLABUS

curriculum development /kəˈrɪkjǔləm dɪˈveləpmənt/ *n*
also **curriculum design** /kəˈrɪkjǔləm dɪˈzaɪn/

the study and development of the goals, content, implementation, and evaluation of an educational system. In language teaching, curriculum development (also called **syllabus design**) includes:

a the study of the purposes for which a learner needs a language (NEEDS ANALYSIS)

b the setting of OBJECTIVES, and the development of a SYLLABUS, teaching METHODS, and materials

c the EVALUATION of the effects of these procedures on the learner's language ability.

Further reading Nunan 1988; Pratt 1980; White 1988

cybernetics /ˌsaɪbəˈnetɪks‖-bər-/ *n*
the study of communication and control in natural and artificial information handling systems, particularly how control systems in electronic and mechanical systems compare to those used in biological systems. Cybernetics is a multidisciplinary field of study involving computer science, linguistics, psychology etc.

cyclical approach /ˈsaɪklɪkəl əˈprəʊtʃ/ *n*
another term for SPIRAL APPROACH

D

dactylology /ˌdæktl̩ˈlɒlədʒi‖-ˈlɑː-/ *n*
  another term for FINGER SPELLING

dangling modifier /ˈdæŋɡlɪŋ ˈmɒdl̩faɪəʳ‖ˈmɑː-/ *n*
  (in composition) a phrase or clause that does not modify anything in a
  sentence or which refers to the wrong word in a sentence.
  For example, in the sentence:
> *Walking home from school, the fire engine came screeching around the*
> *corner.*

  The phrase *walking home from school* modifies *fire engine*, making an
  inappropriate sentence. This could be corrected to:
> *Walking home from school, I saw the fire engine come screeching around*
> *the corner.*

  The phrase *walking home from school*, now modifies *I* in the main clause,
  and the sentence is no longer inappropriate

data /ˈdeɪtə, ˈdɑːtə/ *n* (singular **datum** /ˈdeɪtəm, ˈdɑː-/)
  (in research) information, evidence or facts gathered through experiments or studies which can be analyzed in order to better the understanding of a phenomenon or to support a theory.

data-base /ˈdeɪtəˌbeɪs/ *n*
also **data bank** /ˈdeɪtəˌbæŋk/ *n*
  a large body of information or data which is intended to be used for a
  specific purpose. In a language program, a data-base which contains
  information about students tests scores on all tests taken in the
  institution may be established. Later, this data-base may be used to
  determine students' rates of learning or the effectiveness of tests for
  particular purposes. In first or second language acquisition research, a
  data-base may contain examples of sentences produced by learners at
  different stages of learning, which could later be analyzed for a variety
  of purposes.

dative case[1] /ˈdeɪtɪv ˌkeɪs/ *n*
  the form of a noun or noun phrase which usually shows that the noun
  or noun phrase functions as the INDIRECT OBJECT of a verb.
  For example, in the German sentence:
> *Sie gab der Katze eine Schale Milch.*
> She gave the cat a dish (of) milk

  in the noun phrase *der Katze*, the article has the inflectional ending -er
  to show that the noun phrase is in the dative case because it is the
  indirect object of the verb.

  see also CASE[1]
  Further reading Lyons 1968

dative case² *n*

(In CASE GRAMMAR) the noun or noun phrase which refers to the person or animal affected by the state or action of the verb is in the dative case.

For example, in the sentences:

Gregory was frightened by the storm.

I persuaded Tom to go.

Gregory and *Tom* are in the dative case. Both Gregory and Tom are affected by something: Gregory is frightened and Tom experiences persuasion.

The dative case is sometimes called the **experiencer case.**

Further reading Fillmore 1968

daughter (dependency) /ˈdɔːtəʳ dɪˌpendənsi/ *n*

see SISTER (DEPENDENCY)

declarative /dɪˈklærətɪv/ *n*

see SPEECH ACT CLASSIFICATION

declarative knowledge /dɪˈklærətɪv ˈnɒlɪdʒ‖ˈnɑː-/ *n*

also **factual knowledge** (in cognitive psychology and learning theory), one of two ways information is stored in LONG TERM MEMORY. Declarative knowledge is information that consists of consciously known facts, concepts or ideas that can be stored as PROPOSITIONS. For example, an account of the tense system in English can be presented as a set of statements, rules, or facts, i.e., it can be learned as declarative knowledge. This can be contrasted with **procedural knowledge,** that is, knowledge concerning things we know how to do but which are not consciously known, such as "how to ride a bicycle", or "how to speak German". Procedural knowledge is acquired gradually through practice, and underlies the learning of skills. Many aspects of second language learning consist of procedural rather than declarative knowledge.

Further reading Anderson 1985

declarative sentence /dɪˈklærətɪv ˈsentəns/ *n*

a sentence which is in the form of a STATEMENT. For example:

I'm leaving now.

Declarative sentences may or may not have the function of a statement. For example:

I suppose you're coming this evening.

often functions as a question.

I'd like you to leave immediately.

often functions as an order or request.

declension /dɪˈklenʃən/ *n* **decline** /dɪˈklaɪn/ *v*

a list of the case forms (see CASE¹) of a noun phrase in a particular language.

For example, in German:
nominative case: *der Mann* "the man"
accusative case: *den Mann* "the man"
dative case: *dem Mann* "to the man"
genitive case: *des Mannes* "of the man"

decoding /ˌdiːˈkəʊdɪŋ/ *n* decode /ˌdiːˈkəʊd/ *v*

the process of trying to understand the meaning of a word, phrase, or sentence.

When decoding a speech UTTERANCE, the listener must:

a hold the utterance in short term memory (see MEMORY)

b analyse the utterance into segments (see CHUNKING) and identify clauses, phrases, and other linguistic units

c identify the underlying propositions and illocutionary meaning (see SPEECH ACT).

Decoding is also used to mean the interpretation of any set of symbols which carry a meaning, for example a secret code or a Morse signal.

see also ENCODING, MESSAGE, INFORMATION PROCESSING, INFORMATION THEORY

Further reading Littlewood 1984; Clark & Clark 1977

decreolization /diːˌkriːəʊlaɪˈzeɪʃən‖-ləˈzeɪ-/ *n*

the process by which a CREOLE becomes more like the standard language from which most of its vocabulary comes. For example, an English-based creole may become more like Standard English.

If educational opportunities increase in a region where a creole is spoken and the standard language is taught, then there will be a range from the creole spoken by those with little or no education to the standard language spoken by those with high levels of education. This has been happening in countries like Jamaica and Guyana where there is a range from an English-based creole to a variety close to standard educated English.

see also POST-CREOLE CONTINUUM
Further reading Romaine 1988

deduction /dɪˈdʌkʃən/ *n*

in composition, two ways of presenting an argument are sometimes contrasted: reasoning by deduction and by **induction**. Reasoning by deduction proceeds from a generalization to particular facts which support it, whereas reasoning by **induction** involves moving from particular facts to generalizations about them.

see also ESSAY

deductive learning /dɪˈdʌktɪv ˈlɜːnɪŋ‖ ˈlɜːr-/ *n*
also **learning by deduction**

an approach to language teaching in which learners are taught rules and given specific information about a language. They then apply these rules when they use the language. Language teaching methods which emphasize the study of the grammatical rules of a language (for example the GRAMMAR TRANSLATION METHOD) make use of the principle of deductive learning.

This may be contrasted with **inductive learning** or **learning by induction**, in which learners are not taught grammatical or other types of rules directly but are left to discover or induce rules from their experience of using the language. Language teaching methods which emphasize use of the language rather than presentation of information about the language (for example the DIRECT METHOD, COMMUNICATIVE APPROACH, and COUNSELLING LEARNING) make use of the principle of inductive learning.

Further reading Kelly 1969; Steinberg 1982

deep structure /ˈdiːp ˌstrʌktʃəʳ/ n

(in TRANSFORMATIONAL GENERATIVE GRAMMAR) a level of sentence structure which shows the basic form of a spoken or written sentence in the language.

In earlier models of transformational grammar, each sentence was considered to have two levels of structure: the deep structure and the **surface structure**. The surface structure is the syntactic structure of the sentence which a person speaks, hears, reads or writes, e.g. the passive (see VOICE[1]) sentence:

The newspaper was not delivered today.

The deep structure is much more abstract and is considered to be in the speaker's, writer's, hearer's or reader's mind. The deep structure for the above sentence would be something like:

(NEGATIVE) someone (PAST TENSE) deliver the newspaper today (PASSIVE)

The items in brackets are not lexical items but grammatical concepts which shape the final form of the sentence. Rules which describe deep structure are in the first part of the grammar (BASE COMPONENT). Rules which transform these structures into surface structures (trans-formational rules) are in the second part of the grammar (TRANS-FORMATIONAL COMPONENT).

see also D-STRUCTURE
Further reading Chomsky 1965

deficit hypothesis /ˈdefɪsɪt haɪˌpɒθɪsɪs‖-ˌpɑː-/ n
also **verbal deficit hypothesis**

the theory that the language of some children may be lacking in vocabulary, grammar, or the means of expressing complex ideas, and may therefore be inadequate as a basis for success in school. Linguists have criticized this hypothesis and contrasted it with the **difference hypothesis**. This states that although the language of some children (e.g. children from certain social and ethnic groups) may be different from that of middle-class children, all DIALECTS are equally complex and children can use them to express complex ideas and to form a basis for school learning.

see also CULTURAL DEPRIVATION
Further reading Williams 1970

defining relative clause /dɪˈfaɪnɪŋ ˈrelətɪv ˈklɔːz/ n
also **restrictive relative clause**

a CLAUSE which gives additional information about a noun or noun phrase in a sentence. A defining relative clause restricts or helps to define the meaning of the noun. It usually begins with *who, which, whom, whose,* or *that,* and in written English is not separated from the noun by a comma:

  The man *whom you met* is my uncle.
  The woman *that you want to speak to* has left.

This may be contrasted with a **non-defining relative clause** (also called a **non-restrictive relative clause**), which gives additional information but which does not restrict or define the noun or noun phrase. In writing, it is separated by a comma:

  My uncle, *who is 64,* still plays football.

defining vocabulary /dɪˈfaɪnɪŋ vəˈkæbjəläri, vəʊ-‖ -leri/ n

a basic list of words with which other words can be explained or defined. Defining vocabularies are used to write definitions in dictionaries for children and for people studying foreign languages. They are based on research into WORD FREQUENCY. In the *Longman Dictionary of Contemporary English,* all definitions are written using a 2000 word defining vocabulary, so that anyone who knows the meaning of those 2000 words will be able to understand all the definitions in the dictionary.

definite article /ˈdefɪnɪt ˈɑːtɪkəl‖ˈɑːr-/ n

see ARTICLE

definition method /defɪˈnɪʃən ˌmeθəd/ n

see METHODS OF DEVELOPMENT

deictic /ˈdaɪktɪk, deɪˈɪktɪk/ *adj* **deixis** /ˈdaɪksɪs/ *n*

a term for a word or phrase which directly relates an utterance to a time, place, or person(s).
Examples of deictic expressions in English are:
a *here* and *there,* which refer to a place in relation to the speaker:
  The letter is *here.* (near the speaker)
  The letter is *over there.* (farther away from the speaker)
b *I* which refers to the speaker or writer.
  you which refers to the person or persons addressed.
  he/she/they which refer to some other person or persons.
Further reading Lyons 1977

delayed auditory feedback /dɪˈleɪd ˈɔːdɪtəri ˈfiːdbæk‖-tɔːri/ n

a technique which shows how speakers depend on AUDITORY FEEDBACK (i.e. hearing what they have just said) when speaking. In studies of delayed auditory feedback, speakers wear earphones through which they hear what they have just said, but after a short delay. The effect of this on speakers is that it is very difficult for them to speak normally.
Further reading Foss & Hakes 1978

deletion /dɪ'liːʃən/ *n* **delete** /dɪ'liːt/ *v*

When a speaker leaves out a sound, morpheme, or word from what he/she is saying, this is called deletion. For example, in casual or rapid speech, speakers of English often delete the final consonant in some unstressed words, so *a friend of mine* becomes a *friend o' mine*.

demonstrative /dɪ'mɒnstrətɪv‖dɪ'mɑːn-/ *n*

a word (a PRONOUN or a DETERMINER) which refers to something in terms of whether it is near to or distant from the speaker.
The demonstratives in English are: *this, that, these, those.*
For example:
　You take these books (here) *and I'll take those* (there).
Further reading Quirk et al 1985

denotation /ˌdiːnəʊ'teɪʃən/ *n* **denotative** /dɪ'nəʊtətɪv‖'diːnəʊˌteɪtɪv, dɪ'nəʊtə-/ *adj*

that part of the meaning of a word or phrase that relates it to phenomena in the real world or in a fictional or possible world.
For example, the denotation of the English word *bird* is a two-legged, winged, egg-laying, warm-blooded creature with a beak. In a meaning system, **denotative meaning** may be regarded as the "central" meaning or "core" meaning of a lexical item. It is often equated with referential meaning (see REFERENCE) and with **cognitive meaning** and **conceptual meaning** although some linguists and philosophers make a distinction between these concepts.

see also CONNOTATION
Further reading Leech 1981; Lyons 1977

denotative meaning /dɪ'nəʊtətɪv 'miːnɪŋ‖'diːnəʊˌteɪtɪv, dɪ'nəʊtə-/ *n*
see DENOTATION

dental /'dentl/ *adj*

describes a speech sound (a CONSONANT) produced by the front of the tongue touching the back of the upper front teeth.
For example, in French the /t/ in /tɛr/ *terre* "earth" and the /d/ in /du/ *doux* "sweet" are dental STOPS.
In English, /t/ and /d/ are usually ALVEOLAR stops. The use of dental in place of alveolar sounds by non-native speakers of English helps to create a "foreign accent".

see also PLACE OF ARTICULATION, MANNER OF ARTICULATION
Further reading Gimson 1989

dependency grammar /dɪ'pendənsi ˌgræməʳ/ *n*

a grammatical theory in which the verb is considered to be the central and most important unit. Verbs are classified according to the number of noun phrases they require to complete a sentence. This number is called the **valency** of the verb. The English verb *blush*, for instance, would have a valency of one:

blushes   V
  | |
she   N₁

The verb *give*, as in *The salesgirl gave Jane the parcel* would have a valency of three:

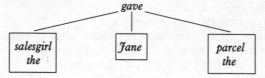

This type of grammar has been developed mainly in France and Germany and is different from many other grammars because of its verb-centred approach.

see also CASE GRAMMAR
Further reading Lyons 1977

dependent clause /dɪ'pendənt 'klɔːz/ n
also subordinate clause

a clause which must be used with another clause to form a complete grammatical construction. It depends on the other clause and is subordinate to it.

A clause which can be used on its own is called an **independent clause**.

For example:

  When it rains, please bring in the washing.
  dependent   independent
  clause   clause
  She told me   that she was going abroad.
  independent   dependent
  clause   clause

Dependent or subordinate clauses are often linked to independent clauses by a subordinating CONJUNCTION like *when, that*, etc., or by a relative pronoun like *who, whose*, etc.

An independent clause (also called a **main clause** or a **principal clause**) does not depend on another clause, although it may be linked to another independent clause, or to a dependent clause. For example:

  I will put the money in the bank or I will spend it.
  independent   independent
  clause   clause
  I am going straight home after I've seen the movie.
  independent   dependent
  clause   clause

Further reading Quirk el at 1985

dependent variable /dɪ'pendənt 'veəriəbəl/ n

(in research) a VARIABLE² which changes or is influenced according to changes in one or more **independent variables**. In empirical studies, one variable (the independent variable) may be studied as a cause or predictor, and another variable (the dependent variable) as the effect or result of the independent variable. For example, we may wish to study the effects of attitudes and motivation on language proficiency. Attitudes and motivation would be the independent variables, while language proficiency would be the dependent variable.

Further reading Seliger & Shohamy 1989

depth interview /'depθ ˌɪntəvjuː‖ˌɪntər-/ *n*
a detailed and extended INTERVIEW covering a wide range of topics in order to obtain as much information as possible and to explore unknown variables which are introduced during the interview.

see also FOCUSSED INTERVIEW, GUIDED INTERVIEW

derivation /ˌderⅈ'veɪʃən/ *n* **derive** /dɪ'raɪv/ *v*
(in MORPHOLOGY and WORD FORMATION) the formation of new words by adding AFFIXES to other words or morphemes.
For example, the noun *insanity* is derived from the adjective *sane* by the addition of the negative prefix *in-* and the noun-forming suffix *-ity*.

see also BACK FORMATION, INFLECTION

derived score /dɪ'raɪvd 'skɔːʳ/ *n*
(in statistics) any type of score other than a RAW SCORE. A derived score is calculated by converting a raw score or scores into units of another scale. For example the number of correct responses in a text (the raw score) may be converted into grades from A to F (a derived score).

see also STANDARD SCORE

description /dɪ'skrɪpʃən/ *n*
see ESSAY

descriptive function /dɪ'skrɪptɪv ˌfʌŋkʃən/ *n*
see FUNCTIONS OF LANGUAGE[1]

descriptive grammar /dɪ'skrɪptɪv 'græməʳ/ *n*
a grammar which describes how a language is actually spoken and/or written, and does not state or prescribe how it ought to be spoken or written.
If a descriptive grammar of a non-prestige variety of English were written, it might show, for example, that speakers of this variety sometimes said:

| I seen 'im. | instead of | I saw him. |
| 'im 'n me done it. | instead of | He and I did it. |

see also PRESCRIPTIVE GRAMMAR

descriptive statistics /dɪ'skrɪptɪv stə'tɪstɪks/ *n*
statistical procedures which are used to describe, organize and summarize the important general characteristics of a set of data. A descriptive statistic is a number that represents some feature of the data, such as measures of CENTRAL TENDENCY and DISPERSION.

see also INFERENTIAL STATISTICS

determiner /dɪ'tɜːmɪ̥nəʳ‖-ɜːr-/ n

a word which is used with a noun, and which limits the meaning of the noun in some way. For example, in English the following words can be used as determiners:

a ARTICLES, e.g. *a pencil, the garden*
b DEMONSTRATIVES, e.g. *this box, that car*
c POSSESSIVES, e.g. *her house, my bicycle*
d QUANTIFIERS, e.g. *some milk, many people*
e NUMERALS, e.g. *the first day, three chairs*
Further reading Close 1975; Quirk et al 1985

developmental error /dɪ'veləpmentl 'erəʳ/ n

an ERROR in the language use of a first or second language learner which is the result of a normal pattern of development, and which is common among language learners. For example, in learning English, first and second language learners often produce verb forms such as *comed, goed,* and *breaked* instead of *came, went,* and *broke.* This is thought to be because they have learned the rule for regular past tense formation and then apply it to all verbs. Later such errors disappear as the learner's language ability increases. These OVERGENERALIZATIONS are a natural or developmental stage in language learning.

see also INTERLANGUAGE, ERROR ANALYSIS
Further reading Dulay, Burt, & Krashen 1982; Ellis 1985

developmental functions of language /dɪ'veləpmentl 'fʌŋkʃənz əv'læŋgwɪdʒ/ n

According to Halliday, a young child in the early stages of language development is able to master a number of elementary functions of language. Each of these functions has a choice of meanings attached to it. He distinguishes seven initial functions:

a **Instrumental** ("I want"): used for satisfying material needs
b **Regulatory** ("do as I tell you"): used for controlling the behaviour of others
c **Interactional** ("me and you"): used for getting along with other people
d **Personal** ("here I come"): used for identifying and expressing the self
e **Heuristic** ("tell me why"): used for exploring the world around and inside one
f **Imaginative** ("let's pretend"): used for creating a world of one's own
g **Informative** ("I've got something to tell you"): used for communication new information.

At about 18 months, the child is beginning to master the adult's system of communication, including grammar, vocabulary and meaning components (see FUNCTIONS OF LANGUAGE²).

Further reading Halliday 1978

developmental interdependence hypothesis /dɪˈveləpmentl
ˌɪntədɪˈpendəns haɪˌpɒθ⁀ləsⱥs‖ˌɪntər-haɪˌpɑː-/ *n*
see THRESHOLD HYPOTHESIS

developmental psychology /dɪˈveləpmentl saɪˈkɒlədʒi‖-ˈkɑː-/ *n*
a branch of psychology which deals with the development of mental,
emotional, psychological, and social processes and behaviour in individuals, particularly from birth to early childhood.
see also GENETIC EPISTEMOLOGY
Further reading Ausubel 1977

developmental sequence /dɪˈveləpmentl ˈsiːkwəns/ *n*
(in second and foreign language learning) a succession of phases in
acquiring new linguistic forms. An important issue in theories of
SECOND LANGUAGE ACQUISITION is whether learners' errors result from
LANGUAGE TRANSFER or are sometimes DEVELOPMENTAL ERRORS. It has
been suggested that a developmental sequence may explain how many
learners acquire the rules for NEGATION in English. Learners may first
produce forms such as *I no like that* (instead of *I don't like that*) and *No
drink some milk* (instead of *I don't want to drink any milk*), even when the
learner's mother tongue has similar negation rules to English. As
language learning progresses, a succession of phases in the development of negation is observed, as *no* gives way to other negative forms
such as *not* and *don't*. A developmental sequence in thus said to occur
with the development of negation in English.
Further reading Ravem 1968; Odlin 1989

deviant /ˈdiːviənt/ *adj*
This term is used to describe any pronunciation, word, or sentence
structure which does not conform to a NORM¹. The norm could be that
of the STANDARD VARIETY or it could be based on the language spoken
by a high status social group.
An example of a sentence which would be deviant in Standard English
is *I seen him* instead of *I saw him*.
Further reading Bailey & Görlach 1982

devoicing /ˌdiːˈvɔɪsɪŋ/ *n*
see VOICE²

diachronic linguistics /daɪəˈkrɒnɪk lɪŋˈgwɪstɪks‖-ˈkrɑː-/ *n*
an approach to linguistics which studies how a language changes over a
period of time, for example the change in the sound system of English
from Early English to Modern British English.
Diachronic linguistics has been contrasted with **synchronic linguistics**
which is the study of a language system at one particular point in time,
for example the sound system of Modern British English.

time 1	description of the sound system of Early English	synchronic study
	description of changes between the two systems	diachronic study
time 2	description of the sound system of Modern British English	synchronic study

The need for diachronic and synchronic descriptions to be kept apart was emphasized by the Swiss linguist Saussure. Not all approaches to linguistic analysis make this distinction (see GENERATIVE PHONOLOGY).

see also COMPARATIVE HISTORICAL LINGUISTICS

Further reading Aitchison 1981; Saussure 1966

diacritic /ˌdaɪəˈkrɪtɪk/ *n*

a mark placed over, under, or through a letter to show that it has a sound value different from that of the same letter without the mark. For example, in Spanish the sign ~ over *n* as in *mañana* "tomorrow" shows that the first *n* represents [nj] whereas the second *n* represents [n].
Diacritics are also used in phonetic script (see NOTATION). For example, [d̪] shows that it is a DENTAL STOP, made with the tongue against the front teeth.

see also ACCENT[2]

diagnostic test /ˈdaɪəgnɒstɪk ˈtest‖-nɑː-/ *n*

a test which is designed to show what skills or knowledge a learner knows and doesn't know. For example a diagnostic pronunciation test may be used to measure the learner's pronunciation of English sounds. It would show which sounds a student is and is not able to pronounce. Diagnostic tests may be used to find out how much a learner knows before beginning a language course.

Further reading Hughes 1989

diagramming /ˈdaɪəgræmɪŋ/ *n*

(in teaching composition), a technique which is sometimes used to show how the parts of a sentence are related. For example:

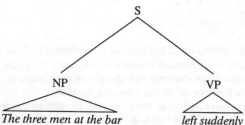

see also BASE COMPONENT

dialect /'daɪəlekt/ *n* **dialectal** /ˌdaɪə'lektl◂/ *adj*

a variety of a language, spoken in one part of a country (**regional dialect**), or by people belonging to a particular social class (**social dialect** or SOCIOLECT), which is different in some words, grammar, and/or pronunciation from other forms of the same language.

A dialect is often associated with a particular ACCENT[3]. Sometimes a dialect gains status and becomes the STANDARD VARIETY of a country.

see also SPEECH VARIETY

Further reading Hughes & Trudgill 1987

dialectology /ˌdaɪəlek'tɒlədʒi||-'tɑː-/ *n*

the study of the regional variations of a language (see DIALECT).

Usually, studies in dialectology have concentrated on different words used in various dialects for the same object or on different pronunciations of the same word in different dialects.

see also AREAL LINGUISTICS

dialogue journal /'daɪəlɒg ˌdʒɜːnl||-lɔːg, -lɑːg -ɜːr-/ *n*

see LEARNING LOG

dialogue /'daɪəlɒg||-lɔːg, -lɑːg/ *n*

(in language teaching) a model conversation, used to practise speaking. Dialogues are often specially written to practise language items, contain simplified grammar and vocabulary, and so may be rather different from real-life conversation.

diary study /'daɪəri ˌstʌdi/ *n*

(in research on first and second language acquisition) a regularly kept journal or written record of a learner's language development, often kept as part of a longitudinal study (see LONGITUDINAL METHOD) of language learning. With a diary study, the researcher records examples of the learner's linguistic production in as much detail as possible, as well as information about the communicative setting involved (i.e. the participants, the purpose etc.). Diary studies are often used to supplement other ways of collecting data, such as through the use of experimental techniques.

Further reading Kastor-Bennet 1988

dichotic listening /daɪ'kɒtɪk 'lɪsənɪŋ||-'kɑː-/ *n*

a technique which has been used to study how the brain controls hearing and language. Subjects wear earphones and receive different sounds in the right and left ear. They are then asked to repeat what they hear. Subjects find it easier to repeat what they heard in one ear than in the other, and this is thought to indicate which brain hemisphere controls language for them (see BRAIN). The ability to perceive language better in the right ear than the left ear is called a **right-ear advantage,** and the ability to perceive language better in the left ear is called **left-ear advantage**.

Further reading Foss & Hakes 1977

dictation /dɪkˈteɪʃən/ n

a technique used in both language teaching and language testing in which a passage is read aloud to students, with pauses during which they must try to write down what they heard as accurately as possible.

Further reading Rivers & Temperley 1978

diction /ˈdɪkʃən/ n

1 a term sometimes used to describe the way in which a person pronounces words, particularly the degree of clarity with which he or she speaks.

2 (in composition), the choice of words employed by the writer, particularly the extent to which the words the writer uses are thought suitable and effective for different kinds of writing.

dicto-comp /ˈdɪktəʊkɒmp‖-kɑːmp/ n

a technique for practising composition in language classes. A passage is read to a class, and then the students must write out what they understand and remember from the passage, keeping as closely to the original as possible but using their own words where necessary.

see also DICTATION

difference hypothesis /ˈdɪfərəns haɪˌpɒθɪ̯sɪ̯s‖-ˌpɑː-/ n

see DEFICIT HYPOTHESIS

digital data /ˈdɪdʒɪ̯tl ˈdeɪtə, ˈdɑːtə/ n

see ANALOGUE DATA

digitized speech /ˈdɪdʒɪ̯taɪzd ˈspiːtʃ/ n

speech which is produced from the digital recording of sounds. This may be contrasted with **synthetic speech**, which is the term applied to sounds produced by a computer through the manipulation of machine-based PHONEMES and not from real speech. Synthetic speech is less realistic than digitized speech. Digitized speech is often used in COMPUTER ASSISTED LEARNING programs.

diglossia /daɪˈglɒsiə‖-ˈglɔː-, -ˈglɑː-/ n

When two languages or language varieties exist side by side in a community and each one is used for different purposes, this is called diglossia. Usually, one is a more standard variety called the **High variety** or **H-variety**, which is used in government, the media, education, and for religious services. The other one is usually a non-prestige variety called the **Low-variety** or **L-variety**, which is used in the family, with friends, when shopping, etc.

An example of diglossia can be found in the German speaking part of Switzerland, where the H(igh) variety is a form of standard German (Hochdeutsch) and the L(ow) variety is called Schwyzertüütsch, which is a range of regional Swiss dialects. Other countries where diglossia exists are, for example, Haiti and the Arab nations.

see also BILINGUALISM, MULTILINGUALISM, CODE SELECTION

Further reading Ferguson 1959; Wardhaugh 1986

diminutive /dɪˈmɪnjʊtɪv/ *n, adj*
    (in MORPHOLOGY) a form which has an AFFIX with the meaning of "little", "small", etc.
    For example, in English, *-let* as in *piglet* and *starlet*, and *-ling* as in *duckling*.

diphthong /ˈdɪfθɒŋ, ˈdɪp-||-θɔːŋ/ *n* **diphthongal** /dɪfˈθɒŋgəl, dɪp-|| -ˈθɔːŋ-/ *adj* **diphthongize** /ˈdɪfθɒŋgaɪz, ˈdɪp-||-θɔːŋ-/ *v*
    a speech sound which is usually considered as one distinctive vowel of a particular language but really involves two vowels, with one vowel gliding to the other.
    For example, the diphthong /aɪ/ in the English word *my* /maɪ/, which consists of the vowel /a/ gliding into the vowel /ɪ/.
    see also GLIDE
    Further reading Gimson 1989

direct access /dɪˈrekt ˈækses, ˌdaɪˈrekt◄/ *n*
    see ACCESS

directive /dɪˈrektɪv, daɪ-/ *n*
    see SPEECH ACT CLASSIFICATION

direct method /dɪˈrekt ˈmeθəd, ˌdaɪˈrekt◄/ *n*
    a method of foreign or second language teaching which has the following features:
    a only the target language should be used in class
    b meanings should be communicated "directly" (hence the name of the method) by associating speech forms with actions, objects, mime, gestures, and situations
    c reading and writing should be taught only after speaking
    d grammar should only be taught inductively (see DEDUCTIVE LEARNING); i.e. grammar rules should not be taught to the learners
    The direct method was developed in the late 19th century as a reaction against the GRAMMAR TRANSLATION METHOD.
    Further reading Titone 1968; Richards & Rodgers 1986

direct object /dɪˈrekt ˈɒbjɪkt, ˌdaɪˈrekt◄||ˈɑːb-/ *n*
    see OBJECT[1]

direct speech /dɪˈrekt ˈspiːtʃ, ˌdaɪˈrekt◄/ *n*
    the style used in writing to report what a speaker actually said, without introducing any grammatical changes. In English the speaker's words may be written between quotation marks. For example:
        actual utterance: *"You are a thief."*
        direct speech: *He said "You are a thief."*
    This may be contrasted with **indirect speech** also called **reported speech,** in which the speaker's words are not reported as they were actually said but are reported, for example, in the form of a *that*-clause. For example:

indirect speech: *He said that you were a thief.*

In English, several grammatical changes occur in indirect speech, including a change of tense that is called **back-shift**. For example:

direct speech	indirect speech
She said "I am tired."	*She said that she was tired.*
He said "The school opened a year ago."	*He said the school had opened a year ago.*

A question as it is reported in indirect speech is called an **indirect question**. For example:

question	indirect question
I asked "Is that your sister?"	*I asked if that was your sister.*
"When are you coming?" he asked.	*He asked when I was coming.*

Further reading Quirk et al 1985

direct teaching /dɨˈrekt ˈtiːtʃɪŋ, ˌdaɪˈrekt◄/ n
also **active teaching**

an approach to teaching which seeks to increase achievement by focussing the teacher's attention on specific, analytical and academic objectives, by coverage of objectives to be tested, by engagement of students in tasks, and by giving feedback which focusses on the degree to which objectives have been achieved. Attention is given to promoting student success in learning through a teacher-directed style of teaching in which the teacher provides a favourable CLIMATE for learning.

see also EFFECTIVE SCHOOLING, TIME ON TASK
Further reading Kindsvatter et al 1988

disambiguation /ˌdɪsæmbɪgjuˈeɪʃən/ n disambiguate
/ˌdɪsæmˈbɪgjueɪt/ v

the use of linguistic analysis to show the different structures of an ambiguous sentence. For example:
The lamb is too hot to eat.
can be analysed as:
a The lamb is so hot that it cannot eat anything
or:
b The cooked lamb is too hot for someone to eat it.

see also AMBIGUOUS

discontinuous constituent /ˈdɪskəntɪnjuəs kənˈstɪtʃuənt/ n
Parts of a sentence which belong to the same CONSTITUENT but which are separated by other constituents are called a discontinuous constituent. For example:
a in French, the negative of the verb is formed with the discontinuous constituent *ne . . .pas* as in:
Paul ne mange pas beaucoup.
"Paul doesn't eat much"
b in English; the phrasal verb *pick up* in

The player picked the ball up.
is a discontinuous constituent.

Further reading Quirk et al 1985

discourse /'dɪskɔːs‖-ɔːrs/ *n*

a general term for examples of language use, i.e. language which has been produced as the result of an act of communication.

Whereas grammar refers to the rules a language uses to form grammatical units such as CLAUSE, PHRASE, and SENTENCE, discourse refers to larger units of language such as paragraphs, conversations, and interviews.

Sometimes the study of both written and spoken discourse is known as DISCOURSE ANALYSIS; some researchers however use discourse analysis to refer to the study of spoken discourse and TEXT LINGUISTICS to refer to the study of written discourse.

discourse accent /'dɪskɔːs ˌæksənt‖-kɔːrs ˌæksent/ *n*

(in writing) those characteristics of writing produced by **non-native writers** which make it different from the writing of **native writers**. For example, non-native patterns of rhetorical organization in a essay or non-native use of cohesive devices, topics, and paragraph organization may contribute to a writer's discourse accent.

see also CONTRASTIVE RHETORIC

discourse analysis /'dɪskɔːs ə,næləˌsɪs‖-kɔːrs/ *n*

the study of how sentences in spoken and written language form larger meaningful units such as paragraphs, conversations, interviews, etc. (see DISCOURSE).

For example, discourse analysis deals with:

a how the choice of articles, pronouns, and tenses affects the structure of the discourse (see ADDRESS FORMS, COHESION)

b the relationship between utterances in a discourse (see ADJACENCY PAIRS, COHERENCE)

c the MOVES made by speakers to introduce a new topic, change the topic, or assert a higher ROLE RELATIONSHIP to the other participants

Analysis of spoken discourse is sometimes called CONVERSATIONAL ANALYSIS. Some linguists use the term TEXT LINGUISTICS for the study of written discourse.

Recent analyses have been carried out on discourse in the classroom. Such analyses can be useful in finding out about the effectiveness of teaching methods and the types of teacher-student relationships.

see also SPEECH EVENT
Further reading Coulthard 1985; Sinclair & Coulthard 1975

discourse competence /'dɪskɔːs ˌkɒmpɨtəns‖-ɔːrs ˌkɑːm-/ *n*

an aspect of COMMUNICATIVE COMPETENCE which describes the ability to produce unified written or spoken discourse that shows COHERENCE and COHESION and which conforms to the norms of different GENRES (e.g. a business letter, a scientific essay etc.). Apart from the ability to produce sentences which are grammatically correct and appropriate to the situation in which they are being used, learners must also be able to produce discourse in which successive sentences are linked through rules of discourse or discourse competence.

see also STRATEGIC COMPETENCE
Further reading Canale 1980

discourse structure /ˈdɪskɔːs ˌstrʌktʃər‖-ɔːrs/ *n*
another term for SCHEME

discovery learning /dɪsˈkʌvəri ˌlɜːnɪŋ‖-ɜːr-/ *n*
(in education) an approach to teaching and learning which is based on the following principles:
a Learners develop processes associated with discovery and inquiry by observing, inferring, formulating hypotheses, predicting and communicating.
b Teachers use a teaching style which supports the processes of discovery and inquiry
c Textbooks are not the sole resources for learning
d Conclusions are considered tentative and not final
e Learners are involved in planning, conducting, and evaluating their own learning with the teacher playing a supporting role.
A number of language teaching approaches make use of discovery-based approaches to learning, particularly communicative language teaching (see COMMUNICATIVE APPROACH) and the SILENT WAY.

discrete /dɪˈskriːt/ *adj* **discreteness** /dɪˈskriːtnʲs/ *n*
(of a linguistic unit) having clearly defined boundaries.
In PHONOLOGY, the distinctive sound units of a language (the PHONEMES) are considered to be discrete units. For example, the English word *pin* would consist of three such units: /p/, /ɪ/, and /n/.

discrete-point test /dɪˈskriːt ˈpɔɪnt ˌtest/ *n*
a language test which measures knowledge of individual language items, such as a grammar test which has different sections on tenses, adverbs, and prepositions. Discrete point tests are based on the theory that language consists of different parts (e.g. grammar, sounds, vocabulary) and different skills (e.g. listening, speaking, reading, and writing) and these are made up of elements that can be tested separately. Tests consisting of MULTIPLE-CHOICE ITEMS are usually discrete point tests. Discrete point tests can be contrasted with **integrative tests**.
An integrative test is one which requires a learner to use several language skills at the same time, such as a dictation test, because it requires the learner to use knowledge of grammar, vocabulary, and listening comprehension.
Further reading Oller 1979

discrimination[1] /dɪˌskrɪmʲˈneɪʃən/ *n*
see STIMULUS-RESPONSE THEORY

discrimination² n
also discrimination power
> (in testing) the degree to which a test or an item in a test distinguishes among better and weaker students who take the test. For example, if all the students who took a test scored around 85%, yet the students were known to be of different degrees of ability, the test would fail to discriminate.
> In ITEM ANALYSIS the CORRELATION, between the answers to an individual item and the scores on the whole test is often used as an estimate of discrimination.
> A measure of the discrimination of a test is known as a **discrimination index.**
> see also ITEM DISCRIMINATION
> *Further reading* Brown 1988

discrimination index /dɪˌskrɪmɪˈneɪʃən ˌɪndeks/ *n*
> see DISCRIMINATION²

discrimination power /dɪˌskrɪmɪˈneɪʃən ˌpaʊəʳ/ *n*
> another term for DISCRIMINATION²

discussion method /dɪsˈkʌʃən ˌmeθəd/ *n*
> an approach to teaching which consists of a goal-focussed group conversation involving either groups of students or the whole class, and which usually involves interaction about subject matter between a teacher and students. Four common types of discussion procedures are used, which differ according to the degree of teacher control.
> 1 **recitation**: a teacher directed and highly structured discussion in which the teacher checks to see if students have learned certain facts.
> 2 **guided discussion**: a less structured discussion in which the teacher seeks to promote understanding of important concepts.
> 3 **reflective discussion**: the least structured form of discussion in which students engage in critical and creative thinking, solve problems, explore issues etc.
> 4 **small group discussion**: The class is divided into small groups, with students assuming responsibility for the discussion.

disjunct /ˈdɪsdʒʌŋkt/ *n*
also sentential adverb
> see ADJUNCT

disk /dɪsk/ *n*
> a flat circular plate with a magnetizable surface layer which stores information for use on a computer. The spelling *disc* is used for video and audio storage media.
> see also DISKETTE HARD DISK

disk drive /ˈdɪsk ˌdraɪv/ *n*
> a device on a COMPUTER which reads information from and writes information on DISKS.

diskette /dɪˈskɛt/ *n*
also **floppy disk**
  a thin, flexible, magnetic disk together with its protective jacket, used
  to record information on a MICROCOMPUTER.

dispersion /dɪˈspɜːʃən‖dɪˈspɜːrʒən/ *n*
  (in testing) the amount of spread among the scores in a group. For
  example if the scores of students on a test were widely spread from
  low, middle to high, the scores would be said to have a large dispersion. Some common statistical measures of dispersion are VARIANCE,
  STANDARD DEVIATION, and RANGE.
  Further reading Hardyck & Petrinovich 1976; Brown 1988

display question /dɪˈspleɪ ˌkwestʃən/ *n*
  a question which is not a real question (i.e. which does not seek information unknown to the teacher) but which serves to elicit language practice. For example:
  It this a book?
  Yes, it's a book.
  It has been suggested that one way to make classes more
  communicative (see COMMUNICATIVE APPROACH) is for teachers to use
  fewer display questions and more REFERENTIAL QUESTIONS.
  see also RHETORICAL QUESTION

distance learning /ˈdɪstəns ˌlɜːnɪŋ‖-ɜːr-/ *n*
  the linking of learners and teachers in different locations and in real
  time, by telephone and telecast, via satellite, or through the use of
  learning packages.

distinctive feature /dɪˈstɪŋktɪv ˈfiːtʃəʳ/ *n*
  (in PHONOLOGY) a particular characteristic which distinguishes one
  distinctive sound unit of a language (see PHONEME) from another or
  one group of sounds from another group.
  For example, in the English sound system, one distinctive feature
  which distinguishes the /p/ in *pin* from the /b/ in *bin* is VOICE². The /b/
  is a voiced STOP whereas the /p/ is a voiceless stop (see VOICE²).
  In GENERATIVE PHONOLOGY, distinctive features play an important part
  in the writing of phonological rules. The features are generally shown
  in the form of a binary opposition, that is the feature is either present
  [+] or absent [−].
  For example, vowels and sounds such as /l/, /n/, and /m/, where the air
  passes relatively freely through the mouth or nose, have the feature
  [+ sonorant] whereas sounds such as /p/, /k/, and /s/, where the air is
  stopped either completely or partially, have the feature [− sonorant].
  see also BINARY FEATURE
  Further reading Hyman 1975

distractor /dɪˈstræktəʳ/ *n*
  see TEST ITEM, MULTIPLE-CHOICE ITEM

distribution[1] /ˌdɪstrɪˈbjuːʃən/ *n*

(in statistics) the pattern of scores or measures in a group. For example the distribution of scores in a test may be displayed in a table:

Test scores	10	20	30	40	50	60	70	80	90	100
Frequency	1	1	3	7	10	6	5	2	2	0

distribution[2] *n*

The range of positions in which a particular unit of a language, e.g. a PHONEME or a word, can occur is called its distribution.

For example, in English, the phoneme /ŋ/, usually written *ng*, cannot occur at the beginning of a word but it can occur in final position, as in *sing*. In other languages, /ŋ/ may occur word initially, as in Cantonese *ngoh* "I".

disyllabic /ˌdaɪsɪˈlæbɪk, ˌdɪ-/ *adj*

consisting of two SYLLABLES, e.g. the English word *garden* /ˈgɑː/ + /dən/.

see also MONOSYLLABIC

ditransitive verb /daɪˈtrænsɪtɪv ˈvɜːb‖ˈvɜːrb/ *n*

see also TRANSITIVE VERB

divergence[1] /daɪˈvɜːdʒəns, dɪ-‖-ɜːr-/ *n*

the process of two or more languages or language varieties becoming less like each other. For example, if speakers of a language migrate to another area, the variety of language spoken by them may become less similar to the variety spoken by those who did not migrate, i.e. there will be divergence. This has been the case with English spoken in the United Kingdom compared with the varieties of English spoken in the USA, Canada, Australia, and New Zealand.

see also CONVERGENCE[1]

divergence[2] *n*

see ACCOMMODATION

divergent question /daɪˈvɜːdʒənt ˈkwestʃən‖-ɜːr-/ *n*

a question that elicits student responses that vary or diverge. For example, divergent questions may be used when a teacher wishes to compare students' ideas about a topic. There are often no right or wrong answers with divergent questions.

see also CONVERGENT QUESTION, EVALUATIVE QUESTION, QUESTIONING TECHNIQUES, CLASSROOM DISCOURSE.

domain[1] /dəˈmeɪn, dəʊ-/ *n*

an area of human activity in which one particular speech variety or a combination of several speech varieties is regularly used. A domain can be considered as a group of related **speech situations** (see SPEECH EVENT). For instance, situations in which the persons talking to one another are members of the family, e.g. mother and children, father and mother, elder sister and younger sister, would all belong to the

Family Domain. In BILINGUAL and MULTILINGUAL communities, one language may be used in some domains and another language in other domains. For example, Puerto Ricans in the USA may use Spanish in the Family Domain and English in the Employment Domain.

see also DIGLOSSIA, SPEECH EVENT
Further reading Fishman 1971; Fasold 1984

domain² *n*

see PROJECTION (PRINCIPLE)

domain³ *n*

in planning goals and OBJECTIVES for an educational programme, the particular area or aspect of learning an objective or set of objectives is designed to address. Three general domains of objectives are often distinguished.

1 **Cognitive domain**: objectives which have as their purpose the development of students' intellectual abilities and skills.

2 **Affective domain**: objectives which have as their purpose the development of students' attitudes, feelings and values.

3 **Psychomotor domain**: objectives which have as their purpose the development of students' motor and coordination abilities and skills.

see also BLOOM'S TAXONOMY
Further reading Kindsvatter, Wilen & Ishler 1988

dominant language /'dɒmɪ̩nənt 'læŋgwɪdʒ||'dɑː-/ *n*
also **dominant dialect** /'dɒmɪ̩nənt 'daɪəlekt||'dɑː-/

see LANGUAGE DOMINANCE

dominate /'dɒmɪ̩neɪt||'dɑː-/ *v*

see NODE

dorsal /'dɔːsəl||'dɔːr-/ *n, adj*

see VELAR

dorsum /'dɔːsəm||'dɔːr-/ *n*

see PLACE OF ARTICULATION

double negative /'dʌbəl 'negətɪv/ *n*

a construction in which two negative words are used.
For example, in NONSTANDARD English
   I never seen nothing.
instead of
   I haven't seen anything.
A double negative does not become a positive. It is used for emphasis. In some languages, e.g. Serbo-Croatian, double negatives are quite usual and are not considered as nonstandard.

drafting /'drɑːftɪŋ||'dræ-/ *n*

see COMPOSING PROCESSES

drill /drɪl/ *n*

a technique commonly used in language teaching for practising sounds or sentence patterns in a language, based on guided repetition or practice. A drill which practises some aspect of grammar or sentence formation is often known as **pattern practice**.

There are usually two parts to a drill.

a The teacher provides a word or sentence as a stimulus (the **call-word** or CUE).

b Students make various types of responses based on repetition, substitution, or transformation. For example:

type of drill	teacher's cue	student
substitution drill	*We bought a book.* *pencil*	*We bought a pencil.*
repetition drill	*We bought a book.* *We bought a pencil.*	*We bought a book.* *We bought a pencil.*
transformation drill	*I bought a book.*	*Did you buy a book?* *What did you buy?*

see also FOUR PHASE DRILL
Further reading Rivers & Temperley 1978

D-structure/'diː ˌstrʌktʃərʲ/ *n*

(in Government/Binding Theory) an abstract level of sentence representation where semantic roles such as agent (the doer of an action) and patient (the entity affected by an action) are assigned to the sentence. *Agent* is sometimes also referred to as the **logical subject** and *patient* as the **theme** of the sentence. For example (in simplified form):

    Vera   *shoot*   *intruder*
 agent or logical   patient or theme
    subject

The next level of sentence representation is the S-STRUCTURE where syntactic/grammatical cases such as nominative/grammatical subject and accusative/grammatical object are assigned. For example (in simplified form):

    Vera (agent)   *shoot*   *intruder* (patient/theme)
 grammatical subject   grammatical object

The **phonetic form** (PF) component and the **logical form** (LF) component are then needed to turn the s-structure into a surface sentence. The phonetic form (PF) component presents the s-structure as sound, and the logical form (LF) component gives the syntactic meaning of the sentence.

The concepts of semantic roles and grammatical cases and their interrelation have been used in first and second language acquisition research (see θ-THEORY)

Further reading Cook 1988; Zobl 1989

dual /ˈdjuːəl‖ˈduːəl/ *adj, n*

see LANGUAGE UNIVERSAL

duality of structure /djuːˈælɪ̩ti əv ˈstrʌktʃəʳ‖duː-/ *n*

a distinctive characteristic of language which refers to the fact that languages are organized in terms of two levels. At one level, language consists of sequences of segments or units which do not themselves carry meaning (such as the letters "g", "d" and "o"). However, when these units are combined in certain sequences, they form larger units and carry meaning (such as *dog, god*).

Further reading Crystal 1980

dyad /ˈdaɪ-æd, -əd/ *n*

two people in communication with each other. A dyad can be considered as the smallest part of a larger communication network. For example, in describing language use within a family, some dyads would be mother-child, grandmother-child, elder sister-younger sister.

dynamic verb /daɪˈnæmɪk ˈvɜːb‖daɪ-, dɪ̩- ˈvɜːrb/ *n*

see STATIC-DYNAMIC DISTINCTION

dysfluency /dɪsˈfluːənsi/ *n* dysfluent /dɪsˈfluːənt/ *adj*

see FLUENCY

dyslexia /dɪsˈleksiə/ *n* dyslexic /dɪsˈleksɪk/ *adj*
also word blindness

a general term sometimes used to describe any continuing problem in learning to read, such as difficulty in distinguishing letter shapes and words. Reading specialists do not agree on the nature or causes of such reading problems however, and both medical and psychological explanations have been made. Because of the very general way in which the term is often used, many reading specialists prefer not to use the term, and describe reading problems in terms of specific reading difficulties.

Further reading Money 1962

dysphasia /dɪsˈfeɪʒə/ *n*

another term for APHASIA

E

EAP /ˌi: eɪ 'pi:/ *n*
an abbreviation for English for Academic Purposes
see ENGLISH FOR SPECIAL PURPOSES

echolalia /ˌekəʊ'leɪlɪə/ *n*
a type of speech disorder or APHASIA in which all or most of a speaker's utterances consist of the simple repetition or echoing of words or phrases which the speaker hears.

eclectic method /ɪ'klektɪk 'meθəd/ *n*
a term sometimes used for the practice of using features of several different METHODS in language teaching, for example, by using both audiolingual and communicative language teaching techniques.
see also AUDIOLINGUAL METHOD, COMMUNICATIVE APPROACH

educational linguistics /edjʊ'keɪʃənəl lɪŋ'gwɪstɪks‖edʒə-/ *n*
a term sometimes used in the USA to refer to a branch of APPLIED LINGUISTICS (2) which deals with the relationship between language and education.
Further reading Spolsky 1978

editing /'edɪtɪŋ/ *n*
see COMPOSING PROCESSES

educational psychology /edjʊ'keɪʃənəl saɪ'kɒlədʒi‖edʒə- -'kɑː-/ *n*
a branch of psychology which studies theories and problems in education, including the application of learning theory to classroom teaching and learning, curriculum development, testing and evaluation, and teacher education.

educational technology /edjʊ'keɪʃənəl tek'nɒlədʒi‖edʒə- tek'nɑː-/ *n*
1 the use of machines and educational equipment of different sorts (e.g. language laboratories, tape recorders, video, etc.) to assist teachers and learners.
2 a system of instruction which contains (a) an analysis of what learners need to know and be able to do (b) a description of these needs as BEHAVIOURAL OBJECTIVES and (c) (1) above.

effective schooling /ɪ'fektɪv 'sku:lɪŋ/ *n*
an educational movement which seeks to make schools more effective through bringing about *effective teaching*. This generally refers to teaching which has the following characteristics:

119

1 Expectations for learning. Students are expected to learn and class activities relate to learning.
2 Student behaviour. Student behaviour and conduct is monitored.
3 Class routines and procedures. Class administrative routines are handled efficiently.
4 Standards. Students, teachers and parents agree on standards.
5 Grouping. Grouping arrangements match instructional needs.
6 Objectives. Objectives are used to focus learning.
7 Instruction and direction. Teachers give clear directions and all students are involved in instruction.
8 Learning time. Class time is used for learning.
9 Reteaching. When students do not learn, they are retaught.
10 Teacher-student Interactions. Teacher-student interactions are positive.
11 Student rewards and incentives. Incentives and rewards are set for learning.

While effective schooling has focussed on the teaching of mainstream subjects, studies of teachers in bilingual classes have also been carried out.

see also TIME ON TASK
Further reading Orlich et al 1985

effective teaching /ɪˈfektɪv ˈtiːtʃɪŋ/ *n*

see EFFECTIVE SCHOOLING

EFL /ˌiː ef ˈel/ *n*

an abbreviation for ENGLISH AS A FOREIGN LANGUAGE

egocentric speech /ˈegəʊsentrɪk ˈspiːtʃ, ˈiːgəʊ-/ *n*

speech which is not addressed to other people. This is one of two types of speech which Piaget observed in the speech of children learning a first language. Egocentric speech serves the purpose of giving pleasure to the child and of expressing the child's thoughts, and provides an opportunity for the child to experiment or play with speech. It may be contrasted with **socialized speech**, or speech which is addressed to other people and which is used for communication.

Further reading Piaget 1955; Vygotsky 1962

egocentric writing /ˈegəʊsentrɪk ˈraɪtɪŋ, ˈiːgəʊ-/ *n*

see READER-BASED PROSE

EGP /ˌiː dʒiː ˈpiː/ *n*

an abbreviation for English for General Purposes
see ENGLISH FOR SPECIAL PURPOSES

elaborated code /ɪˈlæbəreɪt̩d ˈkəʊd/ *n*

see CODE[2]

e-language /ˈiː ˌlæŋgwɪdʒ/ *n*
also **externalized language**

see I-LANGUAGE

elicitation /ɪˌlɪsɪ'teɪʃən/ n

(in language teaching) techniques or procedures which a teacher uses to get learners to actively produce speech or writing.

elicitation procedure /ɪˌlɪsɪ'teɪʃən prəˌsiːdʒəʳ/ n
also **elicitation technique** /ɪˌlɪsɪ'teɪʃən tekˌniːk/

(in linguistics or SECOND LANGUAGE ACQUISITION research) a technique used to obtain information about how someone uses a particular language item. The subject may be asked to describe a picture, tell a story, or finish an incomplete sentence. These procedures are used to get a fuller understanding of linguistic knowledge than the study of naturally occurring speech or writing can provide.

Further reading Quirk & Greenbaum 1970

elicited imitation /ɪ'lɪsɪtɪd ɪmɪ'teɪʃən/ n

an ELICITATION PROCEDURE in which a person has to repeat a sentence which he or she sees or hears. When people are asked to repeat a sentence which uses linguistic rules which they themselves cannot or do not use, they often make changes in the sentence so that it is more like their own speech. Elicited imitation can be used to study a person's knowledge of a language. For example:

stimulus sentence	elicited imitation
Why can't the man climb over the fence?	*Why the man can't climb over the fence?*

Further reading Swain, Dumas, & Naiman 1974

elision /ɪ'lɪʒən/ n **elide** /ɪ'laɪd/ v

the leaving out of a sound or sounds in speech. For example, in rapid speech in English, *suppose* is often pronounced as [spəʊz], *factory* as ['fæktri] and *mostly* as ['məʊsli].

see also ELLIPSIS, EPENTHESIS
Further reading Gimson 1980

ellipsis /ɪ'lɪpsɪs/ n **elliptical** /ɪ'lɪptɪkəl/ adj

the leaving out of words or phrases from sentences where they are unnecessary because they have already been referred to or mentioned. For example, when the subject of the verb in two co-ordinated clauses is the same, it may be omitted to avoid repetition:

The man went to the door and (he) opened it. (subject ellipsis)
Mary ate an apple and Jane (ate) a pear. (verb ellipsis)

see also ELISION
Further reading Quirk et al 1985

ELT /ˌiː el 'tiː/ n

an abbreviation for English Language Teaching. It is used especially in Britain to refer to the teaching of ENGLISH AS A SECOND LANGUAGE or ENGLISH AS A FOREIGN LANGUAGE. In north American usage this is often referred to as TESOL.

embedded sentence /ɪmˈbedɪd ˈsentəns/ *n*

see EMBEDDING

embedding /ɪmˈbedɪŋ/ *n* **embed** /ɪmˈbed/ *v*

(in TRANSFORMATIONAL GENERATIVE GRAMMAR) the occurrence of a
sentence within another sentence.
For example, in:
The news that he had got married surprised his friends.

(1) The news	↑	surprised his friends.
	(2) (that) he had got married	

sentence (2) is embedded in sentence (1) and is therefore an **embedded
sentence**.
Further reading Bach 1974

emotive meaning /ɪˈməʊtɪv ˈmiːnɪŋ/ *n*

another term for CONNOTATION

empathy /ˈempəθi/ *n* **empathize** /ˈempəθaɪz/ *v*

the quality of being able to imagine and share the thoughts, feelings,
and point of view of other people. Empathy is thought to contribute
to the attitudes we have towards a person or group with a different
language and culture from our own, and it may contribute to the
degree of success with which a person learns another language.
Further reading Brown 1980; Gardner & Lambert 1972

emphatic pronoun /ɪmˈfætɪk ˈprəʊnaʊn/ *n*

a pronoun which gives additional emphasis to a noun phrase or which
draws attention to it. In English these are formed in the same way
as REFLEXIVE PRONOUNS, by adding -*self*, -*selves* to the pronouns. For
example:
I myself cooked the dinner.
We spoke to the President herself.

empirical investigation /ɪmˈpɪrɪkəl ɪnˌvestɪˈgeɪʃən/ *n*

see FIELDWORK

empirical validity /ɪmˈpɪrɪkəl vəˈlɪdɪti/ *n*

a measure of the VALIDITY of a test, arrived at by comparing the test
with one or more CRITERION MEASURES. Such comparisons could be
with:
a other valid tests or other independent measures obtained at the same
time (e.g. an assessment made by the teacher) (CONCURRENT
VALIDITY)
b other valid tests or other performance criteria obtained at a later
time (PREDICTIVE VALIDITY).

see also CONSTRUCT VALIDITY.
Further reading Brown 1988

empiricism /ɪmˈpɪrɨsɪzəm/ *n* **empiricist** /ɪmˈpɪrɨsɪst/ *n*

an approach to psychology which states that the development of theory must be related to observable facts and experiments (see BE-HAVIOURISM), or which states that all human knowledge comes from experience. Empiricism contrasts with the view that many forms of human knowledge are in-born or innate (see INNATIST HYPOTHESIS).

Further reading Steinberg 1982

empty word /ˈempti ˈwɜːd‖ˈwɜːrd/ *n*

see CONTENT WORD

enabling skills /ɪˈneɪblɪŋ ˌskɪlz/ *n*

another term for MICRO-SKILLS

encoding /ɪnˈkəʊdɪŋ/ *n* **encode** /ɪnˈkəʊd/ *v*

the process of turning a message into a set of symbols, as part of the act of communication.

In encoding speech, the speaker must:

a select a meaning to be communicated

b turn it into linguistic form using semantic systems (e.g. concepts, PROPOSITIONS), grammatical systems (e.g. words, phrases, clauses), and phonological systems (e.g. PHONEMES, SYLLABLES).

Different systems of communication make use of different types of symbols to encode messages (e.g. pictorial representation, morse code, drum beats).

see also DECODING

Further reading Clark & Clark 1977

endoglossic /ˌendəʊˈɡlɒsɪk◄‖-ˈɡlɔː-, -ˈɡlɑː-/ *adj*

When a language is the NATIVE LANGUAGE of all or most of the population of a region, it is called endoglossic. For example, English is endoglossic for the United Kingdom, Australia, and the USA, but not for nations such as Ghana or Singapore, even though it is an important language and medium of education in these countries.

see also EXOGLOSSIC

endonormative /ˌendəʊˈnɔːmətɪv◄‖-ˈnɔːr-/ *adj*

When a language has a NORM[1] within the area where it is spoken, it is called endonormative. In England and the USA, for example, English is endonormative. This is not the case for English in a country where it is a SECOND LANGUAGE, such as Malaysia, Nigeria, or Hong Kong.

see also EXONORMATIVE

English as a Foreign Language /ˈɪŋɡlɪʃ əz ə ˈfɒrɨn ˈlæŋɡwɪdʒ‖ ˈfɔː-, ˈfɑː-/ *n*

also **EFL**

the role of English in countries where it is taught as a subject in schools but not used as a medium of instruction in education nor as a language of communication (e.g. in government, business, or industry) within the country.

see also ENGLISH AS A SECOND LANGUAGE

English as an International Language /'ɪŋglɪʃ əz ən 'ɪntənæʃənəl 'læŋgwɪdʒ||'ɪntər-/ *n*

the role of English as a language of international communication, for example, when a Brazilian and a Japanese businessman use English to negotiate a business contract. The type of English used on such occasions need not necessarily be based on native speaker varieties of English (e.g. American English or British English) but will vary according to the mother tongue of the people speaking it and the purposes for which it is being used.

see also NON-NATIVE VARIETIES OF ENGLISH
Further reading Smith 1981

English as a Second Dialect /'ɪŋglɪʃ əz ə 'sekənd 'daɪəlekt/ *n*
also ESD

the role of standard English (see STANDARD VARIETY) for those who speak other dialects of English.

see also BIDIALECTAL, BILINGUAL EDUCATION

English as a Second Language /'ɪŋglɪʃ əz ə 'sekənd 'læŋgwɪdʒ/ *n*
also ESL

1 the role of English for immigrant and other minority groups in English-speaking countries. These people may use their mother tongue at home or among friends, but use English at school and at work. This is sometimes called **English for Speakers of other Languages**, or **ESOL**.

2 the role or English in countries where it is widely used within the country (e.g. as a language of instruction at school, as a language of business and government, and of everyday communication by some people) but is not the first language of the population (e.g. in Singapore, the Philippines, India, and Nigeria).

3 in US usage, the role of English in countries where it is not a first language (e.g. Germany and Japan). In British usage, this is called ENGLISH AS A FOREIGN LANGUAGE.

see also ENGLISH AS A FOREIGN LANGUAGE

English as a second language programme /'ɪŋglɪʃ əz ə 'sekənd 'læŋgwɪdʒ ˌprəʊgræm/ *n*
also **ESL/ESOL programme**

a programme for teaching English to speakers of other languages in English-speaking countries. ESL programmes are generally based on particular language teaching methods and teach language skills (speaking, understanding, reading, and writing). They may be school programmes for immigrant and other non-English-speaking children, used together with BILINGUAL EDUCATION or with regular school programmes, or community programmes for adults.

English for Academic Purposes /ˈɪŋglɪʃ fər ˈækədemɪk ˈpɜːpəsᵻz|| ˈpɜːr-/ *n*
also **EAP**

see ENGLISH FOR SPECIAL PURPOSES

English for General Purposes /ˈɪŋglɪʃ fərʳ ˈdʒenərəl ˈpɜːpəsᵻz||ˈpɜːr-/ *n*
also **EGP**

see ENGLISH FOR SPECIAL PURPOSES

English for Science and Technology /ˈɪŋglɪʃ fərʳsaɪəns ən
tekˈnɒl ədʒi||-ˈnɑː-/ *n*
also **EST**

see ENGLISH FOR SPECIAL PURPOSES

English for Speakers of Other Languages /ˈɪŋglɪʃ fərʳ ˈspiːkəz əv
ˈʌðərʳ ˈlæŋgwɪdʒᵻz||-ˈspiːkərz/ *n*
also **ESOL**

see ENGLISH AS A SECOND LANGUAGE (1)

English for Special Purposes /ˈɪŋglɪʃ fərʳ spəˈsɪfɪk ˈpɜːpəsᵻz||-ˈpɜːr-/ *n*
also **English for Specific Purposes, ESP**
the role of English in a language course or programme of instruction in
which the content and aims of the course are fixed by the specific
needs of a particular group of learners. For example courses in **English
for Academic Purposes, English for Science and Technology**, and
English for Nursing. These courses may be compared with those which
aim to teach general language proficiency, **English for General
Purposes**.

see also LANGUAGES FOR SPECIAL PURPOSES
Further reading Robinson 1980

English medium school /ˈɪŋglɪʃ ˌmiːdiəm ˈskuːl/ *n*
a school in which English is used as the major medium of instruction.
This term is usually used in countries where English is a SECOND
LANGUAGE.

enrichment programme /ɪnˈrɪtʃmənt ˌprəʊgræm/ *n*
an educational programme for children who come from backgrounds
with limited social and cultural experiences and whose learning is
thought to benefit from enrichment. Such programmes usually consist
of kindergarten or pre-school programmes which focus on a variety of
basic linguistic, social and interpersonal skills.

entailment /ɪnˈteɪlmənt/ *n*
a relationship between two or more sentences (strictly speaking
PROPOSITIONS). If knowing that one sentence is true gives us certain
knowledge of the truth of the second sentence, then the first sentence
entails the second.

entry

Entailment is concerned with the meaning of the sentence itself (see UTTERANCE MEANING). It does not depend on the context in which a sentence is used.

see also IMPLICATION, UTTERANCE MEANING
Further reading Hurford & Heasley 1983

entry /ˈentri/ *n*
(in teaching) that part of a lesson which begins it. An effective lesson is said to focus learners' attention on the lesson, inform them of the goals of the lesson and what they are expected to learn, and serve as an "organizer", preparing them for an upcoming activity.

see also CLOSURE

epenthesis /ɪˈpenθɪsɪs/ *n* **epenthetic** /ˌepənˈθetɪk◄/ *adj*
the addition of a vowel or consonant at the beginning of a word or between sounds. This often happens in language learning when the language which is being learned has different combinations of vowels or consonants from the learner's first language. For example, Spanish learners of English often say [espiːk] *espeak* for *speak*, as Spanish does not have words starting with the CONSONANT CLUSTER /sp/. Many speakers of other languages do not use combinations like the /lm/ or /lp/ of English and add an epenthetic vowel, for example [fɪləm] *filem* for *film*, and [heləp] *helep* for *help*.

see also ELISION, INTRUSION

episodic memory /ˈepɪsɒdɪk ˈmeməri‖-saː-/ *n*
that part of the MEMORY which is organized in terms of personal experiences and episodes.
For example, if a subject was asked the question "What were you doing on Friday night at 7 pm?" he or she may think of all the things that happened from 5 pm up to 7 pm. The person builds up a sequence of events or episodes to help find the wanted information. Episodic memory may be contrasted with **semantic memory**. Semantic memory is that part of the memory in which words are organized according to semantic groups or classes. Words are believed to be stored in long term memory according to their semantic properties. Thus *canary* is linked in memory to *bird*, and *rose* is linked to *flower*. These links are a part of semantic memory.

Further reading Glucksberg & Danks 1975

equational /ɪˈkweɪʒənəl/ *adj*
another term for EQUATIVE

equative /ɪˈkweɪtɪv/ *adj*
also **equational**
A sentence in which the SUBJECT and COMPLEMENT refer to the same person or thing is called an equative sentence.
For example, the English sentence:

126

> *Susan*   *is the girl I was talking about.*
> subject   complement

equivalent form reliability /ɪˈkwɪvələnt fɔːm rɪˌlaɪəˈbɪl̩tɪ‖ˈfɔːrm/ *n*
another term for ALTERNATE FORM RELIABILITY

equivalent forms /ɪˈkwɪvələnt ˈfɔːmz‖ˈfɔːrmz/ *n*
another term for PARALLEL FORMS

ergative verb /ˈɜːɡətɪv ˈvɜːb‖ˈɜːr-, ˈvɜːr-/ *n*
a verb which can be used both transitively and intransitively with the
same meaning. For example, boil in:
He boiled a kettle of water.
The kettle boiled.

error /ˈerəʳ/ *n*
1 (in the speech or writing of a second or foreign language learner),
the use of a linguistic item (e.g. a word, a grammatical item, a SPEECH
ACT, etc.) in a way which a fluent or native speaker of the language
regards as showing faulty or incomplete learning. A distinction is
sometimes made between an error, which results from incomplete
knowledge, and a **mistake** made by a learner when writing or speaking
and which is caused by lack of attention, fatigue, carelessness, or some
other aspect of PERFORMANCE. Errors are sometimes classified according to vocabulary (**lexical error**), pronunciation (**phonological
error**), grammar, (**syntactic error**), misunderstanding of a speaker's
intention or meaning (**interpretive error**), production of the wrong
communicative effect e.g. through the faulty use of a speech act or one
of the RULES OF SPEAKING (**pragmatic error**).
In the study of second and foreign language learning, errors have been
studied to discover the processes learners make use of in learning and
using a language (see ERROR ANALYSIS).
2 see under SPEECH ERROR.

see also DEVELOPMENTAL ERROR, GLOBAL ERROR
Further reading Richards 1974; Ellis 1985

error analysis /ˈerəʳ əˌnæl̩s̩s/ *n*
the study and analysis of the ERRORS made by second language learners.
Error analysis may be carried out in order to:
a identify strategies which learners use in language learning
b try to identify the causes of learner errors
c obtain information on common difficulties in language learning, as
   an aid to teaching or in the preparation of teaching materials.
Error analysis developed as a branch of APPLIED LINGUISTICS in the
1960s, and set out to demonstrate that many learner errors were not
due to the learner's mother tongue but reflected universal learning
strategies. Error analysis was therefore offered as an alternative to
CONTRASTIVE ANALYSIS. Attempts were made to develop classifications
for different types of errors on the basis of the different processes that

were assumed to account for them. A basic distinction was drawn between intralingual and interlingual errors (see INTERLINGUAL ERROR). Intralingual errors were classified as overgeneralizations (errors caused by extension of target language rules to inappropriate contexts), **simplifications** (errors resulting from learners producing simpler linguistic rules than those found in the target language), **developmental errors** (those reflecting natural stages of development), **communication-based errors** (errors resulting from strategies of communication), **induced errors** (those resulting from **transfer of training**), **errors of avoidance** (resulting from failure to use certain target language structures because they are thought to be too difficult), or **errors of overproduction** (structures being used too frequently). Attempts to apply such categories have been problematic however, due to the difficulty of determining the cause of errors. By the late 1970s, error analysis had largely been superseded by studies of INTERLANGUAGE and SECOND LANGUAGE ACQUISITION.

Further reading Richards 1974; Ellis 1985; Odlin 1989

error gravity /'erəʳ ˌgrævᵻti/ n
a measure of the effect that errors made by people speaking a second or foreign language have on communication or on other speakers of the language. The degree of error gravity of different kinds of errors (e.g. errors of pronunciation, grammar, vocabulary, etc.) varies; some errors have little effect, some cause irritation, while others may cause communication difficulties.
For example, in the sentences below, *a* causes greater interference with communication than *b* and shows a greater degree of error gravity.
a *Since the harvest was good, was rain a lot last year.*
b *The harvest was good last year, because plenty of rain.*
Further reading Svartvik 1973; Burt & Kiparsky 1972

ESD /ˌiː es 'diː/ n
an abbreviation for ENGLISH AS A SECOND DIALECT

ESL /ˌiː es 'el/ n
an abbreviation for ENGLISH AS A SECOND LANGUAGE

ESOL /ˌiː es əu 'el, 'iːsɒl‖-saːl-/ n
an abbreviation for English for Speakers of Other Languages (see ENGLISH AS A SECOND LANGUAGE (1))

ESP /ˌiː es 'piː/ n
an abbreviation for ENGLISH FOR SPECIAL PURPOSES

essay /'eseɪ/ n
(in composition) a longer piece of writing, particularly one that is written by a student as part of a course of study or by a writer writing for publication which expresses the writer's viewpoint on a topic. Essays are often organized according to a number of recognizable

rhetorical forms (see METHODS OF DEVELOPMENT) and usually contain the following sections:

1 the **introduction**: this presents the topic and contains the THESIS STATEMENT.

2 the **body**: this is a series of paragraphs each with a TOPIC SENTENCE. The paragraphs in the body of the body of the essay develop and support the thesis statement.

3 the **conclusion**: this summarises what has been said and often presents a solution or makes a prediction.

essay test /'eseɪ ˌtest/ *n*
a SUBJECTIVE TEST in which a person is required to write an extended piece of text on a set topic.

EST /ˌiː es 'tiː/ *n*
an abbreviation for English for Science and Technology
see ENGLISH FOR SPECIAL PURPOSES

ethnographic research /ˈeθnəgræfɪk rɪ'sɜːtʃ, 'riːsɜːtʃ‖-ɜːr-/ *n*
see ETHNOGRAPHY

ethnography /eθ'nɒgrəfi‖-'naː-/ *n*
the study of the life and culture of a society or ethnic group, especially by personal observation. The related field of **ethnology** studies the comparison of the cultures of different societies or ethnic groups.

In studies of language learning or in descriptions of how a language is used, the term **ethnographic research** is sometimes used to refer to the observation and description of naturally occurring language (e.g. between mother and child, between teacher and students, etc.).

see also ETHNOGRAPHY OF COMMUNICATION

ethnography of communication /eθ'nɒgrəfi əv kəˌmjuːnɪ̩'keɪʃən‖ eθ'naː-/ *n*
the study of the place of language in culture and society. Language is not studied in isolation but within a social and/or cultural setting. Ethnography of communication studies, for example, how people in a particular group or community communicate with each other and how the social relationships between these people affect the type of language they use.

The concept of an ethnography of communication was advocated by the American social anthropologist and linguist Hymes and this approach is important in SOCIOLINGUISTICS and APPLIED LINGUISTICS.

see also COMMUNICATIVE COMPETENCE, ETHNOMETHODOLOGY, ROLE RELATIONSHIP, SPEECH EVENT
Further reading Hymes 1977; Saville-Troike 1982

ethnology /eθ'nɒlədʒi‖-'naː-/ *n*
see ETHNOGRAPHY

ethnomethodology /ˌeθnəʊmeθəˈdɒlədʒi‖-ˈdɑː-/ *n*
ethnomethodologist /ˌeθnəʊmeθəˈdɒlədʒᵻst‖-ˈdɑː-/ *n*
a branch of sociology which studies how people organize and understand the activities of ordinary life. It studies people's relations with each other and how social interaction takes place between people. Ethnomethodologists have studied such things as relationships between children and adults, interviews, telephone conversation, and TURN TAKING in conversation. Language is not the main interest of ethnomethodologists, but their observations on how language is used in everyday activities such as conversation are of interest to linguists and sociolinguists.

see also ETHNOGRAPHY OF COMMUNICATION
Further reading Garfinkel 1976; Turner 1970

etymology /etᵻˈmɒlədʒi‖-ˈmɑː-/ *n* **etymological** /ˌetᵻməˈlɒdʒɪkəl◂‖ -ˈlɑː-/ *adj*
the study of the origin of words, and of their history and changes in their meaning.
For example, the etymology of the modern English noun *fish* can be traced back to Old English *fisc*.
In some cases there is a change in meaning. For example the word *meat*, which now normally means "animal flesh used as food", is from the Old English word *mete* which meant "food in general".

euphemism /ˈjuːfəmɪzəm/ *n*
the use of a word which is thought to be less offensive or unpleasant than another word. For example, *indisposed* instead of *sick*, or *to pass away*, instead of *to die*.

evaluation /ɪˌvæljuˈeɪʃən/ *n*
in general, the systematic gathering of information for purposes of decision making. Evaluation uses both quantitative methods (e.g. tests), qualitative methods (e.g. observations, ratings (see RATING SCALE)) and value judgments. In LANGUAGE PLANNING, evaluation frequently involves gathering information on patterns of language use, language ability, and attitudes towards language. In language teaching programmes, evaluation is related to decisions to be made about the quality of the programme itself, and decisions about individuals in the programmes. The evaluation of programmes may involve the study of CURRICULUM², OBJECTIVES, materials, and tests or grading systems. The evaluation of individuals involves decisions about entrance to programmes, placement, progress, and achievement. In evaluating both programmes and individuals, tests and other measures are frequently used.

see also FORMATIVE EVALUATION
Further reading Popham 1975; Johnson 1989

evaluative comprehension /ɪˈvæljuətɪv ˌkɒmprᵻˈhenʃən‖-jueɪtɪv ˌkɑːm-/ *n*
see READING

evaluative question /ɪ'væljuətɪv 'kwestʃən‖-jueɪtɪv/ *n*
a DIVERGENT QUESTION which requires students to make an evaluation, such as a question which asks students to say why they think a certain kind of behaviour is good or bad.
see also QUESTIONING TECHNIQUES

exact word method /ɪg'zækt 'wɜːd ˌmeθəd‖'wɜːrd/ *n*
see CLOZE PROCEDURE

exclamation[1] /ˌekskləˈmeɪʃən/ *n*
an utterance, which may not have the structure of a full sentence, and which shows strong emotion. For example: *Good God! or Damn!*
see also INTERJECTION

exclamation[2] *n*
also **exclamatory sentence** /ɪk'sklæmətəri 'sentəns‖-tɔːri/
an utterance which shows the speaker's or writer's feelings. Exclamations begin with a phrase using *what* or *how*, but they do not reverse the order of the subject and the auxiliary verb:
How clever she is!
What a good dog!
see also STATEMENT, QUESTION
Further reading Quirk et al 1985

exclusive (first person) pronoun /ɪk'skluːsɪv 'fɜːst 'pɜːsən 'prəʊnaʊn‖'fɜːrst 'pɜːr-/ *n*
a first person pronoun which does not include the person being spoken or written to.
In some languages there is a distinction between first person plural pronouns which include the persons who are addressed (**inclusive pronouns**) and those which do not (exclusive pronouns). For example, in Malay:

exclusive	inclusive
kami	*kita*
"we"	"we"

The lack of this distinction in English occasionally causes problems. For example, *We really must see that film next week* can be ambiguous unless it is clear from the context whether the person addressed is included or not.
see also PERSONAL PRONOUNS

existential /ˌegzɪ'stenʃəl◄/ *adj*
(in linguistics) describes a particular type of sentence structure which often expresses the existence or location of persons, animals, things, or ideas.
In English, a common existential sentence structure is:
There + a form of the verb *be*
For example:
There are four bedrooms in this house.

Another frequently used existential structure uses the verb *to have*. For example:

This house has four bedrooms.

Further reading Lyons 1981

exoglossic /ˌeksəʊˈglɒsɪk◄‖-ˈglɔː-, -ˈglɑː-/ *adj*
when a language is not the NATIVE LANGUAGE of all or most of the population of a region it is called exoglossic.

For example, English is exoglossic in Ghana and Singapore where it is not a native language for many people although it is a medium of education.

see also ENDOGLOSSIC

exonormative /ˌeksəʊˈnɔːmətɪv‖-ˈnɔːr-/ *adj*
When a language has its NORM[1] outside the area where it is spoken or taught, it is called exonormative.

For example, English is exonormative in countries where it is not the NATIVE LANGUAGE but where it is, for instance, a SECOND LANGUAGE, e.g. in Hong Kong.

In some countries such as Australia, there has been a change from an external to an internal norm, i.e. from a British to a local Australian standard.

see also ENDONORMATIVE

expanded pidgin /ɪkˈspændɪd ˈpɪdʒɪn/ *n*
see PIDGIN

expansion /ɪkˈspænʃən/ *n*
see MODELLING

expectancy theory /ɪkˈspektənsi ˌθɪəri/ *n*
the theory that knowledge of a language includes knowing whether a word or utterance is likely to occur in a particular context or situation. For example, in the sentence below, "expected" words in (1) and (2) are *dress* and *change*:

When the girl fell into the water she wet the pretty (1) she was wearing and had to go home and (2) it.

Knowledge of the expectancies of occurrence of language items is made use of in the comprehension of language.

see also PRAGMATICS
Further reading Oller 1979

experiencer case /ɪkˈspɪəriənsərˌkeɪs/ *n*
see DATIVE CASE[2]

experimental design /ɪkˈsperɪmentl dɪˈzaɪn/ *n*
see EXPERIMENTAL METHOD

experimental group /ɪksperɪˈmentl ˌɡruːp/ *n*
see CONTROL GROUP

experimental method /ɪksperɪˈmentl ˌmeθəd/ *n*

an approach to educational research in which an idea or HYPOTHESIS is tested or verified by setting up situations in which the relationship between different subjects or variables can be determined (see DEPENDENT VARIABLE). The description of the purposes of the research, its plan, the statistical procedures used, etc., in an experimental study is called the **experimental design**.

Further reading Bailey 1982

explicit performative /ɪkˈsplɪsɪt pəˈfɔːmətɪv‖pərˈfɔːr-/ *n*

see PERFORMATIVE

exponent /ɪkˈspəʊnənt/ *n*

see FUNCTIONAL SYLLABUS

expressive /ɪkˈspresɪv/ *n*

see SPEECH ACT CLASSIFICATION

expressive function /ɪkˈspresɪv ˈfʌŋkʃən/ *n*

see FUNCTIONS OF LANGUAGE[1]

Extended Standard Theory /ɪkˈstendɪd ˈstændəd ˈθɪəri‖-ərd/ *n*

see TRANSFORMATIONAL GENERATIVE GRAMMAR

extensive reading /ɪkˈstensɪv ˈriːdɪŋ/ *n*

In language teaching, reading activities are sometimes classified as extensive and intensive.

Extensive reading means reading in quantity and in order to gain a general understanding of what is read. It is intended to develop good reading habits, to build up knowledge of vocabulary and structure, and to encourage a liking for reading.

Intensive reading is generally at a slower speed, and requires a higher degree of understanding than extensive reading.

Further reading Mackay et al 1979; Nuttall 1982

external speech /ɪkˈstɜːnəl ˈspiːtʃ‖-ɜːr-/ *n*

see INNER SPEECH

extinction /ɪkˈstɪŋkʃən/ *n*

see STIMULUS-RESPONSE THEORY

extralinguistic /ˌekstrəlɪŋˈgwɪstɪk◄/ *adj*

describes those features in communication which are not directly a part of verbal language but which either contribute in conveying a MESSAGE, e.g. hand movements, facial expressions, etc., or have an influence on language use, e.g. signalling a speaker's age, sex, or social class.

see also PARALINGUISTICS, SIGN LANGUAGE

extraposition /ˌekstrəpəˈzɪʃən/ n
the process of moving a word, phrase, or clause to a position in a sentence which is different from the position it usually has.
For example, the subject of some sentences can be moved to the end of the sentence:

    a <u>Trying to get tickets</u> was difficult.
    b It was difficult <u>trying to get tickets</u>.

In sentence b It is called the **anticipatory subject**, and trying to get tickets is called the **postponed subject**.

Further reading Quirk et al 1985

extrovert (also **extravert**) /ˈekstrəˌvɜːt‖-vɜːrt/ n **extroversion** (also **extraversion**) /ˌekstrəˈvɜːʃən‖-ˈvɜːrʒən/ n
a person whose conscious interests and energies are more often directed outwards towards other people and events than towards the person themself and their own inner experience. Such a personality type is contrasted with an **introvert**, a person who tends to avoid social contact with others and is often preoccupied with his or her inner feelings, thoughts and experiences. Psychologists no longer believe that these are two distinct personality types, since many people show aspects of both. Extroversion and introversion have been discussed as PERSONALITY factors in second language learning, though the contribution of either factor to learning is not clear.

Further reading Brown 1987

eye span /ˈaɪ ˌspæn/ n
see **reading span**

F

face /feɪs/ *n*

In communication between two or more persons, the positive image or impression of oneself that one shows or intends to show to the other PARTICIPANTS is called face. In any social meeting between people, the participants attempt to communicate a positive image of themselves which reflects the values and beliefs of the participants. For example Ms Smith's "face" during a particular meeting might be that of "a sophisticated, intelligent, witty, and educated person". If this image is not accepted by the other participants, feelings may be hurt and there is a consequent "loss of face". Social contacts between people thus involve what the sociologist of language, Goffman, called **face-work**, that is, efforts by the participants to communicate a positive face and to prevent loss of face. The study of face and face-work is important in considering how languages express POLITENESS.

Further reading Goffman 1959, 1967; Levinson 1983

face to face interaction /ˈfeɪs tə ˈfeɪs ɪntərˈækʃən/ *n*
also **face to face communication** /ˈfeɪs tə ˈfeɪs kəmjuːnɪˈkeɪʃən/

communication between people in which the PARTICIPANTS are physically present. In contrast there are some situations where speaker and hearer may be in different locations, such as a telephone conversation.

face validity /ˈfeɪs vəˈlɪdɪti/ *n*

(in testing) the degree to which a test appears to measure the knowledge or abilities it claims to measure, based on the subjective judgment of an observer.

For example, if a test of reading comprehension contains many dialect words which might be unknown to the students the test may be said to lack face validity.

see also VALIDITY
Further reading Heaton 1975

face-work /ˈfeɪswɜːk‖-ɜːr-/ *n*

see FACE

facility value /fəˈsɪlɪti ˈvæljuː/ *n*

another term for ITEM FACILITY

factitive case /ˈfæktɪtɪv ˌkeɪs/ *n*

(In CASE GRAMMAR) the noun or noun phrase which refers to

135

something which is made or created by the action of the verb is in the factitive case.
For example, in the sentence:
  Tony built the shed.
the shed is in the factitive case.
However, in the sentence:
  Tony repaired the shed.
the shed is not in the factitive case as it already existed when the repair work was done. In this sentence, *the shed* is in the OBJECTIVE CASE.
The factitive case is sometimes called the **result** (or **resultative**) case.

Further reading Fillmore 1968

factive verb /'fæktɪv 'vɜːb||-ɜːr-/ *n*

a verb followed by a clause which the speaker or writer considers to express a fact.
For example, in:
  I remember that he was always late.
remember is a factive verb.
Other factive verbs in English include *regret, deplore, know, agree*.

Further reading Lyons 1977

factor analysis /'fæktər ə,næljsįs/ *n*

in statistics, a technique which is used to determine what underlying VARIABLES[2] account for the CORRELATIONS among different observed variables. For example if we give a group of students tests in geometry, algebra, arithmetic, reading and writing, we can find out what factors are common to all the tests, using factor analysis. A factor analysis might show that there are two factors in the tests; one related to mathematics and the other related to language proficiency. These factors may be interpreted as abilities or traits which these tests measure to differing degrees.

Further reading Ebel 1972; Brown 1988

false beginner /'fɔːls bɪ'gɪnəʳ/ *n*

(in language teaching) a learner who has had a limited amount of previous instruction in a language, but who because of extremely limited language proficiency is classified as at the beginning level of language instruction. A false beginner is sometimes contrasted with a **true beginner**, i.e. someone who has no knowledge of the language.

false cognate /'fɔːls 'kɒgneɪt||'kɑːg-/ *n*
also faux amis, false friend /'fɔːls 'frend/

a word which has the same or very similar form in two languages, but which has a different meaning in each. The similarity may cause a second language learner to use the word wrongly. For example the French word *expérience* means "experiment", and not "experience". French learners of English might thus write or say: *Yesterday we performed an interesting experience in the laboratory*.
False cognates may be identified by CONTRASTIVE ANALYSIS.

familiarity /fə͵mɪli'ærɨti/ *n*

a measure of how frequently a linguistic item is thought to be used, or the degree to which it is known. This may be measured by asking people to show on a RATING SCALE whether they think they use a given word or structure *never, sometimes,* or *often.* Word familiarity has been used as a way of selecting vocabulary for language teaching.

Further reading Richards 1970

faux amis /͵fəʊzæ'miː/ *n*

another term for FALSE COGNATE

feature /'fiːtʃəʳ/ *n*

a property of a linguistic item which helps to mark it in certain ways, either singling it out from similar items or classifying it into a group with others.

For example, the English phoneme /b/ has the feature *voice*, it is a voiced stop. By this feature it can be distinguished from /p/, an unvoiced stop, or classified together with /d/ and /g/, other voiced stops. Features can be used in all levels of linguistic analysis, e.g. phonetics, morphology, syntax. They can even form the basis of linguistic theories.

see DISTINCTIVE FEATURE, COMPONENTIAL ANALYSIS

feedback /'fiːdbæk/ *n*

1 any information which provides a report on the result of behaviour. For example, verbal or facial signals which listeners give to speakers to indicate that they understand what the speaker is saying. In DISCOURSE ANALYSIS, feedback given while someone is speaking is sometimes called **back channel cues,** for example comments such as *uh, yeah, really,* smiles, headshakes, and grunts which indicate success or failure in communication.

see also AUDITORY FEEDBACK, DELAYED AUDITORY FEEDBACK, KINES-THETIC FEEDBACK.

2 (in teaching), comments or information learners receive on the success of a learning task, either from the teacher or from other learners.

see also PEER REVIEW

felicity conditions /fɨ'lɪsɨti kən͵dɪʃənz/ *n*

(in SPEECH ACT THEORY) the conditions which must be fulfilled for a speech act to be satisfactorily performed or realized. For example, the sentence *I promise the sun will set today* cannot be considered as a true promise, because we can only make promises about future acts which are under our control. The felicity conditions necessary for promises are:

a A sentence is used which states a future act of the speaker.

b The speaker has the ability to do the act.

c The hearer prefers the speaker to do the act rather than not to do it.

d The speaker would not otherwise usually do the act.

e The speaker intends to do the act.

Further reading Searle 1981

field /fiːld/ *n*

see LEXICAL FIELD

field dependence /'fiːld dɪ'pendəns/ *n* **field dependent** /'fiːld
dɪ'pendənt◄/ *adj*

a learning style in which a learner tends to look at the whole of a
learning task which contains many items. The learner has difficulty in
studying a particular item when it occurs within a "field" of other
items.

A **field independent** learning style is one in which a learner is able
to identify or focus on particular items and is not distracted by other
items in the background or context.

Field dependence and independence have been studied as a difference
of COGNITIVE STYLE in language learning.

Further reading Naiman et al 1975; Brown 1987

field experiences /'fiːld ɪk,spɪəriəns⅃z/ *n*

(in teacher education) opportunities which are provided for student
teachers to participate in real teaching situations, i.e. which involve
student teachers teaching students in a school or classroom and which
enable him or her to assume the role of a teacher, to gain teaching
experience, and to experience teaching as a profession.

field independence /'fiːld ɪndɪ'pendəns/ *n*

see FIELD DEPENDENCE

field method /'fiːld ˌmeθəd/ *n*

see FIELDWORK

field of discourse /ˌfiːld əv 'dɪskɔːs‖-ɔːrs/ *n*

see SOCIAL CONTEXT

field research /'fiːld rɪ'sɜːtʃ, 'riːsɜːtʃ‖-ɜːr-/ *n*

see FIELDWORK

field testing /'fiːld ˌtestɪŋ/ *n*
also **field trial, pilot testing**

in the production of instructional materials, the try-out of materials
before publication or further development in order to determine their
suitability or effectiveness and to determine the reactions of teachers
and learners to the materials.

Further reading Briggs 1977

fieldwork /'fiːldwɜːk‖-wɜːrk/
also **field research**

(In linguistics) the collection of data by observation or recording in as natural a setting as possible. Different procedures (called **field methods**) are used to obtain data. For example:

a the recording of speakers to obtain speech samples for analysis of sounds, sentence structures, lexical use, etc. The people recorded may be native speakers of a particular language or speakers using a SECOND LANGUAGE.

b interviews, e.g. in bilingual or multilingual communities, to obtain information on language choice and/or attitudes to language.

c observation and/or video recording of verbal or non-verbal behaviour in a particular situation (see PARTICIPANT OBSERVATION).

The collection and the use of data (**empirical investigation**) plays an important part in the research work of many applied linguists and sociolinguists.

figure of speech /'fɪgər əv 'spiːtʃ||'fɪgjər/ *n*

a word or phrase which is used for special effect, and which does not have its usual or literal meaning. The two most common figures of speech are the **simile** and the **metaphor** but there are many other less common ones.

A simile is an expression in which something is compared to something else by the use of a FUNCTION WORD such as *like* or *as*. In *Tom eats like a horse*, Tom's appetite is compared to that of a horse. *My hands are as cold as ice* means that my hands are very cold.

In a metaphor, no function words are used. Something is described by stating another thing with which it can be compared.

In *Her words stabbed at his heart*, the words did not actually stab, but their effect is compared to the stabbing of a knife.

filled pause /'fɪld 'pɔːz/ *n*

see PAUSING

final /'faɪnl/ *adj*

occurring at the end of a linguistic unit, e.g. word final, clause final. For example, a group of consonants at the end of a word such as *st* in the English word *list* is called a final CONSONANT CLUSTER.

see also INITIAL, MEDIAL

finger spelling /'fɪŋgər ˌspelɪŋ/ *n*
also **dactylology**

a kind of signing behaviour (see SIGN LANGUAGE) which has been developed to help hearing-impaired persons communicate. Finger-spelling provides a manual alphabet which is used to spell out words using the fingers.

finite verb /'faɪnaɪt 'vɜːb||'vɜːrb/ *n*

a form of a verb which is marked to show that it is related to a subject in PERSON and/or NUMBER, and which shows TENSE[1]. A **non-finite verb** form is not marked according to differences in the person or number of the subject, and has no tense. The INFINITIVE and the PARTICIPLES are non-finite forms of verbs in English. For example:

We	*want*	*to leave.*
She	*wants*	
I	*wanted*	
	finite verb forms	non-finite form

Further reading Quirk et al 1985

first language /ˈfɜːst ˈlæŋgwɪdʒ‖ˈfɜːrst/ *n*
(generally) a person's mother tongue or the language acquired first. In multilingual communities, however, where a child may gradually shift from the main use of one language to the main use of another (e.g. because of the influence of a school language), first language may refer to the language the child feels most comfortable using. Often this term is used synonymously with NATIVE LANGUAGE.
First language is also known as **L1**.

first language acquisition /ˈfɜːst ˈlæŋgwɪdʒ ækwɪˈzɪʃən‖ˈfɜːrst/ *n*
the learning and development of a person's native language. Interest in the processes by which children learn their first language was prompted by the work of Chomsky, who argued that:
a children are born with special language learning abilities
b they do not have to be taught language or corrected for their mistakes
c they learn language by being exposed to it
d linguistic rules develop unconsciously.
Children are said to "acquire" the rules of their mother tongue by being exposed to examples of the language and by using the language for communication.
Early work in first language acquisition concentrated on how children develop a linguistic system which enables them to produce sentences that they have never heard before (i.e. novel sentences). More recent research has studied:
a the relationship between language development and cognitive development
b how children distinguish and develop word meanings
c the development of phonology in the first language
d the effects of interaction (between parents and the child and between a child and other children) on language development (see INTER-ACTIONISM)
Some researchers have suggested that children show evidence of the use of universal rules and principles in language acquisition, which are independent of the particular language they are learning, and pass through similar stages in language development.
Further reading Bennett-Kastor 1988; Fletcher 1985; Brown 1973

fixation pause /fɪk'seɪʃən ˌpɔːz/ n

(in reading) the brief periods when the eyeball is resting and during which the visual input required for reading takes place. The jump from one fixation point to another is known as a **saccade**.

see also READING SPAN

fixed response item /'fɪkst rɪ'spɒns ˌaɪtəm‖-'spɑːns/ n

see TEST ITEM

fixed stress /'fɪkst 'stres/ n

STRESS which occurs regularly on the same syllable in a word in a particular language.

Languages which rigidly follow a fixed stress pattern are rare. There are always exceptions to the rule but Hungarian, for instance, usually stresses the first syllable of a word, and Polish usually stresses the second syllable from the end of a word (the penultimate syllable).

see also FREE STRESS
Further reading Hyman 1975

flap /flæp/ n
also **tap**

a speech sound (a CONSONANT) which is produced by making a single tap, usually by the tongue against a firm surface in the mouth.

For example, for some speakers of English the r-sound in words like *very, sorry,* and *Mary* may be an ALVEOLAR flap, produced by a slight tap with the tip of the tongue against the alveolar ridge, the gum ridge behind the upper front teeth.

see also FRICTIONLESS CONTINUANT, MANNER OF ARTICULATION, PLACE OF ARTICULATION, ROLL
Further reading Gimson 1980

flashcard /'flæʃkɑːd‖-ɑːr-/ n

(in language teaching) a card with words, sentences, or pictures on it, used as an aid or CUE in a language lesson.

FLES /ˌef el iː 'es/ n

an abbreviation for FOREIGN LANGUAGES IN THE ELEMENTARY SCHOOL

fluency /'fluːənsi/ n **fluent** /'fluːənt/ adj

the features which give speech the qualities of being natural and normal, including native-like use of PAUSING, rhythm, INTONATION, STRESS, rate of speaking, and use of interjections and interruptions. If speech disorders cause a breakdown in normal speech (e.g. as with APHASIA or stuttering), the resulting speech may be referred to as **dysfluent**, or as an example of **dysfluency**.

In second and foreign language teaching, fluency describes a level of proficiency in communication, which includes:

a the ability to produce written and/or spoken language with ease
b the ability to speak with a good but not necessarily perfect command of intonation, vocabulary, and grammar

c the ability to communicate ideas effectively
d the ability to produce continuous speech without causing comprehension difficulties or a breakdown of communication.

It is sometimes contrasted with **accuracy**, which refers to the ability to produce grammatically correct sentences but may not include the ability to speak or write fluently.

Further reading Dalton & Hardcastle 1977

focus /ˈfəʊkəs/ n
see FUNCTIONAL SENTENCE PERSPECTIVE

focused interview /ˈfəʊkəst ˈɪntəvjuː‖ˈɪntər-/ n
an interview that explores a particular aspect of an event or situation, particularly with a group of individuals who have had similar experience of the event. For example in language programme evaluation a focussed interview may be held with teachers to find out how well students are reacting to a new set of teaching materials.
see also DEPTH INTERVIEW, GUIDED INTERVIEW

foreground(ed) information /ˈfɔːgraʊndɪd ˌɪnfəˈmeɪʃən‖ ˈfɔːr- ˌɪnfər-/ n
see GROUNDING

foreigner talk /ˈfɒrɪnəʳ ˌtɔːk‖ˈfɔː-, ˈfɑː-/ n
the type of speech often used by native speakers of a language when speaking to foreigners who are not proficient in the language. Some of the characteristics of foreigner talk are:
a it is slower and louder than normal speech, often with exaggerated pronunciation
b it uses simpler vocabulary and grammar. For example, articles, function words, and INFLECTIONS may be omitted, and complex verb forms are replaced by simpler ones.
c topics are sometimes repeated or moved to the front of sentences, for example: *Your bag? Where you leave your bag?*
Native speakers often feel that this type of speech is easier for foreigners to understand.
see also ACCOMMODATION, CARETAKER SPEECH, PIDGIN, INTERLANGUAGE
Further reading Ferguson 1971

foreign language /ˈfɒrɪn ˈlæŋgwɪdʒ‖ˈfɔː-, ˈfɑː-/ n
1 a language which is not a NATIVE LANGUAGE in a country. A foreign language is usually studied either for communication with foreigners who speak the language, or for reading printed materials in the language.
In North American applied linguistics usage, "foreign language" and "second language" are often used to mean the same in this sense.
2 In British usage, a distinction is often made between foreign language and **second language**.

a a foreign language is a language which is taught as a school subject but which is not used as a medium of instruction in schools nor as a language of communication within a country (e.g. in government, business, or industry). English is described as a foreign language in France, Japan, China, etc.

b a second language is a language which is not a native language in a country but which is widely used as a medium of communication (e.g. in education and in government) and which is usually used alongside another language or languages. English is described as a second language in countries such as Fiji, Singapore, and Nigeria.

In *both* Britain and North America, the term "second language" would describe a native language in a country as learnt by people living there who have another FIRST LANGUAGE. English in the UK would be called the second language of immigrants and people whose first language is Welsh.

Foreign Languages in the Elementary School /ˈfɒrɪ�჻n ˈlæŋgwɪdʒɪ̗z ɪn ðiː elɪ̗ˈmentəri ˌskuːl‖ˈfɔː-, ˈfɑː-/ *n*
also **FLES**

1 the teaching of foreign languages in elementary schools.
2 the name of a movement which aims to increase the amount of foreign language teaching in elementary schools in the USA.

Foreign Service Institute Oral Interview /ˈfɒrɪ̗n ˈsɜːvɪ̗s ˈɪnstɪ̗tjuːt ˈɔːrəl ˈɪntəvjuː‖ˈfɔː-, ˈfɑːrɪ̗n ˈsɜːr- -tuːt ˈɪntər-/ *n*
also **FSI**

a technique for testing the spoken language proficiency of adult foreign language learners. The technique was developed by the United States Foreign Service Institute. It consists of a set of RATING SCALES which are used to judge pronunciation, grammar, vocabulary, and fluency during a 30 minute interview between the learner and, usually, two interviewers.
Further reading Oller 1979

form /fɔːm‖fɔːrm/ *n*
the means by which an element of language is expressed in speech or writing. Forms can be shown by the standard writing system for a language or by phonetic or phonemic symbols. For example, in English:

written form	spoken form
house	/haʊs/

Often a distinction is made between the spoken or written form of a linguistic unit and its meaning or function.
For example, in English the written form *-s* and the spoken forms /s/ and /z/ have a common function. They show the plural of nouns:
/kæts/ *cats*   /dɒgz‖dɔːgz/ *dogs*

formal operational stage /ˈfɔːməl ɒpəˈreɪʃənəlˈsteɪdʒ‖ˈfɔːr- ɑːpə-/ *n*
see under GENETIC EPISTEMOLOGY

formal speech /'fɔːməl 'spiːtʃ||'fɔːr-/ *n*
the type of speech used in situations when the speaker is very careful about pronunciation and choice of words and sentence structure. This type of speech may be used, for example, at official functions, and in debates and ceremonies. The English sentence
Ladies and gentlemen, it gives me great pleasure to be present here tonight.
is an example of formal speech.
see also STYLE, COLLOQUIAL SPEECH, STYLISTIC VARIATION

formal universal /'fɔːməl juːnɪ̥'vɜːsəl||'fɔːr- -'vɜːr-/ *n*
see LANGUAGE UNIVERSAL

formative /'fɔːmətɪv||'fɔːr-/ *n*
(in TRANSFORMATIONAL GENERATIVE GRAMMAR) the minimum grammatical unit in a language. For example, in:
The drivers started the engines.
the formatives would be:
the + drive + er + s + start + ed + the + engine + s
see also MORPHEME

formative evaluation /'fɔːmətɪv ɪvælju'eɪʃən||'fɔːr-/ *n*
the process of providing information to curriculum developers during the development of a curriculum or programme, in order to improve it. Formative evaluation is also used in syllabus design and the development of language teaching programmes and materials.
Summative evaluation is the process of providing information to decision makers, after the programme is completed, about whether or not the programme was effective and successful.
see also EVALUATION
Further reading Scriven 1967

formative test /'fɔːmətɪv 'test||'fɔːr-/ *n*
a test which is given during a course of instruction and which informs both the student and the teacher how well the student is doing. A formative test includes only topics which have been taught, and shows whether the student needs extra work or attention. It is usually a pass or fail test. If a student fails he or she is able to do more study and take the test again.
A **summative test** is one given at the end of a course of instruction, and which measures or "sums up" how much a student has learned from the course. A summative test is usually a graded test, i.e. it is marked according to a scale or set of grades.
Further reading Hughes 1989

form class /'fɔːm ˌklɑːs||'fɔːrm ˌklæs/ *n*
(in linguistics) a group of items which can be used in similar positions in a structure.
For example, in the sentence:

The ... is here.
the words *dog, book, evidence,* etc. could be used. They all belong to the same form class of nouns.

see also WORD CLASS, OPEN CLASS

form-function relation /'fɔːm 'fʌŋkʃən rɪ,leɪʃən||'fɔːrm/ *n*
the relationship between the physical characteristics of a thing (i.e. its form) and its role or function. This distinction is often referred to in studying language use, because a linguistic form (e.g. the imperative) can perform a variety of different functions, as the following examples illustrate.

Imperative forms	Communicative functions
Come round for a drink.	*invitation*
Watch out.	*warning*
Turn left at the corner.	*direction*
Pass the sugar.	*request*

form of address /'fɔːm əv ə'dres||'fɔːrm əv ə'dres, 'ædres/ *n*
another term for ADDRESS FORM

formula /'fɔːmjʊlə||-ɔːr-/ *n* (plural **formulae** /'fɔːmjʊliː, -laɪ||-ɔːr-/ *or* **formulas**)
another term for ROUTINE

formulaic speech /'fɔːmjʊleɪ-ɪk 'spiːtʃ||-ɔːr-/ *n*
also **formulaic expression** /'fɔːmjʊleɪ-ɪk ɪk'spreʃən||-ɔːr-/ , **formulaic language** /'fɔːmjʊleɪ-ɪk 'læŋgwɪdʒ||-ɔːr-/
another term for ROUTINE

form word /'fɔːm ,wɜːd||'fɔːrm ,wɜːrd/ *n*
see CONTENT WORD

fortis /'fɔːtɪs||-ɔːr-/ *adj*
describes a CONSONANT which is produced with a relatively greater amount of muscular force and breath, e.g. in English /p/, /t/, and /k/. The opposite to fortis is **lenis,** which describes consonants which are produced with less muscular effort and little or no ASPIRATION, e.g. in English /b/, /d/, and /g/.

see MANNER OF ARTICULATION, VOICE[2]
Further reading Gimson 1989

fossilization /,fɒsɪlaɪ'zeɪʃən||,fɑːsələ-/ *n* **fossilized** /'fɒsɪlaɪzd|| 'fɑː-/ *adj*
(in second or foreign language learning) a process which sometimes occurs in which incorrect linguistic features become a permanent part of the way a person speaks or writes a language. Aspects of pronunciation, vocabulary usage, and grammar may become fixed or

fossilized in second or foreign language learning. Fossilized features of pronunciation contribute to a person's foreign accent.

see also INTERLANGUAGE

Further reading Selinker 1972; Ellis 1985

four phase drill /'fɔːʳ feɪz 'drɪl/ *n*

a type of DRILL used in language teaching materials in a LANGUAGE LABORATORY. A four phase drill has four parts as follows:

a a stimulus on the tape
b a space for the student's response
c the correct response
d a space for the student to repeat the correct response.

fragment /'frægmənt/ *n*

see SENTENCE FRAGMENT

frame /freɪm/ *n*

another term for SCRIPT

framing /'freɪmɪŋ/ *n*

(in teaching) a QUESTIONING TECHNIQUE in which the teacher provides a **frame** for a question by asking a question, pausing, and then calling on a student response. This is said to increase students' attention to the question and thus improve the effectiveness of the question.

see also QUESTIONING TECHNIQUES, WAIT TIME

free composition /'friː kɒmpə'zɪʃən||kɑːm-/ *n*

see COMPOSITION

free form /'friː ˌfɔːm||ˌfɔːrm/ *n*
also free morpheme /'friː 'mɔːfiːm||'mɔːr-/

see BOUND FORM

free practice /'friː 'præktᵻs/ *n*

another term for **production stage**

see STAGE

free response item /'friː rɪ'spɒns ˌaɪtəm||-'spɑːns/ *n*

see TEST ITEM

free stress /'friː 'stres/ *n*

STRESS which does not occur regularly on the same syllable in words in a particular language.

For example, English has free stress. The main stress may occur:

on the first syllable: e.g. '*interval*
on the second syllable: in'*terrogate*
on the third syllable: e.g. *inter*'*ference*

see also FIXED STRESS

Further reading Hyman 1975

free translation /'fri: træns'leɪʃən, trænz-/ *n*

see TRANSLATION

free variation /ˌfri: veəri'eɪʃən/ *n*

When two or more linguistic items occur in the same position without any apparent change of meaning they are said to be in free variation. For example, *who* and *whom* in the English sentence:

$$\text{The man} \left\{ \begin{array}{l} \text{who} \\ \text{whom} \end{array} \right. \text{we saw.}$$

Such variations are now often considered as social variations or stylistic variations.

see also VARIABLE[1], VARIATION

freewriting /'fri:ˌraɪtɪŋ/ *n*
also **timed freewriting, quickwriting, quickwrite**

(in teaching composition) a pre-writing activity (see COMPOSING PROCESSES) in which students write as much as possible about a topic within a given time period (for example, 3 minutes) without stopping. The goal is to produce as much writing as possible without worrying about grammar or accuracy, in order to develop fluency in writing and to produce ideas which might be used in a subsequent writing task.

Further reading Murray 1980

frequency[1] /'fri:kwənsi/ *n*

see SOUND WAVE

frequency[2] *n*

the number of occurrences of a linguistic item in a text or CORPUS. Different linguistic items have different frequencies of occurrence in speech and writing. In English, FUNCTION WORDS (e.g. *a, the, to,* etc.) occur more frequently than verbs, nouns, adjectives, or adverbs. **Word frequency counts** are used to select vocabulary for language teaching, in lexicography, in the study of literary style in STYLISTICS, and in TEXT LINGUISTICS.

The twenty most frequently occurring words in a corpus of over one million words in a study of written American English by Kučera and Francis were:

the, of, and, to, a, in, that, is, was, he, for, it,
with, as, his, on, be, at, by, I.

Further reading Kučera & Francis 1967

frequency count /'fri:kwənsi ˌkaʊnt/ *n*

a count of the total number of occurrences of linguistic items (e.g. syllables, phonemes, words, etc.) in a corpus of language, such as a written text or a sample of spoken language. The study of the frequency of occurrence of linguistic items is known as language statistics and is a part of COMPUTATIONAL and MATHEMATICAL LINGUISTICS. A frequency count of the vocabulary occurring in a text or opus is known as a **word frequency count** or **word frequency list**.

fricative /'frɪkətɪv/ *n*

a speech sound (a CONSONANT) which is produced by allowing the airstream from the lungs to escape with friction. This is caused by bringing the two ARTICULATORS e.g. the upper teeth and the lower lip, close together but not close enough to stop the airstream completely.

For example, in English the /f/ in /fɪt/ *fit* is a fricative.

Some American linguists call a fricative a **spirant**.

see also MANNER OF ARTICULATION, PLACE OF ARTICULATION, SIBILANT, STOP

Further reading Gimson 1989

frictionless continuant /'frɪkʃənləs kən'tɪnjuənt/ *n*

a speech sound (a CONSONANT) which is produced by allowing the airstream from the lungs to move through the mouth and/or nose without friction.

For example, for some speakers of English the /r/ in /rəuz/ *rose* is a frictionless continuant.

In terms of their articulation, frictionless continuants are very like vowels, but they function as consonants.

see also NASAL, LATERAL, FRICATIVE, STOP

Further reading Gimson 1980

front vowel /'frʌnt ˌvauəl/ *n*

see VOWEL

FSI /ˌef es 'aɪ/ *n*

an abbreviation for FOREIGN SERVICE INSTITUTE ORAL INTERVIEW

FSP /ˌef es 'piː/ *n*

an abbreviation for FUNCTIONAL SENTENCE PERSPECTIVE

full verb /'ful 'vɜːb‖'vɜːrb/ *n*

see AUXILIARY VERB

full word /'ful 'wɜːd‖'wɜːrd/ *n*

see CONTENT WORD

function /'fʌŋkʃən/ *n*

the purpose for which an utterance or unit of language is used. In language teaching, language functions are often described as categories of behaviour; e.g. requests, apologies, complaints, offers, compliments. The functional uses of language cannot be determined simply by studying the grammatical structure of sentences. For example, sentences in the imperative form (see MOOD) may perform a variety of different functions:

Give me that book. (Order)
Pass the jam. (Request)
Turn right at the corner. (Instruction)
Try the smoked salmon. (Suggestion)
Come round on Sunday. (Invitation)

In linguistics, the fuctional uses of language are studied in SPEECH ACT theory, SOCIOLINGUISTICS, and PRAGMATICS. In the COMMUNICATIVE APPROACH to language teaching, a SYLLABUS is often organized in terms of the different language functions the learner needs to express or understand.

see also FUNCTIONS OF LANGUAGE[1,2], FUNCTIONAL SYLLABUS, NOTION-AL SYLLABUS, SPEECH ACT, SPEECH ACT CLASSIFICATION
Further reading Wilkins 1976; Richards & Rodgers 1986

functional illiteracy /ˈfʌŋkʃənəl ɪˈlɪtərəsi/ *n*

see LITERACY

functional linguistics /ˈfʌŋkʃənəl lɪŋˈgwɪstɪks/ *n*

an approach to linguistics which is concerned with language as an instrument of social interaction rather than as a system that is viewed in isolation. It considers the individual as a social being and in-vestigates the way in which he or she acquires language and uses it in order to communicate with others in his or her social environment.

see also PRAGMATICS, SOCIAL CONTEXT, SPEECH EVENT
Further reading Halliday 1978

functional literacy /ˈfʌŋkʃənəl ˈlɪtərəsi/ *n*

see LITERACY

functional load /ˈfʌŋkʃənəl ˈləʊd/ *n*

the relative importance of linguistic contrasts in a language. Not all the distinctions or contrasts within the structure of a language are of the same importance. For example the contrast between /p/ and /b/ at the beginning of words in English serves to distinguish many words, such as *pig – big; pack – back; pad – bad*, etc. The distinction /p/ – /b/ is thus said to have high functional load. But other contrasts such as the contrast between /ð/ and /θ/ in words like *wreathe – wreath* are not used to distinguish many words in English and are said to have low functional load.

Further reading Lyons 1981

functional sentence perspective /ˈfʌŋkʃənəl ˈsentəns pəˌspektɪv‖ pər-/ *n*
also FSP

a type of linguistic analysis associated with the Prague School which describes how information is distributed in sentences. FSP deals particularly with the effect of the distribution of known (or given) information and new information in DISCOURSE. The known inform-ation (known as **theme**, in FSP), refers to information that is not new to the reader or listener. The **rheme** refers to information that is new.
FSP differs from the traditional grammatical analysis of sentences because the distinction between subject – predicate is not always the same as the theme – rheme contrast. For example we may compare the two sentences below:

1 *John*	*sat in the front seat.*	2 *In the front seat sat John.*	
Subject	Predicate	Predicate	Subject
Theme	Rheme	Theme	Rheme

John is the grammatical subject in both sentences, but theme in 1 and rheme in 2.

Other terms used to refer to the theme – rheme distinction are topic – comment (see TOPIC²), **background – focus, given – new information**.

Further reading Vachek 1964

functional syllabus /'fʌŋkʃənəl 'sɪləbəs/ n

(in language teaching) a SYLLABUS in which the language content is arranged in terms of functions or SPEECH ACTS together with the language items needed for them. For example, the functions might be identifying, describing, inviting, offering, etc. in different types of DISCOURSE (i.e. speech or writing). The language skills involved might be listening, speaking, reading, or writing. The language items needed for these functions are called **exponents** or realizations.

For example:

Type of discourse	Skill	Function	Exponents	
			Vocabulary	Structures
spoken	speaking listening	asking for directions	*bank* *harbour* *museum*	*Can you tell me where X is?* *Where is X?*

Often this term is used to refer to a certain type of NOTIONAL SYLLABUS.

see also COMMUNICATIVE APPROACH

Further reading Van Ek & Alexander 1975; Wilkins 1976

functions of language¹ /'fʌŋkʃənz əv 'læŋgwɪdʒ/ n
also **language functions**

Language is often described as having three main functions: **descriptive, expressive,** and **social**. The descriptive function of language is to convey factual information. This is the type of information which can be stated or denied and in some cases even tested, for example:

It must be well below ten degrees outside.

The expressive function of language is to supply information about the speaker, his or her feelings, preferences, prejudices, and past experiences.

For example, the utterance:

I'm not inviting the Sandersons again.

may, with appropriate intonation, show that the speaker did not like the Sandersons and that this is the reason for not inviting them again.

The social function of language serves to establish and maintain social relations between people.

For example, the utterance:

Will that be all, Sir?

used by a waiter in a restaurant signals a particular social relationship between the waiter and the guest. The waiter puts the guest in a higher ROLE RELATIONSHIP.

Naturally, these functions overlap at times, particularly the expressive and the social functions.

Further reading Lyons 1977, 1981

functions of language[2]
also **language functions**

The British linguist Halliday considers language as having three main functions:

a the **ideational function** is to organize the speaker's or writer's experience of the real or imaginary world, i.e. language refers to real or imagined persons, things, actions, events, states, etc.

b the **interpersonal function** is to indicate, establish, or maintain social relationships between people. It includes forms of address, speech function, MODALITY, etc.

c the **textual function** is to create written or spoken TEXTS which cohere within themselves and which fit the particular situation in which they are used.

see also DEVELOPMENTAL FUNCTIONS OF LANGUAGE, SOCIAL CONTEXT
Further reading Halliday 1978; de Joia & Stenton 1980

function word /ˈfʌŋkʃən ˌwɜːd‖ˌwɜːrd/ *n*

see CONTENT WORD

functor /ˈfʌŋktəʳ/ *n*

see CONTENT WORD

fundamental frequency /ˈfʌndəmentl ˈfriːkwənsi/ *n*

see SOUND WAVE

fused sentence /ˈfjuːzd ˈsentəns/ *n*

another term for RUN-ON SENTENCE

fusional language /ˈfjuːʒənəl ˈlæŋgwɪdʒ/ *n*

another term for INFLECTING LANGUAGE

future perfect /ˈfjuːtʃəʳ ˈpɜːfɪkt‖-ɜːr-/ *n*

see PERFECT

future tense /ˈfjuːtʃəʳ ˈtens/ *n*

a tense form used to indicate that the event described by a verb will take place at a future time. For example in the French sentence:

Je	partirai	demain.
I	leave+future	tomorrow.

the future tense ending *-ai* has been added to the verb infinitive *partir* (=leave). English has no future tense but uses a variety of different verb forms to express future time (e.g. *I leave tomorrow*; *I am leaving tomorrow*; *I will leave tomorrow*; *I am going to leave tomorrow*). *Will* in English is sometimes used to indicate future time (e.g. *Tomorrow will be Thursday*) but has many other functions, and is usually described as a MODAL verb.

fuzzy /'fʌzi/ *adj*

a term used by some linguists to describe a linguistic unit which has no clearly defined boundary. These units have "fuzzy borders", e.g. the English words *hill* and *mountain*. Another term used for a gradual transition from one linguistic unit to another is **gradience**.

G

gambit /ˈgæmbᵻt/ *n*

(in CONVERSATIONAL ANALYSIS) sometimes used to describe a word or phrase in conversation which signals the function of the speaker's next turn in the conversation (see TURN-TAKING). Gambits may be used to show whether the speaker's contribution adds new information, develops something said by a previous speaker, expresses an opinion, agreement, etc. For example, gambits which signal that the speaker is going to express an opinion include:

The way I look at it . . .
To my mind . . .
In my opinion . . .

These examples can also be considered conversational ROUTINES.

Further reading Coulmas 1981

game¹ /ɡeɪm/ *n*

(in language teaching) an organized activity that usually has the following properties:

a a particular task or objective
b a set of rules
c competition between players
d communication between players by spoken or written language.

game² *n*

(in COMPUTER ASSISTED LANGUAGE LEARNING) rule-based competitive activities usually involving a time limit and/or visual display features in which the player must acquire and/or manipulate knowledge in order to succeed.

Further reading Hope, Taylor & Pusack 1984

GB theory or **G/B theory** /ˌdʒiː ˈbiː ˌθɪəri/ *n*

another term for GOVERNMENT/BINDING THEORY

gender /ˈdʒendəʳ/ *n*

(in some languages) a grammatical distinction in which words such as nouns, articles, adjectives, and pronouns are marked according to a distinction between masculine, feminine, and sometimes neuter. For example, in French, nouns are either masculine or feminine.

Masculine nouns are used with the articles *un* "a", and *le* "the", and feminine nouns are used with *une* and *la*:

une/la table "a/the table" (feminine)
un/le cheval "a/the horse" (masculine)

generalization /ˌdʒenərəlaɪˈzeɪʃən‖-lə-/ *n* **generalize** /ˈdʒenərəlaɪz/ *v*

1 (in linguistics) a rule or principle which explains observed linguistic data.

2 (in learning theory) a process common to all types of learning, which consists of the formation of a general rule or principle from the observation of particular examples. For example a child who sees the English words *book* – *books*, and *dog* – *dogs* may generalize that the concept of plural in English is formed by adding *s* to words.

see also OVERGENERALIZATION
Further reading Gagné 1970; Brown 1987

generate /'dʒenəreɪt/ *v*

see GENERATIVE GRAMMAR, RULE[2]

generative grammar /ˌdʒenərətɪv 'græməʳ/ *n*

a type of grammar which attempts to define and describe by a set of rules all the GRAMMATICAL sentences of a language and no ungrammatical ones. This type of grammar is said to **generate**, or produce, grammatical sentences.
The most important grammar of this type is TRANSFORMATIONAL GENERATIVE GRAMMAR
Further reading Chomsky 1957

generative phonology /'dʒenərətɪv fə'nɒlədʒi||-'nɑː-/ *n*

an approach to phonology which aims to describe the knowledge (COMPETENCE) which a native speaker must have to be able to produce and understand the sound system of his or her language. In generative phonology, the distinctive sounds of a language (the PHONEMES) are shown as groups of sound features (see DISTINCTIVE FEATURES). Each sound is shown as a different set of features. For example, the phoneme /e/ could be shown by the features

$$\begin{bmatrix} \text{-high} \\ \text{-low} \\ \text{+tense} \end{bmatrix}$$

Phonological rules explain how these abstract units combine and vary when they are used in speech.

see also TRANSFORMATIONAL GENERATIVE GRAMMAR, SYSTEMATIC PHONEMICS
Further reading Hyman 1975; Chomsky & Halle 1968

generative semantics /'dʒenərətɪv sᵻ'mæntɪks/ *n*

an approach to linguistic theory which grew as a reaction to Chomsky's syntactic-based TRANSFORMATIONAL GENERATIVE GRAMMAR. It considers that all sentences are generated from a semantic structure. This semantic structure is often expressed in the form of a proposition which is similar to logical propositions in philosophy. Linguists working within this theory have, for instance, suggested that there is a semantic relationship between such sentences as
This dog strikes me as being like her master.
and
This dog reminds me of her master.

because they both have the semantic structure of
   X perceives that Y is similar to Z.

see also INTERPRETIVE SEMANTICS
Further reading Lakoff 1971

generative transformational grammar /ˈdʒenərətɪv trænsfəˈmeɪʃənəl ˈgræməʳ‖-fər-/ *n*

another term for TRANSFORMATIONAL GENERATIVE GRAMMAR

generative transformational theory /ˈdʒenərətɪv trænsfəˈmeɪʃənəl ˈθɪəri‖-fər-/ *n*

another term for TRANSFORMATIONAL GENERATIVE GRAMMAR

generic reference /dʒɪˈnerɪk ˈrefərəns/ *n*

a type of reference which is used to refer to a class of objects or things, rather than to a specific member of a class. For example in English:

specific reference	generic reference
The bird is sick.	*A tiger is a dangerous animal.*
The birds are sick.	*Tigers are dangerous animals.*
There is a bird in the cage.	*The tiger is a dangerous animal.*

Further reading Quirk et al 1985

genetic epistemology /dʒɪˈnetɪk ɪˌpɪstəˈmɒlədʒi‖-ˈmɑː-/ *n*

a term used to describe the theories of DEVELOPMENTAL PSYCHOLOGY of the Swiss psychologist Jean Piaget (1896–1980). Piaget listed several different stages which children pass through in mental development. The first stage is the **sensorimotor stage**, from birth to about 24 months, when children understand their environment mainly by acting on it. Through touch and sight children begin to understand basic relationships which affect them and objects in their experience. These include space, location of objects, and the relationships of cause and effect. But children cannot yet make use of abstract concepts. The next three stages are a movement towards more abstract processes. During the **pre-operational stage**, from around two to seven years, children develop the symbolic function, which includes such skills as language, mental imagery, and drawing. Children also begin to develop the mental ability to use CONCEPTS dealing with number, classification, order, and time, but use these concepts in a simple way. The **concrete operational stage** from about seven to eleven years is the period when children begin to use mental operations and acquire a number of concepts of conservation. During the formal operational stage (from around eleven onwards) children are able to deal with abstract concepts and PROPOSITIONS, and to make hypotheses, inferences, and deductions. Since the mental processes Piaget studied are important for language development, linguists and psycholinguists have made use of Piaget's ideas in studying how mental development and linguistic development are related.

Further reading Piaget 1952

genitive case /ˈdʒenətɪv ˌkeɪs/ *n*

the form of a noun or noun phrase which usually shows that the noun or noun phrase is in a POSSESSIVE relation with another noun or noun phrase in a sentence.

For example, in the German sentence:

Dort drüben ist das Haus des Bürgermeisters.

Over there is   the house of the mayor.

the mayor's house.

in the noun phrase *des Bürgermeisters*, the article has the inflectional ending *-es* and the noun has the inflectional ending *-s* to show that they are in the genitive case because they refer to the owner of *das Haus*.

In the English sentence:

She took my father's car.

some linguists regard *my father's* as an example of the genitive case.

see also CASE[1]

Further reading Lyons 1981

genre /ˈʒɒnrə‖-ɑːn-/ *n*

(in DISCOURSE ANALYSIS) a particular class of SPEECH EVENTS which are considered by the SPEECH COMMUNITY as being of the same type. Examples of genres are: prayers, sermons, conversations, songs, speeches, poems, letters, and novels. They have particular and distinctive characteristics. A group of several genres may be called a complex genre, for example a church service, which contains hymns, psalms, prayers, and a sermon.

see also SCHEME

Further reading Coulthard 1985: Saville-Troike 1982

genre-scheme /ˈʒɒnrə ˌskiːm‖-ɑːn-/ *n*

another term for SCHEME

gerund /ˈdʒerənd/ *n*
also **gerundive** /dʒɨˈrʌndɪv/

a verb form which ends in *-ing*, but which is used in a sentence like a noun.

For example, in the English sentences:

Swimming is good for you.
I don't like smoking.

see also PARTICIPLE

gestalt psychology /gɨˈʃtɑːlt saɪˈkɒlədʒi‖-ˈkɑː-/ *n*
also **gestalt theory** /gɨˈʃtɑːlt ˈθɪəri/

an approach to psychology in which behaviour is studied as undivided wholes or "gestalts". Gestalt psychologists believe that you cannot understand a person's response to a situation in terms of a combination of separate responses to a combination of separate stimuli, but that it should be studied as a whole response to the whole situation. Gestalt psychology is a **holistic approach,** in contrast with the **atomistic approach** of many experimental psychologists.

Further reading Miller 1962

gestalt style /gǝˈʃtɑːlt ˈstaɪl/ *n*
another term for GLOBAL LEARNING

gesture /ˈdʒestʃǝʳ/ *n*
a movement of the face or body which communicates meaning, such as nodding the head to mean agreement. Many spoken utterances are accompanied by gestures which support or add to their meaning. SIGN LANGUAGE is a system of communication based entirely on gestures. The study of the role of gestures in communication is part of the study of non-verbal communication.

see also PARALINGUISTICS

given – new information /ˈgɪvǝn ˈŋjuː ˌɪnfǝˈmeɪʃǝn‖ˈnuː -fǝr-/ *n*
see FUNCTIONAL SENTENCE PERSPECTIVE

glide /glaɪd/ *n*
(in British linguistics) a vowel which is made by the tongue moving, or gliding, from one position to another one. This is the case with DIPHTHONGS, e.g. the English diphthong /aɪ/ as in *my*. Some American linguists use the term glide for the second element in a diphthong. For these elements they use the phonetic symbols /w/, e.g. /bowt/ *boat* and /y/, e.g. /may/ *my*. They also refer to the /w/ in *will* and the /y/ in *yet* as glides, whereas in Britain they are referred to as SEMI-VOWELS.

see also CONSONANT
Further reading Gimson 1989

global error /ˈglǝʊbǝl ˈerǝʳ/ *n*
(in ERROR ANALYSIS) an error in the use of a major element of sentence structure, which makes a sentence or utterance difficult or impossible to understand. For example:
  *I like take taxi but my friend said so not that we should be late for school.
This may be contrasted with a **local error,** which is an error in the use of an element of sentence structure, but which does not cause problems of comprehension. For example:
  *If I heard from him I will let you know.
Further reading Burt & Kiparsky 1972

global learning /ˈglǝʊbǝl ˈlɜːnɪŋ‖ˈlɜːr-/ *n*
also **gestalt style**

a COGNITIVE STYLE in which the learner tries to remember something as a whole. For example, a learner may try to memorize complete sentences in a foreign language.
When a learner remembers something by separating it into parts, this is called an **analytic style,** or **part learning.** For example, a learner may

divide a sentence into words, memorize the words, and then combine them again to make sentences.

see also GESTALT PSYCHOLOGY

global question /ˈgləubəl ˈkwestʃən/ n

(in language teaching) a question used in a reading comprehension exercise. To answer a global question, a student needs a general understanding of the text or passage. A student's understanding of the details of a text can be tested with **specific questions**.

glottal stop /ˈglɒtl ˈstɒp‖ˈglɑːtl ˈstɑːp/ n

a speech sound (a CONSONANT) which is produced by the rapid closing of the **glottis** (the space between the VOCAL CORDS), which traps the airstream from the lungs behind it, followed by a sudden release of the air as the glottis is opened. The phonetic symbol is [ʔ].

In some varieties of British English, a glottal stop is used instead of a /t/ in words like [ˈbɒʔl] *bottle* and [ˈmæʔəʳ] *matter*.

see also STOP, PLACE OR ARTICULATION, MANNER OF ARTICULATION
Further reading Gimson 1989

glottis /ˈglɒtɪs‖ˈglɑː-/ n

see VOCAL CORDS

goal[1] /ˈgəul/ n

(in TRADITIONAL GRAMMAR) a term used by some linguists to refer to the person or thing which is affected by the action expressed by the verb. For example, in the English sentence:
Elizabeth smashed the vase.
vase is the goal.

goal[2] n

(in CASE GRAMMAR) the noun or noun phrase which refers to the place to which someone or something moves or is moved. For example in the sentences:
He loaded bricks on the truck.
He loaded the truck with bricks.
the truck is the goal.
Further reading Fillmore 1971

goal θ-role /ˈgəul ˈθiːtə ˌrəul/ n

see θ-THEORY

government /ˈgʌvənmənt, ˈgʌvəmənt‖ˈgʌvərn-/ n govern /ˈgʌvən‖-ərn/ v

a type of grammatical relationship between two or more elements in a sentence, in which the choice of one element causes the selection of a particular form of another element. In traditional grammar, the term government has typically been used to refer to the relationship between verbs and nouns or between prepositions and nouns. In

German, for example, the preposition *mit* "with" governs, that is requires, the DATIVE CASE[1] of the noun that follows it:

Peter kam mit seiner Schwester.

Peter came with his sister.

Where *sein* "his" has the dative feminine case marker *er*.

In GOVERNMENT/BINDING THEORY the concept of government is based on Traditional Grammar but it has been more strictly defined and structured into a complex system to show the relationship of one element in a sentence to another element.

For example, the verb *give* in the sentence

She will give them to me

governs *them* because:

1 *give* is a LEXICAL CATEGORY and therefore it can be a GOVERNOR
2 they are both within a maximal projection, e.g. a verb phrase (see PROJECTION (PRINCIPLE) and
3 they are in certain structural relationships to each other.

Further reading Cook 1988

government/binding theory /ˈgʌvənmənt ˈbaɪndɪŋ ˌθɪəri, ˈgʌvəmənt ||ˈgʌvərn-/ *n*

a theory of language developed by Chomsky and based on his concept of a UNIVERSAL GRAMMAR. It can be seen as a network of different sub-theories which consist of certain principles and conditions (PARAMETERS) Some of the subtheories are:

1 BINDING THEORY: shows the reference relationship between noun phrases
2 BOUNDING THEORY: places restrictions on movement within a sentence
3 CASE THEORY: assigns cases to the noun phrases in the sentence
4 θ-THEORY: assigns semantic roles to the elements in the sentence
5 X-BAR THEORY: describes the structure of phrases

Some aspects of the Government/Binding Theory and its subtheories have been used in research into first and second language acquisition (see, for example, ADJACENCY PARAMETER, PRO-DROP PARAMETER).

see also PROJECTION (PRINCIPLE)

Further reading Cook, 1988; Gass & Schachter 1989; White 1989a

governor /ˈgʌvənəʳ/ *n*

(in GOVERNMENT/BINDING THEORY) an element in a sentence which **governs**, that is has an influence on, another element. Everything that can be the HEAD of a phrase can function as a governor, e.g. nouns, verbs, adjectives and prepositions.

gradable /ˈgreɪdəbəl/ *adj* **gradability** /ˌgreɪdəˈbɪlǝ̇ti/ *n*

(of objects, people, ideas, etc.) having a certain property to a greater or lesser degree. In English, this property is usually expressed by an adjective, e.g. *hot, cold, rich, poor*.

For example:

gradable adjective

> *Was it really as cold last night as Thursday night?*
> *Your plate is hotter than mine.*

Usually, a comparison is implied, even if it is not expressed. *It's hot in here*, means "compared with outside" or "compared with the room temperature which suits me".

Adjectives which refer to something which can be described in degrees are known as **gradable adjectives**. The negation of a gradable adjective does not necessarily imply the opposite. For example, *not hot* does not necessarily mean *cold*, nor does *not rich* necessarily mean *poor*.

see also ANTONYM
Further reading Lyons 1977

gradable adjective /ˈgreɪdəbəl ˈædʒɪktɪv/ *n*

see GRADABLE

gradable pair /ˈgreɪdəbəl ˈpeəʳ/ *n*

see ANTONYM

gradation /ˌɡrəˈdeɪʃən/ *n*
also **grading, sequencing**

the arrangement of the content of a language course or a textbook so that it is presented in a helpful way. Gradation would affect the order in which words, word meanings, tenses, structures, topics, functions, skills, etc. are presented. Gradation may be based on the complexity of an item, its frequency in written or spoken English, or its importance for the learner.

see also SELECTION
Further reading Mackey 1965; Stern 1983

graded objectives /ˈgreɪdɪd əbˈdʒektɪvz/ *n*

(in language teaching) objectives which describe levels of attainment at different stages within a language programme. These are intended to provide statements of practical short-term goals for learners and to provide practical levels of mastery which they could attain after relatively short periods of study. Graded objectives have been used particularly in programmes for foreign language teaching in the United Kingdom.

Further reading Clark 1987

graded reader /ˈgreɪdɪd ˈriːdəʳ/ *n*
also **simplified reader**

a text written for children learning their mother tongue, or for second or foreign language learners, in which the language content is based on a language grading scheme (see GRADATION). A graded reader may use a restricted vocabulary or set of grammatical structures.

gradience /ˈgreɪdɪəns/ *n*

see FUZZY

grading /'greɪdɪŋ/ *n*
another term for GRADATION

grammar[1] /'græmə^r/ *n*
a description of the structure of a language and the way in which linguistic units such as words and phrases are combined to produce sentences in the language. It usually takes into account the meanings and functions these sentences have in the overall system of the language. It may or may not include the description of the sounds of a language (see PHONOLOGY, PHONEMICS).
see also MORPHOLOGY, SEMANTICS, SYNTAX

grammar[2]
(in TRANSFORMATIONAL GRAMMAR) a grammar which describes the speaker's knowledge of the language. It looks at language in relation to how it may be structured in the speaker's mind, and which principles (see UNIVERSAL GRAMMAR) and PARAMETERS are available to the speaker when producing the language.
see also UNIVERSAL GRAMMAR, CORE GRAMMAR, I-LANGUAGE

grammar checker /'græmə^r ˌtʃekə^r/ *n*
(in COMPUTER ASSISTED LANGUAGE LEARNING) a program which checks certain grammatical and mechanical aspects of writing (see MECHANICS) such as the use of passive forms, CONCORDE, and punctuation.

Grammar Translation Method /'græmə^r træns'leɪʃən ˌmeθəd, trænz-/ *n*
a method of foreign or second language teaching which makes use of translation and grammar study as the main teaching and learning activities. The Grammar Translation Method was the traditional way Latin and Greek were taught in Europe. In the 19th Century it began to be used to teach "modern" languages such as French, German, and English, and it is still used in many countries today. A typical lesson consists of the presentation of a grammatical rule, a study of lists of vocabulary, and a translation exercise. Because the Grammar Translation Method emphasizes reading rather than the ability to communicate in a language there was a reaction to it in the 19th century (see NATURAL APPROACH, DIRECT METHOD), and there was later a greater emphasis on the teaching of spoken language.
Further reading Howatt 1983; Kelly 1969

grammatical[1] /grə'mætɪkəl/ *adj* **grammaticality** /grəˌmætɪ'kælɪti/ *n*
A phrase, clause, or sentence which is ACCEPTABLE because it follows the rules of a grammar (see GRAMMAR[1]), is described as grammatical. For example, the English sentence:
They walk to school.
would be a grammatical sentence according to a grammar of Standard English, but the sentence:

They walks to school.
would be considered **ungrammatical** according to such a grammar.

grammatical[2] *adj* **grammaticalness** /grə'mætɪkəlnɪ̜s/ *n*
In TRANSFORMATIONAL GENERATIVE GRAMMAR, a sentence is grammatical if it follows the rules of a native speaker's COMPETENCE. For example:
The teacher who the man who the children saw pointed out is a cousin of Joan's.
would be a grammatical sentence because it can be generated by the rules of the grammar. However, it could be regarded as **unacceptable** because of its involved structure which makes it difficult for a listener to understand easily.

see also ACCEPTABLE

grammatical ambiguity /grə'mætɪkəl æmbɪ̜'gjuːɪ̜ti/ *n*
see AMBIGUOUS

grammatical category[1] /grə'mætɪkəl 'kætɪ̜gəri‖-gɔːri/ *n*
a class or group of items which fulfil the same or similar functions in a particular language. For example, CASE[1], PERSON, TENSE[1], and ASPECT are grammatical categories.
Some linguists also refer to related groups of words such as nouns, verbs, and adjectives as grammatical categories but these groups are usually referred to in TRADITIONAL GRAMMAR as PARTS OF SPEECH.

grammatical category[2] *n*
(in TRANSFORMATIONAL GENERATIVE GRAMMAR) a concept such as a SENTENCE, a NOUN PHRASE, a VERB. Grammatical categories are shown by **category symbols** such as S, NP, and V.

grammatical function /grə'mætɪkəl 'fʌŋkʃən/ *n*
the relationship that a CONSTITUENT in a sentence has with the other constituents. For example, in the English sentence:
Peter threw the ball.
Peter has the function of being the SUBJECT of the verb *throw*, and *the ball* has the function of being the OBJECT of the verb.

grammatical meaning /grə'mætɪkəl 'miːnɪŋ/ *n*
see CONTENT WORD

grammatical morpheme /grə'mætɪkəl 'mɔːfiːm‖-ɔːr-/ *n*
see MORPHEME

grammatical word /grə'mætɪkəl ˌwɜːd‖ˌwɜːrd/ *n*
see CONTENT WORD

grave accent /'grɑːv 'æksənt‖'æksent/ *n*
the accent, e.g. on French *près* "near".
see also ACCENT[2]

grounding /'graʊndɪŋ/ n

an aspect of the INFORMATION STRUCTURE of a sentence in which in an act of communication, speakers assume that some information is more important than other information. Information which is needed for the listener to understand new information is **background information**, and information which is new or considered more important is **foregrounded** or **foreground information**. For example, in the sentence *As I was coming to school this morning, I saw an accident, I saw an accident this morning* is foregrounded information and *As I was coming to school* is background information. The foregrounded information is contained in the main clause of the sentence, which comes after the clause containing background information.

group discussion /'gruːp dɪ'skʌʃən/ n

a teaching activity which has the following characteristics:

1 A small number of students (four to twelve) meet together.

2 They choose, or are given, a common topic or problem and a goal or objective.

3 They exchange and evaluate information or ideas about the topic.

see also COOPERATIVE LEARNING

group dynamics /'gruːp daɪ'næmɪks/ n

the interactions which take place within a group and the study of how such factors as leadership, interaction and decision making affect the structure of a group. Group dynamics is an important consideration in forming classroom groups (see COOPERATIVE LEARNING) and in designing learning tasks and classroom materials.

see also SMALL-GROUP INTERACTION

grouping /'gruːpɪŋ/ n

(in teaching) arranging students into groups to help them learn better. Choosing suitable grouping arrangements which match different kinds of learning tasks is thought to be an important aspect of effective teaching (see EFFECTIVE SCHOOLING). Group size is an important factor which influences learner participation in group work. Different group arrangements for teaching include:

1 **Whole-group instruction**: The class is taught as a whole.

2 **Small-group discussion**: A group of between six and eight students working on a discussion topic.

3 **Tutorial discussion group**: A small group of usually less than five students focussing on a narrow range of materials, often to help remedy a learning difficulty.

An important issue in grouping is whether students learn better in mixed-ability groups or in groups of about the same proficiency level.

see also COOPERATIVE LEARNING, SMALL-GROUP INTERACTION

Further reading Orlich et al 1985

group work /'gruːp ˌwɜːk||ˌwɜːrk/ n

(in language teaching) a learning activity which involves a small group

guided discussion

of learners working together. The group may work on a single task, or on different parts of a larger task. Tasks for group members are often selected by the members of the group.

see also PAIR WORK

guided discussion /ˈgaɪdɨd dɪˈskʌʃən/ *n*
see DISCUSSION METHOD

guided interview /ˈgaɪdɨd ˈɪntəvjuː‖-tər-/ *n*
an interview in which the interviewer makes use of a set of questions which have been prepared in advance and which are used to guide and structure the interview. The list of questions used by the interviewer is known as an **interview schedule**. Usually the interviewer records answers to the questions onto the schedule during the interview.

see also FOCUSED INTERVIEW, DEPTH INTERVIEW

H

habit /'hæbɪt/ *n*

a pattern of behaviour that is regular and which has become almost automatic as a result of repetition. Linguists and psychologists disagree about how much habit formation is involved in language learning. The habit view of language learning is found in BEHAVIOURISM and contrasting views are found in COGNITIVE PSYCHOLOGY and in research in LANGUAGE ACQUISITION.

half-close vowel /'hɑːf kləʊs 'vaʊəl||'hæf/ *n*

see VOWEL

half-open vowel /'hɑːf ˌəʊpən 'vaʊəl||'hæf/ *n*

see VOWEL

halo effect /'heɪləʊ ɪˌfekt/ *n*

(in research) the effect of a feature which is not being tested, but which changes or influences the results. For example, a teacher who is rating a child according to "interest in learning English" may give the child a higher rating because he or she is well behaved in class.

hard copy /'hɑːd 'kɒpi||'hɑːrd 'kɑːpi/ *n*

a printed copy of a text or other information from a computer.

hard disk /'hɑːd 'dɪsk||'hɑːrd/ *n*

a device for storing information on a computer, based on an aluminium disk coated with magnetic oxide. A hard disk can hold more information and retrieve and record information more quickly than a floppy disk (see DISKETTE).

hard palate /'hɑːd 'pælɪt||'hɑːrd/ *n*

see PLACE OF ARTICULATION

hardware /'hɑːdweəʳ||'hɑːrd-/ *n*

the physical equipment which may be used in an educational system, such as a computer, video-cassette player, film projector, tape-recorder, casette or record player.

The materials used in such equipment such as a programs, tapes, and films are called **software.**

Hawthorn effect /'hɔːθɔːn ɪˌfekt||-ɔːrn/ *n*

(in research) the effect produced by the introduction of a new element into a learning situation. For example, if a new teaching method is used, there may be an improvement in learning which is due not to the method, but to the fact that it is new. Later on, the improvement may disappear.

head /hed/ *n*

the central part of a phrase. Other elements in the phrase are in some grammatical or semantic relationship to the head. For example, in the English noun phrase:

the fat lady in the floral dress

the noun *lady* is the head of the phrase.

see also MODIFIER, CLASSIFIER[2]

head parameter /ˈhed pəˈræmɪtər/ *n*

see PARAMETER

hearing impaired /ˈhɪərɪŋ ɪmˈpeəd‖-eərd/ *adj*

a term used to describe hearing loss, which recognizes that nearly all deaf people have some degree of hearing, known as **residual hearing**. The degree of hearing impairment may vary across speech frequencies (see SOUND WAVE), at different levels of intensity. With the use of hearing aids, people with hearing impairment often learn to use residual hearing to maintain or improve their communication skills.

hemisphere /ˈhemɪsfɪər/ *n*

see BRAIN

hesitation phenomena /hezɪˈteɪʃən fɪˌnɒmɪnə‖-ˌnɑː-/ *n*

another term for PAUSING

heuristic /hjʊəˈrɪstɪk/ *adj* **heuristics** *n*

1 (in education) teaching procedures which encourage learners to learn through experience or by their own personal discoveries.

2 (in learning) processes of conscious or unconscious inquiry or discovery. For example, in trying to discover the meanings of words in a foreign language, a learner may repeat aloud a sentence containing the word, several times, in an attempt to work out its meaning.

In FIRST-LANGUAGE learning these heuristic processes are sometimes known as **operating principles,** i.e. ways in which learners work out the meaning of utterances based on what they understand about the structure of the TARGET LANGUAGE[1]. For example, among the operating principles a child may use are:

a word which ends in *ing* is a verb.

in a sequence of two nouns (e.g. Jane's doll) the first noun is the possessor and the second noun is the thing possessed.

Further reading Slobin 1973

heuristic function /hjʊəˈrɪstɪk ˈfʌŋkʃən/ *n*

see DEVELOPMENTAL FUNCTIONS OF LANGUAGE

high-inference category /ˈhaɪ ˈɪnfərəns ˌkætɪgəri‖-gɔːri/ *n*

also **high inference behaviour** /ˈhaɪ ˈɪnfərəns bɪˌheɪvjər/ *n* (in research on teaching or other aspects of classroom behaviour) a category of behaviour which cannot be observed directly but which has to be inferred. For example, the fact that students are "interested in a lesson", or "making use of higher level thinking during a lesson" cannot be observed directly and hence is a high-inference category of classroom behaviour. On the other hand a category such as "asking questions during a lesson" is easily observed and can be readily quantified (i.e. counted or measured). It is an example of a **low-inference category** of classroom behaviour. The distinction between high-inference and low-inference categories is an important one in research on classroom behaviour, particularly when the researcher wishes to quantify such behaviour.

Further reading Chaudron 1988

highlighting /'haɪlaɪtɪŋ/ *n* **highlight** /'haɪlaɪt/ *v*
(in reading) marking key words or sections in a passage with the use of a coloured pen, making them easier to identify or remember when studying or reviewing.

High variety /'haɪ və'raɪəti/ *n*
see DIGLOSSIA

high vowel /'haɪ ˌvaʊəl/ *n*
another term for **close vowel**
see VOWEL

historical linguistics /hɪ'stɒrɪ̩kəl lɪŋ'gwɪstɪks‖-'stɔː-, -'stɑː-/ *n*
another term for COMPARATIVE HISTORICAL LINGUISTICS

historic present /hɪ'stɒrɪk 'prezənt‖-'stɔː-, -'stɔː-/ *n*
a present tense used in a context where a past tense would normally be used, to create a more vivid effect, to show informality, or to show a sense of "friendliness" between speaker and hearer.
For example:
Do you know what happened to me last night? I'm sitting in a restaurant when this guy comes up and pours water over me.

holistic approach /həʊ'lɪstɪk ə'prəʊtʃ/ *n*
see GESTALT PSYCHOLOGY

holistic evaluation /həʊ'lɪstɪk ɪˌvælju'eɪʃən/ *n*
(in teaching composition) a method of evaluating writing in which the composition is viewed as a whole rather than as distinct parts.

holophrase /'hɒləfreɪz‖'həʊl-, 'hɑː-/ *n* **holophrastic** /ˌhɒlə'fræstɪk◄‖ ˌhəʊl-, ˌhɑː-/ *adj*
a single word which functions as a complex idea or sentence. Holophrastic speech is one of the first stages in children's acquisition of speech.

167

For example:

holophrases	intended meaning
Water!	*I want some water.*
More.	*Give me some more.*

Further reading Dale 1975

home-school language switch /ˈhəʊm ˈskuːl ˈlæŋgwɪdʒ ˌswɪtʃ/ *n*
used in referring to the language used in a school setting to describe the need to change ("switch") from one language spoken at home to another used as the MEDIUM OF INSTRUCTION at school.

see also BILINGUAL EDUCATION, IMMERSION PROGRAMME

homographs /ˈhɒməgrɑːfs, ˈhəʊ-‖ˈhɑːməgræfs, ˈhəʊ-/ *n*
words which are written in the same way but which are pronounced differently and have different meanings.
For example, the English words *lead* /liːd/ in *Does this road lead to town?* and *lead* /led/ in *Lead is a heavy metal*, are homographs.
Homographs are sometimes called **homonyms**.
see also HOMOPHONES

homonyms[1] /ˈhɒmənɪmz, ˈhəʊ-‖ˈhɑː-, ˈhəʊ-/ *n*
see HOMOGRAPHS

homonyms[2] *n*
see HOMOPHONES

homonyms[3] *n* **homonymy** /hɒˈmɒnɪmi, həʊ-‖hɑːˈmɑː-, həʊ-/ *n*
words which are written in the same way and sound alike but which have different meanings.
For example, the English verbs *lie* in *You have to lie down* and *lie* in *Don't lie, tell the truth!*
It is a well-known problem in SEMANTICS to tell the difference between homonymy (several words with the same form but different meanings) and POLYSMEY (a single word with more than one meaning).
Further reading Lyons 1981

homophones /ˈhɒməfəʊnz, ˈhəʊ-‖ˈhɑː-, ˈhəʊ-/ *n*
words which sound alike but are written differently and often have different meanings.
For example, the English words *no* and *know* are both pronounced /nəʊ/ in some varieties of British English.
Homophones are sometimes called **homonyms**.
see also HOMOGRAPHS
Further reading Fromkin & Rodman 1983

homorganic /ˌhɒmɔːˈgænɪk◄‖ˌhɑːmɔːr-/ *adj*
describes speech sounds which have the same PLACE OF ARTICULATION.

For example, the sounds /p/ and /m/ are both produced with the two lips (i.e. are BILABIAL), although one is a STOP and the other a NASAL.

see also ASSIMILATION, MANNER OF ARTICULATION
Further reading Gimson 1980

honorifics /ˌɒnəˈrɪfɪks‖ˌɑːnə-/ *n*
politeness formulas in a particular language which may be specific affixes, words, or sentence structures. Languages which have a complex system of honorifics are, for instance, Japanese, Madurese (a language of Eastern Java), and Hindi. Although English has no complex system of honorifics, expressions such as *would you ...*, *may I ...*, and polite ADDRESS FORMS fulfil similar functions.

Further reading Neustupny 1978

humanistic approach /ˈhjuːmənɪstɪk əˈprəʊʃ/ *n*
(in language teaching) a term sometimes used for what underlies METHODS in which the following principles are considered important:
a the development of human values
b growth in self-awareness and in the understanding of others
c sensitivity to human feelings and emotions
d active student involvement in learning and in the way learning takes place (for this last reason such methods are also said to be STUDENT CENTRED).

The SILENT WAY and COMMUNITY LANGUAGE LEARNING are examples of "humanistic approaches".

see also APPROACH
Further reading Stevick 1980

H-variety /ˈeɪtʃ vəˌraɪəti/ *n*
see DIGLOSSIA

hypercorrection[1] /ˌhaɪpəkəˈrekʃən‖-pər-/ *n*
overgenalization of a rule in language use. For example, the rule that an ADVERB modifies a VERB may be overextended and used in cases where an adjective would normally be used, as in *This meat smells freshly instead of This meat smells fresh.

see also COPULA

hypercorrection[2] *n*
extreme care in speech or writing, especially in an attempt to speak or write in an educated manner.
For example, a speaker of a non-standard variety of English, when speaking formally, may practise more self-correction and use more formal vocabulary than speakers of a standard variety of English.

Further reading Wardhaugh 1986

hyponymy /haɪˈpɒnɪmi, hɪ-‖-ˈpɑː-/ *n* **hyponym** /ˈhaɪpənɪm/ *n*
a relationship between two words, in which the meaning of one of the words includes the meaning of the other word.

For example, in English the words, *animal* and *dog* are related in such a way that *dog* refers to a type of *animal*, and *animal* is a general term that includes dog and other types of animal.

The specific term, *dog*, is called a hyponym, and the general term, *animal*, is called a **superordinate**.

A superordinate term can have many hyponyms. For example:

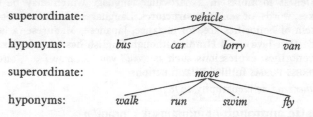

superordinate: *vehicle*

hyponyms: *bus*   *car*   *lorry*   *van*

superordinate: *move*

hyponyms: *walk*   *run*   *swim*   *fly*

see also SYNONYM
Further reading Lyons 1981

hypothesis /haɪˈpɒθəsɪs‖-ˈpɑː-/ *n*

(in research using quantitative methods and statistical techniques for the analysis of data) a speculation concerning either observed or expected relationships among phenomena. For example, "Teaching method A is better than teaching method B". If for the purposes of research the speculation is translated into a statement which can be tested by quantitative methods, the statement is known as a **statistical hypothesis**.

The hypothesis that method A is better than method B can be regarded as a statistical hypothesis because it can be tested by studying the DISTRIBUTION[1] of test scores (obtained by giving a test to students taught by A and B) in a POPULATION (the students who take the test). For each statistical hypothesis that there is a relationship (e.g. a coefficient of CORRELATION) between two features (e.g. method A and good test scores), there is a corresponding, but often unstated, **null hypothesis** that there is no relationship between these two features. The statistical analysis of research results is frequently designed to determine whether this hypothesis of no relationship can be rejected, thus providing support for the preferred hypothesis.

Note that the plural of *hypothesis* is *hypotheses* /haɪˈpɒθəsiːz‖-ˈpɑː-/.

Further reading Ebel 1972; Seliger & Shohamy 1989

hypothesis formation /haɪˈpɒθəsɪs fɔːˌmeɪʃən‖-ˈpɑː- -ɔːr-/ *n*

(in language learning) the formation of ideas ("hypotheses") about a language. These hypotheses may be conscious or unconscious. Most people would agree that at least some of these ideas come from the language we see and hear around us. But scholars (e.g. Chomsky) holding the INNATIST HYPOTHESIS have claimed that some of our most important and basic ideas about language in general are present at birth, and furthermore that this innate knowledge enables children learning their FIRST LANGUAGE to avoid forming ideas about it that could not possibly be true of any human language because such false ideas would violate LANGUAGE UNIVERSALS.

see also HYPOTHESIS TESTING
Further reading Elliott 1981

hypothesis testing /haɪˈpɒθɪ̩sɪ̩s ˌtestɪŋ‖-ˈpɑː-/ *n*
(in language learning) the testing of ideas ("hypotheses") about a language to see whether they are right or wrong.
The most obvious way of doing this is to use the hypotheses to produce new utterances and see whether they work. But one can also compare one's own utterances with those of other people speaking the language, or imagine what other people would say in a particular situation and then see whether they actually say it.
Scholars who hold the INNATIST HYPOTHESIS have claimed, in effect, that the number of hypotheses about a new language that need to be tested is not infinite. Some hypotheses are simply never formed, because of knowledge of LANGUAGE UNIVERSALS present in every normal human being at birth.

see also HYPOTHESIS FORMATION, DEDUCTIVE LEARNING
Further reading Elliot 1981

I

ideal speaker/hearer /aɪˈdɪəl ˈspiːkəʳ ˈhɪərəʳ/ n

see COMPETENCE

ideational function /aɪdiˈeɪʃənəl ˌfʌŋkʃən/ n

see FUNCTIONS OF LANGUAGE[2]

ideogram /ˈɪdɪəgræm/ n

see IDEOGRAPHIC WRITING

ideographic writing /ˌɪdiəgræfɪk ˈraɪtɪŋ/ n

a WRITING SYSTEM using symbols (**ideograms**) to represent whole words or concepts ("ideas"). The Chinese writing system is often considered to be ideographic.
For example, in Chinese the ideogram 水 represents "water".

Chinese can create new LEXEMES by combining existing ideograms to form COMPOUND WORDS. It can also combine existing ideograms into a sequence whose pronunciation is like that of a foreign word the Chinese wish to borrow, thus "transliterating" the foreign word into Chinese characters.

idiolect /ˈɪdɪəˌlekt/ n **idiolectal** /ˌɪdiəˈlektl◄/ adj

the language system of an individual as expressed by the way he or she speaks or writes within the overall system of a particular language.
In its widest sense, someone's idiolect includes their way of communicating; for example, their choice of utterances and the way they interpret the utterances made by others. In a narrower sense, an idiolect may include those features, either in speech or writing, which distinguish one individual from others, such as VOICE QUALITY, PITCH, and SPEECH RHYTHM.

see also DIALECT, SOCIOLECT
Further reading Wardhaugh 1986

idiom /ˈɪdiəm/ n **idiomatic** /ˌɪdiəˈmætɪk◄/ adj

an expression which functions as a single unit and whose meaning cannot be worked out from its separate parts.
For example:
She washed her hands of the matter.
means
"She refused to have anything more to do with the matter".

I-language /ˈaɪ ˌlæŋgwɪdʒ/ n
also **internalized language**

an approach to language which sees it as an internal property of the human mind and not as something external. Linguists who subscribe to this approach, e.g. Chomsky, attempt to construct grammars showing the way the human mind structures language and which (universal) principles are involved (see UNIVERSAL GRAMMAR, CORE GRAMMAR).
They believe that other approaches to language deal with **E-language (externalized language)**. E-language research collects and analyses actual language samples and constructs grammars which describe the general structures and patterns which emerge.
According to the I-language linguists, the externalized language approach is part of the American structuralists tradition. They claim it also includes a large section of sociolinguistic and discourse analysis research as this deals with social and not with mental phenomena.
The division between the two approaches, I-Language and E-Language, is important for language acquisition research and language teaching.
Further reading Cook 1988

illiteracy /ɪˈlɪtərəsi/ *n*
see LITERACY

illocutionary act /ˌɪləˈkjuːʃənəri ˈækt/ *n*
see LOCUTIONARY ACT

illocutionary force /ˌɪləˈkjuːʃənəri ˈfɔːs‖-ɔːr-/ *n*
see SPEECH ACT, LOCUTIONARY ACT, PERFORMATIVE

imagery /ˈɪmɪdʒəri/ *n*
mental pictures or impressions (" images") created by, or accompanying, words or sentences.
Words or sentences that produce strong picture-like images may be easier to remember than those without visual imagery. For example, in the following pair of sentences, (a) may be easier to remember than (b) because it creates a stronger mental image.
a *The gloves were made by a tailor.*
b *The gloves were made by a machine.*
In second language learning, imagery may be used as a *learning strategy*. For example when reading a passage about agricultural machinery, a student may think of a farm scene in which people are using different kinds of machines. Later when trying to recall the passage he or she read, the student may think of the image or picture and use this to trigger recollection of the information in the text.
see AUDIO-VISUAL METHOD
Further reading Glucksberg & Danks 1975; O'Malley & Chamot 1989

imaginative function /ɪˈmædʒɪnətɪv ˌfʌŋkʃən/ *n*
see DEVELOPMENTAL FUNCTIONS OF LANGUAGE

imitation /ɪmɪ̩'teɪʃən/ *n*
(in language learning) the copying of the speech of another person. Traditional views of language learning placed a high emphasis on the role of imitation and it has been considered basic to many methods of teaching foreign languages (see AUDIOLINGUAL METHOD, SITUATIONAL LANGUAGE TEACHING). However, research on first and second language acquisition has offered alternative views on the role of imitation. A basic assumption of such research is that learners use language productively and creatively and do not simply imitate the utterances of others. After the initial phases of learning, the learner's linguistic system or INTERLANGUAGE does not simply result from imitating what is heard in the INPUT but illustrates that learners acquire the ability to create syntactic and morphological combinations that could not have been heard before, resulting in many novel constructions. These should not be regarded as errors but are evidence of successful learning.
see also MODELLING, CREATIVE CONSTRUCTION HYPOTHESIS
Further reading Ellis 1985

immersion programme /ɪ'mɜːʃən ˌprəʊgræm, -ʒən‖-ɜːr-/ *n*
a form of BILINGUAL EDUCATION in which children who speak only one language enter a school where a second language is the MEDIUM OF INSTRUCTION for all pupils.
For example, there are schools in Canada for English-speaking children, where French is the language of instruction.
If these children are taught in French for the whole day it is called a **total immersion programme**, but if they are taught in French for only part of the day it is called a **partial immersion programme**.
see also SUBMERSION PROGRAMME
Further reading Swain 1978; Genesee 1987

imperative /ɪm'perətɪv/ *n*
see MOOD

imperative sentence /ɪm'perətɪv 'sentəns/ *n*
a sentence which is in the form of a command. For example:
Pick up the book!
Imperative sentences do not, however, always have the function of an order. For example:
Look what you've done now!
often functions as an expression of annoyance.
see also DECLARATIVE SENTENCE, INTERROGATIVE SENTENCE
Further reading Lyons 1977

impersonal construction /ɪm'pɜːsənəl kən'strʌkʃən‖-ɜːr-/ *n*
a type of sentence in which there is no mention of who or what does or experiences something. Examples include English *It's cold, It's raining*, and French *Ici on parle anglais* (literally, "Here one speaks English") "English is spoken here".

implication /ˌɪmplɪ'keɪʃən/

In everyday communication, a great deal of information is implied by the speaker rather than asserted. For example, if somebody said:

Rita was on time this morning.

it could imply that Rita was usually late.

Often the hearer would understand the implication of the utterance in the way that the speaker intends (see UTTERANCE MEANING) and give a suitable response but, of course, there may be misunderstandings and misinterpretations:

A: *I'm rather short of cash at the moment.*
   (meaning: I'd like you to pay for the lunch)
B: *Oh, I'm sure they accept credit cards here.*

Further reading Hurford & Heasley 1983; Lyons 1981

implicational scaling /ˌɪmplɪ'keɪʃənəl 'skeɪlɪŋ/ *n*

a method of showing relationships by means of an implicational table or **scalogram**. For example, a group of students learning English may acquire the rule for using the DEFINITE ARTICLE before the rule for the INDEFINITE ARTICLE and they may acquire those two rules before the rule for marking the PLURAL of nouns. This can be shown by investigating their spoken or written language and presenting the results in a table. The symbol + means 100% correct use of the rule and the symbol × means that the rule is applied sometimes but not at other times (variable use).

student	noun plural	indefinite article	definite article
C	×	×	×
A	×	×	+
D	×	×	+
B	×	+	+
F	×	+	+
E	+	+	+

The symbol + in any row in the table implies a + symbol in any column to the right of it in the same row or in any row below it. In this way the students are ranked from Student C through to Student E, who is the best student, because he or she has 100% correct use of all the rules.

Implicational scaling has been used to show the order of acquisition of rules by FOREIGN-LANGUAGE and SECOND-LANGUAGE learners, and by people who are moving from a CREOLE towards a STANDARD VARIETY.

see also VARIABLE[1]

Further reading Hatch & Farhady 1982

implicational universal /ˌɪmplɪ'keɪʃənəl ˌjuːnɪ'vɜːsəl‖-ɜːr-/ *n*

see LANGUAGE UNIVERSAL

implicature /ɪmˈplɪkətʃəʳ/ *n*
see CONVERSATIONAL MAXIM

implicit performative /ɪmˈplɪsɪt pəˈfɔːmətɪv‖pərˈfɔːr-/ *n*
see PERFORMATIVE

inalienable possession /ɪnˈeɪliənəbəl pəˈzeʃən/ *n*
In many languages, there is a distinction between those objects which can change ownership, such as houses, or animals, and those which typically cannot, such as body parts, one's shadow, and one's footprints.
The first type of possession is called **alienable possession** and the latter type is called inalienable.
For example, in English, the verb *own* is typically not used with inalienable possessions: *George owns a car* but not **George owns a big nose* (if it is his own nose). On the other hand the verb *have* can be used with both types of possession: *George has a car* and *George has a big nose*.

inanimate noun /ɪnˈænɪmɪt ˈnaʊn/ *n*
see ANIMATE NOUN

inchoative verb /ɪnˈkəʊətɪv ˈvɜːb‖ˈvɜːrb/ *n*
a verb which expresses a change of state. For example:
yellowed in *The leaves yellowed*.
and
matured in *The cheese matured*.
as the leaves "became yellow" and the cheese "became mature".
see also CAUSATIVE VERB

inclusive (first person) pronoun /ɪŋˈkluːsɪv ˈfɜːst ˈpɜːsən ˈprəʊnaʊn‖ ˈfɜːrst ˈpɜːr-/ *n*
see EXCLUSIVE (FIRST PERSON) PRONOUN

indefinite article /ɪnˈdefənɪt ˈɑːtɪkəl‖ˈɑːr-/ *n*
see ARTICLE

indefinite pronoun /ɪnˈdefənɪt ˈprəʊnaʊn/ *n*
a pronoun that refers to something which is not thought of as definite or particular, such as *somebody, something, anybody, anyone, one, anything, everybody, everything*.

independent clause /ˈɪndɪpendənt ˈklɔːz/ *n*
see DEPENDENT CLAUSE

independent variable /ˈɪndɪpendənt ˈveəriəbəl/ *n*
see DEPENDENT VARIABLE

indexical information /ɪnˈdeksɪkəl ɪnfəˈmeɪʃən‖fər-/ *n*
(in communication) information which is communicated, usually

indirectly, about the speaker or writer's social class, age, sex, nationality, ethnic group, etc., or his or her emotional state (e.g. whether excited, angry, surprised, bored, etc.).

Further reading Lyons 1977

indicative /ɪnˈdɪkətɪv/ *n*
see MOOD

indigenization /ɪnˌdɪdʒɪnaɪˈzeɪʃən‖-nə-/ *n*
another term for NATIVIZATION

indirect object /ˈɪndɪrekt ˈɒbdʒɪkt, ˈɪndaɪ-‖ˈɑːb-/ *n*
see OBJECT[1]

indirect question /ˈɪndɪrekt ˈkwestʃən, ˈɪndaɪ-/ *n*
see DIRECT SPEECH

indirect speech /ˈɪndɪrekt ˈspiːtʃ, ˈɪndaɪ-/ *n*
see DIRECT SPEECH

indirect speech act /ˈɪndɪrekt ˈspiːtʃ ˌækt, ˈɪndaɪ-/ *n*
see SPEECH ACT

individualized instruction /ˌɪndɪˈvɪdʒuəlaɪzd ɪnˈstrʌkʃən/ *n*
also **individualized learning** /ˌɪndɪˈvɪdʒuəlaɪzd ˈlɜːnɪŋ‖ˈlɜːr-/
an approach to teaching in which:
  a OBJECTIVES are based on the needs of individual learners
  b allowances are made in the design of a CURRICULUM for indivdual differences in what students wish to learn, how they learn, and the rate at which they learn.
Individualized instruction attempts to give learners more control over what they learn and how they learn it.
Further reading Disick 1975

Indo-European languages /ˈɪndəʊ ˌjʊərəˈpiːən ˈlæŋgwɪdʒɪz/ *n*
languages which are related and which are supposed to have had a common ancestor language, called "Proto Indo-European".
Languages in this group include most European languages, e.g. English, French, German, and the Celtic and Slavonic languages. They also include the ancient Indian languages Sanskrit and Pali and such languages as Hindi, Urdu, Bengali, Sinhala, and Farsi.

induced error /ɪnˈdjuːst ˈerəʳ‖-ˈduːst/ *n*
also **transfer of training**
(in language learning) an ERROR which has been caused by the way in which a language item has been presented or practised.
For example, in teaching *at* the teacher may hold up a box and say *I'm looking at the box*. However, the learner may infer that *at* means *under*. If

induction

later the learner uses *at* for *under* (thus producing **The cat is at the table* instead of *The cat is under the table*) this would be an induced error.

see also ERROR ANALYSIS, INFERENCING, INTERLANGUAGE
Further reading Stenson 1974

induction /ɪn'dʌkʃən/ *n*
see DEDUCTION

inductive learning /ɪn'dʌktɪv 'lɜːnɪŋ‖'lɜːr-/ *n*
also **learning by induction**
see DEDUCTIVE LEARNING

inferencing /'ɪnfərənsɪŋ/ *n*
(in learning) the process of arriving at a hypothesis, idea, or judgment on the basis of other knowledge, ideas, or judgments (that is, making inferences or inferring). In language learning, inferencing has been discussed as a LEARNING STRATEGY used by learners to work out grammatical and other kinds of rules.
Further reading Carton 1971

inferential comprehension /ˌɪnfə'renʃəl ˌkɒmprɪ'henʃən‖ˌkɑːm-/ *n*
see READING

inferential statistics /ˌɪnfə'renʃəl stə'tɪstɪks/ *n*
also **inductive statistics** /ɪn'dʌktɪv stə'tɪstɪks/ *n*
statistical procedures which are used to make inferences or generalizations about a population from a set of data.
Statistical inference is based upon the theory of probability. A variety of different statistical techniques are used to determine the probable degree of accuracy of generalizations about the population from which a sample or set of data was selected.
see also DESCRIPTIVE STATISTICS, T-TEST, ANALYSIS OF VARIANCE

infinitive /ɪn'fɪnɪtɪv/ *n*
the BASE FORM of a verb (e.g. go, *come*).
In English the infinitive usually occurs with the infinitive marker *to* (e.g. *I want to go*) but can occur without *to* as with AUXILIARY VERBS (e.g. *Do come! You may go*). The infinitive without *to* is known as the **bare infinitive** or **simple form**. The infinitive with *to* is sometimes called the "*to*-infinitive".
The infinitive is a non-finite form of the verb (see FINITE VERB).

infix /'ɪnfɪks/ *n*
a letter or sound or group of letters or sounds which are added within a word, and which change the meaning or function of the word.
see also AFFIX

inflecting language /ɪn'flektɪŋ 'læŋgwɪdʒ/ *n*
also **fusional language** *n*

178

a language in which the form of a word changes to show a change in meaning or grammatical function. Often there is no clear distinction between the basic part of the word and the part which shows a grammatical function such as number or tense.

For example:

mice (=*mouse* + plural)

came (=*come* + past tense)

Greek and Latin are inflecting languages, although there is no clear-cut distinction between inflecting languages, AGGLUTINATING LANGUAGES, and ISOLATING LANGUAGES.

Sometimes inflecting languages and agglutinating languages are called **synthetic languages**.

see also INFLECTION

Further reading Fromkin & Rodman 1983

inflection/inflexion /ɪnˈflekʃən/ *n* **inflect** /ɪnˈflekt/ *v*

(in MORPHOLOGY) the process of adding an AFFIX to a word or changing it in some other way according to the rules of the grammar of a language.

For example, in English, verbs are inflected for 3rd-person singular: *I work, he/she works* and for past tense: *I worked*. Most nouns may be inflected for plural: *horse – horses, flower – flowers, man – men*.

see also DERIVATION, CONJUGATION²

informal speech /ɪnˈfɔːməl ˈspiːtʃ‖-ɔːr-/ *n*

another term for COLLOQUIAL SPEECH

informant /ɪnˈfɔːmənt‖-ɔːr-/ *n*

(in research) a person who provides the researcher with data for analysis. The data may be obtained, for instance, by recording the person's speech or by asking him or her questions about language use.

see also FIELD WORK

information content /ˌɪnfəˈmeɪʃən ˌkɒntent‖ˌɪnfər-ˌkɑːn-/ *n*

see INFORMATION THEORY

information gap /ˌɪnfəˈmeɪʃən ˌgæp‖ˌɪnfər-/ *n*

(in communication between two or more people) a situation where information is known by only some of those present.

In "communicative language teaching" (see COMMUNICATIVE APPROACH) it is said that in order to promote real communication between students, there must be an information gap between them, or between them and their teacher. Without such a gap the classroom activities and exercises will be mechanical and artifical.

Further reading Johnson 1982; Widdowson 1978

information processing /ˌɪnfəˈmeɪʃən ˌprəʊsesɪŋ‖ˌɪnfər-ˌprɑː-/ *n*

(in psychology and PSYCHOLINGUISTICS) a general term for the processes by which meanings are identified and understood in communication, the processes by which information and meaning are stored, organized, and retrieved from MEMORY, and the different kinds of DECODING which take place during reading or listening. The study of information processing includes the study of memory, decoding, and HYPOTHESIS TESTING, and the study of the processes and strategies (see STRATEGY) which learners use in working out meanings in the TARGET LANGUAGE[1].

see also HEURISTIC, HYPOTHESIS TESTING, INFORMATION THEORY, INPUT
Further reading McDonough 1981

information science /ˈɪnfəmeɪʃən ˈsaɪəns‖ˈɪnfər-/ *n*

the study of the generation, organization, communication and use of information. Information science is interdisciplinary and draws on work in linguistics, engineering, computer science, physics, communications etc.

information structure /ˈɪnfəmeɪʃən ˈstrʌktʃʳ‖ˌɪnfər-/ *n*

the use of WORD ORDER, INTONATION, STRESS and other devices to indicate how the message expressed by a sentence is to be understood.
Information structure is communicated by devices which indicate such things as:

a which parts of the message the speaker assumes the hearer already knows and which parts of the message are new information (see FUNCTIONAL SENTENCE PERSPECTIVE)

b contrasts, which may be indicated by stressing one word and not another (e.g. *I broke MY pen*; *I broke my PEN*; *I BROKE my pen*).

see also GROUNDING
Further reading Lyons 1977

information theory /ˈɪnfəmeɪʃən ˈθɪəri‖ˈɪnfər-/ *n*
also communication theory

a theory which explains how communication systems carry information and which measures the amount of information according to how much choice is involved when we send information.

The **information content** of a unit (e.g. of a word or a sentence) is measured according to how likely it is to occur in a particular communication. The more predictable a unit is, the less information it is said to carry. The unit of information used in information theory is the "binary digit", or BIT. The related concept of REDUNDANCY refers to the degree to which a message contains more information than is needed for it to be understood.

A well-known model for describing the sending of information in human or man-made communication systems, proposed by Shannon and Weaver, is known as the Mathematical Model of Communication. It describes communication as a process consisting of the following elements. The information **source** (e.g. a speaker) selects a desired message out of a possible set of messages. The "transmitter" changes the messages into a **signal** which is sent over the communication CHANNEL (e.g. a telephone wire) where it is received by the RECEIVER (e.g. a telephone or earphones) and changed back into a MESSAGE which is sent to the "destination" (e.g. a listener). In the process of transmission certain unwanted additions to the signal may occur which are not part of the message (e.g. interference from a poor telephone line) and these are referred to as NOISE[2]. The different elements in the system may be shown as:

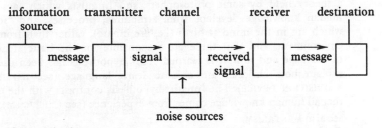

Communication system

In face-to-face communication, the speaker can be both information source and transmitter, while the listener can be both receiver and destination.

Further reading Sager, Dungworth, & McDonald 1980; DeVito 1970

informative function /ɪnˈfɔːmətɪv ˌfʌŋkʃən‖-ɔːr-/ n

SEE DEVELOPMENTAL FUNCTIONS OF LANGUAGE

inhibition /ˌɪnhɪˈbɪʃən/ n

SEE PROACTIVE INHIBITION

initial /ɪˈnɪʃəl/ adj

occurring at the beginning of a linguistic unit, e.g. as word-initial, clause-initial.

For example, a group of consonants at the beginning of a word, such as /spr/ in the English word *spray*, is an initial CONSONANT CLUSTER

SEE ALSO MEDIAL, FINAL

Initial Teaching Alphabet /ɪˈnɪʃəl ˈtiːtʃɪŋ ˌælfəbet/ n
also **ITA**

a system which is used to teach beginners to read English. ITA uses 43 alphabetic characters and tries to make reading easier by reducing the amount of irregularity in the English spelling system. It is designed as an introduction to the normal alphabet and is not a replacement for it.

> Sœ when it's tiem for fœd, ov cors,
> hee ʃhouts, "ħɷrra,
> ie cœd eet a hors!"
> but ʃhis is whot hee has insted:
> milk, ʧhees and frœt,
> and gœd broun bred.

Further reading Downing 1967

innateness position /ɪ'neɪtnɪs pə'zɪʃən/ *n*
another term for INNATIST HYPOTHESIS

innatist hypothesis /ɪ'neɪtɪst haɪ'pɒθɪsɪs||-'pɑː-/ *n*
also **innatist position** /ɪ'neɪtɪst pə'zɪʃən/ , **nativist position**,
innateness position, rationalist position
a theory held by some philosophers and linguists which says that
human knowledge develops from structures, processes, and "ideas"
which are in the mind at birth (i.e. are innate), rather than from the
environment, and that these are responsible for the basic structure
of language and how it is learned. This hypothesis has been used to
explain how children are able to learn language (see LANGUAGE
ACQUISITION DEVICE). The innatist hypothesis contrasts with the belief
that all human knowledge comes from experience (see EMPIRICISM).

see also MENTALISM
Further reading Chomsky 1968

inner speech /ˌɪnəʳ 'spiːtʃ/ *n*
a type of "speech" discussed by the Russian psychologist Vygotsky,
who distinguished between **external speech** and inner speech.
External speech is spoken or written speech, and is expressed in words
and sentences. Inner speech is speech for oneself. It takes place inside
one's own mind and often takes place in "pure word meanings" rather
than in words or sentences, according to Vygotsky.

Further reading Vygotsky 1962

input /'ɪmpʊt/ *n*
1 (in language learning) language which a learner hears or receives and
from which he or she can learn. The language a learner produces is by
analogy sometimes called **output**.
2 In second or foreign language learning, a distinction is sometimes
made between input (above) and **intake**. Intake is input which is
actually helpful for the learner. Some of the language (i.e. the input)
which a learner hears may be too rapid or difficult for the learner to
understand, and therefore cannot be used in learning (i.e. cannot serve
as intake).
3 (in computer systems) information from the outside world which
must be entered into the computer in order to carry out a particular
task. Data which come out of the computer are known as **output**. Any
part of a computer system that is used mainly to put information into
the computer (e.g. a keyboard or a light pen) is known as an **input
device**.

see also INFORMATION PROCESSING
Further reading Davies, Criper, & Howatt 1984; Dulay, Burt, & Krashen
1982

input hypothesis /'ɪmpʊt haɪ'pɒθɪsɪs||-'pɑː-/ *n*
a hypothesis proposed by Krashen, which states that in second or
foreign language learning, for language ACQUISITION to occur, it is
necessary for the learner to understand INPUT language which contains

linguistic items that are slightly beyond the learners' present linguistic COMPETENCE. Learners understand such language using cues in the situation. Eventually the ability to produce language is said to emerge naturally, and need not be taught directly.

see also MONITOR HYPOTHESIS
Further reading Krashen 1981, 1985

input-output /'ɪnpʊt 'aʊtpʊt/ *n*

terms often used in applied linguistics, psychology, cognitive psychology and related disciplines to refer to information that a person receives (**input**), behaviour which results from it (**output**) and the relationships between them.

inquiry learning /ɪnˈkwaɪəri ˌlɜːnɪŋ‖ˈɪŋkwəri ˌlɜːr- ɪnˈkwaɪə-/ *n*

see DISCOVERY LEARNING

insertion sequence /ɪnˈsɜːʃən ˌsiːkwəns‖-ɜːr-/ *n*

In conversation, speakers may interrupt themselves and insert an utterance which is not related to the main conversation. This utterance is often referred to as an insertion sequence.

There may be numerous reasons for the sequence. Often it may be caused by an external event, e.g. a ring/knock at the door, a ringing telephone:

> A: ... *and I actually told her that* ... (doorbell rings)
> *Excuse me, that must be Al. He's probably forgotten his key.*
> A: (returns) Now, *what was I saying before? Ah, yes. She said* ...

In many cases, the original conversation is continued after the insertion sequence. Sometimes it is referred to briefly with utterances such as:

> *Sorry for the interruption. Now where were we? What was I saying?* etc.

see also SEQUENCING[1], SIDE SEQUENCE
Further reading Schegloff 1972; Wardhaugh 1985

inservice education /'ɪnsɜːvɪs edjʊˈkeɪʃən‖-ɜːr- edʒə-/ *n*

see PRESERVICE EDUCATION

instructional objective /ɪnˈstrʌkʃənəl əbˈdʒektɪv/ *n*

another term for BEHAVIOURAL OBJECTIVE

instrumental case /ˌɪnstrəˈmentl ˌkeɪs/ *n*

(In CASE GRAMMAR) the noun or noun phrase that refers to the means by which the action of the verb is performed is in the instrumental case.

For example, in the sentences:

> *He dug the hole with a spade.*
> *The hammer hit the nail.*

a spade and *the hammer* are in the instrumental case.
Further reading Fillmore 1968

instrumental function /ˌɪnstrəˈmentl ˌfʌŋkʃən/ *n*

see DEVELOPMENTAL FUNCTIONS OF LANGUAGE

instrumental motivation /ˌɪnstrəmentl ˌməʊtɬˈveɪʃən/ *n*

see MOTIVATION

intake /ˈɪnteɪk/ *n*

see INPUT

integrated approach /ˈɪntɬgreɪtɬd əˈprəʊtʃ/ *n*

(in language teaching) the teaching of the language skills of reading, writing, listening, and speaking, in conjunction with each other, as when a lesson involves activites that relate listening and speaking to reading and writing.

see also LANGUAGE ARTS

integrated whole language approach /ˈɪntɬgreɪtɬd həʊl ˈlæŋgwɪdʒ əˌprəʊtʃ/ *n*

see WHOLE LANGUAGE APPROACH

integrative motivation /ˈɪntɬgreɪtɪv ˌməʊtɬˈveɪʃən/ *n*

see MOTIVATION

integrative test /ˈɪntɬgreɪtɪv ˈtest/ *n*

see DISCRETE-POINT TEST

intelligibility /ɪnˌtelɬdʒɬˈbɪlɬti/ *n*

the degree to which a message can be understood. Studies of speech PERCEPTION have found that the intelligibility of speech is due to various factors including ACCENT[3] and INTONATION, the listener's ability to predict parts of the message, the location of PAUSES in the utterance, the grammatical complexity of sentences, and the speed with which utterances are produced.

Further reading Foss & Hakes 1978

intensifier /ɪnˈtensɬfaɪəʳ/ *n*

a class of words, generally adverbs, which are used to modify gradable adjective, adverbs, verbs, or -ed- PARTICIPLES, as in:

It is very good
It was completely destroyed.
I absolutely detest it.

see also GRADABLE
Further reading Close 1975

intensive reading /ɪnˈtensɪv ˈriːdɪŋ/ *n*

see EXTENSIVE READING

interactional function /ɪntərˈækʃənəl ˈfʌŋkʃən/ *n*

see DEVELOPMENTAL FUNCTIONS OF LANGUAGE

interaction analysis /ɪntər'ækʃən ə,næl̩s̩s/ *n*
also **interaction process analysis** /ɪntər'ækʃən 'prəʊses ə,næl̩s̩s‖'prɑː-/
any of several procedures for measuring and describing the behaviour
of students and teachers in classrooms, (a) in order to describe what
happens during a lesson (b) to evaluate teaching (c) to study the
relationship between teaching and learning (d) to help teacher-trainees
learn about the process of teaching. In interaction analysis, classroom
behaviour is observed and the different types of student and teacher
activity are classified, using a classification scheme. Several such
schemes have been proposed.
Further reading Flanders 1970

interactionism /ɪntər'ækʃənɪzəm/ *n*
also **interactionist position** /ɪntər'ækʃən̩st pə,zɪʃən/ *n*
(in psychology, linguistics, and research on language acquisition) the
view that language development and social development are associated
and that one cannot be understood without the other. Researchers who
believe in interactionism focus on the social context of language
development and how the relationship between the language learner
and the persons with whom he or she interacts influences language
acquisition. This perspective is sometimes contrasted with a linguistic
approach, which holds that language acquisition can be understood
through analysis of the learner's utterances, independently of his or
her cognitive development or social life.
Further reading Wells 1985; Bennett-Kastor 1989

interactive /ˌɪntər'æktɪv/ *adj*
(in COMPUTER ASSISTED INSTRUCTION) describes the ability of a user
to "communicate" (or "interact") with a computer. Lessons in CAI
materials may involve a question on the computer, a response from the
student, and feedback from the computer telling the student if the
answer is correct. In CAI such activities are said to be "interactive".

interactive audio /'ɪntəræktɪv 'ɔːdiəʊ/ *n*
the use of a computer linked with a tape recorder or other form of
audio equipment for instructional purposes, allowing a learner to
interact with the audio equipment. The use of a computer allows for
better ACCESS, precise control of playing and replaying, as well as ON
LINE facilities.
Further reading Flint Smith 1989

interactive video /'ɪntəræktɪv 'vɪdiəʊ/ *n*
the use of a computer linked with a videodisc or videoplayer for instructional purposes, allowing a learner to interact with the video equipment. The computer allows for different forms of display of material
on the video or videodisc, ONLINE facilities, and allows for BRANCHING

interdental /ˌɪntə'dentl◂‖-tər-/ *adj*
describes a speech sound (a CONSONANT) produced with the tip of the

tongue between the upper and lower teeth, e.g. /θ/ and /ð/ in the English words /θɪk/ *thick* and /ðɪs/ this.

see also MANNER OF ARTICULATION, PLACE OF ARTICULATION

interference /ˌɪntəˈfɪərəns‖-tər-/ *n*

see LANGUAGE TRANSFER

intergroup communication /ˈɪntəgruːp kəˌmjuːnɫˈkeɪʃən‖-tər-/ *n*

communication between different groups, especially those which are socially, ethnically, or linguistically different. Intergroup communication is often by means of a LINGUA FRANCA, a language known by speakers of both groups.

For example, in Indonesia, where many different languages are spoken, Bahasa Indonesia, the national language, is the language most frequently used for intergroup communication.

see also INTRAGROUP COMMUNICATION

interim grammar /ˈɪntərɪm ˌgræməʳ/ *n*

a temporary grammatical system used by children learning their first language at a particular stage in their language development.

Children's grammatical systems change as they develop new grammatical rules; hence they may be said to pass through a series of interim grammars.

see also INTERLANGUAGE

interjection /ˌɪntəˈdʒekʃən‖-tər-/ *n*

a word such as *ugh!*, *gosh!*, *wow!*, which indicates an emotional state or attitude such as delight, suprise, shock, and disgust, but which has no referential meaning (see REFERENCE).

Interjections are often regarded as one of the PARTS OF SPEECH.

see also EXCLAMATION[1]

interlanguage /ˈɪntəˌlæŋgwɪdʒ‖-tər-/ *n*

the type of language produced by second- and foreign-language learners who are in the process of learning a language.

In language learning, learners' errors are caused by several different processes. These include:

a borrowing patterns from the mother tongue (see LANGUAGE TRANSFER)

b extending patterns from the target language, e.g. by analogy (see OVERGENERALIZATION)

c expressing meanings using the words and grammar which are already known (see COMMUNICATION STRATEGY)

Since the language which the learner produces using these processes differs from both the mother tongue and the TARGET LANGUAGE[1], it is sometimes called an interlanguage, or is said to result from the learner's interlanguage system or **approximative system**.

see also INTERIM GRAMMAR

Further reading Davies, Criper, & Howatt 1984; Selinker 1972; Ellis 1985

interlingual error /ˈɪntəlɪŋgwəl ˈerəʳ‖-tər-/ *n*

(in ERROR ANALYSIS) an error which results from LANGUAGE TRANSFER, that is, which is caused by the learner's native language. For example, the incorrect French sentence *Elle regarde les* ("She sees them"), produced according to the word order of English, instead of the correct French sentence *Elle les regarde* (Literally, "She them sees").

An **intralingual error** is one which results from faulty or partial learning of the TARGET LANGUAGE[1], rather than from language transfer. Intralingual errors may be caused by the influence of one target-language item upon another. For example a learner may produce *He is comes*, based on a blend of the English structures *He is coming, He comes*.

Further reading Richards 1974

interlingual identification /ˈɪntəlɪŋgwəl aɪˌdentɪfɪˈkeɪʃən‖ˈɪntər-/ *n*

(in second or foreign language learning) a judgment made by learners about the identity or similarity of structures in two languages. For example, in learning the sound system of a new language, a learner may have to decide whether the '*d*' sound in the new language is the same or different from the '*d*' sound in his or her native language. Learners often categorize sounds in terms of the phonemic systems of their first language, making acquisition of new target language sounds difficult.

see also PHONEME, LANGUAGE TRANSFER
Further reading Odlin 1989

interlocutors /ˌɪntəˈlɒkjʊtəz‖ˌɪntərˈlaːkjʊtərz/ *n*

people who are actively engaged in conversation. Normally, the exchange is in the form of a dialogue or a number of dialogues. Apart from the interlocutors there may be other people present who are just silent participants, such as an audience.

The form and style of the conversation may be affected by the presence of these "silent participants".

internal consistency reliability /ɪnˈtɜːnl kənˈsɪstənsi rɪˌlaɪəˈbɪlᵻti‖ -ˈtɜːr-/ *n*

(in testing) a measure of the degree to which the items or parts of a test are homogeneous or consistent with each other.

Internal consistency reliability is often estimated by comparing the two halves of a test (SPLIT-HALF RELIABILITY) or by a KUDER-RICHARDSON RELIABILITY COEFFICIENT.

internalized language /ɪnˈtɜːnəlaɪzd ˈlæŋgwɪdʒ‖-ɜːr-/ *n*

another term for I-LANGUAGE

international language /ˈɪntənæʃənəl ˈlæŋgwɪdʒ‖-tər-/ *n*

a language in widespread use as a FOREIGN LANGUAGE or SECOND LANGUAGE, i.e. as a language of international communication. English is the most widely used international language.

International Phonetic Alphabet /ˈɪntənæʃənəl fəˈnetɪk ˈælfəbet‖ -tər-/ *n*
also IPA

a system of symbols for representing the pronunciation of words in any language according to the principles of the International Phonetic Association. The symbols consist of letters and DIACRITICS. Some letters are taken from the Roman alphabet (see ALPHABETIC WRITING), e.g. /p/, /e/, and /n/ as in the English word /pen/ *pen*. Others are special symbols, e.g. /ʃ/, /ə/, and /ʊ/ as in the English word /ʃəʊ/ *show*.

interpersonal function /ˈɪntəpɜːsənəl ˈfʌŋkʃən‖ˈɪntərpɜːr-/ *n*
see FUNCTIONS OF LANGUAGE²

interpretation /ɪnˌtɜːprɪˈteɪʃən‖-ˌtɜːr-/ *n*

the translation by an "interpreter" of what someone is saying into another language, to permit a speaker to communicate with people who do not understand the speaker's language.

If the interpretation takes place as the speaker is talking, providing a continuous translation which parallels the speaker's speech, it is called **simultaneous interpretation**.

If the speaker pauses during speaking to give the interpreter time to provide a translation of everything said up to that point, the result is called **consecutive interpretation**.

interpretive error /ɪnˈtɜːprɪtɪv ˈerər‖-ˈtɜːr-/ *n*
see ERROR

interpretive semantics /ɪnˈtɜːprɪtɪv sɪˈmæntɪks‖-ˈtɜːr-/ *n*

a theory about the place of meaning in a model of TRANSFORMATIONAL GENERATIVE GRAMMAR. It considers a meaning component, called the **semantic component**, as part of the grammar. This component contains rules which interpret the meaning of sentences.

This theory differs from GENERATIVE SEMANTICS, which insists that the semantic component is the most basic part of a grammar from which all sentences of a language can be "generated" (see GENERATIVE GRAMMAR, RULE²).

In generative semantics, syntactic rules operate on the meaning of a sentence to produce its form. In interpretive semantics, semantic rules operate on the words and syntactic structure of a sentence to reveal its meaning.

Further reading Katz & Fodor 1963

inter-rater reliability /ˈɪntəˌreɪtər rɪˌlaɪəˈbɪlɪti/ *n*

(in testing) the degree to which different examiners or judges making different subjective ratings of ability (e.g. of language proficiency) agree in their evaluations of that ability. If different judges rank students in approximately the same order, using a RATING SCALE which measures different aspects of proficiency, the rating scale is said to have high inter-rater reliability.

Intra-rater reliability is the degree to which a teacher or examiner making subjective ratings of ability gives the same evaluation of that ability when he or she makes an evaluation on two or more different occasions.

Further reading Seliger & Shohamy 1989

interrogative pronoun /ˌɪntəˈrɒgətɪv ˈprəʊnaʊn‖-ˈrɑː-/ *n*
Wh-pronouns (*who, which, what, whose, who(m)* etc.), which are used to form questions, e.g.:
  Which is your book?
  What is your name?
see also WH-QUESTION
Further reading Quirk et al 1985

interrogative sentence /ˌɪntəˈrɒgətɪv ˈsentəns‖-ˈrɑː-/ *n*
A sentence which is in the form of a question. For example:
  Did you open the window?
Interrogative sentences do not, however, always have the function of a question. For example:
  Could you shut the window?
may be a request for someone to shut the window and not a question about whether or not the person is able to do so.
see also DECLARATIVE SENTENCE, IMPERATIVE SENTENCE
Further reading Lyons 1981

interval scale /ˈɪntəvəl ˈskeɪl‖-tər-*n*
see SCALE

interview /ˈɪntəvjuː‖-tər-/ *n*
a directed conversation between an investigator and an individual or group of individuals in order to gather information.
Interviews are used to gather data for linguistic analysis (see FIELDWORK) and may be used in needs analysis.
see DEPTH INTERVIEW, FOCUSED INTERVIEW, GUIDED INTERVIEW, INTERVIEW GUIDE

interview guide /ˈɪntəvjuː ˌgaɪd‖-tər-/ *n*
a list of topics used by an interviewer during an interview. An interview guide helps the interviewer make sure that the important topics have been covered during the interview, but it differs from an interview schedule (see GUIDED INTERVIEW) in that it contains only the topics to be asked about and not the actual questions which will be asked.

interview schedule /ˈɪntəvjuː ˌʃedjuːl‖-tər- ˌskedʒʊl, -dʒəl/
see GUIDED INTERVIEW

intervocalic /ˌɪntəvəˈkælɪk◄, -vəʊ-‖-tər-/ *adj*
(of CONSONANTS) occurring between two vowels.
For example, English /d/ in /ˈleɪdi/ *lady* is an intervocalic CONSONANT.

intonation /ˌɪntə'neɪʃən/ *n*

When speaking, people generally raise and lower the PITCH of their voice, forming pitch patterns. They also give some syllables in their utterances a greater degree of loudness and change their SPEECH RHYTHM. These phenomena are called intonation. Intonation does not happen at random but has definite patterns (see INTONATION PATTERNS) which can be analysed according to their structure and functions. Intonation is used to carry information over and above that which is expressed by the words in the sentence.

see also KEY², PITCH LEVEL, TONE UNIT

intonation contour /ˌɪntə'neɪʃən ˌkɒntʊəʳ‖ˌkɑː-/ *n*

see TONE UNIT

intonation patterns /ˌɪntə'neɪʃən ˌpætənz‖-tərnz/ *n*

patterns in the spoken form of a language which are usually expressed by variations in pitch (see TONE UNIT), loudness, syllable length, and sometimes SPEECH RHYTHM.

Intonation patterns may, for instance:

a have grammatical functions, e.g. they may show that an utterance is a question and not a statement:
R͜eady?

b give additional information to that given by the words of an utterance:
I G͜OT the job. (it was doubtful whether I would)

c indicate the speaker's attitude to the matter discussed or to the listener:
But I T͜OLD you.

Intonation patterns often differ between languages or even between varieties of the same language, e.g. between Australian English and American English. In some communities, there is a difference in the intonation patterns of different age groups or speakers of different sex.

see also INTONATION

Further reading Brazil, Coulthard, & Johns 1980; Halliday 1970

intragroup communication /'ɪntrəˌgruːp kəˌmjuːnɪ̩'keɪʃən/ *n*

communication among members of a group.

In some multi-ethnic countries or communities, a language may be used for communication within a particular ethnic group although it is not known or used by the majority of the population; for example, Spanish in parts of the USA among some Mexican-Americans.

see also COMMUNITY LANGUAGE, INTERGROUP COMMUNICATION

intralingual error /'ɪntrəlɪŋgwəl 'erəʳ/ *n*

see INTERLINGUAL ERROR

intransitive verb /ɪn'trænsɪ̩tɪv 'vɜːb‖'vɜːrb/ *n*

see TRANSITIVE VERB

190

intra-rater reliability /ˈɪntrəˌreɪtəʳ rɪˌlaɪəˈbɪlɪ̹ti/ *n*
see INTER-RATER RELIABILITY

introduction /ɪntrəˈdʌkʃən/ *n*
see ESSAY

introspection /ɪntrəˈspekʃən/ *n*
see VERBAL REPORTING

introvert /ˈɪntrəvɜːt‖-vɜːrt/ *n*
see EXTROVERT

intrusion /ɪnˈtruːʒən/ *n* **intrusive** /ɪnˈtruːsɪv/ *adj*
When an extra consonant is added at the end of a word to link it to a following word starting with a vowel, this is known as intrusion. In English, an intrusive /r/ is often added, especially before *and*. For example:
  China and Japan /ˈtʃaɪnər ən dʒəˈpæn/
  Lena and Sue /ˈliːnər ən ˈsuː/
Further reading Gimson 1989

IPA /ˌaɪ piː ˈeɪ/ *n*
an abbreviation for
1 *I*nternational *P*honetic *A*ssociation
2 INTERNATIONAL PHONETIC ALPHABET

irregular verb /ɪˈregjl̹əʳ ˈvɜːb‖ˈvɜːrb/ *n*
see REGULAR VERB

isolating language /ˈaɪsəleɪtɪŋ ˈlæŋgwɪdʒ/ *n*
also **analytic language**
  a language in which word forms do not change, and in which grammatical functions are shown by WORD ORDER and the use of FUNCTION WORDS.
  For example, in Mandarin Chinese:
  júzi   wǒ chī̄ le
  orange I   eat (function word
                    showing completion)
  "I ate the orange"

  wǒ chī̄ le   júzi   le
  I   eat (function orange (function
            word)   word)
  "I have eaten an orange"
  Languages which are highly isolating include Chinese and Vietnamese, although there is no clear-cut distinction between isolating languages, INFLECTING LANGUAGES, and AGGLUTINATING LANGUAGES. English is more isolating than many other European languages, such as French, German, and Russian, but is also an inflecting language.
Further reading Fromkin & Rodman 1983

ITA /ˌaɪ tiː 'eɪ/ *n*
an abbreviation for INITIAL TEACHING ALPHABET

item analysis /'aɪtəm əˌnæləsɪs/ *n*
(in testing) the analysis of the responses to the items in a test, in order to find out how effective the test items are and to find out if they indicate differences between good and weak students.
see also ITEM FACILITY, ITEM DISCRIMINATION

item difficulty /'aɪtəm ˌdɪfɪkəlti/ *n*
another term for ITEM FACILITY

item discrimination /'aɪtəm dɪˌskrɪmɪ'neɪʃən/ *n*
(in testing) a measure of the extent to which a test item is sensitive to differences in ability among those who take the test. If a particular item in a test was answered in the same way by both the students who did well on the test as a whole and by those who did poorly, the item would be said to have poor discrimination: it could not discriminate between good students and bad students.

item facility /'aɪtəm fəˌsɪləti/ *n*
also **facility value, item difficulty**
(in testing) a measure of the ease of a test item. It is the proportion of the students who answered the item correctly, and may be determined by the formula:

$$\text{Item Facility(IF)} = \frac{R}{N}$$

where R = number of correct answers, N = number of students taking the test.
The higher the ratio of R to N, the easier the item.

IVI /ˌaɪ viː 'aɪ/ *n*
an abbreviation for **Interactive Videodisc Instruction**.
see INTERACTIVE VIDEO

ℐ

jargon /ˈdʒɑːgən‖-ɑːr-/ *n*

speech or writing used by a group of people who belong to a particular trade, profession, or any other group bound together by mutual interest, e.g. *the jargon of law, medical jargon.*

A jargon has its own set of words and expressions, which may be incomprehensible to an outsider. The term jargon is typically not used by the group itself but by those unfamiliar with that particular type of language, and/or by those who dislike it.

Jargon is sometimes also used for the first (developmental) stage of a PIDGIN language, where there is a great deal of individual variation, a simple sound system, very short sentences and a restricted number of words.

jigsaw /ˈdʒɪgsɔːʳ/ *n*

see CO-OPERATIVE LEARNING

journal /ˈdʒɜːnl‖-ɜːr-/ *n*

see LEARNING LOG

juncture /ˈdʒʌŋktʃəʳ/ *n*

a type of BOUNDARY between two PHONEMES. Often, juncture helps the listener to distinguish between pairs such as *I scream* and *ice cream.*

Further reading Robins 1980

K

key¹ /kiː/ n

the tone, manner, or spirit in which a SPEECH ACT is carried out, for example whether mockingly or seriously. The key chosen would depend on the situation and the relationship of the speakers to each other. For example, the statement *If you do that I'll never speak to you again* may be either a real threat or a mock threat. The signalling of key may be verbal (e.g. by INTONATION) or non-verbal (e.g. by a wink, a gesture, or a certain posture).

Further reading Coulthard 1985; Hymes 1977

key² n

(in INTONATION) a level of PITCH chosen by the speaker together with an intonation contour (see TONE UNIT) in order to convey a particular kind of meaning to the listener.

In English, a difference can be made between high key, mid key, and low key.

For example, the choice of a high key often signals a contrast as in:

But she's Peter's *WIFE* (where *wife* also has a fall in pitch)

This could be a reply to someone who had just stated that the person concerned was Peter's sister.

see also PITCH LEVEL

Further reading Brazil, Coulthard, & Johns 1980

keyword technique /ˈkiːwɜːd tekˌniːk‖-wɜːrd/ n

(in second language learning) a learning strategy in which the learner thinks of a homophone (HOMOPHONES) (the "key word") in the native language for the word he or she is trying to remember in the target language. The learner then imagines a situation in which the homophone and the target language word are interacting in some way. In remembering the target word, the learner recalls the homophone and the situation in which it was used. For example in learning the French word for "door" – *porte* – a learner might think of a near homophone in English, such as "a porter". Then the learner thinks of a situation involving a porter – such as a porter opening a door to carry in a bag. When the learner wants to remember the French word for door, he or she thinks of the situation and the key word – *porter*. This helps recall the French word – *porte*.

kinesics /kɪˈniːsɪks/ n kinesic adj

see PARALINGUISTICS

kinesthetic feedback /ˈkɪniːsθetɪk ˈfiːdbæk/ n

(in speaking or writing) feedback we receive which comes from the movement and positions of the muscles, organs etc. which are used to produce speech or writing. The ability to feel where our tongues are in the mouth, for example, is an important factor in being able to speak clearly. If this kinesthetic feedback is interfered with (e.g. as a result of a dental injection which causes the tongue to lose sensation), our speech may become slurred. The other kind of feedback which is used to monitor our communication is *auditory feedback*.

Further reading Crystal 1980

KR21 /'keɪ ɑːˈ 'twenti 'wʌn/ n

another term for KUDER-RICHARDSON RELIABILITY COEFFICIENT

K through 12 /'keɪ θruː 'twelv/ n

in the US, the period of schooling from kindergarten through to grade 12 – the final year of high school.

Kuder-Richardson Reliability Coefficient /'kuːdəˈ 'rɪtʃədsən rɪˌlaɪ əˈbɪlᶾti kəʊᶾˌfiʃənt‖-ərd-/ n
also KR 21

a statistical formula used as one estimate of the RELIABILITY of a test. It is based on the number of items in the test, the MEAN score, and its STANDARD DEVIATION.

A similar reliability formula, based on information about the difficulty of the individual items, the test mean, and the standard deviation, is known as **KR 20**.

L

L1 /'el 'wʌn/ n

see FIRST LANGUAGE

L2 /'el 'tuː/ n

another term for a TARGET LANGUAGE¹ or a SECOND LANGUAGE.

labial /'leɪbiəl/ adj

(in PHONETICS) describes a pronunciation in which either one or both lips are used. The term comes from Latim *labia* "lip".

see also BILABIAL, LABIO-DENTAL

labialization /ˌleɪbiəlaɪ'zeɪʃən‖-lə-/ n **labialize** /'leɪbiəlaɪz/ v

rounding of the lips in the pronunciation of a speech sound. For example, in English, this may happen in the pronunciation of /r/ so that words like *very* and *red* are pronounced /'vewi/ and /wed/.

This type of pronunciation is heard mainly from children before they are able to produce an *r* sound but it may remain as a feature of adult speech.

Further reading Gimson 1989

labio-dental /ˌleɪbiəʊ'dentl◄/ adj

describes a speech sound (a CONSONANT) which is produced by the lower lip touching or nearly touching the upper teeth.

For example, in English the /f/ in /fæt/ *fat*, and the /v/ in /væt/ *vat* are labio-dental FRICATIVES.

see also PLACE OF ARTICULATION, MANNER OF ARTICULATION

Further reading Gimson 1989

LAD /'el eɪ 'diː/ n

an abbreviation for LANGUAGE ACQUISITION DEVICE

laminal /'læm̩nəl/ adj

describes a speech sound (a CONSONANT) which is produced by the front upper surface of the tongue (the blade or **lamina**) touching the upper teeth or the gum ridge behind the upper teeth (the **alveolar ridge**).

In English, the /ʃ/ in /ʃuː/ *shoe* is a laminal FRICATIVE.

see also PLACE OF ARTICULATION, MANNER OF ARTICULATION

Further reading Gimson 1989

language¹ /'læŋgwɪdʒ/ n

the system of human communication which consists of the structured arrangement of sounds (or their written representation) into larger units, e.g. MORPHEMES, WORDS, SENTENCES, UTTERANCES.

196

In common usage it can also refer to non-human systems of communication such as the "language" of bees, the "language" of dolphins.

language² *n*

any particular system of human communication (see LANGUAGE¹), for example, the French language, the Hindi language. Sometimes a language is spoken by most people in a particular country, for example, Japanese in Japan, but sometimes a language is spoken by only part of the population of a country, for example Tamil in India, French in Canada.

Languages are usually not spoken in exactly the same way from one part of a country to the other. Differences in the way a language is spoken by different people are described in terms of regional and social variation (see DIALECT, SOCIOLECT). In some cases, there is a continuum from one language to another. Dialect A of Language X on one side of the border may be very similar to Dialect B of Language Y on the other side of the border if language X and language Y are related. This is the case between Sweden and Norway and between Germany and the Netherlands.

see also REGISTER

language achievement /ˈlæŋgwɪdʒ əˈtʃiːvmənt/ *n*

a learner's proficiency in a SECOND LANGUAGE and FOREIGN LANGUAGE as the result of what has been taught or learned after a period of instruction. Language achievement may be contrasted with LANGUAGE APTITUDE, which is measured before a course of instruction begins.

Further reading Carroll 1981

language acquisition /ˈlæŋgwɪdʒ ækwᵻˈzɪʃən/ *n*

the learning and development of a person's language. The learning of a native or first language is called FIRST LANGUAGE ACQUISITION, and of a second or foreign language, SECOND LANGUAGE ACQUISITION. The term "acquisition" is often preferred to "learning" because the latter term is sometimes linked to a behaviourist theory of learning (see BEHAVIOURISM). Language acquisition is studied by linguists, psychologists and applied linguists to enable them to understand the processes used in learning a language, to help identify stages in the developmental process, and to give a better understanding of the nature of language. Techniques used include longitudinal studies of language learners as well as experimental approaches, and focus on the study of the development of phonology, grammar, vocabulary, and communicative competence.

Further reading Elliot 1981; Fletcher 1985

language acquisition device /ˈlæŋgwɪdʒ ækwᵻˈzɪʃən dɪˌvaɪs/ *n*
also **LAD**

the capacity to acquire one's FIRST LANGUAGE, when this capacity is pictured as a sort of mechanism or apparatus.

In the 1960s and 1970s Chomsky and others claimed that every normal human being was born with an LAD (see INNATIST HYPOTHESIS). The LAD included basic knowledge about the nature and structure of human language.

The LAD was offered as an explanation of why children develop COMPETENCE in their first language in a relatively short time, merely by being exposed to it.

see also ACQUISITION
Further reading McNeill 1966

language across the curriculum /ˈlæŋgwɪdʒ əˈkrɒs ðə kəˈrɪkjᵿləm‖ əˈkrɔːs/ *n*

(in the teaching of English and in LANGUAGE ARTS) an approach that emphasises the teaching of language skills in relation to their uses in the total school curriculum, particularly in the CONTENT AREAS rather than in isolation from the school curriculum. This approach reflects a functional view of language and one which seeks to teach language through activities which are linked to the teaching of other school subjects. A similar approach to the teaching of reading and writing is known as **writing across the curriculum** and **reading across the curriculum**.

language aptitude /ˈlæŋgwɪdʒ ˈæptᵻjuːd‖-tuːd/ *n*

the natural ability to learn a language, not including intelligence, MOTIVATION, interest, etc.

Language aptitude is thought to be a combination of various abilities, such as the ability to identify sound patterns in a new language, the ability to recognize the different grammatical functions of words in sentences, ROTE-LEARNING ability, and the ability to infer language rules (see INFERENCING, DEDUCTIVE LEARNING). A person with high language aptitude can learn more quickly and easily than a person with low language aptitude, all other factors being equal.

see also LANGUAGE APTITUDE TEST
Further reading Carroll 1981

language aptitude test /ˈlæŋgwɪdʒ ˈæptᵻtjuːd ˌtest‖-tuːd/ *n*

a test which measures a person's aptitude for SECOND LANGUAGE or FOREIGN LANGUAGE learning and which can be used to identify those learners who are most likely to succeed (see LANGUAGE APTITUDE). Language aptitude tests usually consist of several different tests which measure such abilities as:

a sound coding ability – the ability to identify and remember new sounds in a foreign or second language
b grammatical coding ability – the ability to identify the grammatical functions of different parts of sentences
c inductive learning ability – the ability to work out meanings without explanation in a new language (see INDUCTIVE LEARNING)
d memorization – the ability to remember words, rules, etc. in a new language.

Two well-known language aptitude tests are *The Modern Language*

Aptitude Test (Carroll and Sapon 1958) and the *Pimsleur Language Aptitude Battery* (Pimsleur 1966).

Further reading Carroll 1981

language arts /'læŋgwɪdʒ 'ɑːts‖'ɑːrts/ *n*
those parts of an educational CURRICULUM which involve the development of skills related to the use of language, such as reading, writing, spelling, listening, and speaking. The term is used principally to describe approaches used in FIRST LANGUAGE teaching which try to develop LANGUAGE SKILLS together rather than separately.

language attitudes /'læŋgwɪdʒ 'æt̪tjuːdʒ‖-tuːdʒ/ *n*
the attitudes which speakers of different languages or language varieties have towards each other's languages or to their own language. Expressions of positive or negative feelings towards a language may reflect impressions of linguistic difficulty or simplicity, ease or difficulty of learning, degree of importance, elegance, social STATUS, etc. Attitudes towards a language may also show what people feel about the speakers of that language.

Language attitudes may have an effect on SECOND LANGUAGE or FOREIGN LANGUAGE learning. The measurement of language attitudes provides information which is useful in language teaching and LANGUAGE PLANNING.

see also LANGUAGE EGO, MATCHED GUISE TECHNIQUE, MOTIVATION, SEMANTIC DIFFERENTIAL

Further reading Fasold 1984; Ryan & Giles 1982

language attrition /'læŋgwɪdʒ ə'trɪʃən/ *n*
language loss that is gradual rather than sudden. This may refer to the loss of a second or foreign language after instruction, such as often occurs in settings where the language is not used in the community, or to the loss of a first language in situations where the community speaks a different language, as in language loss among immigrants. Language attrition may also refer to the loss of a first or second language due to ageing. Research on second language attrition has attempted to identify which aspects of a language are forgotten after a period of disuse, the rate at which these aspects are lost, whether the sequence of forgetting parallels the sequence in which the language was initially learned, and whether the conditions under which the language was initially learned affect retention.

language change /'læŋgwɪdʒ 'tʃeɪndʒ/ *n*
change in a language which takes place over time. All living languages have changed and continue to change.

For example, in English, changes which have recently been occurring include the following:

a the distinction in pronunciation between words such as *what* and *Watt* is disappearing

b *hopefully* may be used instead of *I hope, we hope, it is to be hoped*

199

c new words and expressions are constantly entering the language, e.g. *drop-out, alternative society, culture shock.*

Language change should not be confused with LANGUAGE SHIFT.

see also COMPARATIVE HISTORICAL LINGUISTICS, DIACHRONIC LINGUISTICS, NEOLOGISM

language comprehension /'læŋgwɪdʒ ˌkɒmprɪ'henʃən||ˌkɑːm-/ *n*

the processes involved in understanding the meaning of written or spoken language. Theories of language comprehension are an important aspect of psycholinguistics, cognitive psychology, and second language acquisition. Among the different processes involved are:

a **Perceptual processing**: attention is focussed on the oral or written text and parts of it are retained in SHORT TERM MEMORY. Some initial analysis of the text may begin and attention is focussed on CUES which will help identify constituents or meaningful sections of the text. These cues may be pauses and acoustic emphasis in spoken text or punctuation or paragraph separation in written text.

b **Parsing**: Words are identified and matched with representations in long term memory (see MEMORY) creating basic units of meaning called PROPOSITIONS. Knowledge of the grammatical structure of the target language is used to help identify constituents and arrive at propositions.

c **Utilization or elaboration**: propositions are related to other information and concepts in long term memory and connections are formed with existing concepts and schema (see SCHEME).

see also LANGUAGE PRODUCTION, INFORMATION PROCESSING, LISTENING COMPREHENSION
Further reading Clark and Clark 1977; Anderson 1985

language contact /'læŋgwɪdʒ 'kɒntækt||'kɑːn-/ *n*

contact between different languages, especially when at least one of the languages is influenced by the contact. This influence takes place typically when the languages are spoken in the same or adjoining regions and when there is a high degree of communication between the people speaking them. The influence may affect PHONETICS, SYNTAX, SEMANTICS, or communicative strategies such as ADDRESS FORMS and greetings.

Language contact occurs or has occurred in areas of considerable immigration such as the USA, Latin America, Australia and parts of Africa, as well as in language border areas such as parts of India.

see also **contact language** under PIDGIN
Further reading Fishman 1971

language distance /'læŋgwɪdʒ 'dɪstəns/ *n*

the relative degree of similarity between two languages. Some languages have similar linguistic features and are said to be "close". Others have very different linguistic feautures and are said to "distant". For example, two languages may have similar word order rules and similar rules for certain syntactic or phonological structures. There is said to be a greater degree of linguistic distance between English and French, for example, than between French and Spanish. Language distance is thought to be one factor which influences the ease or difficulty with which learners acquire new languages.

Further reading Odlin 1989

language dominance /ˈlæŋgwɪdʒ ˈdɒmɪnəns‖ˈdɑ:-/ *n*

greater ability in, or greater importance of, one language than another.

1 For an individual, this means that a person who speaks more than one language or dialect considers that he or she knows one of the languages better than the other(s) and/or uses it more frequently and with greater ease. The **dominant language** may be his or her NATIVE LANGUAGE or may have been acquired later in life at school or a place of employment.

2 For a country or region where more than one language or dialect is used, this means that one of them is more important than the other(s). A language may become the dominant language because it has more prestige (higher STATUS) in the country, is favoured by the government, and/or has the largest number of speakers.

language ego /ˈlæŋgwɪdʒ ˈiːgəu, ˈegəu/ *n*

(in SECOND LANGUAGE or FOREIGN LANGUAGE learning) the relation between people's feelings of personal identity, individual uniqueness, and value (i.e. their ego) and aspects of their FIRST LANGUAGE.

Guiora and others have suggested that a person's self-identity develops as he or she is learning the first language, that some aspects of language, especially pronunciation, may be closely linked to one's ego, and that this may hinder some aspects of second or foreign language learning.

Further reading Guiora et al 1972

language enrichment /ˈlæŋgwɪdʒ ɪnˈrɪtʃmənt/ *n*

a term sometimes used to describe language teaching as part of a programme of COMPENSATORY INSTRUCTION.

language experience approach /ˈlæŋgwɪdʒ ɪkˈspɪəriəns əˌprəutʃ/ *n*

an approach used in the teaching of reading to young children which draws on the experiences children have in their personal lives as well as on the language skills and vocabulary they have developed outside the classroom. In this approach, children may recount stories and experiences orally to the teacher, who writes words on charts or other visual devices and uses them as a basis for teaching reading.

language functions /ˈlæŋgwɪdʒ ˈfʌŋkʃənz/ *n*

another term for FUNCTIONS OF LANGUAGE[1,2]

language laboratory /ˈlæŋgwɪdʒ ləˌbɒrətri‖ˌlæbrətɔːri/ *n*
also **language lab** /ˈlæŋgwɪdʒ ˌlæb/

a room that contains desks or individual booths with tape or cassette recorders and a control booth for teacher or observer and which is used for language teaching. The recorders usually have recording, listening, and playback facilities; students can practise recorded exercises and follow language programmes either individually or in groups, and the teacher can listen to each student's performance through earphones. Language laboratories are associated particularly with the AUDIO-LINGUAL METHOD.

Further reading Dakin 1973

language learning /'læŋgwɪdʒ 'lɜːnɪŋ||'lɜːr-/ n

see FIRST LANGUAGE ACQUISITION, LANGUAGE ACQUISITION, SECOND LANGUAGE ACQUISITION

language loss /'læŋgwɪdʒ 'lɒs||'lɔːs/ n

the process of losing one's ability to speak, write or understand a particular language or dialect.

This often occurs through lack of opportunity to use it. Language loss is frequently experienced by immigrants to a country where their mother tongue is not spoken or not valued (see LANGUAGE MAINTENANCE, LANGUAGE ATTRITION). Language loss may also be pathological, as a result of accident, disease or old age (see APHASIA).

language loyalty /'læŋgwɪdʒ 'lɔɪəlti/ n

retention of a language by its speakers, who are usually in a minority in a country where another language is the dominant language (see LANGUAGE DOMINANCE).

For example, some immigrant groups in the USA, such as Estonians, have shown a high degree of language loyalty.

language maintenance /'læŋgwɪdʒ 'meɪntənəns/ n

the degree to which an individual or group continues to use their language, particularly in a BILINGUAL or MULTILINGUAL area or among immigrant groups. Many factors affect language maintenance, for example:

a whether or not the language is an official language (see NATIONAL LANGUAGE)
b whether or not it is used in the media, for religious purposes, in education
c how many speakers of the language live in the same area. In some places where the use of certain languages has greatly decreased there have been attempts at revival, e.g. of Welsh in Wales and Gaelic in parts of Scotland.

see also DIGLOSSIA, LANGUAGE SHIFT, LANGUAGE REVITALIZATION PROGRAMME

Further reading Fasold 1984

language minority group /'læŋgwɪdʒ maɪ'nɒrɪ̩ti ˌgruːp||mɪ̩'nɔː-, mɪ̩'nɑː-/ n

also **minority language group**

a group of people in a country or community who have a language other than the major or dominant language of the country or community.

see also COMMUNITY LANGUAGE, MAJORITY LANGUAGE

language mixing /ˈlæŋgwɪdʒ ˈmɪksɪŋ/ n

see CODE MIXING

language norm /ˈlæŋgwɪdʒ ˈnɔːm‖ˈnɔːrm/ n

see NORM

language pathology /ˈlæŋgwɪdʒ pəˈθɒlədʒi‖-ˈθɑː-/ n

see SPEECH PATHOLOGY

language pedagogy /ˈlæŋgwɪdʒ ˈpedəgɒdʒi‖-gəʊ-/ n

a general term sometimes used to describe the teaching of a language as a FIRST LANGUAGE, a SECOND LANGUAGE or a FOREIGN LANGUAGE.

language planning /ˈlæŋgwɪdʒ ˈplænɪŋ/ n

planning, usually by a government or government agency, concerning choice of national or official language(s), ways of spreading the use of a language, spelling reforms, the addition of new words to the language, and other language problems. Through language planning, an official **language policy** is established and/or implemented. For example, in Indonesia, Malay was chosen as the national language and was given the name Bahasa Indonesia (Indonesian language). It became the main language of education. There were several spelling reforms and a national planning agency was established to deal with problems such as the development of scientific terms.

see also LANGUAGE TREATMENT, SOCIOLINGUISTICS, SOCIOLOGY OF LANGUAGE
Further reading Fasold 1984

language policy /ˈlæŋgwɪdʒ ˈpɒlˌsi‖ˈpɑː-/ n

see LANGUAGE PLANNING

language production /ˈlæŋgwɪdʒ prəˈdʌkʃən/ n

the processes involved in creating and expressing meaning through language. Numerous theories in psycholinguistics and cognitive psychology attempt to account for the different processes involved in language production. Among the different stages involved are:
Construction: the speaker or writer selects communicative goals, and creates PROPOSITIONS which express intended meanings.
Transformation or articulation: meanings are encoded in linguistic form according to the grammar of the target language.
Execution: the message is expressed in audible or visible form through speech or writing.

An important issue in theories of language production is whether the processes involved are analogous to those involved in language comprehension (though in reverse order).

see also LANGUAGE COMPREHENSION
Further reading Anderson 1985; Littlewood 1984; Ellis 1986

language proficiency /ˈlæŋgwɪdʒ prəˈfɪʃənsi/ *n*

a person's skill in using a language for a specific purpose. Whereas LANGUAGE ACHIEVEMENT describes language ability as a result of learning, proficiency refers to the degree of skill with which a person can use a language, such as how well a person can read, write, speak, or understand language. Proficiency may be measured through the use of a PROFICIENCY TEST.

language programme design /ˈlæŋgwɪdʒ ˈprəʊgræm dɪˈzaɪn/ *n*

another term for COURSE DESIGN

language revitalization programme /ˈlæŋgwɪdʒ riː,vaɪtəl-aɪˈzeɪʃən ,prəʊgræm‖-tələ-/ *n*

a programme intended to help to revive or strengthen a language which is in danger of dying out, such as programmes for the teaching of Irish in Ireland or several American Indian languages.

languages for special purpose /ˈlæŋgwɪdʒ̩z fəʳ ˈspeʃəl ˈpɜːpəs̩z‖ ˈpɜːr-/ *n*

also **languages for specific purposes** /ˈlæŋgwɪdʒ̩z fəʳ spḷˈsɪfɪk ˈpɜːpəs̩z‖ˈpɜːr-/, **LSP**

second or foreign languages used for particular and restricted types of communication (e.g. for medical reports, scientific writing, air-traffic control) and which contain lexical, grammatical, and other linguistic features which are different from ordinary language (see REGISTER). In language teaching, decisions must be made as to whether a learner or group of learners requires a language for general purposes or for special purposes.

see also ENGLISH FOR SPECIAL PURPOSES
Further reading Sager, Dungworth, & McDonald 1980

language shift /ˈlæŋgwɪdʒ ˈʃɪft/ *n*

a change ('shift') from the use of one language to the use of another language. This often occurs when people migrate to another country where the main language is different, as in the case of immigrants to the USA and Australia from non-English-speaking countries. Language shift may be actively encouraged by official government policy, for example by restricting the number of languages used as media of instruction. It may also occur because another language, usually the main language of the region, is needed for employment opportunities and wider communication. Language shift should not be confused with LANGUAGE CHANGE.

see also LANGUAGE PLANNING, MEDIUM OF INSTRUCTION, HOME-SCHOOL LANGUAGE SWITCH

Further reading Fasold 1984

language skills /'læŋgwɪdʒ ˌskɪlz/ *n*
also skills

(in language teaching) the mode or manner in which language is used. Listening, speaking, reading, and writing are generally called the four language skills. Sometimes speaking and writing are called the active/**productive skills** and reading and listening, the passive/**receptive skills**. Often the skills are divided into subskills, such as discriminating sounds in connected speech, or understanding relations within a sentence.

see also MICRO-SKILLS

Further reading Munby 1978

language survey /'læŋgwɪdʒ 'sɜːveɪ‖'sɜːr-/ *n*

investigation of language use in a country or region. Such a survey may be carried out to determine, for example:

a which languages are spoken in a particular region
b for what purposes these languages are used
c what proficiency people of different age-groups have in these languages.

A language survey may also be conducted in order to find out about the USAGE[1] of a language. For example, The Survey of English Usage at University College London has been accumulating evidence about the way Standard British English (see STANDARD VARIETY) is used in many different situations.

see also LANGUAGE PLANNING

language transfer /'læŋgwɪdʒ 'trænsfɜːʳ/ *n*

the effect of one language on the learning of another. Two types of language transfer may occur. **Negative transfer**, also known as **interference**, is the use of a native-language pattern or rule which leads to an ERROR or inappropriate form in the TARGET LANGUAGE[1]. For example, a French learner of English may produce the incorrect sentence *I am here since Monday* instead of *I have been here since Monday*, because of the transfer of the French pattern *Je suis ici depuis lundi* ("I am here since Monday"). **Positive transfer** is transfer which makes learning easier, and may occur when both the native language and the target language have the same form. For example, both French and English have the word *table*, which can have the same meaning in both languages.

see also COMMUNICATIVE INTERFERENCE, ERROR ANALYSIS, INTER-LANGUAGE

Further reading James 1980; Brown 1980; Odlin 1989

language treatment /'læŋgwɪdʒ 'triːtmənt/ *n*
any kind of action which people take about language problems. This includes LANGUAGE PLANNING by governments and government-appointed agencies, but also includes such things as: language requirements for employment in a private company, company policy on style in business letters, trade-name spelling, publishers' style sheets, and the treatment of language in dictionaries and usage guides (see USAGE²).

language typology /'læŋgwɪdʒ taɪ'pɒlədʒi‖-'pɑː-/ *n*
see TYPOLOGY

language universal /'læŋgwɪdʒ juːn̩'vɜːsəl‖-ɜːr-/ *n*
(in general linguistic use) a language pattern or phenomenon which occurs in all known languages.
For example, it has been suggested that:
a if a language has **dual** number for referring to just two of something, it also has PLURAL number (for referring to more than two). This type of universal is sometimes called an **implicational universal**.
b there is a high probability that the word referring to the female parent will start with a NASAL consonant, e.g. /m/ in English *mother*, in German *Mutter*, in Swahili *mama*, in Chinese (Mandarin) *mǔqin*.
see also BIOPROGRAM, UNIVERSAL GRAMMAR
Further reading Greenberg 1966; Fromkin & Rodman 1983

language variation /'læŋgwɪdʒ ˌveərɪ'eɪʃən/ *n*
see VARIATION

langue /lɒŋg, lɑːŋg‖lɑːŋg/ *n*
the French word for "language". The term was used by the linguist Saussure to mean the system of a language, that is the arrangement of sounds and words which speakers of a language have a shared knowledge of or, as Saussure said, "agree to use". Langue is the "ideal" form of a language. Saussure called the actual use of language by people in speech or writing "parole".
Saussure's distinction between "langue" and "parole" is similar to Chomsky's distiction between COMPETENCE and PERFORMANCE. But whereas for Saussure the repository of "langue" is the SPEECH COMMUNITY, for Chomsky the repository of "competence" is the "ideal speaker/hearer". So Saussure's distinction is basically sociolinguistic (see SOCIOLINGUISTICS) whereas Chomsky's is basically psycholinguistic (see PSYCHOLINGUISTICS).
see also USAGE¹
Further reading Saussure 1966

larynx /'lærɪŋks/ *n* **laryngeal** /ˌlærən'dʒɪəl, lə'rɪndʒəl/ *adj*
a casing of cartilage and muscles in the upper part of the windpipe (in the throat) which contains the VOCAL CORDS.

see also PLACE OF ARTICULATION
Further reading Gimson 1989

lateral /'lætərəl/ *n*
a speech sound (a CONSONANT) which is produced by partially blocking the airstream from the lungs, usually by the tongue, but letting it escape at one or both sides of the blockage.
For example, in English the /l/ in /laɪt/ *light* is a lateral.

see also MANNER OF ARTICULATION, PLACE OF ARTICULATION
Further reading Gimson 1989

lateralization /ˌlætərəlaɪˈzeɪʃən‖-lə-/ *n*
see BRAIN

Latin alphabet /ˌlætɪn ˈælfəbet‖ˈlætn/ *n*
another term for ROMAN ALPHABET

lax /læks/ *adj*
describes a speech sound (especially a VOWEL) which is produced with comparatively little movement of any part or parts of the VOCAL TRACT, for example the tongue. The vowels /ɪ/ in English *hit* and /ʊ/ in English *put* are lax vowels, as there is comparatively little movement of the tongue when these two vowels are articulated. In GENERATIVE PHONOLOGY, lax sounds are sometimes marked [-tense] to distinguish them from TENSE[2] sounds.
Further reading Hyman 1975

learner training /'lɜːnəʳ 'treɪnɪŋ‖-ɜːr-/ *n*
see STRATEGY TRAINING

learning /'lɜːnɪŋ‖'lɜːr-/ *n*
see FIRST LANGUAGE ACQUISITION, LANGUAGE ACQUISITION, SECOND LANGUAGE ACQUISITION

learning by deduction /'lɜːnɪŋ baɪ dɪ'dʌkʃən‖'lɜːr-/ *n*
another term for DEDUCTIVE LEARNING

learning by induction /'lɜːnɪŋ baɪ ɪn'dʌkʃən‖'lɜːr-/ *n*
another term for **inductive learning**
see DEDUCTIVE LEARNING

learning curve /'lɜːnɪŋ ˌkɜːv‖'lɜːnɪŋ ˌkɜːrv/ *n*
also **acquisition curve**
a graphic representation of a learner's progress in learning new material over time. The following graph shows the development of negation in Spanish-speaking learner of English. It shows the proportion of the negating devices *no* + v (e.g. *I no want*) and *don't* + *v* (e.g. *I don't want*) over time as found in taped samples taken over 20 different time periods.

learning disability

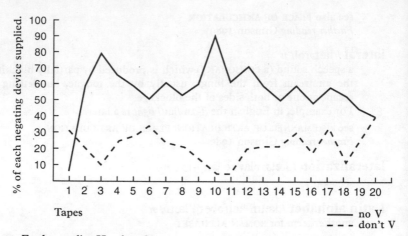

Tapes

— no V
- - - don't V

Further reading Hatch 1983

learning disability /'lɜːnɪŋ dɪsəˌbɪlɪ̩ti‖-ɜːr-/ *n*

a learning difficulty which affects a particular aspect of learning on the part of a learner whose other learning abilities are considered normal. For example, specific difficulties in learning to read (DYSLEXIA) or to write (**dysgraphia**).

learning log /'lɜːnɪŋ ˌlɒg‖-ɜːr- ˌlɔːg, ˌlɑːg/ *n*
also **journal, learning journal**

the use of a notebook or book in which students write about experiences both in and out of school or record responses and reactions to learning and to learning activities. Learning logs provide students with an opportunity to reflect on learning, and are usually shared with the teacher on a regular basis but not graded. In this way, the teacher may be able to find out how the student is progressing and the students gain additional opportunities to practice writing. In writing classes, learning logs may be used as a prewriting activity (see COMPOSING PROCESSES) and also as a way of encouraging students to develop fluency in writing through writing regularly on topics of their own choice. When learning logs are used as a way of establishing a dialogue between teacher and student (through comments, questions and reactions), they are sometimes referred to as **dialogue journals** or diaries.

learning plateau /'lɜːnɪŋ ˌplætəʊ‖-ɜːr- plæˌtəʊ/ *n*
a temporary period that sometimes occurs in learning, when after making initial progress a learner makes little or no further progress (as seen by a flat part on a LEARNING CURVE). After a period of time the learning plateau is followed by further learning. Learning plateaus are often observed in second and foreign language learning.

learning strategy /'lɜːnɪŋ ˌstrætɪ̩dʒi‖'lɜːr-/ *n*
1 (in language learning) a way in which a learner attempts to work out the meanings and uses of words, grammatical rules, and other aspects

of a language, for example by the use of GENERALIZATION and INFERENCING.

In FIRST LANGUAGE learning, a child may not pay attention to grammatical words in a sentence, but in trying to understand a sentence may use the learning strategy that the first mentioned noun in a sentence refers to the person or thing performing an action. The child may then think that the sentence *The boy was chased by the dog* means the same thing as *The boy chased the dog.*

see also COMMUNICATION STRATEGY, COGNITIVE STYLE, HEURISTIC

Further reading Brown 1973

2 (in second language learning, studying, reading etc.) intentional behaviour and thoughts that learners make use of during learning in order to better help them understand, learn or remember new information. These may include focusing on certain aspects of new information, analyzing and organizing information during learning to increase comprehension, evaluating learning when it is completed to see if further action is needed. Learning strategies may be applied to simple tasks such as learning a list of new words, or more complex tasks involving language comprehension and production. The effectiveness of second language learning is thought to be improved by teaching learners more effective learning strategies (see STRATEGY TRAINING.)

Further reading O'Malley & Chamot 1989; Wenden & Rubin 1987

learning style /ˈlɜːnɪŋ ˈstaɪl‖ˈlɜːr-/ n
another term for COGNITIVE STYLE

left branching direction /ˈleft ˈbrɑːntʃɪŋ dɨˌrekʃən, daɪ-‖ˈbræn-/ n
see BRANCHING DIRECTION

left dislocation /ˈleft dɪsləˈkeɪʃən/ n
the occurrence of a linguistic form to the left of its normal position in a sentence. For example in the sentence:
   Madge made the pizza.
pizza is in its normal object position in the sentence. But in the less common sentence:
   The pizza, Madge made it.
the pizza is now a left dislocation. Left dislocation is a WORD ORDER device which is often used to signal a new topic (TOPIC[2]) or to give special emphasis.

With **right dislocation**, a linguistic form appears to the right of its normal position. For example:
   She made the pizza, Madge did.

Further reading Odlin 1989

left-ear advantage /ˈleft ɪər ədˈvɑːntɪdʒ‖-ˈvæn-/ n
see DICHOTIC LISTENING

left hemisphere /ˈleft ˈhemɨsfɪər/ n
see BRAIN

lenis /'liːnᵻs/ *adj*

see FORTIS

LES /ˌel iː 'es/ *n*

an abbreviation for LIMITED ENGLISH SPEAKER

lesson plan /'lesən ˌplæn/ *n*

a description or outline of (a) the OBJECTIVES a teacher has set for a lesson (b) the activities and procedures the teacher will use to achieve them and the order to be followed, and (c) the materials and resources which will be used.

level[1] /'levəl/ *n*

a layer in a linguistic system, e.g. word level, phrase level. Often, these levels are considered to form a scale or hierarchy from lower levels containing the smaller linguistic units to higher levels containing larger linguistic units, e.g. MORPHEME level – WORD level – PHRASE level – CLAUSE level, etc.

It is also sometimes said that the items on each level consist of items on the next lower level: clauses consist of phrases, phrases of words, words of morphemes, etc.

see also RANK, TAGMENICS

level[2] *n*

see PITCH LEVEL

lexeme /'leksiːm/ *n*
also **lexical item**

the smallest unit in the meaning system of a language that can be distinguished from other similar units. A lexeme is an abstract unit. It can occur in many different forms in actual spoken or written sentences, and is regarded as the same lexeme even when inflected (see INFLECTION).

For example, in English, all inflected forms such as *give, gives, given, giving, gave* would belong to the one lexeme *give*.

Similarly, such expressions as *bury the hatchet, hammer and tongs, give up,* and *white paper* would each be considered a single lexeme. In a dictionary, each lexeme merits a separate entry or sub-entry.

Further reading Lyons 1981

lexical access /'leksɪkəl 'ækses/ *n*

(in speech production) the retrieval of words from the speaker's lexicon (LEXICON[4]). According to psycholinguistic models of speech production, vocabulary is stored in some form in the speaker's lexicon and must be accessed in order to be used during the process of communication. Researchers in BILINGUALISM have investigated whether the bilingual person stores words in different lexicons for each language. Speed of access to the lexicon may be faster in one language than the other.

Further reading Romaine 1989

lexical ambiguity /'leksɪkəl ˌæmbɪ'gjuːɪti/ *n*

SEE AMBIGUOUS

lexical category /'leksɪkəl 'kætɪgəri||-gɔːri/ *n*

the four main lexical categories are *n* (noun), *v* (verb), *a* (adjective) and *p* (preposition). Entries in a lexicon (see LEXICON[2]) or dictionary usually show, among other information, the lexical category of a particular word, e.g.

lexical   *a*

lexicon   *n*

see also LEXICAL ENTRY

lexical density /'leksɪkəl 'densɪti/ *n*
also **Type-Token Ratio**

a measure of the ratio of different words to the total number of words in a text, sometimes used as a measure of the difficulty of a passage or text. Lexical density is normally expressed as a percentage and is calculated by the formula:

$$\text{Lexical density} = \frac{\text{number of separate words}}{\text{total number of words in the text}} \times 100$$

For example, the lexical density of this definition is:

$$\frac{29 \text{ separate words}}{57 \text{ total words}} \times 100 = 50.88$$

see also TYPE
Further reading Ure 1971

lexical entry /'leksɪkəl 'entri/ *n*

a term widely used in TRANSFORMATIONAL GENERATIVE GRAMMAR for a word or phrase listed in the lexicon (see LEXICON[3]) of the grammar.

The information given in a lexical entry usually includes:

a its pronunciation (see DISTINCTIVE FEATURE)

b its meaning, which may be given in a formalized way, e.g. ⟨+human⟩ ⟨+male⟩ (see SEMANTIC FEATURES)

c its LEXICAL CATEGORY, e.g. *n*(oun), *v*(erb), *a*(djective)

d other linguistic items it may co-occur with in a sentence, e.g. whether or not a verb can be followed by an object (see OBJECT[1])

In later models of TG Grammar, a lexical entry would also contain semantic roles such as *agent, patient and goal* which can be assigned to noun phrases in the sentence (see θ-THEORY).

see also PROJECTION PRINCIPLE
Further reading Leech 1981; Cook 1988

lexical field /'leksɪkəl 'fiːld/ *n*
also **semantic field**

the organization of related words and expressions (see LEXEME) into a system which shows their relationship to one another.

For example, kinship terms such as *father, mother, brother, sister, uncle, aunt* belong to a lexical field whose relevant features include generation, sex, membership of the father's or mother's side of the family, etc.

The absence of a word in a particular place in a lexical field of a language is called a **lexical gap**.

For example, in English there is no singular noun that covers both *cow* and *bull* as *horse* covers *stallion* and *mare*.

Further reading Lyons 1977

lexical gap /'leksɪkəl 'gæp/ *n*
see LEXICAL FIELD

lexical item /'leksɪkəl 'aɪtəm/ *n*
another term for LEXEME

lexical meaning /'leksɪkəl 'miːnɪŋ/ *n*
see CONTENT WORD

lexical verb /'leksɪkəl 'vɜːb||'vɜːrb/ *n*
see AUXILIARY VERB

lexical word /'leksɪkəl 'wɜːd||'wɜːrd/ *n*
see CONTENT WORD

lexicogrammar /ˌleksɪkəʊˈgræməʳ/ *n*
see SYSTEMIC LINGUISTICS

lexicography /ˌleksɪˈkɒɡrəfi||-ˈkɑː-/ *n* **lexicographic(al)**
/ˌleksɪkəˈgræfɪkəl◄/ *adj* **lexicographer** /ˌleksɪˈkɒɡrəfəʳ||-ˈkɑː-/ *n*
the compiling of dictionaries.
see also LEXICOLOGY

lexicology /ˌleksɪˈkɒlədʒi||-ˈkɑː-/ *n* **lexicological** /ˌleksɪkəˈlɒdʒɪkəl◄||
-ˈlɑː-/ *adj* **lexicologist** /ˌleksɪˈkɒlədʒɪst||-ˈkɑː-/ *n*
the study of the vocabulary items (LEXEMES) of a language, including their meanings and relations (see LEXICAL FIELD), and changes in their form and meaning through time. The discoveries of lexicologists may be of use to lexicographers.
see also ETYMOLOGY, LEXICOGRAPHY

lexicon[1] /'leksɪkən/ *n*
the set of all the words and idioms of any language (see LEXEME).
see also LEXICOGRAPHY, LEXICOLOGY

lexicon[2] *n*
a dictionary, usually of an ancient language such as Latin and Greek.

lexicon[3] *n*
the words and phrases listed in the BASE COMPONENT of a TRANS-FORMATIONAL GENERATIVE GRAMMAR and information about them.
see also LEXICAL ENTRY

lexicon[4] *n*
a mental system which contains all the information a person knows

about words. According to psycholinguists, people's knowledge of a word includes

a knowing how a word is pronounced

b the grammatical patterns with which a word is used

c the meaning or meanings of the word.

The total set of words a speaker knows forms his or her mental lexicon. The content of the mental lexicon and how a mental lexicon is developed are studied in psycholinguistics and language acquisition.

see also LEXICAL ACCESS

Further reading Clark & Clark 1977

lexis /'leksɨs/ *n* **lexical** /'leksɪkəl/ *adj*

the vocabulary of a language in contrast to its grammar (SYNTAX).

see also LEXEME

liaison /li'eɪzən||'lɪəzɑːn, li'eɪ-/ *n*

the linking of words in speech, in particular when the second word begins with a vowel.

For example, in English, the phrase *an egg* is often pronounced [ə'neg] with no noticeable break between the two words.

LF component /'el 'ef kəm,pəʊnənt/

see D-STRUCTURE

Likert Scale /'laɪkət ,skeɪl||-ərt/ *n*

see ATTITUDE SCALE

limited English proficiency /'lɪmɨtɨd 'ɪŋglɪʃ prə'fɪʃənsi/ *n*

see LIMITED ENGLISH SPEAKER

limited English speaker /'lɪmɨtɨd 'ɪŋglɪʃ 'spiːkəʳ/ *n*
also **LES**

(in BILINGUAL EDUCATION or an ENGLISH AS A SECOND LANGUAGE PROGRAMME) a person who has some proficiency in English but not enough to enable him or her to take part fully and successfully in a class where English is the only MEDIUM OF INSTRUCTION.

Such a person may be said to have **limited English proficiency**.

limited English proficient /'lɪmɨtɨd 'ɪŋglɪʃ prə'fɪʃənt/ *n*
also **LEP**

used to describe a MINORITY STUDENT in an English speaking country, whose English language proficiency is not at the level of native speakers of English. Special instruction in English is therefore needed to prepare the student to enter a regular school programme.

see also MAINSTREAMING, SHELTERED ENGLISH, SUBMERSION EDUCATION

linear programme /'lɪniəʳ 'prəʊgræm/ *n*

see PROGRAMMED LEARNING

linear syllabus /ˈlɪniəˠ ˈsɪləbəs/ n

see SPIRAL APPROACH

lingua franca /ˈlɪŋgwə ˈfræŋkə/ n

a language that is used for communication between different groups of people, each speaking a different language. The lingua franca could be an internationally used language of communication (e.g. English), it could be the NATIVE LANGUAGE of one of the groups, or it could be a language which is not spoken natively by any of the groups but has a simplified sentence structure and vocabulary and is often a mixture of two or more languages (see PIDGIN). The term *lingua franca* (Italian for "Frankish tongue") originated in the Mediterranean region in the Middle Ages among crusaders and traders of different language backgrounds.

The term **auxiliary language** is sometimes used as a synonym for lingua franca.

Further reading Wardhaugh 1986

linguistically disadvantaged /lɪŋˈgwɪstɪkli ˌdɪsədˈvɑːntɪdʒd‖-ˈvæn-/ adj

a term sometimes used to refer to a person who has an insufficient command of the dominant language in a country. This term is not favoured by linguists since it suggests the person's home language is not useful or is unimportant.

see also DEFICIT HYPOTHESIS

linguistic analysis /lɪŋˈgwɪstɪk əˈnælɪsɪs/ n

investigation into the structure and functions of a particular language or language variety (see LANGUAGE²) or of language in general as a system of human communication (see LANGUAGE¹).

linguistic insecurity /lɪŋˈgwɪstɪk ɪnsɪˈkjʊərɪti/ n

a feeling of insecurity experienced by speakers or writers about some aspect of their language use or about the variety of language they speak. This may result, for instance, in MODIFIED SPEECH, when speakers attempt to alter their way of speaking in order to sound more like the speakers of a prestige variety.

see also SOCIOLECT

linguistic method /lɪŋˈgwɪstɪk ˈmeθəd/ n

a term used to refer to several methods of teaching first-language reading which claim to be based on principles of linguistics, and in particular to methods which reflect the views of two American linguists, Leonard Bloomfield and Charles Fries.

They argued that since the written language is based on the spoken language, the relationship between speech and written language should be emphasized in the teaching of reading. This led to reading materials which made use of words which had a regular sound-spelling correspondence and in which there was a systematic introduction to regular and irregular spelling patterns. In recent years linguists have not supported any particular method for the teaching of reading.

Further reading Wardhaugh 1969

linguistic relativity /lɪŋ'gwɪstɪk ˌrelə'tɪvɪ̧ti/ *n*

a belief which was held by some scholars that the way people view the world is determined wholly or partly by the structure of their NATIVE LANGUAGE. As this hypothesis was strongly put forward by the American anthropological linguists Sapir and Whorf, it has often been called the **Sapir-Whorf hypothesis** or **Whorfian hypothesis**.

see also ANTHROPOLOGICAL LINGUISTICS

linguistics /lɪŋ'gwɪstɪks/ *n* linguist /'lɪŋgwɪst/ *n* linguistic /lɪŋ'gwɪstɪk/ *adj*

the study of language as a system of human communication. Although studies of language phenomena have been carried out for centuries, it is only fairly recently that linguistics has been accepted as an independent discipline. Linguistics now covers a wide field with different approaches and different areas of investigation, for example sound systems (PHONETICS, PHONOLOGY), sentence structure (SYNTAX), and meaning systems (SEMANTICS, PRAGMATICS, FUNCTIONS OF LANGUAGE).

In recent years, new branches of linguistics have developed in combination with other disciplines, e.g. ANTHROPOLOGICAL LINGUISTICS, PSYCHOLINGUISTICS, SOCIOLINGUISTICS.

see also APPLIED LINGUISTICS, COMPARATIVE LINGUISTICS, COMPUTATIONAL LINGUISTICS, CONTRASTIVE ANALYSIS, DIACHRONIC LINGUISTICS, TRANSFORMATIONAL GENERATIVE GRAMMAR, STRUCTURAL LINGUISTICS, SYSTEMIC LINGUISTICS, TAGMEMICS, TEXT LINGUISTICS

linguistic units /lɪŋ'gwɪstɪk 'juːnɪ̧ts/ *n*

parts of a language system. Linguistic units can be the distinctive sounds of a language (PHONEMES), words, phrases, or sentences, or they can be larger units such as the UTTERANCES in a conversation.

see also CHUNKING, DISCOURSE, DISCOURSE ANALYSIS

linking verb /'lɪŋkɪŋ ˌvɜːrb||ˌvɜːrb/ *n*

another term for COPULA

lipreading /'lɪpˌriːdɪŋ/ *n* lipread /'lɪpˌriːd/ *v* also **speech reading**

a method used by deaf people and others to identify what a speaker is saying by studying the movements of the lips and face muscles.

liquid /'lɪkwɪ̧d/ *n, adj*

(used particularly by American linguists) a speech sound (a CONSONANT) such as /l/ in /laɪt/ *light* and /r/ in /red/ *red*. Liquids are FRICTIONLESS CONTINUANTS but not NASALS.

see also LATERAL

Further reading Hyman 1975

listening comprehension /ˈlɪsənɪŋ ˌkɒmprɪˈhenʃən‖ˌkɑːm-/ *n*
the process of understanding speech in a second or foreign language. Similar processes are referred to in PSYCHOLINGUISTICS as speech recognition or **speech perception** (see PERCEPTION). The study of listening comprehension processes in second language learning focusses on the role of individual linguistic units (e.g. PHONEMES, WORDS, grammatical structures) as well as the role of the listener's expectations, the situation and context, background knowledge and the topic. It therefore includes both TOP DOWN PROCESSING and **bottom up processing.** While traditional approaches to language teaching tended to underemphasize the importance of teaching listening comprehension, more recent approaches emphasize the role of listening in building up language competence and suggest that more attention should be paid to teaching listening in the initial stages of second or foreign language learning.
see also COMPREHENSION APPROACH, NATURAL APPROACH
Further reading Brown and Yule 1983; Rost 1990

literacy /ˈlɪtərəsi/ *n* **literate** /ˈlɪtərɪt/ *adj*
the ability to read and write in a language. The inability to read or write is known as **illiteracy.**
Functional literacy refers to the ability to use reading and writing skills sufficiently well for the purposes and activities which normally require literacy in adult life or in a person's social position. An inability to do this is known as **functional illiteracy.** People who are functionally illiterate are illiterate for all practical purposes. They may be able to write their names and read simple signs, but they can do little else. A person who is able to read and write in two languages is sometimes called (a) **biliterate.**
Further reading Hillerich 1978

literal comprehension /ˈlɪtərəl ˌkɒmprɪˈhenʃən‖ˌkɑːm-/ *n*
see READING

literal translation /ˈlɪtərəl trænsˈleɪʃən, trænz-/ *n*
see TRANSLATION

literary culture /ˈlɪtərəri ˈkʌltʃəʳ‖ˈlɪtəreri/ *n*
see ORAL CULTURE

loan blend /ˈləʊn ˌblend/ *n*
a type of BORROWING in which one part of a word is borrowed from a second language and the other part belongs to the speaker's native language. For example, in the German spoken by some people in Australia, *gumbaum* means gumtree.

loan translation /ˈləʊn trænsˈleɪʃən, trænz-/ *n*
also **calque**
a type of BORROWING, in which each morpheme or word is translated into the equivalent morpheme or word in another language.

For example, the English word *almighty* is a loan translation from the Latin *omnipotens*:

> omni   +   potens
> all   mighty = *almighty*

A loan translation may be a word, a phrase, or even a short sentence, e.g. the English *beer garden* and *academic freedom* are loan translations of the German *Biergarten* and *akademische Freiheit*.

loan word /ˈləʊn ˌwɜːd||ˌwɜːrd/ *n*

see BORROWING

local error /ˈləʊkəl ˈerəʳ/ *n*

see GLOBAL ERROR

locative case /ˈlɒkətɪv ˌkeɪs||ˈlɑː-/ *n*

(In CASE GRAMMAR) the noun or noun phrase which refers to the location of the action of the verb is in the locative case.
For example, in the sentence:
> *Irene put the magazines on the table.*

the table is in the locative case.

Further reading Fillmore 1968

locutionary act /ləʊˈkjuːʃənəri ˈækt||-neri/ *n*

A distinction is made by Austin in the theory of SPEECH ACTS between three different types of act involved in or caused by the utterance of a sentence.
A locutionary act is the saying of something which is meaningful and can be understood.
For example, saying the sentence *Shoot the snake* is a locutionary act if hearers understand the words *shoot, the, snake* and can identify the particular snake referred to. An **illocutionary act** is using a sentence to perform a function. For example *Shoot the snake* may be intended as an order or a piece of advice.
A **perlocutionary act** is the results or effects that are produced by means of saying something. For example, shooting the snake would be a perlocutionary act.
Austin's three-part distinction is less frequently used than a two-part distinction between the propositional content of a sentence (the PRO-POSITION(S) which a sentence express or implies) and the **illocutionary force** or intended effects of speech acts (their function as requests, commands, orders etc.).

Further reading Austin 1962; Searle 1981

locutionary meaning /ləʊˈkjuːʃənəri ˈmiːnɪŋ||-neri/ *n*

see SPEECH ACT

logical form component /ˈlɒdʒɪkəl ˈfɔːm kəmˈpəʊnənt||ˈlɑː- ˈfɔːrm/ *n*

see D-STRUCTURE

logical subject /'lɒdʒɪkəl 'sʌbdʒɪkt||'lɑː-/ *n*

a NOUN PHRASE[1] which describes, typically, the performer of the action. Some linguists make a distinction between the grammatical subject (see SUBJECT) and the logical subject.

For example, in the passive sentence:

The cake was eaten by Vera.

the cake is the grammatical subject but *Vera* is the logical subject as she is the performer of the action. In:

Vera ate the cake.

Vera would be both the grammatical and the logical subject.

see also VOICE[1]

log /lɒg||lɔːg, lɑːg/ *n*

see LEARNING LOG

longitudinal method /ˌlɒndʒɨ'tjuːdənəl 'meθəd||ˌlɑːndʒɨ'tuː-/ *n*
also **longitudinal study** /ˌlɒndʒɨ'tjuːdənəl 'stʌdi||ˌlɑːndʒɨ'tuː-/

see CROSS-SECTION(AL) METHOD

long term memory /'lɒŋtɜːm 'meməri||'lɔːŋtɜːrm/ *n*

see MEMORY

look-and-say method /'lʊk ən 'seɪ ˌmeθəd/ *n*

a method for teaching children to read, especially in the FIRST LANGUAGE, which is similar to the WHOLE-WORD-METHOD except that words are always taught in association with a picture or object and the pronunciation of the word is always required.

low inference category /'ləʊ 'ɪnfərəns ˌkætɨgəri||-gɔːri/ *n*

see HIGH INFERENCE CATEGORY

low variety /'ləʊ və'raɪəti/ *n*

see DIGLOSSIA

low vowel /'ləʊ 'vaʊəl/ *n*

another term for **open vowel**

see VOWEL

Lozanov method /'ləʊzənɒf 'meθəd||-ɑːf/ *n*

another term for SUGGESTOPAEDIA

LSP /ˌel es 'piː/ *n*

an abbreviation for LANGUAGES FOR SPECIAL PURPOSES

L-variety /'el vəˌraɪəti/ *n*

see DIGLOSSIA

M

machine translation /məˈʃiːn trænsˈleɪʃən, trænz-/ n
also **mechanical translation**
> the use of machines (usually computers) to translate texts from one language to another.
> Linguists and specialists in COMPUTATIONAL LINGUISTICS have worked on machine translation for 30 years with limited results, but many advances have been made in the development of some areas relevant to machine translation (e.g. analysis of texts for different lexical, semantic, and grammatical characteristics).

macro-sociolinguistics /ˈmækrəʊ ˌsəʊsiəʊlɪŋˈgwɪstɪks, ˌsəʊʃəʊ-/ n
> see SOCIOLINGUISTICS

macro-structure /ˈmækrəʊ ˌstrʌktʃəʳ/ n
> another term for SCHEME

main clause/ˈmeɪn ˈklɔːz/ n
> see DEPENDENT CLAUSE

mainframe computer /ˈmeɪnfreɪm kəmˈpjuːtəʳ/ n
> a central computer where each user works from a terminal linked by cable or telephone line to the computer, and shares it with other users.
> see also COMPUTER, MICROCOMPUTER

mainstreaming /ˈmeɪnstriːmɪŋ/ n **mainstream** /ˈmeɪnstriːm/ v
> the entry into a regular school programme (i.e. mainstream programme) of students for whom the language spoken in that school is a second language. In many countries where there are significant numbers of immigrant students for whom English is a second language, school ESL programmes seek to prepare students to enter mainstream classes, that is, classes where English is medium of instruction in the CONTENT AREAS.

maintenance bilingual education /ˈmeɪntənəns baɪˈlɪŋgwəl ˌedjᵿˈkeɪʃən‖ˌedʒə-/ n
> see BILINGUAL EDUCATION

majority language /məˈdʒɒrᵻti ˈlæŋgwɪdʒ‖məˈdʒɔː-, -ˈdʒɑː-/ n
> the language spoken by the majority of the population in a country, such as English in the USA. A language spoken by a group of people who form a minority within a country is known as a **minority language**, such as Italian and Spanish in the USA.
> see also COMMUNITY LANGUAGE, NATIONAL LANGUAGE

manner of articulation /'mænəʳ əv aːˌtɪkjŭ'leɪʃən||aːr-/ *n*

the way in which a speech sound is produced by the speech organs. There are different ways of producing a speech sound. With CONSONANTS the airstream may be:

a stopped and released suddenly (a STOP), e.g. /t/

b allowed to escape with friction (a FRICATIVE), e.g. /f/

c stopped and then released slowly with friction (an AFFRICATE), e.g. /dʒ/ as in /dʒem/ *gem*.

The vocal cords may be vibrating (a voiced speech sound) or not (a voiceless speech sound) (see VOICE²).

With VOWELS, in addition to the position of the tongue in the mouth, the lips may be:

a rounded, e.g. for /uː/ in /ʃuː/ *shoe*; or

b spread, e.g. for /iː/ in /miːn/ *mean*.

see also FRICTIONLESS CONTINUANT, LATERAL, NASAL, PLACE OF ARTICULATION

Further reading Gimson 1989

manualist /'mænjuəlɪ̥st/ *n*

see SIGN LANGUAGE

manual method /'mænjuəl ˌmeθəd/ *n*

a method for teaching the deaf, based on the use of SIGN-LANGUAGE. There are many different manual communication systems; some, such as American Sign Language (A.S.L.) have their own linguistic rules which do not resemble the grammar of English. Those who are entirely dependent on A.S.L. or similar manual codes may therefore have difficulty reading, writing, or lip-reading English. Some manual codes such as Signed English or the Pagett-Gorman system are based on English, and learning to read and write English is easier for those who have learned these codes. Those who have learned a manual method of communication normally cannot speak, and therefore have difficulty communicating with those who cannot use their particular sign language.

A third group of manual codes, e.g. Amerind, are based on universal gestural codes.

mapping /'mæpɪŋ/ *n*

see BRAINSTORMING

markedness /'maːkɪ̥dnɪ̥s||'maːr-/ *n* **marked** /maːkt||maːrkt/ *adj*

the theory that in the languages of the world certain linguistic elements are more basic, natural, and frequent (**unmarked**) than others which are referred to as "marked". For example, in English, sentences which have the order:

Subject – Verb – Object: *I dislike such people.*

are considered to be unmarked, whereas sentences which have the order:

Object – Subject – Verb: *Such people I dislike.*

are considered to be marked.

The concept of markedness has been discussed particularly within GENERATIVE PHONOLOGY. Chomsky and Halle suggest that /p, t, k, s, n/ are the least marked consonants and that they occur in most languages. Other consonants such as /v, z/ are considered as more highly marked and less common.

see also NATURALNESS
Further reading Hyman 1975; Chomsky & Halle 1968

marker /ˈmɑːkəʳ‖ˈmɑːr-/ *n*
see SPEECH MARKER

mass noun /ˈmæs ˌnaʊn/ *n*
see COUNTABLE NOUN

mastery learning /ˈmɑːstəri ˌlɜːɪŋ‖ˈmæ- ˌlɜːr-/ *n*
an individualized and diagnostic approach to teaching in which students proceed with studying and testing at their own rate in order to achieve a prescribed level of success. Mastery learning is based on the idea that all students can master a subject given sufficient time. For example in an ESL reading programme, students might be assigned graded reading passages to read in their own time. Test questions after each passage allow the learner to discover what level of comprehension they reached, and re-read the passage if necessary. They must reach a specific comprehension level before they move on to the next passage.

matched guise technique /ˌmætʃt ˈgaɪz tekˌniːk/ *n*
(in studies of LANGUAGE ATTITUDES) the use of recorded voices of people speaking first in one dialect or language and then in another; that is, in two "guises". For example, BILINGUAL French Canadians may first speak in French and then in English. The recordings are played to listeners who do not know that the two samples of speech are from the same person and who judge the two guises of the same speaker as though they were judging two separate speakers each belonging to a different ethnic or national group. The reactions of the listeners to the speakers in one guise are compared to reactions to the other guise to reveal attitudes towards different language or dialect groups, whose members may be considered more or less intelligent, friendly, co-operative, reliable, etc.
Further reading Fasold 1984; Lambert 1967

mathematical linguistics /ˌmæθɪˈmætɪkəl lɪŋˈgwɪstɪks/ *n*
a branch of linguistics which makes use of statistical and mathematical methods to study the linguistic structure of written or spoken texts. This includes the study of the frequency of occurrence of linguistic items (see FREQUENCY COUNT) and the study of literary style.
see also COMPUTATIONAL LINGUISTICS
Further reading Herdan 1964

matrix /'meɪtrɪks/ *n*

a table consisting of rows and columns which is used in linguistics to display data or results of an analysis.

For an example, see the matrix used in this dictionary under the entry for IMPLICATIONAL SCALING.

The plural of *matrix* is *matrices* /'meɪtrɪˌsiːz/.

maximal projection /'mæksɪ̩məl prə'dʒekʃən/ *n*

see PROJECTION (PRINCIPLE)

mean /miːn/ *n*
also **meanscore, X̄**

the arithmetic average of a set of scores. The mean is the sum of all the scores divided by the total number of items. The mean is the most commonly used and most widely applicable measure of the CENTRAL TENDENCY of a distribution.

If the scores on a test of four items are as follows:

2, 5, 7, 10,

the mean is

$$\frac{2 + 5 + 7 + 10}{4} = \frac{24}{4} = 6.$$

see also MEDIAN, MODE

meaning /'miːnɪŋ/ *n*

(in linguistics) what a language expresses about the world we live in or any possible or imaginary world.

The study of meaning is called SEMANTICS. Semantics is usually concerned with the analysis of the meaning of words, phrases, or sentences (see CONNOTATION, DENOTATION, LEXICAL FIELD, SEMANTIC FEATURE) and sometimes with the meaning of utterances in discourse (see DISCOURSE ANALYSIS) or the meaning of a whole text.

see also FUNCTIONS OF LANGUAGE[1, 2], PRAGMATICS

meaningful drill /'miːnɪŋfəl 'drɪl/ *n*

In language teaching, a distinction between different types of DRILLS is made according to the degree of control the drill makes over the response produced by the student.

A **mechanical drill** is one where there is complete control over the student's response, and where comprehension is not required in order to produce a correct response. For example:

Teacher	Student
book	*Give me the book.*
ladle	*Give me the ladle.*

A meaningful drill is one in which there is still control over the response, but understanding is required in order for the student to produce a correct response. For example:

Teacher reads a sentence	Student chooses a response
I'm hot.	*I'll get you something to eat.*
I'm cold.	*I'll turn on the air conditioning.*
I'm thirsty.	*I'll get you something to drink.*
I'm hungry.	*I'll turn on the heater.*

A **communicative drill** is one in which the type of response is controlled but the student provides his or her own content or information. For example in practising the past tense, the teacher may ask a series of questions:

Teacher	Student completes cues
What time did you get up on	
Sunday?	*I got up* ___
What did you have for	
breakfast?	*I had* ___
What did you do after	
breakfast?	*I* ___

Further reading Paulston 1980

meaningful learning /ˈmiːnɪŋfəl ˈlɜːnɪŋ‖ˈlɜːr-/ n

(in COGNITIVE PSYCHOLOGY) learning in which learned items become part of a person's mental system of concepts and thought processes. The psychologist Ausubel contrasted meaningful learning with ROTE LEARNING and other types of learning in which learned items are not integrated into existing mental structures. Meaningful learning is said to be important in classroom language learning.

Further reading Ausubel 1968; Brown 1980

meaning potential /ˈmiːnɪŋ pəˌtenʃəl/ n

a term used by Halliday to refer to the semantic system in language. The "semantic system" means the range of meaning alternatives which are open to a speaker when he or she wishes to communicate with others. Grammar and vocabulary (the "lexicogrammatical" system) express this meaning in words and these are then turned into sounds or writing through the phonological system or the orthographical system.

see also DEVELOPMENTAL FUNCTIONS OF LANGUAGE, FUNCTIONS OF LANGUAGE[2], SYSTEMIC LINGUISTICS
Further reading Halliday 1978

mean length of utterance /ˈmiːn ˈleŋθ əv ˈʌtərəns/ n
also MLU, mean utterance length

(in LANGUAGE ACQUISITION research) a measure of the linguistic complexity of children's utterances, especially during the early stages of FIRST LANGUAGE learning. It is measured by counting the average length of the utterances a child produces, using the MORPHEME rather than the word as the unit of measurement. As a simple countable measure of grammatical development the MLU has been found to be a more reliable basis for comparing children's language development than the age of the children.

Further reading Brown 1973

meanscore /'miːnskɔːʳ/ *n*
another term for MEAN

means-ends model /'miːnz 'endz ˌmɒdl||ˌmɑːdl/ *n*
an approach to CURRICULUM DEVELOPMENT or to teaching in which a distinction is made between ends (e.g. objectives and content) and means (i.e. the process of instruction) and which generally employs a cycle of planning activities involving:
a specification of goals
b formulation of objectives
c selection of content
d organization of content
e selection of learning experiences
f evaluation of learning
Further reading White 1988

mean utterance length /'miːn 'ʌtərəns ˌleŋθ/ *n*
another term for MEAN LENGTH OF UTTERANCE

mechanical drill/mɪ'kænɪkəl 'drɪl/ *n*
see MEANINGFUL DRILL

mechanical translation /mɪ'kænɪkəl træns'leɪʃən, trænz-/ *n*
another term for MACHINE TRANSLATION

mechanics /mɪ'kænɪks/ *n*
(in composition) those aspects of writing such as spelling, use of apostrophes, hyphens, capitals, abbreviations and numbers, which are often dealt with in the revision or editing stages of writing (see COMPOSING PROCESSES). These may be compared with more global or higher level dimensions of writing, such as organization, COHERENCE, or rhetorical structure. (see SCHEME)

media /'miːdiə/ *n*
a general term for television, radio and newspapers considered as a whole and as ways of entertaining or spreading news or information to a large number of people. In language teaching, teaching materials which involve the use of different kinds of media such as visual and printed media, are sometimes known as **multi media** or **mixed media**.

medial /'miːdiəl/ *adj*
occurring in the middle of a linguistic unit.
For example, in English the /ɪ/ in /pɪt/ *pit* is in a medial position in the word.
see also INITIAL, FINAL

median /'miːdiən/ *n*
the value of the middle item or score when the scores in a SAMPLE are arranged in order from lowest to highest. The median is therefore the

score which divides the sample into two equal parts. It is the most appropriate measure of CENTRAL TENDENCY for data arranged in an "ordinal scale" or a "rank scale" (see SCALE). For example the median of the following set of scores is 5:

2 4 5 7 10

see also MEAN, MODE

mediation theory /ˌmiːdiˈeɪʃən ˌθɪəri/ n

(in psychology) a theory which explains certain types of learning in terms of links which are formed between a "stimulus" and a "response" (see STIMULUS-RESPONSE THEORY). A simple model of mediation learning is shown below, where Stimulus A becomes linked to Response C, through the mediation of B.

	Stimulus	Response
Learn	A	.... B
Then learn	B	 C
Test whether	A	 C

Mediation theories exist in many complex forms and have been used to explain different aspects of VERBAL LEARNING, thought, and language learning. Such theories are particularly associated with BEHAVIOURISM.

Further reading Osgood 1957; Mowrer 1960

medium /ˈmiːdiəm/ n

the means by which a message is conveyed from one person to another. For example, an invitation to a party can be made in writing or in speech.

The plural of *medium* is *media* /ˈmiːdɪə/ or *mediums*.

see also MESSAGE, DECODING, ENCODING

medium of instruction /ˈmiːdiəm əv ɪnˈstrʌkʃən/ n

the language used in education. In many countries, the medium of instruction is the STANDARD VARIETY of the main or NATIONAL LANGUAGE of the country, e.g. French in France. In some countries, the medium of instruction may be different in various parts of the country, as in Belgium where both French and Dutch are used. In MULTI-LINGUAL countries or regions there may be a choice, or there may be schools in which some subjects are taught in one language and other subjects in another.

The plural of *medium of instruction* is *media of instruction* or *mediums of instruction*.

see also BILINGUAL EDUCATION

membershipping /ˈmembəʃɪpɪŋ||-ər-/ n membership /ˈmembəʃɪp||-ər-/ v

classifying a person as a member of a group or category, e.g. shop assistant, student, or residents of a particular town. Once a category has been assigned to a person, conversation with that person may be affected.

For example, a visitor to a town may ask a passer-by whom he or she, correctly or incorrectly, memberships as a local resident: *Could you please tell me how to get to the station?* Wrong membershipping may result in misunderstanding or may cause annoyance, e.g. if a customer in a department store is wrongly membershipped as a shop assistant.

Further reading Coulthard 1985; Schegloff 1972

memorizing /'meməraızıŋ/ *n* **memorize** *v* **memorization** /ˌmeməraı'zeıʃən‖-rə-/ *n*
the process of establishing information etc. in memory. The term "memorizing" usually refers to conscious processes. Memorizing may involve ROTE LEARNING, practice, ASSOCIATIVE LEARNING, etc.

memory /'meməri/ *n*
the mental capacity to store information, either for short or long periods. Two different types of memory are often distinguished:

a **Short-term memory** refers to that part of the memory where information which is received is stored for short periods of time while it is being analysed and interpreted. Once the message or information in an utterance is understood the data may become part of permanent memory (or **long-term memory**). The utterance itself is now no longer needed and may fade from short-term memory.

b **Long-term memory** is that part of the memory system where information is stored more permanently. Information in long-term memory may not be stored in the same form in which it is received. For example, a listener may hear sentence A below, and be able to repeat it accurately immediately after hearing it. The listener uses short-term memory to do this. On trying to remember the sentence a few days later the listener may produce sentence B, using information in long-term memory which is in a different form from the original message.

A *The car the doctor parked by the side of the road was struck by a passing bus.*
B *The doctor's car was hit by a bus.*

see also EPISODIC MEMORY
Further reading Clark & Clark 1977

mentalism /'mentəl-ızəm/ *n* **mentalist** /'mentəl-ɪst/ *adj*
the theory that a human being possesses a mind which has consciousness, ideas, etc., and that the mind can influence the behaviour of the body.

see also INNATIST HYPOTHESIS

menu /'menjuː/ *n*
(in a computer program) a list of alternatives presented to the user from which he/she must select an option. The menu guides the inexperienced user through choices, giving lists of options to choose from at each stage.

mesolect /'mesəlekt,-səʊ-/ *n*
see POST CREOLE CONTINUUM, SPEECH CONTINUUM

message /'mesɪdʒ/ *n*
what is conveyed in speech or writing from one person to one or more
other people. The message may not always be stated in verbal form but
can be conveyed by other means, e.g. wink, gestures. A distinction can
be made between message form and message content. In a spoken
request, for example, the message form is how the request is made (e.g.
type of sentence structure, use or non-use of courtesy words, type of
intonation) and the message content is what is actually requested (e.g.
the loan of some money).
see also DECODING, ENCODING, KEY[1]
Further reading, Hymes 1977

metacognitive knowledge /'metə̩kɒgnɪ̩tɪv 'nɒlɪdʒ||-̩kɑːg- 'nɑː-/ *n*
also **metacognition** /̩metəkɒg'nɪʃən||-kɑːg-/ *n*
(in cognition and learning) knowledge of the mental processes which
are involved in different kinds of learning. Learners are said to be
capable of becoming aware of their own mental processes. This
includes recognizing which kinds of learning tasks cause difficulty,
which approaches to remembering information work better than
others, and how to solve different kinds of problems. Metacognitive
knowledge is thought to influence the kinds of learning strategies
learners choose.
see also LEARNING STRATEGY, METACOGNITIVE STRATEGY
Further reading Nisbet & Shucksmith 1986; Oxford 1990; O'Malley
& Chamot 1989

metacognitive strategy /'metə̩kɒgnɪ̩tɪv 'strætədʒi||-̩kɑːg-/ *n*
one of two general kinds of LEARNING STRATEGY (the other being
COGNITIVE STRATEGIES) which learners may use in learning. Metacognitive strategies involve thinking about the mental processes used
in the learning process, monitoring learning while it is taking place,
and evaluating learning after it has occurred. For example, metacognitive strategies a learner may use when he or she is beginning to
learn a new language include:
1 planning ways of remembering new words encountered in
conversations with native speakers
2 deciding which approaches to working out grammatical rules are
more effective
3 evaluating his or her own progress and making decisions about what
to concentrate on in the future
Further reading O'Malley & Chamot 1989

meta-language /'metə̩læŋgwɪdʒ/ *n*
the language used to analyse or describe a language. For example, the
sentence: *In English, the phoneme /b/ is a voiced bilabial stop* is in
meta-language. It explains that the *b*-sound in English is made with
vibration of the vocal cords and with the two lips stopping the
airstream from the lungs.

metalinguistic knowledge /ˈmetəlɪŋˌgwɪstɪk ˈnɒlɪdʒ‖ˈnɑː-/ *n*
(in language learning) knowledge of the forms, structure and other aspects of a language, which a learner arrives at through reflecting on and analyzing the language. In linguistic analysis, researchers sometimes make use of a native speaker's metalinguistic knowledge as one source of information about the language.
Further reading O'Malley & Chamot 1989

metaphor /ˈmetəfəʳ, -fɔːʳ/ *n*
see FIGURE OF SPEECH

metathesis /mɪˈtæθɪsɪs/ *n* **metathesize** /mɪˈtæθəsaɪz/ *v*
change in the order of two sounds in a word, e.g. /flɪm/ for /fɪlm/ *film*. Metathesis sometimes occurs in the speech of language learners but it may also occur with native speakers. When a metathesized form becomes commonly and regularly used by most native speakers of a language, it may lead to a change in the word. For example, Modern English *bird* developed by metathesis from Old English *brid* "young bird".

method /ˈmeθəd/ *n*
(in language teaching) a way of teaching a language which is based on systematic principles and procedures, i.e., which is an application of views on how a language is best taught and learned.
Different methods of language teaching such as the DIRECT METHOD, the AUDIOLINGUAL METHOD, the AUDIO-VISUAL METHOD, the GRAMMAR TRANSLATION METHOD, the SILENT WAY and COMMUNICATIVE APPROACH result from different views of:
a the nature of language
b the nature of language learning
c goals and OBJECTIVES in teaching
d the type of SYLLABUS to use
e the role of teachers, learners, and instructional materials
f the techniques and procedures to use.
see also APPROACH
Further reading Richards & Rodgers 1986

methodology /ˌmeθəˈdɒlədʒi‖-ˈdɑː-/ *n*
1 (in language teaching) the study of the practices and procedures used in teaching, and the principles and beliefs that underlie them.
Methodology includes:
a study of the nature of LANGUAGE SKILLS (e.g. reading, writing, speaking, listening) and procedures for teaching them
b study of the preparation of LESSON PLANS, materials, and textbooks for teaching language skills
c the evaluation and comparison of language teaching METHODS (e.g. the AUDIOLINGUAL METHOD)
2 such practices, procedures, principles, and beliefs themselves. One

can for example criticize or praise the methodology of a particular language course.

see also CURRICULUM, SYLLABUS

3 (in research) the procedures used in carrying out an investigation, including the methods used to collect and analyze data.

see also EXPERIMENTAL METHOD, SCIENTIFIC METHOD

Further reading Rivers 1981; Omaggio 1986; Richards 1990

methods of development /ˌmeθədz əv dɪˈveləpmənt/ *n*

(in composition) the ways in which a paragraph or extended piece of writing is developed. A number of methods of development are often used, either individually, or sometimes within other methods of development. These are:

1 **Process Method**: the writer describes something by breaking a complex whole down into its different parts and describing them in order.

2 **Definition Method**: the writer defines a term or object by identifying it within a general class and then distinguishing it from all other members of the class.

3 **Classification Method**: the writer groups people, things or ideas according to some principle order, in this way both classifying and explaining them.

4 **Comparison and Contrast Method**: the writer describes the similarities or differences between two sets of items.

5 **Cause-Effect Method**: the writer describes why things are the way they are or why something happened, by describing causes and effects. A cause-effect paragraph is usually developed by inductive reasoning.

Further Reading Herman 1982

microcomputer /ˌmaɪkrəʊkəmˈpjuːtəʳ/ *n*

a small computer that is a free standing self contained unit operated by a single user. Microcomputers use a **microprocessor**, an integrated circuit that is capable of functioning as a CENTRAL PROCESSING UNIT.

see also MAINFRAME COMPUTER

micro-skills /ˈmaɪkrəʊ ˌskɪlz/ *n*
also **enabling skills, part skills**

(in language teaching) a term sometimes used to refer to the individual processes and abilities which are used in carrying out a complex activity.

For example, among the micro-skills used in listening to a lecture are: identifying the purpose and scope of the lecture; identifying the role of conjunctions, etc., in signalling relationships between different parts of the lecture; recognizing the functions of PITCH and INTONATION. For the purposes of SYLLABUS DESIGN, reading, writing, speaking, and listening may be further analyzed into different microskills.

see also LANGUAGE SKILLS

Further reading Munby 1978

micro-sociolinguistics /ˈmaɪkrəʊ ˌsəʊsiəʊlɪŋˈgwɪstɪks, ˌsəʊʃəʊ-/ *n*
see SOCIOLINGUISTICS

microteaching /ˈmaɪkrəʊˌtiːtʃɪŋ/ *n*
a technique used in the training of teachers, in which different teaching skills are practised under carefully controlled conditions. It is based on the idea that teaching is a complex set of activities which can be broken down into different skills. These skills can be practised individually, and later combined with others. Usually in micro-teaching, one trainee teacher teaches a part of a lesson to a small group of his or her classmates. The lesson may be recorded on tape or videotape and later discussed in individual or group tutorials. Each session generally focusses on a specific teaching task. Microteaching thus involves a scaling-down of teaching because class size, lesson length, and teaching complexity are all reduced.

mid vowel /ˈmɪd ˈvaʊəl/ *n*
see VOWEL

mim-mem method /ˌmɪm ˈmem ˌmeθəd/ *n*
a term for the AUDIOLINGUAL METHOD, because the method uses exercises such as pattern practice (see DRILL) and dialogues which make use of the *mim*icry (imitation) and *mem*orization of material presented as a model.

minimal-distance principle /ˈmɪnɪməl ˈdɪstəns ˌprɪnsɪpəl/ *n*
the principle that in English, a COMPLEMENT or a NON-FINITE VERB refers to the NOUN PHRASE[1] which is closest to it (i.e. which is minimally distant from it). For example in the following sentences:
John wants Mary to study.
Penny made the children happy.
the non-finite verb *to study* refers to *Mary* (not *John*) and the complement *happy* to *the children* (not *Penny*).
Some sentences do not follow the principle, however. For example, in:
John promised Mary to wash the clothes.
the non-finite verb phrase *to wash the clothes* refers to *John* (not *Mary*). Such sentences are believed to cause comprehension problems for children learning English.
Further reading Chomsky 1969

minimal pair /ˈmɪnɪməl ˈpeəʳ/ *n*
two words in a language which differ from each other by only one distinctive sound (one PHONEME) and which also differ in meaning. For example, the English words *bear* and *pear* are a minimal pair as they differ in meaning and in their initial phonemes /b/ and /p/.
The term "minimal pair" is also sometimes used of any two pieces of language that are identical except for a specific feature or group of related features.

For example, the sentences:
The boy is here.
The boys are here.
may be called a minimal pair because they are the same except for the contrast between singular and plural expressed in both noun and verb.

minimal pair drill /ˌmɪnˑməl 'peəʳ ˌdrɪl/ *n*
a DRILL in which MINIMAL PAIRS are practised together, especially in order to help students to learn to distinguish a sound contrast. For example if a teacher wanted to practise the contrast between /b/ and /p/, the teacher could (a) explain how the sounds differ; (b) present pairs of words containing the contrast, for listening practice; e.g. *bore – pour*, *big – pig, buy – pie*; (c) get the students to show that they know which member of the pair they have heard; (d) get them to pronounce such pairs themselves.

Minimal Terminable Unit /'mɪnˑməl 'tɜːmɪnəbəl 'juːnˑt‖-ɜːr-/ *n*
another term for T-UNIT

minority language /maɪ'nɒrˑti 'læŋgwɪdʒ‖mˑ'nɔː-, mˑ'nɑː-/ *n*
see MAJORITY LANGUAGE

minority language group /maɪ'nɒrˑti 'læŋgwɪdʒ ˌgruːp‖mˑ'nɔː-, mˑ 'nɑː-/ *n*
another term for LANGUAGE MINORITY GROUP

minority students /maɪ'nɒrˑti 'stjuːdənts‖mˑ'nɔː-, mˑ'nɑː- 'stuː-/ *n*
in countries where English is a first language, often used to refer to students whose first language is a language other than English, for whom special instruction in English may be needed.

miscue /mɪs'kjuː/ *n*
see MISCUE ANALYSIS

miscue analysis /mɪs'kjuː əˌnælˑsˑs/ *n*
the analysis of errors or unexpected responses which readers make in reading, as part of the study of the nature of the reading process in children learning to read their mother tongue.
Among the different types of **miscue** which occur are:
a insertion miscue: the adding of a word which is not present in the text (e.g. the child may read *Mr Barnaby was a busy old man* instead of *Mr Barnaby was a busy man*).
b reversal miscue: the reader reverses the order of words (e.g. the child reads *Mrs Barnaby was a rich kind old lady* instead of *Mrs Barnaby was a kind rich old lady*).
Further reading Goodman & Goodman 1977

mistake /mɪ'steɪk/ *n*
see ERROR

231

MLAT /ˌem el eɪ 'tiː/ *n*

an abbreviation for the *Modern Language Aptitude Test*, a test of LANGUAGE APTITUDE

MLU¹ /ˌem el 'juː/ *n*

an abbreviation for MEAN LENGTH OF UTTERANCE

MLU²

an abbreviation for *Multi-Word Lexical Unit*, a LEXEME consisting of more than one word. For example, COMPOUND NOUNS and PHRASAL VERBS are MLUs.

modal /'məʊdl/ *n*
also **modal verb** /ˌməʊdl 'vɜːb‖'vɜːrb/, **modal auxiliary** /ˌməʊdl ɔːg'zɪl jəri, ɔːk-‖ɔːg'zɪljəri, -'zɪləri/

any of the AUXILIARY VERBS which indicate attitudes of the speaker/ writer towards the state or event expressed by another verb, i.e. which indicate different types of **modality**. The following are modal verbs in English:

may, might, can, could, must, have (got) to, will, would, shall, should
Modal meanings are shown in the following examples; all are in contrast to simple assertion:

I *may* be wrong. (*may* = possibility)
That *will* be Tom at the door. (*will* = prediction)
You *can* smoke here. (*can* = permission)
I *can* play the piano. (*can* = ability)
Modality can be expressed in other ways, too:
I *may* be wrong. = *Perhaps* I'm wrong.

modality /məʊ'dælᵻti/ *n*
see MODAL

mode /məʊd/ *n*

the most frequently occurring score or scores in a SAMPLE. It is a measure of the CENTRAL TENDENCY of a DISTRIBUTION. For example, in the following test scores, the mode is equal to 20.

score	number of students with the score
10	2
20	10
30	3
40	4
50	3

A frequency distribution with two modes is known as a **bimodal distribution,** as when the two most frequently occurring scores are 60 and 40. The mode(s) of a distribution can be pictured graphically as the "peaks" in the distribution. A NORMAL DISTRIBUTION has only one peak. The following shows a bimodal distribution:

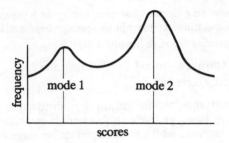

model /ˈmɒdl‖ˈmɑːdl/ *n*

(in language teaching) someone or something which is used as a standard or goal for the learner, e.g. the pronunciation of an educated native speaker.

see also MODELLING

modelling[1] /ˈmɒdəlɪŋ‖ˈmɑː-/ *n*

providing a model (e.g. a sentence, a question) as an example for someone learning a language.

In SECOND LANGUAGE and FOREIGN LANGUAGE learning, some teaching methods emphasize the need for teachers to provide accurate models for learners to imitate, for example the AUDIO-LINGUAL METHOD. In FIRST LANGUAGE learning, parents sometimes provide correct sentences for children to repeat, and this may be referred to as modelling. The effect of modelling on children's language development has been compared with that of **expansion** and **prompting**.

In expansion the parent repeats part of what the child has said, but expands it. The expansion usually contains grammatical words which the child did not use. This is thought to be one of the ways children develop their knowledge of the rules of a language. For example:

Child: *Doggy sleeping.*
Parent: *Yes, the doggy is sleeping.*

Prompting refers to stating a sentence in a different way. For example:

Parent: *What do you want?*
Child: (no answer)
Parent: *You want what?*

By presenting the question in two different forms the parent may assist the child in understanding the structure of questions and other language items.

Further reading Dale 1975

modelling[2]

a learning process in which a person observes someone's behaviour and then consciously or unconsciously attempts to imitate that behaviour. For example, many of the teaching practices a new teacher uses may have been modelled from teachers he or she has observed. Students may also model behaviours from their teachers. For example, if a student sees that the teacher is not punctual and is poorly organized, he or she may decide that punctuality and organization are not important and thus not attempt to develop these qualities.

Further reading Good & Brophy 1987

mode of discourse /'məʊd əv 'dɪskɔːs||-ɔːrs-/ n
see SOCIAL CONTEXT

modern language /'mɒdn 'læŋgwɪdʒ||'maːdərn/ n
in foreign language teaching this term is sometimes used to refer to a foreign language which is an important language today such as French or Italian, as compared to an ancient language such as Latin or ancient Greek.

modified speech /'mɒdɪ̥faɪd 'spiːtʃ||'maː/ n
a term used by linguists to describe speech which is deliberately changed in an attempt to make it sound more educated or refined. The change is usually temporary and the speaker lapses back to his or her normal speech pattern.

modifier /'mɒdɪ̥faɪəʳ||'maː-/ n modification /ˌmɒdɪ̥fɪ̥'keɪʃən||ˌmaː-/ n modify /'mɒdɪ̥faɪ||'maː-/ v
a word or group of words which gives further information about ("modifies") another word or group of words (the HEAD).
Modification may occur in a NOUN PHRASE[1], a VERB PHRASE, an ADJECTIVAL PHRASE, etc.
  a Modifiers before the head are called **premodifiers**, for example *expensive* in *this expensive camera*.
  b Modifiers after the head are called **postmodifiers**, for example *with a stumpy tail* in *The cat with a stumpy tail*.
Halliday restricts the term "modifier" to premodifiers and calls postmodifiers QUALIFIERS.
In earlier grammars, the term "modifier" referred only to words, phrases, or clauses which modified verbs, adjectives, or other adverbials, but not to those which modified nouns.
Further reading Quirk et al 1985; Halliday 1982

monitor /'mɒnɪ̥təʳ||'maː-/ n
the part of a computer which contains a screen on which information is presented to the user.

monitor hypothesis /'mɒnɪ̥təʳ haɪˌpɒθ̥sɪ̥s||'maː- -ˌpaː-/ n
also **monitor model of second language development** /'mɒnɪ̥təʳ 'mɒdl əv 'sekənd 'læŋgwɪdʒ dɪˌveləpmənt||'maː- 'maːdl/
a theory proposed by Krashen which distinguishes two distinct processes in second and foreign language development and use. One, called "acquisition", is said to be a subconscious process which leads to the development of "competence" and is not dependent on the teaching of grammatical rules. The second process, called "learning", refers to the conscious study and knowledge of grammatical rules. In producing utterances, learners initially use their acquired system of

rules. Learning and learned rules have only one function: to serve as a monitor or editor of utterances initiated by the acquired system, and learning cannot lead to acquisition.

see also INPUT HYPOTHESIS
Further reading Ellis 1985; Krashen 1978

monitoring /'mɒnɪ̯tərɪŋ||'mɑː-/ *n* **monitor** *v*
listening to one's own UTTERANCES to compare what was said with what was intended, and to make corrections if necessary. People generally try to speak fluently (see FLUENCY) and appropriately (see APPRO-PRIATENESS), and try to make themselves understood. The inter-jections and self-corrections that speakers make while talking show that monitoring is taking place, and are usually for the purposes of making meaning clearer. For example:
    He is, *well*, rather difficult.
    Can I have, *say*, a glass of beer.
    They own, *I mean rent*, a lovely house.

see also AUDITORY FEEDBACK, PAUSING
Further reading Clark & Clark 1977

monolingual /ˌmɒnə'lɪŋgwəl◄||ˌmɑː-/ *n, adj* **monolingualism** /ˌmɒnə'lɪŋgwəlɪzəm||ˌmɑː-/ *n*
1 a person who knows and uses only one language.
2 a person who has an active knowledge of only one language, though perhaps a passive knowledge of others.

see also ACTIVE/PASSIVE LANGUAGE KNOWLEDGE, BILINGUAL, MULTI-LINGUAL

monophthong /'mɒnəfθɒŋ||'mɑːnəfθɔːŋ/ *n* **monophthongal**/ˌmɒnəf'θɒŋgəl◄||ˌmɑːnəf'θɔːŋ-/ *adj*
also **pure vowel**
a vowel which is produced without any noticeable change in vowel quality. For example, in English:
    /ʌ/ as in /hʌt/ *hut*
is a monophthong.

see also DIPHTHONG
Further reading Gimson 1980

monosyllabic /ˌmɒnəsɪ̯'læbɪk◄||ˌmɑː-/ *adj* **monosyllable** /'mɒnəˌsɪləbəl||'mɑː-/ *n*
consisting of one SYLLABLE, e.g. the English word *cow*.

see also DESYLLABIC

mood /muːd/ *n*
a set of contrasts which are often shown by the form of the verb and which express the speaker's or writer's attitude to what is said or written. Three moods have often been distinguished:
1 **indicative** mood: the form of the verb used in DECLARATIVE SENTENCES or QUESTIONS. For example:

She sat down.
Are you coming?
2 **imperative** mood: the form of the verb in IMPERATIVE SENTENCES.
For example:
Be quiet!
Put it on the table!
In English, imperatives do not have tense or perfect aspect (see ASPECT)
but they may be used in the progressive aspect. For example:
Be waiting for me at five.
3 **subjunctive** mood: the form of the verb often used to express
uncertainty, wishes, desires, etc. In contrast to the indicative mood, the
subjunctive usually refers to non-factual or hypothetical situations. In
English, little use of the subjunctive forms remains. The only
remaining forms are:
a be (present subjunctive), *were* (past subjunctive) of *be*
b the stem form, e.g. *have, come, sing* of other verbs (present
subjunctive only).
The use of the subjunctive forms is still sometimes found in:
a that clauses after certain verbs. For example:
It is required that she be present.
I demand that he come at once.
b past subjunctive of *be* in *if* clauses. For example:
If I were you, I'd go there.
c in some fixed expressions. For example:
So be it.
Further reading Quirk et al 1985

morpheme /'mɔːfiːm‖'mɔːr-/ *n* **morphemic** /mɔːˈfiːmɪk‖mɔːr-/ *adj*
the smallest meaningful unit in a language. A morpheme cannot be
divided without altering or destroying its meaning. For example, the
English work *kind* is a morpheme. If the *d* is removed, it changes to
kin, which has a different meaning. Some words consist of one
morpheme, e.g. *kind*, others of more than one. For example, the
English word *unkindness* consists of three morphemes: the STEM[1] *kind*,
the negative prefix *un-*, and the noun-forming suffix *-ness*. Morphemes
can have grammatical functions. For example, in English the *-s* in *she
talks* is a **grammatical morpheme** which shows that the verb is the
third-person singular present-tense form.

see also AFFIX, ALLOMORPH, BOUND FORM, COMBINING FORM
Further reading Fromkin & Rodman 1983

morpheme boundary /'mɔːfiːm 'baʊndəri‖-ɔːr-/ *n*
the boundary between two MORPHEMES.
For example, in *kindness* there is a clear morpheme boundary between
the STEM[1] *kind* and the suffix *-ness*. On the other hand, in the adverb
doubly (from *double* + *-ly*) it is hard to establish the boundary. Does the
l go with *double*, with *-ly*, or with both?

see also AFFIX, COMBINING FORM

morphology /mɔːˈfɒlədʒi‖mɔːrˈfɑː-/ *n* **morphological** /ˌmɔːfəˈlɒdʒɪkəl ‖ˌmɔːrfəˈlɑː-/ *adj*

1 the study of MORPHEMES and their different forms (ALLOMORPHS), and the way they combine in WORD FORMATION. For example, the English word *unfriendly* is formed from *friend*, the adjective-forming suffix *-ly* and the negative prefix *un-*.

2 a morphemic system: in this sense, one can speak of "comparing the morphology of English with the morphology of German".

see also AFFIX, COMBINING FORM

morphophonemics /ˌmɔːfəʊfəˈniːmɪks‖ˌmɔːr-/ *n* **morphophonemic** *adj*

variation in the form of MORPHEMES because of PHONETIC factor, or the study of this variation.

For example, in spoken English, the regular past tense is formed by adding /d/, /t/ or /ɪd/ to the stem of the verb according to the final sound in the stem: *begged* /begd/, *tripped* /trɪpt/, *needed* /ˈniːdɪd/

see also MORPHOLOGY

morphosyntax /ˌmɔːfəʊˈsɪntæks‖ˌmɔːr-/ *n* **morphosyntactic** /ˌmɔːfə ʊsɪnˈtæktɪk◄‖ˌmɔːr-/ *adj*

an analysis of language which uses criteria from both MORPHOLOGY, the combining of morphemes to form words, and syntax (see SYNTAX[1]), the structuring and functioning of words in sentences.

For example, in English, the plural morpheme /s/ is added to nouns to show that more than one item is being discussed:

Those pears are pretty expensive, aren't they?

The *s*, *ed*, and *ing* of *lives*, *lived*, and *living*, are all morphemes but, at the same time, they have meanings beyond the word they are attached to. We can really say that their meaning only becomes apparent when they are used in a sentence, e.g.

Peter lives in Paris.

Anita lived in Paris a couple of years ago.

Is she still living in Paris?

All these morphemes can be referred to as inflectional morphemes (see INFLECTION) and in order to discuss them, criteria both from morphology and syntax (**morphosyntactic** criteria) have to be used.

Other inflectional morphemes would be the case markers in some languages (see CASE[1]) which show whether a noun phrase is used as the subject or the object of a sentence, and morpheme endings on adjectives to show comparison, e.g.

These vegetables are fresher than those at the other stall.

Further reading Fromkin & Rodman 1983

motherese /ˌmʌðərˈiːz/ *n*

another term for CARETAKER SPEECH

mother talk /ˈmʌðəˌr ˌtɔːk/ *n*

another term for CARETAKER SPEECH

mother tongue /'mʌðəʳ ˌtʌŋ/ *n*
(usually) a FIRST LANGUAGE which is acquired at home.

motivation /ˌməʊtɪ̥'veɪʃən/ *n*
the factors that determine a person's desire to do something. In SECOND
LANGUAGE and FOREIGN LANGUAGE learning, learning may be affected
differently by different types of motivation. Two types of motivation
are sometimes distinguished:
a **instrumental motivation**: wanting to learn a language because it will
  be useful for certain "instrumental" goals, such as getting a job,
  reading a foreign newspaper, passing an examination.
b **integrative motivation**: wanting to learn a language in order to
  communicate with people of another culture who speak it.
Further reading Gardner & Lambert 1972

move /muːv/ *n*
(in DISCOURSE ANALYSIS) a unit of DISCOURSE which may be smaller
than an UTTERANCE.
For example, a teacher's utterance: *That's right, Jessica, and can you give
me another example?* would consist of two moves:
a *That's right, Jessica,* which gives the teacher's reaction to a correct
  answer by the student
b *can you give me another example?* which attempts to elicit another
  response from the student.
see also SPEECH ACT
Further reading Coulthard 1985

multicultural education /ˌmʌlti'kʌltʃərəl ˌedjʊ̥'keɪʃən‖ˌedʒə-/ *n*
see CULTURAL PLURALISM

multilingual /ˌmʌlti'lɪŋgwəl/ *n, adj*
a person who knows and uses three or more languages. Usually, a multilingual does not know all the languages equally well. For example,
he or she may:
a speak and understand one language best
b be able to write in only one
c use each language in different types of situation (DOMAINS), e.g. one
  language at home, one at work, and one for shopping
d use each language for different communicative purposes, e.g. one
  language for talking about science, one for religious purposes, and
  one for talking about personal feelings.
see also BILINGUAL, MULTILINGUALISM

multilingualism /ˌmʌlti'lɪŋgwəlɪzəm/ *n*
the use of three or more languages by an individual (see MULTI-
LINGUAL) or by a group of speakers such as the inhabitants of a
particular region or a nation. Multilingualism is common in, for

example, some countries of West Africa (e.g. Nigeria, Ghana), Malaysia, Singapore, and Israel.

see BILINGUALISM, NATIONAL LANGUAGE

multiple-choice item /ˈmʌːltəpəl ˈtʃɔɪs ˌaɪtəm/ n

a TEST ITEM in which the examinee is presented with a question along with four or five possible answers from which one must be selected. Usually the first part of a multiple choice item will be a question or incomplete statement. This is known as the **stem**. The different possible answers are known as **alternatives**. The alternatives contain (usually) one correct answer and several wrong answers or **distractors**. For example:

> Yesterday I _____ several interesting magazines. (a) have bought (b) buying (c) was bought (d) bought

Further reading Heaton 1975

multiple correlation /ˈmʌltəpəl kɒrəˈleɪʃən‖kɔː- kɑː-/ n

a coefficient of CORRELATION among three or more VARIABLES[2]. For example, if we wish to study the correlation between a DEPENDENT VARIABLE (e.g. the level of students' language proficiency) and several other variables (the independent variables, e.g. the amount of homework the students do each week, their knowledge of grammar, and their motivation) the multiple correlation is the correlation between the dependent variable and all the predictors (the independent variables).

multiple regression /ˈmʌltəpəl rɪˈgreʃən/ n

see REGRESSION ANALYSIS

multivariate analysis /ˈmʌltəˌveərɪ-ət əˈnæləsəs/ n

a general term for various statistical techniques which are used to analyse MULTIVARIATE DATA, such as FACTOR ANALYSIS and REGRESSION ANALYSIS.

multivariate data /ˈmʌltəˌveərɪ-ət ˈdeɪtə, ˈdɑːtə/ n

(in statistics) data which contain measurements based on more than one VARIABLE[2]. For example, if we were measuring a student's language proficiency and tests were given for reading, writing, and grammar, the resulting information would be multivariate data because it is based on three separate scores (three variables).

mutation /mjuːˈteɪʃən/ n

a change in a sound, as in the formation of some irregular noun plurals in English by a change in an internal vowel, e.g. *foot – feet, man – men, mouse – mice*.

The term "mutation" is used when the sound change is due to the PHONETIC environment of the sound that changes. In the examples, mutation was due to other vowels that were present in earlier forms of the words but have since disappeared.

N

N /en/ *n*

(in testing and statistics) a symbol for the number of students, subjects, scores, or observations involved in a study (as in e.g., N = 15).

N' /'en 'baːʳ/ *n*
also **N-bar**

see BAR NOTATION

N'' /'en 'dʌbl 'baːʳ/ *n*
also **N-double bar**

see BAR NOTATION

narrow notation /'nærəʊ nəʊ'teɪʃən/ *n*
also **narrow transcription** /'nærəʊ træn'skrɪpʃən/

see NOTATION

nasal /'neɪzəl/ *adj*

describes a speech sound (consonant or vowel) which is produced by stopping the airstream from the lungs at some place in the mouth (for example by closing the lips) and letting the air escape through the nose.

The English nasal consonants are /m/, /n/, and /ŋ/.

see also MANNER OF ARTICULATION, ORAL², PLACE OF ARTICULATION, NASALIZATION

Further reading Gimson 1989, Hyman 1975

nasal cavity /'neɪzəl 'kævɪ̩ti/ *n*

see VOCAL TRACT, PLACE OF ARTICULATION

nasalization /ˌneɪzəlaɪ'zeɪʃ̩n‖-zələ-/ *n* **nasalize** /'neɪzəlaɪz/ *v*

(in the production of speech sounds) letting the air from the lungs escape through the nose and the mouth. This can be done by lowering the soft palate (the **velum**) at the back of the mouth. In a number of languages, some of the VOWELS are nasalized, as in French *un bon vin blanc* /œ̃ bɔ̃ vɛ̃ blã/ "a good white wine".

see also MANNER OF ARTICULATION, PLACE OF ARTICULATION

national language /'næʃənəl 'læŋgwɪdʒ/ *n*

a language which is usually considered to be the main language of a nation.

For example, German is the national language of Germany.

A government may declare a particular language or dialect to be the national language of a nation, e.g. Bahasa Malaysia (standard Malay) in Malaysia and Pilipino in the Philippines.

Usually, the national language is also the **official language**; that is the language used in government and courts of law, and for official business. However, in multilingual nations, there may be more than one official language, and in such cases the term "official language" is often used rather than "national language". For example, the Republic of Singapore has four official languages; English, Chinese (Mandarin), Malay, and Tamil.

see also STANDARD VARIETY

native language /'neɪtɪv 'læŋgwɪdʒ/ *n*

(usually) the language which a person acquires in early childhood because it is spoken in the family and/or it is the language of the country where he or she is living. The native language is often the first language a child acquires but there are exceptions. Children may, for instance, first acquire some knowledge of another language from a nurse or an older relative and only later on acquire a second one which they consider their native language. Sometimes, this term is used synonymously with FIRST LANGUAGE.

native speaker (of a language) /'neɪtɪv 'spiːkə^r/ *n* natively
/'neɪtɪvli/ *adv*

a person considered as a speaker of his or her NATIVE LANGUAGE. The intuition of a native speaker about the structure of his or her language is one basis for establishing or confirming the rules of the grammar. A native speaker is said to speak his or her native language "natively".

nativist position /'neɪtɪ̹vɨ̹st pə,zɪʃən/ *n*

another term for INNATIST HYPOTHESIS

nativization /,neɪtɪ̹vaɪ'zeɪʃən‖-və-/ *n* nativize /'neɪtɪ̹vaɪz/ *v*
also **indigenization**

the adaptation a language may undergo when it is used in a different cultural and social situation. English in India, for example, is said to have undergone nativization because changes have occurred in aspects of its phonology, vocabulary, grammar, etc. so that it is now recognized as a distinct variety of English – Indian English.

Further reading Kachru 1981

natural approach /'nætʃərəl ə'prəʊtʃ/ *n*
also **natural method**

1 a term for a number of language-teaching METHODS which were developed in the 19th century as a reaction to the GRAMMAR TRANS-LATION METHOD. These methods emphasized:

a the use of the spoken language
b the use of objects and actions in teaching the meanings of words and structures
c the need to make language teaching follow the natural principles of first language learning.

These methods lead to the DIRECT METHOD.

2 a term for an APPROACH proposed by Terrell, to develop teaching principles which:

a emphasize natural communication rather than formal grammar study

b are tolerant of learners' errors

c emphasize the informal ACQUISITION of language rules.

Further reading Rivers 1981; Richards & Rogers 1986; Terrell 1977

natural language /'nætʃərəl 'læŋgwɪdʒ/ n

a language which has NATIVE SPEAKERS, in contrast with an ARTIFICIAL LANGUAGE.

natural language processing /'nætʃərəl ˌlæŋgwɪdʒ 'prəʊsesɪŋ‖ 'prɑː-/ n

the analysis of human language by a computer, for example, the automatic analysis of a text in order to determine the kinds of grammatical structures used, or the processing of spoken input for acoustic analysis.

Further reading Leech & Candlin 1986

natural method /'nætʃərəl 'meθəd/ n

another term for NATURAL APPROACH

naturalness /'nætʃərəlnn̩s/ n natural /'nætʃərəl/ adj

(in GENERATIVE PHONOLOGY), the probability that particular sounds, classes of sounds, or phonological rules occur in any language. For example, the VOWELS [i] and [u] are considered to be more frequent and therefore more "natural" than the vowels [y] (an [i] pronounced with rounded lips) and [ɯ] (an [u] pronounced with spread lips). In general, a language will have a [y], as in German /'ryːmən/ *rühmen* "to praise", only if it has an [i], as in German /'riːmən/ *Riemen* "strap".

Further reading Hyman 1975

natural order hypothesis /'nætʃərəl 'ɔːdəʳ haɪˌpɒθl̩sl̩s‖'ɔːr- haɪˌpɑː-/ n

the hypothesis that children acquiring their first language acquire linguistic forms, rules, and items in a similar order. For example, in English children acquire progressive *-ing*, plural *-s*, and active sentences before they acquire third person *-s* on verbs, or passive sentences. This is said to show a natural order of development. In SECOND LANGUAGE and FOREIGN LANGUAGE learning grammatical forms may also appear in a natural order, though this is not identical with the ORDER OF ACQUISITION in FIRST LANGUAGE learning.

Further reading Brown 1973; Dulay & Burt 1974

needs analysis /'niːdz əˌnæll̩sl̩s/ n
also needs assessment /'niːdz əˌsesmənt/

(in language teaching) the process of determining the needs for which a learner or group of learners requires a language and arranging the needs according to priorities. Needs assessment makes use of both subjective and objective information (e.g. data from questionnaires, tests, interviews, observation) and seeks to obtain information on:

a the situations in which a language will be used (including *who* it will be used *with*)

b the OBJECTIVES and purposes for which the language is needed

c the types of communication that will be used (e.g. written, spoken, formal, informal)

d the level of proficiency that will be required.

Needs assessment is a part of CURRICULUM DEVELOPMENT and is normally required before a SYLLABUS can be developed for language teaching.

Further reading Johnson 1989; Munby 1978

negation /nɪˈɡeɪʃən/ *n*

contradicting the meaning or part of the meaning of a sentence. The main NEGATOR in English is *not*, often in its contracted form *n't* and combined with an auxiliary, for example:

She isn't going / hasn't gone / didn't go / doesn't want to go.

but there are other negators, e.g. *never*:

Although he lived quite close, he never visited us.

Negation can be expressed by NEGATIVE PRONOUNS, e.g:

There was nobody there.

or by negative affixes, e.g.:

That was really unkind!

Some varieties of English may use a DOUBLE NEGATIVE, such as:

I haven't done nothing.

This does not mean that the two negators cancel themselves out and make the sentence again a positive statement. Double negation is merely used for emphasis. Often double negation is frowned on as being non-standard. However, it is typically used in a number of English DIALECTS and it follows a definite pattern, e.g. the use of *no-* instead of *any-*:

We didn't hurt nobody!

In recent grammatical theory, interest has been shown in the scope of the negator, that is, how much of the sentence is actually negated and in what way the meaning of the sentence can change if the negator is put in a different place, for instance, do the two sentences:

She didn't think he could do it

    and

She thought he couldn't do it

really mean the same?

negative politeness strategies /ˈneɡətɪv pəˈlaɪtnɪs ˌstrætɪdʒiz/ *n*

see POLITENESS

negative pronoun /ˈneɡətɪv ˈprəʊnaʊn/ *n*

a PRONOUN which stands for a negative NOUN PHRASE[1]. The following words in English are negative pronouns:

nobody, no one, none, neither, nothing
For example:
Nobody has passed the test.
That's none of your business.
Negative pronouns can function as NEGATORS.

negative question /'negətɪv 'kwestʃən/ *n*
a question which includes a negative word or PARTICLE. For example,
Can't you drive?
Isn't it awful?
In English, negative questions are answered in the same way as
positive questions:

	If you can drive	If you can't drive
Can you drive? *Can't you drive?*	*Yes, I can.*	*No, I can't.*

negative reinforcement /'negətɪv ˌriːɪn'fɔːsmənt‖-ɔːr- / *n*
see OPERANT CONDITIONING, STIMULUS-RESPONSE THEORY

negative transfer /'negətɪv 'trænsfɜːʳ / *n*
see LANGUAGE TRANSFER

negator /nɪ'geɪtəʳ / *n*
a word which makes a sentence a negative sentence. For example,
English negators include *not, hardly ever, never, seldom, neither, nothing.*
see also NEGATIVE PRONOUN

negotiation /nɪˌgəʊʃi'eɪʃən/ *n*
(in conversation) what speakers do in order to achieve successful
communication. For conversation to progress naturally and for
speakers to be able to understand each other it may be necessary for
them to:
a indicate that they understand or do not understand, or that they
   want the conversation to continue (see FEEDBACK)
b help each other to express ideas (see FOREIGNER TALK)
c make corrections when necessary to what is said or how it is said
   (see REPAIR).
These aspects of the work which speakers do in order to make
successful conversation is known as negotiation, in CONVERSATIONAL
ANALYSIS.
see also ACCOMMODATION, CONVERSATIONAL MAXIM, ETHNOMETHOD-
OLOGY
Further reading Garfinkel 1967

neologism /ni'ɒlədʒɪzəm‖-'ɑːl-/ *n*
a new word or expression which has come into a language. It is often
difficult to pinpoint the exact year when a neologism appears in a
language but it has been suggested that, in English, the word *non-
standard* has been used regularly since about 1923 and the word *null-
hypothesis* since about 1935.
Often neologisms are the result of the opening up of new areas of art,

science or technology. For example, the field of computer science brought about a large range of neologisms such as *user-friendly*, *software*, *floppy disk*.

network /'netwɜːk‖-ɜːr-/ *n*

a group of people within a larger community who are in a relatively fixed relationship to one another and who communicate among themselves in certain more or less predictable ways, e.g. a family group, a tutorial group at a university, the staff in an office. Recognition of networks and their structures is of importance for studies of language variation, language use, and language learning. There are two differences between a network and a PEER GROUP:

a in a peer group all members have equal STATUS, but in a network members may be of unequal status (e.g. parents and children in a family).

b in a network all members know one another, but in a peer group this need not be so. For example, a lexicographer may consider all lexicographers to be his or her peer group without knowing them all personally.

Nevertheless, most peer groups are networks and many networks are peer groups.

Further reading Milroy 1987

neurolinguistics /ˌnjʊərəʊlɪŋ'gwɪstɪks‖ˌnʊərə-/ *n* **neurolinguistic** *adj*

the study of the function the BRAIN performs in language learning and language use. Neurolinguistics includes research into how the structure of the brain influences language learning, how and in which parts of the brain language is stored (see MEMORY), and how damage to the brain affects the ability to use language (see APHASIA).

Further reading Lamendella 1979

neutralization /ˌnjuːtrəlaɪ'zeɪʃən‖ˌnuːtrələ-/ *n* **neutralize** /'njuːtrəlaɪz ‖'nuː-/ *v*

the process which takes place when two distinctive sounds (PHONEMES) in a language are no longer distinctive (i.e. in contrast). This usually occurs in particular positions in a word. For example, in German /t/ and /d/ are neutralized at the end of a word. *Rad* "wheel" and *Rat* "advice" are both pronounced /raːt/.

node /nəʊd/ *n*

(in TRANSFORMATIONAL GENERATIVE GRAMMAR) each position in a **tree diagram** where lines ("branches") meet. At each node is a symbol for a GRAMMATICAL CATEGORY[2].

For example, in the tree diagram for a noun phrase, *the child*:

the category symbols NP (NOUN PHRASE[1]), Det (DETERMINER), N (NOUN) are all at nodes in the diagram.

The NP node is said to **dominate** the Det node and the N node.

see also BASE COMPONENT

noise[1] /nɔɪz/ *n*

When speech sounds are produced, the moving particles of air from the lungs may form regular patterns (see SOUND WAVE) or irregular patterns. These irregular patterns are called noise and occur in the production of certain consonants such as /s/.

Further reading Gimson 1980

noise[2] *n*

(in INFORMATION THEORY) any disturbance or defect which interferes with the transmission of the message from one person to another. In speech, this interference could be caused by other sounds, e.g. a pneumatic drill, a voice on the radio. Because of the presence of noise, a certain degree of REDUNDANCY is necessary in any communication.

nominal /ˈnɒmɪnəl||ˈnɑ:-/ *n*

1 a term used instead of NOUN

2 a term for a linguistic unit which has some but not all characteristics of a noun, e.g. *wounded* in *The wounded were taken by helicopter to the hospital*.

Although *wounded* is the HEAD of the noun phrase *the wounded* and is preceded by an article, it would not be modified by an adjective but by an adverb, e.g. *the seriously wounded*.

nominal clause /ˈnɒmɪnəl ˌklɔ:z||ˈnɑ:-/ *n*
also noun clause

a clause which functions like a noun or noun phrase; that is, which may occur as subject, object COMPLEMENT, in APPOSITION, or as prepositional COMPLEMENT. For example:

nominal clause as subject: *What she said is awful*.

nominal clause as object: *I don't know what she said*.

nominalization /ˌnɒmɪnəlaɪˈzeɪʃən||ˌnɑ:mɪnələ-/ *n* nominalize
/ˈnɒmɪnəl-aɪz||ˈnɑ:-/ *v*

the grammatical process of forming nouns from other parts of speech, usually verbs or adjectives. For example, in English: nominalized forms from the verb *to write*: *writing, writer* as in: *His writing is illegible. Her mother is a writer*.

nominal scale /ˈnɒmɪnəl ˌskeɪl||ˈnɑ:-/ *n*

see SCALE

nominative case /ˈnɒmɪnətɪv keɪs, ˈnɒmnə-||ˈnɑ:-/ *n*

the form of a NOUN or noun phrase (see NOUN PHRASE[1]) which usually shows that the noun or noun phrase can function as the subject of the sentence.

For example, in the German sentence:

Der Tisch ist sehr groß

The table is very big.

the article has the ending *-er* to show that the noun phrase is in the nominative case because it is the subject of the sentence.

see also CASE[1]

non-defining relative clause /'nɒndɪˌfaɪnɪŋ 'relətɪv 'klɔːz||'nɑːn-/ *n*
also **non-restrictive relative clause**

see DEFINING RELATIVE CLAUSE

nondirective interview /'nɒndɪ̡rektɪv 'ɪntəvjuː, daɪ-||'nɑːn- -tər-/ *n*

an INTERVIEW which is not directed or structured and in which the interviewer allows the person being interviewed to speak freely about a range of topics of his or her own choice, with a minimum amount of questioning by the interviewer.

see also DEPTH INTERVIEW, FOCUSED INTERVIEW, GUIDED INTERVIEW, INTERVIEW GUIDE

non-finite verb /'nɒnˌfaɪnaɪt 'vɜːb||'nɑːn- 'vɜːrb/ *n*

see FINITE VERB

non-literate /ˌnɒn'lɪtər̡t◄||ˌnɑːn-/ *n*

a culture or group which has no written language, i.e. which possesses an ORAL CULTURE.

non-native varieties of English /'nɒn ˌneɪtɪv və'raɪətiz əv 'ɪŋglɪʃ|| 'nɑːn-/ *n*

a term sometimes used for varieties of English used in countries where English is a SECOND LANGUAGE, such as Singapore English, Nigerian English, Indian English.

see also NATIVIZATION

Further reading Kachru 1981; Platt, Weber & Ho 1984

non-past /ˌnɒn'pɑːst||ˌnɑːn'pæst/ *n, adj*

a term sometimes used for the PRESENT TENSE form of a verb in languages such as English. It emphasizes that this verb form is generally used to describe time periods other than the past, but not necessarily the present. For example:

I leave tomorrow. (future reference)

The sun rises in the east. (general truth)

¬-pro-drop language /ˌnɒn 'prəʊ drɒp 'læŋgwɪdʒ||ˌnɑːn drɑːp/ *n*

see PRO-DROP PARAMETER

non-punctual /ˌnɒn ˈpʌŋktʃuəl‖ˌnɑːn/ *adj*
see PUNCTUAL-NONPUNCTUAL DISTINCTION

non-restrictive relative clause /ˈnɒn rɪˌstrɪktɪv ˈrelətɪv ˈklɔːz‖ˌnɑːn/ *n*
another term for **non-defining relative clause**
see DEFINING RELATIVE CLAUSE

nonstandard /ˌnɒnˈstændəd◄‖ˌnɑːnˈstændərd◄/ *adj*
used of speech or writing which differs in pronunciation, GRAMMAR, or vocabulary from the STANDARD VARIETY of the language. Sometimes the expression SUBSTANDARD is used but linguists prefer the term nonstandard as it is a more neutral term.

see also NORM, STANDARD VARIETY

non-verbal communication /nɒnˈvɜːbəl kəˌmjuːnᵻˈkeɪʃən‖nɑːnˈvɜːr-/ *n*
communication without the use of words. This could be done, for instance, by gestures (see PARALINGUISTICS) or signs (see SIGN LANGUAGE).

norm[1] /nɔːm‖nɔːrm/ *n* **normative** /ˈnɔːmətɪv‖-ɔːr-/ *adj*
that which is considered appropriate in speech or writing for a particular situation or purpose within a particular group or community. The norm for an informal situation may be very different from the norm for a formal one.
For example, in English, a first name (*Joe*) may be the norm for addressing people in an informal situation but title and surname (*Mr Smith*) for a formal one.

see also STANDARD VARIETY, STYLE
Further reading Richards 1982

norm[2] *n*
(in testing and statistics) the scores or typical performance of a particular group (the "norm group") as measured in some way. Norms may be used to compare the performance of an individual or group with the norm group. Norms may be expressed by reference to such factors as age, length of previous instruction, or PERCENTILE rank on a test.

normal distribution /ˈnɔːməl ˌdɪstrᵻˈbjuːʃən‖ˈnɔːr-/ *n*
(in statistics) a commonly occurring DISTRIBUTION of scores in a SAMPLE, in which scores rise and fall gradually from a single peak. It forms a symmetrical bell-shaped curve. In a normal distribution the MEAN, MEDIAN, and MODE all coincide, and the information necessary for describing the distribution is given in the mean and the STANDARD DEVIATION (SD).

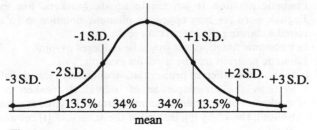

The normal curve

normalized standard score /ˈnɔːməlaɪzd ˈstændəd ˈskɔːʳ‖ˈnɔːr--dərd/ *n*

(in statistics) a STANDARD SCORE which has been converted to a NORMAL DISTRIBUTION through a statistical procedure. For example a PERCENTILE ranking is a normalized standard score.

normative grammar /ˈnɔːmətɪv ˈgræməʳ‖ˈnɔːr-/ *n*

a grammar which contains rules for what is considered to be correct or appropriate usage. The rules may be based on classical literary works or the speech of those people who are considered as models for others to copy. In a nation in which many different DIALECTS are spoken, a NATIONAL LANGUAGE may be developed and a normative grammar and dictionary produced.

see also PRESCRIPTIVE GRAMMAR, STANDARD VARIETY

norm referenced test /ˈnɔːm ˈrefərənst ˈtest‖-ɔːr-/ *n*

see CRITERION REFERENCED TEST

notation /nəʊˈteɪʃən/ *n* **notate** /nəʊˈteɪt/ *v*
also **transcription**

the use of symbols (see PHONETIC SYMBOLS) to show sounds or sound sequences in written form. There are different systems of phonetic symbols. One of the most commonly used is that of the International Phonetic Association.

A distinction is made between two types of notation:

1 **Phonemic notation** uses only the distinctive sounds of a language (PHONEMES). It does not show the finer points of pronunciation. Phonemic notation is written within slanting brackets.

For example, the English word *foot* may appear in phonemic notation as /fʊt/. /f/, /ʊ/, and /t/ are phonemes of English. Phonemic notation may be used, for example:

a for languages which have no writing system of their own

b for teaching purposes, to show differences in pronunciation, e.g. /hed/ *head* and /hæt/ *hat*.

2 **Phonetic notation** (also **phonetic script**) uses phonetic symbols for various sounds, including symbols to show in detail how a particular sound is pronounced. It is used to show finer points of pronunciation.

249

Phonetic notation is written in square brackets. For example, the English word *pin* may appear in phonetic notation as [pʰɪn] with the raised *h* showing the ASPIRATION of the [p].

In phonemic notation, *pin* would be rendered as /pɪn/.

Phonetic notation may be used, for example:

a to show the different pronunciation of closely related dialects

b to show the pronunciation of individual speakers or groups of speakers. For example, students learning English may use a DENTAL t-sound, shown by [t̪], instead of the ALVEOLAR [t] commonly used in English.

Phonemic notation is sometimes referred to as **broad notation** and phonetic notation as **narrow notation**.

see also INTERNATIONAL PHONETIC ALPHABET

Further reading Gimson 1989

notion /ˈnəʊʃən/ *n*

see NOTIONAL SYLLABUS

notional-functional syllabus /ˈnəʊʃənəl ˈfʌŋkʃənəl ˈsɪləbəs/ *n*

another term for NOTIONAL SYLLABUS

notional grammar[1] /ˈnəʊʃənəl ˈgræməʳ/ *n*

a grammar which is based on the belief that there are categories such as TENSE, MOOD, GENDER, NUMBER, and CASE which are available to all languages although not all languages make full use of them. For example, a case system (see CASE[1]) is found in German, Latin, and Russian, but not in modern English.

TRADITIONAL GRAMMAR was often notional in its approach and sometimes attempted to apply some categories to a language without first investigating whether they were useful and appropriate for describing that language.

Further reading Lyons 1981

notional grammar[2] *n*

a grammar based on the meanings or concepts that people need to express through language (e.g. time, quantity, duration, location) and the linguistic items and structures needed to express them.

Further reading Leech & Svartvik 1975

notional syllabus /ˈnəʊʃənəl ˈsɪləbəs/ *n*
also notional-functional syllabus

(in language teaching) a SYLLABUS in which the language content is arranged according to the meanings a learner needs to express through language and the functions the learner will use the language for.

The term NOTIONAL is taken from NOTIONAL GRAMMAR[2]. A notional syllabus is contrasted with a grammatical syllabus or STRUCTURAL SYLLABUS (one which consists of a sequence of graded language items) or a situational syllabus (one which consists of situations and the relevant language items (see SITUATIONAL METHOD)).

A notional syllabus contains:

a the meanings and concepts the learner needs in order to communicate (e.g. time, quantity, duration, location) and the language needed to express them. These concepts and meanings are called **notions**.

b the language needed to express different functions or SPEECH ACTS (e.g. requesting, suggesting, promising, describing).

These notions and functions are then used to develop learning/ teaching units in a language course.

see also COMMUNICATIVE APPROACH

Further reading Wilkins 1976

noun /naʊn/ *n*

a word which (a) can occur as the subject or object of a verb or the object (COMPLEMENT) of a preposition (b) can be modified by an adjective (c) can be used with DETERMINERS.

Nouns typically refer to people, animals, places, things, or abstractions.

see also ADJECTIVAL NOUN, ANIMATE NOUN, COLLECTIVE NOUN, CONCRETE NOUN, COUNTABLE NOUN, PROPER NOUN, PARTS OF SPEECH

noun clause /'naʊn ˌklɔːz/ *n*

another term for NOMINAL CLAUSE

noun phrase[1] /'naʊn ˌfreɪz/ *n*
also NP

(in STRUCTURALIST LINGUISTICS, TRANSFORMATIONAL GENERATIVE GRAMMAR and related grammatical theories) a group of words with a noun or pronoun as the main part (the HEAD).

The noun phrase may consist of only one word (for example *Gina* in *Gina arrived yesterday*) or it may be long and complex (for example, all the words before *must* in: *The students who enrolled late and who have not yet filled in their cards must do so by Friday*).

noun phrase[2] *n*

(in some TRADITIONAL GRAMMARS) a participial (see PARTICIPLES) or INFINITIVE phrase which could be replaced by a noun or pronoun.

For example, the participial phrase *mowing the lawn* in:

  George just hates mowing the lawn.

could be replaced by *it*:

  George just hates it.

NP /ˌen 'piː/ *n*

an abbreviation for NOUN PHRASE[1]

nucleus /'njuːkliəs||'nuː-/ *n*

see SYLLABLE

null hypothesis /'nʌl haɪ'pɒθɪˌsɪs||-'pɑː-/ *n*

see HYPOTHESIS

null subject parameter /'nʌl ˌsʌbdʒɪkt pə'ræmɪ̯təʳ/ n

another term for PRO-DROP PARAMETER

number[1] /'nʌmbəʳ/ n

a grammatical distinction which determines whether nouns, verbs, adjectives, etc. in a language are singular or plural. In English this is seen particularly in NOUNS and DEMONSTRATIVES.

For example:

	singular	plural
count noun	*book*	*books*
demonstrative	*this*	*these*

number[2] n

numbers are used either as **cardinal numbers** (or **cardinals**) or **ordinal numbers** (or **ordinals**).

Cardinal numbers are used when counting; e.g. *6 boys*, *200 dollars*, *a million years*, and they may be used as nouns (e.g. *count up to ten*)

Ordinal numbers are used when we put things in a numerical order; e.g. *first, second, third, fourth, fifth*, etc.

Both cardinal numbers and ordinal numbers can be written with figures (e.g. *6, 6th*) or with words (*six, sixth*).

number concord /'nʌmbəʳ ˌkɒŋkɔːd‖ˌkɑːŋkɔːrd/ n

see CONCORD

numeral /'njuːmərəl‖'nuː-/ n

a word or phrase which is used to name a number.

In English, numerals may be **cardinal numbers** – *one, two, three*, etc. – or **ordinal numbers** – *first, second, third*, etc.

see also DETERMINER, QUANTIFIER, NUMBER[2]

Further reading Quirk et al 1985

O

object[1] /'ɒbdʒɪkt||'ɑːb-/ *n*
the noun, noun phrase or clause, or pronoun in sentences with
TRANSITIVE VERBS, which is traditionally described as being affected by
the action of the verb. The object of a verb can be affected by the verb
either directly or indirectly.
If it is affected directly, it may be called the **direct object**. In English,
the direct object of a verb may be:
a created by the action of the verb, as in:
  Terry baked a cake.
b changed in some way by the action of the verb as in:
  Terry baked a potato.
c perceived by the SUBJECT of the verb, as in:
  Terry saw the cake.
d evaluated by the subject of the verb, as in:
  Terry liked the cake.
e obtained or possessed by the subject of the verb, as in:
  Terry bought the cake.
If the object of a verb is affected by the verb indirectly, it is usually
called the **indirect object**. In English, the indirect object may be:
a the receiver of the direct object, as in:
  Terry gave me the cake. (= "Terry gave the cake *to* me")
b the beneficiary of the action of the verb, as in:
  Terry baked me the cake. (= "Terry baked the cake *for* me")
In English, direct objects and many indirect objects can become
subjects when sentences in the active voice are changed to the passive
voice (see VOICE[1]):
  The cake was given (to) me.
  I was given the cake.
see also GOAL[1], OBJECT OF RESULT

object[2] **(of a preposition)** *n*
another term for **prepositional complement**
see COMPLEMENT

object case /'ɒbdʒɪkt ˌkeɪs||'ɑːb-/ *n*
another term for OBJECTIVE CASE

object complement /'ɒbdʒɪkt 'kɒmplɪmənt||'ɑːb- 'kɑːm-/ *n*
see COMPLEMENT

objective /əb'dʒektɪv/ *n*
a goal of a course of instruction. Two different types of objectives may
be distinguished.

253

General objectives, or **aims**, are the underlying reasons for or purposes of a course of instruction. For example, the aims of the teaching of a foreign language in a particular country might be: to teach students to read and write a foreign language, to improve students' knowledge of a foreign culture, to teach conversation in a foreign language, etc. Aims are long-term goals, described in very general terms.

Specific objectives (or simply objectives), are descriptions of what is to be achieved in a course. They are more detailed descriptions of exactly what a learner is expected to be able to do at the end of a period of instruction. This might be a single lesson, a chapter of a book, a term's work, etc. For instance, specific objectives of a classroom lesson might be: Use of the linking words *and, but, however, although*. These specific objectives contribute to the general objective of paragraph writing. A description of specific objectives in terms which can be observed and measured is known as a BEHAVIOURAL OBJECTIVE.

Further reading Pratt 1980

objective case /ɒbˈdʒektɪv ˌkeɪs‖ɑːb-/ n
also object case

(In CASE GRAMMAR) the noun or noun PHRASE[1] that refers to whoever or whatever has the most neutral relationship to the action of the verb is in the objective case.

The noun or noun phrase in the objective case neither performs the action, nor is the instrument of the action.

For example, in the sentences:

They sliced <u>the sausage</u> with a knife.
<u>*The sausage*</u> *sliced easily.*
<u>*The sausage*</u> *was thick.*

the sausage is neither agent (like *they*) nor instrument (like a *knife*). It is in the objective case.

The notion of the objective case is related to the traditional notion of OBJECT[1]. But not everything in the objective case would be an object, and nor all objects would be considered to be in the objective case.

see also CASE GRAMMAR
Further reading Fillmore 1968

objective test /əbˈdʒektɪv ˈtest/ n

see SUBJECTIVE TEST

objective test item /əbˈdʒektɪv ˈtest ˌaɪtəm/ n

a TEST ITEM which requires the choice of a single correct answer, such as a MULTIPLE-CHOICE ITEM or a TRUE-FALSE ITEM.

see also SUBJECTIVE TEST

object of result /ˈɒbdʒɪkt əv rɪˈzʌlt‖ˈɑːb-/ n
also affected object

an object of a verb which refers to something that is produced through the action indicated by the verb, e.g. *a cake* in:

Terry baked a cake.

as the cake is the result of the baking.
However, in:
> *Terry baked a potato.*

a potato is not an object of result as it is not produced by baking. It is, however, affected by baking, and so may be called an **affected object**.

see also FACTITIVE CASE
Further reading Quirk et al 1985

observational methods /ˈɒbzəveɪʃənəl ˈmeθədz||ˈɑːbzɚr-/ n

(in research) procedures and techniques that are based on systematic observation of events, e.g. using audio and video recorders, check lists, etc. Observational methods are often used in studying language use and classroom events.

see also ETHNOGRAPHY OF COMMUNICATION, EXPERIMENTAL METHOD

obstruent /ˈɒbstruənt||ˈɑːb-/ n, adj

a speech sound (a CONSONANT) where the passage of the air from the lungs is obstructed in some way or other (e.g. the /p/ in *pin*, the /s/ in *sing*). Sounds such as /n/ and /m/ are not usually considered obstruents because although the air is stopped in the mouth, it is allowed free passage through the nose.

In GENERATIVE PHONOLOGY, obstruents are often marked [-sonorant] to distinguish them from sounds such as VOWELS, NASALS, etc., which are marked [+ sonorant].

see also DISTINCTIVE FEATURE
Further reading Hyman 1975

official language /əˈfɪʃəl ˈlæŋgwɪdʒ/ n

see NATIONAL LANGUAGE

off-task behaviour /ˈɒf tɑːsk bɪˈheɪvjəʳ||ˈɔːftæsk/ n

see on-task behaviour

online/ ˈɒnlaɪn||ˈɔːn-,ˈɑːn-/ adj

1 in a computer system, a device is said to be online (i.e. on) or offline (i.e. off) at any given time.
2 An online system in a computer is a system that allows the user to link with it by means of computer. The user gains access to the ·computer through telecommunication links or using his or her own computer.

onomatopoeia /ˌɒnəmætəˈpiːə||ˌɑː-/ n onomatopoeic /ˌɒnəmætəˈpiːɪk||ˌɑː-/ adj

imitation of natural sounds by means of words or groups of words, as in English *moo, baa, cuckoo*. There are other words which are examples of "semi-onomatopoeia", such as the English words *swish, growl, splash*. Languages differ in their choice of onomatopoeic words. An English cock goes *cock-a-doodle-do*; a Japanese one goes *kokekokko*.

onset /'ɒnset‖'ɔːn-, 'ɑːn-/ *n*

see SYLLABLE, TONE UNIT

on-task behaviour /'ɒn taːsk bɪ'heɪvjəʳ‖'ɔːn-, 'ɑːn tæsk/ *n*

(in a lesson or learning activity) learner behaviour which is directed towards the lesson or activity. For example, during a class in which students have been asked to read a passage and answer questions about it, students may not give their full attention to the task during the lesson. Behaviour not related to the task (i.e. **off-task behaviour**) may include getting up and talking to a classmate or doodling. The goal of an effective teacher is said to be to increase the amount of time students are engaged in on-task behaviour in order to provide them with maximum opportunities for learning.

see also TIME ON TASK, EFFECTIVE TEACHING

Further reading Kindsvatter, Wilen & Ishler 1988

ontogeny /ɒn'tɒdʒ₁ni‖ɑːn'tɑː-/ *n* **ontogentic** /ˌɒntədʒ₁'netɪk‖ˌɑːn-/ *adj*

also **ontogenesis** /ˌɒntə'dʒen₁s₁s‖ˌɑːn-/

In studies of child LANGUAGE ACQUISITION, the development of language in an individual is sometimes referred to as ontogeny, and the historical development of language in a speech community as **phylogeny**. Linguists are interested in whether the ontogeny of language in the child shows similar stages to those which a language has gone through in its historical development. In other words, they are interested in the famous question whether ontogeny recapitulates phylogeny.

open class /ˌəupən 'klaːs◄‖'klæs◄/ *n*

also **open set**

a group of words (a WORD CLASS), which contains an unlimited number of items.

Nouns, verbs, adjectives, and adverbs are open-class words. New words can be added to these classes, e.g. *laser, Chomskyan*.

The word classes conjunctions, prepositions, and pronouns consist of relatively few words, and new words are not usually added to them. These are called **closed classes,** or **closed sets**.

Further reading Quirk et al 1985

open-ended question /'əupən end₁d 'kwestʃən/ *n*

a TEST ITEM which allows the person taking the test to answer in his or her own way, in contrast to questions with limited multiple-choice possibilities.

open-ended response /'əupən end₁d rɪ'spɒns‖-'spaːns/ *n*

see TEST ITEM

openings /'əupənɪŋz/ *n*

see CONVERSATIONAL OPENINGS

open set /ˌəʊpən 'set◀/ *n*
another term for OPEN CLASS

open syllable /'əʊpən 'sɪləbəl/ *n*
see SYLLABLE

open vowel /'əʊpən 'vaʊəl/ *n*
also **low vowel**
see VOWEL

operant /'ɒpərənt||'ɑ:-/ *n*
see OPERANT CONDITIONING

operant conditioning /'ɒpərənt kən'dɪʃənɪŋ||'ɑ:-/ *n*
a learning theory proposed by the American psychologist Skinner, and an important aspect of behaviourist psychology (see BEHAVIOURISM). It is a type of conditioning (see CONDITIONED RESPONSE) in which an organism (e.g. a child learning its first language) produces an action (e.g. an UTTERANCE) which achieves an outcome or purpose for the child (e.g. to get food). This action is called the **operant**. If the outcome is favourable the operant is likely to occur again, and is said to be reinforced. It is positively reinforced (**positive reinforcement**) if the operant is followed by something pleasant, and negatively reinforced (**negative reinforcement**) if it is followed by the removal of something unpleasant. If there is no outcome (i.e. no reinforcement), or if the outcome is unpleasant, the operant is less likely to occur again. Skinner believed that children learn language according to the principle of operant conditioning.
Further reading Skinner 1957; Elliot 1981

operating principle /'ɒpəreɪtɪŋ 'prɪnsḷpəl||'ɑ:pə-/ *n*
see HEURISTIC

operating system /'ɒpəreɪtɪŋ ˌsɪstḷm||'ɑ:p-/ *n*
the main program used in a computer to schedule and organize the processing resources. The operating system manages the storage and retrieval of information on the computer and keeps order among the various files and programs. A common operating system used for word processing (see WORD PROCESSOR) is known as **DOS**.

operational definition /ɒpə'reɪʃənəl defʒ'nɪʃən||ɑ:-/ *n*
operationalize /ɒpə'reɪʃənəlaɪz||ɑ:-/ *v*
a definition of a concept in terms which can be observed and measured. In language teaching and language testing, many linguistic concepts need to be operationalized. For example, terms such as "competence" and "proficiency" need to be operationalized in preparing programme goals, OBJECTIVES, and test items.

operator /'ɒpəreɪtər||'ɑ:-/ *n*
(in English) the first AUXILIARY VERB to occur in a verb phrase, so

257

opposition

called because it is the verb which "operates" as the question-forming word, by moving to the initial position in the sentence in questions. For example:

a *He will   be   coming*
    aux 1   aux 2
    (operator)
b *She   couldn't   have   been   there.*
    aux 1   aux 2 aux 3
    (operator)
a becomes <u>*Will*</u> *he be coming?*
b becomes <u>*Couldn't*</u> *she have been there?*

Further reading Quirk et al 1985

opposition /ɒpə'zɪʃən‖ɑːpə-/ n

the relationship between pairs of elements in a language, such as the distinctive sounds (PHONEMES).

For example, the opposition between /k/ and /g/ in English distinguishes between the MINIMAL PAIR *cut* /kʌt/ and *gut* /gʌt/.

In general, the term "opposition" is used when two elements differ in only one feature. So English /k/ and /g/ are said to be in opposition because they differ only in that /g/ is **voiced** and /k/ is **voiceless** (see VOICE²). One is less likely to speak of the opposition between /k/ and /b/ (as in *cut* /kʌt/ and *but* /bʌt/), because they differ in several ways involving both PLACE OF ARTICULATION and VOICING.

see MARKEDNESS

optimum age hypothesis /'ɒptɪ̩məm 'eɪdʒ haɪˌpɒθɪ̩sɪ̩s‖ 'ɑːp- haɪˌpɑː-/ n

the hypothesis that there is an ideal or optimal age (below puberty) during which languages can be learned relatively easily, and after which language learning is more difficult. This hypothesis has not been supported by direct evidence but is based on the observation that children often learn a second or foreign language more easily than older learners.

see also BRAIN
Further reading Penfield & Lamar Roberts 1959

oral¹ /'ɔːrəl/ adj

a term used to stress that a spoken form of language is used as opposed to a written form, as in *an oral test, an oral examination.*

oral² adj, n

(of) a speech sound which is produced while the soft palate (the **velum**) at the back of the mouth is raised so that the airstream from the lungs cannot escape through the nose.

In English, all vowels, and all consonants except /m/, /n/, and /ŋ/ as in /sɪŋ/ *sing*, are oral.

In GENERATIVE PHONOLOGY, oral sounds are marked [-nasal] to distinguish them from NASAL sounds.

see also MANNER OF ARTICULATION, PLACE OF ARTICULATION
Further reading Hyman 1975

oral approach /'ɔːrəl ə'prəʊtʃ/ *n*
another term for SITUATIONAL LANGUAGE TEACHING

oral cavity /'ɔːrəl 'kævʲti/ *n*
see VOCAL TRACT, PLACE OF ARTICULATION

oral culture /'ɔːrəl ˌkʌltʃəʳ/ *n*
the culture of a society in which culture and cultural values are communicated through spoken language rather than through writing. A society in which written language plays an important part in culture and cultural values is said to have a **literary culture.**

see also NON-LITERATE

oralist /'ɔːrəlɪst/ *n*
see SIGN LANGUAGE

oral language /'ɔːrəl ˌlæŋgwɪdʒ/ *n*
see AURAL LANGUAGE

oral method /'ɔːrəl ˌmeθəd/ *n*
a method for teaching the deaf, based on lip-reading and carefully articulated speech. This method is now less commonly used than the AUDITORY/ORAL METHOD.

oral reading /'ɔːrəl 'riːdɪŋ/ *n*
see READING

order of acquisition /'ɔːdər əv ˌækwʲ'zɪʃən||'ɔːr-/ *n*
also **acquisition order**
the order in which linguistic forms, rules, and items are acquired in first- or second-language learning.

see also LANGUAGE ACQUISITION, NATURAL ORDER HYPOTHESIS
Further reading Brown 1973

ordinal number /'ɔːdʲnəl 'nʌmbəʳ||'ɔːr-/ *n*
also **ordinal**
see NUMBER²

ordinal scale /'ɔːdʲnəl 'skeɪl||'ɔːr-/ *n*
see SCALE

orthography /ɔː'θɒgrəfi||ɔːr'θɑː-/ *n* **orthographic** /ˌɔːθə'græfɪk◄||ˌɔːr-/ *adj*
The term "orthography" is used:
1 for spelling in general.
2 for correct or standard spelling.

259

For some languages, the orthography is based on generally accepted usage and is not prescribed by an official body. For other languages, e.g. Swedish, it is laid down by official or semi-official organizations. Like the term "spelling" itself, the term "orthography" is more likely to be used of alphabetic writing than of syllabic writing, and is unlikely to be used of ideographic writing (see WRITING SYSTEMS).

other repair /ˈʌðəʳ rɪˌpeəʳ/ *n*
see REPAIR

outline /ˈaʊtlaɪn/ *n* **outlining** /ˈaʊtlaɪnɪŋ/ *v*
(in composition) a plan for an essay or piece of writing which presents the main points the essay will cover and the order in which they will be mentioned. In an outline, main points are distinguished from supporting details, sometimes using systems of numerals and letters. Several kinds of outlines are often used.

1 **Topic Outline**: each entry is a word or group of words.

2 **Sentence Outline**: similar to a topic outline except that the words are replaced by sentences.

3 **Paragraph Outline**: this contains only a list of TOPIC SENTENCES for each paragraph.

Further reading Herman 1982

output /ˈaʊtpʊt/ *n*
see INPUT

over-extension /ˈəʊvər ɪkˈstenʃən/ *n*
another term for OVERGENERALIZATION

overgeneralization /ˈəʊvəʳˌdʒenərəlaɪˈzeɪʃən‖-rələ-/ *n*
overgeneralize /ˌəʊvəˈdʒenərəlaɪz‖-vər-/ *v*
also **over-extension, over-regularization, analogy**
a process common in both first- and second-language learning, in which a learner extends the use of a grammatical rule of linguistic item beyond its accepted uses, generally by making words or structures follow a more regular pattern. For example, a child may use *ball* to refer to all round objects, or use *mans* instead of *men* for the plural of *man*.

see also LANGUAGE TRANSFER, ERROR ANALYSIS, INTERLANGUAGE
Further reading Dulay, Burt, & Krashen 1982

over-regularization /ˈəʊvəʳˌregjʊləraɪˈzeɪʃən‖-lərə-/ *n*
another term for OVERGENERALIZATION

P

paired-associate learning /ˈpeəd əˈsəʊʃi-ɪ̩t ˈlɜːnɪŋ,-ʃɪ̩t ‖ˈpeərd ˈlɜːr-/ *n*

a type of learning task used in studies of VERBAL LEARNING. Pairs of words or other learning items are presented and the learner is required to make associations between them. For example:

horse – brown
bird   – blue
table – white

The learner is tested with the first member of the pair to see if the second item can be remembered.

see also ASSOCIATIVE LEARNING

Further reading Gagné 1970

pair work /ˈpeəʳ ˌwɜːk‖ˌwɜːrk/ *n*
also **pair practice** /ˈpeəʳ ˌpræktɪ̩s/

(in language teaching) a learning activity which involves learners working together in pairs.

see also GROUP WORK

palatal /ˈpælətl/ *adj*

describes a speech sound (typically a CONSONANT) which is produced by the front upper surface of the tongue touching or nearly touching the hard palate at the top of the mouth.

For example, in German the /ç/ in /ɪç/ *ich* "I", and in /nɪçt/ *nicht* "not" is a palatal FRICATIVE. And in English, the /j/ in /jes/ "yes" may be called an unrounded palatal SEMI-VOWEL.

see also PLACE OF ARTICULATION, MANNER OF ARTICULATION

Further reading Gimson 1989

palatalization /ˌpælətəlaɪˈzeɪʃən‖-tələ-/ *n* **palatalize** /ˈpælətəlaɪz/ *v*

the raising of the front upper surface of the tongue towards the hard palate at the top of the mouth. Palatalization of speech sounds may occur when the sound is followed by a close front vowel such as /i/ (see VOWEL).

For example, in the Paris dialect of French, the /k/ is palatalized in /ki/ *qui* "who".

see also PLACE OF ARTICULATION, MANNER OF ARTICULATION

Further reading Gimson 1980

palate /ˈpælɪ̩t/ *n*

see PLACE OF ARTICULATION

261

paradigm /'pærədaɪm/ *n* **paradigmatic** /,pærədɪg'mætɪk◄/ *adj*

a list or pattern showing the forms which a word can have in a grammatical system. For example, in English:

singular	plural
boy	*boys*
boy's	*boys'*
(of the boy)	(of the boys)

Paradigms may be used to show the different forms of a verb. For example, in French:

singular	plural
je parle "I speak"	*nous parlons* "we speak"
tu parles "you speak"	*vous parlez* "you speak"
il parle "he speaks"	*ils parlent* "they speak"
elle parle "she speaks"	*elles parlent* "they speak"

Paradigms typically show a word's INFLECTIONS rather than its derivatives (see DERIVATION).

paradigmatic relations /'pærədɪg,mætɪk rɪ'leɪʃənz/ *n*
also **paradigmatic relationships**

see SYNTAGMATIC RELATIONS

paragraph /'pærəgrɑːf||-græf/ *n*

a unit of organization of written language, which serves to indicate how the main ideas in a written text are grouped. In TEXT LINGUISTICS, paragraphs are treated as indicators of the macro-structure of a text (see SCHEME). They group sentences which belong together, generally, those which deal with the same topic. A new paragraph thus indicates a change in topic or sub-topic. In English a paragraph begins on a new line and the opening sentence of a new paragraph is usually set in from the margin (i.e. is indented).

see also DISCOURSE ANALYSIS
Further reading Van Dijk 1977

paragraph outline /'pærəgrɑːf 'aʊtlaɪn||-græf/ *n*

see OUTLINE

paralinguistic features /'pærəlɪŋ,gwɪstɪk 'fiːtʃəz||-ərz/ *n*

see PARALINGUISTICS

paralinguistics /,pærəlɪŋ'gwɪstɪks/ *n* **paralinguistic** *adj*

the study or use of non-vocal phenomena such as facial expressions, head or eye movements, and gestures, which may add support, emphasis, or particular shades of meaning to what people are saying. These phenomena are known as **paralinguistic features**.

For example, in many English-speaking countries, nodding the head could be used instead of various spoken ways of showing agreement, such as *yes*, *that's right*, or *agreed*. Sometimes head-nodding accompanies and emphasizes verbal agreement.

The use of paralinguistic features in this sense is also called **kinesics**.

For some linguists, paralinguistic features would also include those vocal characteristics such as TONE OF VOICE which may express the speaker's attitude to what he or she is saying.

see also PROXEMICS

parallel construction /'pærəlel kən'strʌkʃən/ n

a sentence containing words, phrases, clauses or structures which are repeated.
For example:
Michael *smiled* at the baby, *touched* her arm, then *winked* at her.

parallel distributed processing /'pærəlel dɪs'trɪbjʊ̈t̬d 'prəʊsesɪŋ|| 'prɑː-/ n
also PDP

A theory in COGNITIVE SCIENCE that assumes that the individual components of human information processing are highly interactive and that knowledge of events, concepts and language is represented diffusely in the cognitive system and distributed throughout the system. The theory has been applied to models of speech processing and second language acquisition. It provides a mathematical model that tries to capture both the essence of information processing, learning, and thought processes. The basic assumptions of the theory are:

1 Information processing takes place through the interactions of a large number of simple units operating in parallel.
2 Learning takes place through the strengthening and weakening of the interconnections in a particular network in response to examples encountered in the INPUT.
3 The result of learning is a network of simple units that acts as though it knew the rules, although the rules themselves exist only in the form of association strengths distributed across the entire network.

Further reading Schmidt 1988; Rumelhart & McClelland 1986; Sampson 1987

parallel form reliability /'pærəlel fɔːm rɪ,laɪə'bɪl̥ti||-ɔːr-/ n
another term for ALTERNATE FORM RELIABILITY

parallel forms /'pærəlel 'fɔːmz||-ɔːr-/ n
also equivalent forms, alternate forms

different forms of a test which try to measure exactly the same skills or abilities, which use the same methods of testing, and which are of equal length and difficulty.
In general, if people get similar scores on parallel forms of a test, this suggests that the test is reliable (see RELIABILITY).

parallel processing /'pærəlel 'prəʊsesɪŋ||'prɑː-/ n
information processing in which two or more processing operations are carried out at the same time or in parallel, such as when people try to

remember a word and search for its meaning, spelling and pronunciation at the same time. This may be compared with **sequential processing**, where the two pieces of information are processed in sequence, such as when one tries to listen to two simultaneous conversations by attending to both but going back and forth rapidly from one to the other.

parameter /pə'ræm‚tə‖-tər/ *n*

(in Government/Binding Theory) a general condition or rule which is part of the CORE GRAMMAR but which may vary, within certain limits, from one language to another.

An example is the **headparameter** which stipulates the position of the HEAD (main element) within each phrase.

In English, the head is first in a phrase, for example:

<u>with</u> the car   (prepositional phrase)
<u>counted</u> the money   (verb phrase)

In Japanese, the head is last in the phrase, for example:

(*Watashi wa*)	*nihonjin*	<u>*desu*</u>	"I'm Japanese/a Japanese person"
I	Japanese	<u>am</u>	
	Nihon	<u>*ni*</u>	"In Japan"
	Japan	<u>in</u>	

Although the position of the head is different in the two languages, it is claimed that there are universal limits on the variation, namely that a language has the head in the same place in *all* its phrases.

There have been a number of investigations in the field of language acquisition into **parameter settings,** that is how children learn to "set" a parameter so that it fits their particular language. In second language acquisition the investigations have centred around the 'resetting' of parameters. For example, Japanese speakers acquiring English would need to 'reset' the headparameter from a 'head-last' to a 'head-first' position.

see also PRO-DROP PARAMETER
Further reading Cook 1988, Flynn 1989, White 1989a, 1989b

parameter settings /pə'ræm‚təʳ ˌsetɪŋz/ *n*

see PARAMETER

paraphrase /'pærəfreɪz/ *n, v*

an expression of the meaning of a word or phrase using other words or phrases, often in an attempt to make the meaning easier to understand.

For example, *to make (someone or something) appear or feel younger* is a paraphrase of the English verb *rejuvenate*.

Dictionary definitions often take the form of paraphrases of the words they are trying to define.

parsing /'pɑːzɪŋ‖'pɑːrsɪŋ/ *n* **parse** /pɑːz‖pɑːrs/ *v*

the identification of parts of a sentence as SUBJECT, VERB, OBJECT[1], etc. and of words in a sentence as noun (plural), verb (past tense), etc.

For example, in English:

	subject		verb	object
The	*noisy*	*frogs*	*disturbed*	*us*
definite article	adjective	noun (plural)	verb (past tense)	pronoun (1st-person plural)

Parsing is a well-established technique of TRADITIONAL GRAMMAR. Attempts are now being made to carry out parsing with the help of a computer.

participant /pɑːˈtɪsɪ�჻pənt‖pɑːr-/ *n*
a person who is present in a SPEECH EVENT and whose presence may have an influence on what is said and how it is said. He or she may actually take part in the exchange of speech or be merely a silent participant; for example, as part of an audience to whom a political speech is made.

see also INTERLOCUTORS
Further reading Hymes 1977

participant observation /pɑːˈtɪsɪ̗pənt ˌɒbzəˈveɪʃən‖pɑːr- ˌɑːbzər-/ *n*
participant observer /pɑːˈtɪsɪ̗pənt əbˈzɜːvəʳ‖pɑːr- -ɜːr-/ *n*
a research procedure used in different types of research, including language research, in which the researcher or observer takes part in the situation he or she is studying as a way of collecting data for further study.
It is claimed that an observer who is also a participant can understand a situation more fully than an observer who is merely looking on from the outside.

participle /ˈpɑːtɪ̗sɪpəl‖ˈpɑːr-/ *n* **participial** /ˌpɑːtɪ̗ˈsɪpiəl‖ˌpɑːr-/ *adj*
a non-finite verb form (see FINITE VERB) which functions as an adjective, and is used in passive sentences (see VOICE[1]) and to form PERFECT and PROGRESSIVE ASPECT. There are two participles in English, the **present participle** and the **past participle**.
The present participle is formed by adding *-ing* to a verb base. It functions as an adjective (e.g. a *smiling* girl, a *self-winding* watch); it is used with *BE* to form the PROGRESSIVE (e.g. *It is raining*); it occurs in constructions such as *Let's go shopping*.
The past participle is usually formed by adding *-ed* to a verb base; exceptions are the *-en*-suffix (*break – broken*; *fall – fallen*) and some irregular verbs (e.g. *build – built*). It is used as an adjective (e.g. *a broken window*); it is used with *BE* to form the passive (e.g. *I was amused by her*); it is used to form the PERFECT ASPECT (e.g. *She has finished*).

particle /ˈpɑːtɪkəl‖ˈpɑːr-/ *n*
a term sometimes used for a word which cannot readily be identified with any of the main PARTS OF SPEECH (i.e. as a noun, verb, adverb etc.). The word *not* and the *to* used with INFINITIVES are sometimes called particles for this reason, as well as *up*, *down* and similar adverbs when they function as ADVERB PARTICLES.

partitive

partitive /'pɑːtɪ̬tɪv||'pɑːr-/ *n*
also **partitive construction** /'pɑːtɪ̬tɪv kənˈstrʌkʃən||'pɑːr-/
a phrase used to express quantity and used with an uncountable noun
(see COUNTABLE NOUN). There are three types of partitive in English:
a measure partitives, e.g. *a yard of cloth, an acre of land, two pints of milk*
b typical partitives (i.e. where a particular partitive collocates with a
particular noun), e.g. *a slice of cake, a stick of chalk, a lump of coal*
c general partitives (i.e. those which are not restricted to specific
nouns), e.g. *a piece of paper/cake, a bit of cheese/cloth.*
see also COLLOCATION
Further reading Quirk et al 1985

part learning /'pɑːt ˌlɜːnɪŋ||'pɑːrt ˌlɜːr-/ *n*
see GLOBAL LEARNING

part skills /'pɑːt ˌskɪlz||-ɑːr-/ *n*
another term for MICRO-SKILLS

parts of speech /'pɑːts əv 'spiːtʃ||-ɑːr-/ *n*
a traditional term to describe the different types of word which are
used to form sentences, such as noun, pronoun, verb, adjective, adverb,
preposition, conjunction, interjection. From time to time other parts of
speech have been proposed, such as DETERMINER.
Parts of speech may be identified by:
a their meaning (e.g. a verb is the name of a state or event: *go*)
b their form (e.g. a verb has an *-ing*-form, a past tense, and a past
participle: *going, went, gone*)
c their function (e.g. a verb may form or be part of the PREDICATE of a
sentence: *They went away*).
These criteria will identify the most typical representatives of each part
of speech. However, many problems still remain. For example, in the
sentence:
Their going away surprised me.
is *going* a verb or a noun?
see also GERUND, PARTICIPLE, PARTICLE

passive language knowledge /'pæsɪv 'læŋgwɪdʒ ˌnɒlɪdʒ||ˌnɑː-/ *n*
see ACTIVE/PASSIVE LANGUAGE KNOWLEDGE

passive vocabulary /'pæsɪv vəˈkæbjᵿləri, vəʊ-||-leri/ *n*
see ACTIVE/PASSIVE LANGUAGE KNOWLEDGE

passive voice /'pæsɪv 'vɔɪs/ *n*
see VOICE[1]

past continuous /'pɑːst kənˈtɪnjuəs||'pæst/ *n*
see PROGRESSIVE

266

past participle /'pɑːst 'pɑːtᵼsɪpəl||'pæst 'pɑːr-/ *n*
see PARTICIPLE

past perfect /'pɑːst 'pɜːfɪkt||'pæst 'pɜːr-/ *n*
see PERFECT

past tense /'pɑːt 'tens||'pæst/ *n*
the form of a verb which is usually used to show that the act or state
described by the verb occurred at a time before the present.
For example, in English:

present tense	past tense
is	*was*
walk	*walked*
try	*tried*

The form of the past which is used without an AUXILIARY VERB (e.g. I
left, he *wept*) is sometimes known as the **simple past** or **preterite**.

patient θ-role /'peɪʃənt 'θiːtə ˌrəʊl/ *n*
see θ-THEORY/THETA THEORY

pattern practice /'pætn ˌpræktᵼs||-tərn/ *n*
see DRILL

pausing /'pɔːzɪŋ/ *n*
also **hesitation phenomena**
a commonly occurring feature of natural speech in which gaps or
hesitations appear during the production of utterances. The commonest types of pauses are:
a **silent pauses**: silent breaks between words
b **filled pauses**: gaps which are filled by such expressions as *um, er,
mm*.
People who speak slowly often use more pauses than people who speak
quickly. When people speak, up to 50% of their speaking time may be
made up of pauses.

see also FLUENCY
Further reading Clark & Clark 1977

peak (of a syllable) /piːk/ *n*
see SYLLABLE

PDP /ˌpiː diː 'piː/ *n*
an abbreviation for PARALLEL DISTRIBUTED PROCESSING

pedagogic grammar /ˈpedəɡɒdʒɪk 'ɡræməʳ||-ɡɑː-, -ɡəʊ-/ *n*
also **pedagogical grammar**
a grammatical description of a language which is intended for
pedagogical purposes, such as language teaching, syllabus design, or
the preparation of teaching materials. A pedagogic grammar may be
based on:

a grammatical analysis and description of a language

b a particular grammatical theory, such as TRANSFORMATIONAL GENERATIVE GRAMMAR

c the study of the grammatical problems of learners (see ERROR ANALYSIS)

or on a combination of approaches. An example of a pedagogic grammar of English is Close's *A reference grammar for students of English* (Close 1975).

peer editing /ˈpɪəʳ ˌedɪtɪŋ/ *n*
another term for PEER REVIEW

peer feedback /ˈpɪəʳ ˌfiːdbæk/ *n*
another term for PEER REVIEW

peer group /ˈpɪəʳ ˌgruːp/ *n*
a group of people with whom a person associates or identifies, e.g. neighbourhood children of the same age, or members of the same class at school or of the same sports team.

see also NETWORK

peer review/ ˈpɪəʳ rɪˌvjuː/ *n*
also **peer feedback, peer editing**
(in the teaching of composition, particularly according to the PROCESS APPROACH) an activity in the revising stage of writing (see COMPOSING PROCESSES) in which students receive FEEDBACK about their writing from other students – their peers. Typically students work in pairs or small groups, read each other's compositions and ask questions or give comments or suggestions.

peer teaching /ˈpɪəʳ ˌtiːtʃɪŋ/ *n*
also **peer mediated instruction** /ˈpɪəʳ ˈmiːdieɪtᵻd ɪnˈstrʌkʃən/
classroom teaching in which one student teaches another, particularly within an individualized approach to teaching (see INDIVIDUALIZED INSTRUCTION). For example, when students have learnt something, they may teach it to other students, or test other students on it.

peer tutoring /ˈpɪəʳ ˌtjuːtərɪŋ‖ˌtuː-/ *n*
see CO-OPERATIVE LEARNING

percentile /pəˈsentaɪl‖pər-/ *n*
(in statistics) a term indicating the position of a given score or test-taker in a distribution divided into 100 ranks. For example, a score at the 9th percentile will be among the top 10% of all the scores. The higher one's percentile score, the better, on most tests.

see also DISTRIBUTION[1]

perception /pəˈsepʃən‖pər-/ *n*
the recognition and understanding of events, objects, and stimuli

through the use of senses (sight, hearing, touch, etc.). Several different types of perception are distinguished:

a **Visual perception**: the perception of visual information and stimuli

b **Auditory perception**: the perception of information and stimuli received through the ears. Auditory perception requires a listener to detect different kinds of acoustic signals, and to judge differences between them according to differences in such acoustic characteristics as their frequency, amplitude, duration, order of occurrence, and rate of presentation.

c **Speech perception**: the understanding or comprehension of speech (see CHUNKING, HEURISTIC (2)).

perceptual salience /pəˈseptʃuəl ˈseɪliəns‖pər-/ *n*

another term for SALIENCE

perfect /ˈpɜːfɪkt‖ˈpɜːr-/ *n*

(in grammar) an ASPECT which shows a relationship between one state or event and a later state, event, or time. In English the perfect is formed from the AUXILIARY VERB *have* and the past PARTICIPLE. For example:

I have finished. She has always loved animals.

If the auxiliary is in the present tense, the verb group is described as the **present perfect** (e.g. *They have eaten*) and if the auxiliary is in the past tense, the verb group is described as the **past perfect** (e.g. *They had finished*).

English also has a fairly rare **future perfect** (*They will have finished before noon tomorrow*).

In English the perfect generally refers

a to a state or event that extends up to a point in time (e.g. *I have lived here for six years* – up to now)

b to an event that occurred within a time period (e.g. *Have you ever been to Paris* – in your life up to now)

c to an event that has results which continue up to a point in time (e.g. *I have broken my watch* – and it's still broken now).

Further reading Leech 1971

performance /pəˈfɔːməns‖pərˈfɔːr-/ *n*

(in TRANSFORMATIONAL GENERATIVE GRAMMAR) a person's actual use of language. A difference is made between a person's knowledge of the language (COMPETENCE) and how a person uses this knowledge in producing and understanding sentences (performance). The difference between linguistic competence and linguistic performance can be seen, for example, in the production of long and complex sentences (see RECURSIVE RULE). People may have the competence to produce an infinitely long sentence but when they actually attempt to use this knowledge (to "perform") there are many reasons why they restrict the number of adjectives, adverbs, and clauses in any one sentence. They may run out of breath, or their listeners may get bored or forget what has been said if the sentence is too long. Psycholinguists attempt to describe how competence is used in the actual production and understanding of sentences (performance). In second and foreign language learning, a learner's performance in a language may indicate his or her competence (see PERFORMANCE ANALYSIS).

There is also a somewhat different way of using the term "performance". In using language, people make errors (see SPEECH ERRORS) or false starts. These may be due to **performance factors** such as fatigue, lack of attention, excitement, nervousness. Their actual use of language on a particular occasion may not reflect their competence. The errors they make are described as examples of performance.

see also USAGE[1]

Further reading Fromkin & Rodman 1983; Chomsky 1965

performance analysis /pə'fɔːməns ə,næl̩s̩s̩||pər'fɔːr-/ *n*
(in SECOND LANGUAGE ACQUISITION research) an approach to the study of a learner's COMPETENCE in a language, based on the study of a learner's total linguistic performance (i.e. what the learner is able to say and do in the language) and not just the learner's errors (see ERROR ANALYSIS).

Further reading Svartvik 1973

performance factors /pə'fɔːməns ,fæktəz||pər'fɔːr- -tərz/ *n*
see PERFORMANCE

performance grammar /pə'fɔːməns ,græməʳ||pər'fɔːr-/ *n*
a description of the rules or strategies which people use when they produce and understand sentences. A performance grammar may be contrasted with a competence grammar (see COMPETENCE), which is a description of the linguistic knowledge of speakers and hearers, but not an explanation of how they use that knowledge in speaking and listening.

Further reading Carroll 1973

performance objective /pə'fɔːməns əb'dʒektɪv||pər'fɔːr-/ *n*
another term for BEHAVIOURAL OBJECTIVE

performative /pə'fɔːmətɪv||pər'fɔːr-/ *n*
(in SPEECH ACT theory) an utterance which performs an act, such as *Watch out* (= a warning), *I promise not to be late* (= a promise). The philosopher Austin distinguished between performatives and **constatives**. A constative is an utterance which asserts something that is either true or false; for example, *Chicago is in the United States.* Austin further distinguished between **explicit performatives** (those containing a "performative verb", such as *promise, warn, deny*, which names the speech act or **illocutionary force** of the sentence) and **implicit performatives**, which do not contain a performative verb, e.g. *There is a vicious dog behind you* (= an implied warning).

It has even been suggested that there is no real difference between constatives and implicit performatives, because the sentence *Chicago is* in the United States can be understood to mean (*I state that*) *Chicago is in the United States*, with the implicit performative verb *state*.

Further reading Austin 1962; Searle 1981

periphery /pəˈrɪfəri/ *n*
also **peripheral grammar** /pəˈrɪfərəl ˈɡræməʳ/
    see CORE GRAMMAR

perlocutionary act /ˈpɜːləʊˌkjuːʃənəri ˈækt‖ˈpɜːrləʊˌkjuːʃəneri/ *n*
    see LOCUTIONARY ACT

perseveration error /pəˌsevəˈreɪʃən ˌerəʳ‖pər-/ *n*
    see SPEECH ERRORS

person /ˈpɜːsən‖ˈpɜːr-/ *n*
a grammatical category which determines the choice of pronouns in a sentence according to such principles as:

a whether the pronoun represents or includes the person or persons actually speaking or writing ("first person", e.g. *I, we*)

b whether the pronoun represents the person or persons being addressed ("second person", e.g. *you*)

c whether the pronoun represents someone or something other than the speaker/writer or the listener/reader ("third person", e.g. *he, she, it, they*).

personal function /ˈpɜːsənəl ˈfʌŋkʃən‖ˈpɜːr-/ *n*
    see DEVELOPMENTAL FUNCTIONS OF LANGUAGE

personality /ˌpɜːsəˈnælˌti‖ˌpɜːr-/ *n*
those aspects of an individual's behaviour, attitudes, beliefs, thought, actions and feelings which are seen as typical and distinctive of that person and recognized as such by that person and others. Personality factors such as self-esteem, inhibition, anxiety, RISK-TAKING and extroversion (see EXTROVERT), are thought to influence second language learning because they can contribute to MOTIVATION and the choice of learner strategies.

Further reading Brown 1987

personal pronouns /ˈpɜːsənəl ˈprəʊnaʊnz‖ˈpɜːr-/ *n*
the set of pronouns which represent the grammatical category of PERSON, and which in English is made up of *I, you, he, she, it, we, they*, and their derived forms (e.g. *me, mine, yours, him, his, hers*, etc.).

PF component /ˌpiː ˈef kəmˌpəʊnənt/ *n*
also **phonetic component**
    see D-STRUCTURE

pharyngeal /ˌfəˈrɪndʒiəl, ˌfærˌnˈdʒiəl/ *n, adj*
a speech sound (a CONSONANT which is produced by pushing the very

back of the tongue (the **root**) towards the back of the throat (the PHARYNX). The airstream from the lungs can be either completely blocked and then released, or allowed to escape with friction (a pharyngeal FRICATIVE).

Pharyngeal sounds are used, for example, in some dialects of Arabic.

see also PLACE OF ARTICULATION, MANNER OF ARTICULATION
Further reading Gimson 1989

pharynx /ˈfærɪŋks/ n

that part of the throat which extends from above the VOCAL CORDs up to the soft palate (**velum**) at the back of the mouth. The pharynx is like a large chamber and in the production of speech sounds its shape and volume can be changed in various ways:

a by tightening the muscles which enclose it
b by movement of the back of the tongue
c by either raising or lowering the soft palate.

Changes in the shape of the pharynx affect the quality of the sounds produced.

see also PLACE OF ARTICULATION

phatic communion /ˈfætɪk kəˈmjuːnjən/ n

a term used by the British-Polish anthropologist Malinowski to refer to communication between people which is not intended to seek or convey information but has the social function of establishing or maintaining social contact. Examples of phatic communion in English include such expressions as *How are you?* and *Nice day, isn't it?*

philology /fɪˈlɒlədʒi||-ˈlɑː-/ n philological /ˌfɪləˈlɒdʒɪkəl◄||-ˈlɑː-/ adj

another term for COMPARATIVE HISTORICAL LINGUISTICS

phone /fəʊn/ n phonic /ˈfɒnɪk||ˈfɑː-/ adj

individual sounds as they occur in speech. Phones are grouped by PHONEMIC ANALYSIS into the distinctive sound units (PHONEMES) of a language.

For example, in English, the different ways of pronouncing the vowel in the word *can* , e.g. long [æː], shorter [æ], with nasalization [æ̃], are all phones of the phoneme /æ/.

see also ALLOPHONE, PHONEMICS, PHONOLOGY

phoneme /ˈfəʊniːm/ n phonemic /fəˈniːmɪk/ adj

the smallest unit of sound in a language which can distinguish two words. For example:

a in English, the words *pan* and *ban* differ only in their initial sound: *pan* begins with /p/ and *ban* with /b/
b *ban* and *bin* differ only in their vowels: /æ/ and /ɪ/.

Therefore, /p/, /b/, /æ/, and /ɪ/ are phonemes of English. The number of phonemes varies from one language to another. English is often considered to have 44 phonemes: 24 CONSONANTS and 20 VOWELS.

see also ALLOPHONE, MINIMAL PAIR, PHONEMICS, PHONOLOGY
Further reading Gimson 1989

phoneme synthesis /ˈfəʊniːm ˈsɪnθ⸱s⸱s/ n

the conversion of a digital representation of phonemes into sounds by a
speech synthesizer (see SPEECH SYNTHESIS)

phonemic analysis /fəˈniːmɪk əˈnæl⸱s⸱s/ n

the grouping of words and sounds (PHONES) in a particular language in
order to decide which are the distinctive sound units (PHONEMES) of
that language and which are only variants of these.
For example, the two English words *nip* and *nib* differ only because *nip*
ends with /p/ and *nib* with /b/. So /p/ and /b/ are two separate English
phonemes.
On the other hand, pronouncing *nip* with an aspirated /p/, [pʰ], does
not make it into another word. So [pʰ] is a variant (an ALLOPHONE) of
/p/ and not a separate phoneme.
There are different approaches to phonemic analysis (see DISTINCTIVE
FEATURES, MINIMAL PAIRS).
see also ALLOPHONE, ASPIRATION, PHONEMICS, PHONOLOGY

phonemic notation /fəˈniːmɪk nəʊˈteɪʃən/ n

see NOTATION

phonemics /fəˈniːmɪks/ n phonemic adj

1 the study or description of the distinctive sound units (PHONEMES) of
a language and their relationship to one another.
2 procedures for finding the phonemes of a language (see PHONEMIC
ANALYSIS).
The term "phonemics" has been used by American linguists,
particularly in STRUCTURAL LINGUISTICS. Lately, the term PHONOLOGY
has been preferred.
3 the phonemic system of a language, as in a phrase like "the
phonemics of English".
see also MORPHOPHONEMICS

phonetic component /fəˈnetɪk kəmˈpəʊnənt/ n

another term for **PF component**
see D-STRUCTURE

phonetic method /fəˈnetɪk ˈmeθəd/ n

another term for PHONICS

phonetic notation /fəˈnetɪk nəʊˈteɪʃən/ n

also **phonetic script**
see NOTATION, PHONETIC SYMBOLS

phonetics /fəˈnetɪks/ n phonetic adj

the study of speech sounds. There are three main areas of phonetics:

1 **Articulatory phonetics** deals with the way in which speech sounds are produced. Sounds are usually classified according to the position of the lips and the tongue, how far open the mouth is, whether or not the VOCAL CORDS are vibrating, etc.

2 **Acoustic phonetics** deals with the transmission of speech sounds through the air. When a speech sound is produced it causes minor air disturbances (SOUND WAVES). Various instruments are used to measure the characteristics of these sound waves.

3 **Auditory phonetics** deals with how speech sounds are perceived by the listener.

For example, a listener may perceive:

a differences ASPIRATION e.g. between the aspirated /p/ of [pʰɪt] *pit* and the unaspirated /p/ of [tɪp] *tip*.

b other differences in sound quality, e.g. between the "clear" /I/ of [laɪt] *light* and the "dark" /I/ of [hɪɫ] *hill*.

see also PHONEMICS, PHONOLOGY
Further reading Gimson 1989; Denes & Pinson 1973

phonetic script /fə'netɪk 'skrɪpt/ *n*
another term for **phonetic notation**
see NOTATION, PHONETIC SYMBOLS

phonetic symbols /fə'netɪk 'sɪmbəlz/ *n*
special symbols which express the sounds of an actual spoken utterance in writing. A transcription of such an utterance in phonetic symbols is said to be in **phonetic notation** or **script**.

For example, the sound which is written *sh* in English, *sch* in German and *ch* in French can be expressed by symbols [ʃ] or [š], e.g. English [ʃɪp] *ship*, German [ʃɪf] *Schiff* "ship", French [ʃik] *chic* "smart, stylish".

see also INTERNATIONAL PHONETIC ALPHABET, NOTATION, PHONETICS

phonics /'fɒnɪks||'fɑː-/ *n*
also **phonetic method**
a method of teaching children to read. It is commonly used in teaching reading in the mother tongue.

Children are taught to recognize the relationship between letters and sounds. They are taught the sounds which the letters of the alphabet represent, and then try to build up the sound of a new or unfamiliar word by saying it one sound at a time.

see also ALPHABETIC METHOD
Further reading Smith 1971

phonological component /ˌfɒnə'lɒdʒɪkəl kəm'pəunənt|| ˌfɑːnə'lɑː-/ *n*
see TRANSFORMATIONAL GENERATIVE GRAMMAR

phonological rule /ˌfɒnəˈlɒdʒɪkəl ˈruːl||ˌfɑːnəˈlɑː-/ *n*
see GENERATIVE PHONOLOGY

phonology /fəˈnɒlədʒi||-ˈnɑː-/ *n* **phonological** /ˌfɒnəˈlɒdʒɪkəl||ˌfɑːnə
ˈlɑː-/ *adj*
1 another term for PHONEMICS.
2 (for some linguists) a cover term for both PHONETICS and PHONEMICS.
3 the establishment and description of the distinctive sound units of a
language (PHONEMES) by means of DISTINCTIVE FEATURES.
Each phoneme is considered as consisting of a group of these features
and differing in at least one feature from the other phonemes, e.g.

/iː/	/uː/
+ high	+ high
– low	– low
– back	+ back
– round	+ round

where the features + or – *high*, + or – *low*, + or – *back* refer to the
position of the tongue in the mouth and + or – *round* to whether the
lips are rounded or not.
Phonology is also concerned with:
a the study of word-to-word relations in sentences; that is, how sound
patterns are affected by the combination of words. For example, /gɪv/
give and /hɪm/ *him* may combine to /gɪvɪm/ *give him*.
b the investigation of INTONATION PATTERNS.
see also BOUNDARIES, GENERATIVE PHONOLOGY, SUPRASEGMENTAL

phonotactics /ˌfəʊnəˈtæktɪks/ *n* **phonotactic** *adj*
(in PHONOLOGY) the arrangements of the distinctive sound units
(PHONEMES) in a language.
For example, in English, the consonant groups (CONSONANT CLUSTERS)
/spr/ and /str/ can occur at the beginning of a word, as in *sprout, strain,*
but they cannot occur at the end of a word. A description of the
phonotactics of English consonant clusters would include this information.

phrasal-prepositional verb /ˈfreɪzəl ˌprepəˈzɪʃənəl ˈvɜːb||ˈvɜːrb/ *n*
see PHRASAL VERB

phrasal verb /ˈfreɪzəl ˈvɜːb||ˈvɜːrb/ *n*
a verbal construction consisting of a verb plus an ADVERB PARTICLE. A
distinction may be made between phrasal verbs, **prepositional verbs,**
and **phrasal-prepositional verbs,** according to the different grammatical patterns in which they occur. For example:

	phrasal verb		prepositional verb
Particle	*Turn OFF the*	Verb may	*I'll APPLY for the*
may be	*light.*	be stressed	*job.*
stressed			

275

phrase

Particle can occur after the object	*Turn the light off.*	Particle cannot occur after the object	(**I'll apply the job for*)
short pronouns occur between the verb and the particle	*Turn it off.* (**Turn off it*)	Pronouns occur after the verb+ particle	*I'll apply for it.* (**I'll apply it for*)

A phrasal-prepositional verb consists of a verb, an adverb particle, and a PREPOSITION:

> *We must cut down on expenses.*
> *They put their failure down to bad advice.*

The meaning of some of these verbal constructions can be guessed from the meanings of their parts (*e.g. cut down on*). But the meaning of others is idiomatic (e.g. *put down to*).

Nowadays the term "phrasal verb" is often used to include phrasal verbs, prepositional verbs, and phrasal-prepositional verbs.

see also IDIOM
Further reading Quirk et al 1985

phrase /freɪz/ *n*
see CLAUSE

phrase marker /'freɪz ˌmɑːkəʳ||ˌmɑːr-/ *n*
also **P-marker**

(in TRANSFORMATIONAL GENERATIVE GRAMMAR) the representation of the structure of a sentence. This could be its basic syntactic structure (DEEP STRUCTURE) or the structure after the application of transformational rules.

see also BASE COMPONENT, TRANSFORMATIONAL COMPONENT
Further reading Chomsky 1965

phrase-structure component /'freɪz 'strʌktʃəʳ kəm'pəʊnənt/ *n*
another term for BASE COMPONENT

phrase-structure grammar /'freɪz 'strʌktʃəʳ 'græməʳ/ *n*
a grammar which analyses the structure of different sentence types in a language. It consists of phrase-structure rules (see BASE COMPONENT) which show how a sentence can be broken up into its various parts (CONSTITUENTS) and how each part can be expanded. The structure of a sentence can be illustrated by a diagram called a **tree diagram**. For example, the structure of the English sentence:

> *The parrot shrieked noisily.*

can be shown by the simplified diagram:

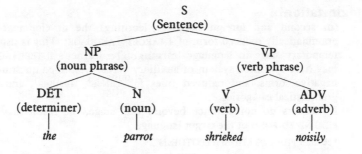

A phrase-structure grammar is a major part of the BASE COMPONENT of a TRANSFORMATIONAL GENERATIVE GRAMMAR.

see also TRANSFORMATIONAL GENERATIVE GRAMMAR
Further reading Chomsky 1957

phrase-structure rule /'freɪz 'strʌktʃəʳ 'ruːl/ *n*

see BASE COMPONENT

phylogeny /fɪ'lɒdʒ³₂ni||-'lɑː-/ *n*
also **phylogenesis** /ˌfaɪləʊ'dʒenₗsₗs/

see ONTOGENY

pidgin /'pɪdʒ³₂n/ *n*

a language which develops as a **contact language** when groups of people who speak different languages try to communicate with one another on a regular basis. For example, this might occur where foreign traders have to communicate with the local population or groups of workers from different language backgrounds on plantations or in factories. A pidgin usually has a limited vocabulary and a reduced grammatical structure which may expand when a pidgin is used over a long period and for many purposes. For example, Tok Pisin (New Guinea Pidgin):

yu	ken	kisim	long	olgeta	bik	pela	stua
you	can	get(it)	at	all	big	(noun marker)	stores

Usually pidgins have no native speakers but there are **expanded pidgins**, e.g. Tok Pisin in Papua New Guinea and Nigerian Pidgin English in West Africa, which are spoken by some people in their community as first or PRIMARY LANGUAGE. Often expanded pidgins will develop into CREOLE languages.

Research has shown that there are some similarities between the structures of pidgin and creole languages and the INTERLANGUAGES of second language learners (seel PIDGINIZATION[2])

see also PIDGINIZATION[1], SUBSTRATUM INTERFERENCE/INFLUENCE, SUPER-STRATUM/SUBSTRATE LANGUAGE
Further reading Muhlhausler 1986; Romaine 1988

pidginization[1] /ˌpɪdʒ³₂naɪ'zeɪʃən||-nə-/ *n*

the process by which a PIDGIN develops.

pidginization[2] *n*

(in second and foreign language learning) the development of a grammatically reduced form of a TARGET LANGUAGE[1]. This is usually a temporary stage in language learning. The learner's INTERLANGUAGE may have a limited system of auxiliary verbs, simplified question and negative forms, and reduced rules for TENSE[1], NUMBER[1], and other grammatical categories.

If learners do not advance beyond this stage, the result may be a PIDGINIZED FORM of the target language.

see also PIDGINIZATION HYPOTHESIS

pidginization hypothesis /ˌpɪdʒˌnaɪˈzeɪʃən haɪˌpɒθˌsˌs||-nə- -ˌpiː-/ *n*

(in SECOND LANGUAGE ACQUISITION theory) the hypothesis that a PIDGINIZED FORM of a language may develop (*a*) when learners regard themselves as socially separate from speakers of the TARGET LANGUAGE[1] (*b*) when a language is used for a very limited range of functions.

see also PIDGINIZATION[2]

Further reading Schumann 1978

pidginized form (of a language) /ˈpɪdʒˌnaɪzd ˌfɔːm||-ɔːr-/ *n*

a variety of a language in which the sentence structure and the vocabulary of the original language have been greatly reduced.

Generally, elements from another language have been absorbed, either in the form of vocabulary items or in the way sentences are structured (see PIDGIN).

An example is Bahasa Pasar (Bazaar Malay), a pidginized form of Malay, which was spoken extensively by Chinese and other non-Malays in Malaysia and Singapore.

pilot testing /ˈpaɪlət ˈtestɪŋ/ *n*

see FIELD TESTING

pitch /pɪtʃ/ *n*

When we listen to people speaking, we can hear some sounds or groups of sounds in their speech to be relatively higher or lower than others. This relative height of speech sounds as perceived by a listener is called "pitch".

For example, in the English question Ready? meaning "Are you ready?" the second syllable -*dy* will be heard as having a higher pitch than the first syllable, though pitch movement upwards will begin on the first syllable *rea*- (see TONE[2]). What we can hear as pitch is produced by the VOCAL CORDS vibrating. The faster the vocal cords vibrate, the higher the pitch.

see also SOUND WAVES

Further reading Fromkin & Rodman 1983

pitch level /ˈpɪtʃ ˌlevəl/ *n*

the relative height of the PITCH of a speaker's voice, as this is perceived by the listener.

For English, three pitch levels have often been recognized: normal pitch level, higher than normal level, lower than normal level.

These three levels cannot be identified in absolute terms. One person's high pitch will not be the same as another person's high pitch. Differences in pitch level are therefore relative (see KEY[2]).

see also TONE UNIT
Further reading Brazil, Coulthard, & Johns 1980; Crystal 1969

pitch movement /'pɪtʃ ˌmuːvmənt/ *n*
another term for TONE[2]

pitch range[1] /'pɪtʃ ˌreɪndʒ/ *n*
variations in PITCH height that an individual speaker is able to produce.

Differences in the pitch of individual speakers are related to differences in the size of their VOCAL CORDS and the structure of their VOCAL TRACT. Usually, women can speak with a higher pitch than men, but there are exceptions.

pitch range[2] *n*
variations in height which are used by a speaker or group of speakers in communication. Whether the pitch range used by individuals in a speech community is wide or narrow often depends on social or cultural conventions and may be a convention of a whole speech community.

For example, the pitch range of the average Australian when speaking English is narrower than that of many British English speakers.

When speakers are in certain emotional states, they may either extend their normal pitch range, e.g. to express anger or excitement, or narrow it, e.g. to express boredom or misery.

Further reading Brazil, Coulthard, & Johns 1980

pivot grammar /'pɪvət ˌgræməʳ/ *n*
a term for a now-discarded theory of grammatical development in first-language learning. Children were said to develop two major grammatical classes of words: a pivot class (a small group of words which were attached to other words, e.g. *on, allgone, more*) and an "open class' (e.g. *shoe, milk*) to which pivot words were attached. The child's early grammar was thought to be a set of rules which determined how the two classes of words could be combined to produce utterances such as *allgone milk, shoe on*.

Further reading McNeill 1970

PLAB /ˌpiː el eɪ 'biː/ *n*
an abbreviation for the *P*imsleur *L*anguage *A*ptitude *B*attery, a test of LANGUAGE APTITUDE.

placement test /'pleɪsmənt ˌtest/ *n*
a test which is designed to place students at an appropriate level in

a programme or course. The term "placement test" does not refer to what a test contains or how it is constructed, but to the purpose for which it is used. Various types of test or testing procedure (e.g. dictation, an interview, a grammar test) can be used for placement purposes.

Further reading Hughes 1989

place of articulation /ˈpleɪs əv ɑːtɪkjʊˈleɪʃən‖ɑːr-/ *n*

there are many parts of the mouth and throat (the **oral cavity**) that are used in the production of speech sounds. The main ones for the articulation of English CONSONANTS are:

a the two lips (BILABIAL), e.g. /p/

b the lower lip touching the upper teeth (LABIODENTAL), e.g. /f/

c the tongue touching the upper teeth (INTERDENTAL), e.g. /θ/ *th* in *thick*

d the tongue touching the **alveolar ridge** (**alveolum**) (ALVEOLAR), e.g. /t/

e the back of the tongue touching the soft palate (**velum**) (VELAR), e.g. /k/

The production of VOWELS is conditioned by the position of the tongue in the mouth, e.g. front vowels, back vowels, high vowels, low vowels (see VOWEL).

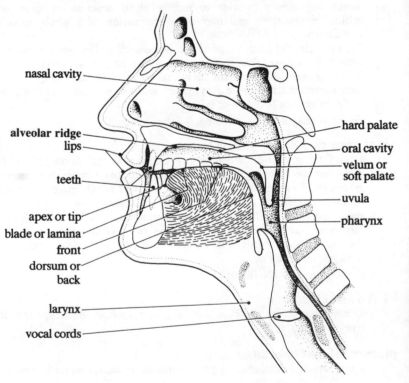

see also CARDINAL VOWELS, MANNER OF ARTICULATION
Further reading Gimson 1989

planning /ˈplænɪŋ/ *n*

see COMPOSING PROCESSES

plosive /ˈpləʊsɪv/ *n*

another term for STOP

plural /ˈplʊərəl/ *n*

(with English COUNTABLE NOUNS, and PRONOUNS,) the form referring
to more than one. For example, *books*, *geese*, *they* are the plurals of *book*,
goose, and *he/she/it*.

P-marker /ˈpiː ˌmɑːkəʳ‖-ɑːr-/ *n*

an abbreviation for PHRASE MARKER

point of view /ˌpɔɪnt əv ˈvjuː/ *n*

(in composition) the position from which the writer presents an idea or
topic. Good writing is said to be written from a consistent point of
view, that is, without any unnecessary shifts of point of view. In the
following example, an inconsistent point of view is used because the
writer shifts from referring to teachers impersonally (using "teachers"
and "they") to referring to them personally (using "you").

> *Teachers should always prepare carefully for lessons. They should never
> walk into class without knowing what they are going to teach, and you
> should never arrive late for class.*

Further reading Herman 1982

politeness /pəˈlaɪtn̩s/ *n*

(in language study) (a) how languages express the SOCIAL DISTANCE
between speakers and their different ROLE RELATIONSHIPS; (b) how
face-work (see FACE), that is, the attempt to establish, maintain, and
save face during conversation, is carried out in a speech community.
Languages differ in how they express politeness. In English, phrases
like *I wonder if I could ...* can be used to make a request more polite.
In other languages the same effect can be expressed by a word or
PARTICLE.

Politeness markers include differences between FORMAL SPEECH and
COLLOQUIAL SPEECH, and the use of ADDRESS FORMS. In expressing
politeness, the anthropologists Brown and Levinson distinguished
between **positive politeness strategies** (those which show the close-
ness, intimacy, and rapport between speaker and hearer) and **negative
politeness strategies** (those which indicate the social distance between
speaker and hearer).

Further reading Brown & Levinson 1978

politeness formula /pəˈlaɪtn̩s ˌfɔːmjʊləʳ‖ˌfɔːr-/ *n*

see ROUTINE

polysemy /pə'lɪsɨmi/ *n* **polysemous** /pə'lɪsɨməs/ *adj*
    (of a word) having two or more closely related meanings, e.g. *foot* in:
    He hurt his foot.
    She stood at the foot of the stairs.
    The foot is the lowest part of the stairs just as the foot is the lowest part
    of the human body.
    A well known problem in SEMANTICS is how to decide whether we are
    dealing with a single polysemous word (like *foot*) or with two or more
    HOMONYMS[3].
    Further reading Hurford and Heasley 1983

polysyllabic /ˌpɒlɪsɨ'læbɪk◄||ˌpɑː-/ *adj*
    (of a word) consisting of more than one SYLLABLE.
    For example, in English:
    baby: *ba-by*
    telephone: *tel-e-phone*
    are polysyllabic words.

population /ˌpɒpjʊ'leɪʃən||ˌpɑːp-/ *n*
    (in statistics) any set of items, individuals, etc. which share some
    common and observable characteristics and from which a SAMPLE can
    be taken. Thus, one can speak of comparing test scores across a sample
    of a population of students.

portmanteau word /pɔːt'mæntəʊ 'wɜːd||pɔːrt- 'wɜːrd/ *n*
also blend
    a word formed by combining parts of other words. For example *brunch*,
    which is formed from *breakfast* and *lunch*.

positive politeness strategies /'pɒzɨtɪv pə'laɪtnɨs ˌstrætɨdʒiz||
'pɑː-/ *n*
    see POLITENESS

positive reinforcement /'pɒzɨtɪv ˌriːɪn'fɔːsmənt||'pɑː- -'fɔːrs-/ *n*
    see OPERANT CONDITIONING, STIMULUS-RESPONSE THEORY

positive transfer /'pɒzɨtɪv 'trænsfɜːʳ||'pɑː-/ *n*
    see LANGUAGE TRANSFER

possessive /pə'zesɪv/ *n*
    a word or part of a word which is used to show ownership or pos-
    session. In English, there are many kinds of possessives, for example:
    a possessive pronouns, such as *my, her, your, mine, hers, yours*, etc.
    b *'s*, as in *Helen's shoes*, and *s'*, as in *the three boys' books*
    c the *of* construction, as in *the home of the doctor*
    The possessive pronouns that are used before a noun (e.g. *my, her, your*)
    are often called "possesive adjectives" to distinguish them from those

that are used after a verb (e.g. *mine, hers, yours*). The distinction can be seen in a pair of sentences like:

My book is here. This book is mine.

see also DETERMINER

Further reading Quirk et al 1985

post-creole continuum /ˈpəʊst ˈkriːəʊl kənˈtɪnjuəm/ *n*

When people in a CREOLE-SPEAKING community are taught in the standard language to which the creole is related, they form a post-creole continuum.

For example, in Jamaica and Guyana, an English-based creole is spoken and Standard English is taught in schools. Those with higher levels of education speak something close to Standard English, the **acrolect**. Those with little or no education speak the creole or something close to it, the **basilect**, and the rest speak a range of varieties in between, the **mesolects**.

speech varieties	speakers
acrolect	higher education and social status
mesolects	
basilect	little or no education, low social status

see also DECREOLIZATION, SPEECH CONTINUUM

postmodifier /ˌpəʊstˈmɒdᵻfaɪəʳ‖-ˈmɑː-/ *n*

see MODIFIER

postponed subject /pəsˈpəʊnd ˈsʌbdʒɪkt/ *n*

see EXTRAPOSITION

postposition /ˌpəʊstpəˈzɪʃən/ *n*

a word or MORPHEME which follows a noun or NOUN PHRASE[1] and indicates location, direction, possession, etc.

For example, in Japanese:

Tokyo – kara

"Tokyo" "from"

"from Tokyo"

English prefers PREPOSITIONS to postpositions, but a word like *notwithstanding* can be used in either way:

The plan went ahead, notwithstanding my protests.

(prepositional use)

The plan went ahead, my protests notwithstanding.

(postpositional use)

post-test /ˈpəʊst ˌtest/ *n*

a test given after learning has occurred or is supposed to have occurred. A test given before learning has occurred is a pre-test. In teaching, the comparison of pre-test and post-test results measures the amount of progress a learner has made.

postverbal negation /'pəʊst,vɜːbəl nɪ'geɪʃən‖-ɜːr-/ *n*
the use of a NEGATOR following a verb, as in German *Ingrid kommt nicht.* (Ingrid comes not = Ingrid isn't coming), where *nicht* is the negator.

postwriting /'pəʊst,raɪtɪŋ/ *n*
see COMPOSING PROCESSES

preverbal negation /'priː,vɜːbəl nɪ'geɪʃən‖-ɜːr-/
the use of a negator preceding the verb, as in Spanish *Juan no va* (Juan not goes = Juan isn't going), where *no* is the negator.

practice effect /'præktɪs ɪ,fekt/ *n*
the effect of previous practice on later performance. For example, in testing how much grammar improvement had occurred in students after a grammar course, if the same items appeared on a pre-test and a post-test (see POST-TEST), students might perform better on the post-test simply because they had already had practice on the items during the pre-test, rather than because of what they had learned from the course.

practice stage /'præktɪs ,steɪdʒ/ *n*
also **repetition stage**
see STAGE

practice teaching /'præktɪs ,tiːtʃɪŋ/ *n*
also **practicum** /'præktɪkəm/, **teaching practice**
(in teacher education) opportunities provided for a student teacher to gain teaching experience, usually through working with an experienced teacher – the CO-OPERATING TEACHER – for a period of time by teaching that teacher's class. Practice teaching experiences may include MICROTEACHING, teaching an individual lesson from time to time, or regular teaching over a whole term or longer, during which the student teacher has direct and individual control over a class. Practice teaching is intended to give student teachers experience of classroom teaching, an opportunity to apply the information and skills they have studied in their teacher education programme, and a chance to acquire basic teaching skills.
Further reading Richards & Nunan 1990

pragmatic error /præg'mætɪk 'erəʳ/ *n*
see ERROR

pragmatics /præg'mætɪks/ *n* **pragmatic** *adj*
the study of the use of language in communication, particularly the relationships between sentences and the contexts and situations in which they are used. Pragmatics includes the study of:
a how the interpretation and use of UTTERANCES depends on knowledge of the real world

b how speakers use and understand SPEECH ACTS

c how the structure of sentences is influenced by the relationship between the speaker and the hearer.

Pragmatics is sometimes contrasted with SEMANTICS, which deals with meaning without reference to the users and communicative functions of sentences.

see also USAGE[2]

Further reading Leech 1983; Levinson 1983; Palmer 1981

predeterminer /ˌpriːdɪˈtɜːmɪnəʳ‖-ɜːr-/ *n*

a word which occurs before DETERMINERS in a NOUN PHRASE[1]. For example, in English the QUANTIFIERS *all, both, half, double, twice,* etc. can be predeterminers.

all the bread

determiner

predeterminer

Further reading Quirk et al 1985

predicate /ˈpredɪkɪt/ *n* predicate /ˈpredɪkeɪt/ *v*

that part of a sentence which states or asserts something about the SUBJECT and usually consists of a verb either with or without an OBJECT[1], COMPLEMENT, or ADVERB. For example:

Joan is tired.

The children saw the play.

The sun rose.

Adjectives, nouns, etc. which occur in the predicate are said to be used "predicatively". For example:

Her behaviour was friendly. (PREDICATIVE ADJECTIVE)

These books are dictionaries. (predicative noun)

see also ATTRIBUTIVE ADJECTIVE

predication /ˌpredɪˈkeɪʃən/ *n*

see PROPOSITION

predicative adjective /prɪˈdɪkətɪv ˈædʒɪktɪv/ *n*

an adjective that is used after a verb

see also ATTRIBUTIVE ADJECTIVE

predictive validity /prɪˈdɪktɪv vəˈlɪdɪti/ *n*

a type of VALIDITY based on the degree to which a test accurately predicts future performance. A LANGUAGE APTITUDE test, for example, should have predictive validity, because the results of the test should predict the ability to learn a second or foreign language.

prefabricated language /priːˈfæbrɪkeɪtɪd ˈlæŋgwɪdʒ/ *n*
also prefabricated speech /priːˈfæbrɪkeɪtɪd ˈspiːtʃ/

another term for ROUTINE

preferred language /prɪˈfɜːd ˈlæŋgwɪdʒ‖-ɜːrd/ *n*
    see PRIMARY LANGUAGE

prefix /ˈpriːfɪks/ *n*
    a letter or sound or group of letters or sounds which are added to the beginning of a word, and which change the meaning or function of the word.
    Some COMBINING FORMS can be used like prefixes. For example, the word *pro-French* uses the prefix *pro-* "in favour of", and the word *Anglo-French* uses the combining form *Anglo-* "English".
    see also AFFIX

premodifier /priːˈmɒdɪ̬faɪəʳ‖-ˈmɑː-/ *n*
    see MODIFIER

pre-operational stage /ˌpriːɒpəˈreɪʃənəl ˌsteɪdʒ‖-ɑːpə-/ *n*
    see GENETIC EPISTEMOLOGY

preposition /ˌprepəˈzɪʃən/ *n*
    a word used with NOUNS, PRONOUNS and GERUNDS to link them grammatically to other words. The phrase so formed, consisting of a preposition and its COMPLEMENT, is a **prepositional phrase**. In English, a prepositional phrase may be "discontinuous", as in:
    Who(m) did you speak to?
    Prepositions may express such meanings as possession (e.g. *the leg of the table*), direction (e.g. *to the bank*), place (e.g. *at the corner*), time (e.g. *before now*). They can also mark the cases discussed in CASE GRAMMAR. For example, in the sentence:
    Smith killed the policeman with a revolver.
    the preposition *with* shows that a revolver is in the INSTRUMENTAL CASE.
    In English, too, there are groups of words (e.g. *in front of, owing to*) that can function like single-word prepositions.
    see also POSTPOSITION
    Further reading Quirk et al 1985

prepositional adverb /ˈprepəˌzɪʃənəl ˈædvɜːb‖-ɜːr-/ *n*
    another term for ADVERB PARTICLE

prepositional complement /ˈprepəˌzɪʃənəl ˈkɒmplɪ̬mənt‖ˈkɑːm-/ *n*
also **prepositional object** /ˈprepəˌzɪʃənəl ˈɒbdʒɪkt‖ˈɑːb-/, **object (of a preposition)**
    see COMPLEMENT

prepositional phrase /ˈprepəˌzɪʃənəl ˈfreɪz/ *n*
    see PREPOSITION

prepositional verb /ˈprepəˌzɪʃənəl ˈvɜːb‖ˈvɜːrb/ *n*
    see PHRASAL VERB

prescriptive grammar /prɪˈskrɪptɪv ˈgræməʳ/ *n*

a grammar which states rules for what is considered the best or most correct usage. Prescriptive grammars are often based not on descriptions of actual usage but rather on the grammarian's views of what is best. Many TRADITIONAL GRAMMARS are of this kind.

see also DESCRIPTIVE GRAMMAR, NORMATIVE GRAMMAR

presentation stage /ˌprezənˈteɪʃən ˌsteɪdʒ/ *n*

see STAGE

present continuous /ˈprezənt kənˈtɪnjuəs/ *n*

see PROGRESSIVE

present participle /ˈprezənt ˈpɑːt̬sɪpəl‖ˈpɑːr-/ *n*

see PARTICIPLE

present perfect /ˈprezənt ˈpɜːfɪkt‖ˈpɜːr-/ *n*

see PERFECT

present perfect continuous /ˈprezənt ˈpɜːfɪkt kənˈtɪnjuəs‖ˈpɜːr-/ *n*

see PROGRESSIVE

present tense /ˈprezənt ˈtens/ *n*

a tense which typically relates the time of an action or state to the present moment in time. In English the present tense can also be used to refer to future time (e.g. *We leave tomorrow*) or to timeless expressions (e.g. *Cats have tails*), and for this reason it is sometimes called the NON-PAST tense.

see also ASPECT

preservice education /ˈpriːsɜːvɪ̯s edjʊ̯ˈkeɪʃən‖-ɜːr- edʒə-/ *n*
also **preservice training** /ˈpriːsɜːvɪ̯s ˈtreɪnɪŋ‖-ɜːr-/

(in teacher education) a course or programme of study which student teachers complete before they begin teaching. This may be compared with INSERVICE EDUCATION, which refers to experiences which are provided for teachers who are already teaching and which form part of their continued professional development. Preservice education often sets out to show future teachers basic teaching techniques and give them a broad general background in teaching and in their subject matter. Inservice education or training usually takes place for a specific purpose and often involves the following cycle of activities:

1 assess participants' needs
2 determine objectives for inservice programme
3 plan content
4 choose methods of presentation and learning experiences
5 implement
6 evaluate effectiveness
7 provide follow-up assistance

Inservice programmes for language teachers are sometimes referred to as **Continuing Education for Language Teachers (CELT)**.

Further reading Richards & Nunan 1990

presupposition /ˌpriːsʌpəˈzɪʃən/ *n* presuppose /ˌpriːsəˈpəʊz/ *v*

what a speaker or writer assumes that the receiver of the message already knows.

For example:

speaker A: *What about inviting Simon tonight?*

speaker B: *What a good idea; then he can give Monica a lift.*

Here, the presuppositions are, amongst others, that speakers A and B know who Simon and Monica are, that Simon has a vehicle, most probably a car, and that Monica has no vehicle at the moment. Children often presuppose too much. They may say:

. . . and he said "let's go" and we went there.

even if their hearers do not know who *he* is and where *there* is.

see also COHERENCE, COHESION

pre-teaching /ˈpriː ˈtiːtʃɪŋ/ *n*

selecting new or difficult items that students will meet in a future classroom activity, and teaching such items before the activity. For example, difficult words in a listening-comprehension exercise may be taught before students do the exercise.

preterite /ˈpretərɪ̩t/ *n*

see PAST TENSE

pre-test /ˈpriːˌtest/ *n* pre-test /ˌpriːˈtest/ *v*

the try-out phase of a newly written but not yet fully developed test. Tests under development may be revised on the basis of the ITEM ANALYSIS obtained from the results of pre-testing.

see also POST-TEST

pretonic /priːˈtɒnɪk‖-ˈtɑː-/ *n, adj*

see TONE UNIT

preverbal negation /ˈpriːvɜːbəl nɪˈgeɪʃən‖-ɜːr-/ *n*

see POSTVERBAL NEGATION

pre-writing /ˈpriː ˌraɪtɪŋ/ *n*

see COMPOSING PROCESSES

primary cardinal vowel /ˈpraɪməri ˈkɑːdɪ̩nəl ˈvaʊəl‖-meri ˈkɑːr-/ *n*

see CARDINAL VOWEL

primary language /ˈpraɪməri ˈlæŋgwɪdʒ‖-meri/ *n*
also **preferred language**

People speaking more than one language (see BILINGUAL, MULTI-LINGUAL) may not necessarily be most fluent in the first language they acquired as a child (the mother tongue). The terms primary language or **preferred language** are used to refer to the language which bilingual or multilingual speakers are most fluent in or which they prefer using for most everyday communicative functions.

primary language instruction /'praɪmərɪ ˌlæŋgwɪdʒ ɪnˈstrʌkʃən‖ -merɪ/ *n*

an approach to the teaching of **limited English proficient** (see LIMITED ENGLISH SPEAKER) students in which instruction in the students' primary language – i.e. the native language of the students – is used for subjects which are the most cognitively demanding.

primary stress /'praɪmərɪ 'stres‖-merɪ/ *n*

see STRESS

principal clause /'prɪnsᵻpəl 'klɔːz/ *n*

see DEPENDENT CLAUSE

principle of subjacency /'prɪnsᵻpəl əv sʌbˈdʒeɪsənsɪ/ *n*

see BOUNDING THEORY

principles /'prɪnsᵻpəlz/ *n*

see UNIVERSAL GRAMMAR

PRO /prəʊ/ *n*
also **BIG PRO**

This term is used in GOVERNMENT/BINDING THEORY when discussing embedded sentences with infinitives, e.g.

 a I wanted to leave
 b I wanted Anita to leave
 c It is time to leave

The proposed D-STRUCTURE for these sentences would be

 d I wanted [PRO *to leave*]
 e I wanted Anita [PRO *to leave*]
 f It is time [PRO *to leave*]

In *d* and *e* the element PRO behaves like an anaphor. In *d* it refers to *I* and in *e* it refers to *Anita*. In *f* PRO does not behave like an anaphor but more like a pronoun referring to someone or some people outside the sentence (see BINDING PRINCIPLE).

Further reading Cook 1988

pro
also **little pro**

This term is used in GOVERNMENT/BINDING THEORY when discussing declarative sentences which do not have an overt subject (see PRO-DROP PARAMETER).

proactive inhibition /prəʊˈæktɪv ˌɪnhᵻˈbɪʃən/ *n*
also **proactive interference** /prəʊˈæktɪv ɪntəˈfɪərəns‖-tər-/

the interfering effect of earlier learning on later learning. For example, if a learner first learns how to produce questions which require AUXILIARY VERB inversion (e.g. *I can go → Can I go?*) this may interfere with the learning of patterns where auxiliary inversion is not required. The learner may write *I don't know where can I find it* instead of *I don't know where I can find it*. By contrast, **retroactive inhibition/interference** is the effect of later learning on earlier learning. For example, children learning English may learn irregular past-tense forms such as *went, saw*. Later, when they begin to learn the regular *-ed* past-tense inflection, they may stop using *went* and *saw* and produce **goed* and **seed*.

problem posing activities /ˈprɒbləm ˈpəʊzɪŋ ækˌtɪvᵻtiz||ˈprɑː-/ *n*

see PROBLEM SOLVING ACTIVITIES

problem solving /ˈprɒbləm ˌsɒlvɪŋ||ˈprɑː- ˌsɑːl-ˌsɔːl-/ *n*

a learning STRATEGY which involves selecting from several alternatives in order to reach a desired goal. In second and foreign language learning, problem-solving strategies are often used, for example, in choosing whether to use *a* or *the* before a noun.

problem solving activities /ˈprɒbləm ˈsɒlvɪŋ ækˌtɪvᵻtiz||ˈprɑː- ˈsɑːl-, ˈsɔːl-/ *n*

also problem-posing activities

learning activities in which the learner is given a situation and a problem and must work out a solution. Such activities are said to require higher-order thinking. Many activities in COMPUTER ASSISTED LANGUAGE LEARNING involve problem solving and offer feedback while the student is trying to solve the problem.

procedural knowledge /prəˈsiːdʒərəl ˈnɒlɪdʒ||ˈnɑː-/ *n*

see DECLARATIVE KNOWLEDGE

procedural syllabus /prəˈsiːdʒərəl ˈsɪləbəs/ *n*

another term for TASK SYLLABUS

process approach /ˈprəʊsəs əˌprəʊtʃ||ˌprɑː-/ *n*

(in teaching composition) an approach which emphasizes the composing processes writers make use of in writing (such as planning, drafting and revising) and which seeks to improve students' writing skills through developing their use of effective COMPOSING PROCESSES. This approach is sometimes compared with a **product approach** or a **prose model approach**, that is, one which focuses on producing different kinds of written products and which emphasises imitation of different kinds of model paragraphs or essays.

Further reading Murray 1980

process method /ˈprəʊsəs ˌmeθəd||ˈprɑː-/ *n*

see METHODS OF DEVELOPMENT

process-product research /ˈprəʊses ˈprɒdʌkt rɪˌsɜːtʃ, ˌriːsɜːtʃ‖ ˈpraːses ˈpraː- -ɜːr-/ *n*

an approach to educational research (particularly research on the effects of classroom teaching or teaching methods), which attempts to measure the relationship between teacher behaviour or processes (i.e. what the teacher does in class, such as presenting and practising grammar points, setting up problem solving tasks, or asking questions) and pupil learning or products (e.g. as demonstrated by performance on a test). The assumption behind process-product research is that the process of teaching can be characterized by recurring patterns of teacher behaviour, which can be linked to particular learning outcomes.

Further reading Chaudron 1988

proclaiming tone /prəˈkleɪmɪŋ ˌtəʊn/ *n*

see REFERRING TONE

pro-drop language /ˈprəʊ drɒp ˌlæŋgwɪdʒ‖draːp/ *n*

see PRO-DROP PARAMETER

pro-drop parameter /ˈprəʊ drɒp pəˌræmᵻtəʳ‖draːp/ *n*
also **null subject parameter**

(in UNIVERSAL GRAMMAR) a parameter which determines whether the subject in declarative sentences may be deleted.

Parameters vary in different languages within certain defined limits. Languages such as Italian and Arabic can have subject-less declarative sentences, e.g. Italian *parla* 'he/she speaks/talks', and are referred to as **pro-drop languages**. However, languages such as English, French and German do not typically omit the subject in declarative sentences. They are referred to as **non-pro-drop languages**, e.g.:

	Subject	Verb	
Italian	(*lui*)	*parla*	pro-drop
Arabic	(*huwa*)	*yatakalamu*	pro-drop
English	*he*	*speaks*	non-pro-drop
French	*il*	*parle*	non-pro-drop
German	*er*	*spricht*	non-pro-drop

(adapted from Cook 1988)

The term *pro-drop* is used because in the D-STRUCTURE of the grammar, the empty subject position is filled by the element *pro*, e.g.

pro parla

The pro-drop parameter and other parameters of Universal Grammar have attracted the interest of researchers working in the fields of child language acquisition and language teaching. For example, the question has been raised: How do children 'set' a UG parameter to fit their particular language?

Researchers in second language acquisition have investigated what happens if a parameter in the speaker's native language is different from that of their target language, making it necessary to 'reset' the parameter. This would happen, for example, in the acquisition of Spanish (a pro-drop language) by speakers of non-pro-drop languages such as English and French.

see also PARAMETER

Further reading Chomsky 1988; Cook 1988; Liceras 1989

product approach /ˈprɒdʌkt əˌprəʊtʃ||ˈprɑː-/ *n*

see PROCESS APPROACH

production stage /prəˈdʌkʃən ˌsteɪdʒ/ *n*
also **transfer stage, free practice**

see STAGE

productive/receptive language knowledge /prəˈdʌktɪv rɪˈseptɪv ˈlæŋgwɪdʒ ˌnɒlɪdʒ||-ˌnɑː-/ *n*

another term for ACTIVE/PASSIVE LANGUAGE KNOWLEDGE

productive skills /prəˈdʌktɪv ˈskɪlz/ *n*

see LANGUAGE SKILLS

product-process distinction /ˈprɒdʌkt ˈprəʊses dɪˌstɪŋkʃən|| ˈprɑːdʌkt ˈprɑː-/ *n*

(in language teaching and SECOND LANGUAGE ACQUISITION research) a distinction sometimes made between completed acts of communication or language output (products) and the underlying abilities and skills used in producing them (processes).

For example: in writing, letters, compositions, and long essays are examples of the products of writing. But in order to write a long essay, a number of processes are involved, such as collecting information, note-taking, outlining, drafting, and revising. These are among the processes of writing the essay (the product). Language teaching and the study of language learning are concerned both with products, and with underlying processes.

Further reading Murray 1980

proficiency /prəˈfɪʃənsi/ *n*

see LANGUAGE PROFICIENCY

proficiency test /prəˈfɪʃənsi ˌtest/ *n*

a test which measures how much of a language someone has learned. The difference between a proficiency test and an ACHIEVEMENT TEST is that the latter is usually designed to measure how much a student has learned from a particular course or SYLLABUS. A proficiency test is not linked to a particular course of instruction, but measures the learner's general level of language mastery. Although this may be a result of previous instruction and learning the latter are not the focus of attention. Some proficiency tests have been standardized for worldwide use, such as the American TOEFL TEST which is used to measure the English language proficiency of foreign students who wish to study in the USA. A proficiency test measures what the student has learned relative to a specific purpose, e.g. does he or she know enough English to follow a lecture in English.

see also ACHIEVEMENT TEST
Further reading Hughes 1989

profile /ˈprəʊfaɪl/ *n*

(in testing, statistics, etc.) a graphic representation of scores or VARIABLES² of an individual or group on a number of tests or measures for the purposes of comparison. For example, the profile below is based on PERCENTILE scores of a student in English, French, and Mathematics.

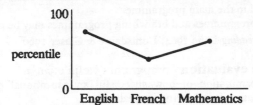

pro-forms /ˈprəʊˌfɔːmz‖-ɔːr-/ *n*

forms which can serve as replacements for different elements in a sentence. For example:
a A: *I hope you can come.*
   B: *I hope so.* (*so* replaces *that I can come*)
b A: *Mary is in London.*
   B: *John is there too.* (*there* replaces *in London*)
c *We invited Mary and John to eat with us because we liked them.* (*them* replaces *Mary and John*)
d A: *I like coffee.*
   B: *We do too.* (*do* replaces *like coffee*)

see also PRONOUN, PRO-VERB
Further reading Quirk et al 1985

program /ˈprəʊɡræm/ *n*

the sequence of instructions and routines designed to make a computer carry out a given task. The task of writing a computer program involves:
1 defining a problem or task in as much detail as possible
2 devising a procedure for carrying out the task
3 checking that the procedure will work under all circumstances
4 writing the instructions that form the actual program. These are written in a **programming language** consisting of a set of characters and rules with specific meanings and functions.

293

programme design /ˈprəʊgræm dɪˌzaɪn/ *n*
another term for COURSE DESIGN

programmed learning /ˈprəʊgræmd ˈlɜːnɪŋ‖ ˈlɜːr-/ *n*
also **programmed instruction** /ˈprəʊgræmd ɪnˈstrʌkʃən/
an APPROACH to the design of teaching/learning in which the subject matter to be learned is presented as an ordered sequence of items, each of which requires a response from the learner. The student then compares his or her response with the correct response which is provided.
In a **linear programme** students work through learning material which is presented in graded units, at their own pace.
In a **branching programme** a student who has difficulty with a particular item is directed to supplementary or revision material in a separate part (a "branch") of the programme. Then the student is returned to the main programme.
Linear programmes and branching programmes may be combined.
Further reading Lane 1964; Lumsdaine & Glaser 1960

programme evaluation /ˈprəʊgræm ɪˌvæljuˈeɪʃən/ *n*
the determination of how successful an educational programme or curriculum is in achieving its goals.
see also EVALUATION, FORMATIVE EVALUATION

programming language /ˈprəʊgræmɪŋ ˌlæŋgwɪdʒ/ *n*
see PROGRAM

progressive /prəˈgresɪv/ *n, adj*
also **continuous**
a grammatical ASPECT which indicates that an action is incomplete, in progress, or developing. The progressive in English is formed with the AUXILIARY VERB BE and the *-ing* form of the verb (e.g. *She is wearing contact lenses. They were crossing the road when the accident occurred*). The progressive aspect may be used (a) with the present tense (*Today I am wearing glasses*: present tense; progressive aspect) – this is called the **present continuous,** (b) with the past tense (*Yesterday I was wearing glasses*: past tense; progressive aspect) – this is called the **past continuous,** (c) with PERFECT aspect: (*I have been wearing glasses for six years*: present tense; perfect and progressive aspects). This is called the **present perfect continuous.** Verbs which describe states in English (e.g. *know, believe*) are not usually used in the progressive.
see also STATIVE VERB
Further reading Comrie 1976

progressive assimilation /prəˈgresɪv əˌsɪmᵻˈleɪʃən/ *n*
see ASSIMILATION[1]

progress test /'prəʊgres ˌtest‖'prɑː-/ *n*

an ACHIEVEMENT TEST linked to a particular set of teaching materials or a particular course of instruction. Tests prepared by a teacher and given at the end of a chapter, course, or term are progress tests. Progress tests may be regarded as similar to achievement tests but narrower and much more specific in scope.

They help the teacher to judge the degree of success of his or her teaching and to identify the weakness of the learners.

Further reading Heaton 1975

progressivism /prə'gresɪvɪzəm/ *n*

see RECONSTRUCTIONISM

projection (principle) /prə'dʒekʃən ˌprɪnsɪpəl/ *n*

In some models of TRANSFORMATIONAL GRAMMAR, e.g. Chomsky's UNIVERSAL GRAMMAR, a lexical item in the lexicon (see LEXICON[3]) of a grammar, e.g. a verb, has specific information about syntactic categories (complements) which it 'projects' onto the structure of the sentence. For example, the English verb *give* has two complement noun phrases:

give [-NP₁, NP₂]

which it can project, e.g.:

She gave the accountant the file.

The influence of the properties of lexical entries only goes up to a certain structure in the sentence, e.g. a *verb* would have influence on the whole verb phrase (VP) but not beyond it. This is often called **maximal projection**. Points of maximal projection are often shown by "(two bars) (see BAR NOTATION), e.g. V" (VP), N" (NP), P" (PP = prepositional phrase).

The DOMAIN of an element in a sentence is considered to be the area within its particular maximal projection. For example, in the sentence:

Bill took her to an expensive restaurant.

the domain of the verb take (*took*) would be the whole verb phrase (V"), including *her to an expensive restaurant*, the domain of the preposition *to* would be the whole prepositional phrase (P"), including *an expensive restaurant*.

The concepts of maximal projection and domain are important when discussing GOVERNMENT.

Further reading Cook 1988

project work /'prɒdʒekt ˌwɜːk‖'prɑː- ˌwɜːrk/ *n*

(in teaching) an activity which centres around the completion of a task, and which usually requires an extended amount of independent work either by an individual student or by a group of students. Much of this work takes place outside the classroom. Project work often involves three stages:

1 Classroom planning. The students and teacher discuss the content and scope of the project, and their needs.

2 Carrying out the project. The students move out of the classroom to complete their planned tasks (e.g. conducting interviews, collecting information).
3 Reviewing and monitoring. This includes discussions and feedback sessions by the teacher and participants, both during and after the project.

In language teaching, project work is thought to be an activity which promotes CO-OPERATIVE LEARNING, reflects the principles of STUDENT-CENTRED TEACHING, and promotes language learning through using the language for authentic communicative purposes.

Further reading Fried-Booth 1986

prominence /ˈprɒmɪ̈nəns||ˈprɑː-/ *n* **prominent** /ˈprɒmɪ̈nənt||ˈprɑː-/ *adj*

(in DISCOURSE), greater STRESS on the words or syllables which the speaker wishes to emphasize. Prominence may be given to different words according to what has been said before by another speaker, e.g.:

He may come to MORRow.
(as a reply to "*When is Mr Jones coming?*")
He MAY come tomorrow.
(as a reply to "*Is Mr Jones likely to come tomorrow?*")

Prominence may be accompanied by pitch movement (see TONE²) on the **prominent syllable.**

Further reading Brazil, Coulthard, & Johns 1980

prominent syllable /ˈprɒmɪ̈nənt ˈsɪləbəl||ˌprɑː-/ *n*

see PROMINENCE

prompting /ˈprɒmptɪŋ||ˈprɑː-/ *n*

see MODELLING

pronoun /ˈprəʊnaʊn/ *n*

a word which may replace a noun or noun phrase (e.g. English *it*, *them*, *she*).

see also PERSONAL PRONOUNS, POSSESSIVE, DEMONSTRATIVE, INTERROGATIVE PRONOUN, REFLEXIVE PRONOUN, INDEFINITE PRONOUN, RELATIVE CLAUSE

pronunciation /prəˌnʌnsiˈeɪʃən/ *n* **pronounce** /prəˈnaʊns/ *v*

the way a certain sound or sounds are produced. Unlike ARTICULATION, which refers to the actual production of speech sounds in the mouth, pronunciation stresses more the way sounds are perceived by the hearer, e.g.:

You haven't pronounced this word correctly.

and often relates the spoken word to its written form, e.g.:

In the word knife, the k is not pronounced.

proper noun /ˈprɒpəʳ ˈnaʊn‖ˈprɑː-/ *n*

a noun which is the name of a particular person, place, or thing. Proper nouns are spelt with a capital letter. For example: *London, Richard*.

A noun which is not the name of a particular person, place or thing is called a **common noun**. For example, *book, woman, sugar*. In English, common nouns are spelt with a lower-case (small) letter.

see also NOUN, ABSTRACT NOUN, ADJECTIVAL NOUN, ANIMATE NOUN, COLLECTIVE NOUN, CONCRETE NOUN, COUNTABLE NOUN

proposition /ˌprɒpəˈzɪʃən‖ˌprɑː-/ *n* **propositional** *adj*

(in philosophy, LINGUISTICS and SEMANTICS) the basic meaning which a sentence expresses. Propositions consist of (a) something which is named or talked about (known as the **argument**, or entity) (b) an assertion or **predication** which is made about the argument.

A sentence may express or imply (see PRESUPPOSITION) more than one proposition. For example:

sentence	underlying propositions
Maria's friend, Tony, who is a dentist, likes apples.	*Maria has a friend.*
	The friend's name is Tony.
	Tony is a dentist.
	Tony likes apples.

In SPEECH ACT theory a distinction is made between the propositional meaning of a sentence, and its **illocutionary force** (i.e. the use made of the sentence in communication, e.g. as a request, a warning, a promise).

Further reading Austin 1962; Lyons 1977

propositional network /ˈprɒpəzɪʃənəl ˈnetwɜːrk‖ˈprɑː- -wɜːrk/ *n*

the simpler PROPOSITIONS on which the truth of a main proposition rests. For example, the proposition:

The woman gave the man an expensive ring, which contained a large ruby.

contains the following propositional network:

There was a woman.
There was a man.
There was a ring.
The ring was expensive.
The ring contained a ruby.
The ruby was large.
The woman gave the ring to the man.

The process of identifying the propositional networks underlying sentences or texts is thought to be a basic part of LANGUAGE COMPREHENSION.

Further reading Anderson 1985

proprioceptive feedback /ˈprəʊpriəʊˌseptɪv ˈfiːdbæk, -priə-/ *n*

FEEDBACK involving muscular movements which are used in the production of speech and which can be used in MONITORING speech.

Deaf people make use of this ·form of feedback rather than AUDITORY FEEDBACK.

Further reading Dalton & Hardcastle 1977

prose-model approach /'prəuz ˌmɒdl əˌprəutʃ||ˌmɑːdl/ *n*
see PROCESS APPROACH

prosodic features /prə'sɒdɪk 'fiːtʃəz||-'sɑː- -ərz/ *n*
sound characteristics which affect whole sequences of syllables. They may involve, for instance, the relative loudness or duration of syllables, changes in the pitch of a speaker's voice (see TONE[2]) and the choice of pitch level (see KEY[2]).

see also INTONATION PATTERNS, PROMINENCE, SUPRASEGMENTALS

prosody /'prɒsədi||'prɑː-/ *n* prosodic /prə'sɒdɪk||-'sɑː-/ *adj*
(in PHONETICS) a collective term for variations in loudness, PITCH and SPEECH RHYTHM.

protocol /'prəutəkɒl||-kɔːl/ *n*
a sample containing observation(s) of a phenomenon which is being described, observed, or measured. For example, if a researcher were studying the use of a grammatical feature, and recorded a person's speech for purposes of analysis, a transcription of the recording could be called a protocol. A completed test script and responses of subjects to an experiment are also sometimes called protocols. Nowadays the term "protocol" is often used for a person's own account of his or her thoughts and ideas while doing a task. Such protocol can give information of value in the study of PSYCHOLINGUISTICS and COGNITIVE PROCESS*ES*.

protocol materials /'prəutəkɒl məˌtɪəriəlz||-kɔːl/ *n*
(in teacher development) a recorded or filmed segment of a lesson or classroom event. In teacher education programmes, video protocols of teachers in classrooms carrying out normal classroom activities are sometimes used to illustrate different aspects of teaching. It is often more convenient to use protocol materials than to observe actual classes.

Further reading Nunan 1989a

prototype /'prəutətaɪp/ *n*
a person or object which is considered (by many people) to be typical of its class or group.

The **prototype theory** suggests that many mental concepts we have are really prototypes. People often define a concept by reference to typical instances. For example, a prototype of a bird would be more like a small bird which flies than, for instance, a large flightless bird like an emu or a New Zealand kiwi.

Prototype theory has been useful in investigations into how concepts are formed, e.g. what is considered a typical item of furniture, a typical vegetable, a typical house, and to what extent certain concepts can be considered universal or specific to certain cultures/languages.

It has also been suggested that prototype theory may account for our ability to communicate appropriately in social situations. That would mean, for example, that we learn to associate certain words, phrases, or general communicative behaviour with people who typically use them or situations where they are typically used.

Further reading Hudson 1981; Wardhaugh 1986

prototype theory /ˈprəʊtətaɪp ˌθɪəri/ *n*

see PROTOTYPE

pro-verb /ˈprəʊ ˌvɜːb‖-ɜːr-/ *n*

a verb form that may be used instead of a full verb phrase. For example, in English, various forms of *do* can be pro-verbs, as in:

A: *I like coffee*   A: *She broke the window.*
B: *I do too.*   B: *So she did.*
   So do I.
   Alan does too.

see also PRO-FORMS

proxemics /prɒkˈsiːmɪks‖prɑːk-/ *n* proxemic *adj*

the study of the physical distance between people when they are talking to each other, as well as their postures and whether or not there is physical contact during their conversation. These factors can be looked at in relation to the sex, age, and social and cultural background of the people involved, and also their attitudes to each other and their state of mind.

see also PARALINGUISTICS, SOCIAL DISTANCE

pseudo-cleft sentence /ˈsjuːdəʊ ˈkleft ˈsentəns‖ˈsuː-/ *n*

see CLEFT SENTENCE

psycholinguistics /ˌsaɪkəʊlɪŋˈgwɪstɪks/ n psycholinguistic adj

the study of (a) the mental processes that a person uses in producing and understanding language, and (b) how humans learn language. Psycholinguistics includes the study of speech PERCEPTION, the role of MEMORY, CONCEPTS and other processes in language use, and how social and psychological factors affect the use of language.

Further reading Clark & Clark 1977; Foss & Hakes 1978; Hatch 1983

psychometrics /ˌsaɪkəʊˈmetrɪks/ n

1 A branch of psychology concerned with measurement.
2 The application of the principles of mathematics and statistics to the analysis of data.

psychomotor domain /ˈsaɪkəʊˌməʊtəʳ dəˈmeɪn,dəʊ-/ n

see DOMAIN³

pull-out programme /ˈpʊl aʊt ˌprəʊgræm/ n

in English speaking countries, a programme for LIMITED ENGLISH PROFICIENT students in which students are placed in a regular class-room but are "pulled out" for instruction in English for part of the day. Usually no native language instruction is provided and the goal is for the student to learn English through ESL instruction and submersion (see SUBMERSION EDUCATION).

punctual-nonpunctual distinction /ˈpʌŋktʃuəl ˌnɒnˈpʌŋktʃuəl dɪsˈtɪŋkʃən‖nɑːn-/ n

A distinction is sometimes made between verbs which refer to actions that occur briefly and only once (punctual), for example:
She kicked the burglar down the stairs.
and verbs which refer to repeated actions or actions/states which take place or exist over a period of time (non-punctual), for example:
She sold flowers at the market.
Verbs referring to a state, such as *seem, like, know,* (see STATIC-DYNAMIC) are, by nature, non-punctual but many other verbs can be used either punctually or non-punctually, for example:
Look! He waved to me just now. (punctual use)
The branches of the trees were waving in the breeze. (non-punctual use)
It has been claimed (see BIOPROGRAM HYPOTHESIS) that in situations where a CREOLE changes to the standard language (see POST-CREOLE CONTINUUM), verbs used punctually are more likely to be marked for past tense then verbs used non-punctually. Similar patterns have been found in investigations of second language acquisition, such as a large scale investigation into English language acquisition which was carried out in Singapore. When the speech of speakers of Singapore English was analysed in detail, it was found that of all the past tense verbs used, on average only 23% were marked for past tense when the verbs were used non-punctually, but 56% were marked for past tense when used punctually.
Marking verbs for past tense

	when used punctually	*when used non-punctually*
Guyana Creole	38%	12%
Hawaiian Creole English	53%	7%
Singapore English	56%	23%

Further reading Bickerton 1981; Platt & Ho 1991; Quirk et al 1985

pure vowel /ˈpjʊəʳ ˈvaʊəl/ *n*
another term for MONOPHTHONG

Q

qualifier[1] /ˈkwɒlɪ̩faɪəʳ‖ˈkwɑː-/ *n* **qualify** /ˈkwɒlɪ̩faɪ‖ˈkwɑː-/ *v*

(in TRADITIONAL GRAMMAR) any linguistic unit (e.g. an adjective, a phrase, or a clause) that is part of a NOUN PHRASE[1] and gives added information about the noun.

For example, *her, expensive,* and *from Paris* are qualifiers in the noun phrase:

her expensive blouse from Paris

see also MODIFIER[1]

qualifier[2] *n* **qualify** *v*

(in Halliday's FUNCTIONAL GRAMMAR) any linguistic unit that is part of a group, gives added information about the HEAD of the group, and follows the head.

For example, *from Paris* is a qualifier in the noun group

her expensive blouse from Paris

see also MODIFIER[2]

Further reading Freeborn 1987

qualitative data /ˈkwɒlɪ̩tətɪv ˈdeɪtə, ˈdɑːtə‖ˈkwɑːlɪ̩teɪtɪv/ *n*

data that are not in numerical form, such as a written account of what happened during a lesson or an interview. Data collected in qualitative form can often be converted into quantitative form.

see also QUANTITATIVE DATA

qualitative research /ˈkwɒlɪ̩tətɪv rɪˈsɜːsɜːtʃ, ˈriːsɜːtʃ‖ˈkwɑːlɪ̩teɪtɪv -ɜːr-/ *n*

research which uses procedures that make use of QUALITATIVE DATA, such as observations, interviews, or PARTICIPANT OBSERVATION.

see also CASE STUDY, ETHNOGRAPHY

quantifier /ˈkwɒntɪ̩faɪəʳ‖ˈkwɑːn-/ *n*

a word or phrase which is used with a noun, and which shows quantity. Some quantifiers in English are: *many, few, little, several, much, a lot of, plenty of, a piece of, a loaf of, three kilograms of,* etc.

see also NUMERAL, DETERMINER

Further reading Quirk et al 1985

quantitative data /ˈkwɒntɪ̩tətɪv ˈdeɪtə, ˈdɑːtə‖ˈkwɑːntɪ̩tətɪv/ *n*

data that are in numerical form, obtained through counting and measurement. Quantitative data may be collected directly or derived from QUALITATIVE DATA.

quantitative research /ˈkwɒntɪ̩tətɪv rɪˈsɜːtʃ, ˈriːsɜːtʃ‖ˈkwɑːntɪ̩teɪtɪv -ɜːr-/ *n* research which uses procedures which gather data in numerical form.

see also EXPERIMENTAL METHOD

question /'kwestʃən/ *n*

a sentence which is addressed to a listener/reader and asks for an expression of fact, opinion, belief etc. In English, questions may be formed:

a by the use of a **question word** such as *what, how, when, where, why*

b by the use of an OPERATOR in the first position in a sentence, as in *Can she come?*

c through the use of intonation, as in:
She isn't married?

d by the use of a **question tag** such as *isn't it, is it, can he, won't she, do you* etc. For example:
Patricia is a student isn't she?

questioning techniques /'kwestʃənɪŋ tek,niːks/ *n*

(in teaching) the different procedures teachers use in asking questions and the different kinds of questions they ask. Since questioning is one of the most frequently used teaching techniques, the study of teachers' questions and questioning behaviours has been an important issue in classroom research in both first and second language classrooms. Among the factors which have been examined are:

a the frequency of low-level versus high-level questions

b the degree to which students are encouraged to ask questions

c the amount of WAIT-TIME teachers allow after a question

d the choice of CONVERGENT or DIVERGENT QUESTIONS

e how often teachers answer their own questions.

see also DISPLAY QUESTION, EVALUATIVE QUESTION, REFERENTIAL QUESTION

questionnaire /,kwestʃə'neəʳ/ *n*

a set of questions on a topic or group of topics designed to be answered by a respondent. Other formats for questionnaires include check lists and rating scales. Designing questionnaires which are valid, reliable and unambiguous is a very important issue. Questionnaires are used in many branches of applied linguistics, such as in LANGUAGE SURVEYS, the study of attitudes and motivation, and in NEEDS ANALYSIS.

Further reading Oppenheim 1966

question tag /'kwestʃən ,tæg/ *n*

see QUESTION

question word /'kwestʃən ,wɜːd‖,wɜːrd/ *n*

see QUESTION

R

r² /ˈɑːʳ ˈtuː/
an abbreviation for COEFFICIENT OF DETERMINATION

random access /ˈrændəm ˈækses/ *n*
see ACCESS

random sample /ˈrændəm ˈsɑːmpəl‖ˈsæm-/ *n*
see SAMPLE

range /reɪndʒ/ *n*
1 In statistics, the DISPERSION of a DISTRIBUTION. The range of a sample is the distance between the smallest and the largest values in a set of measurements or observations. For example if the top score in a test is 80 and the bottom score is 32, the range is 48. Since the range does not take the distribution of scores into account it is usually supplemented in statistical reports by the STANDARD DEVIATION.
2 In a FREQUENCY COUNT, a measure of the distribution of linguistic items throughout a sample, and generally expressed as a measure of the number of texts or samples in which a linguistic item occurs.

rank /ræŋk/ *n*
a term used in a type of linguistic analysis in which linguistic units (e.g. sentences, clauses, words) are arranged in a certain order (**rank scale**) to show that higher units include lower ones.
For example, on the rank scale below, each unit consists of one or more units of the next lower rank.

higher rank

↑   clause
        group (verbal, nominal, etc.)
        word (verb, noun, etc.)
↓   morpheme

lower rank

The term was first used by Halliday (see SYSTEMIC GRAMMAR, SYSTEMIC LINGUISTICS).
Further reading Freeborn 1987; Halliday 1978

rank correlation /ˈræŋk kɒrɪˌleɪʃən‖kɔː-, kɑː-/ *n*
a type of coefficient of CORRELATION in which the two VARIABLES[1] are measured in ranks, or on ordinal scales (see SCALE). For example, a rank correlation could be determined between the frequency of occurrence of words in two different texts based on their ranks in each text.

TEXT A		TEXT B	
rank frequency	word	rank frequency	word
1st	*a*	1st	*the*
2nd	*the*	2nd	*and*
3rd	*and*	3rd	*a*

In this data there is a negative correlation between the "rank order" of the words in Text A and Text B.

rank scale /ˈræŋk ˌskeɪl/ *n*

see RANK

rapid reading /ˈræpɪd ˈriːdɪŋ/ *n*

another term for SPEED READING

rate of articulation /ˈreɪt əv ɑːtɪkjʊˈleɪʃən‖ɑːr-/ *n*

see RATE OF SPEECH

rate of reading /ˈreɪt əv ˈriːdɪŋ/ *n*

another term for READING SPEED

rate of speech /ˈreɪt əv ˈspiːtʃ/ *n*
also **rate of utterance, speech rate**

the speed at which a person speaks. This may depend on a number of factors, such as the speaker's personality, the type of topic, the number of people present, and the speaker's reactions to them. Another factor is the speaker's familiarity with the language or dialect he or she is using.

A distinction is often made between the rate of speech, measured by the number of syllables per minute, and the **rate of articulation**, measured by the number of syllables per minute minus the time taken up by PAUSING. Usually, the longer and more frequent the pauses, the slower the speech rate.

Further reading Goldman-Eisler 1968

rate of utterance /ˈreɪt əv ˈʌtərəns/ *n*

another term for RATE OF SPEECH

rating scale /ˈreɪtɪŋ ˌskeɪl/ *n*

(in language testing) a technique for measuring language proficiency in which aspects of a person's language use are judged using scales that go from worst to best performance in a number of steps.

For example, the components of FLUENCY in a foreign language could be rated on the following scales:

naturalness of language	unnatural	1 2 3 4 5 natural
style of expression	foreign	1 2 3 4 5 native-speaker-like
clarity of expression	unclear	1 2 3 4 5 clear

For each component skill, the listener rates the speaker on a scale of 1 to 5. Overall fluency can then be measured by taking account of the three scores for each speaker.

see also SCALE
Further reading Cohen 1980

rationalist position /'ræʃənəl̩st pə'zɪʃən/ *n*
another term for INNATIST HYPOTHESIS

ratio-scale /'reɪʃiəʊ ˌskeɪl/ *n*
see SCALE

raw-score /'rɔː 'skɔːʳ/ *n*
(in testing, statistics, etc.) a score that is presented in terms of its original numerical value, not converted into some other value. For example, raw scores may be the number of correct answers in a test, or, in some cases, the number of errors. Usually it is necessary to convert such values into percentages, PERCENTILES, ranks, or some other form (e.g. STANDARD SCORES), in order to make the scores easier to interpret.

readability /ˌriːdə'bɪl̩ti/ *n*
how easily written materials can be read and understood. Readability depends on many factors, including (a) the average length of sentences in a passage (b) the number of new words a passage contains (c) the grammatical complexity of the language used. Procedures used for measuring readability are known as "readability formulae".

see also LEXICAL DENSITY
Further reading Klare 1978

reader-based prose /'riːdəʳ beɪst ˌprəʊz/ *n*
writing in which the audience is another person rather than the writer himself or herself. Inexperienced writers are often said to choose themselves as audience for their writing, producing **writer-based prose** or **egocentric writing**, rather than providing the background knowledge, information and organization that other readers may need. In the composing process, writers often begin with writer-based prose and then revise it to make it easier for another reader to read, that is, to make it reader-based.

reading /'riːdɪŋ/ *n*
1 perceiving a written text in order to understand its contents.
This can be done silently (**silent reading**). The understanding that results is called reading comprehension.
2 saying a written text aloud (**oral reading**). This can be done with or without an understanding of the contents.
Different types of reading comprehension are often distinguished, according to the reader's purposes in reading and the type of reading used. The following are commonly referred to:
a **literal comprehension**: reading in order to understand, remember, or recall the information explicitly contained in a passage.
b **inferential comprehension**: reading in order to find information which is not explicitly stated in a passage, using the reader's experience and intuition, and by inferring (INFERENCING)

c **critical** or **evaluative comprehension**: reading in order to compare information in a passage with the reader's own knowledge and values

d **appreciative comprehension**: reading in order to gain an emotional or other kind of valued response from a passage.

see also SCANNING, READING SPEED, EXTENSIVE READING
Further reading Alderson & Urquhart 1983

reading across the curriculum /'riːdɪŋ əˈkrɒs ðə kəˈrɪkjᵿləm‖ əˈkrɔːs/ *n*

see LANGUAGE ACROSS THE CURRICULUM

reading age /'riːdɪŋ ˌeɪdʒ/ *n*

the usual age at which a child is expected to begin learning to read or to benefit from instruction in reading.

reading approach /'riːdɪŋ əˌprəʊtʃ/ *n*
also **reading method** /'riːdɪŋ ˌmeθəd/

in foreign language teaching, a programme or method in which reading comprehension is the main objective. In a reading approach (a) the foreign language is generally introduced through short passages written with simple vocabulary and structures (b) comprehension is taught through translation and grammatical analysis (c) if the spoken language is taught, it is generally used to reinforce reading and limited to the oral reading of texts.

Further reading Mackey 1965

reading log /'riːdɪŋ ˌlɒg‖lɔːg, lɑːg/

see LEARNING LOG

reading readiness /'riːdɪŋ 'redinᵻs/ *n*

the degree to which a child is ready to benefit from instruction in reading. The specific factors which contribute to reading readiness are not clear, but are thought to include perceptual, cognitive, social, emotional and motivational factors. Reading readiness is not always indicated by a child's chronological age.

reading span /'riːdɪŋ ˌspæn/ *n*
also **eye span, visual span**

the amount of printed text that a person can perceive within a single FIXATION PAUSE, usually described as being between seven and ten letter spaces.

reading speed /'riːdɪŋ ˌspiːd/ *n*
also **rate of reading**

The speed which a person reads depends on
a the type of reading material (e.g. fiction or non-fiction)
b the reader's purpose (e.g. to gain information, to find the main ideas in a passage)

c the level of comprehension required (e.g. to extract the main ideas or to gain complete understanding)

d the reader's individual reading skills.

The following are typical reading speeds:

speed	purpose	good reader
slow	study reading, used when material is difficult and/or high comprehension is required	200–300 words per minute (wpm) 80–90% comprehension
average	used for everyday reading of magazines, newspapers, etc.	250–500 wpm 70% comprehension
fast	skimming, used when highest speed is required comprehension is intentionally lower	800 + wpm 50% comprehension

Further reading Fry 1965

reading vocabulary /ˈriːdɪŋ vəˈkæbjŭləri, vəʊ-‖-leri/ *n*
see ACTIVE/PASSIVE LANGUAGE KNOWLEDGE

realia /riˈɑːliə‖-ˈæ-/ *n plural*
(in language teaching) actual objects and items which are brought into a classroom as examples or as aids to be talked or written about and used in teaching. Realia may include such things as photographs, articles of clothing, and kitchen objects.

reality principle /riˈælɪ̥ti ˌprɪnsɪ̥pəl/ *n*
(in SPEECH ACT theory) the principle that in conversation, people are expected to talk about things that are real and possible if there is no evidence to the contrary.

For example, in the following exchange:

A: *How are you going to New York?*

B: *I'm flying.*

A understands B to mean that B is travelling by plane and not literally flying through the air.

see also CONVERSATIONAL MAXIM

realization /ˌrɪəlaɪˈzeɪʃən‖-lə-/ *n* realize /ˈrɪəlaɪz/ *v*
the actual occurrence in speech or writing of an abstract linguistic unit. For example, the PHONEME /ɪ/ as in /bɪg/ *big* can be realized with more or less length, e.g. as [ɪ], [ɪː] or [ɪːː], where : means "with some length" and :: means "particularly long". The last example may be used when someone wants to put special emphasis on the word *big*, or to suggest by the duration of the vowel the size of the "big" thing:

It's really bíg!

received pronunciation /rɪˈsiːvd prəˌnʌnsiˈeɪʃən/ *n*
also **RP**

the type of British STANDARD ENGLISH pronunciation which has been regarded as the prestige variety and which shows no REGIONAL VARIATION. It has often been popularly referred to as "BBC English" because it was the standard pronunciation used by most British Broadcasting Corporation newsreaders.

RP differs from Standard American English pronunciation in various ways. For example, it uses the PHONEME /ɒ/ where most Americans would use another phoneme, as in *hot* /hɒt‖haːt/. Speakers of RP do not have an *r* sound before a CONSONANT, though most Americans do, as in *farm* /faːm‖faːrm/.

receiver /rɪˈsiːvəʳ/ *n*

see COMMUNICATION

receptive language knowledge /rɪˈseptɪv ˈlæŋgwɪdʒ ˌnɒlɪdʒ‖ˌnɑː-/ *n*

see ACTIVE/PASSIVE LANGUAGE KNOWLEDGE

receptive skills /rɪˈseptɪv ˈskɪlz/ *n*

see LANGUAGE SKILLS

reciprocal pronoun /rɪˈsɪprəkəl ˈprəʊnaʊn/ *n*

a PRONOUN which refers to an exchange or mutual interaction between people or groups.

English uses the phrases *each other* and *one another* like reciprocal pronouns. For example, the sentence *X and Y smiled at each other* implies that X smiled at Y and that Y smiled at X.

reciprocal verb /rɪˈsɪprəkəl ˈvɜːb‖ˈvɜːrb/ *n*.

A verb is called reciprocal when it suggests that the people or things represented by the SUBJECT of the sentence are doing something to one another.

For example, the sentence *Jeremy and Basil were fighting* may imply that Jeremy and Basil were fighting each other. In that case, the sentence uses *fight* as a reciprocal verb.

recitation /ˌresɪˈteɪʃən/ *n*

see DISCUSSION METHOD

recognition vocabulary /ˌrekəgˈnɪʃən vəˌkæbjʊləri, vəʊ-‖-leri/ *n*
another term for **passive vocabulary**

see ACTIVE/PASSIVE LANGUAGE KNOWLEDGE

reconstructionism /ˌriːkənˈstrʌkʃənɪzəm/ *n*
this term is sometimes used to describe an approach to curriculum development which emphasizes the importance of planning, efficiency, and rationality and which stresses the practical aspects of education. In foreign language teaching this approach emphasizes the promotion of practical skills, makes use of objectives or mastery learning, and

advocates a systematic approach to needs analysis, programme development, and syllabus design. Reconstructionism is contrasted with **progressivism**, which emphasizes that education is a means of providing people with learning experiences which enable them to learn from their own efforts. It advocates a learner-centred approach to education, sees the learner as a "whole person", promotes the learner's individual development, and leads to a focus on the process of learning rather than mastery of discrete learning items.

Further reading Clark 1987

record keeping /ˈrekɔːd ˌkiːpɪŋ‖-kərd/ *n*

(in a language programme) the maintenance of a file of data, usually numerical, on student performance.

recursive rule /rɪˈkɜːsɪv ˌruːl‖-ˈkɜːr-/ *n*

a rule which can be applied repeatedly without any definite limit. For example, a recursive rule for the addition of relative clauses could produce:

The man saw the dog which bit the girl who was stroking the cat which had caught the mouse which had eaten the cheese which . . .

reduction /rɪˈdʌkʃən/ *n* reduce /rɪˈdjuːs‖-ˈduːs/ *v*

(in PHONETICS and PHONOLOGY) change in a vowel to a centralized vowel when it is in an unstressed position.

For example, *could* /kʊd/ is often reduced to /kəd/ in a sentence like:

We could go to the park this afternoon.

see also ELISION

redundancy /rɪˈdʌndənsi/ *n* redundant /rɪˈdʌndənt/ *adj*

the degree to which a message contains more information than is needed for it to be understood. Languages have built-in redundancy, which means that utterances contain more information than is necessary for comprehension.

For example, in English, PLURAL may be shown on the demonstrative, the noun, and the verb, as in:

These books are expensive.

However, if the *s* on *books* is omitted, the message would still be understood. Therefore, the *s* is redundant in this context. 50% of normal language is said to be redundant.

reduplication /rɪˌdjuːplɪˈkeɪʃən‖rɪˌduː-/ *n*

repetition of a syllable, a MORPHEME, or a word. For example:

a in Tagalog (a Philippine language) *tatlo* "three", *tatatlo* "only three"

b in Malay *anak* "child", *anak anak* "children".

reference /ˈrefərəns/ *n* referent /ˈrefərənt/ *n* refer /rɪˈfɜːʳ/ *v*
referential /ˌrefəˈrenʃəl◄/ *adj*

(in SEMANTICS) the relationship between words and the things, actions, events, and qualities they stand for.

Reference in its wider sense would be the relationship between a word or phrase and an entity in the external world (see DENOTATION). For example, the word *tree* refers to the object 'tree' (the referent).

Reference in its narrower sense is the relationship between a word or phrase and a specific object, e.g. a particular tree or a particular animal. For example, *Peter's horse* would refer to a horse which is owned, ridden by, or in some way associated with Peter.

Further reading Lyons 1981

referential question /ˈrefərenʃəl ˈkwestʃən/ n

a question which asks for information which is not known to the teacher, such as *What do you think about animal rights?*

see also DISPLAY QUESTION, QUESTIONING TECHNIQUES

referring expression /rɪˈfɜːrɪŋ ɪkˌspreʃən/ n

see BINDING PRINCIPLE

referring tone /rɪˈfɜːrɪŋ ˌtəʊn/ n

an intonation pattern which indicates that something that is said is part of the knowledge shared between the speaker and the listener. In Standard British English, the referring tone (r) is often a fall and then a rise in PITCH \↗ or a rise in pitch ⟶ whereas the **proclaiming tone** (p), often shown by a fall in pitch ⟶↘, suggests that the speaker is introducing information which is new to the listener:

a (r) He'll be twenty (p) in August.
b (p) He'll be twenty (r) in August.

In example (a) the new information is *August*. In example (b) the new information is the age of the person discussed.

see also KEY², TONE², TONE UNIT
Further reading Brazil, Coulthard, & Johns 1980

reflective discussion /rɪˈflektɪv dɪˈskʌʃən/ n

see DISCUSSION METHOD

reflective teaching¹ /rɪˈflektɪv ˈtiːtʃɪŋ/ n

an activity sometimes used in teacher preparation programmes which aims to provide student teachers with a controlled teaching experience and a chance to consider the nature of teaching thoughtfully and objectively. The process involves the following stages:

1 student teachers are divided into small groups of four to six
2 each is given an identical lesson to teach, based on content or a subject area they are not familiar with (e.g. language teachers might be asked to teach a geography lesson). The lesson takes not more than 15 minutes
3 a few days later each person teaches the lesson to the group. There is an observable outcome to determine whether learning took place, such as a paper and pencil test

4 teaching is followed by a reflective session which focuses on the quality and effects of the teaching experienced

Further reading Cruickshank & Applegate 1981

reflective teaching[2] *n*

an approach to teaching and to teacher education which is based on the assumption that teachers can improve their understanding of teaching and the quality of their own teaching by reflecting critically on their teaching experiences.

In teacher education programmes, activities which seek to develop a reflective approach to teaching aim to develop the skills of considering the teaching process thoughtfully, analytically and objectively, as a way of improving classroom practices. This may involve the use of:

1 journals in which student teachers or practising teachers write about and describe classroom experiences and use their descriptions as a basis for review and reflection

2 audio and video taping of a teacher's lesson by the teacher, for purposes of later review and reflection

3 group discussion with peers or a supervisor in order to explore issues that come out of classroom experience.

Further reading Bartlett 1990; Richards 1990

reflexive pronoun /rɪˈfleksɪv ˈprəʊnaʊn/ *n*

a form of a PRONOUN which is used when the direct or indirect OBJECT in a sentence refers to the same person or thing as the subject of the sentence. In English these are formed in the same way as EMPHATIC PRONOUN*s*, i.e. by adding, *-self, -selves* to the pronoun, as in:

I hurt myself.

reflexive verb /rɪˈfleksɪv ˈvɜːb‖-ɜːr-/ *n*

a verb used so as to imply that the subject is doing something to himself or herself.

In English, this is typically expressed by means of a REFLEXIVE PRONOUN added to the verb, e.g. *They hurt themselves.* But the same meaning may be expressed by the verb on its own, as in *I was shaving.*

regional dialect /ˈriːdʒənəl ˈdaɪəlekt/ *n*

see DIALECT

regional variation /ˈriːdʒənəl veəriˈeɪʃən/ *n*

variation in speech according to the particular area where a speaker comes from (see DIALECT). Variation may occur with respect to pronunciation, vocabulary, or syntax.

For example, in the southwest of England and in the American Midwest, many speakers use an /r/ sound in words such as *her, four, part,* whereas speakers from some other places, such as the London region and New England, do not.

register /ˈredʒɪstər/ *n*

1 see STYLE

2 a SPEECH VARIETY used by a particular group of people, usually sharing the same occupation (e.g. doctors, lawyers) or the same interests (e.g. stamp collectors, baseball fans).

A particular register often distinguishes itself from other registers by having a number of distinctive words, by using words or phrases in a particular way (e.g. in tennis: *deuce, love, tramlines*), and sometimes by special grammatical constructions (e.g. legal language).

regression /rɪˈgreʃən/ n

a backward movement of the eye along a line of print when reading. Poor readers tend to make more regressions than good readers. In reading aloud, a regression is the repetition of a syllable, word, or phrase that has already been read.

regression analysis /rɪˈgreʃən əˌnælɪsɪs/ n

a statistical technique for estimating or predicting a value for a DEPENDENT VARIABLE from a set of INDEPENDENT VARIABLES. For example, if a student scored 60% on a test of reading comprehension and 70% on a grammar test (the independent variables) regression analysis could be used to predict his or her likely score on a test of language proficiency (the dependent variable). When two or more independent variables are present, as in this example, the statistical technique is called **multiple regression**.

regressive assimilation /rɪˈgresɪv əˌsɪmɪˈleɪʃən/ n

see ASSIMILATION[1]

regular verb /ˈregjələr ˈvɜːb‖-ɜːr-/ n

a verb which has the most typical forms in its language for grammatical categories such as TENSE or PERSON. In written English regular verbs form the past tense (a) by adding *-ed* to the verb base; *walk* → *walked*; (b) by adding *-d* to the base; *smile* → *smiled*; (c) by changing *-y* → *-ied*; *cry* → *cried*. A verb which does not have regular forms for tense, person, etc. is known as an **irregular verb**. Irregular verbs in English may form the past tense (a) by using the same form as the present tense; *upset* → *upset*; *put* → *put* (b) by having an irregular past tense form which is also used as past participle; *keep* → *kept*; *catch* → *caught* (c) by having an irregular past tense form which is different from the past participle; *drive* → *drove* → *driven*.

regulatory function /ˈregjələtəri ˈfʌŋkʃən‖-tɔːri/ n

see DEVELOPMENTAL FUNCTIONS OF LANGUAGE

rehearsal /rɪˈhɜːsəl‖-ɜːr-/ n

a LEARNING STRATEGY which involves saying a new word or sentence to oneself (usually silently) in order to memorize it. Rehearsal is sometimes described as a 'surface' approach to learning, since it deals primarily with the form of an item and not its underlying meaning. It is a technique sometimes used to keep information in short-term memory (see MEMORY).

rehearsing /rɪˈhɜːsɪŋ‖-ɜːr-/ *n*
see COMPOSING PROCESSES

reinforcement /ˌriːɪnˈfɔːsmənt‖-ɔːr-/ *n*
see STIMULUS-RESPONSE THEORY

relative clause /ˈrelətɪv ˈklɔːz/ *n*
a CLAUSE which modifies a noun or noun phrase. For example in English:
  People who smoke annoy me.
  The book which I am reading is interesting.
The pronoun which introduces a relative clause is known as a **relative pronoun**, e.g. *who, which, that.*

see also DEFINING RELATIVE CLAUSE

relative pronoun /ˈrelətɪv ˈprəʊnaʊn/ *n*
see RELATIVE CLAUSE

relativity /ˌreləˈtɪvɪti/ *n*
see LINGUISTIC RELATIVITY

reliability /rɪˌlaɪəˈbɪlɪti/ *n* **reliable** /rɪˈlaɪəbəl/ *adj*
(in testing) a measure of the degree to which a test gives consistent results. A test is said to be reliable if it gives the same results when it is given on different occasions or when it is used by different people.

see also PARALLEL FORMS, ALTERNATE FORM RELIABILITY, SPLIT-HALF RELIABILITY, INTERNAL CONSISTENCY RELIABILITY, SPEARMAN-BROWN FORMULA

remedial grammar /rɪˈmiːdiəl ˈgræməʳ/ *n*
(in language teaching) a term sometimes used to describe grammatical explanation, teaching, etc. which is intended to remedy, correct, or compensate for the learner's inadequate understanding or use of any aspect of the grammar of a language.

repair /rɪˈpeəʳ/ *n, v*
(in CONVERSATIONAL ANALYSIS) a term for ways in which errors, unintended forms, or misunderstandings are corrected by speakers or others during conversation. A repair which is made by the speaker (i.e. which is self-initiated) is known as a **self repair**. For example:
  I bought a, uhm . . . what do you call it . . . a floor polisher.
A repair made by another person (i.e. which is other-initiated) is known as **other repair**. For example:
  A: *How long you spend?*
  B: *Hmm?*
  A: *How long did you spend there?*
B's response serves to indicate that a repair is needed to A's original utterance.
Further reading Schegloff, Jefferson, & Sacks 1977

repertoire /'repətwɑːʳ||-pər-/ *n*
see SPEECH REPERTOIRE

repetition drill /ˌrepɪ̩'tɪʃən ˌdrɪl/ *n*
see DRILL

repetition stage /ˌrepɪ̩'tɪʃən ˌsteɪdʒ/ *n*
another term for **practice stage**
see STAGE

reported speech /rɪ'pɔːtɪ̩d 'spiːtʃ||-ɔːr-/ *n*
see DIRECT SPEECH

representative /ˌreprɪ'zentətɪv◄/ *n*
see SPEECH ACT CLASSIFICATION

representative sample /'reprɪzentətɪv 'sɑːmpəl||'sæm-/ *n*
see SAMPLE

research /rɪ'sɜːtʃ,'riːsɜːtʃ||-ɜːr-/ *n*
the study of an event, problem or phenomenon using systematic and objective methods, in order to understand it better and to develop principles and theories about it.
see also ACTION RESEARCH, DATA, EXPERIMENTAL METHOD, HYPOTHESIS, THEORY

residual hearing /rɪ'zɪdʒuəl 'hɪərɪŋ/ *n*
see HEARING IMPAIRED, AUDITORY/ORAL METHOD

response /rɪ'spɒns||-'spɑːns/ *n*
1 see STIMULUS-RESPONSE THEORY, BEHAVIOURISM
2 see CUE

restricted code /rɪ'strɪktɪ̩d 'kəʊd/ *n*
see CODE²

restrictive relative clause /rɪ'strɪktɪv 'relətɪv 'klɔːz/ *n*
another term for DEFINING RELATIVE CLAUSE

result(ative) case /rɪ'zʌltətɪv ˌkeɪs/ *n*
see FACTITIVE CASE

retention /rɪ'tenʃən/ *n*
the ability to recall or remember things after an interval of time. In language teaching, retention of what has been taught (e.g. grammar rules, vocabulary) may depend on the quality of teaching, the interest of the learners, or the meaningfulness of the materials.

retroactive inhibition interference /'retrəʊæktɪv ɪnhɪ̩'bɪʃən/ *n*
also **retroactive** /'retrəʊæktɪv ɪntə'fɪərəns||ɪntər-/
see PROACTIVE INHIBITION

retroflex /'retrəfleks/ *adj*

describes a speech sound (a CONSONANT) which is produced with the tip of the tongue curled back to touch or nearly touch the hard palate at the top of the mouth.

Many Indian languages use retroflex /t/ and /d/, – [ʈ] and [ɖ] – and many native speakers of these languages continue to use these sounds when they speak English.

The /r/ used by some speakers in the south-west of England, and in many varieties of American English, is a retroflex sound.

see also PLACE OF ARTICULATION, MANNER OF ARTICULATION
Further reading Gimson 1989

retrospective syllabus /'retrəspektɪv 'sɪləbəs/ *n*

see A PRIORI SYLLABUS

retrospection /,retrə'spekʃən/ *n*

see VERBAL REPORTING

reversal error /rɪ'vɜːsəl ,erəʳ||-ɜːr-/ *n*

see SPEECH ERRORS

reverse stress /rɪ'vɜːs 'stres||-ɜːr-/ *n*

see STRESS SHIFT

revising /rɪ'vaɪzɪŋ/

see COMPOSING PROCESSES

rewrite rule /'riːraɪt ,ruːl/ *n*

see BASE COMPONENT

rheme /riːm/ *n*

see FUNCTIONAL SENTENCE PERSPECTIVE

rhetoric /'retərɪk/ *n*

the study of how effective writing achieves its goals. The term "rhetoric" in this sense is common in North American college and university courses in rhetoric or "rhetorical communication", which typically focus on how to express oneself correctly and effectively in relation to the topic of writing or speech, the audience, and the purpose of communication.

In traditional grammar, rhetoric was the study of style through grammatical and logical analysis. Cicero, the ancient Roman orator and writer, described rhetoric as "the art or talent by which discourse is adapted to its end".

rhetorical question /rɪ'tɒrɪkəl 'kwestʃən||-'tɔː-, -'tɑː-/ *n*

a forceful statement which has the form of a question but which does not expect an answer. For example, *"What difference does it make?"*, which may function like the statement, *"It makes no difference"*.

rhetorical structure /rɪ'tɒrɪkəl 'strʌktʃəʳ‖-'tɔː-, -'tɑː-/ *n*
another term for SCHEME

rhotic /'rəʊtɪk/ *adj*
In some varieties of English an /r/ sound can be heard after the vowel in such words as *far, bird, early*. These varieties are sometimes referred to as rhotic.
Most varieties of English spoken in Midwest USA are rhotic, whereas most varieties of English spoken in the south of England are **non-rhotic**.
Further reading Ladefoged 1982

rhythm /'rɪðəm/ *n*
see SPEECH RHYTHM

right branching direction /'raɪt 'brɑːntʃɪŋ dʒ,rekʃən, daɪ-‖'bræn-/ *n*
see BRANCHING DIRECTION

right dislocation /'raɪt dɪslə'keɪʃən/ *n*
see LEFT DISLOCATION

right-ear advantage /'raɪt 'ɪər əd'vɑːntɪdʒ‖-'væn-/ *n*
see DICHOTIC LISTENING

right hemisphere /'raɪt 'hemɪsfɪəʳ/ *n*
see BRAIN

risk-taking /'rɪsk ,teɪkɪŋ/ *n*
a PERSONALITY factor which concerns the degree to which a person is willing to undertake actions that involve a significant degree of risk. Risk-taking is said to be an important characteristic of successful second language learning, since learners have to be willing to try out hunches about the new language and take the risk of being wrong.
see also COGNITIVE VARIABLE
Further reading Brown 1987

ritual /'rɪtʃuəl/ *n*
a SPEECH EVENT which follows a more or less strictly defined pattern, e.g. part of a religious service, an initiation ceremony. Often UTTERANCES must follow each other in a particular sequence and may have to be of a particular kind.

role /rəʊl/ *n*
1 the part taken by a participant in any act of communication. Some roles are more or less permanent, e.g. that of teacher or student, while other roles are very temporary, e.g. the role of someone giving advice. The same person could have a number of different roles in his or her daily activities. For example, a man may be father, brother, son, husband in his family life but colleague, teacher, employee, treasurer,

317

counsellor in his working life. Roles affect the way people communicate with each other (see ROLE RELATIONSHIPS).

2 people also sometimes talk of the "roles" of *speaker* or *listener* in a SPEECH EVENT.

Further reading Hymes 1977

role-play /ˈrəʊl ˌpleɪ/ *n, v*
also role playing *n*
drama-like classroom activities in which students take the ROLES of different participants in a situation and act out what might typically happen in that situation. For example, to practise how to express complaints and apologies in a foreign language, students might have to role-play a situation in which a customer in a shop returns a faulty article to a salesperson.

see also SIMULATION

role relationship /ˈrəʊl rɪˌleɪʃənʃɪp/ *n*
the relationship which people have to each other in an act of communication and which influences the way they speak to each other. One of the speakers may have a ROLE which has a higher STATUS than that of the other speaker(s), e.g. school principal ←→ teacher, teacher ←→ student(s), lieutenant ←→ sergeant. Sometimes people temporarily take on superior roles, either because of the situation, e.g. bank manager ←→ loan seeker, or because one of them has a stronger personality, e.g. student A ←→ student B.

roll /rəʊl/ *n*
also trill
a speech sound (a CONSONANT) which is produced by a series of rapid closures or taps by a flexible speech organ, e.g. the tip of the tongue, against a firm surface, e.g. the gum ridge behind the upper teeth (the **alveolar ridge**).
For example, in some varieties of Scottish English the /r/ in /əˈgriːd/ *agreed* is a roll.

see also MANNER OF ARTICULATION, PLACE OF ARTICULATION, FLAP
Further reading Gimson 1989

Roman alphabet /ˈrəʊmən ˈælfəbet/ *n*
also Latin alphabet
an alphabetic writing system used for many languages, including English. It consists of letters which may represent different sounds or sound combinations in different languages. For example, the letter *w* represents /w/ in English as /ˈwɔːtəʳ/ *water* but /v/ in German /ˈvasər/ *Wasser* "water".

see also ALPHABET

romance languages /rəʊˈmæns ˌlæŋgwɪdʒɪz, rə-/ *n*
a group of languages which are derived from Latin. French, Italian, Spanish, Portuguese and Romanian are all romance languages. Their

common ancestry can still be seen in some of their words and structures, for example:

French	Italian	Spanish	English
pere	*padre*	*padre*	*father*
poisson	*pesce*	*pescado*	*fish*
champ	*campo*	*campo*	*field*

Romance languages are part of the wider INDO-EUROPEAN LANGUAGE group.

root /ruːt/ *n*
also base form

a MORPHEME which is the basic part of a word and which may, in many languages, occur on its own (e.g. English *man, hold, cold, rhythm*). Roots may be joined to other roots (e.g. English *house + hold → household*) and/or take AFFIX*ES* (e.g. *manly, coldness*) or COMBINING FORM*S* (e.g. *biorhythm*).

see also STEM[1]

rote learning /ˈrəʊt ˌlɜːnɪŋ||ˌlɜːr-/ *n*

the learning of material by repeating it over and over again until it is memorized, without paying attention to its meaning.

rounded vowel /ˈraʊnd̩d ˈvaʊəl/ *n*

see VOWEL

routine /ruːˈtiːn/ *n*
also formula, formulaic speech/expressions/language,
conventionalized speech, prefabricated language/speech

(generally) a segment of language made up of several morphemes or words which are learned together and used as if they were a single item. For example *How are you? With best wishes, To Whom it May Concern, You must be kidding.* Researchers use different names for these routines. A routine or formula which is used in conversation is sometimes called a **conversational routine**, (e.g. *that's all for now, How awful!, you don't say, the thing is . . . Would you believe it!*) and one used to show politeness, a **politeness formula** (e.g. *Thank you very much*).

see also GAMBIT, IDIOM, UTTERANCE
Further reading Coulmas 1981

RP /ˌɑːr ˈpiː/ *n*

an abbreviation for RECEIVED PRONUNCIATION

rule[1] /ruːl/ *n*

(in TRADITIONAL GRAMMAR) a statement
1 about the formation of a linguistic unit, e.g. how to form the PAST TENSE of VERBS, or
2 about the CORRECT usage of a linguistic unit or units, e.g. that verbs are modified by adverbs (*Come here quickly*) and not by adjectives (**Come here quick*).

rule² *n*

(in TRANSFORMATIONAL GENERATIVE GRAMMAR) a statement about the formation of a linguistic unit or about the relationship between linguistic units. Rules describe and analyse (**generate**) structures in a language and change the structures into sentences.

see also BASE COMPONENT, GENERATIVE GRAMMAR, TRANSFORMATIONAL COMPONENT

rule-governed behaviour /ˈruːlˌgʌvənd bɪˈheɪvjəʳ‖-vərnd/ *n*

A person's knowledge of a language (COMPETENCE) can be described as a system made up of rules for linguistic units such as MORPHEMES, words, clauses, and sentences. Although speakers of a language may not be able to explain why they construct sentences in a particular way in their language, they generally use their language in a way which is governed by the rules of this linguistic system. Language is thus described as "rule-governed behaviour".

rules of speaking /ˈruːlz əv ˈspiːkɪŋ/ *n*

see CONVERSATION RULES

run-on-sentence /ˈrʌn ɒn ˈsentəns‖ɔːn, ɑːn/ *n*
also fused sentence

(in composition) an error in punctuation where one or more full stops are omitted between sentences or independent clauses (see DEPENDENT CLAUSE). For example:

Mrs Lee is a great teacher she always explains things very clearly.

This could be rewritten as two independent clauses separated by a comma followed by the coordinating CONJUNCTION *and*.

Mrs Lee is a great teacher, and she always explains things very clearly.

S

saccade /sæˈkɑːd, -ˈkeɪd/ *n*

see FIXATION PAUSE

salience /ˈseɪliəns/ *n* **salient** /ˈseɪliənt *adj*
also **perceptual salience**

(in language learning, speech PERCEPTION, and INFORMATION PROCESS-ING) the ease with which a linguistic item is perceived. In language learning, the salience of linguistic items has been studied to see if it affects the order in which the items are learned. For example, the salience of a spoken word may depend on:

a the position of a phoneme in the word

b the emphasis given to the word in speech, i.e. whether it is STRESSED or unstressed

c the position of the word in a sentence.

see also NATURAL ORDER HYPOTHESIS
Further reading Dulay, Burt, & Krashen 1982

sample /ˈsɑːmpəl‖ˈsæm-/ *n*

(in statistics and testing) any group of individuals which is selected to represent a POPULATION.

A sample in which every member of the population has an equal and independent chance of being selected is known as a **random sample**.

A sample in which the population is grouped into several strata (e.g. of high, medium, and low scores), and a selection drawn from each level, is known as a **stratified sample**.

A sample which contains a good representation of the population from which it is selected is known as a **representative sample**.

sampling /ˈsɑːmplɪŋ‖ˈsæm-/ *n*

the procedure of selecting a SAMPLE. This selection can be done in various ways, e.g. by selecting a random sample or a stratified sample.

Sapir-Whorf hypothesis /ˈsæpɪəʳ ˈwɔːf haɪˌpɒθ⅟₂s⅟₂s‖-ɔːr- -ˌpɑː-/ *n*

see LINGUISTIC RELATIVITY

scaffolding /ˈskæfəldɪŋ/ *n*

(in language learning) the building up of a target language structure over several TURNS in an interaction. Initially in language learning, learners may be unable to produce certain structures within a single utterance, but may build them through interaction with another speaker. For example, in the following exchange, the learner produces the structure *"Oh, this an ant"*, across five turns:

Child: *Oh!*
Mother: *What?*
Child: *This* (points to an ant)
Mother: *It's an ant*
Child: *Ant*

Later, the child is able to produce the structure within a single turn:
Oh, this an ant.
Scaffolding is thought to be one way in which learners acquire new linguistic structures.

scale /skeɪl/ *n*

(in statistics and testing) the level or type of quantification produced by a measurement. Four different scales are often used:

a a **nominal scale** is used to assign values to items or individuals which belong to different groups or categories. For example, we may assign the number 1 to all students in one class, 2 to those in another, 3 to students in another class, and so on.

b An **ordinal scale** makes use of ORDINAL NUMBERS (e.g. first, second, third). It ranks things in order (e.g. because the examiner judges that there is a greater amount of skill required by one task than another, without knowing precisely how much). The difference between the values on the scale are not necessarily the same (e.g. the difference in points between being first or second on a test may not be the same as the difference between being 21st or 22nd).

c An **interval scale** is similar to an ordinal scale except that it has the additional quality that the intervals between the points on the scale are equal (as on the centigrade scale). The difference between 6 and 8 on the centigrade scale is the same as the difference between 26 and 28.

d A **ratio-scale** is similar to an interval scale except that it has an absolute zero, enabling actual scores to be compared rather than the intervals between scores. A scale for measuring distance or time would be a "ratio-scale".

scalogram /ˈskeɪləgræm/ *n*

see IMPLICATIONAL SCALING

scanning /ˈskænɪŋ/ *n*

(in READING) a type of SPEED READING technique which is used when the reader wants to locate a particular piece of information without necessarily understanding the rest of a text or passage. For example, the reader may read through a chapter of a book as rapidly as possible in order to find out information about a particular date, such as when someone was born.

Scanning may be contrasted with **skimming** or **skim-reading**, which is a type of rapid reading which is used when the reader wants to get the main idea or ideas from a passage. For example a reader may skim-read a chapter to find out if the writer approves or disapproves of something.

see also READING SPEED

scatter diagram /'skætə^r ˌdaɪəgræm/ *n*
also **scattergram** /'skætəˌgræm‖-tər-/, **scatterplot** /'skætəˌplɒt‖
-tərˌplɑːt/
> a representation on a graph of two separate variables, in such a way as
> to display their relationship as shown below:

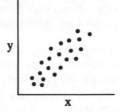

Y *axis*: scores on test Y
X *axis*: scores on test X
> see also CORRELATION

scheme /skiːm/ *n*
also **schema** /'skiːmə/, **macro-structure, genre-scheme, discourse
structure, rhetorical structure**
> (in TEXT LINGUISTICS and DISCOURSE ANALYSIS) the underlying
> structure which accounts for the organization of a TEXT or DISCOURSE.
> Different kinds of texts and discourse (e.g. stories, descriptions, letters,
> reports, poems) are distinguished by the ways in which the TOPIC,
> PROPOSITIONS, and other information are linked together to form a
> unit. This underlying structure is known as the "scheme" or "macro-
> structure". For example the scheme underlying many stories is:
> *Story = Setting(= state + state +. . .) + Episodes(= Event(s) + Reaction)*
> i.e. stories consist of a setting in which the time, place, and characters
> are identified, followed by episodes leading towards a reaction. A text
> or discourse in which a suitable underlying scheme or macro-structure
> is used is said to be "coherent" (see COHERENCE).
> Note that the plural of *scheme* is *schemes*, but the plural of *schema* is
> either *schemes* or *schemata*.
>
> see also SCRIPT
> *Further reading* van Dijk 1977

school-based curriculum development /'skuːl beɪst kəˈrɪkjᵘləm
dɪˌveləpmənt/ *n*
> an educational movement which argues that the planning, designing,
> implementation and evaluation of a programme of students' learning
> should be carried out by the educational institutions of which these
> students are members (i.e. schools) rather than by an external
> institution, such as a state department of education or a national
> curriculum centre. The movement towards school-based curriculum
> development is an attempt to develop learning programmes that are
> more relevant to students' interests and needs by involving schools,
> learners, and teachers in the planning and decision making. In second

language teaching such attempts have also been described as leading to a **learner-centred-curriculum.**

Further reading Sillbeck 1984

schwa /ʃwɑː/ *n*
also **shwa**

a short vowel usually produced with the tongue in a central position in the mouth and with the lips unrounded. The phonetic symbol for a schwa is [ə].

In English, it occurs very frequently in unaccented syllables, e.g. *-mous* in /ˈfeɪməs/ *famous*, *-ment* in /ˈmuːvmənt/ *movement* and in unstressed words in rapid speech, e.g. *to* in /tə ˈteɪk/ *to take*.

see also MANNER OF ARTICULATION, PLACE OF ARTICULATION
Further reading Gimson 1989

scientific method /ˈsaɪəntɪfɪk ˈmeθəd/ *n*

(in research) an approach to the study of knowledge which uses observation, experimentation, generalization and verification, and which involves using facts to develop theories. The following stages are usually involved in research based on a scientific method:

1 A problem is defined.
2 The problem is related to previous knowledge.
3 A HYPOTHESIS is developed.
4 Procedures needed to collect data to test the hypothesis are selected.
5 DATA is collected.
6 The data is analyzed to see if the hypothesis can be accepted or rejected (see NULL HYPOTHESIS).
7 The conclusions are related to the existing body of scientific knowledge, which is modified according to the new findings.

The question of whether the scientific method is appropriate to research in language teaching and learning has often been discussed by researchers. Some have argued that such research should be made more scientific; others have argued that teaching is not a science and that other research traditions are more suitable.

see also QUALITATIVE RESEARCH

scope /skəup/ *n*

see NEGATION

scoring /ˈskɔːrɪŋ/ *n*

procedures for giving numerical values or scores to the responses in a test.

script /skrɪpt/ *n*
also **frame**

(in COGNITIVE PSYCHOLOGY) units of meaning consisting of sequences of events and actions that are related to particular situations. For example a "restaurant script" is our knowledge that a restaurant is a place where waitresses, waiters, and cooks work, where food is served to customers, and where customers sit at tables, order food, eat, pay the bill, and depart. A person's knowledge of this "script" helps in understanding the following paragraph:

Tom was hungry. He went into a restaurant. At 8 p.m. he paid the bill and left.

Although Tom was most probably shown to a table, sat down, ordered a meal, and ate it, these facts are not mentioned in the paragraph. The reader's knowledge of a restaurant script, i.e. the usual sequence of events for this situation, provides this information. Script theory has been used in studies of problem solving, reading, memory, and comprehension.

see also SCHEME
Further reading Schank & Abelson 1977

SD¹ /ˌes ˈdiː/ *n*
an abbreviation for STANDARD DEVIATION

SD² *n*
an abbreviation for STRUCTURAL DESCRIPTION

SE /ˌes ˈiː/ *n*
an abbreviation for STANDARD ERROR

secondary cardinal vowel /ˈsekəndəri ˈkaːdɪ̯nəl ˈvauəl‖-deri ˈkaːr-/ *n*
see CARDINAL VOWEL

secondary stress /ˈsekəndəri ˈstres/ *n*
see STRESS

second language /ˈsekənd ˈlæŋgwɪdʒ/ *n*
see FOREIGN LANGUAGE

second language acquisition /ˈsekənd ˈlæŋgwɪdʒ ˌækwɨˈzɪʃən/ *n*
(in APPLIED LINGUISTICS) the processes by which people develop proficiency in a second or foreign language. These processes are often investigated with the expectation that information about them may be useful in language teaching. The term "second language acquisition" has been used particularly in the USA by researchers interested in:

a longitudinal studies and case studies of the development of syntax and phonology in second and foreign language learners (see CROSS-SECTIONAL METHOD, CASE STUDY)

b analysis of the spoken and written discourse of second and foreign language learners (see DISCOURSE ANALYSIS)

c the study of other aspects of language development.

Further reading Hatch 1978, Ellis 1985

segment /ˈsegmənt/ *n* segment /segˈment/ *v*
any linguistic unit in a sequence which may be isolated from the rest of the sequence, e.g. a sound in an UTTERANCE or a letter in a written text.

segmental error /seg'mentl 'erə^r/ *n*

(in SECOND LANGUAGE ACQUISITION) an error of pronunciation which involves individual vowels or consonants. Segmental errors often contribute to a learner's accent (see ACCENT[3]) in a second or foreign language.

Further reading Odlin 1989

segmental phonemes /seg'mentl 'fəuni:mz/ *n*

Sometimes a distinction is made between the segmental phonemes (i.e. the vowels and consonants of a language) and the supra-segmentals, i.e. such sound phenomena as accent (see ACCENT[1]) and INTONATION, which may stretch over more than one segment.

selection /sɪ'lekʃən/ *n*

(in language teaching) the choice of linguistic content (vocabulary, grammar, etc.) for a language course, textbook, etc. Procedures for selecting language items to include in a language course include the use of FREQUENCY COUNTS, NEEDS ANALYSIS, and PEDAGOGIC GRAMMARS.

see also SYLLABUS
Further reading Mackey 1965

selective branching /sɪ'lektɪv 'brɑːntʃɪŋ||'bræn-/ *n*

see BRANCHING

self /self/ *n*

an aspect of PERSONALITY that consists of a person's view of their own identity and characteristics. A person's sense of his or her self is formed as a result of contact and experiences with other people and how they view and treat the invidividual. Self has been discussed as a personality variable in second language learning.

see also COGNITIVE VARIABLE

self-access /'self 'ækses/ *adj*

(of instructional materials) the capacity of materials to be used independently by learners without the guidance or direction of a teacher.

see also SELF-ACCESS LEARNING CENTRE

self-access learning centre /'self 'ækses 'lɜːnɪŋ ˌsentə^r||-ɜːr-/ *n*

a room or area in an educational institution containing learning resources of different kinds which students can use under supervision. It may contain computers for individual student use, video and TV monitors and audio facilities, as well as more conventional learning resources. Students may be directed to certain learning materials (e.g. grammar reviews) designed to complement and support regular teaching activities in a language programme.

self concept /'self ˌkɒnsept||ˌkɑːn-/ *n*

the image a person has of himself or herself. A measure of a person's self concept is sometimes included in the study of affective variables (see COGNITIVE VARIABLE) in language learning.

self-evaluation /'self ɪˌvælju'eɪʃən/ *n*
also **self-assessment** /'self ə'sesmənt/
checking one's own performance on a language learning task after it has been completed or checking one's own success in using a language. Self-evaluation is an example of a METACOGNITIVE STRATEGY in language learning.

see also SELF-RATING

self-instruction /'self ɪn'strʌkʃən/ *n* **self-instructional** /ˌself ɪn'strʌk ʃənəl◂/ *adj*
(in education) approaches to learning in which a learner works alone or with other learners, without the control of a teacher. The use of self-instructional activities in language teaching helps to give learners a greater degree of control over their own learning. It is based on the belief that learning is sometimes more effective if learners can make choices about the kinds of things they wish to learn, the strategies they use, and the amount of time they can spend on a learning task.
Further reading Dickinson 1987

self-monitoring /'self 'mɒnɪtərɪŋ||'mɑː-/ *n*
also **self-observation** /'self ɒbzə'veɪʃən||ɑːbzər-/
1 Observing and recording information about one's own behaviour for the purpose of achieving a better understanding of and control over one's behaviour. In TEACHER EDUCATION, teachers may be taught procedures for self-monitoring as an aspect of their on-going professional development. Techniques used include keeping a journal of their teaching experiences, regular and systematic use of self-reports (see SELF REPORTING), or through making audio or video recordings of their own lessons.
2 Checking one's performance during a learning task as a METACOGNITIVE STRATEGY during language learning.
Further reading Richards 1990

self-rating /'self 'reɪtɪŋ/ *n*
also **self report**
(in language testing) an individual's own evaluation of their language ability, generally according to how good they are at particular language skills (e.g. reading, speaking), how well they are able to use the language in different DOMAINS or situations (e.g. at the office, at school) or how well they can use different styles of the language (e.g. a formal style or an informal style). Self-ratings are a way of obtaining indirect information about a person's proficiency in a language.

self repair /'self rɪ'peə ʳ/ *n*
see REPAIR

self report /ˈself ˈrɪpɔːt‖-ɔːrt/ *n*
another term for SELF-RATING

self-reporting /ˈself rɪˈpɔːtɪŋ‖-ɔːr-/ *n*
(in teaching) the use of an inventory or check list of teaching behaviour used during a lesson, which is completed after the lesson has
been taught. The self-report form indicates which teaching practices
were used during a lesson and how often they were employed and may
be completed by an individual teacher or by a group of teachers in a
group session. Self-reporting is intended to assist teachers assess their
own classroom practices.
Further reading Richards 1990

semantic component /sɪˈmæntɪk kəmˈpəʊnənt/ *n*
see TRANSFORMATIONAL GENERATIVE GRAMMAR, INTERPRETIVE SEMAN-
TICS

semantic components /sɪˈmæntɪk kəmˈpəʊnənts/ *n*
another term for SEMANTIC FEATURES

semantic differential /sɪˈmæntɪk ˌdɪfəˈrenʃəl/ *n*
a technique for measuring people's attitudes or feelings about words.
The semantic differential makes use of a RATING SCALE which contains
pairs of adjectives with opposite meanings (**bi-polar adjectives**) which
are used to rate different impressions of meaning. The following scale,
for example, could be used to measure the subjective meanings of
words:

WORD (e.g. *democracy*)

good	—	—	—	—	*bad*
weak	—	—	—	—	*strong*
rough	—	—	—	—	*smooth*
active	—	—	—	—	*passive*

Subjects rate the word on each dimension. The ratings of different
words can be compared. The semantic differential has been used in
SEMANTICS, PSYCHOLINGUISTICS, and in the study of LANGUAGE ATTI-
TUDES.
Further reading Osgood 1964

semantic feature /sɪˈmæntɪk ˈfiːtʃə‖-ər/ *n*
also **semantic component, semantic properties**
the basic unit of meaning in a word. The meanings of words may be
described as a combination of semantic features.
For example, the semantic feature ⟨+ male⟩ is part of the meaning of
father, and so is the feature ⟨+ adult⟩ but other features are needed to
give the whole concept or sense of *father*.
The same feature may be part of the meaning of a number of words.
For example, ⟨+ movement⟩ is part of the meaning of a whole group of
verbs and nouns, e.g. *run, jump, walk, gallop*.

Sometimes, semantic features are established by contrasts and can be stated in terms of ⟨+⟩ or ⟨–⟩, e.g.

child ⟨+ human⟩ ⟨– adult⟩
man ⟨+ human⟩ ⟨+ adult⟩ ⟨+ male⟩
boy ⟨+ human⟩ ⟨– adult⟩ ⟨+ male⟩

see also BINARY FEATURE, COMPONENTIAL ANALYSIS
Further reading Fromkin & Rodman 1983

semantic field /sɪ'mæntɪk 'fiːld/ *n*
another term for LEXICAL FIELD

semantic memory /sɪ'mæntɪk 'meməri/ *n*
see EPISODIC MEMORY

semantic property /sɪ'mæntɪk 'prɒpəti‖'prɑːpər-/ *n*
another term for SEMANTIC FEATURE

semantics /sɪ'mæntɪks/ *n* semantic *adj*
the study of MEANING. There are many different approaches to the way in which meaning in language is studied. Philosophers, for instance, have investigated the relation between linguistic expressions, such as the words of a language, and persons, things and events in the world to which these words refer (see REFERENCE, SIGNS). Linguists have investigated, for example, the way in which meaning in a language is structured (see COMPONENTIAL ANALYSIS, LEXICAL FIELD, SEMANTIC FEATURES) and have distinguished between different types of meanings (see CONNOTATION, DENOTATION). There have also been studies of the semantic structure of sentences (see PROPOSITIONS).
In recent years, linguists have generally agreed that meaning plays an important part in grammatical analysis but there has been disagreement on how it should be incorporated in a grammar (see BASE COMPONENT, GENERATIVE SEMANTICS, INTERPRETIVE SEMANTICS).

see also PRAGMATICS
Further reading Leech 1981; Lyons 1977; Palmer 1981

semi-consonant /'semi ˌkɒnsənənt‖ˌkɑːn-/ *n*
see CONSONANT

semilingual /ˌsemɪ'lɪŋgwəl ◂/ *adj* semilingualism /ˌsemɪ'lɪŋgwəlɪzəm/ *n*
a term sometimes used for people who have acquired several languages at different periods of their lives, but who have not developed a nativespeaker level of proficiency in any of them. This issue is regarded as controversial by many linguists.
Further reading Skutnabb-Kangas & Toukomaa 1976

semiotics /ˌsemi'ɒtɪks‖-'ɑːtɪks/ *n* semiotic *adj*
1 the theory of SIGNS.
2 the analysis of systems using signs or signals for the purpose of

communication (**semiotic systems**). The most important semiotic system is human language, but there are other systems, e.g. Morse code, SIGN LANGUAGE, traffic signals.

semiotic systems /ˈsemiɒtɪk ˈsɪstn̩mz‖-ɑːtɪk/ *n*

see SEMIOTICS

semi-vowel /ˈsemi ˌvaʊəl/ *n*

a speech sound (a CONSONANT) which is produced by allowing the airstream from the lungs to move through the mouth and/or nose with only very slight friction.

For example, in English the /j/ in /jes/ *yes* is a semi-vowel.

In terms of their articulation, semi-vowels are very like vowels, but they function as consonants in the sound system of a language.

see also CONSONANT

Further reading Gimson 1980

sender /ˈsendəʳ/ *n*

see COMMUNICATION

sense /sens/ *n*

the place which a word or phrase (a LEXEME) holds in the system of relationships with other words in the vocabulary of a language. For example, the English words *bachelor* and *married* have the sense relationship of *bachelor* = *never married*.

A distinction is often made between sense and REFERENCE.

see also CONNOTATION, DENOTATION

Further reading Lyons 1981

sensorimotor stage /ˌsensəriˈməʊtəʳ ˌsteɪdʒ/ *n*

see GENETIC EPISTEMOLOGY

sentence /ˈsentəns/ *n*

(in GRAMMAR[1, 2]) the largest unit of grammatical organization within which parts of speech (e.g. nouns, verbs, adverbs) and grammatical classes (e.g. word, phrase, clause) are said to function. In English a sentence normally contains one independent clause (see DEPENDENT CLAUSE) with a FINITE VERB. Units which are larger than the sentence (e.g. paragraph) are regarded as examples of DISCOURSE.

sentence combining /ˈsentəns kəmˌbaɪnɪŋ/ *n*

a technique used in the teaching of grammar and writing, in which the student combines basic sentences to produce longer and more complex sentences and paragraphs. For example:

The teacher has doubts.
The doubts are grave.
The doubts are about Jackie.

↓

The teacher has grave doubts about Jackie.

sentence fragment /ˈsentəns ˌfrægmənt/ *n*

(in composition) an incomplete sentence which cannot stand on its own. For example:

Whenever I try to hold a conversation with my parents about my career
is a sentence fragment because it is a DEPENDENT CLAUSE which contains a SUBORDINATING CONJUNCTION (see CONJUNCTION) and should therefore be connected to an INDEPENDENT CLAUSE (see DEPENDENT CLAUSE). For example:

Whenever I try to hold a conversation with my parents about my career, they get angry with me.

Further reading Herman 1982

sentence meaning /ˈsentəns ˈmiːnɪŋ/ *n*

see UTTERANCE MEANING

sentence method /ˈsentəns ˌmeθəd/ *n*

a method used to teach reading in the mother tongue, which uses sentences as the basic units of teaching, rather than words or sounds (see PHONICS, WHOLE-WORD METHOD). The reading material uses whole sentences from the beginning, and less importance is given to letter names or sounds.

Further reading Goodacre 1978

sentence outline /ˈsentəns ˈaʊtlaɪn/ *n*

see OUTLINE

sentence pattern /ˈsentəns ˌpætn‖-tərn/ *n*

(in language teaching) a structure which is considered a basic grammatical pattern for sentences in the language being taught, and which can be used as a model for producing other sentences in the language. For example:

		sentence pattern				
Determiner	+ Noun	+ Verb	+ Article	+ Adjective	+ Noun	
Our	*house*	*has*	*a*	*large*	*garden.*	
My	*dog*	*has*	*a*	*big*	*tail.*	

sentential adverb /senˈtenʃəl ˈædvɜːb‖-ɜːr-/ *n*

another term for **disjunct**

see ADJUNCT

sequencing[1] /ˈsiːkwənsɪŋ/ *n*

(in CONVERSATIONAL ANALYSIS) the relationship between UTTERANCES, that is, which type of utterance may follow another one. Sequencing is governed by rules known as **sequencing rules**, which may be different for different languages or different varieties of the same language. In some cases, the sequence of utterances is quite strictly regulated, as in greetings and leave-takings (see ADJACENCY PAIRS) but often there is a range of possibilities depending on the situation, the topic, the speakers, and their intentions at the moment.

331

For example, a question is usually followed by an answer but can, in certain circumstances, be followed by another question:

A: *What are you doing tonight?*
B: *Why do you want to know?*

see also TURN-TAKING

Further reading Coulthard 1985; Schegloff 1972

sequencing²

another term for GRADATION

sequencing rules /'siːkwənsɪŋ ˌruːlz/ n

see SEQUENCING¹

sequential access /sɪ'kwenʃəl 'ækses/ n

see ACCESS

sequential processing /sɪ'kwenʃəl 'prəʊsesɪŋ||'prɑː-/ n

see PARALLEL PROCESSING

serial learning /'sɪəriəl ˌlɜːnɪŋ||ˌlɜːr-/ n

also **serial-order learning** /ˌsɪəriəl 'ɔːdəʳ ˌlɜːnɪŋ||'ɔːr- ˌlɜːr-/

the learning of items in a sequence or order, as when a list of words is memorized. In PSYCHOLINGUISTICS, serial-order learning theories (also known as "linear" or "left-to-right" theories) have been compared with **top-to-bottom** or hierarchical theories of how people produce sentences. For example in producing the sentence *The dog chased the cat*, in a serial-order model each word the speaker produces determines the word which comes after it:

The + dog + chased + the + cat.

In a top-to-bottom model, items which build the PROPOSITION are produced before other items. For example:

a *dog, cat, chase* (unordered)
b *dog + chase + cat* (ordered)
c *the + dog + chased + the + cat* (modified)

Further reading Foss & Hakes 1978

setting /'setɪŋ/ n

the time and place of a SPEECH EVENT.

For example, a conversation can take place in a classroom, a garden, a church, and it can take place at any hour of the day. The setting of a speech event may have an effect on what is being said and how it is said.

see also COMMUNICATIVE COMPETENCE

Further reading Hymes 1977

sheltered English /'ʃeltəd 'ɪŋglɪʃ||-tərd/ n

an approach to the teaching of LIMITED ENGLISH PROFICIENT students based on the Canadian model of immersion education (see IMMERSION PROGRAMME), in which content is taught in English and made comprehensible to the students by special instructional techniques. The goal of the approach is to enable the LEP student to acquire high levels of oral English proficiency while at the same time achieving in the CONTENT AREAS, i.e. to teach academic subject matter and language simultaneously until the student is ready for MAINSTREAMING.

short-term memory /'ʃɔːt ˌtɜːm 'meməri‖-ɔːr- -ɜːr-/ *n*
see MEMORY

shwa /ʃwaː/ *n*
another spelling of SCHWA

sibilant /'sɪbɨlənt/ *n*
a speech sound (a CONSONANT) which is produced with friction and which has an s-like quality.
For example, in English the /s/ in /siː/ *sea* and the /z/ in /heɪz/ *haze* are sibilants.
A sibilant is a type of FRICATIVE.
Further reading Gimson 1989

side sequence /'saɪd ˌsiːkwəns/ *n*
In a conversation, one of the speakers may break the main course of the conversation to check up on a particular point. Usually the other speaker(s) would supply the answer. After this exchange, the side sequence, the main conversation is often taken up again.
For example, A and B are arranging to meet:
A: I'll be there at six.
B: *Aren't you working late?*
A: *Not on Thursdays.*
B: Fine, see you at six then.
The B/A exchange in the middle of the conversation is the side sequence.
see also INSERTION SEQUENCE, REPAIR, SEQUENCING
Further reading Jefferson 1972; Wardhaugh 1986

sight method /'saɪt ˌmeθəd/ *n*
another term for WHOLE-WORD METHOD

sight vocabulary /'saɪt vəˌkæbjɨləri, vəʊ-‖-leri/ *n*
(in teaching reading in the mother tongue) those words which a child can recognize at sight in a reading passage or text and which he or she does not need to decode using phonic or other reading skills (see PHONICS).

signal /'sɪgnəl/ *n*
see INFORMATION THEORY

signal converter /'sɪgnəl kənˌvɜːtəʳ‖-ɜːr-/ *n*
(in COMPUTER ASSISTED LANGUAGE LEARNING) a device which turns a

tape on or off after receiving appropriate instructions from a computer.
see also INTERACTIVE AUDIO

signification /ˌsɪgnɪ̩fɪ̩ˈkeɪʃən/ *n*
see SIGNS, USAGE²

signify /ˈsɪgnɪ̩faɪ/ *v*
see SIGNS

sign language /ˈsaɪn ˌlæŋgwɪdʒ/ *n* **sign** *v*
a language used by many deaf people and by some who communicate with deaf people, which makes use of movements of the hands, arms, body, head, face, eyes, and mouth to communicate meanings. Different sign languages have developed in different parts of the world, for example American Sign Language or **Ameslan**, British Sign Language, Danish Sign Language, French Sign Language. These are true languages with their own grammars and are not simply attempts to "spell out" the language spoken in the country where they are used. The visual-gestural units of communication used in sign languages are known as "signs".

Within the deaf community and those concerned with the education of the hearing-impaired, there is a controversy between those who are in favour of signing (people arguing this position are referred to as **manualists**) and those who oppose it (the **oralists**). Oralists argue that teaching the hearing-impaired sign language prevents them from communicating with the outside world and limits their interaction to other people who know sign language.

Further reading Baker & Cokely 1980; Deuchar 1984

signs /saɪnz/ *n*
in linguistics, the words and other expressions of a language which **signify**, that is, "stand for", other things. In English, the word *table*, for instance, stands for a particular piece of furniture in the real world. Some linguists and philosophers include a third item in the process of **signification**, that is, an abstract CONCEPT of the thing for which the sign stands, e.g.:

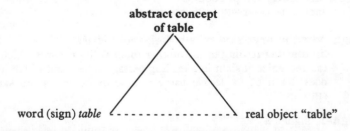

abstract concept of table

word (sign) *table* ⟵ - - - - - - - - - - - - - - ⟶ real object "table"

Further reading Lyons 1977; Ogden & Richards 1923

silent pause /ˈsaɪlənt ˈpɔːz/ *n*
see PAUSING

silent reading /'saɪlənt 'riːdɪŋ/ *n*

see READING

silent way /'saɪlənt ˌweɪ/ *n*

a METHOD of foreign-language teaching developed by Gattegno which makes use of gesture, mime, visual aids, wall charts, and in particular Cuisinière rods (wooden sticks of different lengths and colours) that the teacher uses to help the students to talk. The method takes its name from the relative silence of the teacher using these techniques.

Further reading Gattegno 1976; Richards & Rogers 1986

simile /'sɪmɬli/ *n*

see FIGURE OF SPEECH

simple form /'sɪmpəl ˌfɔːm‖-ɔːr-/ *n*

see INFINITIVE

simple past /'sɪmpəl 'pɑːst‖'pæst/ *n*

see PAST TENSE

simple sentence /'sɪmpəl 'sentəns/ *n*

see COMPLEX SENTENCE

simplification[1] /ˌsɪmplɬfɬ'keɪʃən/ *n*

(in the study of SECOND LANGUAGE ACQUISITION and ERROR ANALYSIS) a term sometimes used to describe what happens when learners make use of rules which are grammatically (or morphologically/phonologically, etc.) less complex than TARGET-LANGUAGE[1] rules, often as a result of an OVERGENERALIZATION. For example, a learner may have a single rule for forming the past tense (by adding *-ed* to the verb base) ignoring exceptions and producing incorrect forms such as *breaked, standed*. In studies of the INTERLANGUAGE of second- and foreign-language learners, simplifications may by contrasted with errors which result from other processes, such as LANGUAGE TRANSFER.

simplification[2] *n*

(in language teaching) the rewriting or adaptation of original texts or materials, generally using a WORD LIST and sometimes also a structure list or grammatical SYLLABUS, to produce simplified reading or other materials suitable for second- or foreign-language learners.

see also GRADED READER

simplified reader /'sɪmplɬfaɪd 'riːdər/ *n*

another term for GRADED READER

simulation /ˌsɪmjʊ'leɪʃən/ *n*

classroom activities which reproduce or simulate real situations and which often involve dramatization and group discussion (see ROLE-PLAY, which does not include group discussion). In simulation activities, learners are given roles in a situation, TASKS, or a problem to be solved, and are given instructions to follow (for example, an employer-employee discussion over wage increases in a factory). The participants then make decisions and proposals. Consequences are "simulated" on the basis of decisions the participants take. They later discuss their actions, feelings, and what happened.

simultaneous interpretation /ˌsɪməl'teɪnɪəs ɪnˌtɜːprɨ'teɪʃən||saɪ-ˌtɜːr-/ *n*

see INTERPRETATION

singular /ˈsɪŋɡjʊləʳ/ *n, adj*

the form of nouns, verbs, pronouns, etc. used to refer to only one in number.

For example:

singular	plural
machine	machines
it	they/them

sister dependency /ˈsɪstəʳ dɪˌpendənsi/ *n*

In some syntactic analyses, if two constituents of a sentence are on the same level of structure, they are considered to be *sisters*.
For example, in the English sentence:

All the children were laughing

the noun phrase *all the children* is a 'sister' to the verb phrase *were laughing*. They are mutually dependent on each other (sister-dependent). In a diagram, they would both be under the same NODE for example:

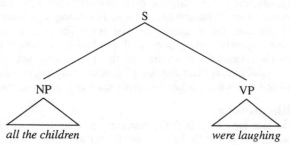

Both phrases would be DAUGHTERS of S which "immediately dominates them". That means that S is the NODE or point in the tree diagram which is immediately above them. They are daughter-dependent on S.

Further reading Burton-Roberts 1986

Situational Language Teaching /ˌsɪtʃu'eɪʃənəl 'læŋɡwɪdʒ ˌtiːtʃɪŋ/ *n*
also **oral approach**

a language teaching METHOD developed by British language teaching specialists between 1940 and 1960. Situational Language Teaching is a grammar-based method in which principles of grammatical and lexical GRADATION are used and new teaching points presented and practised through situations. Although no longer in fashion, techniques derived from Situational Language Teaching are found in many widely used language teaching textbooks.

Further reading Richards & Rodgers 1986

situational method /ˌsɪtʃuˈeɪʃənəl ˌmeθəd/ *n*

(in language teaching) a term sometimes used to refer to a programme or method in which the selection, organization, and presentation of language items is based on situations (e.g. *at the bank, at the supermarket, at home*). A SYLLABUS for such a language course or textbook may be referred to as a **situational syllabus.** Many methods make use of simulated situations as a way of practising language items, but use other criteria for selecting and organizing the content of the course (see NOTIONAL SYLLABUS, FUNCTIONAL SYLLABUS, for example). Only if situations are used to select, organize, and practise language would the term "situational method" strictly apply.

situational syllabus /ˌsɪtʃuˈeɪʃənəl ˈsɪləbəs/ *n*

see SITUATIONAL METHOD

skills /skɪlz/ *n*

(in language teaching) another term for LANGUAGE SKILLS

skimming /ˈskɪmɪŋ/ *n*
also **skim-reading** /ˈskɪm ˌriːdɪŋ/

see SCANNING

slang /slæŋ/ *n*

casual, very informal speech, using expressive but informal words and expressions (**slang words/expressions**).

For some people, slang is equivalent to COLLOQUIAL SPEECH but for others, it means 'undesirable speech'. Usually, 'colloquial speech' refers to a speech variety used in informal situations with colleagues, friends or relatives, and 'slang' is used for a very informal speech variety which often serves as an 'in-group' language for a particular set of people such as teenagers, army recruits, pop-groups etc. Most slang is rather unstable as its words and expressions can change quite rapidly, for example:

Beat it! Scram! Rack off!   (for 'leave')

see also JARGON

slang words /ˈslæŋ wɜːdz‖-ɜːr-/ *n*
also **slang expressions** /ˈslæŋ ɪkˈspreʃənz/ *n*

see SLANG

small-group discussion /ˈsmɔːl gruːp dɪˈskʌʃən/ *n*

see DISCUSSION METHOD

small-group interaction /ˈsmɔːl gruːp ɪntərˈækʃən/ *n*

(in teaching) the factors which explain the interactions occurring

337

within small groups. These include whether the interactions in the group are verbal or non-verbal, the kind of TASK involved, the roles of the group members, the leadership and the cohesion of the group.

see also GROUPING

social context /ˈsəʊʃəl ˈkɒntekst‖ˈkɑːn-/ *n*
the environment in which meanings are exchanged. (According to Halliday) the social context of language can be analysed in terms of three factors:

a The **field of discourse** refers to what is happening, including what is being talked about.

b The **tenor of discourse** refers to the participants who are taking part in this exchange of meaning, who they are and what kind of relationship they have to one another (see ROLE RELATIONSHIP).

c The **mode of discourse** refers to what part the language is playing in this particular situation, for example, in what way the language is organized to convey the meaning, and what CHANNEL is used – written or spoken or a combination of the two.

Example: A foreign language lesson in a secondary school.

field: language study, a defined area of information about the foreign language, e.g. the use of tenses. Teacher imparting, students acquiring knowledge about tenses and their use.

tenor: participants: teacher – students. Fixed role relationships defined by the educational institution. Teacher in higher role. Temporary role relationships between students, depending on personality.

mode: language used for instruction and discussion. Channel: spoken (e.g. questions eliciting information, answers supplying information, acted dialogues by students) and written (e.g. visual presentation on blackboard, textbooks, additional reading material).

see also FUNCTIONS OF LANGUAGE[2], SYSTEMIC LINGUISTICS
Further reading Halliday 1978

social dialect /ˈsəʊʃəl ˈdaɪəlekt/ *n*
another term for SOCIOLECT

social dialectal variation /ˈsəʊʃəl daɪəˈlektl veəriˈeɪʃən/ *n*
another term for **sociolectal variation**
see SOCIOLECT

social distance /ˈsəʊʃəl ˈdɪstəns/ *n*
the feeling a person has that his or her social position is relatively similar to or relatively different from the social position of someone else. The social distance between two different groups or communities influences communication between them, and may affect the way one group learns the language of another (for example, an immigrant group, learning the language of the dominant group in a country). Social distance may depend on such factors as differences in the size,

ethnic origin, political STATUS, social status of two groups, and has been studied in SECOND LANGUAGE ACQUISITION research.

see also PIDGINIZATION HYPOTHESIS, ASSIMILATION², ACCULTURATION
Further reading Schumann 1978

social function /ˈsəʊʃəl ˈfʌŋkʃən/ *n*

see FUNCTIONS OF LANGUAGE¹

socialized speech /ˈsəʊʃəl-aɪzd ˈspiːtʃ/ *n*

see EGOCENTRIC SPEECH

social psychology of language /ˈsəʊʃəl saɪˈkɒlədʒi əv ˈlæŋgwɪdʒ‖ -ˈkɑː-/ *n*

the study of how society and its structures affect the individual's language behaviour. The term is used particularly in that branch of psychology known as social psychology. Investigations in this field deal, for instance, with attitudes to different languages or language varieties and to their speakers.

Further reading Giles & St Clair 1979

sociolect /ˈsəʊʃiəlekt/ *n* sociolectal /ˌsəʊʃiəˈlektl◄/ *adj*
also social dialect

a variety of a language (a DIALECT) used by people belonging to a particular social class. The speakers of a sociolect usually share a similar socioeconomic and/or educational background. Sociolects may be classed as high (in STATUS) or low (in status).
For example:

He and I were going there. (higher sociolect)
'Im'n me was goin' there. (lower sociolect)

The sociolect with the highest status in a country is often the STANDARD VARIETY.

The difference between one sociolect and another can be investigated by analysing the recorded speech of large samples of speakers from various social backgrounds. The differences are referred to as **socio-lectal variation** or **social dialectal variation**.

see also DIALECT, ACCENT³, SPEECH VARIETY

sociolectal variation /ˈsəʊʃiəlektl veəriˈeɪʃən/ *n*
also social dialectal variation

see SOCIOLECT

sociolinguistics /ˌsəʊsiəʊlɪŋˈgwɪstɪks, ˌsəʊʃəʊ-/ *n* sociolinguistic adj

the study of language in relation to social factors, that is, social class, educational level and type of education, age, sex, ethnic origin, etc. Linguists differ as to what they include under sociolinguistics. Many would include the detailed study of interpersonal communication, sometimes called **micro-sociolinguistics**, e.g. SPEECH ACTS, SPEECH EVENTS, SEQUENCING¹ of UTTERANCES, and also those investigations which relate variation in the language used by a group of people to social factors (see SOCIOLECT). Such areas as the study of language choice in BILINGUAL or MULTILINGUAL communities, LANGUAGE PLANNING, LANGUAGE ATTITUDES, etc. may be included under sociolinguistics and are sometimes referred to as **macro-sociolinguistics**, or they are considered as being part of the SOCIOLOGY OF LANGUAGE or the SOCIAL PSYCHOLOGY OF LANGUAGE.

see also ETHNOGRAPHY OF COMMUNICATION
Further reading Trudgill 1983; Wardhaugh 1986

sociology of language /səʊsiˈɒlədʒi əv ˈlæŋgwɪdʒ, səʊʃi-‖-ˈɑːlə-/ *n*

the study of language varieties and their users within a social framework, for example the study of language choice in BILINGUAL or MULTILINGUAL nations, LANGUAGE PLANNING, LANGUAGE MAINTENANCE and LANGUAGE SHIFT.

The sociology of language is considered either as including the branch of linguistics called SOCIOLINGUISTICS or as an extension of socio-linguistics.

Further reading Fishman 1971

soft palate /ˈsɒft ˈpælᵻt‖ˈsɔːft/ *n*

another term for **velum**

see PLACE OF ARTICULATION, VELAR

software /ˈsɒft‚weəʳ‖ˈsɔːft-/ *n*

see HARDWARE

sonorant /ˈsɒnərənt‖ˈsɑː-/ *n*

a speech sound which is produced with a relatively free passage of air from the lungs, either through the mouth or through the nose. For example, /e/ in *bed,* /l/ in *lid* and /n/ in *nose* are sonorants. In GENERATIVE PHONOLOGY these sounds are marked [+sonorant] to distinguish them from OBSTRUENTS, which are marked [−sonorant].

see also DISTINCTIVE FEATURES
Further reading Hyman 1975

sound change /ˈsaʊnd ˌtʃeɪndʒ/ *n*

change in the pronunciation of words over a period of time. For example, there has been a sound change from Middle English /aː/ to Modern English /eɪ/:

Middle English /naːmə/   Modern English /neɪm/ *name.*

Such sound changes are still continuing and often differences can be observed between the pronunciation of older and younger speakers in a community.

Further reading Aitchison 1981; Fromkin & Rodman 1983

sound generator /ˈsaʊnd ˌdʒenəreɪtəʳ/ *n*

(in a computer system) a device which can produce musical or sound effects.

sound wave /ˈsaʊnd ˌweɪv/ *n*

wave-like movements of air which transmit sounds. In speech, sound waves are caused by the vibration of the VOCAL CORDS.

The rate at which the air in a sound wave moves backwards and forwards in a given time is called **frequency**. The faster the movement, the higher the frequency. A speech sound is a combination of simple sound waves vibrating at different frequencies and forming a complex sound wave. e.g.:

a simple sound wave

a complex sound wave

The lowest frequency in a complex sound wave is called the **fundamental frequency**. It is the same frequency as that at which the vocal cords are vibrating.

Further reading Denes & Pinson 1973

source[1] /sɔːs‖sɔːrs/ *n*

see INFORMATION THEORY

source[2] *n*

(in CASE GRAMMAR) the place from which someone or something moves or is moved.

For example, *the station* in:

  He came from the station.

Further reading Fillmore 1971

source language[1] /ˈsɔːs ˌlæŋgwɪdʒ‖-ɔːr-/ *n*

(in language BORROWING) a language from which words have been taken into another language. French was the source language for many words which entered English after the Norman Conquest (1066), e.g. *prince, just, saint, noble,* as well as for words which entered English at a later stage, e.g. *garage, restaurant.*

source language[2] *n*

the language out of which a translation is made (e.g. in a bilingual dictionary).

see also TARGET LANGUAGE[2]

SOV language /ˌes əʊ ˈviː ˌlæŋgwɪdʒ/ *n*

see TYPOLOGY

Spearman-Brown Formula /'spɪəmən 'braʊn ˌfɔːmjᵘlə||

'spɪər- ˌfɔːr-/ *n*

a formula for estimating the RELIABILITY of a test by calculating the reliability of a shorter or longer version of the same test. This formula is most frequently used in estimating the reliability of two independent halves of a test (see SPLIT-HALF RELIABILITY).

special languages /'speʃəl 'læŋgwɪdʒɪz/ *n*

a term used for the varieties of language used by specialists in writing about their subject matter, such as the language used in botany, law, nuclear physics or linguistics. The study of special languages includes the study of TERMINOLOGY (the special LEXEMES used in particular disciplines) and REGISTER (2) the distinctive linguistic features which occur in special languages.

see also ENGLISH FOR SPECIAL PURPOSES
Further reading Sager, Dungworth, & McDonald 1980

specific question /spᵊ'sɪfɪk 'kwestʃən/ *n*

see GLOBAL QUESTION

spectrogram /'spektrəgræm/ *n*

see SPECTROGRAPH

spectrograph /'spektrəgrɑːf||-græf/ *n*

an instrument used in acoustic phonetics (see PHONETICS). It gives a visual representation of a sound, showing its component frequencies. The spectrograph 'prints' out a SPECTROGRAM on special paper. A time scale is shown along the horizontal axis and a scale of frequencies along the vertical axis. The greater the intensity (i.e. the louder the sound), the darker the ink.

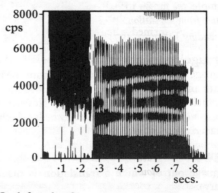

Further reading Ladefoged 1982

speech act /'spiːtʃ ˌækt/ *n*

an UTTERANCE as a functional unit in communication. In speech act theory, utterances have two kinds of meaning:

342

a propositional meaning (also known as **locutionary meaning**). This is the basic literal meaning of the utterance which is conveyed by the particular words and structures which the utterance contains (see PROPOSITION, LOCUTIONARY ACT).

b illocutionary meaning (also known as **illocutionary force**). This is the effect the utterance or written text has on the reader or listener.

For example, in *I am thirsty* the propositional meaning is what the utterance says about the speaker's physical state. The illocutionary force is the effect the speaker wants the utterance to have on the listener. It may be intended as a request for something to drink. A speech act is a sentence or utterance which has both propositional meaning and illocutionary force.

There are many different kinds of speech acts, such as requests, orders, commands, complaints, promises (see SPEECH ACT CLASSIFICATION).

A speech act which is performed indirectly is sometimes known as an **indirect speech act**, such as the speech act of requesting above. Indirect speech acts are often felt to be more polite ways of performing certain kinds of speech act, such as requests and refusals.

In language teaching, and SYLLABUS design, speech acts are often referred to as "functions" or "language functions" (see NOTIONAL SYLLABUS, FUNCTIONAL SYLLABUS).

see also PERFORMATIVE, PRAGMATICS, UPTAKE

Further reading Austin 1962; Searle 1981

speech act classification /ˈspiːtʃ ˌækt ˌklæsɨfɨˈkeɪʃən/ *n*

The philosopher Searle established a five-part classification of SPEECH ACTS:

a **commissive**: a speech act that commits the speaker to doing something in the future, such as a promise or a threat. For example:
  If you don't stop fighting I'll call the police. (threat)
  I'll take you to the movies tomorrow. (promise)

b **declarative**: a speech act which changes the state of affairs in the world. For example, during the wedding ceremony the act of marriage is performed when the phrase *I now pronounce you man and wife* is uttered.

c **directive**: a speech act that has the function of getting the listener to do something, such as a suggestion, a request, or a command.
  For example:
  Please sit down.
  Why don't you close the window.

d **expressive**: a speech act in which the speaker expresses feelings and attitudes about something, such as an apology, a complaint, to thank someone, to congratulate someone. For example:
  The meal was delicious.

e **representative**: a speech act which describes states or events in the world, such as an assertion, a claim, a report. For example, the assertion:
  This is a German car.

Further reading Searle 1965

343

speech community /'spiːtʃ kə,mjuːnᵻ̩ti/ *n*

a group of people who form a community, e.g. a village, a region, a nation, and who have *at least* one SPEECH VARIETY in common.

In BILINGUAL and MULTILINGUAL communities, people would usually have more than one speech variety in common (see SPEECH REPERTOIRE).

Further reading Hymes 1977; Wardhaugh 1986

speech continuum /'spiːtʃ kən,tɪnjuəm/ *n*

a range of speech varieties (see SPEECH VARIETY). Although it is common to think of a language as being divided into separate regional DIALECTS or social dialects (see SOCIOLECT), there is often no clear division between them but rather a continuum from one to another.

"Speech continuum" is used particularly when referring to varieties spoken by those with varying levels of proficiency in a second language (see FOREIGN LANGUAGE), e.g. English in Singapore. The sub-variety used by those with high levels of English medium education is frequently called the **acrolect**. The **basilect** is the sub-variety used by those with rather low levels of education and the **mesolects** are the sub-varities in between. Naturally there are no clear-cut boundaries between these "lects".

Educated speakers of a more established ESL variety may use the acrolect or an upper mesolect in more formal situations and something close to the basilect in a more informal context.

see also POST CREOLE CONTINUUM

Further reading Platt & Weber 1980; Platt & Ho 1991

speech defect /'spiːtʃ ,diːfekt/ *n*

also **speech disorder** /'spiːtʃ dɪs,ɔːdəʳ‖-,ɔːr-/

any abnormality in the production of speech which interferes with communication, such as APHASIA, or stuttering.

speech errors /'spiːtʃ ,erəz‖-ərz/ *n*

faults made by speakers during the production of sounds, words, and sentences.

Both NATIVE SPEAKERS and non-native speakers of a language make unintended mistakes when speaking. Some of the commonest speech errors include:

a **anticipation error**: when a sound or word is brought forward in a sentence and used before it is needed. For example:
I'll put your c̲at in the c̲upboard instead of *I'll put your h̲at in the cupboard.*

b **perseveration error**: when a sound or word which has already been uttered reappears. For example:
the p̲resident of P̲rance instead of *the p̲resident of France*

c **reversal error**, also **spoonerism**: when the position of sounds, syllables, or words is reversed, For example:
let's have c̲hish and f̲ips instead of *let's have fish and c̲hips*
Speech errors have been studied by psycholinguists in order to find

out how people store language items in long term memory and how they select items from memory when speaking.

see also MEMORY

Further reading Clark & Clark 1977

speech event /'spiːtʃ ɪ,vent/ *n*

a particular instance when people exchange speech, e.g. an exchange of greetings, an enquiry, a conversation. For example:

Child: *Mum, where's my red jumper?*
Mother: *Bottom drawer in your bedroom.*
Child: *Right, I'll have a look.*

Speech events are governed by rules and norms for the use of speech, which may be different in different communities. The structure of speech events varies considerably according to the GENRE they belong to.

The components of a speech event are its SETTING, the PARTICIPANTS and their ROLE RELATIONSHIPS, the MESSAGE, the key (see KEY[1]) and the CHANNEL.

The term **speech situation** is sometimes used instead of speech event, but usually it refers to any situation which is associated with speech, e.g. a classroom lesson, a party.

A speech situation may consist of just one speech event, e.g. two people meeting in the street and having a brief conversation, or it may contain a number of speech events, some going on at the same time, e.g. a large dinner party.

Further reading Coulthard 1985; Hymes 1977

speech marker /'spiːtʃ ,maːkəʳ‖,maːr-/ *n*

a linguistic feature which may give an indication of the speaker's age, sex, ethnicity or social group.

A speech marker could be a particular sound, e.g. the pronunciation of /r/ in New York, or /ei/ in *today* in Australia. It could be a syntactic structure, e.g. *between my husband and I/me*, or a word or expression.

see also VARIABLE[1]

speech pathology /'spiːtʃ pə,θɒlədʒi‖-,θaːl-/ *n*

the study of abnormalities in the development and use of language in children and adults (such as STUTTERING and APHASIA). Speech pathology includes the diagnosis of such disorders and the development of techniques (including clinical techniques) to treat them. Speech therapists (see SPEECH THERAPY) are sometimes called **speech pathologists** or **speech-language pathologists**, especially in the USA.

Further reading Crystal 1980

speech perception /'spiːtʃ pə'sepʃən‖pər-/ *n*

see PERCEPTION

speech rate /'spiːtʃ ,reɪt/ *n*

another term for RATE OF SPEECH

345

speech reading /'spiːtʃ ˌriːdɪŋ/ *n*

another term for LIPREADING

speech repertoire /'spiːtʃ ˌrepətwɑːʳ‖-ər-/ *n*

the languages or language varieties that a person knows and uses within his or her SPEECH COMMUNITY in everyday communication. A particular group of speakers may use not just one language or language variety to communicate with one another but several, each appropriate for certain areas of everyday activity (see DOMAIN). The speech repertoire of a French Canadian in Montreal could include Standard Canadian French, Colloquial Canadian French and English (perhaps in more than one variety).

see also DIGLOSSIA, VERBAL REPERTOIRE

speech rhythm /'spiːtʃ ˌrɪðəm/ *n*

rhythm in speech is created by the contracting and relaxing of chest muscles (pulses). This causes changes in air pressure. There are two different patterns of pulses:

a a more regular type of contraction with regular rises in air pressure (**chest pulses**)

b less frequent but stronger contractions with more sudden rises in air pressure (**stress pulses**).

The way these two systems operate together in any one language is said to cause different types of speech rhythm.

see also STRESS-TIMED RHYTHM, SYLLABLE-TIMED RHYTHM

Further reading Ladefoged 1982

speech situation /'spiːtʃ sɪtʃuˌeɪʃən/ *n*

see SPEECH EVENT

speech styles /'spiːtʃ ˌstaɪlz/ *n*

alternative ways of speaking within a community, often ranging from more colloquial to more formal. Usually, the range of styles available to a person varies according to his or her own background and the type of SPEECH COMMUNITY. The choice of a particular style has social implications. For example, choosing a formal style in a casual context may sound funny and using a very colloquial style in a formal context, such as in a sermon at a funeral service, may offend. Generally, a native speaker knows when a certain speech style is or is not appropriate (see APPROPRIATENESS).

Two types of rules which are connected with speech styles are **co-occurrence rules** and **alternation rules**. Co-occurrence rules determine which linguistic unit may follow or precede, that is, "co-occur with", another unit or units. For example:

formal style: *I should most certainly like to attend your ball, Sir Reginald.*

colloquial style: *I'd love to come to your do, Reg.*

Alternation rules determine the possible choice of "alternatives" from a number of speech styles or stylistic features which are at the speaker's disposal, e.g.

formal style: *Good morning, Mrs Smith* . . .
semi-formal style: *Hullo*. . .
colloquial style: *Hi, Penny*. . .

Further reading Coulthard 1985; Ervin-Tripp 1972

speech synthesis /'spiːtʃ 'sɪnθ⸜sɪs/ *n*

the automatic synthesis of speech-like sounds by a computer using a **speech synthesizer** or **voice synthesizer**, such as when a computer takes printed text as input and produces a spoken version of it. Many of the recorded messages heard on the telephone are not natural language but are produced by speech synthesis.

see also DIGITIZED SPEECH, COMPUTATIONAL LINGUISTICS

speech synthesizer /'spiːtʃ 'sɪnθ⸜saɪzəʳ/ *n*

see VOICE SYNTHESIZER

speech therapy /'spiːtʃ ˌθerəpi/ *n*

activities and exercises which are designed to help to alleviate or cure a language or speech defect (e.g. stuttering) or to help someone to regain their use of speech after having suffered speech loss (e.g. after a stroke). A person who works in the field of speech therapy is called a **speech therapist**.

see also SPEECH PATHOLOGY

speech variety /'spiːtʃ vəˌraɪəti/ *n*

a term sometimes used instead of LANGUAGE², DIALECT, SOCIOLECT, PIDGIN, CREOLE, etc. because it is considered more neutral than such terms. It may also be used for different varieties of one language, e.g. American English, Australian English, Indian English.

speed reading /'spiːd ˌriːdɪŋ/ *n*
also rapid reading

techniques used to teach people to read more quickly and to achieve a greater degree of understanding of what they read. Readers are usually trained to use more effective eye movements when reading (see REGRESSION*S*), and to use better ways of understanding words and meanings in written texts.

see also READING, TACHISTOSCOPE

spelling checker /'spelɪŋ ˌtʃekəʳ/ *n*

(in COMPUTER ASSISTED LANGUAGE LEARNING), a program which checks a text for misspelt words by comparing each word in a file with the entries in an ONLINE dictionary.

spelling pronunciation /'spelɪŋ prənʌnsiˌeɪʃən/ *n*

a way of pronouncing a word which is based on its spelling and which may differ from the way the word is generally pronounced. For example, a non-native speaker of British English might pronounce *yacht* as /jɒkt/ instead of /jɒt/. Native speakers also sometimes use spelling pronunciations, and some have become acceptable ways of pronouncing words, such as /'ɒftən/ for *often* rather than /'ɒfən/.

spiral approach /'spaɪərəl ə,prəʊtʃ/ *n*
also cyclical approach
a SYLLABUS in which items recur throughout the syllabus but are treated in greater depth or in more detail when they recur. This may be contrasted with a **linear syllabus,** in which syllabus items are dealt with once only.

Further reading Howatt 1974

spirant /'spaɪərənt/ *n*
a term used by some American linguists for a FRICATIVE

split construction /'splɪt kən'strʌkʃən/ *n*
(in composition) a sentence in which the subject has been separated from the verb, making it awkward to read. For example:

Teresa, after gathering together her clothes, books, and papers, left.

A less awkward sentence would be:

After gathering together her clothes, books and papers, Teresa left.

split-half reliability /'splɪt ,hɑːf rɪ,laɪə'bɪlˌti‖,hæf/ *n*
(in TESTING and statistics) an estimate of RELIABILITY based on the coefficient of CORRELATION between two halves of a test (e.g. between the odd and even scores or between the first and second half of the items of the test). Usually the SPEARMAN-BROWN FORMULA is applied to the results in order to estimate the reliability of the full test rather than its separate halves.

split infinitive /'splɪt ɪn'fɪnˌtɪv/ *n*
(in composition) a sentence in which the word *to* in an infinitive has been separated from the base of the verb making the sentence awkward to read. For example:

She asked me to as quickly as possible drop over to her house.

Without the split infinitive this would be:

She asked me to drop over to her house as quickly as possible.

In some sentences however, the split infinitive is appropriate. For example:

We expect to more than double profits this year.

Further reading Herman 1982

spoonerism /'spuːnərɪzəm/ *n*
see SPEECH ERROR

SQ3R technique /'es 'kjuː θriː 'ɑːʳ tek,niːk/ *n*
an acronym for Survey – Question – Read – Recite – Review, a reading strategy often recommended for students who are reading for study purposes which makes use of the following procedures:

Survey: The student looks through the chapter or text, looks at headings, pictures, summaries etc. to get an overall idea of what the chapter might contain.

2 **Question**: The student turns headings and subheadings into questions.

3 **Read**: The student reads to find answers to the questions, and marks any sections which are unclear.

4 **Recite**: The student covers the chapter and tries to remember the main ideas, saying them to him or herself.

5 **Review**: The student reviews the chapter and looks at the sections marked to see if they can now be understood.

S-R theory /ˈes ˈɑːʳ ˌθɪəri/ *n*

an abbreviation for STIMULUS-RESPONSE THEORY

stage /steɪdʒ/ *n*

In language teaching, a lesson is sometimes divided into three stages:

a **presentation stage**: the introduction of new items, when their meanings are explained, demonstrated, etc., and other necessary information is given

b **practice stage** (also **repetition stage**): new items are practised, either individually or in groups. Practice activities usually move from controlled to less controlled practice.

c **production stage** (also **transfer stage, free practice**): students use the new items more freely, with less or little control by the teacher.

standard /ˈstændəd‖-dərd/ *n* standard *adj*

another term for STANDARD VARIETY

Standard American English /ˈstændəd əˈmerɪkən ˈɪŋglɪʃ‖-dərd/ *n*

see STANDARD VARIETY

Standard British English /ˈstændəd ˈbrɪtɪʃ ˈɪŋglɪʃ‖-dərd/ *n*

see STANDARD VARIETY

standard deviation /ˈstændəd ˌdiːviˈeɪʃən‖-dərd/ *n*
also **SD**

(in statistics) the commonest measure of the DISPERSION of a DISTRIBUTION^2, that is, of the degree to which scores vary from the MEAN. It is defined as the square root of the VARIANCE.

$$SD = \sqrt{\frac{\Sigma x^2}{N}}$$

x = a score minus the mean
N = the number of items
Σ = the sum of

standard dialect /'stændəd 'daɪəlekt||-dərd/ *n*
another term for STANDARD VARIETY

Standard English /'stændəd 'ɪŋglɪʃ||-dərd/ *n*
see STANDARD VARIETY

standard error /'stændəd 'erəʳ||-dərd/ *n*
also **SE**
(in TESTING and statistics) a statistic used for determining the degree to which the estimate of a POPULATION PARAMETER is likely to differ from the computed sample statistic. The standard error of a statistic provides an indication of how accurate an estimate it is of the population parameter. One commonly used standard error is the standard error of the MEAN, which indicates how close the mean of the observed sample is to the mean of the entire population.

standardization /ˌstændədaɪ'zeɪʃən||-dərdə-/ *n* **standardize** /'stændə daɪz||-dər-/ *v*
the process of making some aspect of language USAGE[1] conform to a STANDARD VARIETY. This may take place in connection with the WRITING SYSTEM or the spelling system of a particular language and is usually implemented by a government authority. For example, a standardized system has been introduced in Malaysia and Indonesia, which provides a common standard for the spelling of Malay and Indonesian.

	Indonesian	Malay	
old spelling	*tjantik*	*chantek*	"pretty, good-
new spelling	*cantik*	*cantik*	looking"
old spelling	*burung*	*burong*	"bird"
new spelling	*burung*	*burung*	

standardized test /'stændədaɪzd 'test||-dər-/ *n*
a test
a which has been developed from tryouts and experimentation to ensure that it is reliable and valid (see RELIABILITY, VALIDITY)
b for which NORMS[2] have been established
c which provides uniform procedures for administering (time limits, response format, number of questions) and for scoring the test.

standard language /'stændəd 'læŋgwɪdʒ||-dərd/ *n*
another term for STANDARD VARIETY

standard nine /'stændəd 'naɪn||-dərd/ *n*
another term for STANINE

standard score /'stændəd 'skɔːʳ||-dərd/ *n*
(in TESTING and statistics) a type of DERIVED SCORE by which scores or values from different measures can be reported or compared using a common scale. For example, in order to compare a student's scores on two tests of different lengths, a standard score might be used. A

standard score expresses a RAW SCORE as a function of its relative position in a DISTRIBUTION[1] of scores, and is thus usually easier to interpret than the raw score. Commonly used standard scores are the Z-SCORE and the T-SCORE.

Standard Theory /'stændəd 'θɪəri‖-dərd/ n

see TRANSFORMATIONAL GENERATIVE GRAMMAR

standard variety /'stændəd və'raɪəti‖-dərd/ n
also **standard dialect, standard language, standard**

the variety of a language which has the highest STATUS in a community or nation and which is usually based on the speech and writing of educated native speakers of the language.

A standard variety is generally:

a used in the news media and in literature

b described in dictionaries and grammars (see NORMATIVE GRAMMAR)

c taught in schools and taught to non-native speakers when they learn the language as a foreign language.

Sometimes it is the educated variety spoken in the political or cultural centre of a country, e.g. the standard variety of French is based on educated Parisian French.

The standard variety of American English is known as **Standard American English** and the standard variety of British English is **Standard British English**.

A standard variety may show some variation in pronunciation according to the part of the country where it is spoken, e.g. Standard British English in Scotland, Wales, Southern England. **Standard English** is sometimes used as a cover term for all the national standard varieties of English. These national standard varieties have differences in spelling, vocabulary, grammar, and particularly pronunciation, but there is a common core of the language. This makes it possible for educated native speakers of the various national standard varieties of English to communicate with one another.

see also RECEIVED PRONUNCIATION, NATIONAL LANGUAGE
Further reading Trudgill 1983; Wardhaugh 1986

stanine /'steɪnaɪn/ n
also **standard nine**

a NORMALIZED STANDARD SCORE sometimes used in testing, in which standardized scores are arranged on a nine-step scale. A stanine equals one ninth of the range of the standard scores of a DISTRIBUTION[1].

statement /'steɪtmənt/ n

an utterance which describes a state of affairs, action, feeling or belief, e.g.

It's very cold here in winter; I don't think she looks very well.

A statement occurs in the form of a DECLARATIVE SENTENCE but not all declarative sentences make statements. For example:

I suppose you'll be there.

could be said to be more a question than a statement.

static-dynamic distinction /'stætɪk daɪ'næmɪk dɪs,tɪŋkʃən/ n

Verbs are sometimes divided into two groups: **stative verbs** and **dynamic verbs**.

Stative verbs usually refer to a state (an unchanging condition). They express emotion, knowledge, belief, (e.g. *love, hate, know*) and show relationships, (e.g. *belong to, equal, own*). As stative verbs describe a state of affairs, they do not occur in the progressive form, for example:

not   *Monica owns a house.*
    *Monica is owning a house.

Dynamic verbs express activity and processes, (e.g. *run, come, buy, read*). When they express something that is actually in progress, the progressive form of the verb can be used, for example:

She is reading the paper.

Some English verbs such as *have* and *think*, can be used statively, describing a state, or dynamically, describing an action or activity, for example:

statively: *I have a really bad headache.* (state)
dynamically: *We are having a party tonight.* (activity)
statively: *I think it's going to rain.* (opinion, mental state)
dynamically: *I'm thinking hard about how to solve this problem.* (mental activity)

see also PUNCTUAL-NONPUNCTUAL DISTINCTION
Further reading Leech 1987; Platt & Ho 1991

statistical hypothesis /stə'tɪstɪkəl haɪ'pɒθ_bsɪ̥s||-'pɑː-/ n

see HYPOTHESIS

statistical significance /stə'tɪstɪkəl sɪg'nɪfɪkəns/ n

a term used when testing a statistical hypothesis (see HYPOTHESIS), which refers to the likelihood that an obtained sample MEAN can be expected to represent the mean of the population. The level of significance, symbolized as p (for probability) is expressed as a proportion of 1. The most common levels of significance are $p < .05$ and $p < .01$ (where the symbol < means "less than"). If the difference between two means, for instance, is given as significant at the $p < .05$ or at the 0.05 level, this indicates that such a difference could be expected to occur by chance in only 5 out of 100 samplings. A level of significance of 0.01 means that the difference can be expected to occur by chance only one time in 100 samplings. Thus, the *lower* the probability of chance occurrence (p), the *higher* the level of significance, and the *greater* the probability that the observed difference is a true one and not due to chance.

stative verb /'steɪtɪv 'vɜːb||-ɜːr-/ n

a verb which usually refers to a state (i.e. an unchanging condition), for example *believe, have, belong, contain, cost, differ, own*, as in:

This contains calcium.
She believes in God.

Stative verbs are not usually used in the PROGRESSIVE ASPECT.

A verb which can be used in the progressive aspect is known as a **dynamic verb**, for example *read, wear.*
I am reading a good book.
She is wearing dark glasses.
Further reading Quirk et al 1985

status /'steɪtəs‖'steɪtəs, 'stæ-/ *n*
higher, lower, or equal position, particularly in regard to prestige, power, and social class.
Speech varieties (see SPEECH VARIETY) may have different statuses in a SPEECH COMMUNITY. For example, a variety which is limited to use in markets and for very informal situations would have a low status whereas another variety which is used in government, education, administration, etc., would have a high status (see DIGLOSSIA).
The status of people, when they are communicating in speech or writing, is also important, as it may affect the SPEECH STYLE they use to each other, e.g. ADDRESS FORMS, courtesy formulae.
see also ROLE RELATIONSHIP

stem[1] /stem/ *n*
also **base form**
that part of a word to which an inflectional AFFIX is or can be added.
For example, in English the inflectional affix *-s* can be added to the stem *work* to form the plural *works* in *the works of Shakespeare.*
The stem of a word may be:
a a simple stem consisting of only one morpheme (ROOT), e.g. *work*
b a root plus a derivational affix, e.g. *work + -er = worker*
c two or more roots, e.g. *work + shop = workshop.*
Thus we can have *work + -s = works, (work + -er) + -s = workers,* or *(work + shop) + -s = workshops.*
see also DERIVATION, INFLECTION.

stem[2] *n*
see MULTIPLE-CHOICE ITEM

stereotype /'steriəʊtaɪp/ *n*
a popular concept of the speech of a particular group of people, e.g. Irish, New Yorkers, Australians.
For example:
New Yorkers: /boid/ for *bird*
/toititoid/ for *thirtythird*
Australians: /woin/ for *wine*
/dai/ for *day*
Stereotypes are usually highly exaggerated and concentrate on only a few features of the speech patterns of a particular group.

stimulus /'stɪmjʊləs/ *n*
see STIMULUS-RESPONSE THEORY, BEHAVIOURISM

stimulus-response theory /ˈstɪmjŭləs rɪˈspɒns ˌθɪəri‖-ˈspaːns/ *n*
also **S-R theory**
a learning theory associated particularly with the American psychologist B.F. Skinner (1904–1990) (see BEHAVIOURISM), which describes learning as the formation of associations between responses. A **stimulus** is that which produces a change or reaction in an individual or organism. A **response** is the behaviour which is produced as a reaction to a stimulus. **Reinforcement** is a stimulus which follows the occurrence of a response and affects the probability of that response occurring or not occurring again. Reinforcement which increases the likelihood of a response is known as **positive reinforcement**. Reinforcement which decreases the likelihood of a response is known as **negative reinforcement**. If no reinforcement is associated with a response the response may eventually disappear. This is known as **extinction**. If a response is produced to similar stimuli with which it was not originally associated this is known as "stimulus generalization". Learning to distinguish between different kinds of stimuli is known as **discrimination**.
There are several S-R theories which contain these general principles or variations of them, and they have been used in studies of VERBAL LEARNING and language learning.

see also OPERANT CONDITIONING
Further reading Gagné 1970

stop /stɒp‖staːp/ *n*
also **plosive**
a speech sound (a CONSONANT) which is produced by stopping the airstream from the lungs and then suddenly releasing it.
For example, /p/ is a BILABIAL stop, formed by stopping the air with the lips and then releasing it.

see also CONSONANT, MANNER OF ARTICULATION, PLACE OF ARTICULATION
Further reading Gimson 1989

story grammar /ˈstɔːri ˌgræməʳ/ *n*
schemata (see SCHEME) which represent the discourse organization of stories, fables and narratives. Just as sentences are constructed according to grammatical rules, stories have structures which can be described by a set of rules. These describe the elements common to most stories, the kinds of situations, events, actors, actions and goals that occur in stories and the interrelationships among the elements of a story.

strategic competence /strəˈtiːdʒɪk ˈkɒmpĭtəns‖ˈkaːm-/ *n*
an aspect of COMMUNICATIVE COMPETENCE which describes the ability of speakers to use verbal and non-verbal communication strategies (see COMMUNICATION STRATEGY) to compensate for breakdowns in communication or to improve the effectiveness of communication. For example, a learner may lack a particular word or structure and have to

use a PARAPHRASE or circumlocution to compensate, or a speaker may use a deliberately slow and soft manner of speaking to create a particular effect on a listener.

see also DISCOURSE COMPETENCE
Further reading Canale 1980

strategy /'strætɪdʒi/ *n*
procedures used in learning, thinking, etc. which serve as a way of reaching a goal. In language learning, learning strategies (see LEARNING STRATEGY) and communication strategies (see COMMUNICATION STRATEGY) are those conscious or unconscious processes which language learners make use of in learning and using a language.

see also HEURISTIC, HYPOTHESIS TESTING, OVERGENERALIZATION, SIMPLIFICATION[1]

strategy training /'strætədʒi ˌtreɪnɪŋ/ *n*
also **learner training**
training in the use of learning strategies in order to improve a learner's effectiveness. A number of approaches to strategy training are used, including:
Explicit or **direct training**: learners are given information about the value and purpose of particular strategies, taught how to use them, and how to monitor their own use of the strategies.
Embedded strategy training: the strategies to be taught are not taught explicitly but are embedded in the regular content of an academic subject area, such as reading, maths or science.
Combination strategy training: explicit strategy training is followed by embedded training.
Further reading O'Malley & Chamot 1989

stratified sample /'strætɪfaɪd 'sɑːmpəl||'sæm-/ *n*
see SAMPLE

stress /stres/ *n*
the pronunciation (see ARTICULATION) of a word or syllable with more force than the surrounding words or syllables. A stressed word or syllable is produced by using more air from the lungs.
A listener often hears a stressed word or syllable as being louder than the surrounding words or syllables. A stressed word or syllable is often on a higher PITCH and/or it has a longer duration, i.e. the vowel appears to be longer. In writing or printing, stress may be shown by a small raised line in front of the stressed syllable, e.g. '*syllable*.
In a word, the basic difference is between stressed and unstressed syllables. A distinction used to be made in long words between stressed syllables of varying degree, i.e. it was said that the syllable with the greatest prominence had the **primary stress** and the next stressed syllable the **secondary stress**. Now it is felt that such distinctions are often only relevant when words are used in isolation. In an UTTERANCE, the overall intonation tends to neutralize the degree of stress within the individual word.

Stress has two main semantic functions:

a It may distinguish between two words (e.g. a verb and a noun) which are alike, e.g. 'import (noun) and im'port (verb) (see also ACCENT[1])

b The speaker wishes to emphasize the syllable or word, for example:

I said in<u>duce</u>, not de<u>duce</u>.

I prefer <u>small</u> apples, those are far too large.

see also CONTRASTIVE STRESS, STRESS SHIFT

Further reading Ladefoged 1982

stress shift /'stres ˌʃɪft/ also reverse stress

In English, a change in the stress patterns of certain words or phrases when they are used in connected speech.

A stress shift depends on whether or not the word or phrase is followed by a noun which has a strong stress.

Usually, these words and phrases have a low (**secondary**) stress, shown here as /ˌ/, followed by a high (**primary**) stress, shown here as /'/

For example:

ˌinde'pendent

ˌplate'glass

When, in connected speech, the word or phrase itself has the TONIC STRESS, the most important stress of the sentence, (shown here by ＼) these words and phrases keep their usual stress pattern, e.g.:

She was 'very ˌindep̀endent

This window is ˌplate glàss

They may be followed by a noun with a low stress, e.g.:

They are ˌplate glàss ̧manu ̧facturers

However, before a noun that has either a high stress or the tonic stress, the strong (primary) stresses on the third syllable of *independent* and on the word *glass* in 'plate glass' are lost and the secondary stress on the first syllable of *independent* and on *plate* in 'plate glass' now becomes a primary stress, e.g.:

He has 'independent mèans

It's a 'plate glass wìndow

The 'plate glass 'window is bròken

Words or phrases which may have a stress shift are followed by the symbol /◄/ in this and some other dictionaries.

stress-timed rhythm /'stres ˌtaɪmd 'rɪðəm/ *n*

a SPEECH RHYTHM in which the stressed syllables are said to recur at equal intervals of time. English has often been called stress-timed.

For example, in:

Álison didn't/fínish her/éssay

    I   2   3

each of the three segments (marked 1, 2, 3) would take the same time to utter, although each segment has a different number of syllables. The effect is that the stressed syllables (marked') occur at equal intervals.

However, recorded speech of British English shows that, although English has a tendency to stress-timed rhythm, it is not strictly stress-timed.

see also SYLLABLE-TIMED RHYTHM
Further reading Brazil, Coulthard, & Johns 1980; Ladefoged 1982

strong form /'strɒŋ ˌfɔːm||'strɔːŋ ˌfɔːrm/ *n*
one of the possible forms in which a word appears in speech. If a word is said in isolation or if it is stressed (e.g. *he cán pay us*), the strong form is used (e.g. /kæn/ *can*). If a word is unstressed, it often appears in its **weak form**. For example, the vowel sound in *can* does not have the same quality in the weak form and is reduced in length (e.g. /kən/).

strong verb /'strɒŋ 'vɜːb||'strɔːŋ 'vɜːrb/ *n*
(in grammar) a term sometimes used to refer to a verb which forms the past tense and the past participle by a change in a vowel (e.g. *begin-began-begun, sing-sang-sung*). A regular verb which forms the past tense and participle by adding *-ed* is known as a **weak verb** (e.g. open-opened).

structural description /'strʌktʃərəl dɪ'skrɪpʃən/ *n*
also **SD**
(in TRANSFORMATIONAL GENERATIVE GRAMMAR) a complete grammatical analysis of a sentence typically in the form of tree-like structures (**tree diagram**) or strings of labelled constituents. The structural description shows the most abstract syntactic form of the sentence (DEEP STRUCTURE) and the changes made to it by various rules ("transformational rules").
see also BASE COMPONENT, TRANSFORMATIONAL COMPONENT

structural global method /'strʌktʃərəl 'gləʊbəl ˌmeθəd/ *n*
another term for AUDIO-VISUAL METHOD

structural(ist) linguistics /'strʌktʃərəlɪst lɪŋ'gwɪstɪks/ *n*
an approach to linguistics which stresses the importance of language as a system and which investigates the place that linguistic units such as sounds, words, sentences have within this system.
Structural linguists, for example, studied the distribution of sounds within the words of a language; that is, whether certain sounds appear only at the beginning of words or also in the middle or at the end. They defined some sounds in a language as distinctive and used in the identification of words (see PHONEME), and some as variants (see ALLOPHONE). Similar studies of distribution and classification were carried out in MORPHOLOGY and SYNTAX.
In its widest sense, the term has been used for various groups of linguists, including those of the Prague School, but most often it is used to refer to a group of American linguists such as Bloomfield and Fries, who published mainly in the 1930s to 1950s. The work of these linguists was based on the theory of BEHAVIOURISM and had a considerable influence on some language teaching methods (see AUDIOLINGUAL METHOD).
Further reading Bolinger 1975

357

structural syllabus /'strʌktʃərəl 'sɪləbəs/ n

a SYLLABUS for the teaching of a language which is based on a selection of the grammatical items and structures (e.g. tenses, grammatical rules, sentence patterns) which occur in a language and the arrangement of them into an order suitable for teaching. The order of introducing grammatical items and structures in a structural syllabus may be based on such factors as frequency, difficulty, usefulness, or a combination of these.

see also NOTIONAL SYLLABUS, SITUATIONAL METHOD
Further reading Alexander et al 1975

structural word /'strʌktʃərəl ˌwɜːd‖-ɜːr-/ n

see CONTENT WORD

structure /'strʌktʃəʳ/ n

(in linguistics) the term often refers to a sequence of linguistic units that are in a certain relationship to one another.

For example, one of the structures of a NOUN PHRASE[1] may be "article + adjective + noun" as in *the friendly ape*. One of the possible SYLLABLE structures in English is CVC (consonant + vowel + consonant) as in *concert*.

see also SYNTAGMATIC RELATIONS

structure dependency /'strʌktʃəʳ dɪˌpendənsi/ n

see UNIVERSAL GRAMMAR

structured interview /'strʌktʃəd 'ɪntəvjuː‖-tʃərd -tər-/ n

an interview in which the organization and procedure of the interview, as well as the topics to be asked about, the questions, and the order in which they will be presented, have all been determined in advance.

structured response item /'strʌktʃəd rɪ'spɒns ˌaɪtəm‖-tʃərd -'spaːns/n

see TEST ITEM

structure word /'strʌktʃəʳ ˌwɜːd‖-ɜːr-/ n

see CONTENT WORD

structuring /'strʌktʃərɪŋ/ n
also **structure**

(in describing a lesson) the degree to which a lesson has a recognizable purpose, organization, and development. A lesson which has a good degree of structure is said to be one in which:

1 both teacher and students understand what the goals of the lesson are

2 the tasks and activities employed during the lesson occur in a logical sequence

3 the directions which students are asked to follow are clear

4 students have a clear understanding of what they are supposed to accomplish during the lesson

The concept of structuring has been referred to in studies of effective teaching (see EFFECTIVE SCHOOLING). Students are believed to pay more attention and learn more effectively if a lesson is well structured.

Further reading Berliner 1984

student-centred learning /'stjuːdənt ˌsentəd 'lɜːnɪŋ||'stuː- -tərd 'lɜːr-/ *n*

(in education) learning situations in which:

a students take part in setting goals and OBJECTIVES

b there is a concern for the student's feelings and values (see HUMANISTIC APPROACH)

c there is a different role of the teacher; the teacher is seen as a helper, adviser, or counsellor.

Language-teaching methods such as COMMUNITY LANGUAGE LEARNING and SILENT WAY give the students an active role in learning and are hence said to be less teacher-centred and more student-centred than many traditional methods.

student-centred teaching /'stjuːdənt ˌsentəd 'tiːtʃɪŋ||'stuː- -tərd/ *n*

methods of teaching which (a) emphasise the active role of students in learning (b) try to give learners more control over what and how they learn and (c) encourage learners to take more responsibility for their own learning. This may be contrasted with more traditional teacher-centred approaches, in which control rests with the teacher.

study skills[1] /'stʌdi ˌskɪlz/ *n*

abilities, techniques, and strategies (see MICRO-SKILLS) which are used when reading, writing, or listening for study purposes. For example, study skills needed by university students studying from English-language textbooks include: adjusting reading speeds according to the type of material being read (see READING SPEED), using the dictionary, guessing word meanings from context, interpreting graphs, diagrams, and symbols, note-taking and summarizing.

study skills[2] *n*

(in reading) those specific abilities that help a student understand a reading assignment, such as surveying the material, skimming for main ideas, paying attention to headings, interpreting graphs and illustrations, and identifying key vocabulary.

see also SQ3R TECHNIQUE

stuttering /'stʌtərɪŋ/ *n* **stutter** /'stʌtər/ *v*

a speech disorder which results from one or more of the following factors and which leads to disfluent speech;

1 abnormal repetition of segments of speech (sounds, syllables, words). For example:

d-d-d-don't

I've gota-gota-gota-cold

2 excessive pausing between words

3 abnormal lengthening of sounds. For example:

I fffffffeel cold.

4 introduction of extra words or sounds at points of difficulty, such as *oh*, or *gosh*.

Stutterers vary in the precise nature of their stuttering and in the situations which cause them to stutter. Serveral theories have been suggested to account for stuttering but no single cause has been identified.

Further reading Crystal 1980

style /staɪl/ *n* stylistic /staɪˈlɪstɪk/ *adj*

1 variation in a person's speech or writing. Style usually varies from casual to formal according to the type of situation, the person or persons addressed, the location, the topic discussed, etc. A particular style, e.g. a formal style or a colloquial style, is sometimes referred to as a **stylistic variety**.

Some linguists use the term "register" for a stylistic variety whilst others differentiate between the two (see REGISTER).

2 style can also refer to a particular person's use of speech or writing at all times or to a way of speaking or writing at a particular period of time, e.g. Dickens' style, the style of Shakespeare, an 18th-century style of writing.

see also STYLISTIC VARIATION

style checker /ˈstaɪl ˌtʃekəʳ/ *n*

(in COMPUTER ASSISTED LANGUAGE LEARNING) a program which analyzes a text for possible problems of style, such as the overuse of particular words or the inclusion of sexist language.

style shift /ˈstaɪl ʃɪft/ *n*

a change in STYLE during a verbal or written communication. Uusally, a style shift takes place if the writer reassesses or redefines a particular situation. For example, a writer may add an informal note at the end of a formal invitation because he or she is on familiar terms with the person the invitation is addressed to. In a job interview, an applicant may change his or her formal style to a less formal style if the interviewer adopts a very informal manner.

see also STYLISTIC VARIATION

stylistics /staɪˈlɪstɪks/ *n*

the study of that variation in language (STYLE) which is dependent on the situation in which the language is used and also on the effect the writer or speaker wishes to create on the reader or hearer. Although stylistics sometimes includes investigations of spoken language, it usually refers to the study of written language, including literary texts. Stylistics is concerned with the choices that are available to a writer and the reasons why particular forms and expressions are used rather than others.

see also DISCOURSE ANALYSIS
Further reading Bolinger 1975

stylistic variation /staɪˈlɪstɪk veərɪˈeɪʃən/ *n*

differences in the speech or writing of a person or group of people according to the situation, the topic,.the addressee(s) and the location. Stylistic variation can be observed in the use of different speech sounds, different words or expressions, or different sentence structures. For example, in English:

a Pronunciation: People are more likely to say /'sɪtn/ *sitt'n* /'meɪkɪ̯n/ *mak'n* instead of /'sɪtɪŋ/ *sitting* /'meɪkɪŋ/ *making* if the style is more informal.

b Words and sentence structures:

more formal: *We were somewhat dismayed by his lack of*
              response to our invitation.

less formal: *We were rather fed up that she didn't answer*
              when we invited her.

The stylistic variation of an individual or group can be measured by analysing recorded speech and making comparisons.

see also STYLE

stylistic variety /staɪ'lɪstɪk və'raɪəti/ *n*

see STYLE

subject /'sʌbdʒɪkt/ *n*

(in English grammar) generally the noun, pronoun or NOUN PHRASE[1] which:

a typically precedes the main verb in a sentence and is most closely related to it

b determines CONCORD

c refers to something about which a statement or assertion is made in the rest of the sentence.

That part of the sentence containing the verb, or VERB GROUP (and which may include OBJECTS, COMPLEMENTS, or ADVERBIALS) is known as the PREDICATE. The predicate is that part of the sentence which predicates something of the subject. For example:

subject	predicate
The woman	*smiled.*
Fish	*is good for you.*

see also OBJECT[1]

subject complement /'sʌbdʒɪkt 'kɒmplɪ̯mənt‖'kɑːm-/ *n*

see COMPLEMENT

subjective test /səb'dʒektɪv 'test/ *n*

a test which is scored according to the personal judgment of the marker, such as an essay examination. A subjective test may be contrasted with an **objective test** which is a test that can be marked without the use of the examiner's personal judgment. TRUE-FALSE and MULTIPLE-CHOICE tests are examples of objective tests.

Subject-Prominent language /'sʌbdʒɪkt 'prɒmɪ̯nənt 'læŋgwɪdʒ‖ 'prɑː-/ *n*

a language in which the grammatical units of SUBJECT and PREDICATE are basic to the structure of sentences and in which sentences usually have subject-predicate structure. English is a Subject-Prominent language, since sentences such as the following are a usual sentence type:

I   *have already seen Peter.*

(Subject) (Predicate)

A language is which the grammatical units of topic and comment (see TOPIC²) are basic to the structure of sentences is known as a **Topic-Prominent language**. Chinese is a Topic-Prominent language, since sentences with Topic-Comment structure are a usual sentence type in Chinese. For example:

Zhāngsān wǒ yǐjīng jiàn guo   le
Zhangsan I   already see aspect particle
                            marker
ie *Zhangsan, I have already seen (him).*

(Topic)   (Comment)

Further reading Li & Thompson 1981

subjunctive /səb'dʒʌŋktɪv/ *n*
see MOOD

submersion education /səb'mɜːʃən edjʊ̯ˌkeɪʃən||-'mɜːrʒən edʒə-/ *n*
a term which is sometimes used to describe a situation in which LIMITED ENGLISH PROFICIENT students are placed in regular classrooms and compete with native speakers, and are given no special assistance with English – i.e. a kind of "sink or swim approach". Few adaptations are made to meet the students' special needs and the goal is to ensure that the students learn English as quickly as possible.

submersion programme /səb'mɜːʃən ˌprəʊgræm||-'mɜːrʒən/ *n*
a form of BILINGUAL EDUCATION in which the language of instruction is not the FIRST LANGUAGE of some of the children, but *is* the first language of others. This happens in many countries where immigrant children enter school and are taught in the language of the host country.
see also IMMERSION PROGRAMME
Further reading Swain 1978

subordinate clause /sə'bɔːdɪ̯nət 'klɔːz||-'bɔːr-/ *n*
another term for DEPENDENT CLAUSE

subordinating conjunction /sə'bɔːdɪ̯neɪtɪŋ kən'dʒʌŋkʃən||-ɔːr-/ *n*
see CONJUNCTION

subordination /sə'bɔːdɪ̯'neɪʃ ən||-ɔːr-/*n*
see CONJUNCTION

subordinator /səˌbɔːdɪ̯neɪtəʳ||-ɔːr-/ *n*
see CONJUNCTION

substandard /ˌsʌb'stændəd◄||-dərd/ *adj*
a term which expresses a negative value judgment on any part of the

speech or writing of a person or group that does not conform to the STANDARD VARIETY of a language and is therefore thought to be undesirable.

For example, the double negative used in some dialects of English:

I don't know nothing.

would be considered by some people as substandard. A more neutral term used by linguists for forms which do not belong to the standard variety of a language is NONSTANDARD.

substantive /səb'stæntɪv‖'sʌbstəntɪv/ *n*

a term sometimes used for a NOUN or any word which can function as a noun, such as a pronoun, an adjective (e.g. in *the old*), a GERUND, etc.

substantive universal /səb'stæntɪv juːnɪ̩'vɜːsəl‖'sʌbstəntɪv -ɜːr-/ *n*

see LANGUAGE UNIVERSAL

substitution /ˌsʌbstɪ̩'tjuːʃən‖-'tuː-/ *n*

(in SECOND LANGUAGE ACQUISITION) an ERROR in which the learner substitutes a form from one language (usually the learner's first language) for a form in the TARGET LANGUAGE[1]. For example a French speaker may say "*I'll be leaving demain*" instead of "*I'll be leaving tomorrow*".

substitution drill /ˌsʌbstɪ̩'tjuːʃən ˌdrɪl‖-'tuː-/ *n*

see DRILL

substitution table /ˌsʌbstɪ̩'tjuːʃən ˌteɪbəl‖-'tuː-/ *n*

(in language teaching) a table which shows the items that may be substituted at different positions in a sentence. A substitution table can be used to produce many different sentences by making different combinations of items. For example:

The post office	is	behind	the park.
The bank		near	the hotel.
The supermarket		across from	the station.

substrate language /'sʌbstreɪt 'læŋgwɪdʒ/ *n*

see SUBSTRATUM LANGUAGE

substratum influence /'sʌbstrɑːtəm 'ɪnfluəns‖-streɪ-/ *n*

the influence of a speaker's original language on the acquisition of another language, whether taught formally or acquired informally (as in the case of PIDGIN languages).

The influence may be on pronunciation, sentence structures, vocabulary or various aspects of COMMUNICATIVE COMPETENCE.

For example, it is common in a number of ESL varieties to use the verbs *open* and *close* for turning radios and lights on and off. This can often be seen as a substratum influence:

Philippine English	Tagalog
"open the radio"	*buksan mo ang radyo* open you the radio
"close the light"	*isara mo ang ilaw* close you the light

Further reading Platt, Weber & Ho 1984

substratum interference /ˈsʌbstrɑːtəm ˌɪntəˈfɪərəns‖-streɪtəm ɪntər-/ *n*

see SUBSTRATUM INFLUENCE

substratum language /ˈsʌbstrɑːtəm ˈlæŋgwɪdʒ‖-streɪ-/

the original language of those who have acquired another language. The term was first used for speakers of PIDGIN and CREOLE languages. For example, the substratum languages of West African Pidgins were the various local West African languages, e.g. Akan, Ewe, Ga, Hausa, Igbo, Yoruba. Lately, the term substratum language has been extended to include the first language of those acquiring a second/foreign language.

see also SUBSTRATUM INFLUENCE/INTERFERENCE, SUPERSTRATUM LANGUAGE

Further reading Romaine 1988

subtest /ˈsʌbˌtest/ *n*

a test which is given as a part of a longer test. For example, a language-proficiency test may contain subtests of grammar, writing, and speaking.

subtractive bilingual education /səbˈtræktɪv baɪˈlɪŋgwəl edjʊ̩ˈkeɪʃən‖edʒə-/ *n*

also subtractive bilingualism /səbˈtræktɪv baɪˈlɪŋgwəlɪzəm/

see ADDITIVE BILINGUAL EDUCATION

subvocalization /sʌbˌvəʊkə-laɪˈzeɪʃən‖-kələ-/ *n*

see SUBVOCAL READING

subvocal reading /ˈsʌbvəʊkəl ˈriːdɪŋ/ *n*

also subvocalization

a type of reading said to be characteristic of all readers (by some researchers) and of poor readers (by other researchers), in which the reader pronounces words silently while reading, sometimes also making slight movements of the tongue, lips, and vocal cords.

suffix /ˈsʌfɪks/ *n*

a letter or sound or group of letters or sounds which are added to the end of a word, and which change the meaning or function of the word.

see also AFFIX

suggestopaedia /sə,dʒestəʊ'piːdiə, -stə-/ *n*
also **suggestopedia, suggestopedy** /sə,dʒe'stɒpədi‖-'staː-/, **Lozanov method**

a METHOD of foreign-language teaching developed by the Bulgarian Lozanov. It makes use of dialogues, situations, and translation to present and practise language, and in particular, makes use of music, visual images, and relaxation exercises to make learning more comfortable and effective. Suggestopaedia is said to be a pedagogical application of "Suggestology", the influence of suggestion on human behaviour.

Further reading Lozanov 1979; Richards & Rogers 1986

summative evaluation /'sʌmətɪv ɪ,vælju'eɪʃən/ *n*
see FORMATIVE EVALUATION

summative test /'sʌmətɪv 'test/ *n*
see FORMATIVE TEST

superlative /suːˈpɜːlətɪv, sjuː-‖sʊˈpɜːr-/ *n*, *adj*
also **superlative degree** /suːˈpɜːlətɪv dɪˈgriː, sjuː-‖sʊˈpɜːr-/
see COMPARATIVE

superordinate /ˌsuːpərˈɔːdn̩t, ˌsjuː-‖-ˈɔːr-/ *n*, *adj*
see HYPONYMY

superstratum language /'suːpəstraːtəm 'læŋgwɪdʒ, 'sjuː-‖'suːpər streɪ-/ *n*

the language from which most of the lexical items of a PIDGIN or CREOLE have been derived. Usually the superstratum language is the language of the former colonial power in the region where the pidgin or creole is spoken.

For example, English is the superstratum language of Jamaican Creole and of Tok Pisin, spoken in Papua New Guinea.

see also SUBSTRATUM/SUBSTRATE LANGUAGE(S)

supervision /ˌsuːpəˈvɪʒən,ˌsjuː-‖ˌsuːpər-/ *n*

(in teacher education) the monitoring and evaluation of a student teacher's teaching performance by a supervisor. Current approaches to supervision differ with respect to whether the supervisor's primary role is seen to be as an evaluator of teaching performance or as a facilitator or consultant. When the former is the case, the supervisor seeks to point out the differences between actual teaching performance and ideal teaching behaviour, guiding the student teacher's development and offering suggestions for improvement. When the supervisor acts more as a consultant or facilitator, the goal is to explore aspects of teaching that have been determined through negotiation, and to encourage teacher self-development through reflection and self-observation.

see also REFLECTIVE TEACHING[2], CLINICAL SUPERVISION
Further reading Acheson & Gall 1987; Gebhard 1990

suppletion /səˈpliːʃən/ *n*

(in MORPHOLOGY) a type of irregularity in which there is a complete change in the shape of a word in its various inflected forms (see INFLECTION).

For example, English *good* – *better* – *best* does not follow the normal pattern as in *tall* – *taller* – *tallest* but uses different forms for the comparative and the superlative (see COMPARATIVE) of the adjective *good*.

supporting sentences /səˈpɔːtɪŋ ˌsentənsɪ̩z‖-ɔːr-/ *n*

(in composition) sentences in a paragraph which support, illustrate or explain the TOPIC SENTENCE.

suprasegmental /ˌsuːprəsegˈmentl ˌsjuː-‖ˌsuː-/ *n*

(in PHONETICS and PHONOLOGY) a unit which extends over more than one sound in an utterance, e.g. STRESS and tone (see TONE[1], TONE[2]). The term suprasegmental is used particularly by American linguists. See also INTONATION, PROMINENCE, SEGMENTAL PHONEMES

Further reading Ladefoged 1982

surface structure /ˈsɜːfɪ̩s ˌstrʌktʃəʳ‖ˈsɜːr-/ *n*

see DEEP STRUCTURE, BASE COMPONENT, TRANSFORMATIONAL GENERATIVE GRAMMAR

surrender value /səˈrendəʳ ˌvæljuː/ *n*

(in language teaching) a term borrowed from life insurance and sometimes used to refer to the functional skills which a learner has acquired at any given point in a language course, and which the learner would be able to use even if he or she did not continue learning beyond that point.

SVO language /ˌes viː ˈəʊ ˌlæŋgwɪdʒ/ *n*

see TYPOLOGY

syllabic writing /sɪ̩ˈlæbɪk ˈraɪtɪŋ/ *n*

a WRITING SYSTEM in which each symbol represents a SYLLABLE e.g. the Japanese syllabic systems Katakana and Hiragana:
Examples from Katakana:

イギリス

Igirisu (Great Britain)

トランプ

toranpu (playing cards)

see also ALPHABETIC WRITING, IDEOGRAPHIC WRITING

syllabification /sᵻˌlæbᵻfᵻ'keɪʃən/ n **syllabify** /sᵻ'læbᵻfaɪ/ v
dividing a word up into SYLLABLES.
For example, *locomotive* can be divided up into four syllables:
lo-co-mo-tive.
The syllabification of the spelling of a word can differ from the
syllabification of its pronunciation. For example, in
styl-is-tics /staɪ'lɪstɪks/
the first syllable of the spelling is *styl*, but the first syllable of the
pronunciation is /staɪ-/.

syllable /'sɪləbəl/ n **syllabic** /sᵻ'læbɪk/ adj
a unit in speech which is often longer than one sound and smaller than
a whole word. For example, the word *terminology* consists of five
syllables: *ter-mi-no-lo-gy.*
In PHONETICS, the syllable is often related to chest pulses. These are the
contractions of certain chest muscles. Each chest pulse is accompanied
by increased air pressure. This air pressure is most noticeable in the
"central" part, the **peak** of a syllable. The hearer may distinguish
the central part of a syllable because it has more sound quality than the
surrounding sounds, but people often have difficulty in hearing when
one syllable ends and another one begins. For example, the word *bitter*
may be heard as *bi-tter, bit-ter* or *bitt-er.*
In PHONOLOGY, the syllable is defined by the way in which VOWELS and
CONSONANTS combine to form various sequences. Vowels can form a
syllable on their own or they can be the "centre" of a syllable, e.g. /e/
in /bed/ *bed.* Consonants are at the beginning or the end of syllables
and, with a few exceptions, do not usually form syllables on their own.
Syllables may be classified according to whether they end in a vowel
(**open syllables**) or in a consonant (**closed syllables**). For example, in
English, *to, try, show* are open syllables and *bet, ask* and *snap* are closed
syllables.
A syllable can be divided into three parts:
a the beginning, called the **onset**
b the central part, called the **nucleus** or **peak**
c the end, called the **coda.**
In the English word bed, /bed/, /b/ would be the onset, /e/ the nucleus
and /d/ the coda.
Speech sounds which can be in the nucleus of a syllable are sometimes
called **syllabic** or [+syllabic]. Speech sounds which cannot be in the
nucleus are called **asyllabic** or [-syllabic].
Further reading Gimson 1980; Ladefoged 1982

syllable-timed rhythm /'sɪləbəl ˌtaɪmd 'rɪðəm/ n
a SPEECH RHYTHM in which all syllables are said to recur at equal
intervals. French is usually referred to as syllable-timed. For example,
in :
Il / est / ar/ri/vé / à / six/ heures/
1 2   3 4 5 6 7 8
"he arrived (is arrived) at six o' clock"

367

the segments marked 1_2 2, 3, etc. would each take the same time to utter, and each segment consists of a single syllable.

However, recorded speech of French speakers shows that although French has a tendency towards syllable-timed rhythm, it is usually not strictly syllable-timed.

see also STRESS-TIMED RHYTHM
Further reading Brazil, Coulthard, & Johns 1980; Ladefoged 1982

syllabus /'sɪləbəs/ *n*
also **curriculum**

a description of the contents of a course of instruction and the order in which they are to be taught. Language-teaching syllabuses may be based on (a) grammatical items and vocabulary (see STRUCTURAL SYLLABUS) (b) the language needed for different types of situations (see SITUATIONAL METHOD) (c) the meanings and communicative functions which the learner needs to express in the TARGET LANGUAGE[1] (see NOTIONAL SYLLABUS).

see also CURRICULUM[2], GRADATION, LANGUAGES FOR SPECIAL PURPOSES, SPIRAL APPROACH, SYNTHETIC APPROACH
Further reading Johnson 1989; Nunan 1988; Wilkins 1976

syllabus design /'sɪləbəs dɪˌzaɪn/ *n*

see COURSE DESIGN, CURRICULUM DEVELOPMENT

syllogism /'sɪlədʒɪzəm/ *n*

an argument (see PROPOSITION) in the form of two premises and a conclusion drawn from them. For example:
Major premise: All boys like sports.
Minor premise: John is a boy.
Conclusion: John likes sports.

synchronic /sɪn'krɒnɪk‖-'krɑː-/ *adj*

see DIACHRONIC LINGUISTICS

synchronic linguistics /sɪn'krɒnɪk lɪŋ'gwɪstɪks‖-'krɑː-/ *n*

see DIACHRONIC LINGUISTICS

synonym /'sɪnənɪm/ *n* synonymous /sɪ'nɒnɪməs‖-'nɑː-/ *n* synonymy /sɪ'nɒnɪmi‖-'nɑː-/ *n*

a word which has the same, or nearly the same, meaning as another word.
For example, in English *hide* and *conceal* in:
He hid the money under the bed.
He concealed the money under the bed.
Often one word may be more appropriate than another in a particular situation, e.g. *conceal* is more formal than *hide*.
Sometimes two words may be synonymous in certain sentences only.
For example, in the sentences:
I must buy some more stamps at the post office.
I must get some more stamps at the post office.

buy and *get* are synonyms, as it would usually be thought that *get* in the second sentence means *buy* and not *steal*.

see also ANTONYM, HYPONYMY

Further reading Palmer 1981

syntactic /sɪnˈtæktɪk/ *adj*

see SYNTAX

syntactic structure /sɪnˈtæktɪk ˈstrʌktʃəʳ/ *n*

the arrangement of words and MORPHEMES into larger units (PHRASES, CLAUSES and SENTENCES). Languages may be compared for differences in syntactic structure.

For example, in English, the word order in a NOUN PHRASE[1] is usually:

demonstrative + adjective + noun
this   *big*   *house*

whereas in Malay the order is:

noun + adjective + demonstrative
rumah besar   ini
house   big   this

syntagm /ˈsɪntæm/ *n*

also syntagma /sɪnˈtægmə/ syntagmatic /ˌsɪntægˈmætɪk◄/ *adj*

a structurally significant combination of two or more units in a language. For example, a syntagm may consist of:

a two or more morphemes forming a word, e.g.

re- + write = rewrite

or

b combinations of words forming PHRASES, CLAUSES, and SENTENCES, e.g.:

the + train + is + leaving + now

see also SYNTAGMATIC RELATIONS, SYNTAX

syntagmatic relations /ˈsɪntægmætɪk rɪˈleɪʃənz/ *n*

the relationship that linguistic units (e.g. words, clauses) have with other units because they may occur together in a sequence. For example, a word may be said to have syntagmatic relations with the other words which occur in the sentence in which it appears, but **paradigmatic relations** with words that could be substituted for it in the sentence.

For example:

I ⟷ gave ⟷ Tracy ⟷ the ⟷ book
　　　↕
　　passed
　　　↕
　　handed　　　　　　⟷ = *syntagmatic relations*
　　　↕　　　　　　　　↕ = *paradigmatic relations*
　　threw

see also STRUCTURE

syntax[1] /'sɪntæks/ *n* **syntactic** /sɪn'tæktɪk/ *adj*

the study of how words combine to form sentences and the rules which govern the formation of sentences.

In TRANSFORMATIONAL GENERATIVE GRAMMAR, the syntactic component is one of the three main parts of the grammar. This component contains the rules for forming syntactic structures (see BASE COMPONENT) and rules for changing these structures (see TRANSFORMATIONAL COMPONENT).

see also MORPHOLOGY, PHONOLOGY, SYNTACTIC STRUCTURE

syntax[2]

the rules which determine how the commands of a COMPUTER LANGUAGE are used and how they fit together.

synthetic approach /sɪn'θetɪk ə'prəʊtʃ/ *n*

(in language teaching) a term sometimes used to refer to procedures for developing a SYLLABUS or a language course, in which the language to be taught is first analysed into its basic parts (e.g. the grammar is analysed into parts of speech and grammatical constructions) and these are taught separately. The learner's task is to put the individual parts together again (i.e. to synthesize them). A syllabus which consisted of a list of grammatical items arranged in order of difficulty would be part of a synthetic approach to language teaching. In this sense, many traditional syllabuses would be called "synthetic".

This may be contrasted with an **analytic approach** in which units of language behaviour are the starting point in syllabus and course design (e.g. descriptions, requests, apologies, enquiries, and other SPEECH ACTS). At a later stage, if necessary, the vocabulary and grammar used for different functions can be analysed. In this sense, a NOTIONAL SYLLABUS would be called "analytic".

Further reading Wilkins 1976

synthetic language /sɪn'θetɪk 'læŋgwɪdʒ/ *n*

a cover term for AGGLUTINATING LANGUAGE or INFLECTING LANGUAGE

synthetic speech /sɪn'θetɪk 'spiːtʃ/

see DIGITIZED SPEECH, SPEECH SYNTHESIS

systematic phonemics /ˌsɪstɪmætɪk fə'niːmɪks/ *n*

a theory that a native speaker's knowledge of a language includes knowledge of the phonological relationships between different forms of words. It is claimed that the forms of words as they occur in actual speech (e.g. the English words *serene* and *serenity*) are produced from an underlying abstract level called the "systematic phonemic level". The abstract form, called the **underlying form,** for both *serene* and *serenity* is said to be //serēn//, with //ē// representing a long //e// SEGMENT. This form does not exist in actual speech.

see also GENERATIVE PHONOLOGY

Further reading Hyman 1975; Chomsky & Halle 1968

systemic grammar /sɪˈstiːmɪk ˈgræməʳ, -ˈstemɪk/ n

an approach to grammatical analysis which is based on a series of systems. Each system is a set of options of which one must be chosen at each relevant point in the production of an UTTERANCE. For example, in English, the speaker or writer makes choices among the systems of NUMBER[1]: singular or plural; TENSE[1]: past, present, or future; MOOD: declarative, interrogative, or imperative, and many others.
Choices made in the sentence:
  She jumped.
include:
  singular, third person, and feminine (for *she*)
  past, active, and action process (for *jumped*)
see also SYSTEMIC LINGUISTICS, TRANSITIVITY[2]
Further reading Berry 1975; Fawcett & Halliday 1985

systemic linguistics /sɪˈstiːmɪk lɪŋˈgwɪstɪks, -ˈstemɪk/ n

an approach to linguistics developed by Halliday which sees language in a social context. The theory behind this approach is functional rather than formal, that is, it considers language as a resource used for communication and not as a set of rules. In this way, the scope of systemic linguistics is wider than that of many other linguistic theories (see TRANSFORMATIONAL GENERATIVE GRAMMAR). PHONOLOGY and **lexicogrammar** (words and grammatical structures) are closely related to meaning and cannot be analysed without reference to it. An essential concept of the theory is that each time language is used, no matter in what situation, the user is making constant choices. These choices are essentially choices in meaning but are expressed, for instance, by INTONATION, words, and GRAMMATICAL structures.
see also SOCIAL CONTEXT, SYSTEMIC GRAMMAR, TRANSITIVITY[2]
Further reading de Joia & Stenton 1980; Fawcett & Halliday 1985

systems approach /ˈsɪstə̧mz əˈprəʊtʃ/ n

(in education, language teaching, and COURSE DESIGN) an approach to analysis, planning and development in which (a) all the different elements involved are identified (e.g. society, parents, teachers, learners, time, materials, etc.) (b) their interactions are analysed and studied (c) a plan or system is developed which enables OBJECTIVES to be reached.

T

tachistoscope /tə'kɪstə‚skəʊp/ *n*

a mechanical apparatus which presents printed material (e.g. words, sentences) very briefly when a shutter or similar device is opened and closed rapidly, and which is used in research on PERCEPTION and READING, and sometimes in SPEED READING courses.

tag /tæg/ *n*

a word, phrase, or clause added to a sentence in order to give emphasis or to form a question.
For example:
> They're lovely and juicy, *these oranges.*
> Jill's coming tomorrow, *isn't she?*

The latter is called a **tag question**.
Further reading Quirk et al 1985

tagmeme /'tægmiːm/ *n* **tagmemic** /tæg'miːmɪk/ *adj*

(in TAGMEMICS) the basic unit of grammatical analysis. A tagmeme is a unit in which there is a relationship between the GRAMMATICAL FUNCTION, for instance the function of SUBJECT, OBJECT[1] or PREDICATE, and a class of **fillers**.
For example, in the sentence:
> The baby bit Anthea.

the subject tagmeme is filled by the NOUN PHRASE[1] *the baby*, the predicate tagmeme is filled by the TRANSITIVE VERB *bite* in its past tense form *bit*, and the object tagmeme is filled by the proper noun *Anthea*.

tagmemics /tæg'miːmɪks/ *n*

a theory of language originated by Pike. In tagmemic analysis there are three hierarchies or systems: grammatical, phonological, and lexical. In each of these systems there are a number of levels. For example, in the grammatical system there are: the morpheme level, the word level, the phrase level, the clause level, the sentence level, the paragraph level. On each level of the grammatical system there are TAGMEMES displaying relationships between grammatical functions and classes of linguistic items which can fill these functions (**fillers**).
Further reading Pike 1967

tag question /'tæg ‚kwestʃən/ *n*

see TAG

tap /tæp/ *n*

another term for FLAP

372

target language[1] /ˈtɑːgᵻt ˌlæŋgwɪdʒ‖ˈtɑːr-/ *n*
also **L2**
> (in language teaching) the language which a person is learning, in
> contrast to a FIRST LANGUAGE or mother tongue.

target language[2] *n*
> the language into which a translation is made (e.g. in a bilingual
> dictionary).
> see also SOURCE LANGUAGE[2]

task /tɑːsk‖ˈtæsk/ *n*
> (in teaching) an activity which is designed to help achieve a particular
> learning goal. A number of dimensions of tasks influence their use in
> language teaching. These include:
> **goals** – the kind of goals teachers and learners identify for a task
> **procedures** – the operations or procedures learners use to complete a
> task
> **order** – the location of a task within a sequence of other tasks
> **pacing** – the amount of time that is spent on a task
> **product** – the outcome or outcomes students produce, such as a set of
> questions, an essay, or a summary as the outcome of a reading task
> **learning strategy** – the kind of strategy a student uses when
> completing a task
> **assessment** – how success on the task will be determined
> **participation** – whether the task is completed individually, with a
> partner, or with a group of other learners
> **resources** – the materials and other resources used with a task
> **language** – the language learners use in completing a task (e.g. the
> mother tongue or English, or the particular vocabulary, structures or
> functions the task requires the learners to use).
> The concept of task is central to many theories of classroom teaching
> and learning, and the school curriculum is sometimes described as a
> collection of tasks. From this viewpoint, school work is defined by a
> core of basic tasks that recur across different subjects in the curri-
> culum. The teacher's choice of tasks determines learning goals, how
> learning is to take place, and how the results of learning will be
> demonstrated. In second language teaching, the use of a variety of
> different kinds of tasks is said to make teaching more communicative
> (see COMMUNICATIVE APPROACH) since it provides a purpose for a
> classroom activity which goes beyond the practice of language for its
> own sake.
> *Further reading* Johnson 1982; Doyle 1983; Nunan 1989b

task syllabus /ˈtɑːsk ˌsɪləbəs‖ˈtæsk/ *n*
also **task-based syllabus** /ˈtɑːsk beɪst ˌsɪləbəs‖ˈtæsk/, **procedural
syllabus**
> (in language teaching) a SYLLABUS which is organized around TASKS,
> rather than in terms of grammar or vocabulary. For example the

syllabus may suggest a variety of different kinds of tasks which the learners are expected to carry out in the language, such as using the telephone to obtain information; drawing maps based on oral instructions; performing actions based on commands given in the target language; giving orders and instructions to others, etc. It has been argued that this is a more effective way of learning a language since it provides a purpose for the use and learning of a language other than simply learning language items for their own sake.

Further reading Prabhu 1983; Johnson 1982

taxonomic /ˌtæksəˈnɒmɪk◄‖-ˈnɑː-/ *adj* **taxonomy** /tækˈsɒnəmi‖ -ˈsɑː-/ *n*

(in linguistics) classification of items into classes and sub-classes. Taxonomic approaches have been used in PHONOLOGY, SYNTAX and SEMANTICS.

For example, in taxonomic PHONEMICS, the distinctive speech sounds of a language are classified as VOWELS and CONSONANTS, the consonants are classified as STOPS, FRICATIVES, NASALS, etc., the stops are classified as voiced or voiceless (see VOICE[2]) and so on.

see also CLASS

teacher directed instruction /ˈtiːtʃəʳ dɨˌrektɨd ɪnˈstrʌkʃən, daɪ-/ *n*
also **teacher fronted instruction**

a teaching style in which instruction is closely managed and controlled by the teacher, where students often respond in unison to teacher questions, and where whole-class instruction is preferred to other methods. Many current teaching approaches try to encourage less teacher-directed interaction through the use of individualized activities or group work.

see also CO-OPERATIVE LEARNING, COMMUNICATIVE APPROACH, GROUP WORK

teacher education /ˈtiːtʃər edjʊˈkeɪʃən‖edʒə-/ *n*
also **teacher training**

the field of study which deals with the preparation and professional development of teachers. Within the field of teacher education, a distinction is sometimes made between **teacher training** and **teacher development**.

Teacher training deals with basic teaching skills and techniques, typically for novice teachers in a PRESERVICE EDUCATION programme. These skills include such dimensions of teaching as preparing lesson plans, classroom management, teaching the four skills (i.e. reading, writing, listening, speaking), techniques for presenting and practising new teaching items, correcting errors, etc.

Teacher development looks beyond initial training and deals with the on-going professional development of teachers, particularly in IN-SERVICE EDUCATION programmes. This includes a focus on teacher self-evaluation, investigation of different dimensions of teaching by the teacher (see ACTION RESEARCH), and examination of the teacher's approach to teaching.

Further reading Richards & Nunan 1990

teacher fronted instruction /'tiːtʃəʳ ˌfrʌntɪd ɪn'strʌkʃən/ *n*

another term for TEACHER DIRECTED INSTRUCTION

teacher self-evaluation /'tiːtʃəʳ ˌself ɪvælju'eɪʃən/ *n*

the evaluation by a teacher of his or her own teaching. Procedures used in self-evaluation include the video or audio-recording of a teacher's lesson for the purpose of subsequent analysis or evaluation, the use of self-report forms on which a teacher records information about a lesson after it was taught, as well as the keeping of journal or diary accounts of lessons in which a teacher records information about teaching which is then used for reflection and development.

Further reading Richards & Nunan 1990

teacher talk /'tiːtːʃəʳ ˌtɔːk/ *n*

that variety of language sometimes used by teachers when they are in the process of teaching. In trying to communicate with learners, teachers often simplify their speech, giving it many of the characteristics of FOREIGNER TALK and other simplified styles of speech addressed to language learners.

see also CARETAKER SPEECH

Further reading Sinclair & Brazil 1982

teacher training /'tiːtʃəʳ 'treɪnɪŋ/ *n*

another term for TEACHER EDUCATION

teaching practice /'tiːtʃɪŋ ˌpræktɪs/ *n*

see PRACTICE TEACHING

team teaching /'tiːm ˌtiːtʃɪŋ/ *n*

a term used for a situation in which two teachers share a class and divide instruction between them. Team teaching is said to offer teachers a number of benefits: it allows for more creative teaching, allows teachers to learn through observing each other, and gives teachers the opportunity to work with smaller groups of learners.

technique /tek'niːk/ *n*

see APPROACH

TEFL /'tefəl/ *n*

an acronym for *T*eaching *E*nglish as a *F*oreign *L*anguage, used to describe the teaching of English in situations where it is a FOREIGN LANGUAGE.

telegraphic speech /'telɪgræfik 'spiːtʃ/ *n*

a term sometimes used to describe the early speech of children learning their first language, so called because children's early speech lacks the same sorts of words which adults leave out of telegrams (e.g. prepositions, AUXILIARY VERBS, articles). For example:

Baby no eat apple.

tenor of discourse /ˈtenər əv ˈdɪskɔːs‖-ɔːrs/ *n*

see SOCIAL CONTEXT

tense¹ /tens/ *n*

the relationship between the form of the verb and the time of the action or state it describes.

In English, verbs may be in the PAST or PRESENT TENSE. However, the present tense form of the verb is also used in:

a timeless expressions: *The sun rises in the east.*
b for future events: *I leave/am leaving next Monday.*
c past events for dramatic effect: *Suddenly she collapses on the floor.*

The past tense form of the verb may also occur in conditional clauses (see CONDITIONAL): *If you worked harder, you would pass the exam.*

see also MOOD
Further reading Quirk et al 1985

tense² *adj*

describes a speech sound which is produced with a comparatively greater degree of movement and muscular tension in the VOCAL TRACT. The vowel /iː/ as in English /siːp/ *seep* is a tense vowel as the lips are spread and the tongue moves towards the roof of the mouth.

Further reading Hyman 1975

terminology /ˌtɜːmɪˈnɒlədʒi‖ˌtɜːrmɪˈnɑː-/ *n*

1 the special lexical items which occur in a particular discipline or subject matter. For example *clause, conjunction,* and *aspect* are part of the terminology of English grammar.
2 the development or selection of lexical items for concepts in a language. Terminology is often a part of LANGUAGE PLANNING, since when languages are being adapted or developed for different purposes (e.g. when a NATIONAL LANGUAGE is being developed) new terms are often needed for scientific or technical concepts.

see also SPECIAL LANGUAGES, STANDARDIZATION
Further reading Sager, Dungworth, & McDonald 1980

term of address /ˈtɜːm əv əˈdres‖ˈtɜːrm əv əˈdres, ˈædres/ *n*

another term for ADDRESS FORM

TESL /ˈtesəl/ *n*

an acronym for *T*eaching *E*nglish as a *S*econd *L*anguage, used either to describe the teaching of English in situations where it is a SECOND LANGUAGE or to refer to any situation where English is taught to speakers of other languages.

TESOL /'tesəl, 'tiːsɒl‖'tiːsɑːl/ *n*

an acronym for *T*eaching *E*nglish to *S*peakers of *O*ther *L*anguages, used, particularly in the USA, to describe the teaching of English in situations where it is either a SECOND LANGUAGE or a FOREIGN LANGUAGE. In British usage this is usually referred to as ELT, i.e. *E*nglish *L*anguage *T*eaching.

test /test/ *n*

any procedure for measuring ability, knowledge, or performance.
see also ACHIEVEMENT TEST, CLOZE PROCEDURE, DISCRETE POINT TEST, LANGUAGE APTITUDE TEST, PLACEMENT TEST, PROFICIENCY TEST, PROGRESS TEST, STANDARDIZED TEST, TOEFL TEST

test battery /'test ˌbætəri/ *n*

another term for BATTERY OF TESTS

testing /'testɪŋ/ *n*

the use of TESTS, or the study of the theory and practice of their use, development, evaluation, etc.

test item /'test ˌaɪtəm/ *n*

a question or element in a test which requires an answer or response. Several different types of test item are commonly used in language tests, including:

a **alternate response item**: one in which a correct response must be chosen from two alternatives, such as True/False, Yes/No, or A/B.

b **fixed response item**, also **closed-ended response**: one in which the correct answer must be chosen from among several alternatives. A MULTIPLE-CHOICE ITEM is an example of a fixed response item.
For example:
Choose (a), (b), (c), or (d).
Yesterday we _____ a movie. (a) has seen (b) saw (c) have seen (d) seen.
(*b*) is the correct response, while (*a*), (*b*) and (*d*) are called **distractors**.

c **free response item**, also **open-ended response**: one in which the student is free to answer a question as he or she wishes without having to choose from among alternatives provided.

d **structured response item**: one in which some control or guidance is given for the answer, but the students must contribute something of their own. For example, after a reading passage, a comprehension question such as the following:
What is astrology?
Astrology is the ancient _____ of telling what will _____ in the future by studying the _____ of the stars and the planets.
Further reading Cohen 1980

test-retest reliability /'test 'riːtest rɪˌlaɪəˈbɪləti/ *n*

an estimate of the RELIABILITY of a test determined by the extent to which a test gives the same results if it is administered at two different

377

times. It is estimated from the coefficient of CORRELATION which is obtained from the two administrations of the test.

test-wisenesss /'test ˌwaɪznɬs/ *n* **test-wise** /'test ˌwaɪz/ *adj*

a test-taking skill which enables a person to do well on certain kinds of test by using their familiarity with the characteristics and formats of tests to help them guess the correct answer. For example, in taking a reading comprehension test based on multiple choice questions, a student may analyze the alternatives given, eliminating unlikely choices, until only one remains, and then choose this as the correct answer. Test writers try to avoid test items which can be answered in this way.

text /tekst/ *n* **textual** /'tekstʃuəl/ *adj*

a piece of spoken or written language. A text may be considered from the point of view of its structure and/or its functions, e.g. warning, instructing, carrying out a transaction.

A full understanding of a text is often impossible without reference to the context in which it occurs.

A text may consist of just one word, e.g. *DANGER* on a warning sign, or it may be of considerable length, e.g. a sermon, a novel, or a debate.

see also CONTEXT, DISCOURSE, TEXT LINGUISTICS

text editor /'tekst ˌedɪtər/ *n*

a computer PROGRAM that stores, edits, manipulates and performs other operations on text.

text linguistics /'tekst lɪŋˌgwɪstɪks/ *n*

a branch of linguistics which studies spoken or written TEXT*s*, e.g. a descriptive passage, a scene in a play, a conversation. It is concerned, for instance, with the way the parts of a text are organized and related to one another in order to form a meaningful whole.

Some linguists prefer to include the study of all spoken texts, particularly if they are longer than one sentence, under DISCOURSE ANALYSIS.

textual function /'tekstʃuəl ˌfʌŋkʃən/ *n*

see FUNCTIONS OF LANGUAGE[2]

TG grammar /'tiː dʒiː 'græmər/ *n*

another term for TRANSFORMATIONAL GENERATIVE GRAMMAR

thematic roles /θiːˈmætɪk 'rəʊlz/ *n*

see θ–THEORY/THETA THEORY

theme /θiːm/ *n*

see FUNCTIONAL SENTENCE PERSPECTIVE

378

theory /'θɪəri/ *n*

1 a statement of a general principle, based upon reasoned argument and supported by evidence, that is intended to explain a particular fact, event, or phenomenon. A theory is more strongly supported by evidence than a HYPOTHESIS.

2 the part of a science or art that deals with general principles and methods as opposed to practice: a set of rules or principles for the study of a subject.

thesaurus /θɪ'sɔːrəs/ *n*

an arrangement of the words and phrases of a language not in alphabetical order but according to the ideas they express. A thesaurus is different from a dictionary. Whereas a dictionary aims at explaining the meaning of words and expressions, a thesaurus suggests a range of words and phrases associated with an idea. For example, an excerpt from *Roget's Thesaurus of English Words and Phrases* shows under *"Amusement"* expressions such as:

fun, frolic, merriment, whoopee, jollity, joviality, laughter

thesis statement /'θiːsɪs ˌsteɪtmənt/ *n*

(in composition) a sentence which states the central idea of an essay. A thesis statement comes at the beginning of the essay – usually in the introductory paragraph. It describes the aim or purpose of the essay, and contains the main ideas that will be developed in the *topic sentences* of the paragraphs which make up the rest of the essay. For example, the underlined sentence in the following introductory paragraph of an essay is the thesis statement.

Reading is the process of getting meaning from printed material. Reading is a complex process and depends upon learning specific skills. The purpose of <u>*teaching reading in school is both to teach children to become independent*</u> <u>*active readers and to introduce them to the pleasure and knowledge which*</u> <u>*effective reading makes possible.*</u>

θ–roles /'θiːtə ˌrəʊlz/ *n*
also **thematic roles**

see θ-THEORY/THETA THEORY

θ–theory/theta theory /'θiːtə ˌθɪəri/ *n*

(in UNIVERSAL GRAMMAR) a sub-theory which deals with semantic relationships. In the lexicon of the grammar (see LEXICON[3]), each LEXICAL ENTRY for a verb shows the semantic roles (θ–roles or thematic roles) that go with it. For example, the English verb *smash* would have the θ–roles:

AGENT (the person or thing carrying out the action)
and
PATIENT (the person or thing affected by the action)
The θ–roles are assigned to the relevant noun phrases in the sentence, e.g.:

Rose	smashed	the vase
agent		patient

The theory of Universal Grammar draws a distinction between these thematic roles, such as agent and patient, sometimes also called **themes**, and grammatical cases, such as grammatical subject and grammatical object (see CASE THEORY). In the example above, *Rose* is the grammatical subject and *the vase* is the grammatical object, but in the sentence:

The vase broke.

the vase still has the patient or theme role but it is now the grammatical subject of the sentence. There is no agent role in this sentence. In second language acquisition research, Theta roles and their relationship to grammatical cases have been used, for example when distinguishing between verb groups which require an agent role (e.g. *hit, walk, work*) and those which do not (e.g. *fall, occur, suffer*).

see also D-STRUCTURE

Further reading Cook 1988; Zobl 1989

think aloud procedure /'θɪŋk ə'laʊd prə,siːdʒəʳ/ *n*

a technique used in investigating *learner strategies*, in which learners think aloud as they are completing a task, in order that the researcher can discover what kinds of thinking processes or strategies they are making use of. For example, while writing a composition, a student may record his or her thoughts into a tape recorder during the planning, drafting, and revising of the composition. Later, the recording may be used to determine the planning or revision processes used by the student.

see also VERBAL REPORTING

threshold hypothesis /'θreʃhəʊld haɪ,pɒθɪ̩sɪ̩s, -ʃəʊld‖-,pɑː-/ *n*

a hypothesis first proposed by Cummins which states that in learning a second language, a certain minimum "threshold" level of proficiency must be reached in that language before the learner can benefit from the use of the language as a medium of instruction in school. This hypothesis is related by Cummins to the **developmental interdependence hypothesis** which says that the development of proficiency in a second language depends upon the level of proficiency the child learner has reached in the first language at the time when extensive exposure to the second language begins.

Further reading Cummins 1979

threshold level /'θreʃhəʊld ,levəl, -ʃəʊld/ *n*

a term used by the European regional organization, The Council of Europe, to refer to the minimal level of language proficiency which is needed to achieve functional ability in a foreign language. It serves as an OBJECTIVE for foreign language teaching. The threshold level is defined according to the situations in which the language will be used, the activities it will be used for, the topics to be referred to, the functions the language will be used for, and the language forms (e.g. vocabulary and grammar) which will be needed.

see also NOTIONAL SYLLABUS
Further reading Van Ek 1975

timbre /'tæmbəʳ, 'tɪm/ *n*
another term for VOICE QUALITY

timed freewriting /'taɪmd 'friːraɪtɪŋ/ *n*
another term for FREEWRITING

time on task /'taɪm ɒn 'taːsk‖'ɔːn, aːn 'tæsk/ *n*
also **on-task time**
(in teaching) the amount of time within a lesson in which students are actively thinking about and working with the content of a lesson. The amount of time that students spend "on task" in a lesson is one of the most basic predictors of learning. Research has distinguished several ways in which time is used within a lesson:

1 **allocated time**: the amount of time provided by the teacher for student learning within a lesson. In secondary schools with a 50 minute class period, teachers typically allocate between 30–35 minutes for instruction.

2 **time on task or engagement rate**: time during which students are working on learning tasks.

3 **academic learning time**: a category of time on task which consists of "high-quality" use of time, i.e. when students devote themselves to, and succeed in, meaningful tasks.

Time-on task rates vary greatly in lessons and may be as low as 30% in some lessons and as high as 90% in others. Effective teachers are said to be successful in maintaining high rates of time on task and academic learning time in lessons.

Further reading Kindsvatter, Wilen & Ishler 1988

t-list /'tiː ˌlɪst/ *n*
a form of notetaking in which the main ideas from a passage are noted on the left side of a page and the corresponding details are listed on the right. The "T" is derived from the fact that the learner makes a vertical line to separate the main ideas from the details and a horizontal line at the top of the page on which to write the words "main ideas" and "details".

see also OUTLINE

TOEFL test /'təʊfəl ˌtest/ *n*
a name containing an acronym for the *T*est *O*f *E*nglish as a *F*oreign *L*anguage, a STANDARDIZED TEST of English proficiency administered by the Educational Testing Service, and widely used to measure the English-language proficiency of foreign students wishing to enter American universities.

token /'təʊkən/ *n*

see TYPE

tone[1] /təʊn/ *n*

height of PITCH and change of pitch which is associated with the pronunciation of syllables or words and which affects the meaning of the word.

A **tone language** is a language in which the meaning of a word depends on the tone used when pronouncing it.

For example, Mandarin Chinese, a tone language, makes a distinction between four different tones:

mā (high level tone)	"mother"
má (high rising tone)	"hemp"
mǎ (fall-rise)	"horse"
mà (high falling tone)	"scold"

Other tone languages are spoken in Vietnam, Thailand, West Africa, and Central America.

tone[2] *n*
also pitch movement

a change in PITCH which affects the meaning and function of utterances in discourse.

In English, linguists have distinguished four or five different tones:

Tone 1 fall in pitch ↘

Tone 2 rise in pitch ↗

Tone 3 a slight rise in pitch ➔

Tone 4 fall in pitch followed by a rise ↘↗

Tone 5 rise in pitch followed by a fall ↗↘

In a unit of intonation (see TONE UNIT) the syllable on which pitch movement begins is often called the **tonic** or the **tonic syllable**. The tonic syllable is often the last prominent syllable in the unit.

For example, in:

They flew to Frankfurt.

the pitch of the speaker's voice begins to fall on the syllable *Frank*.

see also KEY[2], REFERRING TONE

Further reading Brazil, Coulthard, & Johns 1980; Halliday 1970

tone group /'təʊn ˌgruːp/ *n*

another term for TONE UNIT

tone language /'təʊn ˌlæŋgwɪdʒ/ *n*

see TONE[1]

tone unit /'təʊn ˌjuːnɪt/ *n*
also tone group

the basic unit of INTONATION in a language. A tone unit is usually divided into several parts. The most important part contains the syllable on which a change of pitch begins: the **tonic syllable**. The ways in which linguists have divided the tone unit into its different parts and the terms they have used for these parts are not always the same. The simplified diagram below shows the main parts of a tone unit together with different divisions and terms which have been used.

	unstressed syllables	*onset* first stressed syllable	*tonic syllable* where major pitch movement begins	continuation and completion of pitch movement
Crystal 1969	(prehead)	head	nucleus	(tail)
Halliday 1967, 1970	pretonic		tonic	
Brazil et al, 1980	(proclitic segment)		tonic segment	(enclitic segment)

e.g.   *That's a*   VERY TALL   STO   *ry*

where the first syllable of *very* is the **onset**, the first prominent syllable in the tone unit, and the first syllable of *story* is the tonic syllable, where the pitch of the speaker's voice begins to fall.

Some linguists refer to a tone unit as an **intonation contour**.

see also PROMINENCE, TONE[2]

Further reading Brazil, Coulthard, & Johns 1980; Crystal 1969, 1975; Halliday 1967, 1970

tonic /ˈtɒnɪk‖ˈtɑː-/ *n, adj*
    see TONE[2]

tonicity /təˈnɪsᵻti, təʊ-, tɒ-‖təˈ-, təʊ-/ *n*
    the choice of the places in an utterance or part of an utterance where a movement in pitch begins (see **tonic syllable** under TONE UNIT). The choice depends on what the speaker wishes to emphasize. For example, in *She came last SATurday* the change in pitch would often be placed on the *SAT* of *Saturday* but in a dialogue such as:
    A: *She never comes on Saturdays.*
    B: *But she came LAST Saturday.*
    a change in pitch would start on *LAST*.
    Further reading Halliday 1970

tonic segment /ˈtɒnɪk ˈsegmənt‖ˈtɑː-/ *n*
    see TONE UNIT

tonic syllable /ˈtɒnɪk ˈsɪləbəl‖ˈtɑː-/ *n*
    see TONE[2], TONE UNIT

top-down process /ˌtɒp ˈdaʊn ˌprəʊses‖ˌtɑːp ˌprɑː-/ *n*
    in PSYCHOLINGUISTICS, COGNITIVE PSYCHOLOGY, and INFORMATION

PROCESSING, a contrast is made between two different ways in which humans analyse and process language as part of the process of comprehension and learning. One way, known as a top-down process or approach, makes use of previous knowledge ("higher-level knowledge") in analysing and processing information which is received (words, sentences, etc.). The other way, a **bottom-up process**, makes use principally of information which is already present in the data (i.e. the words, sentences etc.). As applied to reading comprehension for example, bottom-up processing would be understanding a text mainly by analysing the words and sentences in the text itself. Top-down processing on the other hand would make use of the reader's previous knowledge, his or her expectations, experience, SCRIPTS, and SCHEMES, in reading the text.

The term "top-down process" should not be confused with the term "top-to-bottom" (see SERIAL LEARNING).

topic[1] /'tɒpɪk||'tɑː-/ *n*

what is talked about or written about. In different speech communities (see SPEECH COMMUNITY) there are different rules about what topics may or may not be discussed. For example, in some communities, illness, death, a person's income, and a person's age may be considered unsuitable topics for conversation.

Further reading Coulthard 1985

topic[2] *n*

in describing the INFORMATION STRUCTURE of sentences, a term for that part of a sentence which names the person, thing, or idea about which something is said (the **comment**). The concept of Topic and Comment is not identical with SUBJECT and PREDICATE. Subject-Predicate refers to the grammatical structure of a sentence rather than to its information structure (see SUBJECT-PROMINENT LANGUAGE). The difference is illustrated in the following example:

As for your drycleaning, I will bring it tomorrow.

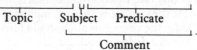

In some sentences in English, however, Topic-Comment and Subject-Predicate are identical. For example:

Hilary	*is a dancer.*
Subject	Predicate
Topic	Comment

topic outline /'tɒpɪk ˌaʊtlaɪn||'tɑː-/ *n*

see OUTLINE

Topic-Prominent language /'tɒpɪk ˌprɒmɪ̩nənt 'læŋgwɪdʒ||'tɑː- ˌprɑː-/ *n*

see SUBJECT-PROMINENT LANGUAGE

topic sentence/'tɒpɪk ˌsentəns‖'taː-/ *n*
(in composition) a sentence which describes the topic, purpose or main
idea of a paragraph, i.e. which states what the paragraph is about.
A topic sentence may be the first sentence in a paragraph, with the
other sentences adding illustrative or supporting details (a paragraph
which follows deductive reasoning – see DEDUCTION) or it may be the
final sentence of a paragraph (a paragraph which follows inductive reasoning – see INDUCTION). Sometimes the topic sentence in a
paragraph may be unstated but implied. An effective topic sentence
usually contains an opinion that will be proved or supported in the
paragraph or a statement which the writer will explain in more detail
in the paragraph. For example, the first sentence in the following
paragraph is the topic sentence.
In order to get a summer job, there are a number of things you should do.
You should first decide on the kind of job you want. You should check all
relevant sources for jobs. You should also start looking early. It is also useful
to prepare a short resume. Above all, be confident and don't be discouraged
by any refusals you may get.
Further reading Herman 1982

top-to-bottom /'tɒp tə 'bɒtəm‖'taːp 'baː-/ *adj*
see SERIAL LEARNING
see also TOP-DOWN PROCESS

total communication /'təʊtl kəˌmjuːnɪ̩'keɪʃən/ *n*
a method of teaching hearing impaired children which is based on the
simultaneous use of both SIGN LANGUAGE and spoken language. This
allows the child to use both vision and residual hearing. The results
achieved may depend on the MANUAL METHOD employed and the skill
of the teacher in matching the two systems of communication.
Acquisition of spoken language is said to be limited by this approach.

Total Physical Response /'təʊtl 'fɪzɪkəl rɪ'spɒns‖-'spaːns/ *n*
also **TPR** /'tiː piː ˌɑːr/
a language teaching METHOD developed by Asher in which item are
presented in the foreign language as orders, commands, and instructions requiring a physical response from the learner (e.g. opening a
window or standing up). This is thought to lead to more meaningful
and effective learning.
Further reading Asher 1977; Richard & Rogers 1986

trace /treɪs/ *n*
see D-STRUCTURE

traditional grammar /trə'dɪʃənəl 'græməʳ/ *n*
a grammar which is usually based on earlier grammars of Latin or
Greek and applied to some other language, often inappropriately. For
example, some grammarians stated that English had six CASES[1] because
Latin had six cases. These grammars were often notional and pre-

scriptive in their approach (see NOTIONAL GRAMMAR, PRESCRIPTIVE GRAMMAR). Although there has been a trend towards using grammars which incorporate more modern approaches to language description and language teaching, some schools still use traditional grammars.

transaction /træn'zækʃən/ n

an event or series of actions which involves interactions between two or more people and has a particular goal. In describing language use (particularly for the purpose of developing language programmes), the term "transaction" is sometimes used to refer to the activities people carry out in specific situations, for example, the activities of a waiter or waitress in a restaurant. The language demands of particular transactions such as "serving a customer and taking the customer's order" may be a focus of NEEDS ANALYSIS. The term TASK is sometimes used with a similar meaning. A transaction between a worker and a customer is sometimes known as a **service encounter**.

transcription /træn'skrɪpʃən/ n

another term for NOTATION

transfer /'trænsfɜː^r/ n

(in learning theory) the carrying over of learned behaviour from one situation to another. **Positive transfer** is learning in one situation which helps or facilitates learning in another later situation. **Negative transfer** is learning in one situation which interferes with learning in another later situation.

see also LANGUAGE TRANSFER, PROACTIVE INHIBITION
Further reading Brown 1980

transfer of training /'trænsfɜːr əv 'treɪnɪŋ/ n

see INDUCED ERROR

transfer stage /'trænsfɜː^r ˌsteɪdʒ/ n

another term for **production stage**

see STAGE

transformational component /'trænsfəˌmeɪʃənəl kəm'pəʊnənt‖ -fər-/ n

the part of a TRANSFORMATIONAL GENERATIVE GRAMMAR which contains the **transformational rules**. These are rules which change a basic syntactic structure (see BASE COMPONENT) into a sentence-like structure. Another part of the grammar (the "phonological component") is needed to supply the rules for pronouncing a sentence (phonetic interpretation).

Further reading Chomsky 1965

transformational-generative grammar /'trænsfəˌmeɪʃənəl 'dʒenərətɪv 'græmə^r‖-fər-/ n

also **transformational grammar, TG grammar, generative-transformational grammar, generative transformational theory**

a theory of grammar which was proposed by the American linguist Chomsky in 1957. It has since been developed by him and many other linguists. Chomsky attempted to provide a model for the description of all languages. A transformational generative grammar tries to show, with a system of rules, the knowledge which a native speaker of a language uses in forming grammatical sentences (see COMPETENCE).

Chomsky has changed his theory over the years. The most well-known version was published in his book *Aspects of the Theory of Syntax* in 1965. It is often referred to as the **Aspects Model** or **Standard Theory**. This model consists of four main parts:

a the BASE COMPONENT, which produces or generates basic syntactic structures called DEEP STRUCTURES.

b the TRANSFORMATIONAL COMPONENT, which changes or transforms these basic structures into sentences called **surface structures**.

c the **phonological component**, which gives sentences a phonetic representation so that they can be pronounced (see GENERATIVE PHONOLOGY).

d the **semantic component**, which deals with the meaning of sentences (see INTERPRETATIVE SEMANTICS).

The relationship of the four components to one another can be seen in the simplified diagram below:

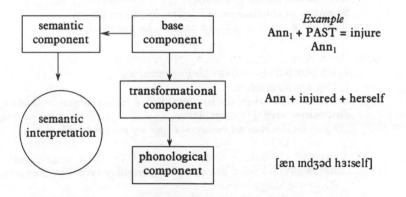

Chomsky and others later modified the Aspects Model. They felt that not only the base component but also the transformational and phonological components had some effect on the semantic interpretation of a sentence (**Extended Standard Theory**).

see also PERFORMANCE

Further reading Chomsky 1965

transformational grammar /'trænsfə,meɪʃənəl 'græmər||-fər-/ *n*
another term for TRANSFORMATIONAL GENERATIVE GRAMMAR

transformational rules /ˈtrænsfəˌmeɪʃənəl ˈruːlz‖-fər-/ *n*

see TRANSFORMATIONAL COMPONENT

transformation drill /ˌtrænsfəˈmeɪʃən ˌdrɪl‖-fər-/ *n*

see DRILL

transitional bilingual education /trænˈzɪʃənəl baɪˈlɪŋgwəl edjʊˈkeɪ
ʃən, trænˈsɪ-‖edʒə-/ *n*

see BILINGUAL EDUCATION

transition words /trænˈzɪʒən ˌwɜːdz, -ˈsɪ-‖-ɜːr-/ *n*
also **transitions, transition devices**

(in composition) adverbs which are used to indicate relations or
transitions between sentences in a paragraph or piece of writing. These
may be either single words or phrases. Transition words often give
COHERENCE to a composition. Different transition words are used to
signal different kinds of relations between sentence. For example:

Time: *after a while, afterwards, later*
Place: *nearby, there*
Addition: *also, besides, furthermore*
Result: *accordingly, hence, therefore*
Comparison: *likewise, similarly*
Contrast: *however, nevertheless, otherwise*
Concession: *naturally, of course*
Summary or conclusion: *in brief, finally, to sum up*
Illustration and example: *for example, for instance, indeed*

transitive verb /ˈtrænsɪtɪv ˈvɜːb, -zɪ̆-‖ˈvɜːrb/ *n*

a verb which takes an OBJECT[1]. For example:

They saw the accident.

A verb which takes an indirect and a direct object is known as
ditransitive verb. For example:

I gave the money to my mother. = I gave my mother the money.
　　　　　DO　　IO　　　　　　IO　　DO

A verb which takes a direct object and an object complement (see
COMPLEMENT) is known as a **complex transitive verb.** For example:

We elected Mary chairman.
　　　　DO　object complement

A verb which does not take an object is an **intransitive verb.** For
example:

The children danced.

see also COMPLEMENT

transitivity[1] /ˌtrænsɪˈtɪvəti, -zɪ̆-/ *n*

the state of being a TRANSITIVE VERB. In this sense, one can speak of the
transitivity of the verb *saw* in the sentence:

They saw the accident.

transitivity² *n*

(in SYSTEMIC GRAMMAR) a choice between the three main processes that can be represented in a sentence:

a a physical or "material" process as in *Fred cut the lawn.*
b a "mental" process as in *David saw Rosemary.*
c a "relational" process as in *This view is magnificent.*

Related to this choice of processes is:

a the choice of participants. A participant is someone or something involved in the process, e.g., in the above examples, *Fred* and *the lawn, David* and *Rosemary* and
b the choice of circumstances, e.g. David saw Rosemary *yesterday/in the garden/by accident.*

Further choices associated with transitivity would be which roles the participants had in a process and how processes, participants, and circumstances are combined.

see also SYSTEMIC LINGUISTICS

Further reading Berry 1975; Halliday 1967; de Joia & Stenton 1980

translation /træns'leɪʃən, trænz-/ *n*

the process of changing speech or writing from one language (the SOURCE LANGUAGE²) into another (the TARGET LANGUAGE²), or the target-language version that results from this process. A translation which reproduces the general meaning and intention of the original but which does not closely follow the grammar, style, or organization of it is known as a **free translation**. A translation which approximates to a word-for-word representation of the original is known as a **literal translation.**

see also INTERPRETATION

translation equivalence /træns'leɪʃən ɪ'kwɪvələns, trænz-/ *n*

the degree to which linguistic units (e.g. words, syntactic structures) can be translated into another language without loss of meaning. Two items with the same meaning in two languages are said to be **translation equivalents.**

tree diagram /'triː ˌdaɪəgræm/ *n*

see BASE COMPONENT, CONSTITUENT STRUCTURE, NODE, PHRASE-STRUCTURE GRAMMAR

trill /trɪl/ *n*

another term for ROLL

triphthong /'trɪfθɒŋ, 'trɪp-‖-θɔːŋ/ *n*

(in PHONETICS) a term sometimes used for a combination of three vowels. For example, in English:

/aɪə/ as in /faɪəʳ/ *fire*

is a triphthong.

see also DIPHTHONG, MONOPHTHONG

true beginner /'truː bɪ'gɪnəʳ/ *n*

see FALSE BEGINNER

true-false item /ˌtruː 'fɔːls ˌaɪtm̩/ *n*

an item in a test which requires "true" or "false" as the answer or response.

T-score /'tiː ˌskɔːʳ/ *n*

(in statistics) a STANDARD SCORE whose DISTRIBUTION has a MEAN of 50 and a STANDARD DEVIATION of 10.

T-test /'tiː ˌtest/ *n*

(in testing and statistics) a quantitative procedure for determining the STATISTICAL SIGNIFICANCE of the difference between the MEANS on two sets of scores.

see also CHI-SQUARE

T-unit /'tiː ˌjuːnɪt/ *n*
also **Minimal Terminable Unit**

a measure of the linguistic complexity of sentences, defined as the shortest unit (the Terminable Unit, Minimal Terminable Unit, or T-Unit) which a sentence can be reduced to, and consisting of one independent clause together with whatever DEPENDENT CLAUSES are attached to it. For example the sentence *After she had eaten, Kim went to bed* would be described as containing one T-Unit.

Compound sentences (see COMPLEX SENTENCE) contain two or more T-Units. The study of T-Units in written language has been used in the study of children's language development.

Further reading Hunt 1966

turn /tɜːn‖tɜːrn/ *n*

see TURN-TAKING

turn-taking /'tɜːn ˌteɪkɪŋ‖'tɜːrn/ *n*

In conversation, the roles of speaker and listener change constantly. The person who speaks first becomes a listener as soon as the person addressed takes his or her **turn** in the conversation by beginning to speak.

The rules for turn-taking may differ from one community to another as they do from one type of SPEECH EVENT (e.g. a conversation) to another (e.g. an oral test). Turn-taking and rules for turn-taking are studied in CONVERSATIONAL ANALYSIS and DISCOURSE ANALYSIS

see also SEQUENCING[1]
Further reading Coulthard 1985; Sacks et al 1974

type /taɪp/ *n*

In linguistics, a distinction is sometimes made between classes of linguistic items (e.g. PHONEMES, WORDS, UTTERANCES) and actual occurrences in speech or writing of examples of such classes. The class of linguistic units is called a **type** and examples or individual members of the class are called **tokens**.

For example, *hello, hi, good morning* are three different tokens of the type "Greeting".

In MATHEMATICAL LINGUISTICS the total number of words in a text may be referred to as the number of text tokens, and the number of different words as the number of text types. The ratio of *different* words in a text to *total* words in the text is known as the LEXICAL DENSITY or **Type-Token Ratio** for that text.

see also LEXICAL DENSITY

Further reading Mackey 1965

Type-Token Ratio /'taɪp 'təʊkən ˌreɪʃiəʊ‖ˌreɪʃəʊ/ *n*
another term for LEXICAL DENSITY

typology /taɪˈpɒlədʒi‖-ˈpɑː-/ *n*
classification of languages into types.

For example, languages may be classified according to whether or not they are tone languages (see TONE[1]) or according to their most typical SYNTACTIC STRUCTURES, e.g. whether they are **SVO languages** (Subject – Verb – Object languages) like English or **SOV languages** (Subject – Object – Verb languages) like Japanese.

U

UG /ˌuː ˈdʒiː/ *n*
    an abbreviation for UNIVERSAL GRAMMAR

unacceptable /ˌʌnəkˈseptəbəl◄/ *adj*
    see ACCEPTABLE

unaspirated /ʌnˈæspɪ̥reɪt̥d/ *adj*
    see ASPIRATION

uncountable noun /ʌnˈkaʊntəbəl ˈnaʊn/ *n*
    see COUNTABLE NOUN

underlying form /ˈʌndəlaɪ-ɪŋ ˈfɔːm‖-dər- ˈfɔːrm/ *n*
    see SYSTEMATIC PHONEMICS

underlying structure /ˈʌndəlaɪ-ɪŋ ˈstrʌktʃəʳ‖-dər- / *n*
    another term for DEEP STRUCTURE

ungrammatical /ˌʌngrəˈmætɪkəl◄/ *adj*
    see GRAMMATICAL[1]

unit-credit system /ˈjuːn̩t ˈkredɪ̩t ˌsɪst̩m/ *n*
    a language-learning system suggested by the European regional
    organization The Council of Europe in connection with their
    THRESHOLD LEVEL. In this system the OBJECTIVES for a foreign
    language programme are divided into portions or units. Each of these
    units represents a selection of the learner's language needs and is
    related to all the other units in the programme. If after successful
    completion of each unit the learners receive some sort of official
    recognition, the system is known as a unit-credit system.
    Further reading Van Ek & Alexander 1975; Van Ek 1976

universal /ˌjuːn̩ˈvɜːsəl◄‖-ˈvɜːr-/ *n*
    see LANGUAGE UNIVERSAL

universal grammar /ˈjuːn̩vɜːsəl ˈgræməʳ‖-ɜːr-/ *n*
also **UG**
    a theory which claims to account for the grammatical competence of
    every adult no matter what language he or she speaks.
    It claims that every speaker knows a set of **principles** which apply to
    all languages and also a set of PARAMETERS that can vary from one
    language to another, but only within certain limits.
    The theory was proposed by Noam Chomsky and has been stated more
    specifically in his model of GOVERNMENT/BINDING THEORY.

392

According to UG theory, acquiring a language means applying the principles of UG grammar to a particular language, e.g. English, French or German, and learning which value is appropriate for each parameter.

For example, one of the principles of UG is **structure dependency**. It means that a knowledge of language relies on knowing structural relationships in a sentence rather than looking at it as a sequence of words, e.g.:

not *The /policeman/raised/his/revolver*
but

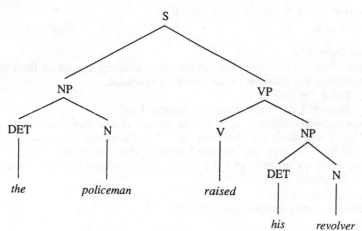

One of the parameters in Universal Grammar which may vary, within certain limits, from one language to another, is the **head parameter**. It concerns the position of HEADS (principal elements) within each phrase.

In English, the head is first in a phrase, for example:

<u>with</u> the car (prepositional phrase)

In Japanese, the head is last in the phrase:

Nihon <u>ni</u>
Japan <u>in</u>

The role of Universal Grammar (UG) in second language acquisition is still under discussion. Three possibilities are emerging:

1 UG operates in the same way for L2 as it does for L1 (see CORE GRAMMAR). The learner's knowledge of L1 is irrelevant

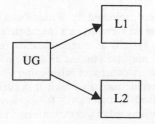

2 The learner's Core Grammar is fixed and UG is no longer available to the L2 learner, particularly not to the adult learner.

3 UG is partly available but it is only one factor in the acquisition of L2. There are other factors and they may interfere with the UG influence.

Further reading Cook 1988; Hyams 1986; White 1989a

unmarked /ˌʌnˈmɑːkt◄||-ɑːr-/ *adj*

see MARKEDNESS

unrounded vowel /ʌnˈraʊndɨd ˈvaʊəl/ *n*

see VOWEL

uptake /ˈʌpteɪk/ *n*

the illocutionary force (see SPEECH ACT) a hearer interprets from an utterance. For example in the following exchange:

Child: *I'm tired.*

Mother: *You can stop doing your homework now.*

the uptake or interpretation by the mother is as if the child had said "Can I stop doing my homework now?" But sometimes there may be a difference between the intended uptake (what the speaker wants the hearer to understand) and the actual uptake (what the hearer actually understands).

see also PRAGMATICS

Further reading Austin 1962

usage[1] /ˈjuːsɪdʒ, ˈjuːzɪdʒ/ *n*

the ways people actually speak and write. In this sense, usage is closely related to PERFORMANCE, and can be studied by the analysis of specimens of AUTHENTIC language and by experiments of various kinds. The study of usage can reveal, for example, that the passive voice (see VOICE[1]) is more than ordinarily frequent in scientific writing, or that the spellings *all right* and *alright* both occur.

It is also possible to study reactions to usage, and on this basis to make recommendations when usage is divided. **Usage guides** attempt to do this. They may say, for example, that people write both *all right* and *alright*, but that there are still strong feelings against the spelling *alright*, and that therefore it is better to write *all right* as two words.

Further reading Haegeman 1982; Ilson 1982, 1984

usage[2] *n*

a distinction has been proposed by Widdowson between the function of a linguistic item as an element in a linguistic system (**usage**) and its function as part of a system of communication (**use**). For example the PROGRESSIVE ASPECT may be studied as an item of grammar or usage (i.e. to consider how it compares with other ASPECTS and TENSES in English and the constructions in which it occurs) and in terms of its use (i.e. how it is used in DISCOURSE for performing such communicative acts as descriptions, plans, commentaries, etc.).

394

The meaning a linguistic item has as an example of usage is called its **signification**, and the meaning it has as an example of use is called its **value**.

see also SPEECH ACT, UPTAKE
Further reading Widdowson 1978

use /juːs/ *n*

see USAGE²

utterance /ˈʌtərəns/ *n*

(in DISCOURSE) what is said by any one person before or after another person begins to speak.

For example, an utterance may consist of:

a one word, e.g. B's reply in:
   A: *Have you done your homework?*
   B: *Yeah.*
b one sentence, e.g. A's question and B's answer in:
   A: *What's the time?*
   B: *It's half past five.*
c more than one sentence, e.g. A's complaint in:
   A: *Look, I'm really fed up. I've told you several times to wash your hands before a meal. Why don't you do as you're told?*
   B: *But Mum, listen …*

see also MOVE, SEQUENCING¹
Further reading Coulthard 1985

utterance meaning /ˈʌtərəns ˈmiːnɪŋ/ *n*

the meaning a speaker conveys by using a particular utterance in a particular context situation.

For example:

My watch has stopped again.

could convey, according to the context situation:

a I can't tell you the time.
b This is the reason for my being late.
c I really have to get it repaired.
d What about buying me another one?

see also ILLOCUTIONARY FORCE, IMPLICATION, PRAGMATICS, SENTENCE MEANING

uvula /ˈjuːvjᵿlə/ *n*

see PLACE OF ARTICULATION, UVULAR

uvular /ˈjuːvjᵿləʳ/ *adj*

describes a speech sound (a CONSONANT) which is produced by the back of the tongue against the very end of the soft palate (the **uvula**), or by a narrowing in the VOCAL TRACT near the uvula.

The /r/ used by some speakers in the northeast of England, and by some speakers of Scottish English, is a uvular ROLL [R].

see also PLACE OF ARTICULATION, MANNER OF ARTICULATION
Further reading Gimson 1980

V

V', V" /'viː 'bɑːʳ/, /'viː 'dʌbl ˌbɑːʳ/ *n*
see BAR NOTATION

valency /'veɪlənsi/ *n*
see DEPENDENCY GRAMMAR

validity /vəˈlɪdɪti/ *n*
(in testing) the degree to which a test measures what it is supposed to measure, or can be used successfully for the purposes for which it is intended. A number of different statistical procedures can be applied to a test to estimate its validity. Such procedures generally seek to determine what the test measures, and how well it does so.

see also CONSTRUCT VALIDITY, CONTENT VALIDITY, CRITERION MEASURE, CRITERION-RELATED VALIDITY, EMPIRICAL VALIDITY, FACE VALIDITY, PREDICTIVE VALIDITY

value /'væljuː/ *n*
see USAGE[2]

values clarification /'væljuːz klærɪfɪˌkeɪʃən/ *n*
an instructional activity which requires students to explore their values and attitudes towards a topic, and in so doing discover the positive and negative aspects of their own value systems as well as learn about the values of others. For example, questions such as the following might be posed:
What would you do if you discovered a family member was shop lifting?
a inform the police
b ask the person to return the stolen property to the store
c talk to other family members about it
d nothing
Values clarification activities are often used as a communicative activity in COLLABORATIVE LEARNING and communicative language teaching (see COMMUNICATIVE APPROACH).

variable[1] /'veəriəbəl/ *n*
a linguistic item which has various forms (**variants**). The different forms of the variable may be related to differences in STYLE or to differences in the socio-economic background, education, age, or sex of the speakers (see SOCIOLECT). There are variables in the PHONOLOGY, MORPHOLOGY, SYNTAX, and LEXICON[1] of a language.
Examples in English include:
a the *ng* variable as in *coming, working*. In careful formal speech it often

occurs as /ɪŋ/, e.g. /'kʌmɪŋ/ *coming*, /'wɜːkɪŋ/ *working*, but in informal or regional speech it often occurs as /'kʌmn/ *com'n*, /'wɜːkn/ *work'n*

b the marker on verb forms for 3rd-person singular present tense (as in *He works here*), which is a variable because in some NON-STANDARD and some new varieties of English a variant without the ending (as in *He work here*) may occur.

Linguistic rules which try to account for these variables in language are referred to as **variable rules**.

Further reading Trudgill 1983; Wardhaugh 1986

variable[2]

(in testing and statistics) a property whereby the members of a set or group differ from one another. In comparing teaching methods, for example, different variables may be (a) the level of interest each creates, (b) the amount of teaching time each method is used for, and (c) how difficult each method is to use.

see also DEPENDENT VARIABLE

variable rule /'veəriəbəl 'ruːl/ n

see VARIABLE[1]

variance /'veəriəns/ n

(in testing and statistics) a statistical measure of the DISPERSION of a SAMPLE. The variance of a set of scores on a test, for example, would be based on how much the scores obtained differ from the MEAN, and is the square of the STANDARD DEVIATION.

variant /'veəriənt/ n, adj

see VARIABLE[1]

variation /veəri'eɪʃən/ n
also language variation

differences in pronunciation, grammar, or word choice within a language. Variation in a language may be related to region (see DIALECT, REGIONAL VARIATION), to social class and/or educational background (see SOCIOLECT) or to the degree of formality of a situation in which language is used (see STYLE).

see also FREE VARIATION

variety /və'raɪəti/ n

see SPEECH VARIETY

velar /'viːləʳ/ adj

describes a speech sound (a CONSONANT) which is produced by the back of the tongue touching the soft palate (the **velum**) at the back of the mouth.

For example, in English the /k/ in /kɪn/ *kin* and the /g/ in /get/ *get* are velars, or, more precisely, velar STOPS.

Because the back of the tongue is called the **dorsum,** these sounds are sometimes called **dorsal.**

see also PLACE OF ARTICULATION, MANNER OF ARTICULATION
Further reading Gimson 1980

velum /'viːləm/ *n*
also **soft palate**

see PLACE OF ARTICULATION, VELAR

verb /vɜːb||vɜːrb/ *n*
(in English) a word which, (a) occurs as part of the PREDICATE of a sentence (b) carries markers of grammatical categories such as TENSE, ASPECT, PERSON, NUMBER[1] and MOOD, and (c) refers to an action or state. For example:

He opened the door.
Jane loves Tom.

see also AUXILIARY VERB, FINITE VERB, INCHOATIVE VERB, MODAL, PHRASAL VERB, REGULAR VERB, STATIVE VERB, TRANSITIVE VERB, VERB GROUP, VERB PHRASE

verbal /'vɜːbəl||-ɜːr-/ *n*
(in TRANSFORMATIONAL GENERATIVE GRAMMAR) a WORD CLASS including VERB*s* and AJECTIVE*s.*
The reason for considering verbs and adjectives as belonging to one class is that they have many properties in common.
For example, some verbs and adjectives in English can occur in IMPERATIVE SENTENCE*s:* *Throw the ball! Be quiet!* while other verbs and adjectives normally cannot: **Resemble me!* **Be tall!*

verbal association /'vɜːbəl əˌsəʊsi'eɪʃən, əˌsəʊʃi-||-ɜːr-/ *n*
see VERBAL LEARNING
see also WORD ASSOCIATION

verbal deficit hypothesis /'vɜːbəl 'defⵣsⵣt haiˌpɒθⵣsⵣs||-ɜːr- -ˌpɑː-/ *n*
another term for DEFICIT HYPOTHESIS

verbal learning /'vɜːbəl 'lɜːnɪŋ || 'vɜːr- 'lɜːr-/ *n*
(in behaviourist psychology) the learning of language. Also used to refer to studies of the learning and remembering of linguistic items. The forming of associations between words is known as **verbal-association.**

see also ASSOCIATIVE LEARNING, BEHAVIOURISM, WORD ASSOCIATION

verbal repertoire /'vɜːbəl 'repətwɔːʳ || 'vɜːr- -pər-/ *n*
the speech varieties (LANGUAGE*s*[2], DIALECT*s*, SOCIOLECT*s*, STYLE*s*, REGISTER*s*) which an individual knows.
Sometimes a language may be part of someone's verbal repertoire although he or she has no chance to use it.
For example, a person who knows English and Welsh and moves from

Wales to New Zealand may not be able to continue using Welsh. It would still be part of his or her verbal repertoire but it does not belong to the SPEECH REPERTOIRE of the community, in this case, New Zealand.

Further reading Wardhaugh 1986

verbal reporting /ˈvɜːbəl rɪˈpɔːtɪŋ||-ɜːr- -ɔːr-/ *n*

(in research) a procedure used for collecting data about the processes a person employs in carrying out a task. Verbal reporting involves the subject giving an oral description of the processes they are using while they are completing a task. Verbal reporting attempts to gather information about the cognitive and linguistic aspects involved in different kinds of tasks. For example, in order to learn how someone writes a summary of a text, a person may be asked to describe the decisions and judgements they make as they complete a summary task. Several different kinds of verbal reporting techniques have been used in studies of second language learning. These include; THINK-ALOUD PROCEDURES. These involve saying aloud everything that occurs while performing a task. For example; in studying how a person revises a piece of writing (such as a draft of a term paper), the learner describes everything that occurs to them as they revise the paper.

Introspection. This involves the subject reflecting on the kinds of decisions they make and the kinds of strategies they use while carrying out a task, and reporting them as they occur.

Retrospection. This involves reflecting on how a task or activity was carried out after it occurred. This requires the subject to infer his or her own mental processes or strategies from their memory of a particular mental event under observation.

Further reading Seliger & Shohamy 1989

verb group /ˈvɜːb ˌgruːp||ˈvɜːrb/ *n*

a VERB, together with an associated MODAL VERB or AUXILIARY VERB(*s*).

For example:
He didn't come.
She can't have been there.

verb phrase /ˈvɜːb ˌfreɪz||ˈvɜːrb/ *n*
also **VP**

(in TRANSFORMATIONAL GENERATIVE GRAMMAR) the part of a SENTENCE which contains the main verb and also any OBJECT^2(*s*), COMPLEMENT(*s*) and ADVERBIAL(*s*).

For example, in:
Tom gave a watch to his daughter.
all the sentence except *Tom* is the verb phrase.

see also NOUN PHRASE

vernacular /vəˈnækjʊ̈ləʳ||vər-/ *n, adj*

a term used of a language or language variety:

a when it is contrasted with a classical language, such as Latin, e.g.:
Church services in the Roman Catholic church used to be conducted in Latin, but now they are in the vernacular. (e.g., in English, Italian, Swahili, etc.)

b when it is contrasted with an internationally used language such as English, e.g.:
If you want to teach English in that country, it will be useful to know the vernacular.

c in BILINGUAL and MULTILINGUAL countries, when it is spoken by some or most of the population but when it is not the official or the NATIONAL LANGUAGE of a country, e.g.:
In addition to schools that teach in the national language, there are also vernacular schools.

see also BLACK ENGLISH, DIGLOSSIA, DOMAIN

VESL /ˈvesəl/ *n*

see VOCATIONAL ENGLISH

videodisc /ˈvɪdiəuˌdɪsk/ *n*

a storage device similar in size to a long-player record, containing pre-recorded video and audio information suitable for playback through a standard television receiver or monitor connected to a videodisc player. Videodiscs have many applications in education and in language teaching.

see also INTERACTIVE VIDEO
Further reading Flint Smith 1989

video teleconferencing /ˈvɪdiəu ˈteliˌkɒnfərənsɪŋ‖-ˌkɑːn-/ *n*

the linking of students and teachers in different locations via satellite and television, to provide interaction between native speakers of a language and students learning the language as well as cultural exchange.

visual perception /ˈvɪʒuəl pəˈsepʃən‖pər-/ *n*

see PERCEPTION

visual span /ˈvɪʒuəl ˈspæn/ *n*

see READING SPAN

vocabulary /vəˈkæbjⁱləri, vəu-‖-leri/ *n*

a set of LEXEMES, including single words, COMPOUND WORDS and IDIOMS.

see also ACTIVE/PASSIVE LANGUAGE KNOWLEDGE, CONTENT WORD, FREQUENCY[2], TYPE

vocabulary control /vəˈkæbjⁱləri kənˌtrəul, vəu-‖-leri/ *n*

(in the preparation of materials for language teaching, reading, etc.) the practice of using a limited vocabulary based on a WORD LIST or other source. GRADED READERS are often written using vocabulary control.

vocal cords /ˈvəʊkəl ˌkɔːdz‖-ɔːr-/ n
also **vocal chords**

> the folds of tough, flexible tissue in the LARYNX extending from back to front. The space between the vocal cords is the **glottis**. When the vocal cords are pressed together, the air from the lungs is completely sealed off. During speech, the vocal cords open and close the air passage from the lungs to the mouth.
>
> In the production of vowels and voiced consonants (see VOICE²) the vocal cords vibrate.

glottis
wide open for breathing

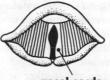
vocal cords
loosely together and vibrating as for a voiced sound

> see also PITCH, PLACE OF ARTICULATION
> *Further reading* Denes & Pinson 1973; Gimson 1989

vocal tract /ˈvəʊkəl ˌtrækt/ n

> (in phonetics) the air passages which are above the VOCAL CORDS and which are involved in the production of speech sounds.
>
> The vocal tract can be divided into the **nasal cavity**, which is the air passage within and behind the nose, and the **oral cavity**, which is the air passage within the mouth and the throat.
>
> The shape of the vocal tract can be changed, e.g. by changing the position of the tongue or the lips. Changes in the shape of the vocal tract cause differences in speech sounds.

vocational english /vəʊˈkeɪʃənəl ˈɪŋglɪʃ/ n
also **vocational ESL** /vəʊˈkeɪʃənəl ˌiː es ˈel/, **VESL**

> English taught for use in a particular job or occupation.
>
> see also LANGUAGE FOR SPECIAL PURPOSES

vocative /ˈvɒkətɪv‖ˈvɑː-/ n

> a NOUN PHRASE¹ which is an optional part of a sentence, and which names or indicates one being addressed.
>
> For example:
> *Really <u>dear</u>, do you think so?*
> *That's a pretty dress, <u>Mrs Johnson</u>.*

voice¹ /vɔɪs/ n

> the ways in which a language expresses the relationship between a verb and the noun phrases which are associated with it. Two sentences can differ in voice and yet have the same basic meaning. However, there

may be a change in emphasis and one type of sentence may be more appropriate (see APPROPRIATENESS).
For example, in:
   The wind damaged the fence.
the wind is the subject of the verb *damaged*, which is in the **active voice**, while in:
   The fence was damaged by the wind.
the fence is the subject of the verb *was damaged*, which is in the **passive voice**.
The first sentence would be a suitable answer to the question:
   Did the wind damage anything?
while the second sentence would be a suitable answer to the question:
   How did the fence get damaged?
The so-called "agentless" passive, e.g.:
   The fence has been damaged.
is used when the speaker or writer does not know or wish to state the cause, or when the cause is too obvious to be stated.

voice² *n*

Speech sounds which are produced with the VOCAL CORDS vibrating are called "voiced". Such vibration can be felt when touching the neck in the region of the LARYNX.
For example, VOWELS are usually voiced, and, in English:
a the /d/ in /den/ *den* is a voiced STOP
b the /z/ in /zɪŋk/ *zinc* is a voiced FRICATIVE.
Speech sounds which are produced without vibration of the vocal cords are called "voiceless".
For example, in English:
a the /t/ in /tɪn/ *tin* is a voiceless stop
b the /s/ in /sæd/ *sad* is a voiceless fricative.
When a speech sound which is normally voiced is pronounced without vibration or only slight vibration, this is called **devoicing**. Devoicing of voiced consonants often occurs in English when they are at the end of a word, e.g. *lid* is pronounced [lɪd̥] where the mark ̥ under the /d/ means devoicing.

see also INTERNATIONAL PHONETIC ALPHABET, MANNER OF ARTICU-LATION, PLACE OF ARTICULATION
Further reading Gimson 1989

voice onset time /ˈvɔɪs ˈɒnset ˌtaɪm‖ˈɑːn-/ *n*

When pronouncing STOPS, such as /p/, /b/ in *pin*, *bin*, the two articulators (i.e. the lips) are closed and then opened again. With /b/ the VOCAL CORDS are vibrating to produce a voiced stop (see VOICE²). The voice onset time is a relationship between these two factors. It is the point in time at which the voicing starts in relation to the opening of the two articulators. For example, the voice onset time for French, Spanish and Thai /b/ is generally earlier than that for English /b/.
Further reading Ladefoged 1982

voice quality /'vɔɪs ˌkwɒlɪ̩ti‖ˌkwɑː-/ *n*

the overall impression that a listener obtains of a speaker's voice. It is also sometimes called TIMBRE, and refers to those characteristics of a particular voice that enable the listener to distinguish one voice from another, such as when a person is able to identify a telephone caller.

Systematic research into voice quality has been hampered by a lack of suitable terminology.

Further reading Crystal 1969, 1975

voice synthesizer /'vɔɪs 'sɪnθɪ̩saɪzəʳ/ *n*

see SPEECH SYNTHESIS

vowel /'vaʊəl/ *n*

a speech sound in which the airstream from the lungs is not blocked in any way in the mouth or throat, and which is usually pronounced with vibration of the VOCAL CORDS, e.g. English /iː/ in /siː/ *see* and /uː/ in /tuː/ *too*.

The type of vowel sound which is produced depends largely on the position of the tongue:

a which part of the tongue (the front, the middle, or the back) is raised
b how far the tongue is raised.

A division of vowels can be made into **front, central,** and **back vowels** (according to which part of the tongue is raised) and **close, half-close, half-open,** and **open vowels** (according to how far ·the tongue is raised).

For example, /iː/ in /tiː/ *tea* is a close front vowel and /ɑː/ in /'fɑːðəʳ/ *father* is an open back vowel.

Sometimes, instead of the four-way division for tongue height, a three-way division is made: **high, mid,** and **low vowels.** Thus /iː/ would be described as a high front vowel and /ɑː/ as a low back vowel.

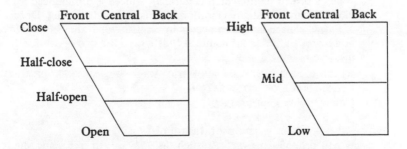

Vowel sounds also depend on the shape of the lips. The lips are rounded for **rounded vowels,** e.g. /uː/ in /ʃuː/ *shoe,* and the lips are spread for **unrounded vowels,** e.g. /iː/ in /biː/ *bee.*

see also CARDINAL VOWEL, MANNER OF ARTICULATION, NASAL, PLACE OF ARTICULATION, SEMI-VOWEL

Further reading Fromkin & Rodman 1983; Gimson 1989

vowel harmony /ˈvaʊəl ˈhɑːməni‖ˈhɑːr-/ *n*

a modification (ASSIMILATION) of the pronunciation of vowels in a word so that one agrees or "harmonizes" with another one.

For example, in Turkish the word for the number *1* is *bir* and for the number *10* is *on*. When suffixes are added to them, the vowel of the suffix must be either a front vowel or a back vowel, depending on the vowel that precedes it, e.g.:

   bir + *de* = *birde* "at one"
   both /i/ and /e/ are front vowels
   on + *da* = *onda* "at ten"
   both /o/ and /a/ are back vowels.

Further reading Ladefoged 1982

vowel length /ˈvaʊəl ˈleŋθ/ *n*

the duration of a vowel sound.

In phonetic script (see NOTATION), vowel length is often shown by /ː/ after the vowel.

Many languages have pairs of similar vowels that differ in length and usually also in VOWEL QUALITY. For example, in English, /iː/ (as in /siːt/ *seat*) may be longer than /ɪ/ (as in /sɪt/ *sit*), but it is also higher and tenser, and may have the quality of a DIPHTHONG.

vowel quality /ˈvaʊəl ˈkwɒlɪti‖ˈkwɑː-/ *n*

features other than length which distinguish one vowel from another. Vowel quality is determined by the shape of the mouth when the particular vowel is produced. The shape of the mouth varies according to the position of the tongue and the degree of lip rounding (see VOWEL).

VP /ˌviː ˈpiː/ *n*

an abbreviation for VERB PHRASE

W

wait time /'weɪt ˌtaɪm/ n

(in questioning) the pause after a teacher has asked a question before a student is asked to respond. The effectiveness of questioning is said to be partly dependent on the use of wait time. Teachers tend to use insufficient wait time and to either answer questions themselves or call on another student to answer the question. Increasing wait time both before calling on a student to respond and after a student's initial response (i.e. before the teacher comments on the response) often increases the length of students' responses, increases the number of questions asked by students, and increases student involvement in learning.

Further reading Rowe 1978

weak form /'wiːk ˌfɔːm‖ˌfɔːrm/ n

see STRONG FORM

weak verb /'wiːk 'vɜːb‖'vɜːrb/ n

see STRONG VERB

weighting /'weɪtɪŋ/ n
also **weighted scoring** /'weɪtɪd 'skɔːrɪŋ/

(in testing) determining the number of points to be given to correct responses in a test, when not all of the responses in a test receive the same number of points. Such a SCORING procedure is known as **weighted scoring**.

Wernicke's area /'veənɪkəz ˌeəriə‖'veər-/ n

see BRAIN

whole-group instruction /'həʊl gruːp ɪn'strʌkʃən/ n

instruction in which an entire class is taught together rather than in groups

see also GROUPING

whole language approach /'həʊl 'læŋgwɪdʒ ə,prəʊtʃ/ n
also **integrated whole language approach**

an approach to both first and second language teaching which is said to reflect principles of both first and second language acquisition and which is based on the following principles:

1 Language is presented as a whole and not as isolated pieces. The approach is thus **holistic** rather than **atomistic**, attempts to teach language in real contexts and situations, and emphasizes the purposes for which language is used.

405

2 Learning activities move from whole to part, rather than from part to whole. For example; students might read a whole article rather than part of it or an adapted version of it.

3 All four modes of language are used, thus lessons include all four skills of listening, speaking, reading and writing, rather than a single skill.

4 Language is learned through social interaction with others, hence students often work in pairs or groups instead of individually.

In ESL situations, the whole language approach is sometimes used to prepare students for MAINSTREAMING.

Further reading Freeman & Freeman 1989

whole-word method /'həʊl 'wɜːd ˌmeθəd||-ɜːr-/ n
also word method, sight method

a method for teaching children to read, commonly used in teaching reading in the MOTHER TONGUE, in which children are taught to recognize whole words rather than letter-names (as in the ALPHABETIC METHOD) or SOUNDS (as in PHONICS). It usually leads to the use of a SENTENCE METHOD, where whole sentences are used.

Whorfian hypothesis /'wɔːfiən haɪ'pɒθ⅟ₛ⅟ₛs||'wɔːr- -'pɑː-/ n

see LINGUISTIC RELATIVITY

wh-question /'dʌbəljuː 'eɪtʃ ˌkwestʃən/ n

(in English) a question that begins with *what, who(m), when, where, which, why* or *how.*

see also YES-NO QUESTION

word /wɜːd||wɜːrd/ n

the smallest of the LINGUISTIC UNITS which can occur on its own in speech or writing.

It is difficult to apply this criterion consistently. For example, can a FUNCTION WORD like *the* occur on its own? Is a CONTRACTION like *can't* ("can not") one word or two? Nevertheless, there is evidence that NATIVE SPEAKERS of a language tend to agree on what are the words of their language.

In writing, word boundaries are usually recognized by spaces between the words. In speech, word boundaries may be recognized by slight pauses.

see also BOUNDARIES, CONTENT WORD, LEXEME

word association /'wɜːd əsəʊsiˌeɪʃən, -səʊʃi- || 'wɜːrd/ n

ways in which words come to be associated with each other and which influence the learning and remembering of words. In a word-association test, a person is given a word or list of words and asked to respond with another word or words. Word associations have been studied in SEMANTICS, VERBAL LEARNING theory and PSYCHO-LINGUISTICS. The following are common associations to words from American college students:

word	response
accident	*car*
airplane	*fly*
American	*flag*
baby	*child*
depression	*recession*

see also ASSOCIATIVE MEANING
Further reading Deese 1965

word bank /'wɜːd ˌbæŋk||-ɜːr-/ *n*
see BRAINSTORMING

word blindness /'wɜːd ˌblaɪndnᵻs||'wɜːrd/ *n*
another term for DYSLEXIA

word boundary /'wɜːd ˌbaʊndəri||-ɜːr-/ *n*
see BOUNDARIES

word class /'wɜːd ˌklɑːs||'wɜːrd ˌklæs/ *n*
a group of words which are similar in function.
Words are grouped into word classes according to how they combine
with other words, how they change their form, etc.
The most common word classes are the PARTS OF SPEECH: NOUN, VERB,
ADJECTIVE, ADVERB, PREPOSITION, PRONOUN, ARTICLE, DEMONSTRATIVE,
CONJUNCTION, INTERJECTION, etc.

see also FORM CLASS, OPEN CLASS

word formation /'wɜːd fɔːˌmeɪʃən||'wɜːrd fɔːr-/ *n*
the creation of new words. There are several ways of doing this,
including:
a the addition of an affix in DERIVATION
b the removal of an affix: BACK FORMATION
c the addition of a COMBINING FORM
d the construction of a COMPOUND WORD
e the shortening of an old word, as when *influenza* becomes *flu*
f the repetition of a word or part of a word: REDUPLICATION
g the invention of a completely new word, such as the mathematical
   term *googal*
In addition, other processes are sometimes regarded as part of word
formation. These include:
h the addition of an affix in INFLECTION
i the use of words as different PARTS OF SPEECH, as when the noun *cap*
   is used as the verb *to cap*.

word frequency /'wɜːd ˌfriːkwənsi||'wɜːrd/ *n*
the frequency with which a word is used in a text or corpus.
see also FREQUENCY²

word frequency count /'wɜːd ˌfriːkwənsi ˌkaʊnt‖'wɜːrd/
also **word frequency list** /'wɜːd 'friːkwənsi ˌlɪst‖'wɜːrd/ *n*

see FREQUENCY COUNT, FREQUENCY²

word list /'wɜːd ˌlɪst‖'wɜːrd/ *n*

a list of the basic and most important words in a language or in a
REGISTER of a language, generally intended for use as a basis for
language teaching or for the preparation of teaching materials. Word
lists are usually based on FREQUENCY COUNTS, often supplemented by
other measures of the importance of words (see COVERAGE).

Further reading Hindmarsh 1980

word method /'wɜːd ˌmeθəd‖'wɜːrd/ *n*

another term for WHOLE-WORD METHOD

word order /'wɜːd ˌɔːdəʳ‖'wɜːrd ˌɔːr-/ *n*

the arrangement of words in a sentence. Languages often differ in their
word order.

For example, the past participle occurs in German at the end of the
main clause rather than after the auxiliary as in English:

Er hat mir das Buch gegeben.

He has to me the book given

"He has given me the book."

In English, the position of a word in a sentence often signals its
function. Thus, in the sentence:

Dogs eat meat.

the position of *dogs* shows that it is the SUBJECT, and the position of
meat shows that it is the OBJECT. In some languages, including English,
a change from the usual word order may often be used to emphasize or
contrast, e.g.

That cheese I really don't like.

where the object of the sentence is shifted to the beginning.

see also FUNCTIONAL SENTENCE PERSPECTIVE

word processor /'wɜːd ˌprəʊsesəʳ‖'wɜːrd ˌprɑː-/ *n*

a computer program that allows for the processing of text and enables
the user to enter, edit, store and print out text in the form of words,
lines, paragraphs or pages. The activity of using a word processor is
known as **word processing**.

Word processors have many applications in education and language
teaching, and are used to teach writing, spelling and other aspects of
composing.

Further reading Flint Smith 1989

word stress /'wɜːd ˌstres‖-ɜːr-/ *n*

see STRESS

working memory /'wɜːkɪŋ 'meməri‖-ɜːr-/ *n*

see MEMORY

writer-based prose /'raɪtəʳ beɪst ˌprəʊz/ *n*
also **egocentric writing**

    see READER-BASED PROSE

writing across the curriculum /'raɪtɪŋ ə'krɒs ðə kə'rɪkjʊ̩ləm||
ə'krɔːs/ *n*

    see LANGUAGE ACROSS THE CURRICULUM

writing conference /'raɪtɪŋ ˌkɒnfərəns||ˌkɑːn-/ *n*

    (in teaching composition) an activity in which the teacher and a
student meet for a short period of time to discuss student writing and
different aspects of the composing process (see COMPOSING PROCESSES).
Through regular conferences with students during a writing programme either in a part of the classroom or elsewhere, the teacher tries
to promote awareness of writing strategies, to personalize writing for
the student, and to make learners more confident about their writing.

writing log /'raɪtɪŋ ˌlɒg||lɔːg, lɑːg/ *n*

    see LEARNING LOG

writing system /'raɪtɪŋ ˌsɪstʰm/ *n*

    a system of written symbols which represent the sounds, syllables, or
words of a language. The three main types of writing system are
ALPHABETIC, based on sounds; SYLLABIC, based on syllables; and
IDEOGRAPHIC, based on words.

X

χ^2 /'kaɪ 'skweə^r/ n
   a symbol for CHI-SQUARE

X-BAR syntax /'eks bɑː^r ˌsɪntæks/ n

see X-BAR THEORY

X-BAR theory /'eks bɑː^r ˌθɪəri/ n

(in UNIVERSAL GRAMMAR), an approach to syntax, **X-BAR syntax**, which attempts to show the general principles of language rather than deal with the structures of one particular language.

The syntax is based on four main lexical categories (see LEXICAL CATEGORY): verbs, nouns, adjectives and prepositions, which become the HEADS of phrases, e.g. the noun *dog* becomes the head of the noun phrase *The dog with black ears*.

To show the structure within each phrase and within the phrase marker of the whole sentence, constituents are marked N, N', N" etc. (see BAR NOTATION)

Further reading Cook 1988

Y

yes-no question /ˌjes ˈnəʊ ˌkwestʃən/ *n*

(in English) a question that can be answered with Yes or No, such as a question formed with a MODAL verb or an AUXILIARY VERB. For example:

Can you swim?
Are you hungry?

see also WH-QUESTION

Z

zero anaphora /ˈzɪərəʊ əˈnæfərə‖ˈziːrəʊ/ *n*

a type of ANAPHORA in which a form may be omitted because its referent (see REFERENCE) is known or can be guessed. For example in:

Kim went down town and met Kenji.

the verb *met* has a "zero" subject: neither a noun nor a pronoun appears as subject, but the referent "Kim" can be inferred.

zero article /ˈzɪərəʊ ˈɑːtɪkəl‖ˈziːrəʊ ˈɑːr-/ *n*

see ARTICLE

Z-score /ˈzed ˌskɔːʳ‖ˈziː/ *n*

(in statistics) a STANDARD SCORE expressed in units of STANDARD DEVIATION.

FURTHER READING

Acheson, K. A. and M. D. Gall 1987 (2nd edition) *Techniques in the clinical supervision of teachers*. New York: Longman.

Ahmad, K., G. Corbett, M. Rogers, and R. Sussex 1985 *Computers, language learning and language teaching*. Cambridge: Cambridge University Press.

Aitchison, J. 1981 *Language change: progress or decay?* London: Fontana Paperbacks.

Alderson, J. and A. Urquhart 1983 *Reading in a foreign language*. London: Longman.

Alexander, L. G., W. Stannard Allen, R. A. Close, and R. J. O'Neill 1975 *English grammatical structure*. London: Longman.

Anderson, J. R. 1985 *Cognitive psychology and its implications* (2nd edition). New York: W. H. Freeman.

Anthony, E. M. 1963 "Approach, method, and technique". *English Language Teaching* 17: 63–67.

Appel, R. and P. Muysken 1987 *Language contact and bilingualism*. London: Arnold.

Ardener, E. (ed) 1971 *Social anthropology and language*. London: Tavistock Publications.

Asher, J. 1977 *Learning another language through actions: the complete teacher's guidebook*. Los Gatos, CA: Sky Oaks Productions.

Austin, J. L. 1962 *How to do things with words*. Cambridge, Mass.: Harvard University Press.

Ausubel, D. P. 1968 *Educational psychology – a cognitive view*. New York: Holt, Rinehart, and Winston.

Ausubel, D. P. 1977 *Developmental psychology*. New York: Grune and Stratton.

Bach, E. 1974 *Syntactic theory*. New York: Holt, Rinehart, and Winston.

Baetens Beardsmore, H. 1986 (2nd edition) *Bilingualism: basic principles*. Clevedon: Tieto (Multilingual Matters).

Bailey, K. D. 1982 (2nd edition) *Methods of social research*. New York: The Free Press.

Bailey, R. W. and M. Gorlach (eds) 1982 *English as a world language*. Ann Arbor: University of Michigan Press.

Baker, C. and D. Cokely 1980 *American sign language: a teacher's resource text on grammar and culture*. Maryland: TJ Publishers.

Bartlett, L. 1990 "Teacher development through reflective teaching". In J. C. Richards and D. Nunan (eds) *Second language teacher education*. New York: Cambridge University Press.

Bennett-Kastor, T. 1988 *Analyzing children's language*. Oxford: Blackwell.

Berliner, D. C. 1984 "The half-full glass: a review of research on teaching". In P. L. Horsford (ed) *Using what we know about teaching*. Alexandria, Va. Association for Supervision and Curriculum Development.

Bernstein, B. 1971 *Class, codes and control: theoretical studies towards a sociology of language*. London: Routledge and Kegan Paul.

Berry, M. 1975 *An introduction to systemic linguistics: structures and systems*. London: Batsford.

Bickerton, D. 1981 *Roots of language*. Ann Arbor: Karoma.

Bley-Vroman, R. 1989 "What is the logical problem of foreign language learning?" In S. M. Gass and J. Schachter (eds) *Linguistic perspectives on second language acquisition*. Cambridge: Cambridge University Press.

Bloom, B. (ed) 1956 *A taxonomy of educational objectives. Handbook 1: Cognitive domain*. New York: McKay.

Further Reading

Bolinger, D. 1975 (2nd edition) *Aspects of language*. New York: Harcourt, Brace, and World.

Boone, Daniele R. 1987 *Human communication and its disorders*. New Jersey: Prentice-Hall.

Brazil, D. C., M. Coulthard, and C. Johns 1980 *Discourse intonation and language teaching*. London: Longman.

Briggs, L. (ed) 1977 *Instructional design: principles and applications*. Englewood Cliffs, New Jersey: Educational Technology Publications.

Brown, E. K. and J. E. Miller 1980 *Syntax: a linguistic introduction to sentence structure*. London: Hutchinson.

Brown, G. and G. Yule 1983 *Teaching the spoken language*. Cambridge: Cambridge University Press.

Brown, H. D. 1987 (2nd edition) *Principles of language teaching and learning*. New Jersey: Prentice-Hall.

Brown, J. D. 1988 *Understanding research in second language learning*. New York: Cambridge University Press.

Brown, P. and S. Levinson 1978 "Universals in language usage: politeness phenomena". In E. Goody (ed) *Questions and politeness: strategies in social interaction*. Cambridge: Cambridge University Press.

Brown, R. 1973 *A first language: the early stages*. Cambridge Mass.: Harvard University Press.

Brown, R. and A. Gilman 1972 "The pronouns of power and solidarity". Inv P. P. Giglioli (ed) *Language and social context*. Harmondsworth: Penguin.

Burt, M. K. and C. Kiparsky 1972 *The gooficon: a repair manual for English*. Rowley: Newbury House.

Burt, M. K., H. Dulay, and E. Hernández-Chávez 1975 *Bilingual syntax measure 1*. New York: Harcourt, Brace, Jovanovich.

Burton-Roberts, N. 1986 *Analysing sentences: an introduction to English syntax*. London: Longman.

Canale, M. 1980 "From communicative competence to communicative language pedagogy". In J. C. Richards and R. Schmidt (eds) *Language and communication*. Harlow: Longman, pp 2–28.

Carroll, J. B. 1973 "Implications of aptitude test research and psycholinguistic theory for foreign language teaching". *International Journal of Psycholinguistics* 2: 5–14.

Carroll, J. B. 1981 "Twenty-five years of research of foreign language aptitude". In K. C. Diller (ed) *Universals in language learning aptitude*. Rowley: Newbury House.

Carton, S. A. 1971 "Inferencing; a process in using and learning language". In P. Pimsleur and T. Quinn (eds) *The psychology of second language learning*. Cambridge: Cambridge University Press.

Chaudron, C. 1988 *Second language classrooms*. New York: Cambridge University Press.

Chomsky, C. 1969 *Acquisition of syntax in children from 5 to 10*. Cambridge, Mass.: The MIT Press.

Chomsky, N. 1957 *Syntactic structures*. The Hague: Mouton.

Chomsky, N. 1965 *Aspects of the theory of syntax*. Cambridge, Mass.: The MIT Press.

Chomsky, N. 1968 *Language and mind*. New York: Harcourt, Brace, Jovanovich.

Chomsky, N. 1980 *Rules and representations*. Oxford: Basil Blackwell.

Chomsky, N. 1988 *Language and problems of knowledge. The Nicaraguan lectures*. Cambridge, Mass.: The MIT Press.

Chomsky, N. and M. Halle 1968 *The sound pattern of English*. New York: Harper and Row.

Clark, H. H. and E. Clark 1977 *Psychology and language*. New York: Harcourt, Brace, Jovanovich.

Clarke, J. L. 1987 *Curriculum renewal in school foreign language learning*. Oxford: Oxford University Press.

Close, R. A. 1975 *A reference grammar for students of English*. London: Longman.

Clyne, M. 1972 *Perspectives on language contact*. Melbourne: The Hawthorn Press.

Clyne, M. 1985 (2nd edition) *Multilingual Australia*. Melbourne: River Seine.

Cohen, A. D. 1980 *Testing language ability in the classroom*. Rowley: Newbury House.

Comrie, B. 1976 *Aspect*. Cambridge: Cambridge University Press.

Cook, V. J. 1988 *Chomsky's Universal Grammar: an introduction*. Oxford: Basil Blackwell.

Coulmas, F. (ed) 1981 *Conversational routine*. The Hague: Mouton.

Coulthard, M. 1985 (2nd edition) *An introduction to discourse analysis*. London: Longman.

Cruickshank, D. R. and J. H. Applegate 1981 "Reflective teaching as a strategy for teacher growth". *Educational Leadership* 38: 553–4.

Crystal, D. 1969 *Prosodic systems and intonation in English*. London: Cambridge University Press.

Crystal, D. 1975 *The English tone of voice*. London: Edward Arnold.

Crystal, D. 1980 *Introduction to language pathology*. London: Edward Arnold.

Cummins, J. 1979 "Linguistic interdependence and the educational development of bilingual children". *Review of Educational Research* 49: 222–251.

Cummins, J. 1980 "The construct of language proficiency in bilingual education". In J. E. Alatis (ed) 1980 *Georgetown Round Table on languages and linguistics*. Washington, DC: Georgetown University Press.

Curran, C. A. 1976 *Counseling–learning in second languages*. Apple River: Apple River Press.

Dakin, J. 1973 *The language laboratory and language learning*. London: Longman.

Dale, P. S. 1975 (2nd edition) *Language development: structure and function*. New York: Holt, Rinehart, and Winston.

Dalton, P. and W. J. Hardcastle 1977 *Disorders of fluency*. London: Edward Arnold.

Davies, A., C. Criper, and A. Howatt 1984 *Interlanguage*. Edinburgh: Edinburgh University Press.

Deese, J. 1965 *The structure of associations in language and thought*. Baltimore: The John Hopkins Press.

de Joia, A. and A. Stenton 1980 *Terms in systemic linguistics: a guide to Halliday*. London: Batsford.

Denes, P. B. and E. N. Pinson 1973 *The speech chain*. Garden City, N.Y.: Anchor Books.

Deuchar, M. 1984 *British sign language*. London: Routledge and Kegan Paul.

de Villiers, J. G. and P. A. de Villiers 1978 *Language acquisition*. Cambridge, Mass.: Harvard University Press.

De Vito, J. 1970 *The psychology of speech and language*. New York: Random House.

Dickinson, L. 1987 *Self-Instruction in Language Learning*. Cambridge: Cambridge University Press.

Disick, R. S. 1975 *Individualization of instruction: strategies and methods*. New York: Harcourt, Brace, Jovanovich.

Downing, J. 1967 *Evaluating the initial teaching alphabet*. London: Cassell.

Doyle, W. 1983 Academic Work. Review of Research in Teacher Education, Vol 5, pp. 163–198.

Dulay, H. and M. Burt 1974 "Errors and strategies in child second language acquisition". *TESOL Quarterly* 8: 129–136.

Dulay, H., M. Burt, and S. Krashen 1982 *Language two*. New York: Oxford University Press.

Ebel, R. L. 1972 *Essentials of educational measurement*. Englewood Cliffs, NJ: Prentice-Hall.

Edwards, J. R. 1979 *Language and disadvantage*. London: Edward Arnold.

Elliot, A. J. 1981 *Child language*. Cambridge: Cambridge University Press.

Ellis, R. 1985 *Understanding second language acquisition*. Oxford: Oxford University Press.

Ervin, S. and C. E. Osgood 1954 "Second language learning and bilingualism". In C. E. Osgood and T. Sebeok (eds) *Psycholinguistics* (Supplement) *Journal of Abnormal and Social Psychology* 49: 139–146.

Ervin-Tripp, S. 1972 "Sociolinguistic rules of address". In J. B. Pride and J. Holmes (eds) *Sociolinguistics*. Harmondsworth: Penguin.

Faerch, C. and G. Kasper 1983 *Strategies of interlanguage communication*. London: Longman.

Further Reading

Fawcett, R. and M. A. K. Halliday (eds) 1985 *New developments in systemic linguistics*. London: Batsford.

Fasold, R. 1984 *The sociolinguistics of society*. Oxford: Basil Blackwell.

Ferguson, C. A. 1959 "Diglossia". *Word* 15: 325–340, also 1972 in P. P. Giglioli (ed) *Language and social context*. Harmondsworth: Penguin.

Ferguson, C. A. 1971 "Absence of copula and the notion of simplicity: a study of normal speech, baby talk, foreigner talk, and pidgins". In D. Hymes (ed) *Pidginization and creolization of languages*. Cambridge: Cambridge University Press.

Fillmore, C. J. 1968 "The case for case". In E. Bach and R. T. Harms (eds) *Universals in linguistic theory*. New York: Holt, Rinehart, and Winston.

Fillmore, C. J. 1971 "Types of lexical information". In D. D. Steinberg and L. A. Jakobovits (eds) *Semantics: an interdisciplinary reader in philosophy, linguistics and psychology*. London: Cambridge University Press.

Flanders, N. T. 1970 *Analyzing teacher behavior*. Reading, Mass.: Addison-Wesley.

Fletcher, P. 1985 *A child's learning of English*. Oxford: Blackwell.

Fletcher, P. and M. Garman (eds) 1979 *Language acquisition*. Cambridge: Cambridge University Press.

Flint Smith, W. (ed) 1989 *Modern technology in foreign language education*. Lincolnwood, Illinois: National Textbook Company.

Flynn, S. 1989 "The role of the head initial/head final parameter in the acquisition of English relative clauses by adult Spanish and Japanese speakers". In S. M. Gass and J. Schachter (eds) *Linguistic perspectives on second language acquisition*. Cambridge: Cambridge University Press.

Foss, D. J. and D. T. Hakes 1978 *Psycholinguistics: an introduction to the psychology of language*. New Jersey: Prentice-Hall.

Freeborn, D. 1987 *A course book in English grammar*. Basingstoke: Macmillan Education.

Freeman, Y. S. and D. Freeman 1989 "Whole language approaches to writing with secondary students of English as a second language". In R. Kindsvatter, W. Wilen, and M. Ishler (eds) *Dynamics of effective teaching*. New York: Longman.

Fromkin, V. and R. Rodman 1983 (2nd edition) *An introduction to language*. New York: Holt, Rinehart, and Winston.

Fry, E. 1965 *Teaching faster reading*. Cambridge: Cambridge University Press.

Gagné, R. M. 1970 (2nd edition) *The conditions of learning*. Holt, Rinehart and Winston.

Gardner, R. C. and W. E. Lambert 1972 *Attitudes and motivation in second-language learning*. Rowley: Newbury House.

Garfinkel, H. 1967 *Studies in ethnomethodology*. Englewood Cliffs: Prentice-Hall.

Gass, S. M. and J. Schachter (eds) 1989 *Linguistic perspectives on second language acquisition*. Cambridge: Cambridge University Press.

Gattegno, C. 1976 *The common sense of teaching foreign languages*. New York: Educational Solutions.

Gebhard, J. 1990 "Models of supervision choices". In J. C. Richards and D. Nunan (eds) *Second language teacher education*. New York: Cambridge University Press.

Genesee, F. 1987 *Learning through two languages*. Rowley, Mass.: Newbury House.

Giles, H. and R. St Clair 1979 *Language and social psychology*, Oxford: Basil Blackwell.

Gimson, A. C. 1980 *An introduction to the pronunciation of English*. London: The English Language Book Society and Edward Arnold.

Gimson, A. C. 1989 (4th edition) *An introduction to the pronunciation of English*. Revised by Susan Ramsaran. London: Edward Arnold.

Glucksberg, S. and J. H. Danks 1975 *Experimental psycholinguistics: an introduction*. New York: John Wiley and Sons.

Goffman, E. 1959 *The presentation of self in everyday life*. New York: Anchor Books.

Goffman, E. 1967 *Interaction ritual: essays on face to face behaviour*. New York: Anchor Books.

Goldman-Eisler, F. 1968 *Psycholinguistics*. London: Academic Press.

Good, T. L. and J. Brophy 1987 *Looking in classrooms*. New York: Harper and Row.

Goodacre, E. J. 1978 "Methods of teaching reading". In J. L. Chapman and

P. Czerniewska (eds) *Reading: from process to practice*. London: Routledge and Kegan Paul.

Goodman, K. and Y. M. Goodman 1977 "Learning about psycholinguistic processes by analyzing oral reading behavior". *Harvard Educational Review* 47, 3: 317–333.

Gougenheim, G. R. Michea, and P. Rivenc 1964 *L'élaboration du français fondamental* (1er degré). Paris: Didier.

Grabe, W. and R. B. Kaplan 1989 "Contrastive rhetoric". In R. Kinsvatter, W. Wilen and M. Ishler (eds) *Dynamics of effective teaching*. New York: Longman.

Greenberg, J. H. 1966 (2nd edition) *Universals of language*. Cambridge, Mass.: The MIT Press.

Grice, H. P. 1967 William James Lectures, Harvard University 1967. Published in part as "Logic in conversation". In P. Cole and J. L. Morgan (eds) 1975 *Syntax and semantics* vol. 3 (Speech Acts): 41–58.

Guiora, A. Z., B. Beit-Hallami, R. C. L. Brannon, C. Dull, and T. Scovel 1972 "The effects of experimentally induced changes in ego states on pronunciation ability in second language: an exploratory study". *Comprehensive Psychiatry* 13: 421–428.

Gumperz, J. 1982 *Discourse strategies*. Cambridge: Cambridge University Press.

Haegman, L. 1982 "English grammar and the Survey of English Usage". *ELT Journal* 36, 4: 248–255.

Halliday, M. A. K. 1967 "Notes on transitivity and theme in English". *Journal of Linguistics* III: 38–81, 199–244, and IV: 179–215.

Halliday, M. A. K. 1970 *A course in spoken English*. London: Oxford University Press.

Halliday, M. A. K. 1978 *Language as social semiotic*. London: Edward Arnold.

Halliday, M. A. K. 1982 *Functional grammar*. London: Edward Arnold.

Halliday, M. A. K. and R. Hasan 1976 *Cohesion in English*. London: Longman.

Hardyck, C. D. and L. F. Petrinovich 1976 (2nd edition) *Introduction to statistics for the behavioral sciences*. Philadelphia: W. B. Saunders.

Hatch, E. (ed) 1978 *Second language acquisition*. Rowley: Newbury House.

Hatch, E. 1983 *Psycholinguistics: a second language perspective*. Rowley: Newbury House.

Hatch, E. and H. Farhady 1982 *Research design and statistics*. Rowley: Newbury House.

Heaton, J. B. 1975 *Writing English language tests*. London: Longman.

Herdan, G. 1964 *Quantitative linguistics*. London: Butterworths.

Herman, W. 1982 (2nd edition) *The portable English handbook*. New York: Holt, Rinehart, and Winston.

Hillerich, R. L. 1978 "Toward an assessable definition of literacy". In L. J. Chapman and P. Czerniewska (eds) *Reading: from process to practice*. London: Routledge and Kegan Paul.

Hindmarsh, R. 1980 *Cambridge English lexicon*. Cambridge: Cambridge University Press.

Hope, G., H. Taylor and J. Pusack 1984 *Using computers in teaching foreign languages*. Orlando, Florida: Harcourt, Brace, Jovanovich.

Howatt, A. 1974 "The background to course design". In J. P. B. Allen and S. P. Corder (eds) *Techniques in applied linguistics: The Edinburgh course in applied linguistics*. Vol. 3. Oxford: Oxford University Press.

Howatt, A. 1983 *A history of English language teaching*. Oxford: Oxford University Press.

Hudson, R. 1981 *Sociolinguistics*. Cambridge: Cambridge University Press.

Hughes, A. 1989 *Testing for language teachers*. Cambridge: Cambridge University Press.

Hughes, A. and P. Trudgill 1987 *English accents and dialects: an introduction to the social and regional varieties of British English*. London: Edward Arnold.

Hunt, K. W. 1966 "Recent measures in syntactic development". *Elementary English* 43: 732–739.

Hurford, J. R. and B. Heasley 1983 *Semantics: a coursebook*. Cambridge: Cambridge University Press.

Hyams, N. 1986 *Language acquisition and the theory of parameters*. Dordrecht: Reidel.

Hyltenstam, K. 1977 "Implicational patterns in interlanguage syntax". *Language Learning* 27, 2: 383–411.

Further Reading

Hyman, L. M. 1975 *Phonology: theory and analysis*. New York: Holt, Rinehart, and Winston.

Hymes, D. (ed) 1964 *Language in culture and society*. New York: Harper and Row.

Hymes, D. 1972 "On communicative competence". In J. B. Pride and J. Holmes (eds) *Sociolinguistics*. Harmondsworth: Penguin.

Hymes, D. 1977 *Foundations in sociolinguistics*. London: Tavistock Publications.

Ilson, R. F. 1982 "The Survey of English Usage: past, present – and future". *ELT Journal* 36, 4: 242–248.

Ilson, R. F. 1984 "The survey, the language, and the teacher". *World Language English* 3, 1.

Jakobovits, L. A. 1970 *Foreign language learning*. Rowley: Newbury House.

James, C. 1980 *Contrastive analysis*. London: Longman.

Jefferson, G. 1972 "Side sequences'. In D. Sudnow (ed) *Studies in social interaction*. New York: Free Press.

Johnson, K. 1982 *Communicative syllabus design and methodology*. Oxford: Pergamon.

Johnson, R. K. 1989 (ed) *The second language curriculum*. Cambridge: Cambridge University Press.

Johnson-Laird, P. N. and P. C. Watson 1977 (eds) *Thinking: readings in cognitive science*. Cambridge: Cambridge University Press.

Kachru, B. B. 1981 "The pragmatics of non-native varieties of English". In L. E. Smith (ed) *English for cross-cultural communication*. London: Macmillan.

Kagan, S. 1987 *Cooperative learning resources for teachers*. Riverside, CA: University of California.

Kastor-Bennett, T. 1988 *Analyzing children's language*. Oxford: Blackwell.

Katz, J. J. and J. A. Fodor 1963 "The structure of a semantic theory". *Language* 39: 170–210. Reprinted in J. A. Fodor and J. J. Katz 1964 *The structure of language: readings in the philosophy of language*. Englewood Cliffs: Prentice-Hall.

Kelly, L. G. 1969 *Twenty-five centuries of language teaching*. Rowley: Newbury House.

Kemmis, S. and R. McTaggart 1988 *The action research planner*. Victoria, Australia: Deakin University Press.

Kindsvatter, R., W. Wilen, and M. Ishler 1988 *Dynamics of effective teaching*. New York: Longman.

Klare, G. R. 1978 "Assessing readability". In J. L. Chapman and P. Czerniewska (eds) *Reading: from process to practice*. London: Routledge and Kegan Paul.

Koch, C. and J. M. Brazil 1978 *Strategies for teaching the composition process*. Urbana, Illinois: National Council for Teachers of English.

Krashen, S. D. 1978 "The monitor model for second-language acquisition". In R. Gringras (ed) *Second language acquisition and foreign language teaching*. Washington: Center for Applied Linguistics.

Krashen, S. D. 1981 *Second language acquisition and second language learning*. Oxford: Pergamon.

Krashen, S. D. 1985 *The input hypothesis: issues and implications*. Harlow: Longman.

Kučera, H. and W. Francis 1967 *Computational analysis of present-day American English*. Providence: Brown University Press.

Labov, W. 1972 *Language in the inner city: studies in the Black English vernacular*. Philadelphia: University of Pennsylvania Press.

Ladefoged, P. 1982 (2nd edition) *A course in phonetics*. New York: Harcourt, Brace, Jovanovich.

Lakoff, G. 1971 "On generative semantics". In D. D. Steinberg and L. A. Jakobovits (eds) *Semantics: an interdisciplinary reader in philosophy, linguistics and psychology*. London: Cambridge University Press.

Lambert, E. E. 1967 "The social psychology of bilingualism". *Journal of Social Issues* 23: 91–109.

Lamendella, J. T. 1979 "Neurolinguistics". *Annual Review of Anthropology* 8: 373–391.

Lane, H. 1964 "Programmed learning of a second language". *IRAL* 2, 4: 249–301.

Leech, G. 1981 (2nd edition) *Semantics*. Harmondsworth; Penguin.

Leech, G. 1983 *Principles of pragmatics*. London: Longman.

Leech, G. 1987 (2nd edition) *Meaning and the English verb*. London: Longman.

Leech, G. and J. Svartik 1975 *A communicative grammar of English*. London: Longman.

Leech, G. and C. Candlin (eds) 1986 *Computers in language teaching and research*. Harlow: Longman.

Lenneberg, E. 1967 *Biological foundations of language*. New York: Wiley.

Levinson, S. 1983 *Pragmatics*. Cambridge: Cambridge University Press.

Li, C. N. and S. A. Thompson 1981 *Mandarin Chinese*. Berkeley: University of California Press.

Liceras, J. M. 1989 "On some properties of the 'pro-drop' parameter: looking for missing subjects in non-native Spanish". In S. M. Gass and J. Schachter (eds) *Linguistic perspectives on second language acquisition*. Cambridge: Cambridge University Press.

Littlewood, W. 1981 *Communicative language teaching: an introduction*. Cambridge: Cambridge University Press.

Littlewood, W. 1984 *Foreign and second language learning*. Cambridge: Cambridge University Press.

Long, M. N. 1980 "Inside the 'black box': methodological issues in classroom research on language learning". *Language Learning* 30, 1: 1–42.

Lozanov, G. 1979 *Suggestology and outlines of suggestopedy*. New York: Gordon and Breach.

Lumsdaine, A. A. and R. Glaser (eds) 1960 *Teaching machines and programmed learning*. Washington, DC: National Education Association.

Lyons, J. 1977 *Semantics I and II*. London: Cambridge University Press.

Lyons, J. 1981 *Language, meaning and context*. London: Fontana.

Mackay, R., R. Barkham, and R. R. Jordan (eds) 1979 *Reading in a second language*. Rowley: Newbury House.

Mackey, W. F. 1965 *Language teaching analysis*. London: Longman.

MacDonough, S. 1981 *Psychology in foreign language teaching*. London: George Allen and Unwin.

McLaughlin, B. 1987 *Theories on second-language learning*. London: Edward Arnold.

McNeill, D. 1966 "Developmental psycholinguistics". In F. Smith and G. A. Miller (eds) *The genesis of language: a psycholinguistic approach*. Cambridge, Mass.: The MIT Press.

McNeill, D. 1970 *The acquisition of language: the study of developmental psycholinguistics*. New York: Harper and Row.

Madsen, H. S. and J. D. Bowen 1978 *Adaptation in language teaching*. Rowley: Newbury House.

Miller, G. A. 1962 *Psychology: the science of mental life*. Harmondsworth: Penguin.

Miller, G. A. and P. N. Johnson-Laird 1976 *Language and perception*. Cambridge: Cambridge University Press.

Milroy, L. 1987 (2nd edition) *Language and social networks*. Oxford: Basil Blackwell.

Money, J. (ed) 1962 *Reading disability: progress and research needs in dyslexia*. Baltimore: The Johns Hopkins Press.

Mowrer, O. H. 1960 *Learning theory and behavior*. New York: Wiley.

Muhlhausler, P. 1986 *Pidgin and creole linguistics*. Oxford: Basil Blackwell.

Munby, J. 1978 *Communicative syllabus design*. Cambridge: Cambridge University Press.

Murray D. M. 1980 "Writing as process: how writing finds its own meaning". In T. R. Donovan and W. McClelland (eds) *Eight approaches to the teaching of composition*. Illinois, Ill.: National Council of Teachers of English.

Naiman, N., M. Frohlich, and H. H. Stern 1975 *The good language learner*. Toronto: Ontario Institute for Studies in Education.

Nation, I. S. P. 1990 *Teaching and learning vocabulary*. New York: Newbury House.

Neisser, U. 1967 *Cognitive psychology*. New York: Appleton-Century Crofts.

Neustupný, J. V. 1978 *Post-structural approaches to language: language theory in a Japanese context*. Tokyo: University of Tokyo Press.

Nisbet, J. and J. Shucksmith 1986 *Learning strategies*. London: Routledge.

Nunan, D. 1988 *Syllabus design*. Oxford: Oxford University Press.

Further Reading

Nunan, D. 1989a *Understanding language classrooms: a guide for teacher initiated action.* New York: Prentice-Hall.

Nunan, D. 1989b *Designing tasks for the communicative classroom.* Cambridge: Cambridge University Press.

Nuttall, C. 1982 *Teaching reading skills in a foreign language.* London: Heinemann.

Odlin, T. 1989 *Language transfer: cross-linguistic influence in language learning.* New York: Cambridge University Press.

Ogden, C. K. 1930 *Basic English.* London: Routledge and Kegan Paul.

Ogden, C. K. and I. A. Richards 1923 (8th edition) *The meaning of meaning.* London: Routledge and Kegan Paul.

Oller, J. W. Jr 1979 *Language tests at school.* London: Longman.

Omaggio, A. L. 1986 *Teaching languages in context.* Boston: Heinle and Heinle.

O'Malley, J. and A. Chamot 1989 *Learning strategies in second language acquisition.* New York: Cambridge University Press.

Oppenheim, A. 1966 *Questionnaire design and attitude measurement.* London: Heinemann.

Orlich, D. C., R. J. Harder, R. C. Callahan, C. H. Kravas, D. Kauchak, R. A. Pendergrass, and A. Keogh 1985 *Teaching strategies.* Lexington, Mass.: D. C. Heath.

Osgood, C. E. 1957 "A behavioristic analysis of perception and language as cognitive phenomena". In *Contemporary approaches to cognition.* Cambridge, Mass.: Harvard University Press.

Osgood, C. E. 1964 "Semantic differential technique in the comparative study of cultures". *American Anthropologist* LXVI 171–200.

Oxford, R. L. 1990 *Language learning strategies.* New York: Newbury House.

Palmer, F. R. 1981 (2nd edition) *Semantics.* Cambridge: Cambridge University Press.

Parker, L. L. 1977 *Bilingual education; current perspectives.* Washington: Center for Applied Linguistics.

Paulston, C. B. 1980 "The sequencing of structural pattern drills". In K. Croft (ed) *Readings on English as a second language.* Cambridge. Mass.: Winthrop.

Penfield, W. and R. Lamar Roberts 1959 *Speech and brain mechanisms.* Princeton: Princeton University Press.

Piaget, J. 1952 *The origins of intelligence in children.* New York: Norton.

Piaget, J. 1955 *The language and thought of the child.* Translated by M. Gabain. Cleveland: Meridian.

Pike, K. L. 1967 *Language in relation to a unified theory of the structure of human behavior.* The Hague: Mouton.

Platt, J. T. and H. Weber 1980 *English in Singapore and Malaysia – status: features: functions.* Kuala Lumpur: Oxford University Press.

Platt, J., H. Weber, and M. L. Ho 1984 *The new Englishes.* London: Routledge and Kegan Paul.

Platt, J. and M. L. Ho 1991 *Dynamics of a contact continuum.* Oxford: Oxford University Press.

Popham, W. J. 1975 *Educational evaluation.* Englewood Cliffs: Prentice-Hall.

Prabhu, N. S. 1983 "Procedural syllabuses". Paper presented at RELC seminar on new trends on language syllabus design. Singapore: RELC.

Pratt, D. 1980 *Curriculum: design and development.* New York: Harcourt, Brace, Jovanovich.

Proett, J. and K. Gill 1986 *The writing process in action.* Urbana, Illinois: National Council of Teachers of English.

Quirk, R. and S. Greenbaum 1970 *Elicitation experiments in English: linguistic studies in use and attitude.* London: Longman.

Quirk, R., S. Greenbaum, G. Leech, and J. Svartik 1985 *A comprehensive grammar of the English language.* London: Longman.

Radford, A. 1988 *Transformational grammar: a first course.* Cambridge: Cambridge University Press.

Ravem, R. 1968 "Language acquisition in a second language environment". *IRAL* 6: 175–185.

Richards, J. C. 1970 "A psycholinguistic measure of vocabulary selection", *IRAL* VII, 2: 87–102.

Richards, J. C. 1974 (ed) *Error analysis: perspectives on second language acquisition.* London: Longman.

Richards, J. C. 1982 "Rhetorical and communicative styles in the new varieties of English". In J. B. Pride (ed) *New Englishes.* Rowley: Newbury House.

Richards, J. C. 1990 *The language teaching matrix.* New York: Cambridge University Press.

Richards, J. C. and D. Nunan 1990 (eds) *Second language teacher education.* New York: Cambridge University Press.

Richards, J. C. and T. Rodgers 1982 "Method: approach, design procedure". *TESOL Quarterly* 16, 2: 153–168.

Richards, J. C. and T. Rodgers 1986 *Approaches and methods in language teaching.* New York: Cambridge University Press.

Rivers, W. M. 1964 *The psychologist and the foreign language teacher.* Chicago: The University of Chicago Press.

Rivers, W. M. 1972 *Speaking in many tongues.* Rowley: Newbury House.

Rivers, W. M. 1981 (2nd edition) *Teaching foreign language skills.* Chicago: University of Chicago Press.

Rivers, W. M. and M. S. Temperley 1978 *A practical guide to the teaching of English.* New York: Oxford University Press.

Robinson, P. 1980 *ESP (English for specific purposes).* Oxford: Pergamon.

Romaine, S. 1988 *Pidgin and creole languages.* London: Longman.

Romaine, S. 1989 *Bilingualism.* Oxford: Blackwell.

Rost, M. 1990 *Listening in language learning.* Harlow: Longman.

Rowe, M. B. 1978 "Wait, wait, wait". *School Science and Mathematics* 78: 207–216.

Rumelhart, D. E. and J. L. McClelland 1986 *Parallel distributed processing: explorations in the microstructure of cognition.* Cambridge, Mass.: The MIT Press.

Ryan, E. B. and H. Giles (eds) 1982 *Attitudes towards language variation: social and applied contexts.* London: Edward Arnold.

Sacks, H., E. A. Schegloff, and G. Jefferson 1974 "A simplest systematics for the organization of turn-taking for conversation". *Language* 50: 696–735.

Sager, J. C., D. Dungworth, and P. McDonald 1980 *English special languages.* Wiesbaden: Brandsetter.

Sampson, G. 1987 "Parallel distributed processing". *Language* 63, 4: 871–886.

Saussure, F. de (1916) 1966 *Course in general linguistics.* New York: McGraw-Hill.

Savard, J-G. and J. C. Richards 1969 *Les indices d'utilité du vocabulaire fondamental français.* Quebec: Les Presses de l'Université Laval.

Saville-Troike, M. 1982 *The ethnography of communication: an introduction.* Oxford: Basil Blackwell.

Schachter, J. 1974 "An error in error analysis". *Language learning* 24, 2: 73–107.

Schachter, J. 1989 "Testing a proposed universal". In S. M. Gass and J. Schachter (eds) *Linguistic perspectives on second language acquisition.* Cambridge: Cambridge University Press.

Schank, R. C. and R. P. Abelson 1977 *Scripts, plans, goals, and understanding.* Hillsdale, NJ: Erlbaum.

Schegloff, E. A. 1972 "Sequencing in conversational openings". In J. J. Gumperz and D. Hymes (eds) *Directions in sociolinguistics.* New York: Holt, Rinehart, and Winston.

Schegloff, E. A., G. Jefferson, and H. Sacks 1977 "The preference for self correction in the organization of repair in conversation". *Language* 53: 361–382.

Schmidt, R. W. 1988 "The potential of parallel distributed processing for SLA theory and research". *University of Hawaii Working Papers in ESL,* 7, 1: 55–66.

Schumann, J. H. 1978 *The pidginization process: a model for second language acquisition.* Rowley: Newbury House.

Scriven, M. 1967 "The methodology of evaluation". In R. W. Tyler, R. M. Gagné, and M. Scriven (eds) *Perspectives on curriculum evaluation.* AERA Monograph Series on Curriculum Evaluation No. 1. Chicago: Rand McNally and Co.

Further Reading

Searle, J. R. 1965 "What is a speech act". In M. Black (ed) *Philosophy in America*. London: Allen and Unwin.

Searle, J. R. 1981 (2nd edition) *Speech acts*. London: Cambridge University Press.

Seliger, H. W. and E. Shohamy 1989 *Second language research methods*. Oxford: Oxford University Press.

Selinker, L. 1972 "Interlanguage". *IRAL* 10: 201–231.

Shiffrin, R. M. and Schneider, W. 1977 "Controlled and automatic human information processing, II: Perceptual learning, automatic attending, and a general theory". *Psychological Review* 84: 127–190.

Sinclair, J. McH. and R. M. Coulthard 1975 *Towards an analysis of discourse*. London: Oxford University Press.

Sinclair, J. McH. and D. Brazil 1982 *Teacher talk*. Oxford: Oxford University Press.

Skilbeck, M. 1984 *School-based curriculum development*. London: Harper and Row.

Skinner, B. F. 1957 *Verbal behavior*. New York: Appleton Century Crofts.

Skutnabb-Kangas, T. and P. Toukomaa 1976 *Teaching migrant children's mother tongue and learning the language of the host country in the context of the sociocultural situation of the migrant family*. Helsinki: The Finnish Commission for UNESCO.

Slobin, D. I. 1973 "Cognitive prerequisites for the acquisition of grammar". In C. A. Ferguson and D. I. Slobin (eds) *Studies of child language development*. New York: Holt, Rinehart, and Winston.

Smith, F. 1971 *Understanding reading*. New York: Holt, Rinehart, and Winston.

Smith, L. E. (ed) 1981 *English for cross-cultural communication*. London: Macmillan.

Snow, C. E. and C. A. Ferguson (eds) 1977 *Talking to children: language input and acquisition*. Cambridge: Cambridge University Press.

Spolsky, B. 1978 *Educational linguistics: an introduction*. Rowley: Newbury House.

Steinberg, D. 1982 *Psycholinguistics: language, mind and world*. London: Longman.

Stenson, N. 1974 "Induced errors". In J. Schumann and N. Stenson (eds) *New frontiers in second language learning*. Rowley: Newbury House.

Stern, H. H. 1983 *Fundamental concepts of language teaching*. Oxford: Oxford University Press.

Stevick, E. 1980 *A way and ways*. Rowley: Newbury House.

Svartik, J. 1973 *Errata: papers in error analysis*. Lund: CWK Gleerup.

Swain, M. 1978 "Home-school language switching". In J. C. Richards (ed) *Understanding second and foreign language learning*. Rowley: Newbury House.

Swain, M., G. Dumas, and N. Naiman 1974 "Alternatives to spontaneous speech: elicited translation and imitation as indicators of second language competence". *Working Papers in Bilingualism* 4: 68–79.

Tarone, E. 1977 "Conscious communication strategies: a progress report". In H. D. Brown, C. Yorio, and R. Crymes (eds) *On TESOL 1977*. Washington DC: TESOL.

Terrell, T. D. 1977 "A natural approach to second language acquisition and learning". *Modern Language Journal* 61: 325–337.

Thakerar, J. N., H. Giles and J. Cheshire 1982 "Psychological and linguistic parameters of speech accommodation theory". In C. Fraser and K. R. Scherer (eds) *Advances in the social psychology of language*. Cambridge: Cambridge University Press.

Titone, R. 1968 *Teaching foreign languages; an historical sketch*. Washington: Georgetown University Press.

Tribble, C. and G. Jones 1990 *Concordances in the classroom*. Harlow: Longman.

Trudgill, P. 1983 (2nd edition) *Sociolinguistics*. Harmondsworth: Penguin.

Turner, R. (ed) 1970 *Ethnomethodology*. Harmondsworth: Penguin.

Ure, J. 1971 "Lexical density and register differentiation". In G. E. Perren and J. L. M. Trim (eds) *Applications of linguistics*. Cambridge: Cambridge University Press.

Vachek, J. (ed) 1964 *A Prague school reader in linguistics*. Bloomington, Indiana: Indiana University Press.

Van Dijk, T. A. 1977 *Text and context: explorations in the semantics and pragmatics of discourse*. London: Longman.

Van Ek, J. A. 1976 *The threshold level*. Strasbourg: Council of Europe.

Van Ek, J. A. and L. G. Alexander 1975 *Threshold level English*. Oxford: Pergamon.

Vygotsky, L. S. 1962 *Thought and language*. Translated by E. Hanfmann and G. Vakar. Cambridge, Mass.: The MIT Press.

Wardhaugh, R. 1969 *Reading: a psycholinguistic perspective*. New York: Harcourt, Brace, and World.

Wardhaugh, R. 1985 *How conversation works*. Oxford: Blackwell.

Wardhaugh, R. 1986 *An introduction to sociolinguistics*. Oxford: Blackwell.

Wells, G. 1982 *Accents of English*. Cambridge: Cambridge University Press.

Wells, G. 1985 *Language development in the preschool years*. Cambridge: Cambridge University Press.

Wenden A. L. and J. Rubin 1987 *Learner strategies in language learning*. Englewood Cliffs, NJ: Prentice-Hall.

West, M. 1953 *A general service list of English words*. London: Longman.

White, L. 1989a *Universal grammar and second language acquisition*. Amsterdam: John Benjamins.

White, 1989b "The adjacency condition on case assignment: do L2 learners observe the subset principle?" In S. M. Gass and J. Schachter (eds) *Linguistic perspectives on second language acquisition*. Cambridge: Cambridge University Press.

White, R. V. 1988 *The ELT curriculum*. Oxford: Blackwell.

Widdowson, H. G. 1978 *Teaching language as communication*. Oxford: Oxford University Press.

Wilkins, D. 1976 *Notional syllabuses*. Oxford: Oxford University Press.

Williams, F. 1970 *Language and poverty*. Chicago: Markham.

Winitz, H. (ed) 1981 *The comprehension approach to foreign language instruction*. Rowley: Newbury House.

Zobl, H. 1989 "Canonical typological structures and ergativity in English L2 acquisition". In S. M. Gass and J. Schachter (eds) *Linguistic perspectives on second language acquisition*. Cambridge: Cambridge University Press.